Juvenile Justice

Third Edition

Robert W. Drowns
Metropolitan State University (late of affiliation)

Kären M. Hess
Normandale Community College

Wadsworth
Thomson Learning™

Australia • Canada • Denmark • Japan • Mexico • New Zealand • Philippines
Puerto Rico • Singapore • South Africa • Spain • United Kingdom • United States

Executive Editor, Criminal Justice: Sabra Horne
Senior Development Editor: Dan Alpert
Assistant Editor: Shannon Ryan
Editorial Assistant: Ann Tsai
Marketing Manager: Christine Henry
Marketing Assistant: Kenneth Baird
Project Editor: Jennie Redwitz
Print Buyer: Karen Hunt
Permissions Editor: Susan Walters
Production Service: Andrea Bednar, Shepherd, Inc.

Text Designer: Harry Voight
Photo Reseacher: Mary Reeg
Copy Editor: Greenleaf Editorial
Illustrator: James W. Daggett
Cover Designer: Liz Harasymczuk
Cover Image: © 1999 Corbis
Cover Printer: Phoenix Color Coporation
Compositor: Shepherd, Inc.
Printer/Binder: R. R. Donnelley/Willard
Indexing: Christine M. H. Orthmann

**Library of Congress
Cataloging-in-Publication Data**
Drowns, Robert W.
    Juvenile justice / Robert W. Drowns, Kären
        M. Hess.—3rd ed.   p.   cm.
    ISBN 0-534-52174-6   OCLC# 4076 2826
    1. Juvenile justice, Administration of—
United States.   2. Juvenile delinquency—
United States.   I. Hess, Kären M.,
II. Title
HV9104.D76   2000
364.36'0973—dc21

Wadsworth/Thomson Learning
10 Davis Drive
Belmont, CA 94002-3098
USA
www.wadsworth.com

International Headquarters
Thomson Learning
290 Harbor Drive, 2nd Floor
Stamford, CT 06902-7477
USA

UK/Europe/Middle East
Thomson Learning
Berkshire House
168-173 High Holborn
London WC1V 7AA
United Kingdom

Asia
Thomson Learning
60 Albert Street #15-01
Albert Complex
Singapore 189969

Canada
Nelson/Thomson Learning
1120 Birchmount Road
Scarborough, Ontario M1K 5G4
Canada

 This book is printed on acid-free recycled
paper.

Contents in Brief

Contents

Foreword

The juvenile justice system—and there are those who would put quotation marks around "system"—has several specialized components. Each component has long been used to autonomy. Each too often has only superficial knowledge of the other components. And the components seldom work together, even though each may be managing the same problem.

The system should be more than this. Our children are entitled to more. Their lives and their parents' lives are greatly affected by the agencies' responses to their problems. Unfortunately the responses often are unintentionally inconsistent and noncomplimentary.

For the system to improve it must know itself. And that means that each professional within each component must know the functions and functioning of all other professionals in the system as they relate to the delinquency, misconduct and neglect of children. At the least the classic function of each component must be recognized.

- *The police*—must protect the safety of children and the public and investigate the behavioral facts.
- *Welfare and probation services*—must investigate the social facts and provide inpatient and outpatient counseling and supervision of children and their parents.
- *Schools*—must educate children academically and, to a great extent, socially and must ensure peace within their walls.
- *Lawyers*—must stand in for their clients, advocating the views of each, whatever they may be.
- *Service providers*—must have treatments that can reunite families and prevent a recurrence of the misconduct that initiated the public's intervention.
- *The court*—must arbitrate and insist on rehabilitative and protective dispositions, and must use force and power within the confines of statutes and the Constitution to ensure due execution of these dispositions.

Each should perform its function knowledgeable of what the others are or may do and of the impact each may have on the others. There needs to be a coordination, a flow, a focus on the child and the family.

Beyond this primary interagency knowledge and respect, there must exist within families—whether the children's own or ones found for them or provided by the streets—solid values, caring and stability. Youths will reflect the values and stability of their families. Therefore the system cannot focus only on the child. It must look at the affective family for its influence on both the causes and the rehabilitation of misconduct, whether it be delinquency, status offenses or inadequate parental care.

Each component must look at the family as it affects its own particular function but, more, it must share its investigation and consider the investigations of others, moving toward a collaborative disposition involving the family that will be the most effective for the children.

And even this is not enough. Each professional working with children must understand children, their behavioral patterns and psychological development, and their changing emotional needs as they mature, seek independence and acquire sexual appetites. They must understand that boys don't truant just because they don't like school and that they join gangs because gangs can better satisfy emotional needs that their families have not. Children are not small adults. Legally, they lack the maturity to make important judgments, under the stress of changing bodies, and with the insistent need for independence.

The juvenile justice system must understand itself and become a system in the true sense of the word, working together toward the common goal of assisting children in trouble and protecting them and the public. The juvenile justice system must know itself. This book can be its primer.

Judge Emeritus Lindsay G. Arthur

Preface

Few social problems arouse public concern more than the problem of juveniles who exhibit antisocial behavior, whether it be minor offenses, such as smoking, or major crimes, such as murder. Any such activities evoke a demand from society for corrective action.

Theories about why juveniles exhibit delinquent behavior, and about how to prevent it, abound. It is an area charged with emotion. Because of this, clear vision is imperative when considering how Americans raise, direct and guide their youths and how they try to make youths' activities conform with social standards, to shape the children's growth and that of the nation.

The causes of problematic youth activity present an intricate puzzle. No easy explanation fits the observed facts. Parents blame social and economic pressures along with a lack of cooperation from the school and social services. The school, police, social agencies and the courts blame parents and each other.

What society is willing to call juvenile violations of the law depends in part on what it thinks it can do about the behavior in question. The effectiveness of rehabilitation facilities, social service placements, the family and youth reform depends on their recognized influence on the control of behavior.

Although the rehabilitation of youthful offenders is a worthy goal, society lacks a proven way to accomplish it. Society is always faced with the difficult task of weighing individual liberties against protecting its members from harm.

To focus on only one part of the youth problem without a knowledge of the system in which it is embedded can result in a distorted or misleading interpretation of the juvenile justice system. Not only must the system concern itself with youths who break the law, it must also be responsible for children who are abandoned, neglected or abused—no small responsibility. The latter children are in dire need of protection and help. Yet often they are placed in the same facilities as juvenile delinquents. Further, such children are at much greater risk of becoming delinquents than are children who have not been mistreated.

Juvenile justice is, indeed, a complex topic, and the literature on it is vast. The purpose of this text is to discuss as many key issues as possible. Each section is but a small window into an extensive, complicated area of debate. An understanding of youths, their protection and control, must be based on an awareness of youth behavior and the total juvenile justice system.

The first section of this text describes the evolution of the juvenile justice system from its historical and philosophical roots through its evolution in the United States in the twentieth century. The second section describes our nation's youths, how they grow and develop, the influence of family, school and community and the major classifications of youths with whom the juvenile justice system interacts: youths who are victims, those who break the law and who victimize and those who belong to gangs. The third section takes an up-close look at our contemporary juvenile justice system and its three major components: law enforcement, the juvenile/family court and corrections. It then places the system within its larger context, the community, and examines the role of that larger community. The fourth and final section goes from the theoretical to everyday practices and programs being conducted in the juvenile justice system. It includes current approaches to prevention and treatment, as well as an examination of innovations in juvenile justice in several other countries. The text concludes with a discussion of the need for rethinking juvenile justice and how it might look and function in the twenty-first century.

Caring for children in need of protection or correction is a proper concern of society, not just the law enforcement community and others within the juvenile justice system. This concern carries with it the need to be informed, to take into account opposing viewpoints and to keep the principles of justice and fairness in the forefront.

How to Use This Book

Juvenile Justice is more than a textbook; it is a planned learning experience. The more actively you participate in it, the better your learning will be. You will learn and remember more if you first familiarize yourself with the total scope of the subject. Read and think about the table of contents; it outlines the many facets of juvenile justice. Then follow these steps as you study each chapter:

1. Read the objectives at the beginning of the chapter. These are stated as "Do You Know?" questions. Assess your current knowledge of each question. Examine any preconceptions you may hold. Glance through the terms presented to see if you can currently define them. Watch for them as you read—in bold print the first time they are defined in the text.

2. Read the chapter, underlining, highlighting or taking notes, whichever is your preferred style.

   a. Pay special attention to all information that is graphically highlighted. For example:

   Juvenile justice currently consists of a "one-pot" jurisdictional approach.

   The key concepts of the chapter are presented this way.

   b. Look up unfamiliar words in the glossary at the back of the book.

3. When you have finished reading a chapter, reread the "Do You Know?" questions at the beginning of the chapter to make sure you can give an educated response to each question. If you find yourself stumped by one, find the appropriate section in the chapter and review it. Do the same thing for the "Can You Define" terms.

4. Finally read the discussion questions and be prepared to contribute to a class discussion of the ideas presented in the chapter.

By following these steps, you will learn more information, understand it more fully and remember it longer. It's up to you. Good learning!

Acknowledgments

We would like to acknowledge those who gave help and encouragement so this text could become a reality: Veronica and Mick Aston; Judy Babcock; Mary Baldwin; Dr. Lyndal Bullock, University of North Texas; Betty Drowns, Tempe Police Department; Lorraine Drowns, a patient and beautiful lady; Romaine Drowns; William A. Drowns; Leonora Drowns-Kissel; "Al" and Susan Campbell; Zvi Eisikovitz, University of Haifa, Israel; Thomas and JoAnn Elwell; Ian Fowler; Paul Gasner; Jacoub Hindiyeh; Dr. Meir Hovav, Ministry of Labour and Social Affairs, Israel; Dr. N. Doran Hunter, Mankato State University; Susan and Rolf Jostad; Lutfis Labon; Dan Laurila; Diane and Gary Lewis; David Lind, Tempe Police Department; Rene Litecky; Senior Sergeant Terry O'Connell, New South Wales (Australia) Police Department; Dr. Robert Pockrass, Mankato State University; Kay Pranis; Jean Raeburn; Chief Andrew Revering, Anoka Police Department and Tiffany Revering; Judge Michael Roith; Mary Ann, Karen and Steve Schmidt, Tempe Police Department; Ira Schwarz, Flint (Michigan) Police Department; Dr. Stanton Samenow, a friend and author of *Before It's Too Late;* Donald Stirling; Kenneth Thompson; and Rose Totino. A special thanks to Lindsay Arthur, retired judge, Juvenile Court, Hennepin County, who formed instead of reformed children.

Since the first edition two great contributors have died: William A. Drowns (1992) and Rose Totino (1994), both of whom had "the best interests of children" in all their works. They are sadly missed.

We would like to add our gratitude to the reviewers of the first and second editions for their constructive suggestions: Kelly J. Asmussen; Steven W. Atchley; Jerald C. Burns; Patrick Dunworth; J. Price Foster; Burt C. Hagerman; Patricia M. Harris; Frederick F. Hawley; James Paul Heuser; Robert Ives; Peter Kratcoski; Matthew C. Leone; Clarence Augustus Martin; Richard H. Martin.

For this third edition we would like to thank these reviewers for their numerous helpful suggestions:

Kelly Asmussen—Peru State College

Steve Atchley—Delaware Technical Community College

J. Price Foster—University of Louisville

James Jengeleski—Shippensburg University

Richard Martin—Elgin Community College

Paul Steele—University of New Mexico—Albuquerque

A heartfelt thank you also to Christine M. H. Orthmann for her hours of research, word processing and indexing; and to Sabra Horne, executive editor; Shannon Ryan, assistant editor; Jennie Redwitz, production editor; and Andrea Bednar, project editor. Thanks to these editors for their attention to detail and their support throughout the revision process.

About the Authors

Robert W. Drowns, MS, *(1931–1996).* Mr. Drowns was a retired police officer and an instructor at Metropolitan State University. In addition to conducting seminars and workshops on various aspects of juvenile justice, he was a consultant to the Office of Juvenile Justice Delinquency and Prevention (OJJDP).

Kären M. Hess, Ph.D. Dr. Hess has written extensively in the field of law enforcement and criminal justice, including these texts for Wadsworth Publishing Company: *Constitutional Law for the Criminal Justice Professional; Corrections for the 21st Century; Criminal Investigation,* 5th ed.; *Criminal Procedure; Introduction to Law Enforcement and Criminal Justice,* 6th ed.; *Introduction to Private Security,* 5th ed.; *Management and Supervision in Law Enforcement,* 2nd ed.; *The Police and the Community: Strategies for the 21st Century,* 2nd ed.; *Police Operations,* 2nd ed.; and *Seeking Employment in Criminal Justice and Related Fields,* 3rd ed.

She is also a frequent instructor for report writing workshops and seminars for law enforcement agencies and is a member of the English department at Normandale Community College and President of the Institute for Professional Development. Dr. Hess belongs to the National Criminal Justice Association and the National Council of Teachers of English.

Chapter **1**	# The Historical and Philosophical Roots of the Juvenile Justice System

History is a vast early warning system.
—Norman Cousins

Do You Know

- What *parens patriae* is and why it is important in juvenile justice?
- What institutions were developed for juveniles in the early nineteenth century?
- When and where the first house of refuge was opened in the United States?
- What reform schools emphasized?
- Who the child savers were and what their philosophy was?
- When and where the first juvenile court was established?
- How the first juvenile courts functioned?
- How Progressive Era proponents viewed crime? What model they refined?
- What resulted from the 1909 White House Conference on Youth?
- What act funded federal programs to aid children and families?
- What effect isolating offenders from their normal environment might have?
- What the Uniform Juvenile Court Act provided?
- What the major impact of the 1970 White House Conference on Youth was?
- What the two main goals of the JJDP Act of 1974 were?
- What the Four Ds of juvenile justice refer to?
- What juvenile delinquency liability should be limited to according to the American Bar Association?
- What was established by the following key cases: *Breed v. Jones, In re Gault, Kent v. United States, McKeiver v. Pennsylvania, Schall v. Martin, In re Winship*?

Can You Define

Bridewell, child, child savers, common law, corporal punishment, custodian, decriminalization, deinstitutionalization, delinquent act, delinquent child, deprived child, deserts, deterrence, diversion, double jeopardy, due process, just deserts, justice model, *lex talionis,* medical model, net widening, *parens patriae,* PINS, poor laws, preventive detention, retaliation, status offense

INTRODUCTION

Our juvenile justice system is a complex, changing network apart from, yet a part of, the broader criminal justice system. It is *apart from* that system in that it is charged with protecting youths from harm, neglect, and abuse, both emotional and physical. This protection frequently involves the criminal justice system as well as numerous public agencies and organizations. The juvenile justice system is *a part of* the criminal justice system in that it is charged with dealing with youths who break the law, and some juveniles end up in the adult system.

A separate system for youthful offenders is, historically speaking, relatively recent. An understanding of how this system evolved is central to understanding the system as it currently exists and the challenges it faces. It has been said that the historian is a prophet looking backward. History reveals patterns and changes in attitudes towards youths and how they are to be treated. The emphasis has changed from punishment to protection and back. As one emphasis achieves prominence, problems persist and critics clamor for change. History also reveals mistakes that can be avoided in the future as well as hopes and promises that remain unfulfilled.

Anthropologists tell us that people have banded together for companionship and protection since the earliest times. As societies developed, they established rules to protect the safety of their members. Those who broke the rules were severely punished. Also since the beginning of recorded history, societies have sought to keep their young under control and have tried to encourage them to conform to society's expectations.

Most early societies treated all wrongdoings and criminal offenses alike. Both children and adults were subject to the same rules and laws. They were tried under the same legal process and, when convicted, suffered the same penalties.

This chapter begins with a brief review of social control in early societies and the development of a juvenile justice system in England. This is followed by a description of the early development of the U.S. juvenile justice system. Next the major periods of the twentieth century are explored: the Progressive Era, the New Deal Era, The Great Society Era and its civil liberties concerns, the 1970s and the 1980s. Figure 1.1 provides a timeline as a guide and an illustration of the overlapping influences at different times in history. The chapter concludes with a discussion of the evolution of child, parent and state relationships and how the juvenile justice system is still evolving.

Social Control in Early Societies

Even the most primitive tribes exercised social control over their members' behavior. In primitive societies, **retaliation** was the accepted way to deal with members of the tribe who broke the rules. Such personal revenge was accepted when victims made their victimizers pay them back.

As tribal leaders emerged, they began to help victims by imposing fines and punishments on wrongdoers. If the wrongdoer refused to pay the fine or accept the punishment, that person was declared an *outlaw,* outside the law, and banished, probably to be eaten by wild animals or killed by the elements. Such social vengeance is the forerunner of our criminal law, taking *public* action against those who do not obey the rules. Ancient societies confined wrongdoers, including children, in dungeons, castle towers and even animal cages.

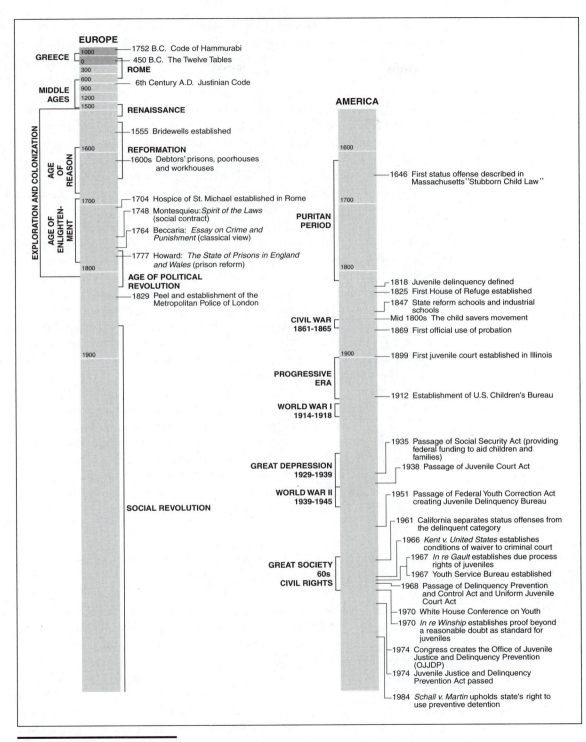

EUROPE

GREECE
— 1752 B.C. Code of Hammurabi
— 450 B.C. The Twelve Tables

MIDDLE
AGES

ROME
— 6th Century A.D. Justinian Code

EXPLORATION AND COLONIZATION

AGE OF REASON

RENAISSANCE
— 1555 Bridewells established

REFORMATION
— 1600s Debtors' prisons, poorhouses
     and workhouses

AGE OF ENLIGHTEN-MENT
— 1704 Hospice of St. Michael established in Rome
— 1748 Montesquieu:*Spirit of the Laws*
     (social contract)
— 1764 Beccaria: *Essay on Crime and
     Punishment* (classical view)
— 1777 Howard: *The State of Prisons in England
     and Wales* (prison reform)

**AGE OF POLITICAL
REVOLUTION**
— 1829 Peel and establishment of the
     Metropolitan Police of London

SOCIAL REVOLUTION

AMERICA

— 1646 First status offense described in
     Massachusetts "Stubborn Child Law"

**PURITAN
PERIOD**

— 1818 Juvenile delinquency defined
— 1825 First House of Refuge established
— 1847 State reform schools and industrial
     schools
— Mid 1800s The child savers movement

**CIVIL WAR
1861-1865**
— 1869 First official use of probation

— 1899 First juvenile court established in Illinois

**PROGRESSIVE
ERA**
— 1912 Establishment of U.S. Children's Bureau

**WORLD WAR I
1914-1918**

— 1935 Passage of Social Security Act (providing
     federal funding to aid children and
     families)

**GREAT DEPRESSION
1929-1939**
— 1938 Passage of Juvenile Court Act

**WORLD WAR II
1939-1945**
— 1951 Passage of Federal Youth Correction Act
     creating Juvenile Delinquency Bureau

— 1961 California separates status offenses from
     the delinquent category

— 1966 *Kent v. United States* establishes
     conditions of waiver to criminal court
— 1967 *In re Gault* establishes due process
     rights of juveniles

**GREAT SOCIETY
60s
CIVIL RIGHTS**
— 1967 Youth Service Bureau established
— 1968 Passage of Delinquency Prevention
     and Control Act and Uniform Juvenile
     Court Act
— 1970 White House Conference on Youth
— 1970 *In re Winship* establishes proof beyond
     a reasonable doubt as standard for
     juveniles
— 1974 Congress creates the Office of Juvenile
     Justice and Delinquency Prevention
     (OJJDP)
— 1974 Juvenile Justice and Delinquency
     Prevention Act passed

— 1984 *Schall v. Martin* upholds state's right to
     use preventive detention

Figure 1.1
**Timeline of Significant
Dates in Juvenile Justice**

As societies developed writing skills, they began to record their laws. Around 1752 B.C. the Babylonian king Hammurabi set forth rules for his kingdom establishing offenses and punishments. Hammurabi, like all kings in his day, was the supreme lawmaker, enforcer and judge. His Code of Hammurabi is viewed by historians as the first comprehensive description of a system to regulate behavior and at the same time take vengeance on those failing to comply. The Code of Hammurabi's main principle was that the strong shall not injure the weak. It established a social order based on individual rights and is the origin of the legal principle of *lex talionis,* that is, an eye for an eye.

In early societies men were the heads of their families, charged with many responsibilities to their wives and children. In such patriarchal societies rebellion against the father, even by adult sons, was not tolerated. Punishment was swift and severe. For example, Item 195 of the Code of Hammurabi states: "If a son strikes his father, one shall cut off his hands" (Kocourek and Wigmore, 1951, p. 427).

Another indication of father-son conflict comes from an essay written by a young man attending a Sumerian academy (located in what is now Iraq). The youths of that time, 1750 B.C., started school at an early age and continued to young manhood. They attended school from sunrise to sunset, every day, year-round. Industriousness was encouraged by the generous use of **corporal punishment** (inflicting bodily pain). In this essay, the father instructs the son to attend school, stand with respect and fear before his professor, complete his assignments and avoid wandering about the public square or standing idly in the streets. In short, the son was to be about the business of getting an education (Kramer, 1963).

The father in ancient Roman culture also exercised unlimited authority over his family. He had the authority to administer corporal punishment and could even sell his children into slavery. One important concept from the Roman civilization that influenced the development of juvenile justice was *patria postestas—* referring to the absolute control fathers had over their children and the children's absolute responsibility to obey. This concept evolved into the doctrine of *parens patriae,* a basic doctrine in our juvenile justice system.

Developments in England

Developments in England had a great influence on the juvenile justice system that would later develop in the United States.

The Middle Ages (A.D. 500–1500)

The earliest legal document written in English contained the laws of King Aethelbert (around A.D. 600). These laws made no special allowance for an offender's age. In fact several cases document children as young as six being hanged or burned at the stake.

Early in English history, how children were viewed was greatly influenced by the Church of Rome. Church doctrine stated that under age seven, children had not yet reached the age of reason and, thus, could not be held liable for sins. English law adopted the same perspective. Under seven years of age, children were not considered legally able to have the required intent to commit a crime. From ages 7 to 14, it was presumed they did not have such intent, but if evidence proved differently, children could be found guilty of committing a crime. After age 14, individuals were considered adults.

The Feudal Period

The Feudal period falls near the end of the Middle Ages, covering roughly the ninth to the fifteenth centuries. In thirteenth-century England **common law** (law of custom and usage) gave the king of England the power of being the "father of his country." The king was perceived as guardian over the person and property of minors, who were considered wards of the state and, as such, received special protection (Rendleman, 1979). The Latin phrase meaning "father of the country" is *parens patriae,* a doctrine critical to the evolution of juvenile justice.

Parens patriae gave the king the right and responsibility to care for minors.

Parens patriae was used to justify the state's intervention in the lives of its feudal lords and their children, and it placed juveniles between the civil and the criminal systems. The chancery courts were one means by which the king maintained control of the wealthier class, and they also enabled the state to act in the best interests of its children. These courts heard issues involving guardianship, for example. The chancery courts did *not* have jurisdiction over children who committed crimes. Such youths were handled within the criminal court system.

The Renaissance

The Middle Ages are generally conceded to have ended with Columbus's discovery of America in 1492. The next two centuries in Europe, the Renaissance, marked the transition from medieval to modern times. The Renaissance was characterized by an emphasis on art and the humanities, as well as a more humanistic approach to criminal justice.

London's **Bridewell** Prison was the first institution of its kind to control youthful beggars and vagrants. The underlying theme for Bridewell was work and severe punishment to provide discipline, deterrence and rehabilitation. Grunhut (1948, p. 15) describes the goals of the institution as follows: "To make

London's Bridewell was similar to a debtor's prison. It confined both children and adult "vagrants."

them earn their keep, to reform them by compulsory work and discipline, and to deter others from vagrancy and idleness."

Because they were so successful, Parliament passed a law in 1576 calling for Bridewell-type institutions in every county. Modeled after the first prison, the Bridewells combined the principles of the workhouse and the poorhouse, as well as the penal institutions' formalities. These Bridewells confined both children and adults who were considered idle and disorderly. Some parents placed their children into these Bridewells believing the emphasis on hard work would benefit the children.

During Elizabeth I's reign, the English passed **poor laws,** which established the appointment of overseers to *indenture* poor and neglected children into servitude. Such children were forced to work for wealthy families who, in turn, trained them in a trade, domestic service or farming. Such involuntary apprenticeships were served until the youths were 21 or older. These Elizabethan poor laws were the model for dealing with poor children for the next 200 years.

In England in 1563, the Statutes of Artificers inaugurated a system of *indenturing* and *apprenticeship* for children over 10 years of age. While the primary aim of the legislation was to ensure an adequate labor supply, the statutes served to provide and promote an approved method of child care (Zietz, 1969, p. 6).

In 1601 England proposed establishing large workhouses where children who could not be supported by their parents would be placed and "bred up to labor, principles of virtue implanted in them at an early age, and laziness be discouraged . . . and, settled in a way serviceable to the public's good and not bred up in all manners of vice" (Webb and Webb, 1927, p. 52). This proposal was finally implemented with the passage of the Gilbert Act of 1782. The act decreed that all poor, aged, sick and those too infirm to work were to be placed in *poorhouses* (almshouses). Under the act, poor infants and children who could not go with their mothers were not placed in the poorhouse but with a "proper person," presumably in a family setting (de Scheveinitz, 1943, pp. 20–21).

The Reform Movement

Historians have labeled the eighteenth and nineteenth centuries the Age of Enlightenment. One important milestone in the development of juvenile justice during this time was the founding of the London Philanthropic Society in 1817. One purpose of this society was the reformation of juvenile offenders. The Society opened the first English house of refuge for children, a major shift from family-oriented discipline to institutional treatment.

An important reformer was John Howard (1726–1790), sheriff of Bedfordshire and often considered the father of prison reform. Howard undertook a study of England's prisons and traveled to other countries to study their prisons. One institution that greatly impressed Howard was the Hospice (hospital) of San Michele in Rome, commonly referred to as St. Michael. Built in 1704 by Pope Clement XI, the Hospice was one of the first institutions designed exclusively for youthful offenders. Incorrigible youths under age 20 ate and worked in silence in a large central hall, but they slept in separate cells.

The emphasis was on reading the Bible and hard work. An inscription placed over the door by the pope is still there: "It is insufficient to restrain the wicked by punishment unless you render them virtuous by corrective discipline." The pope said that the facility's purpose was "For the correction and instruction of profligate youth, that they who when idle were injurious, may when taught become useful to the state" (Griffin and Griffin, 1978, p. 7).

The Early Development of U.S. Juvenile Justice

The justice system developed in England served as the basis for the juvenile justice system in America. A distinctively American system evolved in response to conditions unique to this country.

From the Colonial Period to the Industrial Revolution

The American colonists brought with them much of the English criminal justice system, including poor laws and the forced apprenticeship system for poor and neglected children. Before 1800, under common law, age was a consideration in juvenile justice. Blackstone (1776, p. 23) summarized the law on the responsibility of youths in these words: "Under seven years of age indeed an infant cannot be guilty of a felony; for then a felonious discretion is almost an impossibility in nature; but at eight years old he may be guilty of a felony." He went on to say that under age 14, although by law a youth may be adjudged incapable of discerning right from wrong (*doli incapax*), it appeared to the court and the jury that he *could* discern between good and evil (*doli capax*) (italics in original).

In the early years of colonization, the fundamental mode of juvenile control was the family, with the father given absolute authority over all family matters. Early laws prescribed the death penalty for children who disobeyed their parents.

In 1646 the colonial Puritan philosophy was enacted into law when Massachusetts passed the Stubborn Child Law, which created the first **status offense,** that is, an act that is illegal for minors only. The law stood, unrevised, for over three hundred years.

Until the end of the eighteenth century, the family was also the main economic unit, with family members working together farming or in home-based trades. Children were important contributors to these family-based industries. The privileged classes found apprenticeships for their children so that they could learn marketable skills. The children of the poor, in contrast, were often bound out as indentured servants.

The Industrial Revolution, which began at the end of the eighteenth century, changed forever the face of America. Families flocked to the cities to work in the factories, and child labor in these factories replaced the apprenticeship system.

For the next 20 years child labor was used increasingly. During this period, children made up 47 to 55 percent of the cotton mill workforce (Krisberg and Austin, 1993, p. 15). As the country became more industrialized, the social control once exerted by the family weakened. Children in the workforce had to obey the demands of their bosses, often in conflict with the demands of their parents. In addition, poverty was increasing for many families. This combination of poverty and weakened family control set an "ominous stage," with some Americans fearing a growing "dangerous class" and seeking ways to "control the wayward youth who epitomized this threat to social stability" (Krisberg and Austin, p. 15).

Colonial America handled juveniles much like petty thieves. After a warning, shaming or corporal punishment, the offender would return to the community. If accused of a major criminal act, the juvenile would proceed through the justice system as an adult. Trials and punishment were based on age, and anyone over seven years old was subject to the courts.

Highlights of Colonial Period and Industrial Revolution Reform*

Philosophy

The consensus was that children were inherently sinful and in need of strict control and/or punishment when necessary. Most nonconforming children were of lower-class parentage; middle-class families protected their children from bad influences by controlling the behavior of less fortunate youths.

Treatment

Misbehaving children were generally controlled by familial punishment. External, community punishment and control were necessary only when the parents failed.

Policies

Communal legal sanctions were guided by the British tradition of common law, allowing children over seven years of age to receive public punishment. Children could be punished publicly for several status offenses such as rebelliousness, disobedience and sledding on the Sabbath. Thus, separate systems of justice were set up for children and adults. Institutions created to care for orphaned and neglected children included almshouses and orphanages.

Developments in the Early Nineteenth Century

In the 1700s and the early 1800s, the family, the church and other social institutions were expected to handle juvenile delinquents. Jails, the only form of incarceration, were primarily used for detention pending trial.

As time passed, the traditional forms of social control began to break down. To counteract this, communities created institutions for children where they could learn good work and study habits, live in a disciplined and healthy environment, and develop "character." During the nineteenth century and continuing into the early twentieth century, juveniles were handled by various civil courts and public institutions such as welfare agencies. Increasing industrialization, urbanization and immigration created severe problems for families and their children.

Five distinct, yet interrelated, institutions evolved to handle poor, abused, neglected, dependent and delinquent children brought before a court: (1) indenture and apprenticeship, (2) mixed almshouses (poorhouses), (3) private orphanages, (4) public facilities for dependent children and (5) jails.

---

*Highlights of the several periods of reform discussed are adapted from materials of the Center for the Assessment of the Juvenile Justice System (Hawkins et al., 1980).

The 1800s were marked by rising concern and social reform. The reformers were instrumental in changing laws and public policy as they affected children. New York, Pennsylvania and Massachusetts established the first halfway houses in America in the early 1800s (Keller and Alper, 1970, p. 7). A committee report in 1818 listed "juvenile delinquency" as a major cause of pauperism—the first public recognition of the term *juvenile delinquency.*

Several other significant events occurred in the 1800s that altered the administration of juvenile justice (Griffin and Griffin, p. 20):

1818—Juvenile delinquency defined

1825—First house of refuge established in United States

1847—State reform and industrial schools founded

1869—First official use of probation (Massachusetts)

1870—First use of separate trials for juveniles (Massachusetts)

1877—Separate dockets and records established for juveniles (Massachusetts)

1880—First probation system applicable to juveniles instituted

1898—Segregation of children under 16 awaiting trial (Rhode Island)

1899—First juvenile court established (Illinois)

The institutions created by the reformers were houses of refuge, reform schools and foster homes.

Houses of Refuge

In 1823 the New York Society for the Reformation of Juvenile Delinquents was founded.

In 1825 the New York House of Refuge, the first U.S. reformatory, opened to house juvenile delinquents, defined in its charter as "youths convicted of criminal offenses or found in vagrancy."

The House of Refuge was to care for children who were vagrants or had been convicted of criminal offenses. It was the predecessor of today's training schools. Children were placed there by court order and usually stayed until they reached the age of maturity.

The managers of the House believed children's behavior would change through vigilant instruction. Children who misbehaved were punished by losing certain rewarded positions or by whippings. The managers took the position that the public was responsible for disciplining children where natural parents and guardians refused to do so. The labor of the House was contracted out for a fee to local businesses. Youths were given apprenticeships and training in practical occupations.

The authority of the state to send children to such houses of refuge under the doctrine of *parens patriae* was upheld in 1838 in Pennsylvania in *Ex parte*

At the New York House of Refuge, children learned various trades and also engaged in physical activities.

Crouse. In this case a mother claimed that her daughter was incorrigible and had her committed to the Philadelphia House of Refuge. The girl's father sought her release, but was denied by the court, which stated:

> The object of the charity is reformation, by training its inhabitants to industry; by imbuing their minds with principles of morality and religion; by furnishing them with means to earn a living; and above all, by separating them from the corrupting influence of improper associates. To this end, may not the natural parents, when unequal to the task of education, or unworthy of it, be superseded by the *parens patriae,* or common guardian of the community?

However, many houses of refuge were prisons with harsh discipline, including severe whippings and solitary confinement. Krisberg and Austin (p. 17) note that: "[F]rom the onset, the special institutions for juveniles housed together delinquent, dependent, and neglected children—a practice still observed in most juvenile detention facilities today."

Houses of refuge were operated by private philanthropic societies in many of the largest cities of the northeastern states. A typical day at the house began at sunrise and followed a highly disciplined, regimented routine. Morning prayers were followed by one and one-half hours of school and then by work routines until the noon meal. After eating, youths returned to work until 5:00 P.M., at which time they ate, had one and one-half hours of school followed by prayers, and then returned to their cells and the rule of silence (Pickett, 1969, p. 49). Confinements were lengthy, and escapes were frequent. There was public disapproval of the harsh disciplinary treatment and the health hazards, but by 1860, 20 such institutions had opened in the United States.

Krisberg and Austin (p. 16) suggest: "Although early 19th-century philanthropists relied on religion to justify their good works, their primary motivation was protection of their class privileges. Fear of social unrest and chaos dominated their thinking. The rapid growth of a visible impoverished class, coupled with apparent increases in crime, disease, and immorality, worried those in power."

Reform Schools

By the middle of the nineteenth century, the more progressive states began to develop new institutions—*reform schools*—intended to provide discipline in a "homelike" atmosphere where education was emphasized.

Reform schools emphasized formal schooling, but they also retained large workshops and the contract system of labor.

From 1859 to 1890 many houses of refuge were replaced by reform schools. In many respects, however, reform schools were indistinguishable from the houses of refuge.

Foster Homes

While many states were building reform schools, New York in 1853 emphasized placing neglected and delinquent children in private *foster homes,* frequently located in rural areas. At the time, the city was viewed as a place of crime and bad influences, in contrast with the clean, healthy, crime-free country.

The foster home was to be the family surrogate used in all stages of the juvenile justice process. For a variety of reasons this concept faltered. Personality conflicts between foster parents and juvenile clients often caused disruption. Some foster parents were convicted of various abuses and neglect. In addition, the accreditation and monitoring of foster home licenses was inadequate and sometimes was ignored completely.

The Child Savers

Many reforms swept through the United States in the nineteenth century, including the child-saving movement, which began around the middle of the 1800s. The **child savers** believed that children's environments could make them "bad." These wealthy, civic-minded citizens tried to "save" unfortunate children by placing them in houses of refuge and reform schools.

These reformers were shocked that children could be tried in a criminal court, like adults, and be sentenced to jail with hardened criminals. The reformers believed that society owed more to its children than the guarantee of justice.

The child savers were reformers whose philosophy was that the child was basically good and was to be treated by the state as a young person with a problem.

Children's contact with the justice system should not be a process of arrest and trial, but should seek answers to what the children are, how they have become what they are, and what society should do in the children's, as well as society's, best interests, to save them from wasted lives. The child savers' motivating principles were as follows (Task Force Report, 1976, p. 6):

- Children should not be held as accountable as adult transgressors.
- The objective of juvenile justice is to help the youngster, to treat and rehabilitate rather than punish.
- Dispositions should be predicated on an analysis of the youth's special circumstances and needs.
- The system should avoid the punitive adversary role and formalized trappings of the adult criminal process.

The child savers were not entirely humanitarian, however; they viewed poor children as a threat to society. These children needed to be reformed to conform, to value hard work and to become contributing members of society. Anthony Platt (1968, p. 176), who did extensive research on this period, wrote:

> The child savers should in no sense be considered libertarians or humanists:
>
> 1. Their reforms did not herald a new system of justice but rather expedited traditional policies which had been informally developing during the nineteenth century.
> 2. They implicitly assumed the "natural" dependence of adolescents and created a special court to impose sanctions on premature independence and behavior unbecoming youth.
> 3. Their attitudes toward "delinquent" youth were largely paternalistic and romantic, but their commands were backed up by force.
> 4. They promoted correctional programs requiring longer terms of imprisonment, long hours of labor and militaristic discipline, and the inculcation of middle-class values and lower-class skills.

Highlights of Early 1800s Reform

Philosophy
Poverty was a crime that could be eliminated by removing children from offending environments and reforming their unacceptable conduct.

Treatment
Nonconforming children were controlled by external institutions, such as houses of refuge and reformatories created by paternalistic child savers. Public education was used to "Americanize" foreign and lower-class children. Private groups were organized to rescue children from poor and unfit environments.

Policies
Local and state governments became providers of care and treatment for neglected and delinquent children. The costs of building and supervising juvenile institutions were shared by private and public agencies. The *parens patriae* tradition, correctional policies that separated adult and youthful offenders,

and indeterminate sentencing for juvenile inmates were adopted. Statutory definitions of juvenile delinquency were expanded to include new status offenses, such as begging, cheating and gambling.

Developments in the Late Nineteenth Century

Organizations such as the Young Men's Christian Association (YMCA, 1851) and the Young Women's Christian Association (YWCA, 1861) provided recreation and counseling services to youths to "keep normals normal," thereby preventing delinquency.

The Civil War (1861–1865) was followed by reconstruction and massive industrialization. Many children were left fatherless by the war, and many families moved to the urban areas seeking work. Often children were exploited in sweatshops or roamed the streets in gangs while their parents worked in factories.

In 1866 the first specialized institution for male juveniles was authorized in Washington, DC. This House of Corrections consisted of several cottages containing some 60 or more beds. In 1869 Massachusetts appointed a State Board of Charities to investigate cases involving children who were tried before the courts. At this time state reformatories also came into existence, including the New York State Reformatory at Elmira, which opened in 1877.

By the end of the 1800s, reform schools introduced vocational education, military drill and calisthenics into the institutions' regimens. At the same time, some reform schools changed their names to "industrial schools" and later to "training schools," to emphasize the "treatment" aspect of corrections. For example, the Ohio Reform Farm School opened in 1857, later became the Boy's Industrial School, and was renamed again to the Fairfield School for Boys.

The Juvenile Court Movement

A juvenile court movement in the 1890s provided citizen participation in community-based corrections. This citizen participation through the Parent Teacher Association (PTA), founded in 1897, induced the Cook County Bar Association to write the law to establish a juvenile court in Chicago (Hunt, 1973).

The first juvenile court in the United States was created by the Illinois Juvenile Court Act in 1899, which was entitled an "Act to Regulate the Treatment and Control of Dependent, Neglected and Delinquent Children." Key features of this act included:

- Defining a delinquent as any detainee under age 16.
- Separating children from adults in institutions.
- Setting special, informal procedural rules for juvenile court.
- Providing for the use of probation officers.
- Prohibiting the detention of children under age 12 in a jail or police station.

In 1899 the Illinois legislature passed a law establishing a juvenile court that became the cornerstone for juvenile justice throughout the United States.

In this engraving from an American newspaper of 1868, a six-year-old sentenced to the House of Refuge on Blackwell's Island, New York City, for vagrancy pleads unavailingly for mercy for his first offense.

The Illinois act removed those under age 16 from the jurisdiction of the criminal court, replacing it with a paternalistic system that viewed juvenile delinquents as victims of their environments, not responsible for their offenses. Rehabilitation and the child's welfare were to be of prime concern. As described by Schwartz (1989, p. 150), the newly created juvenile court was:

> . . . a special court in which children were denied due process and adversarial proceedings in exchange for informal and confidential hearings and dispositions based on what was felt to be in the "best interests of the child." It was a court in which the distinctions between dependent, neglected and delinquent children were less important than their common need for state supervision in the manner of a wise and devoted parent.

However, as Flicker (1990, p. 32) states:

> [I]t could be argued that the most reprehensible feature of the Illinois contribution to juvenile justice is the continued erosion of distinctions between juveniles who commit criminal acts, thereby demonstrating objectively that they are a present threat to community safety, and those who are themselves victims as abused, neglected, or dependent children.

Nonetheless, Schwartz (p. 151) suggests: "The creators of the juvenile court envisioned that this special court for children would be less like a court and more like a social welfare agency." Further, "Children who were brought to the attention of the juvenile court were to be helped rather than punished."

The 1899 Juvenile Court Act provided public policy, social reform and a structured way to reform children in trouble. It also provided a way to care for children who needed official protection. The law created a public policy, based on the **medical model**—that is, a treatment model—to retard the social and moral decay of the environment, family and youths. The reformers' efforts were directed at restoring and controlling children. They emphasized parental authority, home education, domesticity and rural values.

The adjudicative process set up within the juvenile court was to be special; it was *not* to function as an adult criminal court. The Juvenile Court Act gave "original jurisdiction in *all* cases coming within the terms of this act," divesting adult criminal courts of all criminal jurisdiction over children under age 16.

The first juvenile courts were administrative agencies of the circuit or district courts. They served a social welfare function embracing the rehabilitative ideal of reforming children rather than punishing them.

Juvenile courts were to be separate, with separate records and informal procedures. Several important parts of a criminal trial, such as the indictment, pleadings and jury, were eliminated.

The adversary function of the criminal court was perceived to be incompatible with the procedural safeguards of the juvenile court reflecting the basic doctrine of *parens patriae.* Since children were legally wards of the state, they were perceived to be without constitutional rights. Despite this, juvenile court was initially perceived to be far more humane than the criminal court. The act was construed liberally, so that the care, custody and discipline of children would approximate as nearly as possible that given by individual parents.

Some scholars contend that the system was set up to take advantage of children. Disputing the benevolent motives of the founders of the juvenile court, especially in the adjudication procedure, scholars have suggested that the civil liberties and privacy rights of juveniles diminished in the process. They accuse the middle class of promoting the child-saving movement to support its own interests.

Other scholars contend that the development of the juvenile courts and the adjudication function represents neither a great social reform in processing juveniles nor an attempt to diminish juveniles' civil liberties and control them arbitrarily. Rather, it represents another example of the trend toward bureaucracy and an institutionalized compromise between social welfare and the law.

The passage of the Illinois juvenile court law marked the first time that probation and a probation officer were formally made *specifically* applicable to juveniles. The Illinois Juvenile Court Act stipulated:

> The court shall have authority to appoint or designate one or more discreet persons of good character to serve as probation officers during the pleasure of the court . . . it shall be the duty of the said probation officer to make such investigation as may be required by the court; to be present in court in order to represent the interests of the child when the case is heard; to furnish to the court such information and assistance as the judge may require; and to take such charge of any child before and after trial as may be directed by the court.

Probation, according to the 1899 Illinois Juvenile Court Act, was to have both an investigative and a rehabilitative function.

In 1899, with the Illinois act, the nation's criminal justice system finally recognized that it owed a different duty to children than to adults and that impressionable, presumably salvageable youths should not be mixed in prisons with hardened criminals. The development of juvenile courts is considered the first transformation of the juvenile justice system.

Highlights of Late Nineteenth-Century Reform

In the nineteenth century, children were protected from confinement in jails, prisons and institutions by the opening of houses of refuge. Responsibilities shifted back and forth between the private and public sectors. Chicago, as early as 1861, provided a local commission to hear and determine petty cases of boys from 6 to 17 years old. Between 1878 and 1898 Massachusetts established a statewide system of probation to aid the court in juvenile matters, a method of corrections currently used in every state in the United States. The same period saw the regulation of child labor, the development of special services for handicapped children and the growth of public education.

There was a growing acceptance of public responsibility for the protection and care of children. However, no legal machinery yet existed to handle juveniles who needed special care, protection and treatment as wards of the state, rather than as criminals.

Philosophies

Youth problems increased as by-products of rapid urbanization: poverty, immigration and unhealthy environments. Individual treatment and control of juvenile offenders could improve their behavior.

Treatment

Several private organizations were created to assimilate foreign and lower-class youths into American culture. Locked facilities were built across the nation. Orphan asylums became popular ways to house and mold the conduct of children left homeless by the Civil War and/or neglected by unfit parents.

Policy

State and local governments expanded their involvement in the lives of neglected and delinquent children through the adoption of new educational/assimilation tools (vocational, industrial and manual training schools) for institutionalized and lower-class youths, the passage of immigration restriction laws and the assumption of a stronger role in creating, financing and administering reform institutions.

Into the Twentieth Century: The Progressive Era

The first quarter of the twentieth century is often referred to as the Progressive Era or the Age of Reform. According to the progressives, children were not bad, but they were made so by society and their environment. Progressives believed that the family was especially influential and that parents were responsible for bringing their children up to be obedient and to work hard.

The reformers were optimistic, college-educated people who believed that individualized treatment based on the juvenile's history was critical. They were also concerned with their own futures, as noted by Krisberg and Austin (p. 27): "During the Progressive Era, those in positions of economic power feared that the urban masses would destroy the world they had built. . . . From all sectors came demands that new action be taken to preserve social order, and to protect private property and racial privilege."

The progressives further developed the medical model, viewing crime as a disease to treat and cure by social intervention.

According to Krisberg and Austin (p. 27): "The times demanded reform, and before the Progressive Era ended, much of the modern welfare state and the criminal justice system were constructed." Further (p. 31): "The thrust of Progressive Era reforms was to found a more perfect control system to restore social stability while guaranteeing the continued hegemony [predominance or authority] of those with wealth and privilege."

The First Juvenile Courts

Although a formalized juvenile justice system was desperately needed, the reformers gained governmental control over a wide range of youthful conduct that previously had been handled informally and would continue to be so handled. The juvenile court received formal sanction for its informal process of dealing with youths.

In an early critique, Breckenridge and Abbott, two prominent progressives, evaluated the records of the first juvenile courts in Cook County, Illinois, from 1899 to 1909. Their report (1912, pp. 42–43) noted: "Children who do wrong can be found in every social stratum, but those who become wards of the court are the children of the poor." Their findings confirmed that the juvenile court constituted a powerful means of social control by the dominant class.

Commonwealth v. Fisher (1905) defended the juvenile court ideal, reminiscent of the holding of the court in the Crouse case of 1838:

> To save a child from becoming a criminal, or continuing in a career of crime, to end in maturer years in public punishment and disgrace, the legislatures surely may provide for the salvation of such a child, if its parents or guardians be unwilling or unable to do so, by bringing it into one of the courts of the state without any process at all, for the purpose of subjecting it to the state's guardianship and protection.

Early juvenile courts believed that:

- Delinquency was preventable and curable.
- Special informal court procedures best served the juveniles involved by providing a supportive atmosphere in which to resolve problems.
- Since both criminal and non-criminal misbehavior were but symptoms of an unhealthy environment, the distinction between them was of minimal significance (Rieffel, 1983, p. 3).

Judge Benjamin Lindsay presided in juvenile court in Denver, Colorado, from 1900 to 1927. These first juvenile courts were informal proceedings focusing on rehabilitation rather than punishment.

The juvenile court was the creation of Progressive Era reformers who believed that children were incapable of being fully responsible for antisocial and criminal behavior. Further, children were thought to be malleable and more capable of rehabilitation than adults. Treatment rather than punishment continued to be the focus. Social workers served the juvenile court as probation officers and held this same philosophy.

Social workers collected facts about youths' misbehavior, including the history of their families, school performance, church attendance and neighborhood. They made recommendations for disposition to the judges and provided community supervision and casework services to the vast majority of children who were adjudicated by the juvenile courts.

Social work and the juvenile justice system movement flourished, focusing on youths and their families. The movement gradually became more concerned with professionalism in the intake process and correctional supervision. This went unnoticed by outsiders until the early 1960s.

Federal Government Concern and Involvement

The earliest federal interest in delinquency was demonstrated by the 1909 White House Conference on Youth. Golden (1997, pp. 120–121) notes:

> Following the 1909 White House Conference on Dependent Children, in which family preservationists won the debate with the children's rights defenders of the charitable private agencies, the foster care population, ironically, increased. Child welfare's policies supported family preservation, but the practice of child removal advanced by the charity workers continued—to the present day.

A direct result of the White House Conference on Youth was the establishment of the U.S. Children's Bureau in 1912.

In addition, in 1912 Congress passed the first child labor laws.

Early Efforts at Diversion: The Chicago Boy's Court

Diversion is the official halting of formal juvenile proceedings against a youthful offender and, instead, treating or caring for the youth outside the formal juvenile justice system. In 1914 diversion from juvenile court began in the Chicago Boy's Court, an extralegal form of probation to process and treat young offenders without labeling them as criminals.

The Boy's Court version of diversion used four community service agencies: the Holy Name Society (a Catholic church agency), the Chicago Church Foundation (predominantly Protestant), the Jewish Social Service Bureau and the Colored Big Brothers. The court released juveniles to the supervision and authority of these agencies. After a sufficient time to evaluate each youth's behavior, the agencies reported back to the court. The court took the evaluation and, if satisfactory, the judge officially discharged the individual. No record was made.

Highlights of Progressive Era Reform

Policy makers and practitioners differed over the most effective treatment for unacceptable behavior and over who should be responsible for organizing and regulating juvenile justice. Clearly, someone or some agency should be responsible, but at what governmental level—local, state or federal? Specialized rules of juvenile procedure were being set forth by a growing number of judicial bodies.

Philosophies
Adolescence was accepted as a unique period of biological and emotional transition from child to adult that required careful control and guidance. Misbehavior by middle-class youths was to be expected and controlled by concerned families, but lower-class youths were to be reformed via public efforts.

Treatment
Children were primarily treated by public efforts guided by new public policies and research.

Policies
State juvenile courts were created to adjudicate youths separately from adults, thereby expanding the *parens patriae* precedent. The federal government began providing direction for youth services by sponsoring conferences, stimulating discussions, passing child-labor legislation and creating the Children's Bureau as the first national child-welfare agency.

The New Deal Era

The aftermath of World War I, the Great Depression and World War II occupied much of the government's attention during the period from 1920 to 1960 as it sought to help citizens cope with the pressures of the times. However, by 1925 all but two states had juvenile court systems, and the U.S. Children's Bureau and the National Probation Association issued a recommendation for *A Standard Juvenile Court Act* in 1925.

In 1937 a group of concerned juvenile court judges founded the National Council of Juvenile and Family Court Judges. According to Schwartz

(p. 91): "One of the most significant sources of power and influence over the lives of children and the formulation of youth policy in practically every community is the juvenile court." He notes that over the years, the National Council of Juvenile and Family Court Judges has "established itself as an influential and respected organization." He also suggests, however: "In recent years the council's reputation has slipped . . . because the council has become dependent upon and corrupted by the availability of federal funds and has lost sight of its mission." Originally, however, its efforts were focused on the best interests of children, as was passage of the Social Security Act in 1935.

Passage of the Social Security Act in 1935 was the beginning of major federal funding for programs to aid children and families.

The National Youth Administration provided work relief and employment for young people ages 16 to 25 years. Then, in 1936, the Children's Bureau began administering the first federal subsidy program, providing child welfare grants to states for the care of dependent, neglected, exploited, abused and delinquent youths.

The federal government passed the Juvenile Court Act in 1938, adopting many features of the original Illinois act. Within 10 years every state had enacted special laws for handling juveniles. Schmalleger (1993, p. 514) contends that the juvenile court movement was based upon five identifiable philosophical principles:

1. The belief that the state is the "higher or ultimate parent" of all the children within its borders.

2. The belief that children are worth saving, and the concomitant belief in the worth of nonpunitive procedures designed to save the child.

3. The belief that children should be nurtured. While the nurturing process is underway, they should be protected from the stigmatizing impact of formal adjudicatory procedures.

4. The belief that justice, to accomplish the goal of reformation, needs to be individualized.

5. The belief that noncriminal procedures give primary consideration to the needs of the child. The denial of due process could be justified in the face of constitutional challenges because the court acted not to punish, but to help.

In the 1940s a number of conferences on children and youths were held, but most of the energy for public support and public programs was directed toward the war and reconstructing families after the war. In 1951 Congress passed the Federal Youth Corrections Act and created a Juvenile Delinquency Bureau (JDB) in the Department of Health, Education and Welfare. The positioning of the JDB within the Department of Health, Education and Welfare reflects the prevalence of the medical model at this time as well as the emphasis on prevention.

The Youth Counsel Bureau

In the early 1950s, developments in youth diversionary programs included New York City's Youth Counsel Bureau. This bureau was established to handle delinquents who were not deemed sufficiently advanced in their misbehavior to be directed to court and adjudicated. Referrals were made directly to the bureau from police, parents, schools, courts and other agencies. The bureau provided a counseling service and discharged those whose adjustments appeared promising. There was no record labeling the youths delinquent.

Highlights of New Deal Era Reform

During this period the juvenile court was perceived to be a means for attaining certain social ends. However, a growing belief developed that the juvenile system carried its own stigma that was harmful to juveniles under its jurisdiction. That stigma was applied by procedures that denied due process of law.

By the late 1940s, the gap between the theoretical assistance given to youths in the juvenile court system and the actual punitive practices had become obvious. Legal challenges to the system's informality and lack of safeguards were brought. Many critics asserted that the courts applied legal sanctions and procedures capriciously.

Philosophies

Controlling and improving societal rather than individual conditions might decrease the incidence of youthful crime. Children were to be gently led back to conformity, not harshly punished.

Treatment

Children were handled primarily by juvenile courts.

Policies

The juvenile court system was adopted by every state. The federal government broadened its role with youths by passing legislation to improve conditions for families and youths during the Depression, creating federal juvenile legislation and supporting the protection of children's basic constitutional rights.

The Great Society Era and Civil Liberties Concerns

The next 20 years in the United States saw radical changes occurring in society as well as in the juvenile justice system, particularly the juvenile courts.

The 1960s

In 1960 the United States attorney general reported that delinquency and crime were costing the American public more than $20 million per year. In addition, the poor, lower-class delinquents were now joined by youths with middle- and upper-class backgrounds and rural youths.

In the 1960s the American family underwent significant changes that directly affected social work and its liaison between the juvenile, the family and the court. Divorces increased, with the result that more children lived in one-parent households. Births to unmarried women increased, and more women started to enter the labor force. This affected the family structure and prompted a reorganization of social work philosophy and service.

During the 1960s Martin Luther King, Jr. led many civil rights marches like this one in Albany, GA. Civil rights of juveniles also came to the forefront during the 1960s with several landmark decisions involving youths' rights in judicial proceedings.

A significant program, Mobilization for Youth, developed in New York City in 1962 based on the theoretical perspective of Richard Cloward and Lloyd Ohlin. These sociologists believed that delinquency resulted from the disparity low-income youths perceived between their aspirations and the social, economic and political opportunities available to achieve them. The Mobilization for Youth project encompassed five areas: work training, education, group work and community organizations, services to individuals and families, and training and personnel (Krisberg and Austin, p. 43).

President Lyndon Johnson's Great Society initiative of the 1960s, known for its "War on Poverty," advanced causes for families and children, providing federal monies to attack poverty, crime and delinquency. Further, the 1960s saw racial tensions at an all-time high with leaders such as Malcolm X and groups such as the Black Muslims and the Black Panthers demanding "power to the people." As noted by Krisberg and Austin (p. 44): "The riots of the mid-1960s dramatized the growing gap between people of color in the United States and their more affluent 'benefactors.'"

Civil rights efforts during the 1960s helped broaden concerns for all children, especially those coming under the jurisdiction of juvenile courts. Rieffel (p. 3) suggests: "Juvenile law, perhaps more than any other aspect of law, reflects the stumbling and confused nature of our society as its values and goals evolve. So it was in the 1960s, when American society put itself through an extraordinary period of self-examination, that a great many problems were identified in the way we handle juvenile crime."

To deal with problems identified within the juvenile justice system, two policies were established—decriminalization and due process.

The American Bar Association supports decriminalizing status offenses such as smoking cigarettes.

Decriminalization

Decriminalization refers to legislation that makes status offenses, such as smoking and violating curfew, noncriminal acts. In 1961 California was the first state to separate status offenses from the delinquent category.

New York followed California. In 1962 the revised New York Family Court Act created a new classification for noncriminal misconduct—**PINS,** Person in Need of Supervision. Other states followed suit, adopting such labels as CINS, CHINS (Children in Need of Supervision), MINS (Minors in Need of Supervision), JINS (Juveniles in Need of Supervision) and FINS (Families in Need of Supervision). These new labels were intended to reduce the stigma of being labeled a delinquent. A broad range of status offenses were decriminalized.

Due Process

Legal challenges to the notion that the juvenile justice system—and the juvenile court in particular—truly was a benign parent, went as far as the U.S. Supreme Court in the 1960s. Society began to demand that children brought before the juvenile court for matters that exposed them to the equivalent of criminal sanctions receive **due process** protection. The due process clause of the U.S. Constitution requires that no person be deprived of life, liberty or property without due process of law. The Supreme Court began protecting juveniles from the court's paternalism. Due process became a clear concern in *Kent v. United States* (1966).

The Kent *Decision*

Morris Kent, a 16-year-old with a police record, was arrested and charged with housebreaking, robbery and rape. Kent admitted the charges and was held at a juvenile detention facility for almost a week. The judge then transferred jurisdiction of the case to an adult criminal court. Kent received no hearing of any kind.

The procedural requirements for waiver to criminal court were articulated by the Supreme Court in *Kent v. United States.*

In reviewing the case, the Supreme Court decreed: "As a condition to a valid waiver order, petitioner [Kent] was entitled to a hearing, including access by his counsel to the social records and probation or similar reports which are presumably considered by the court, and to a statement of the reasons for Juvenile Court's decision."

An appendix to the *Kent* decision contained the following criteria established by the Supreme Court for states to use in deciding whether to transfer juveniles to adult criminal court for trial. The juvenile court was to consider:

- The seriousness of the alleged offense and whether the protection of the community requires waiver.
- Whether the alleged offense was committed in an aggressive, violent, premeditated or willful manner.
- Whether the alleged offense was against persons or against property, greater weight being given to offenses against persons, especially if personal injury resulted.
- The prospective merit of the complaint.
- The desirability of trial and disposition of the offense in one court when the juvenile's associates in the alleged offense are adults who will be charged with crimes in the adult court.
- The sophistication and maturity of the juvenile as determined by a consideration of his or her home, environmental situation, emotional attitude and pattern of living.
- The record and previous history of the juvenile.

The *Kent* decision was a warning to the juvenile justice system that the juvenile court's traditional lack of concern for procedural and evidentiary standards would no longer be tolerated.

The Gault *Decision*

The juvenile court process became a national issue in *In re Gault* (1967). Schwartz (p. 99) suggests: "The *Gault* decision is, by far, the single most important event in the history of juvenile justice." This case was instrumental in changing the adjudication process almost completely into a deliberately adversarial process. *In re Gault* concerned a 15-year-old Arizona boy already on probation who was taken into custody at 10:00 A.M. for allegedly making obscene phone calls to a neighbor. No steps were taken to notify his parents. When Mrs. Gault arrived home about 6:00 P.M., she found her son missing. She went to the detention home and was told why he was there and that a hearing would be held the next day. At the hearing, a petition was filed with the juvenile court that made general allegations of "delinquency." No particular facts were stated.

The hearing was held June 9 in the judge's chambers. The complaining neighbor was not present, no one was sworn in, no attorney was present and no record of the proceedings was made. Gault admitted to making part of the phone call in question. At the end of the hearing, the judge said he would consider the matter.

Gault was held in the detention home for two more days and then released. Another hearing was held on his delinquency on June 15. This hearing also had no complaining witnesses, sworn testimony, counsel or transcript. The probation officer's referral report listed the charge as lewd phone calls and was filed with the court. The report was not made available to Gault or his parents. At the end of the hearing the judge committed him to the state industrial school until age 21. Gault received a six-year sentence for an action for which an adult would have received a fine or a two-month imprisonment. The U. S. Supreme Court overruled Gault's conviction on the grounds that he was deprived of his due process rights.

The *Gault* decision requires that the due process clause of the Fourteenth Amendment apply to proceedings in state juvenile courts, including the right of notice, the right to counsel, the right against self-incrimination and the right to confront witnesses.

In delivering the Court's opinion, Justice Fortas stated:

> Where a person, infant or adult, can be seized by the State, charged and convicted for violating a state criminal law, and then ordered by the State to be confined for six years, I think the Constitution requires that he be tried in accordance with the guarantees of all provisions of the Bill of Rights made applicable to the States by the Fourteenth Amendment. Undoubtedly this would be true of an adult defendant, and it would be a plain denial of equal protection of the laws—an invidious discrimination—to hold that others subject to heavier punishments could, because they are children, be denied these same constitutional safeguards. I consequently agree with the Court that the Arizona law as applied here denied to the parents and their son the right of notice, right to counsel, right against self-incrimination, and right to confront the witnesses against young Gault. Appellants are entitled to these rights, not because "fairness, impartiality and orderliness—in short the essentials of due process"—require them and not because they are "the procedural rules which have been fashioned from the generality of due process," but because they are specifically and unequivocally granted by provisions of the Fifth and Sixth Amendments which the Fourteenth Amendment makes applicable to the States.

Thus, the *Gault* decision provided the standard of due process for juveniles.

*The President's
Commission and
Youth Service Bureaus*

The President's Commission on Law Enforcement and Administration of Justice, in 1967, gave evidence of "disenchantment, with the experience of the juvenile court" (President's Commission, 1967, p. 17). It criticized lack of due process, law enforcement's poor relationship to youths and the handling of juveniles and the corrections process of confining status offenders and children "in need" to locked facilities.

According to the President's Commission (p. 69): "Institutions tend to isolate offenders from society, both physically and psychologically, cutting them off from schools, jobs, families, and other supportive influences and increasing the probability that the label of criminal will be indelibly impressed upon them." The commission, therefore, recommended that community-based corrections should be considered seriously for juvenile offenders.

Isolating offenders from their normal social environment may encourage the development of a delinquent orientation and, thus, further delinquent behavior.

The issues raised by the President's Commission indicated a need to integrate rather than isolate offenders. The resulting community-based correctional programs, such as probation, foster care and group homes, represented attempts to respond to these issues by normalizing social contacts, reducing the stigma attached to being institutionalized and providing opportunities for jobs and schooling.

The President's Commission also strongly endorsed diversion for status offenders and minor delinquent offenses. In addition, the commission recommended establishing a national youth service bureau and local or community youth service bureaus to assist the police and the courts in diverting youths from the juvenile justice system. In 1967 the President's Commission established a federal Youth Service Bureau to coordinate community-centered referral programs.

Local youth service bureaus were to divert minor offenders whose behavior was rooted in problems at home, in school or in the community. While a broad range of services and certain mandatory functions were suggested for youth service bureaus, individually tailored work with troublemaking youngsters was a primary goal.

As envisioned by the commission, youth service bureaus were not part of the juvenile justice system. The bureaus would provide necessary services to youths as a substitute for putting them through the juvenile justice process, thus avoiding the stigma of formal court involvement. The three main functions of local youth service bureaus were diversion, resource development and system modification.

Diversion included accepting referrals from the police, the courts, schools, parents and other sources, and working with the youths in a voluntary, noncoercive manner through neighborhood-oriented services. *Resource development* included offering leadership at the neighborhood level to provide and develop a variety of youth assistance programs, as well as seeking funding for new projects. *System modification* included seeking to change attitudes and practices that discriminate against troublesome youths and, thereby, contribute to their antisocial behavior. To meet the unique needs of each community, the organization and programming of local youth service bureaus were to remain flexible.

Many youth service bureaus did not survive the federal funding cuts during the Carter and Reagan administrations. Those bureaus that have endured have turned their focus to providing employment activities for employable juveniles, particularly during the summer. They have also concentrated on providing health, recreation or educational referrals or services.

The Task Force on Juvenile Delinquency and Youth Crime of the President's Commission on Law Enforcement and Administration of Justice (1967) advocated *prevention* as the most promising and important method of dealing with crime.

The Uniform Juvenile Court Act

In 1968 the historic Delinquency Prevention and Control Act was passed. One provision of this act was to reform the juvenile justice system nationally. Although titled a "court" act, the legislation included provisions that affected law enforcement and corrections, illustrating the interconnectedness of the parts of the system.

The Uniform Juvenile Court Act provided for the care, protection and development of youths, without the stigma of a criminal label, by a program of treatment, training and rehabilitation, in a family environment when possible. It also provided simple judicial and interstate procedures.

The act included the following definitions:

- A **child** is "an individual who is under the age of 18 years or under the age of 21 years who committed an act of delinquency before reaching the age of 18 years."

- A **delinquent act** is "an act designated a crime under the law." It includes local ordinances, but does not include traffic offenses.

- A **delinquent child** is "a child who has committed a delinquent act and is in need of treatment or rehabilitation."

- A **deprived child** is one who "is without proper parental care or control, subsistence, education as required by law, or other care or control necessary for his physical, mental, or emotional health, or morals, and the deprivation is not due primarily to the lack of financial means of his parents, guardian, or other custodian; or who has been placed for care or adoption in violation of the law; or who has been abandoned by his parents, guardian, or other custodian; or is without a parent, guardian, or legal custodian."

- A **custodian** is "a person, other than a parent or legal guardian, who stands *in loco parentis* to the child or a person to whom legal custody of the child has been given by order of a court."

The act described probation services, referees, venue and transfer, custody and detention, petitions and summons, hearings, children's rights, disposition, court files and records, and procedures for fingerprinting and photographing children. These areas are described in detail in the chapters dealing with law enforcement and the courts.

*Highlights of Great
Society Era Reform*

The combination of serious, stigmatizing results achieved without due process safeguards led the U.S. Supreme Court in the 1960s to impose new requirements in determining when a juvenile could be made a ward of the state.

Since its inception, the juvenile court was guided by a welfare concept. When the U.S. Supreme Court took issue with its procedures, the juvenile court environment moved from a simple family atmosphere to a more adversarial system. The treatment of juveniles changed to a criminal approach, dispensing punishment and placing youths in locked facilities.

Philosophies

Dissent arose among professional child-welfare workers and policymakers about the causes of and treatment for juvenile delinquency. Consensus arose among the public and policymakers that the traditional agents of control—family, police, schools and courts—could not curb the rise of delinquency.

Treatment

The juvenile court system was revised to include due process, deinstitutionalization, decriminalization and diversion programs. Community-based therapy, rather than institutionalization, became the preferred method of treatment.

Policies

The federal executive branch expressed its concern about crime and delinquency by appointing the President's Commission on Law Enforcement and Administration of Justice. Large-scale federal financial and programmatic grants-in-aid were made available to states and localities for delinquency prevention and control programs.

While the Supreme Court questioned the juvenile court on due process procedures, the juvenile court also came under severe criticism because its philosophy of helping all juveniles rather than punishing delinquents led to an indiscriminate mixing together of neglected or abused children, status offenders and violent offenders. Public policy has since been developed to separate neglected and abused juveniles from the delinquents, but status offenders have continued to be in contact with violent criminal delinquents.

The 1970s

The 1970s brought further challenges to the juvenile justice system. A growing body of empirical evidence cast serious doubt upon the ability of social casework, the linchpin of correctional treatment along with probation and parole, to help rehabilitate youths (Hellum, 1979).

Rehabilitation was the major premise on which the juvenile justice system rested. Research found that correctional "treatment," especially in institutions, was often unnecessarily punitive and sometimes sadistic. The modern reformers became appalled that noncriminal youths and status offenders could easily find their way into the same institutions as seriously delinquent youths. This spawned a rapid growth in community-based alternatives to institutionalization, or **deinstitutionalization,** as well as national interest in juvenile justice.

The White House Conference on Youth

National interest in youth problems was again expressed in 1970 at the White House Conference on Youth. This conference warned: "Our families and children are in deep trouble. A society that neglects its children and fears its youth cannot care about its future" (*The White House Conference on Youth,* 1972, p. 346). The message from the conference was interpreted as a need for special federal assistance to identify the needs of families.

> The major impact of the 1970 White House Conference on Youth was that it hit hard at the foundation of our system for handling youths, including unnecessarily punitive institutions.

Beginning in 1971 a series of federal cases tried to specify minimum environmental conditions for juvenile institutions. By 1972 there was a cooperative effort among federal administrations to focus on programs for *preventing* delinquency and rehabilitating delinquents outside the traditional criminal justice system.

The Office of Juvenile Justice and Delinquency Prevention and the Juvenile Justice and Delinquency Prevention Act

In 1974 Congress created the Office of Juvenile Justice and Delinquency Prevention (OJJDP) and placed it in the Department of Justice. Congress also passed the Juvenile Justice and Delinquency Prevention (JJDP) Act, by a vote of 329 to 20 in the House and with only one dissenting vote in the Senate. It was signed by a reluctant President Gerald R. Ford. According to Schwartz (p. 124): "The Juvenile Justice and Delinquency Prevention Act of 1974 is the most important piece of federal juvenile justice legislation ever enacted." The intent of the act was "to provide a unified rational program to deal with juvenile delinquency prevention and control within the context of the total law."

The landmark JJDP Act required that in order for states to receive federal funds, incarceration and even temporary detention should be used for young people only as a last resort.

> The Juvenile Justice and Delinquency Prevention Act of 1974 had two key goals: deinstitutionalization of status offenders and separation/removal of juveniles from adult facilities.

The act made funds available to states that removed status offenders from prisons and jails and created alternative voluntary services to which status offenders could be diverted. The act was amended in 1976, 1977 and 1980. According to Decker (1984, pp. 37–38), amendments to the JJDP Act in 1977:

- Boadened the functions of State Planning Agency Advisory groups to include the private business sector.
- Involved alternate youth programs and people with special experience in school violence and vandalism programs, including social workers.
- Gave states the opportunity to participate in grant programs for deinstitutionalization.
- Required monitoring of all states with state juvenile detention and correctional facilities to determine their suitability for status offenders.

The 1980 amendment called for the removal of juveniles from adult jails. Clearly, deinstitutionalization was one of the Four Ds described by sociologist LaMar Empey (1978) as characterizing the second transformation of the juvenile justice system, the first transformation having begun with the 1899 Illinois Juvenile Court Act.

The Four Ds of Juvenile Justice

The "Four Ds" of juvenile justice are deinstitutionalization, diversion, due process and decriminalization.

Deinstitutionalization

Deinstitutionalization refers to providing programs for juveniles in a community-based setting rather than in an institution. Deinstitutionalization of status offenders (DSO) was especially recommended on the theoretical basis that labeling a youth as delinquent could become self-fulfilling. This is discussed in chapter 2.

In the early 1970s, Massachusetts undertook what some considered a "radical" experiment in deinstitutionalization. Jerome Miller, state commissioner of youth services and head of the Massachusetts Department of Youth Services, closed every juvenile institution in the state. As noted by Schmalleger (p. 535):

> Deinstitutionalization was accomplished by placing juveniles in foster care, group homes, mental health facilities, and other programs. Many were simply sent home. The problems caused by hard-core offenders among the released juveniles, however, soon convinced authorities that complete deinstitutionalization was not a workable solution to the problem of delinquency. The Massachusetts experiment ended as quickly as it began.

Although total deinstitutionalization ended in Massachusetts, hundreds of juveniles were successfully moved into community-based programs. The successes of this experiment in deinstitutionalization, as well as the availability of federal funds for such programs, were encouraging to those who wanted to reform the juvenile justice system.

Diversion

The juvenile due process requirements from *Kent* and *Gault,* combined with the rising costs of courts and correctional facilities, resulted in wider use of community-based alternatives to treat youths before and after adjudication. The trend was to make greater use of diversion programs in the 1970s. Young offenders were placed in remedial education, drug abuse programs, foster homes and out-patient health care and counseling facilities.

The justifications for diversion lay with labeling theory and differential association theory. Many studies have focused on the problems produced by labeling and the stigma that comes from a youth's involvement with the juvenile justice system.

Net Widening Diversion does not necessarily mean less state social control over juveniles. It has had the negative effect of transferring state power from juvenile courts to police and probation departments. Many youngsters who earlier would have been simply released were instead referred to the new diversionary programs. This phenomenon was called **net widening,** and it was the opposite of diversion's original purpose, which was to lessen the states' power to exercise control over juveniles.

Critics of Diversion Although diversion programs have greatly expanded during the past decade, the number of young people committed to institutions has not decreased appreciably. Instead of weakening state control, the correctional structure has become stronger.

The diversion apparatus has in many cases become a prevention apparatus, receiving the bulk of its referrals from parents, schools and welfare agencies, as opposed to the police, intake or the courts. The referrals are, by and large, younger juveniles with minor offenses and without prior records, girls and status offenders.

Not only does diversion widen the net, it also increases the risk of violating rights of due process and fundamental fairness because referrals usually occur *before* adjudication. Thus, it is often never established that referred youngsters are actually guilty of any offense that might make them properly the subjects of conditional placement.

For nearly 20 years, juvenile diversion and its labeling-theory orientation have received attention. The philosophical, legal, theoretical and practical strengths and weaknesses of diversion have been debated. Little research has been done to examine the effectiveness of limiting official intervention in the lives of diverted and nondiverted youths. However, one fact exists: diverted youths tend to remain in the justice system longer than nondiverted youths.

Because diversion is personalized, treatment may be inconsistent from one youth to the next. Diversion is also problematic because it may reflect individual class or social prejudices. It removes juveniles from any penalties with no exposure to the judicial process of the juvenile court. Further, informal diversion is usually unsystematic.

Due Process

As in the 1960s, the 1970s saw juveniles' rights being addressed and the juvenile court becoming more like the adult court in several important ways. The juvenile rights addressed were the standard of proof, right to jury trial and double jeopardy. Whether dealing with status offenders, youths who had committed violent crimes or protecting abused or neglected children, the court no longer had free reign.

The Standard of Proof in Juvenile Proceedings In re Winship (1970) concerned a 12-year-old New York boy charged with having taken $112 from a woman's purse. He was adjudicated a delinquent based on a *preponderance of the evidence* submitted at the juvenile hearing. He was committed to a training school for 18 months, with extension possible until he was 18-years old, a total possible sentence of six years. The question raised was whether New York's statute allowing juvenile cases to be decided on the basis of a preponderance of evidence was constitutional.

Gault had already established that due process required fair treatment for juveniles. The Court held that: "The Due Process Clause protects the accused against conviction except upon *proof beyond a reasonable doubt* of every fact necessary to constitute the crime with which he is charged" (italics in original). New York argued that its juvenile proceedings were civil, not criminal; but the Supreme Court said the standard of proof beyond a reasonable doubt not only played a vital role in the criminal justice system, it also ensured a greater degree of safety for the presumption of innocence of those accused of crimes.

In re Winship established proof beyond a reasonable doubt as the standard for juvenile adjudication proceedings, eliminating lesser standards such as a preponderance of the evidence, clear and convincing proof and reasonable proof.

The Right to a Jury Trial   The move toward expanding juveniles' civil rights was slowed by the ruling in *McKeiver v. Pennsylvania* (1971), in which the Court ruled that juveniles do not have the right to a jury trial. This case involved a 16-year-old Pennsylvania boy charged with robbery, larceny and receiving stolen goods, all felonies in Pennsylvania. He was adjudicated a delinquent. The question for the Court to decide was whether the due process clause of the Fourteenth Amendment guaranteeing the right to a jury trial applied to the adjudication of a juvenile court case.

In *McKeiver* the Court held that *Gault* and *Winship* demonstrated concern for the fundamental principle of fairness in justice, with the fact-finding elements of due process necessary and present for this fairness. The Court emphasized in *McKeiver*: "One cannot say that in our legal system the jury is a necessary component of accurate fact finding. There is much to be said for it, to be sure, but we have been content to pursue other ways for determining facts."

McKeiver established that a jury trial is not a required part of due process in the adjudication of a youth as a delinquent by a juvenile court.

The Court realized that juvenile courts had not been successful, but it also concluded that juvenile court should not become fully adversarial like the criminal court. Requiring a jury might put an end to "what has been the idealistic prospect of an intimate informal protective proceeding." Requiring jury trials for juvenile courts could also result in delays, as well as in the possibility of public trials.

Double Jeopardy   **Double jeopardy** was the issue in *Breed v. Jones* (1975). The Supreme Court ruled that defendants may not be tried twice for the same offense. Breed was 17 when apprehended for committing acts with a deadly weapon. He was adjudicated in a California juvenile court, which found the allegation true. A dispositional hearing determined there were not sufficient facilities "amenable to the care, treatment and training programs available through the facilities of the juvenile court," as required by the statute. Breed was transferred to the criminal court where he was again found guilty. Breed argued that he had been tried twice for the same offense, constituting double jeopardy. The Supreme Court agreed and reversed the conviction.

A juvenile cannot be adjudicated in juvenile court and then tried for the same offense in an adult criminal court (*Breed v. Jones,* 1975).

Beginning in 1976 the majority of states enacted legislation that made it easier to transfer youths to adult courts.

Decriminalization

In 1977 the American Bar Association (ABA) Joint Commission on Juvenile Justice Standards voted for the elimination of uniquely juvenile offenses, that is, status offenses, such as cigarette smoking or consuming alcohol.

According to the American Bar Association, juvenile delinquency liability should include only such conduct as would be designated a crime if committed by an adult.

The referral of status offenses to juvenile court has been viewed by many as a waste of court resources. These critics believe that court resources are best used for serious recidivist delinquents.

The Issue of Right to Treatment Also in the 1970s, two conflicting types of cases emerged: one type tried to establish a "right to treatment," the other to establish the "least restrictive alternative." *Martarella v. Kelley* (1972) established that if juveniles who are judged to be "in need of supervision" are not provided with adequate treatment, they are deprived of their rights under the Eighth and Fourteenth Amendments. *Morales v. Turman* (1973) ruled that juveniles in a Texas training school have a statutory right to treatment. And, in *Nelson v. Heyne* (1974), the Seventh U.S. Court of Appeals also confirmed juveniles' right to treatment:

> When a state assumes the place of a juvenile's parents, it assumes as well the parental duties, and its treatment of its juveniles should, so far as can be reasonably required, be what proper parental care would provide. . . . Without a program of individual treatment, the result may be that the juvenile will not be rehabilitated, but warehoused.

The U.S. Supreme Court has not yet declared that juveniles have a right to treatment.

Development of Standards for Juvenile Justice In 1977 a tentative draft of the Institute of Judicial Administration/American Bar Association *Juvenile Justice Standards* was published in 23 volumes. In 1978 the state of Washington began extensive legislative revision of its juvenile justice system based, in part, on these standards. It was found that following implementation of the new legislation (Rieffel, pp. 36–37, italics in original):

- Sentences were considerably more uniform, more consistent and more proportionate to the seriousness of the offense and the prior criminal record of the youth.
- While the overall level of severity of sanctions was reduced during the first two years, there was an increase in the certainty that a sanction of some kind would be imposed.
- There was a marked increase in the use of incarcerative sanctions for the violent and serious/chronic offender, but nonviolent offenders and chronic minor property offenders were less likely to be incarcerated and more apt to be required to pay restitution, do community service, or be on probation.
- Compliance with the sentencing guidelines was extremely high; nevertheless, differential handling of minorities and females still existed.
- There was a better record of holding juveniles accountable for their offenses.
- While the new legislation completely eliminated the referral of *status offenses,* it did not eliminate the referral of *status offenders.* Runaways were more likely to be contacted for delinquent acts, for example.

From 1979 to 1980, 20 volumes of these standards received American Bar Association approval. The standards related to the following: adjudication; appeals and collateral review; architecture of facilities; corrections administration; counsel for private parties; court organization and administration; dispositional procedures; dispositions; interim status; the release, control and detention of accused juvenile offenders between arrest and disposition; juvenile delinquency and sanctions; juvenile probation function; intake and predisposition investigative services; juvenile records and information systems; monitoring; planning for juvenile justice; police handling of juvenile problems; pretrial court proceedings; prosecution; rights of minors; transfer between courts; and youth service agencies. A summary and analysis of the project and the standards was released in 1990, reviewing the progress of the application of the standards (Flicker).

In the 1970s the rising fear of youth crime and rebelliousness coincided with a growing disillusionment with the effectiveness of the juvenile justice system. The result was a much harsher attitude toward youth crime and a call to "get tough" with youthful lawbreakers in the 1980s and 1990s. At the same time, the medical model of viewing unlawful behavior began to shift to what is often called a **justice model.** The issues involved and how they are viewed in each model are summarized in Table 1.1.

Table 1.1 **Comparison of the Medical and Justice Models**	Issue	Medical Model 1930–1974	Justice Model 1974–Present
	Cause of crime	Disease of society or of the individual.	Form of rational adaptation to societal conditions.
	Image of offender	Sick; product of socioeconomic or psychological forces beyond control.	Capable of exercising free will; of surviving without resorting to crime.
	Object of correction	To cure offender and society; to return both to health; rehabilitation.	Humanely control offender under terms of sentence; offer voluntary treatment.
	Agency/institution responsibility	Change offender; reintegrate back into society.	Legally and humanely control offender; adequate care and custody; voluntary treatment; protect society.
	Role of treatment and punishment	Voluntary or involuntary treatment as means to change offender. Treatment is mandatory; punishment used to coerce treatment; punishment and treatment [are] viewed as same thing.	Voluntary treatment only; punishment and treatment not the same thing. Punishment is for society's good, treatment is for offender's good.
	Object of legal sanctions (sentence)	Determine conditions that are most conducive to rehabilitation of offender.	Determine conditions that are just re: wrong done, best protect society and deter offender from future crime.
	Type of sentence	Indeterminate, flexible; adjust to offender changes.	Fixed sentence (less good time).
	Who determines release time?	"Experts" (parole board for adults, institutional staff for juveniles).	Conditions of sentence as interpreted by Presumptive Release Date (PRD) formula.

Source: D. F. Pace, *Community Relations Concepts,* 3rd ed. Copyright © 1993, p. 127. Placerville, CA: Copperhouse. Reprinted by permission.

The 1980s

According to Schwartz (pp. 83–84), the Carter administration was deeply committed to removing juveniles from adult jails, and the Department of Justice recommended a 34 percent increase in fiscal year 1981–82 for the OJJDP, to be targeted at juvenile jail removal. However, when the Reagan administration took office, it significantly reduced this funding level, claiming that the goal of removing children from adult jails had been largely accomplished and that even if not, it was a state and local problem.

By the 1980s the "best interests" of society had gained ascendency over those of youths. In the 1980s the OJJDP became increasingly conservative. Emphasis shifted to dealing with hard-core, chronic offenders. Also in the 1980s, state and federal concerns tended to center on the problems created by procedural informality and the juvenile court's broad discretion. The adversary system of legal process replaced the sedate environment and process of the "family" court that was directed to consider the "best" interest of the child's health, safety and welfare. The courts returned to a focus on what was right according to the law.

According to Krisberg (1990), the conservative swing added two more "Ds" to our juvenile justice system: **deterrence** and **just deserts.** *Deterrence* involves the use of punishment to prevent future lawbreaking. It does so in several ways, the most obvious being locking offenders up so that they can do no further harm to society. Incarceration may result in further deterrence by (1) serving as a lesson to the incarcerated person that crime does not pay and (2) sending the same message to the law-abiding public.

Deserts, or *just deserts* as it is often called, is a concept of punishment as a kind of justified revenge—the offending individual gets what is coming. This is the concept of *lex talionis,* or an "eye for an eye," expressed in the Code of Hammurabi centuries ago.

In 1982, 214 long-term public institutions in the United States were designated either "strict" or "medium" custody training schools. This number included some original training schools, as well as smaller, high-security institutions built to either replace or augment them.

Most schools involved agricultural training, which was thought to be reformative. This training focus required the schools to be located in rural areas. An unanticipated effect of this location policy was to remove the corrections problem from community awareness.

Shall v. Martin *and Preventive Detention*

On December 13, 1977, at 11:30 P.M., Gregory Martin was arrested on charges of robbery, assault and criminal possession of a weapon. Because of the late hour and because he lied about his address, Martin was kept in detention overnight. The next day he was brought before the family court accompanied by his grandmother. The family court judge noted that he had lied to the police about his address, that he was in possession of a loaded weapon and that he appeared to lack supervision at night. In view of these circumstances, the judge ordered Martin detained until trial. New York law authorized such pretrial or **preventive detention** of accused juvenile delinquents if "there is a substantial probability that they will not appear in court on the return date or there is a serious risk that they may before the return date commit an act which if committed by an adult would constitute a crime."

While Martin was in preventive detention, his attorneys filed a habeas corpus petition demanding his release. The petition charged that his detention denied him due process rights under the Fifth and Fourteenth Amendments. The suit was a class action suit on behalf of all youths being held in preventive detention in New York. The New York appellate courts upheld Martin's claim, stating that most delinquents are released or placed on probation; therefore, it was unfair to confine them before trial. Indeed, later at trial, Martin was adjudicated a delinquent and sentenced to two years' probation.

The prosecution appealed the decision disallowing pretrial detention to the Supreme Court for final judgment. The Supreme Court reversed the decision, establishing the right of juvenile court judges to deny youths pretrial release if they perceived them to be dangerous.

In *Schall v. Martin* (1984) the Supreme Court upheld the state's right to place juveniles in preventive detention, fulfilling a legitimate state interest of protecting society and juveniles by detaining those who might be dangerous to society or to themselves.

Pretrial detention need not be considered punishment merely because the juvenile is eventually released or put on probation. In *Schall* the Court reiterated its belief in the fundamental fairness doctrine and the doctrine of *parens patriae,* trying to strike a balance between the juvenile's right to freedom pending trial and the right of society to be protected. All 50 states have similar language allowing preventive detention in their juvenile codes.

Schall also established a due process standard for detention hearings. This standard included procedural safeguards, such as a notice, a hearing and a statement of facts given to juveniles before they are placed in detention.

The Court further stated that detention based on prediction of future behavior did not violate due process. Many decisions made in the justice system, such as the decision to sentence or grant parole, are based partly on predicting future behavior. These decisions have all been accepted by the Court as legitimate exercises of state power.

Some Effects of Preventive Detention

The effects of preventive detention can be tragic. A 15-year-old California girl arrested for assaulting a police officer hanged herself after four days of isolation in a local jail. A 17-year-old boy was taken into custody and detained for owing $73 in unpaid traffic tickets, only to be tortured and beaten to death by his cellmates. In a West Virginia jail a truant was murdered by an adult inmate; in an Ohio jail a teenage girl was raped by a guard. A 15-year-old boy hanged himself in a Kentucky jail where he had been held for only 30 minutes. His offense: arguing with his mother.

The Evolution of Child, Parent and State Relationships

Developments with the evolving juvenile justice system in the United States had a direct effect on the relationships between children and their parents, children and the state and parents and the state. The National Juvenile Justice System Assessment Center has summarized the major developments and influences on these relationships in Table 1.2.

The developments described and neatly categorized in the table are actually fluid, overlapping and ongoing.

Still Evolving

The juvenile justice system continues to evolve. As Krisberg (p. 157) observes: "Although the conservative revolution in juvenile justice was motivated by the concepts of deterrence and deserts, the emergence of a 'get tough' philosophy also produced another 'D' in the world of juvenile justice—disarray." Which direction the system will take in the twenty-first century is unclear.

Table 1.2
Juvenile Justice Developments and Their Impact

Periods	Major Developments	Precipitating Influences	Child/State	Parent/State	Parent/Child
Puritan 1646–1824	Massachusetts Stubborn Child Law (1646)	A. Christian view of child as evil B. Economically marginal agrarian society	Law provides: A. Symbolic standard of maturity B. Support for family as economic unit	Parents considered responsible and capable of controlling child	Child considered both property and spirtual responsibility of parents
Refuge 1824–1899	Institutionalization of deviants; New York House of Refuge established (1824) for delinquent and dependent children	A. Enlightenment B. Immigration and Industrialization	Child seen as helpless, in need of state intervention	Parents supplanted as state assumes responsibility for correcting deviant socialization	Family considered to be a major cause of juvenile deviancy
Juvenile court 1899–1960	Establishment of separate legal system for juveniles–Illinois Juvenile Court Act (1899)	A. Reformism and rehabilitative ideology B. Increased immigration, urbanization, and large-scale industrialization	Juvenile court institutionalizes legal irresponsibility of child	*Parens patriae* doctrine gives legal foundation for state intervention in family	Further abrogation of parents' rights and responsibilities
Juvenile rights 1960–[1980]	Increased "legalization" of juvenile law–*Gault* decision (1966); Juvenile Justice and Delinquency Prevention Act (1974) calls for deinstitutionalization of status offenders	A. Criticism of juvenile justice system on humane grounds B. Civil rights movements by disadvantaged groups	Movement to define and protect rights as well as provide services to children	Reassertion of responsibility of parents and community for welfare and behavior of children	Attention given to children's claims against parents; earlier emancipation of children

Source: J. David Hawkins; Paul A. Pastor, Jr.; Michelle Bell; and Sheila Morrison. *Reports of the National Juvenile Justice Assessment Center: A Topology of Cause-Focused Strategies of Delinquency Prevention*. Washington, DC: U. S. Government Printing Office, 1980.

Summary

A significant influence on the development of juvenile justice was the concept of *parens patriae,* which gave the king the right and responsibility to take care of minors. The first houses of corrections in England were Bridewells that confined both children and adults who were considered to be idle and disorderly.

The American colonists brought with them much of the English criminal justice system and its ways to deal with wayward youth. During this time five distinct, yet interrelated, institutions evolved to handle poor, abused, neglected, dependent and delinquent children brought before a court: (1) indenture and apprenticeship, (2) mixed almshouses (poorhouses), (3) private orphanages, (4) public facilities for dependent children and (5) jails.

In 1825 the New York House of Refuge, the first reformatory, opened to house juvenile delinquents. By the middle of the nineteenth century many states either built reform schools or converted their houses of refuge to reform schools. The reform schools emphasized formal schooling, but they also retained large workshops and continued the contract system of labor.

The middle of the nineteenth century also included the child-saving movement. The child savers were reformers whose philosophy was that the child was basically good and was to be treated by the state as a young person with a problem. They persuaded the 1899 Illinois legislature to pass a law establishing a juvenile court that became the cornerstone for juvenile justice throughout the United States. The first juvenile courts were administrative agencies of the circuit or district courts and served a social service function with the rehabilitative ideal of reforming children rather than punishing them.

In the first quarter of the twentieth century, the progressives further developed the medical model established by the Illinois Juvenile Court Act, approaching crime as a disease that could be treated and cured by social intervention. Federal government concern and involvement also began during this period. A direct result of the White House Conference on Youth was the establishment of the U.S. Children's Bureau in 1912. Passage of the Social Security Act in 1935 was the beginning of major federal funding for programs to aid children and families.

During the 1960s the concern about the due process rights of youths in juvenile proceedings resulted in several landmark cases. The procedural requirements for waiver to criminal court were articulated by the Supreme Court in *Kent v. United States*. The *Gault* decision required that the due process clause of the Fourteenth Amendment be applied to proceedings in state juvenile courts, including the right of notice, the right to counsel, the right against self-incrimination and the right to confront witnesses.

In the 1970s the major impact of the White House Conference on Youth was that it hit hard at the foundation of our system for handling youths, including unnecessarily punitive institutions. Another major change was the assignment of the Office of Juvenile Justice and Delinquency Prevention to the Department of Justice rather than the Department of Health, Education and Welfare.

The Juvenile Justice and Delinquency Prevention (JJDP) Act of 1974 made federal delinquency prevention funds available to states that removed status offenders from prisons and jails and created alternative voluntary services to which status offenders could be diverted. This act had two key goals: deinstitutionalization of status offenders and separation/removal of juveniles from adult facilities.

The 1970s also saw juveniles' rights being addressed. *In re Winship* established proof beyond a reasonable doubt as the standard for juvenile adjudication proceedings, eliminating lesser standards such as a preponderance of the evidence, clear and convincing proof and reasonable proof. *McKeiver* established that a jury trial is not a required part of due process in the adjudication of a youth as a delinquent by a juvenile court. *Breed v. Jones* established that a juvenile cannot be adjudicated in juvenile court and then tried for the same offense in an adult criminal court (double jeopardy).

By 1977 the American Bar Association endorsed the decriminalization of status offenses, urging that juvenile delinquency liability should include only such conduct as would be designated a crime if committed by an adult.

In the 1980s in *Schall v. Martin* (1984), the Supreme Court upheld the state's right to place juveniles in preventive detention. Preventive detention was perceived as fulfilling a legitimate state interest of protecting society and juveniles by detaining those who might be dangerous to society or to themselves.

Discussion Questions

1. The juvenile justice system has been defined as "justice that applies to children and adolescents, with concern for their health, safety, and welfare under sociolegal standards and procedures." Is this definition adequate? Why or why not?
2. Under the principle of *parens patriae,* how does the state (or the court) accept the role of "parent"? Are all households administered and managed alike?
3. Who are the present "child savers"? What states, associations and individuals have contributed to the present child-saver philosophy?
4. What do you consider to be the major milestones in the evolution of juvenile justice?
5. Is it possible for one system to effectively and fairly serve both children who need correction and those who need protection?
6. How may diversion result in "widening the net" of juvenile justice processing?
7. What are the rationales on which police diversion of juveniles is based in your community and state?
8. What are the major types of police diversion programs in your area and state?
9. What evidence suggests that diversion programs are effective in reducing juvenile recidivism? What, if any, findings contradict this evidence? Do you know of a diversion program that is working or one that has failed? Why?
10. What are the advantages and disadvantages of diversion?

References

American Bar Association Joint Commission on Juvenile Justice Standards. Juvenile Justice Section. Washington, DC, n.d.

Blackstone, William. *Commentaries on the Laws of England,* Vol. 4. Oxford: Clarendon, 1776.

Breckenridge, Sophoniska P. and Abbott, Edith. *The Delinquent Child and the Home.* New York: Random House, 1912.

Decker, Scott H. *Juvenile Justice Policy.* Beverly Hills, CA.: Sage Publications, 1984.

de Scheveinitz, Karl. *England's Road to Social Security.* Philadelphia: University of Pennsylvania, 1943.

Empey, LaMar. *American Delinquency: Its Meaning and Construction.* Homewood, IL: Dorsey, 1978.

Flicker, Barbara Danziger. *Standards for Juvenile Justice: A Summary and Analysis,* 2nd ed. New York: Institute for Judicial Administration, 1990.

Golden, Renny. *Disposable Children: America's Child Welfare System.* Belmont, CA: Wadsworth Publishing Company, 1997.

Griffin, Brenda S. and Griffin, Charles T. *Juvenile Delinquency in Perspective.* New York: Harper & Row, 1978.

Grunhut, Max. *Penal Reform.* New York: Clarendon, 1948.

Hawkins, J. David; Pastor, Paul A., Jr.; Bell, Michelle; and Morrison, Sheila. *Reports of the National Juvenile Justice Assessment Center: A Topology of Cause-Focused Strategies of Delinquency Prevention.* Washington, DC: National Institute for Juvenile Justice and Delinquency Prevention, U.S. Government Printing Office, 1980.

Hellum, F. "Juvenile Justice: The Second Revolution." Crime and Delinquency 25, 1979, Vol. 3, pp. 299–317.

Hunt, G. Bowdon. Foreword. In *A Handbook for Volunteers in Juvenile Court,* by Vernon Fox. Special Issue of *Juvenile Justice.* February 1973.

Keller, Oliver J. and Alper, Benedict S. *Halfway Houses: Community-Centered Corrections and Treatment.* Lexington, MA: D.C. Heath, 1970.

Kocourek, Albert and Wigmore, John H. *Source of Ancient and Punitive Law, Evolution of Law, Selected Readings on the Origin and Development of Legal Institutions,* Vol. 1. Boston: Little, Brown, 1951.

Kramer, S. N. *The Sumerians.* Chicago: University of Chicago Press, 1963.

Krisberg, Barry. "The Evolution of the Juvenile Justice System." Appeared in *The World & I,* April 1990, pp. 487–503. Reprinted in *Criminal Justice 92/93,* 16th ed., edited by John J. Sullivan and Joseph L. Victor. Guilford, CT: Dushkin Publishing Group, Inc., 1992, pp. 152–159.

Krisberg, Barry and Austin, James F. *Reinventing Juvenile Justice.* Newbury Park, CA: Sage Publications, 1993.

Pickett, Robert. *House of Refuge: Origins of Juvenile Justice in New York State.* Syracuse, NY: Syracuse University Press, 1969.

Platt, Anthony M. *The Child Savers: The Invention of Delinquency.* Chicago: University of Chicago Press, 1968.

The President's Commission on Law Enforcement and Administration of Justice. *The Task Force Report: Juvenile Delinquency and Youth Crime.* Washington, DC: U.S. Government Printing Office, 1967.

Rendleman, Douglas R. *"Parens Patriae:* From Chancery to the Juvenile Court." In *Juvenile Justice Philosophy,* edited by Frederick L. Faust and Paul J. Branington. St. Paul, MN: West Publishing Company, 1979, pp. 58–96.

Rieffel, Alaire Bretz. *The Juvenile Justice Standards Handbook.* Washington, DC: American Bar Association, 1983.

Schmalleger, Frank. *Criminal Justice Today,* 2nd ed. Englewood Cliffs, NJ: Prentice Hall, 1993.

Schwartz, Ira M. *(In)Justice for Juveniles: Rethinking the Best Interests of the Child.* Lexington, MA: D.C. Heath and Company, 1989.

Task Force Report on Juvenile Justice and Delinquency Prevention. *Juvenile Justice and Delinquency Prevention.* Washington, DC: U.S. Government Printing Office, 1976.

Webb, Sidney and Webb, Beatrice. *English Local Government: English Poor Law History,* Part I. New York: Longmans, Green, 1927.

The White House Conference on Youth. Washington, DC: U.S. Government Printing Office, 1972.

Zietz, Dorothy. *Child Welfare: Services and Perspective.* New York: John Wiley, 1969.

Cases

Breed v. Jones, 421 U.S. 519, 533, 95 S.Ct. 1779, 1787, 44 L.Ed.2d 346 (1975).

Commonwealth v. Fisher, 213 Pa. 48, 62 A. 198, 199, 200 (1905).

Ex parte Crouse, 4 Whart. 9 (Pa. 1838).

In re Gault, 387 U.S. 1, 19–21, 26–28, 87 S.Ct. 1428, 1439–1440, 1442–1444, 18 L.Ed.2d 527 (1967).

Kent v. United States, 383 U.S. 541, 86 S.Ct. 1045, 16 L.Ed.2d 84 (1966).

Martarella v. Kelley, 349 F. Supp. 575 (S.D.N.Y. 1972).

McKeiver v. Pennsylvania, 403 U.S. 528, 547, 91 S.Ct. 1976, 1987, 29 L.Ed.2d 647 (1971).

Morales v. Turman, 364 F.Supp. 166 (E.D. Tex. 1973).

Nelson v. Heyne, 491 F.2d 352 (7th Cir. 1974).

Schall v. Martin, 467 U.S. 253, 104 S.Ct. 2403, 81 L.Ed.2d 207 (1984).

In re Winship, 397 U.S. 358, 90 S.Ct. 1068, 25 L.Ed.2d 368 (1970).

2 Crime, Delinquency and Justice: Theoretical Roots

Injustice anywhere is a threat to
justice everywhere.
—Martin Luther King, Jr. (1929–1968)

Do You Know

- What types of justice exist?
- How crimes were originally differentiated?
- What two theories exist to explain the purpose of the law?
- What function is served by punishment according to the Durkheimian perspective? the Marxist perspective?
- How the contemporary conservative and liberal approaches to juvenile justice differ?
- What two competing world views have existed over the centuries and the concepts important to each view?
- What proponents of the classical view and those of the positivist view advocate for offenders?
- What theories have been developed to explain the cause of crime and delinquency and the major premises of each?
- Whether any single theory provides a complete explanation?
- What behavior correlates highly with delinquency?
- What the terminology of the juvenile justice system emphasizes?

Can You Define

American Dream, anomie, anomie theory, biotic balance, classical world view, concordance, conflict theory, consensus theory, critical theory, determinism, deterrence, differential association theory, distributive justice, ecological model, ecology, folkways, functionalism, incapacitation, labeling theory, *mala in se, mala prohibita,* mores, natural law, norms, phrenology, physiognomy, positivist world view, primary deviance, radical theory, retributive justice, secondary deviance, social contract, social disorganization theory, social ecology theory, social justice, strain theory, symbiosis

INTRODUCTION

The juvenile justice system has evolved slowly, influenced by many circumstances. In addition to its historical evolution, the system has deep roots in theories about justice, crime, delinquency and punishment. This chapter begins with a discussion of how justice has been viewed through the ages, the types of laws instituted to achieve justice and perspectives on punishment. This is followed by an explanation of two competing world views that have influenced the entire criminal justice system, including the juvenile justice system. Next, various theories about the causation of crime and delinquency are explored. Then the link between drugs and delinquency is examined. The chapter concludes with a comparison of the contemporary juvenile justice system and the criminal justice system and a discussion of what the juvenile justice system might look like in the twenty-first century.

Justice

Centuries ago Aristotle warned that no government can stand that is not founded on justice. As a nation, America is firmly committed to "liberty and justice for all." But is this the reality? And what is justice?

Aristotle wrote that the *just* is that which is lawful (universal justice) and that which is fair and equal (particular justice). According to Aristotle (Ross, 1952, pp. 378–379):

> Of particular justice and that which is just in the corresponding sense, one kind is that which is manifested in distributions of honour or money or the other things that fall to be divided among those who have a share in the constitution. . . .
>
>   This, then, is what the just is—the proportional; the unjust is what violates the proportion. Hence one term becomes too great, the other too small, as indeed happens in practice; for the man who acts unjustly has too much, and the man who is unjustly treated too little, of what is good.

Distributive or **social justice** provides an equal share of what is valued in a society to each member of that society. This includes power, prestige and possessions. **Retributive justice** seeks revenge for unlawful behavior.

Distributive justice or social justice is frequently ignored but must certainly be considered in any discussion of justice. Usually, however, the focus is on retributive justice, harkening back to the ancient concept of "an eye for an eye" (*lex talionis*). When distributive and retributive justice are not differentiated, critics may claim that retributive justice has failed when, in effect, it has no power over the failure.

Merton (1957) views crime as being caused by the frustration of the lower socioeconomic levels within an affluent society that denies them legal access to social status and material goods. He views this denial as not only unjust but also as a root of many social ills, including crime. Merton further suggests that this is especially true of our "underprivileged youth" who need not only groceries, but "groceries for growing."

In a paper on justice for juveniles, Springer (1986, p. 76) suggests:

> It is beyond the scope of this paper to discuss social justice, what Aristotle called "distributive justice," but it is within its scope to make mention of the sad

consequences of our inability to provide a decent social environment for what would appear to be a growing segment of our youthful society.

This is not the place to engage in discourse on the dire ends of poverty, class divisions, urbanization, industrialization, urban blight, unemployment, breakdown of religion, breakdown of the family, and all of the other established criminogenic factors. It is the place, however, to recognize, at least, that the criminal justice system is the least effective means of crime prevention and social control. If we are interested in a relatively crime-free society, we must look elsewhere than the courts.

Breed (1990, p. 68) shares Springer's view: "When half of our nation's children live in poverty and one-third grow up ignorant, we have in fact developed a third world underclass within this major nation." Breed, like Springer, suggests (p. 68):

Crime and delinquency will be reduced only to the degree that we are willing to address wider social problems, such as maintaining and supporting the family unit—nurturing, housing, nutrition, education, health care and parent training.

If we are unwilling to address basic prevention issues, then we are not going to reduce crime. Our concern must be to keep children out of harm's way, instead of concentrating on caring for them after they have been harmed. We must recognize that investing in children is not a national luxury and not a national chore, but a national necessity.

Consider finally the statement of Krisberg and Austin (1993, p. 51) at the conclusion of their discussion of historical approaches to juvenile delinquency:

Not surprisingly, juvenile justice reforms have inexorably increased state control over the lives of the poor and their children. The central implication of this historical analysis is that the future of delinquency prevention and control will be determined largely by ways in which the social structure evolves. It is possible that this future belongs to those who wish to advance social justice on behalf of young people rather than to accommodate the class interests that have dominated this history.

This explanation for the existence of crime is discussed in more detail later in this chapter.

Justice and the Law

Every society has **norms,** that is, rules or laws governing the actions and interactions of its people. These are usually of two types: folkways and mores. **Folkways** describe how people are expected to dress, eat and show respect for one another. They encourage certain behaviors. **Mores,** in contrast, are the *critical* norms vital to a society's safety and survival. Mores are often referred to as **natural law**—the rules of conduct that are the same everywhere because they are basic to human behavior.

Some behaviors, such as murder and rape, are deemed by any reasonable person to be inherently bad. Natural law states that certain acts are wrong by their very nature, that behavior that disregards the common decency one human owes to another is morally and legally wrong. Each society has a general idea of what constitutes natural law. Our founding fathers identified such principles when they wrote of the "inalienable rights to life, liberty and the pursuit of happiness" and of "truths held to be self-evident."

Acts considered immoral or wrong in themselves, such as murder and rape, are called *mala in se.* Those acts prohibited because they infringe on others' rights, not because they are necessarily considered evil by nature, such as having more than one wife, are called *mala prohibita.*

Natural laws may be declared to be criminal acts by man-made laws. Natural laws have remained relatively unchanged over the years, while man-made laws are altered nearly every legislative session.

Crimes were originally differentiated as:

mala in se	mala prohibita
wrong in and of itself	a prohibited wrong
origin in mores	origin in folkways
natural law	man-made law
common law	statutory law
stable over time	changes over time

Purposes of Law

According to sociologist Max Weber, the primary purpose of law is to regulate human interactions—that is, to support social order (Rheinstein, 1954). Throughout history, law has served many other purposes, including to protect the interests of society, govern behavior, deter antisocial behavior, enforce moral beliefs, support those in power, regulate human interactions, uphold individual rights, identify lawbreakers, punish lawbreakers and seek retribution for wrongdoing.

Two prominent theories about the underlying purpose of law are consensus theory and conflict theory.

Consensus Theory

Consensus theory holds that individuals within a society agree on basic values, on what is inherently right and wrong. Laws express these values.

This theory dates back at least as far as Plato and Aristotle. Deviant acts are deviant because society, in general, feels they are abnormal and unacceptable behavior. This theory was expanded upon by the French historian and philosopher Montesquieu (1689–1755), a founder of political science. Montesquieu's philosophy centered around the **social contract,** whereby free, independent individuals agree to form a community and to give up a portion of their individual freedom to benefit the security of the group.

This social contract applied to minors as well as adults. Youths were expected to obey the rules established by society and to suffer the consequences if they did not. Centuries later the concept of the social contract was expanded upon by Emile Durkheim.

Emile Durkheim (1858–1917) was a French sociologist and author who established the method and theoretical framework of social science.

Punishment and Social Solidarity— The Durkheimian Perspective

Emile Durkheim (1858–1917), a pioneer in sociology, argued that punishment is a moral process to preserve the shared values of a society, that is, its "collective conscience." When individuals deviate from this collective conscience, society is outraged and seeks revenge to restore the moral order. As Garland (1991, p. 123) notes: "Punishment thus transforms a threat to social order into a triumph of social solidarity." Garland (p. 127) also notes: "As Durkheim makes clear, an act of punishment is also a sign that authorities are in control, that crime is an aberration, and that the conventions that govern social life retain their force and vitality."

The Durkheimian perspective sees punishment as revenge and as a way to restore and solidify the social order.

Two key elements of Durkheim's perspective are (1) that the general population is involved in the act of punishing, giving it legitimacy, and (2) it is marked by deeply emotional, passionate reactions to crime. Durkheim (1933, pp. 73–80) believed:

- Crime is conduct "universally disapproved of by members of each society."
- "An act is criminal when it offends strong and defined states of the collective conscience."

According to Durkheim, criminal law synthesizes society's essential morality and establishes boundaries that cannot be crossed without threatening the society's very existence. Durkheim (1951 [1897], p. 252) developed a concept known as **anomie,** meaning normlessness. Anomie refers to the breakdown of societal norms as a result of society's failure to distinguish between right and wrong.

Although laws usually reflect the majority values of a society, important in a democracy, they rarely represent the views of everyone. This may result in conflict.

Conflict Theory

Conflict theory suggests that laws are established to keep the dominant class in power.

The roots of this theory can be found in the writings of Marx and Engels who wrote in the *Manifesto of the Communist Party* (1848):

> The history of all hitherto existing society is the history of class struggles. Freeman and slave, patrician and plebeian, lord and serf, guild-master and journeyman, in a word, oppressor and oppressed stood in constant opposition to one another, carried on an interrupted, now hidden, now open fight, a fight that each time ended in either a revolutionary reconstruction of society at large, or in the common ruin of the contending classes.

Conflict theory shifts the focus from lawbreaking to lawmaking and law enforcing and how they protect the interests and values of the dominant groups within a society. Walker et al. (1996, p. 19) suggest:

> Conflict theory explains racial disparities in the administration of justice as products of broader patterns of social, economic, and political inequality in U.S. society. These inequalities are the result of prejudicial attitudes on the part of the white majority and discrimination against minorities in employment, education, housing, and other aspects of society. . . . Conflict theory explains the overrepresentation of racial and ethnic minorities in arrest, prosecution, imprisonment, and capital punishment as both the product of these inequalities and an expression of prejudice against minorities.

Punishment and Class Power—
The Marxist Perspective

Rather than viewing punishment as a means of providing social solidarity, Marx (1818–1883) saw punishment as a way to enhance the power of the upper class and an inevitable result of capitalism. Marx referred to the lower class as a "slum proletariat" made up of vagrants, prostitutes and criminals. "In effect, penal policy is taken to be one element within a wider strategy of controlling the poor; punishment should be understood not as a social response to the criminality of individuals but as a mechanism operating in the struggle between social classes" (Garland, p. 128).

The Marxist perspective sees punishment as a way to control the lower class and preserve the power of the upper class.

This rationale was doubtless operating throughout the Middle Ages, the Renaissance, the Reformation and into the nineteenth century. Society was divided into a small ruling class, a somewhat larger class of artisans and a vastly larger class of peasants. Intimidation through a brutal criminal law was an important form of social control.

Flicker (1990, p. 38) sees this rationale operating in the development of our juvenile justice system:

> The unfortunate historical fact is that the juvenile justice system . . . began with the right observation and the wrong conclusion. Manifestly, poor people are more likely to beg, steal, and commit certain other crimes related to their social and economic

status than affluent people. Although socially unacceptable, crime could be seen as a response to poverty. It was a way to get money. The preferred solutions—jobs, vocational training, financial assistance for the unemployable—required a constructive community attitude toward the disadvantaged. But a combination of Calvinism, prejudice, and social Darwinism confused cause and effect—idleness, inferiority, and criminality were seen as causing poverty, rather than the reverse. Therefore progressive elements in the community, the social reformers, felt justified in saving impoverished children from the inexorable path of crime by investigating their homes and families, attempting to imbue them with principles of Christian morality, and, if unsuccessful, removing them to a better environment.

Contemporary Perspectives on Punishment

The *conservative* attitude is to "get tough," "stop babying these kids" and "get them off the streets." This is reminiscent of the child savers' efforts to "contain" certain children.

> The conservative approach to juvenile justice is "get tough on juveniles"—to punish and imprison them.

The conservative philosophy accepts retribution as a purpose of punishment. The conservative view also supports the use of imprisonment to control crime and antisocial behavior. Rehabilitative programs may be provided during incarceration, but it is imprisonment itself, with its attendant deprivations, that must be primarily relied on to prevent crime, delinquency and recidivism. Correctional treatment is not necessary.

In contrast, the *liberal* attitude toward juvenile justice is "treatment, not punishment" for youths who are antisocial and wayward.

> The liberal approach to juvenile justice stresses treatment and rehabilitation, including community-based programs.

The theoretical roots of these two perspectives can be found in the centuries-old competing world views of who or what is responsible for crime.

Two Competing World Views

Two distinct and opposing views exist as to who or what is responsible for crime.

> The two competing world views are the classical view and the positivist view.

The Classical World View

In the eighteenth century, criminologists began to apply the scientific method to explore the causes of crime. A leader of the classical school was Cesare Beccaria (1738–1794), whose *On Crimes and Punishment* was published in 1764.

> The **classical world view** holds that humans have free will and are responsible for their own actions.

Other important principles of the classical theory include the following:

- Individuals have free will. Some choose to commit crime.
- Laws should bring the greatest measure of happiness to the largest number of people.
- Those who break the law should be punished according to penalties established in the law.
- The focus is on crime.

Like Durkheim, Beccaria believed that society functions under a social contract, with individuals giving up certain freedoms to live peacefully together. As noted by Shoham and Hoffmann (1991, p. 17): "People organize in communities in order to ensure their safety and security, and that is the purpose of the state and its laws."

Classical theorists believed that delinquency was the result of free will. Consequently, they advocated harsh and immediate punishment, so that offenders would be "unwilling" to commit future crimes.

Proponents of the classical view advocate punishment for offenders.

Several aspects of the classical view are found in the juvenile justice system. Classical theory suggests that the threat of punishment will lower youths' tendency to delinquency. If the punishment is severe enough, youths will avoid delinquent activity, a process known as **deterrence.** However, the effectiveness of deterrence is uncertain. Many law violators believe they will never be caught, and if they are, they believe they can "beat the rap." Those who violate the law under the influence of drugs may believe they are invincible. Punishment is no threat to them. Juveniles may also resist the threat of punishment because of peer pressure. Being rejected by the gang would be worse than getting caught by the police. Indeed, being arrested and serving time are often seen as rites of passage, endowing a sort of higher status on those who make the journey. Also, many juveniles know the differences between juvenile and adult court and believe they will receive less severe punishment because of their age.

Classical theory also advocates **incapacitation** as a consequence for criminal activity. Institutionalization is intended not to rehabilitate offenders, but to keep them away from law-abiding society. Classical theory holds that criminal offenders should be sanctioned merely because they deserve punishment, and that punishment should be founded on what the offender deserves. Critics say this "just deserts" approach is actually a desire for revenge. Since the first juvenile court in 1899, the juvenile justice system has opposed deserts-based punishment. Incarcerated juveniles were usually given short sentences (one to three years maximum) and sent to a nonpunitive, rehabilitation-oriented institution.

Classical view theorists suggest that deterrence, incapacitation and, in some cases, just deserts punishment is the way to deal with delinquency.

Classical theorists' views conflict with those adhering to the *parens patriae* philosophy, which advocates reform as a more appropriate way to deal with delinquency. In the nineteenth century, another view of criminality was developed in reaction to the classical theory.

The Positivist World View

A leader of the **positivist world view** was Cesare Lombroso (1835–1909), an Italian physician who studied the brains of criminals. Lombroso maintained that criminals were born with a predisposition to crime and needed exceptionally favorable conditions in life to avoid criminal behavior. As the originator of the positivist view of criminality—that is, transferring emphasis from the crime itself to the criminal behavior—Lombroso has been called the father of modern criminology. He firmly believed that criminals were literally "born," not made—that the primary cause of crime was biological. He was writing at the same time that Charles Darwin's theory of evolution was becoming widely circulated, and he was probably greatly influenced by Darwin's ideas. Although some of Lombroso's work was later found to be flawed, he had started people thinking about causes for criminal behavior other than free will.

The positivist world view holds that humans are shaped by their society and are the product of environmental and cultural influences.

Other important principles of the positivist theory include the following:

- Individuals' actions are determined not by free will but by biological and cultural factors.
- The purpose of law is to avert revolution and convince the masses to accept the social order.
- The focus is on the criminal.

The positivist view theorists, who believe delinquent behavior is the result of a youth's biological makeup and life experiences, feel treatment should include altering one or more of the factors that contributed to the unlawful behavior.

Proponents of the positivist view advocate rehabilitation for offenders.

Positivist theorists stress community treatment and rehabilitation rather than incapacitation. For years, the *parens patriae* attitude prevailed, with youths shielded from being labeled and punished as criminals.

Building on Lombroso's idea that environmental influences affected criminal behavior, some scholars developed the positivist view of criminality based on the concept of **determinism.** As noted by Snarr (1992, p. 47):

Determinism maintains that human behavior is the product of a multitude of environmental and cultural influences. The view regards crime as a consequence, not of a single but of many factors. Among the influences considered were the population density, the economic status, and the legal definition of crime. The multiple-factor causation theory brought the positivist view into direct conflict with the complex free-will notion of the rejection of pain and the seeking of pleasure concept.

Throughout the ages, societies have embraced one view or the other, with many people taking a middle position but tending toward one view. And these two world views have profoundly affected the various theories about the causes of crime and delinquency that have been set forth over the years.

Causes of Crime and Delinquency: An Overview

Over time, many theories have been developed to explain why people fail to obey society's laws—why do they become criminals? Other theories take the opposite approach and try to explain why people obey the laws—why do they *not* become criminals? As you explore the theories that follow, keep these questions in mind.

During the first half of the twentieth century, several interpretations of the cause of delinquency gained prominence. The earliest theories explored biological and psychological factors. In fact, physical and psychological examinations of children who were brought before the court were standard orders in the juvenile court process. Judicial disposition often included individual counseling and psychological therapy. In the 1950s, under the influence of therapists such as Carl Rogers, group counseling became common in most juvenile institutions.

Slowly, this approach was replaced with social milieu and environmental explanations for delinquency. Delinquency prevention attempts focused on reorganizing the social environment, both physically, through housing renewal, and socioeconomically, through social welfare. There was a significant philosophical shift of the blame for delinquency from personal to social factors. Consequently, the federal government was increasingly drawn into the process of juvenile delinquency prevention.

Early efforts to explain crime and delinquency were set forth in the classical theory and the positivist theory. Later theories focused on biological, psychological or sociological causes of crime and delinquency. Most recently, critical theories of the causes of crime and delinquency have been developed.

Biological Theories

Some researchers propose biological explanations for crime. They find that some biological characteristics appear more frequently in criminals than in noncriminals. In other words, they believe there are such things as criminal genes.

Biological theories include physiognomy, phrenology, body type and heredity studies, including studies of twins and adoptees.

Physiognomy Studies

Physiognomy assigns character traits to physical features, especially facial features. Curran and Renzetti (1994, p. 39) note that in the Middle Ages the law specified that if "two people were suspected of having committed the same crime, the uglier one should be regarded as more likely the guilty party." Indeed, people tend to have a mental picture of criminals. Some researchers have pointed out that criminals tend toward large, prominent or crooked noses, abnormal ears, lantern jaws, high cheek bones, higher sex drives, lower intelligence, larger body types, longer arms, larger lips or abnormal amounts of body hair. Researchers search for predominant factors among criminals and compare these factors with their presence or absence in the general population.

Phrenology

Phrenology studies the shape of the skull to predict intelligence and character. This was the approach used by Cesare Lombroso, who believed that at birth criminals are recognizable by certain anomalies. Such anomalies do not cause crime, but they indicate a predisposition to criminal behavior. Techniques used in phrenology are sometimes demonstrated at fairs or shopping malls.

Body Type Theories

Going beyond the study of the skull to predict predisposition to criminality, William Sheldon (1898–1977) theorized that humans can be divided into three distinct body types, or somatotypes, corresponding to three distinct personalities: (1) the endomorphic—soft, fat—easygoing; (2) the mesomorphic—athletic, muscular, aggressive; and (3) the ectomorphic—thin, delicate—shy, introverted.

Heredity Studies

Bohm (1997, pp. 39–40) describes studies of twins and of adopted boys that tend to support a biological basis for one's predisposition to crime. More than a half century of using this methodology reveals that identical twins are more likely to demonstrate **concordance** (where both twins have criminal records) than are fraternal twins. This supports the heredity link. A problem with the twin studies, however, is the potential confounding of genetic and environmental influences.

The findings from adoption studies reveal that the percentage of adoptees who are criminal is greater when the biological father has a criminal record than when the adoptive father has one. Thus, like the twin studies, the adoption studies presumably demonstrate the influence of heredity but cannot adequately separate it from the influences of the environment.

Other Approaches Supporting Biological Causation Theories

Some studies have indicated that chromosomal factors may be responsible for criminal behavior. If this is true, certain people are victims of their own heritage. Some researchers believe that nutritional factors are related to abnormal behavior. High testosterone has been associated with aggressive physical and sexual behavior. Testosterone injected into female rats causes them to adopt the male physical characteristics of aggressive physical and sexual behavior.

The environment can shape children's development. Youths growing up in poverty may resort to delinquent acts such as window breaking for entertainment—or to more serious delinquent acts to obtain material possessions.

Some biological studies have indicated that high levels of specific chemicals in the body, as well as allergic reactors, contribute to aggression and perhaps criminality. Abnormal levels of manganese, zinc, copper or chromium may cause antisocial behavior. Abnormal EEG patterns have also been recorded in some prisoners.

As noted by Donohue (1995, p. 1): "The genetics and crime issue is one very hot potato" and results in "a crime-causation hornet's nest." He notes (p. 12): "Many scientists doubt the existence of a so-called 'crime gene,' adding fuel to the age-old 'nature vs. nurture' debate with respect to crime causation." He concludes:

> Scientists say that low levels of serotonin, a neurotransmitter that helps regulate emotions, may cause people to become violent. Since serotonin deficits have been tied to both genetic defects and environmental factors, serotonin studies may help sociologists and scientists find a common ground in the debate on how to reduce violent crime.

Psychological Theories

Exploring psychological causes of crime has produced a number of explanations, including the following:

- Criminals are morally insane; what they do criminally they do not perceive as wrong.
- Personality is developed in early childhood. Future behavior is determined in early childhood. Subsequent sociological and environmental associations do not change this early behavior development.
- Certain people have personalities so deviant that they have little or no control over their impulses.

- There are criminal families in which succeeding generations gravitate toward criminality.
- Mental and moral degeneration cause crime.

***

Psychological theories about crime focus on intelligence and psychoanalysis.

Intelligence and Crime

H. H. Goddard (1866–1957) was one of the earliest psychologists to link intelligence and criminality. Goddard believed that criminals are not necessarily biologically inferior, although they might be intellectually inferior. This correlation was again brought to public attention by Hernstein and Murray (1994), who used the bell-shaped normal curve from statistical studies to promote the idea that individuals' intelligence falls within this curve and may also account for criminality.

Psychoanalysis

The psychoanalytic theory of Sigmund Freud (1859–1939) was a popular explanation for human behavior. It stated that personality imbalances had their roots in abnormal emotional and mental development. A person might become fixed at a certain developmental stage or regress to an earlier stage.

Of most importance to the study of criminality is Freud's explanation of problems that arise from fixation at or regression to the phallic stage (three to six years of age). Fixation or regression to this stage may result in sexual assault, rape or prostitution. It may also result in unresolved oedipal or electra conflicts. According to Bohm (p. 56):

> Individuals who do not successfully resolve the oedipal or electra complex, and thus do not develop a strong superego capable of controlling the id, were called psychopaths by Freud. (Sociologists call them sociopaths.) Many criminal offenders are presumed to be *psychopaths, sociopaths,* or *antisocial personalities* and are characterized by no sense of guilt, no subjective conscience, and no sense of right and wrong.

Sociological Theories

Sociology studies human social structures and their relationships. People start life as members of families and later learn to live with other work and social groups. Some sociologists believe that criminals are molded by social conditions and the environment in which they develop. Not everyone has the same goals or ways to achieve them. Some people choose to reach their goals of financial success and power through illegal acts. To what extent social conditions cause criminal behavior is a subject of much debate.

There are several opinions about the relationship of sociological theories and crime occurrence, including the following:

- Lack of education, poverty-level income, poor housing, slum conditions and conflict within home and family probably increase crime commission. Achievement expectations are low. If all these conditions disappeared, crime would decrease.
- Continual lawbreaking causes an individual to become part of a subculture that advocates crime and violence as a way to achieve goals or solve

problems. It operates outside society's rules. Crimes committed within the subculture are rarely reported to police.

- Behavior is learned. There is good and bad, right and wrong behavior. Identical pressures affect criminals and noncriminals alike.

Sociological theories include ecological models, social disorganization, functionalism, anomie or strain theory, learning theories and social control theories.

The Ecological Model

Ecology studies the relationships between organisms and their environment. Findings from ecology were the basis for the **ecological model,** first described by sociologist Robert Park, University of Chicago. Park et al. (1928) compared the growth of a city and its attendant crime problems with growth in nature. As Shoham and Hoffmann (p. 39) explain:

> Ecologists note that an area of land goes through several stages with regard to its plant life and growth. First there is a period of invasion when a new species of plant attempts to gain a foothold in order to grow and mature. Second, the new plant may take over the area, or come to dominate it. . . . Finally, there is a period of succession in which the environment stabilizes and accepts the inevitable presence of its new dominant organism.
>
> Ecologists also observe what is known as **symbiosis:** the condition of two different organisms living together in a mutually beneficial relationship. A **biotic balance** occurs when the relations between the different species of plants and their necessary conditions for survival (e.g., climate, soil condition) maintain an equilibrium. All of the organisms are thus able to survive and prosper. [emphasis added]
>
> It was in this vein that Park encouraged his colleagues and students to study the dynamics of urban life. Many of the conditions that existed and the problems that plagued cities were believed to be explainable by utilizing this ecological model. Communities could be studied in part by analyzing the invasion, domination, and succession of different ethnic and racial groups. Problems within the community could perhaps be alleviated by studying the symbiosis and biotic balance, or lack of, in a neighborhood. . . .
>
> One can demarcate a city based on its outwardly moving growth pattern. The resulting pattern is one of concentric zones, with each zone representing a particular form of development and community life.

The ecological model stressed that any explanation of criminal behavior cannot be taken out of its social context.

Social Disorganization Theory

Two other Chicago sociologists, Clifford Shaw and Henry McKay (1942), applied the ecological model to a study of delinquency. Their area studies involved 25,000 delinquents from the Juvenile Court of Cook County from 1900 to 1933. They, too, found concentric zones within an area, with transitional inner-city zones having the highest crime rates. Their **social ecology theory** suggested that ecological conditions predicted delinquency and that gang membership is a normal response to social conditions.

Figure 2.1
Social Disorganization Model

Source: Constructed by R. J. Sampson and W. B. Groves. "Community Structure and Crime: Testing Social-Disorganization Theory." *American Journal of Sociology*, 94, 1989, p. 783. Printed in S. Giora Shoham and John Hoffmann. *A Primer in the Sociology of Crime*. New York: Harrow and Heston Publishers, 1991, p. 51. Reprinted by permission.

Shaw and McKay's **social disorganization theory** contended that urban areas produced delinquency directly by weakening community controls and generating a subculture of delinquency passed on from one generation to the next. Their social disorganization theory was built upon by other sociologists, including Sampson and Groves (1989), who developed the social disorganization model shown in Figure 2.1.

Functionalism

Harvard sociologist Talcott Parsons (1902–1979) developed a theory explaining criminal behavior as an integral part of our society. Borrowing from Durkheim, **functionalism** views crime as a necessary part of society. Without crime who would need laws, lawyers, police officers, courts, judges, jails and jailers?

Anomie or Strain Theory

Building on Parsons's theory of functionalism, Robert Merton (1910–) saw a basic conflict between cultural goals in the United States and our social structure. Merton (1938) adopted Durkheim's concept of anomie—the breakdown of social norms, individuals dissociating themselves from the collective conscience of the group—as the basis for his theory. As Shoham and Hoffmann (p. 57) explain:

> Merton identified two elements of the social and cultural structure which were especially important for explaining deviance: *cultural goals* and *institutionalized norms*. Cultural goals are legitimate goals which members of a society wish to obtain. Institutionalized norms or means define the appropriate methods for attaining the cultural goals. Cultural goals and institutionalized means do not hold a constant relationship to one another; rather, during certain periods one may take precedence over the other.

Because most people believe in the **American Dream** (that is, through hard work anyone can become rich), strive for it, and fall short, they experience a strain (Merton, 1938). **Anomie** or **strain theory** is thoroughly explored by Messner and Rosenfeld (1997) in *Crime and the American Dream*. They note (p. 11):

> Our analysis is grounded in the variant of anomie theory associated with the work of the American sociologist Robert K. Merton. Merton combines strategic ideas from Durkheim with insights borrowed from Karl Marx, another founding figure in the social sciences, to produce a provocative and compelling account of the social forces underlying deviant behavior in American society. . . .
>
> Most importantly, we accept Merton's underlying premise that motivations for crime do not result simply from the flaws, failures, or free choices of individuals. A complete explanation of crime ultimately must consider the sociocultural environments in which people are located.

The views of Messner and Rosenfeld are presented in the preface of their text (p. xi):

> The essence of our argument is that the distinctive patterns and levels of crime in the United States are produced by the cultural and structural organizations of American society. American culture is characterized by a strong emphasis on the goal of monetary success and a weak emphasis on the importance of the legitimate means for the pursuit of success. This combination of strong pressures to succeed monetarily and weak restraints on the selection of means is intrinsic to the dominant cultural ethos: the American Dream. The American Dream contributes to crime directly by encouraging people to employ illegal means to achieve goals that are culturally approved. It also exerts an indirect effect on crime through its interconnections with the institutional balance of power in society.
>
> The American Dream promotes and sustains an institutional structure in which one institution—the economy—assumes dominance over all others. The resulting imbalance in the institutional structure diminishes the capacity of other institutions, such as the family, education, and the political system, to curb criminogenic cultural pressures and to impose controls over the behavior of members of society. In these ways, the distinctive cultural commitments of the American Dream and its companion institutional arrangements contribute to high levels of crime.

Cohen (1955) also built upon Merton's work, adapting his anomie/strain theory in an attempt to explain gang delinquency. Cohen replaced Merton's social goals of wealth with acceptance and status. Youths abandoned the middle-class values for their own values—attaining status among their peers. Cohen's study of delinquent subculture, set forth in *Delinquent Boys* (1955), found that delinquency was caused by social and economic limitations, inadequate family support, developmental handicaps and status frustration. The result: short-run hedonism and group autonomy.

Closely related to strain theorists are those who look at the correlation between unemployment and crime. For example, Carlson and Michalowski (1997, pp. 210–211) note:

> The proposition that increases in unemployment will generate increases in crime has long been accepted as a basic tenet of the macro sociology of crime and delinquency. A number of otherwise competing models of crime causation such as conflict theory, Marxian theories, social disorganization theories, and strain theory share the assumption that economic distress generated by rises in unemployment will increase crimes against both persons and property.

Another strain theorist is Agnew (1992) who identified three sources of strain: (1) failure to achieve positively valued goals, (2) the removal of positively valued stimuli and (3) the presentation of negative stimuli.

Learning Theories

In the 1930s and 1940s, Edwin Sutherland (1883–1950) set forth the proposition that criminal behavior is learned through imitation or modeling. In *Principles of Criminology* (1939) with Donald Cressey, he set forth the principles of differential association. Among their propositions are the following (Sutherland and Cressey, 1974, pp. 75–77):

- Criminal behavior is learned in interaction with other persons in a process of communication.
- The principal part of the learning of criminal behavior occurs within intimate personal groups.
- The process of learning criminal behavior by association with criminal and anticriminal patterns involves all the mechanisms involved in any other type of learning.
- A person becomes delinquent because of an excess of definitions favorable to the violation of law over definitions unfavorable to the violation of law. This is the principle of differential association.

Sutherland's **differential association theory** is still an important theory of crime causation. As noted by Bohm (p. 99): "Learning theory explains criminal behavior and its prevention with the concepts of positive reinforcement, negative reinforcement, extinction, punishment, and modeling or imitation." Many of these factors were explored thoroughly during the 1960s and 1970s based on the behavior modification studies initiated by B. F. Skinner.

Social Control Theories

An influential contemporary social control theorist is Travis Hirschi, whose text *Causes of Delinquency* (1969) greatly influenced current thinking. Hirschi's social control theory traces delinquency to the bond that individuals maintain with society. Social controls rather than moral values are what maintain law and order. A lack of attachment to parents and school can result in delinquency. Hirschi believed that delinquency resulted from a lack of proper socialization and particularly ineffective child-rearing practices. As Bohm (p. 104) suggests: "For Hirschi, proper socialization involves the establishment of a strong moral bond between the juvenile and society. This *bond to society* consists of (1) *attachment* to others, (2) *commitment* to conventional lines of action, (3) *involvement* in conventional activities, and (4) *belief* in the moral order and law."

Critical Theories

As the name suggests, some theorists became disenchanted with the failure of existing theories to satisfactorily explain the causes of crime. **Critical theory** combines the classical free-will and positivist determinism views of crime, suggesting that humans are both self-determined and society-determined. As noted by Bohm (p. 110): "Critical theories assume that human beings are the creators of the institutions and structures that ultimately dominate and constrain them."

Critical theories include labeling theory, conflict theory and radical theory.

Labeling Theory

According to Bohm (p. 112), **labeling theory** has its roots in the work of George Herbert Mead (1863–1931), whose ideas can be summarized in three propositions:

- Human beings act toward things on the basis of the meanings that the things have for them.
- The meaning of things arises out of the social interaction that one has with one's fellows.
- These meanings are handled in, and modified through, an interpretative process people use to deal with things they encounter.

A belief in labeling theory can greatly influence how juveniles are treated by the juvenile justice system.

In labeling theory, it is important to differentiate between primary deviance and secondary deviance. **Primary deviance** is the initial criminal act. **Secondary deviance** is accepting the criminal label and consequently committing other crimes. If a person commits a delinquent act and is labeled a delinquent, this may affect the person's chance to make friends or get a good job. It may also become a self-fulfilling prophecy—that is, the person may accept the label and act accordingly.

Messner and Rosenfeld (p. 45) suggest: "The principal contribution of *labeling theory* is to call attention to the interplay between social control and personal identity."

Conflict Theory

Conflict theory has been discussed. To briefly review, as Messner and Rosenfeld (p. 45) summarize: "Conflict theories emphasize the political nature of crime production, posing the question of how the norms of particular groups are encoded into law and how, in turn, law is used as a means of domination of certain groups by others." More specifically: "For conflict theorists, the amount of crime in a society is a function of the extent of conflict generated by *stratification, hierarchical relationships, power differentials,* or the ability of some groups to dominate other groups in that society. Crime, in short, is caused by *relative powerlessness*" (Bohm, p. 119).

Radical Theory

Bohm (pp. 124–125) also describes **radical theory** as a way to explain crime:

> Radical criminologists focus their attention on the social arrangements of society, especially on political and economic structures and institutions (the "political economy") of *capitalism*. . . .
>
> Crime is a product of the political economy that, in capitalist societies, encourages an individualistic competition among wealthy people and among poor people and between rich and poor people (the intra- and inter*class struggle*) and the practice of taking advantage of other people (*exploitation*).

Appendix A provides a comprehensive summary of the most prominent theories on the causation of crime and delinquency.

Conclusion

As noted by Ohlin (1998, p. 143):

> One of the most striking developments in juvenile justice over the past 20 years has been the increasing rapidity and the widening scope of change in theories, goals, and knowledge about delinquency and its prevention or control. Many competing biological, psychological, social, and cultural theories of delinquency have emerged in the past two decades, yet none is sufficient to account for the rate and forms of delinquency today.

No single theory is sufficient to explain why delinquency exists. A reasonable combination of theories must be considered.

The Relationship between Drug Use and Delinquency

Although no single theory can explain the cause of delinquency, one fact *is* clear. The link between the use of drugs and crime has been clearly established in the literature. This link is stressed by Bilchik (1998, p. iii):

> Juvenile drug use . . . has risen significantly over the past several years, with one in two high school seniors in 1996 reporting having used illicit drugs. While this problem is of concern in itself, the clear correlation between substance abuse and other forms of delinquency gives further reason for concern. The prevalence of juvenile drug use, therefore, burdens our juvenile justice system and places the future of our youth at considerable risk.

There is a clear correlation between substance abuse and other forms of delinquency.

Crowe (1998, pp. 3–4) reports: "Not only are more youth using mood-altering substances than in the previous decade, they are beginning to ingest them at increasingly younger ages." She cautions that youths who persistently abuse illegal substances experience an array of problems including academic difficulties, health-related problems, poor peer relationships and involvement with the juvenile justice system.

In a North Philadelphia neighborhood that police call "The Land of Oz," children on their way to a game of sandlot football stop to sort through thousands of empty crack vials dropped by a young dealer as he fled from dealers whom he had robbed.

The Juvenile and Adult Justice Systems Compared

Not only did the juvenile justice system evolve into one separate from the adult system, but also the terms used were tailored to fit the juvenile system.

The terminology of the juvenile justice system underscores its emphasis on protecting youth from harmful labels and their stigmatizing effects.

Youths are not *arrested;* they are *taken into custody.* If the allegations against the youth are true, the youth is called a *delinquent* rather than a *criminal.* Youths sentenced to custodial care upon release receive *aftercare* rather than *parole.*

For 100 years, juveniles have had the benevolent protection of a separate system, particularly a separate juvenile court. Public opposition to such a system, however, appears to be increasing. Sprott (1998, p. 399) notes: "There is evidence in the United States. . . that small but cumulative steps are being taken to eliminate these separate youth systems." Torbet (1997) gives as examples a report from the National Center for Juvenile Justice stating that 40 states have modified their laws to permit easier transfer of youths to adult court and that some states have created mandatory minimum sentence laws for youths and blended sentences whereby sanctions imposed can be a combined juvenile and adult sanction.

Torbet also cites increased pressure to publish the names of young offenders, to lower the minimum age at which a youth is under the jurisdiction of the juvenile justice system and to broaden the scope of cases transferable to adult court. Sprott suggests: "The net result . . . is that the treatment of youth is becoming more similar to that of adults, with a consequent erosion of the youth justice system and the philosophies that underlie it."

Summary

Distributive or social justice provides an equal share of what is valued in a society to each member of that society. This includes power, prestige and possessions. Retributive justice seeks revenge for unlawful behavior. Unlawful behaviors or crimes were originally differentiated in the following two ways: (1) *mala in se,* an act considered wrong in and of itself based on mores, natural law and common law, and stable over time, or (2) *mala prohibita,* a prohibited wrong, originating in folkways and man-made statutory law and changeable over time.

Two prominent theories as to the underlying purpose of law are consensus theory and conflict theory. Consensus theory contends that individuals within a society agree on basic values, on what is inherently right and wrong. Laws express these values. It includes the Durkheimian perspective, which sees punishment as revenge and as a way to restore and solidify the social order.

Conflict theory suggests that laws are established to keep the dominant class in power. It includes the Marxist perspective, which sees punishment as a way to control the lower class and preserve the power of the upper class.

Contemporary views on the treatment of juveniles include the conservative approach—to "get tough on juveniles," to punish and imprison them—and the liberal approach, which stresses treatment and rehabilitation, including community-based programs. These approaches have their roots in two competing world views: the classical view and the positivist view.

The classical world view holds that humans have free will and are responsible for their own actions. Proponents of the classical view advocate punishment for offenders. They suggest that deterrence, incapacitation and, in some cases, "just deserts" punishment is the way to deal with delinquency. The positivist world view holds that humans are shaped by their societies and are the products of environmental and cultural influences. Proponents of the positivist view advocate rehabilitation for offenders.

Early efforts to explain crime and delinquency according to these theories were expanded upon and refined. Later theories focused on biological, psychological or sociological causes of crime and delinquency. Most recently, critical theories of the causes of crime and delinquency have been developed.

Biological theories include physiognomy, phrenology, body type and heredity studies, including studies of twins and adoptees. Psychological theories explaining crime focus on intelligence and psychoanalysis. Sociological theories include ecological models, social disorganization, functionalism, anomie or strain theory, learning theories and social control theories. Critical theories include labeling theory, conflict theory and radical theory.

No single theory is sufficient to explain why delinquency exists. A reasonable combination of theories must be considered. What is *not* theoretical, however, is the clear correlation between substance abuse and other forms of delinquency.

Also of importance are the differences between the adult and the juvenile systems of justice. The terminology of the juvenile justice system underscores its emphasis on protecting youths from harmful labels and their stigmatizing effects.

Discussion Questions

1. Do you take the position of those who hold a classical view or those who hold a positivist view? Do you hold the same view for children as you do for adults?
2. Do you feel that distributive justice is required for the United States to truly provide "liberty and justice for all"?
3. What instances of the Durkheimian or Marxist perspective of punishment can you cite from the historical overview of juvenile justice?
4. Do you support the conservative or the liberal approach toward delinquent youths? Which approach is more prevalent in your community? our country?
5. Which of the theories of the causation of crime and delinquency seem most logical?
6. Can you tell a delinquent youth by his or her appearance?
7. Diagram the ecological model as it might look for a major city.
8. How is the labeling theory of importance to parents? teachers? you?
9. Do you believe you can make the American Dream a reality for yourself? Why or why not?
10. Do you support a separate justice system for juveniles? Why or why not?

References

Agnew, Robert. "Foundation for a General Strain Theory of Crime and Delinquency." *Criminology,* Vol. 30, 1992, pp. 47–87.

Bilchik, Shay. Foreword. In *Drug Identification and Testing in the Juvenile Justice System* by Ann H. Crowe. Washington, DC: Office of Juvenile Justice and Delinquency Prevention, May 1998.

Bohm, Robert M. *A Primer on Crime and Delinquency.* Belmont, CA: Wadsworth Publishing Company, 1997.

Breed, Allen F. "America's Future: The Necessity of Investing in Children." *Corrections Today,* February 1990, pp. 68–72.

Carlson, Susan M. and Michalowski, Raymond J. "Crime, Unemployment, and Social Structures of Accumulation: An Inquiry into Historical Contingency." *Justice Quarterly,* Vol. 14, No. 2, June 1997, pp. 210–241.

Cohen, Albert K. *Delinquent Boys: The Culture of the Gang.* New York: Free Press, 1955.

Crowe, Ann H. *Drug Identification and Testing in the Juvenile Justice System.* Washington, DC: Office of Juvenile Justice and Delinquency Prevention, May 1998.

Curran, Daniel J. and Renzetti, Claire M. *Theories of Crime.* Boston: Allyn & Bacon, 1994.

Donohue, Stephen. "A Crime-Causation Hornet's Nest." *Law Enforcement News,* December 15, 1995, pp. 1, 12.

Durkheim, Emile. *The Division of Labor in Society.* New York: Free Press, 1933.

Durkheim, Emile. *Suicide* (1897). Glencoe, IL: Free Press, 1951.

Flicker, Barbara Danziger. *Standards for Juvenile Justice: A Summary and Analysis,* 2nd ed. New York: Institute for Judicial Administration, 1990.

Garland, David. "Sociological Perspectives on Punishment." In *Crime and Justice: A Review of Research,* Vol. 14, edited by Michael Tonry. Chicago: University of Chicago Press, 1991, pp. 115–165.

Hernstein, Richard J. and Murray, Charles. *The Bell Curve: Intelligence and Class Structure in American Life.* New York: Free Press, 1994.

Hirschi, Travis. *Causes of Delinquency.* Berkeley: University of California Press, 1969.

Krisberg, Barry and Austin, James F. *Reinventing Juvenile Justice.* Newbury Park, CA: Sage Publications, 1993.

Marx, Karl and Engels, Friedrich. *Manifesto of the Communist Party.* Chicago: Encyclopedia Britannica, Inc., 1848, p. 419.

Merton, Robert K. "Social Structure and Anomie." *American Sociological Review,* Vol. 3, 1938, pp. 672–682.

Merton, Robert K. *Social Theory and Social Structure,* rev. ed. New York: Free Press, 1957.

Messner, Steven F. and Rosenfeld, Richard. *Crime and the American Dream,* 2nd ed. Belmont, CA: Wadsworth Publishing Company, 1997.

Ohlin, Lloyd E. "The Future of Juvenile Justice Policy and Research." *Crime & Delinquency,* Vol. 44, No. 1, January 1998, pp. 143–153.

Park, Robert E.; Burgess, Ernest W.; and McKenzie, Roderick D. *The City.* Chicago: University of Chicago Press, 1928.

Rheinstein, Max, ed. *Max Weber on Law in Economy and Society.* Cambridge, MA: Harvard University Press, 1954.

Ross, W. D., trans. "Nicomachean Ethics." *Aristotle: II.* Chicago: Encyclopedia Britannica, 1952.

Sampson, R. J. and Groves, W. B. "Community Structure and Crime: Testing Social-Disorganization Theory." *American Journal of Sociology,* Vol. 94, 1989, pp. 774–802.

Shaw, Clifford and McKay, H. D. *Juvenile Delinquency and Urban Areas.* Chicago: University of Chicago Press, 1942.

Shoham, S. Giora and Hoffmann, John. *A Primer in the Sociology of Crime.* New York: Harrow and Heston, Publishers, 1991.

Snarr, Richard W. *Introduction to Corrections,* 2nd ed. Dubuque, IA: Wm. C. Brown Publishers, 1992.

Springer, Charles E. *Justice for Juveniles.* Washington, DC: U.S. Department of Justice, Office of Juvenile Justice and Delinquency Prevention, 1986.

Sprott, Jane B. "Understanding Public Opposition to a Separate Youth Justice System." *Crime & Delinquency,* Vol. 44, No. 3, July 1998, pp. 399–411.

Sutherland, Edwin H. and Cressey, Donald R. *Principles of Criminology.* Philadelphia: J. B. Lippincott, 1939.

Sutherland, Edwin H. and Cressey, Donald R. *Criminology,* 9th ed. Philadelphia: Lippincott, 1974.

Torbet, Patricia. "States Respond to Violent Juvenile Crime." *National Center for Juvenile Justice in Brief,* 1997, Vol. 1, p. 1.

Walker, Samuel; Spohn, Cassia; and DeLone, Miriam. *The Color of Justice: Race, Ethnicity, and Crime in America.* Belmont, CA: Wadsworth Publishing Company, 1996.

Chapter **3**

Growth and Development:
The First Eighteen Years

There is no characteristic of adolescence
whose germ may not be found in childhood,
and whose consequences may not be traced
in maturity and old age.
—Frederick Tracy

Do You Know

- At what age most individuals legally become adults?
- What ages are most critical in child development?
- What age is the most aggressive?
- What is required for learning?
- What kind of reinforcement is usually best?
- What a self-fulfilling prophecy is?
- What danger occurs by labeling a child as deviant?
- How many children live in poverty?
- What are two of the most serious consequences for children who live in poverty?
- What types of children with special needs may be involved in the juvenile justice system?
- What adolescence is? What occurs during this time?
- What is happening to the American Dream?

Can You Define

attention deficit disorder, crack children, EBD, fetal alcohol syndrome, learning disability, runaways, self-fulfilling prophecy, thrownaways

INTRODUCTION

Before examining our contemporary juvenile justice system, it is important to understand those served by this system—our youths. An extreme challenge facing the system is the "one-pot" approach to juvenile justice, evident throughout history. That is, those who are poor, who are neglected, who commit minor status-type offenses and those who commit vicious, violent crimes are currently lumped into the same judicial "pot." But their needs and the approaches required to meet those needs are drastically different.

The challenges facing today's youths are tremendous, as noted by Louv (1990, p. 5):

> Today's children are living a childhood of firsts. They are the first day-care generation; the first truly multicultural generation; the first generation to grow up in the electronic bubble, the environment defined by computers and new forms of television; the first post-sexual revolution generation; the first generation for which nature is more abstraction than reality; the first generation to grow up in new kinds of dispersed, deconcentrated cities, not quite urban, rural, or suburban.

This chapter begins with a brief overview of the rights our youths ideally enjoy and how they normally grow and develop. Next the effect of poverty on growth and development is described, followed by a look at children with special needs and those at risk of not developing normally. The chapter concludes with a discussion of adolescence and the unique challenges and stresses of this developmental stage, including the problem of teen pregnancy.

Youths and *Parens Patriae*

Under the principle of *parens patriae,* the state is to protect its youths. The age at which a child becomes an adult is legally established by each state.

Eighteen is the age most commonly recognized as the beginning of legal adulthood.

Table 3.1 lists the ages at which young people are officially considered adults in each state. Note the range from 16 to 19 years of age. Until they become adults, it is generally understood that youths need special assistance. In fact, the Joint Commission on Mental Health of Children (1970, pp. 3–4) lists the following as children's *rights:*

- The right to be wanted
- The right to be born healthy
- The right to live in a healthy environment
- The right to satisfaction of basic needs
- The right to continuous loving care
- The right to acquire the intellectual and emotional skills necessary to achieve individual aspirations and to cope effectively in our society

Table 3.1	Age 16	Age 17	Age 18		Age 19
Age at Which U.S. Courts Gain Jurisdiction over Young Offenders	Connecticut New York N. Carolina	Georgia Illinois Louisiana Massachusetts Michigan Missouri S. Carolina Texas	Alabama Alaska Arizona Arkansas California Colorado Delaware D. of Columbia Florida Hawaii Idaho Indiana Iowa Kansas Kentucky Maine Maryland Minnesota Mississippi Montana	Nebraska Nevada New Hampshire New Jersey New Mexico N. Dakota Ohio Oklahoma Oregon Pennsylvania Rhode Island S. Dakota Tennessee Utah Vermont Virginia Washington W. Virginia Wisconsin Federal Districts	Wyoming

Source: Linda A. Szymanski. "Upper Age of Juvenile Court Jurisdiction Statutes Analysis." Washington, DC: National Center for Juvenile Justice, March 1987.

- The right to receive care and treatment through facilities that are appropriate to their needs and that keep them as closely as possible within their normal social settings

Such rights are essential to our youths' growth and development.

Child Development

The study of child development usually deals with children from birth to adolescence and concerns their physical, intellectual, emotional and social growth as they adjust to the demands of society.

The study of child development is relatively new, having begun at the end of the nineteenth century. Pioneers in the field included psychologist John B. Watson, who believed that environment dominated development and that children could be shaped and molded as desired. Another pioneer, Arnold Gesell, held the opposing view, that biology dominated. As the study of child development evolved, many researchers stressed the importance of both. "Development," according to Hall et al. (1986, p. 2), "is an intricate process in which heredity, culture, and personal experience interact to produce the final pattern of a life. . . . No single theory has been able to explain all aspects of the process satisfactorily, but each has contributed to our understanding of human development."

Behavior and sociability are learned very early in life and become ingrained in one's character structure. According to Caticchio (1990, p. 7):

> If the child [during the first 18 months of life] experiences being treasured and important to those around him, then his basic sense of self as having value is repeatedly and predictably reinforced. . . .
>
> If his experiences are primarily ones in which he is related to as a burden—to be seen and not heard—all the successes in his later life will give only brief respite from a basic sense of inferiority and inadequacy which was repeatedly reinforced by thousands of incidents, big and small, over many years, with the most important people who will ever relate to him. . . .
>
> Being treasured during these first few months and years has much more to do with a child's *basic* sense of self-esteem than will all the magnificent structures he may build in later life.

Caticchio (p. 9) also suggests that if very young children are not nurtured by their parents, the children will feel alienated and isolated:

> The non-nurturing patterns, if sustained both in time and substance, lead the child to be withdrawn, or hostile and aggressive. These traits, in turn, make him a less enjoyable person, reinforcing others' lack of interest or caring about him. He begins to *not* be a very nice person.

The Critical First Three Years

Child development experts state that the first three years of life lay the foundation for all that follows.

The period from birth to age three is the most formative time of a child's life.

During this time, with attentive parents or older brothers or sisters, children learn the concept of consequences—rewards and punishments. They also begin to distinguish right from wrong and to develop what is commonly called a *conscience*.

Table 3.2 summarizes some of the basic needs of children if they are to grow and develop. Unfortunately, for too many of our nation's children, this is *not* the reality. Their healthy development is hindered by inadequate medical care, poverty, violence and disintegrating families.

According to a Carnegie study ("Developmental Risk . . . ," 1994, p. A1): "Millions of infants and toddlers are so deprived of medical care, loving supervision and intellectual stimulation that their growth into healthy and responsible adults is threatened." Specifically,

> The report notes that 3 million children, nearly one-fourth of all American infants and toddlers, live in poverty. Divorce rates, births to unmarried women and single-parent households have all soared in the past 30 years, and children in single-parent households, it points out, are more likely to experience behavioral and emotional problems than those in two-parent households. The number of children entering foster care jumped by more than 50 percent from 1987 to 1991, rising to 460,000 from 300,000.

David A. Hamburg, Carnegie president, states ("Developmental Risk . . ."): "What could be more important than a decent start in life? All the rest

Table 3.2
What Children Need for Healthy Growth and Development

Need	Comments
Choices and challenges	Children need the chance to explore and learn, to stretch to their limits.
Healthy and safe surroundings	Children need to feel secure and protected from harm, supported when confronted with strange or frightening experiences.
Independence	Children need to develop their own personality and self-confidence, to know that others have faith in their ability to do things for themselves.
Love	Children need to be loved—physically and emotionally. They need to feel wanted, appreciated, a part of a family unit. They need hugs.
Direction	Children need to know the rules, their boundaries and what will happen if they overstep these boundaries. They need to know how to interact with others and to get along.
Respect and recognition	Children need to be accepted for who they are and to be praised for their accomplishments.
Encouragement	Children need to be supported and helped to grow and develop.
Nurturing	Children need not only nutritious food, but attention to their mental and emotional growth and development as well.

depends on this foundation. . . . If a poor start leaves an enduring legacy of impairment, then high costs follow. They may show up in various systems: health, education, justice. We call them by many names: disease, disability, ignorance, incompetence, hatred, violence. By whatever name, these outcomes involve severe economic and social penalties for the entire society." Other findings of the Carnegie study include the following:

- One in every three abused children is less than one year old.
- More than half of women with children under one year old are working.
- American children are among the least likely in the world to be immunized.
- An increasing number of very young children grow up witnessing knifings, shootings and beatings as *everyday events*.

According to the Carnegie study, scientific evidence points to the criticality of the first three years of life in the development of the human brain. Research in molecular biology and neurology shows that what children experience in the first few years affects how many brain cells develop and how many connections are formed between them. Early environmental stimulation increases the number of cells and interconnections. Research also shows that stress early in life may activate hormones that impair learning and memory.

Between the ages of one and three, normal conflicts arise between parents and their children: toilet training, eating certain vegetables, going to bed at a certain time, staying within prescribed boundaries and the like. How these conflicts are resolved will establish the pattern for how the child will deal with conflict later in life.

Aggression and Violence

Headlines across the nation highlight the ever lowering age at which youths commit horrific, violent crimes. Such behavior most likely has its roots in the critical first years of development. According to Richard Tremblay, who has conducted long-term studies of childhood aggression: "Humans are more physically aggressive between the ages of twenty-four and thirty months than at any other time in their lives" (Ruben, 1998, p. 98). Ruben suggests: "Research shows that the most aggressive age of all, measured in pure frequency, is not 19, 16, 14, or 12."

The most aggressive age in humans is two.

Unfortunately, many parents, relatives and friends attribute hitting, biting and throwing tantrums to the "terrible twos." But ignoring such behavior or reacting in kind with violence such as spanking or otherwise striking a child can have dire consequences.

The Next Ten Years

Building on the foundation of the first three critical years, children continue to grow and develop physically, mentally and emotionally. During this time they are continuously learning.

The Learning Process

Understanding the process of learning, either in groups or individually, requires an understanding of the psychological principles involved and the social conditions under which learning happens.

The basic formation of individual personalities and character usually takes place within the family. Through a series of learning experiences within this intimate circle, individuals form attitudes, values and behaviors that they generally retain throughout life.

Adults often forget about the difficult learning experiences of early childhood. They remember them only by observing the blundering adaptations of children. Everyone has tried to learn a skill and failed without knowing why, or has tried to teach others and found them slow to understand. Remember learning how to tie your shoes or ride a bike—or teaching a child to do these things? Such experiences demonstrate that learning is not automatic. Where the principles of learning are not understood and conditions are not correctly arranged, little learning occurs.

Because most things are not learned on the first try, teaching requires great patience. No one immediately walks, talks or performs motor skills without repeating them time and again. Under appropriate conditions children learn to talk, to walk, to have good manners and to suppress socially unacceptable words heard and behaviors seen in play groups. To learn, children must want something, notice something, do something and get something. What they get can be positive or negative.

Learning requires drive, a cue, a response and reinforcement.

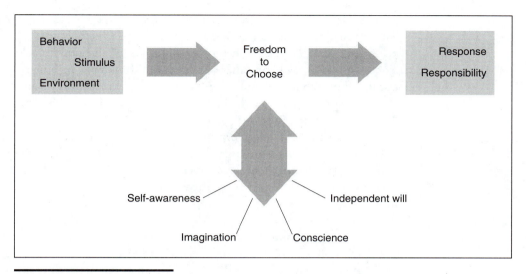

Figure 3.1
Interaction of Behavioral Variables

To use a classic example: a child sees fire, is curious and touches it. The child is burned and learns not to touch fire again.

Learning research suggests that positive reinforcement or rewards are much stronger than negative reinforcement or punishments. Unfortunately, too often inappropriate behaviors are noticed and punished rather than appropriate behaviors noticed and rewarded. Children learn what not to do—or get caught doing—but are often not taught what they should be doing.

> Praise is usually better than punishment when teaching children. Accentuate the positive.

The message for parents, teachers and all adults who work with children is to reward children for doing good things and acting in socially accepted ways.

To go a step further, learning is reflected in behavior. Youths' behavior depends on how they see, interpret and react to the world around them. Physical, psychological and social influences directly affect their behavior. This behavior within a specific environment provides the stimulus for choice. If this choice is achieved through self-awareness, imagination, conscience and independent will, the response is likely to be one that reflects responsibility to self and to society. The complex interaction of these variables is illustrated in Figure 3.1.

A strong advocate of individual responsibility for behavior is Samenow (1989, p. 18), who writes: "The environment from which a person comes is less crucial than the choice the individual makes as he responds to his environment." Samenow supports this position by presenting examples of families in which one child is antisocial, but the other children in the family or in similar circumstances are not. He notes: "Children do not get pressured haplessly into a life of crime. They make deliberate choices to do so."

Smetanka (1993, p. 1A) describes the choices of an eight-year-old girl left alone, supperless, by her mother who went out drinking. The hungry child got out the phone book and looked up the number to order pizza. When it came, she paid for it with money she had saved. The question posed by Smetanka is: "Is she a victim or a survivor?"

The Institute of Child Development at the University of Minnesota is studying children who overcome large obstacles and thrive despite living in poverty or with other large personal problems. Such children are considered *resilient*. A resilient child is one who "has the capacity to spring back, to successfully adapt in the face of adversity" (Smetanka, p. A16). A noted child psychiatrist, E. James Anthony, suggests the following analogy: Imagine three dolls, one made of glass, one of plastic, and one of steel. If struck with a hammer, the glass doll shatters, the plastic doll is scarred, but the steel doll proves invulnerable, reacting only with a metallic ping (Gelman, 1991, p. 44). That's resiliency. A profile of the resilient child suggests that such children are caring, independent, hopeful about the future, good at expressing their feelings and "most of all, they have a strong relationship with at least one caring adult."

The importance of adult support is stressed by U.S. Attorney General Janet Reno: "[I]t is essential that we view a child's life as a continuum and provide a consistent support system for those times when the family is unable to provide that support on its own" (Wilson, 1993, p. 2).

Labeling Revisited
It is human nature to apply labels to *things,* to name them. But when we are dealing with people, it is important to restrict the labeling to specific behaviors rather than to those who exhibit these behaviors. For example, "Hitting is a bad thing" in contrast to "You are a bad child for hitting."

Much has been made of the power of positive thinking. Negative thinking can be just as powerful. People can be talked into believing what or who they are. If children are constantly called stupid, this could retard their intellectual growth. Edwin Lemert (1951, p. 22) formulated some major assumptions of the labeling perspective. He related deviance to processes of social differentiation and social definition, stating:

> We start with the idea that persons and groups are differentiated in various ways, some of which result in social penalties, rejection, and segregation. These penalties and segregative reactions of society or the community are dynamic factors which increase, decrease, and condition the form which the initial differentiation or deviation takes.

Labeling and Self-Fulfilling Prophecies
In a frequently cited research study, psychology majors were given three groups of laboratory rats. They were told in advance how smart each group was. The first set consisted of super-smart rats who would be able to master a maze with no difficulty; therefore, they should have ample rewards along the way and a huge piece of cheese at the end. The second set consisted of rats of average ability

who would not be able to make use of the clues along the way; they should have an average amount of cheese at the end. The third group consisted of rats of below-average intelligence who had little hope of finding their way through the maze; a simple picture of some cheese at the end would do.

At the end of the day, all the super-smart rats were munching away at the cheese at the end of the maze, some of those with average intelligence had found their way to the end, and the below-average rats were aimlessly milling around in the maze, with none of them yet at the end. Imagine the students' surprise when the professor told them the rats were all of the same intelligence. It was how they were treated, based on how they were labeled, that made the difference.

A similar experiment that used three classes of second graders has often been cited to illustrate the effects of labeling. The teachers were told that one group was brilliant, one group was of average intelligence, and one group was below average. The "brilliant" group made tremendous gains in learning during a six-week period; the "average" group made some gains; and the "below-average" group actually lost ground. In reality, all three groups were of the same intelligence, but the teachers treated them differently, expecting large gains from the "brilliant" group and paying little attention to the "below-average" group. What they expected is exactly what they got.

Self-fulfilling prophecy occurs when people live up to the labels they are given.

Consequences of Labeling

Before formalized law enforcement, neighbors watched over neighbors, and if an incident occurred that needed public service, a "hue and cry" was raised. For example, if a neighbor saw a stranger removing a cow, he would pursue the thief yelling, "Stop, thief!" and arouse all the other neighbors to join the chase. If the thief abandoned the animal out of sight of the crowd, and an innocent person stopped to hold the cow and was mistakenly labeled as the thief by the pursuers, he was probably hanged.

The same thing can happen to youths who commit status offenses. They are automatically labeled delinquent and subject to the discipline of the juvenile court. If the court decides to teach such youths "a lesson," they can be placed in a locked facility for something as petty as a curfew violation. The youths are not hanged as was the innocent man with the cow, but the consequences can be almost as devastating.

Regardless of social class or environment, children have a strong natural inclination to believe those they respect. What is said to them makes a difference. A 16-year-old boy who appeared in juvenile court was admonished by the judge who called the youth a "menace" to society. The judge further stated that the boy was the kind of "kid" who gave "good" kids a bad name. This insensitive judge did not know that there was a computer error, and the "kid" was not the ruthless figure he was labeled. The event, however, was so traumatic for the 16-year-old that he wrote in a note, "The judge is right; I am no good." He signed it and then shot himself. It was the third suicide of a youth who appeared before the same judge.

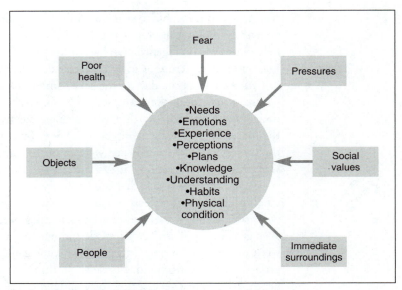

Figure 3.2
Barriers to Achievement

Behavior depends upon how individuals see, interpret and react to the world around them.

The harmful consequences of negative labeling are stressed here because at some point nearly every child gets into trouble, regardless of social status. It is not just inner-city youths or youths living in poverty who break the rules of society. It is almost *all* youths who do so.

Labeling theorists state that when a deviant label is attached to people, they become stigmatized and have little chance to be rewarded for conformist behavior. The label becomes a self-fulfilling prophecy.

Fortunately, it is also a fact that most children grow up to be law-abiding, sociable, productive citizens, having developed responsible behavior through the maturation process.

Barriers to Achievement

Many obstacles can hinder growth and development, not only during the preadolescent period but also throughout life. Some of these barriers are illustrated in Figure 3.2.

Some barriers are the result of a lack of prenatal care. One-fourth of pregnant mothers receive no physical care of any sort during the crucial first trimester of pregnancy. About 20 percent of handicapped children would not be impaired had their mothers had one physical exam during the first trimester, which could have detected potential problems (Hodgkinson, 1991, p. 10). In addition, every year about 350,000 children are born to mothers who were addicted to cocaine during pregnancy. Those who survive birth have strikingly short attention spans, poor coordination and worse, as will be discussed shortly.

Another large barrier to achievement while children are growing up may be fear. Some children are constantly afraid. They may fear not belonging, not being accepted, not meeting adult expectations. Children are especially afraid in school. They fear failing, being kept back, being called stupid, feeling stupid and, nowadays, they may fear physical harm, as will be discussed shortly. Such fears are most pronounced in children from poor families with low social status.

Pressures such as wanting to belong to "the" group, to get good grades or to make an athletic team may mount to the point that they inhibit achievement of any kind. A desire for money and possessions is yet another type of barrier if it becomes too high a priority. Closely related to this is the use of drugs, including alcohol. Substance abuse usually lessens achievement in many areas.

Other barriers to achievement exist in one's immediate surroundings. Youths who grow up in homes without books or magazines, with no nutritious food, and with unsanitary conditions in run-down neighborhoods may have difficulty accomplishing much more than simply surviving. Many of the barriers are a direct result of living in poverty.

Children Living in Poverty

A recent study shows ("Number of Children . . .," 1998, p. A6): "Nationally, nearly one in four preschoolers lived in poverty in the mid-1990s. . . . In 1995, 5.5 million children under 6 were living in poverty, down from the peak in 1993, but still much higher than it was in the early 1980s, when there were 4.4 million."

Nearly one-fourth of our children live in poverty.

According to Cowley (1991, p. 21):

> Poor children are more likely to suffer from low birth weight, more likely to die during the first year of life, more likely to suffer hunger or abuse while growing up and less likely to benefit from immunizations or adequate medical care.

Home conditions of economic deprivation or uncertainty can expose children to ills ranging from malnutrition to extreme psychopathology. This country has pockets of squalor found on tenant farms, in migrant camps and in the tenements of large cities. A report of the Task Force on Juvenile Justice and Delinquency Prevention (1977, p. 794) warned two decades ago:

> [A]n increase in crime is highly probable in the remainder of this century. More crimes may be committed as our population continues to grow; as the process of urbanization continues and more of our largest cities become ghettos composed largely of the poor, the young, and the black; as the inhibitions and restraints imposed by religious morality continue to weaken in an increasingly secularized society; as women and teenagers feel increasingly free to go their own way in a society liberated from the prejudices of the past; as increasing economic affluence brings the difference between the well-to-do and those caught in the "culture of poverty" into sharper focus; as the material goods of a growing middle income group increase and become more vulnerable to criminal acts; as higher professional standards make employment more difficult for millions of inadequately educated citizens and contribute to a widening cultural gulf between white and minority

Children playing in an unsafe, abandoned tenement building in New York City's lower east side.

group citizens; as the employment opportunities for the illiterate, uneducated and undereducated in post-industrialized society decline relative to the opportunities for those trained in professional and technical skills; and as the process of bureaucratization alienates an increasing number of citizens from the administration of justice and makes the larger police departments in urban centers more efficient but less responsive to the needs of the population they serve, and less adaptable to a rapidly changing social environment.

The recitation of trends associated with crime is likely to continue in the twenty-first century and appears to be very accurate. Many of these trends result in increased poverty for millions of youths, which may remove children from the culture at large and deprive them of the stimulation to grow as most children do.

It takes more than economic relief to lift families from a pattern of irresponsibility or depravity. Social agencies in every community know certain families that can be counted on to produce more than their share of school failures, truancy, sexual deviation, alcoholism, disorderliness and disease. They are also all too familiar with the inadequate personalities who become parents of other inadequate personalities in a recurring sequence that led early geneticists to talk about heredity and social incompetence.

It must be remembered, however, that poverty alone cannot be blamed for delinquency. Many children raised in extreme poverty grow up just fine. The Children's Defense Fund has suggested: "We must make it un-American for any child to grow up poor, or without adequate child care, health care, food, shelter, or education" (Kaplan, 1991, p. K1). Unfortunately, as Kaplan notes (p. K7), the universal, gilt-edged rhetorical support for such care is hollow at the core: "[T]he jury of public opinion is still debating whether children are actually a valued national resource or just another neglected minority." Two possible reasons for this lack of action are that children don't vote and they don't contribute to political campaigns.

Two of the most serious consequences of poverty for children are homelessness and increased risk of lead poisoning.

Homelessness

The number of children who are homeless on any given night ranges from 68,000 (U.S. General Accounting Office) to half a million (National Coalition for the Homeless). Being homeless places great stress on families and may result in child neglect or abuse. The homeless children also experience the stress, and they are likely to exhibit some of the following general tendencies (Linehan, 1992, p. 62): "[A]cting out, restlessness, aggressive behavior, depression, school behavioral problems, learning problems, regressive behavior (especially in younger children), inattentiveness, hyperactivity, and persistent tiredness and anxiety." Linehan also notes that: "A child living in a shelter is vulnerable to physical, mental, and emotional maladies because the whole experience tends to erode the child's primary protective structure—the family."

In addition to these general tendencies, four conditions often characterize homeless children's experiences (Linehan, pp. 62–64):

- Constant moving—results in a lack of roots, viewing life as temporary, becoming restless, being easily frustrated, and having limited attention spans.
- Frequent change of schools—results in falling behind academically as well as an unwillingness to form friendships or to participate in extracurricular activities.
- Overcrowded living quarters—results in either withdrawal or aggressiveness.
- Lack of access to basic resources (food, clothing, transportation)—results in deprivations with far-reaching effects.

Some homeless youths are entirely on their own, including **runaways** and **thrownaways** (their family has kicked them out). Stevens and Price (1992, p. 18) report that more than 300,000 school-age children are homeless each year. Difficulties facing such youths are discussed later.

Victims of Lead Poisoning

Children who live in poverty are also much more likely than others to be exposed to lead from old paint and old plumbing fixtures and from the lead in household dust. Other sources of lead are old water systems, lead crystal and some imported cans and ceramics. According to Eitzen (1992, p. 587), 16 percent of white children and 55 percent of black children have high levels of lead in their blood, a condition that leads to irreversible learning disabilities and other problems.

Stevens and Price (p. 18) report that some three to four million children are exposed to damaging levels of lead. The gravity of this problem was stated by the Public Health Service: "[L]ead poisoning remains the most common and societally devastating environmental disease of young children" (Needleman, 1992, p. 35). Babies exposed to low doses of lead before birth often are born underweight and underdeveloped. Even if they overcome these handicaps, when they go to school they face more obstacles (Cowley, p. 20):

> [L]ead-exposed kids exhibit behavioral problems, low IQ and deficiencies in speech and language. And research has shown that teenagers with histories of lead exposure drop out of school seven times as often as their peers.

According to Needleman:

> Being poor increases a child's risk radically. The ATSDR [Agency for Toxic Substances and Disease Registry] estimates that 7% of well-off white children have elevated blood lead levels; for poor whites, the proportion is 25%. Of poor African-American children, 55% have elevated levels. More than half of African-American children who live in poverty begin their education with the potentially handicapping condition. Lead exposure may be one of the most important—and least acknowledged—causes of school failure and learning disorders.

Cowley suggests that according to some experts lead poisoning is the nation's "foremost environmental hazard."

The Underclass

Scholars have used the term *underclass* in reference to the very poor. According to historian Michael Katz (1995, pp. 65–66), this term simply replaces the "unworthy poor" of the late 1800s and the "culture of poverty" of the mid-1900s. Concurring, Golden (1997, p. 65) states: "The language is new; the reality is old. Urban poverty has changed in three ways, however. It is more visible, more concentrated, and more expanded." Golden further suggests (pp. 65–66):

> Urban poor youth are facing a future in which public welfare benefits have been cut, part-time and summer jobs have been cut, health care and services have been cut, schools have become battlegrounds, homelessness is on the rise, there are no more traditional manufacturing jobs, and incarceration has tripled as a response to the "violence of the underclass." Their neighborhoods are isolated, crumbling slums.

Still other obstacles hindering growth and development are faced by children with special needs.

Children with Special Needs

The majority of children in our country are "normal," but thousands of other children have special needs.

Children with special needs include those who are emotionally/behaviorally disturbed, who have learning disabilities, who have an attention deficit disorder, or who have behavior problems resulting from prenatal exposure to drugs, including alcohol, or to the human immunodeficiency virus (HIV).

Emotionally/ Behaviorally Disturbed Children

One challenging segment of youths are emotionally/behaviorally disturbed (**EBD**) children. Emotionally/behaviorally disturbed youths usually have one or more of the following behavior patterns:

- Severely aggressive or impulsive behavior
- Severely withdrawn or anxious behaviors, pervasive unhappiness, depression or wide mood swings
- Severely disordered thought processes that show up in unusual behavior patterns, atypical communication styles and distorted interpersonal relationships

Such children may have limited coping skills and may be easily traumatized.

Youths with Attention Deficit Disorder (ADD)

Attention deficit disorder is a common childhood disruptive behavior disorder. Also called attention deficit hyperactivity disorder (ADHD), this phenomenon is characterized by the following behaviors:

- Heightened motor activity (fidgeting and squirming)
- Short attention span
- Distractibility
- Impulsiveness
- Lack of self-control

Such behaviors can greatly interfere with learning and are usually unnerving for parents, teachers and other adults.

Studies show that between 3 and 5 percent of children in the United States can be diagnosed with ADHD (Dupaul and Stoner, 1994, p. 3). Furthermore, of those children referred to clinics for ADHD treatment, boys outnumber girls by a ratio of nearly 6 to 1 (p. 3). Thompson (1996, p. 434) notes: "To meet the diagnostic criteria of the American Psychiatric Association, the child must have been creating disturbances for at least six months."

According to Smelter et al. (1996, p. 429): "Professionals who serve children must exercise due caution when labeling children as suffering from ADD or ADHD. . . . Likewise, those who work in schools should refrain from implying that such a diagnosis absolves the child from all responsibility for his or her behavior in the school setting."

Some educators, including Armstrong (1996, p. 424), question "the methods used to diagnose attention deficit disorder, the usefulness of a perspective that focuses on disability rather than potential, and the very existence of the disorder in the first place." However, a five-year federal study of boys with ADD revealed abnormalities in brain configuration, "a finding that supports the hotly debated theory that these behavioral disorders are strongly rooted in biology" ("Attention Deficit Disorder . . .," 1996, p. A11).

Attention deficit disorder is often accompanied by a learning disability.

Youths with Learning Disabilities

From 5 to 10 million children in the United States experience some form of **learning disability.** The Association for Children with Learning Disabilities (ACLD) describes a learning disabled child in the following way (p. 4): "A learning disabled person is an individual who has one or more significant deficits in the essential learning processes."

According to the ACLD (p. 3): "The most frequently displayed symptoms are short attention span, poor memory, difficulty following directions, inadequate ability to discriminate between and among letters, numerals, or sounds, poor reading ability, eye-hand coordination problems, difficulties with sequencing, disorganization and numerous other problems." Such children are often discipline problems, are labeled underachievers and are at great risk of becoming dropouts.

Although usually associated with school, the consequences of learning disabilities go well beyond school. Behaviors that may be problematic include:

- Responding inappropriately
- Saying one thing, meaning another
- Forgetting easily
- Acting impulsively
- Demanding immediate gratification
- Becoming easily frustrated and then engaging in disruptive behavior

Other behaviors that often accompany learning disability include (ACLD, p. 8):

- An inability to read and interpret environment and people
- An inability to adequately interpret their problems and needs
- Little thought about the results of their actions—poor judgment
- Inability to set realistic priorities and goals
- Inappropriate conclusions due to deficient reasoning ability
- Illogical reasons for their actions—sometimes even contradicting what was previously stated
- Inability to develop meaningful social relationships with others; usually these children are loners
- Inability to draw appropriate conclusions due to poor reasoning
- Childish and bossy behavior

Youths with learning disabilities are usually frustrated, have experienced failure after failure and lack self-esteem.

Youths Exposed to Drugs or HIV Prenatally

"Intrauterine exposure to drugs is the epidemic of the 1990s. Drug abuse is not new. . . . But the threat today is like a tidal wave" (Brazelton, 1990, p. 1). According to the National Institute on Drug Abuse, as reported in Sautter (1992, p. K2):

- The number of drug-exposed children born each year ranges from 375,000 to 739,000—possibly 18% of all newborns in the United States.
- Nearly 5% have been exposed to cocaine, from which crack is derived.

- Nearly 17% have been exposed to marijuana.
- Nearly 73% have been exposed to alcohol.
- By the year 2000 as many as *four million* drug-exposed children will be attending school.

Children exposed to cocaine while in the womb, the so-called **crack children,** may exhibit social, emotional and cognitive problems. As noted by Downing (1990, p. 9):

> These children, exposed to the damaging effects of cocaine (commonly in its less expensive and highly-addictive crystalized form: crack) while still in the womb, are already showing up in significant numbers in kindergarten classes and preschool programs in New York and Los Angeles. . . .
>
> They may over-react to—or fail to respond to—the stimuli of a classroom. They may have difficulty forming attachments. They may not be capable of structuring their own play or playing with other children.
>
> Typically, these kids don't socialize well, don't work well in groups, and stimulate too easily or do not respond at all—they can be either hyperactive or lethargic.

Griffith (1992, p. 30) cautions against stereotyping such children, however, noting that: "[T]he media have sensationalized the problems these children present and have shown worst-case scenarios as if they were the norm."

A closely related problem is **fetal alcohol syndrome** (FAS). Burgess and Streissguth (1992, p. 24) suggest: "Fetal alcohol syndrome (FAS) is now recognized as the leading known cause of mental retardation in the western world." They estimate that one in 500 to 600 children is born with fetal alcohol syndrome, and one in 300 to 350 children has fetal alcohol effects, including the following:

- Children are impulsive and have poor communication skills.
- Children are not able to predict consequences or to use appropriate judgment in daily life.
- Small children may exhibit a high level of activity and distractibility.
- Adolescents may suffer frustration and depression.

A study by the Centers for Disease Control (CDC) ("More Pregnant Women . . .," 1998, p. E5) puts the incidence of fetal alcohol syndrome at about one per 1,000 live births, yet notes that Ann Streissguth, director of the Fetal Alcohol Syndrome and Drug Unit at the University of Washington Medical Center, believes that "the overall rate of babies affected in some way [by maternal alcohol consumption] is much greater." According to this study: "In 1995, four times as many pregnant women said they frequently consumed alcohol as in 1991." The study also stresses: "Alcohol is the leading known preventable cause of mental retardation. . . . Babies born with fetal alcohol syndrome suffer from a variety of physical and mental defects that can include abnormally formed organs, small brains, poor coordination, short attention span and mental retardation. They are typically small at birth, with similar facial features—tiny eyes, small, flat cheeks, and a short, upturned nose."

Another group of children with special needs are those prenatally exposed to HIV. According to Seidel (1992, p. 39), such children may experience:

- Deficits in both gross and fine motor skills
- Reduced flexibility and muscle strength
- Cognitive impairment including decreased intellectual levels, specific learning disabilities, mental retardation, visual/spatial deficits, and decreased alertness
- Language delays

A great number of these children with special needs entered grade school in the early 1990s and will be adolescents toward the end of the decade. Early intervention and support is imperative.

Adolescence

Adolescence refers to the period from age 12 to age 19 or 20.

In adolescence, children go through puberty, experiencing hormonal changes. During this time adolescents seek independence but can be very much influenced by their peers. Each generation produces a distinct adolescent subculture, with a common language, clothing, music and standards. The result is what is often referred to as a *generation gap*. According to Canning (1992), adolescence is characterized by:

- Rapid growth and sexual maturity—self-image, self-centeredness, wondering about body changes, sexuality, intimacy, and sexual identity.
- Consciousness of self in relation to other people—peer pressure and the shift of the primary support system from parents to friends.
- Mood swings of high and low feelings—changeable, intense and often confused feelings; outlets for high energy are needed.
- Experimentation—examining the myth of invulnerability, beginning to learn from experience (doubt advice), developing abstract thinking vs. concrete thinking, new freedoms.
- Re-evaluation of values—rebelling against "what-is"—search for values that fit lifestyles.
- Search for identity—a negative identity is better than no identity at all, internal vs. external control, recognition as an individual, seeking independence.
- Self-image—the need to be valued, to feel worth, to be viewed as capable and contributing.

Glick (1998) has developed an adolescent development model whose core is "based on the assumption that adolescence is a process of growth during which certain attitudes, beliefs and values are explored, cognitive structuring occurs, and skills are acquired" (see Figure 3.3). That adolescence is no longer typified by the

ADOLESCENT DEVELOPMENT—A DEVELOPMENTAL TASKS MODEL

Early Adolescence (10–12 years)

PHYSICAL DEVELOPMENT

Puberty starts (period of rapid growth; bodily changes; fidgets, squirms, has trouble sitting still; requires lots of physical activity). Puberty usually starts two years earlier for girls than boys. Begins to show bodily changes (pubic hair; hair thickens and darkens; testes and breasts enlarge).

COGNITIVE DEVELOPMENT

Inconsistent thoughts as they adjust to an open mind and body. Shifts from immature to mature thinking. Logic and reasoning are discovered. Able to imagine beyond immediate environment. Conversation leads to exchange of ideas. Spends more time talking to parents. It is important to feel that their opinion counts. Thoughts lead to feelings of self-consciousness. Girls are more communicative than boys.

EMOTIONAL DEVELOPMENT

Seeks independence, establishes individuality. Wants some control in decisions affecting life. Propensity toward awkwardness, self-consciousness, and bouts with low self-esteem. Begins developing mature relationships with siblings. Begins to be self-conscious about appearance. Girls often feel less attractive. Need praise and approval from adults to demonstrate concern and care about their welfare.

SOCIAL DEVELOPMENT

Has a desire to "fit in;" to be well-liked is important. Cliques are formed with others. Wants to be with friends without adult supervision. Feels that peer pressure is constantly present. Begins experimenting with smoking, alcohol and sex. Appreciates conversations that lead to an exchange of ideas to better understand other people's points of view.

Middle Adolescence (13–15 years)

PHYSICAL DEVELOPMENT

Puberty continues (boys begin growth spurts and surpass girls in height and weight by age 15). Acne and body odor are prevalent. Habits are developed that affect lifelong levels of physical fitness. Motor skills increase through physical activity. Clumsiness due to rapid physical development. At-risk habits such as smoking, drinking or drugs are started. Poor eating habits develop. Extremely aware and sensitive to own development and that of peers.

COGNITIVE DEVELOPMENT

Abstract thinking begins. Problem-solving, analytical thinking and writing may be deficient. Learn from doing; expand knowledge; experience through academic activities and performance. Greater separation in school between those who succeed and those who fail. Parents have less influence. Girls may begin failing in school. Decreased evidence of creativity and flexibility. Peer conformity critically important ("belongingness").

EMOTIONAL DEVELOPMENT

Craves freedom. Adept at "masking" true feelings and state of mind. Neutral responses to feelings of happiness and sadness. Intense desire and need for privacy. Rapid hormonal and body changes often lead to low self-esteem and lack of confidence. Seeks independence from, but still needs structure and limits from, parents and adults. Increased sexual desires and experimentation. Needs praise and approval to show that adults are concerned about their welfare.

SOCIAL DEVELOPMENT

Friendships and romance become increasingly important. Realizes that others have different points of view. (Initial perspective-taking critically important to moral reasoning); and that outlook may be influenced by self-interest. Begins to define themselves and develop more concrete self-concept. Shows increased communication and negotiation skills. Experiences increased capacity for meaningful relationships with peers and adults. Explores rights and responsibilities. Wants to hang out with older teens. Same sex groups socialize together. Parents start to have less influence.

Late Adolescence (16+ years)

PHYSICAL DEVELOPMENT

Boys' growth has doubled since age 12. They are taller and heavier than girls. Appropriate physical tasks have been learned and managed. Appetite has increased. Eating disorders may appear (bulimia and anorexia). Life patterns become consistent.

COGNITIVE DEVELOPMENT

Critical thinking and reasoning skills begin. Want to think out their own decisions. Concerned about the purpose and meaning of life. Can manipulate a number of variables at once. Develops beliefs, values, career choices and an identity. Limited evidence of creativity. Increased peer conformity. New challenges and experiences are required.

EMOTIONAL DEVELOPMENT

Develops a sense of personal identity. Self-esteem continues to develop and improve. Competencies such as decision-making, stress management and coping with problems develop. Thoughts and worries about adult life increase. Friendships are based on mature intimacy, and sharing thoughts and feelings—rather than just hanging out and doing things together. Strong sexual feelings are experienced. Generally, strong ties with the family are maintained with increased need for parental love, care and respect.

SOCIAL DEVELOPMENT

Independence developed and demonstrated. Susceptibility to peer pressure declines; parent-teen conflicts decrease. Cooperation and communication increase. Identity formation experienced through exploration and experimentation. Obsessed about appearance. Want to distinguish themselves from the crowd. Begins forming heterosexual groups and pairs up socially. Strong same-sex friendships continue to exist and strengthen. Has large circle of acquaintances and small circle of friends. After-school work prevalent—usually 15 to 20 hours per week. Is involved with social causes and movements (e.g., local community actions; environmental issues; volunteer work; political awareness).

Figure 3.3
Adolescent Development

Source: Barry Glick. "Kids in Adult Correctional Systems." *Corrections Today,* August 1998, p. 97. Reprinted by permission.

carefree lifestyle of the 1950s, depicted in the television program *Happy Days,* is underscored by the large percentage of high school seniors who report worrying about social problems, as shown in Table 3.3.

Crime and violence has been the number one concern of high school seniors since 1984. Ninety percent of the class of 1996 reported worrying about crime and violence. Since 1984, the level of concern about hunger and poverty has also risen considerably among high school students, and worry over race relations has increased steadily to become the number two concern for our nation's high school seniors. Another study reports ("Survey: . . . ," 1998, p. A10) that nearly 60 percent of public school students feel vulnerable to crime and violence while in school, believing not enough is being done to ensure their safety and security. Fear of the chance of nuclear war has greatly lessened, however, reflecting the dramatic changes that have taken place in the world.

Adolescence is a difficult time of life, not only for youths themselves, but also for their families, schools, neighborhoods and, increasingly, the police. It is a period of stress and social strain.

Adolescence brings biological, psychological, emotional and social changes, often resulting in stress.

The influence of social change in shaping adolescent behavior is second in importance only to psychological change. The mind must adjust to the conditions, pleasures and pressures of society that influence growth and development to adulthood. This is seldom done smoothly.

Juveniles often pretend to be adults in various ways, but becoming an emotionally mature, socially accepted adult requires a struggle. From a social standpoint, many never succeed. Adolescents may try to look like adults, talk like adults or take on what they believe to be adult ways, but in general they remain quite immature. At the same time that they imitate adult behavior, juveniles also strive for individuality, independence and freedom, which they believe they can achieve by disassociating themselves from society and their parents. Such a position between imitation and disassociation can generate a great deal of psychological stress.

Typical stressors for adolescents have been suggested by Daniel J. Anderson, President of Hazelden Foundation (1986, p. C5), which provides a wide range of services related to chemical dependency:

- Families with single parents or both parents working, placing more demands on young people
- Children never getting a chance to be bored because they are in every scheduled event possible
- Children who are bored because they watch many hours of television each day
- Families that do not provide nutritionally balanced meals for children

Table 3.3
High School Seniors Reporting That They Worry about Selected Social Problems (United States, 1984–96)

Question, "Of all the problems facing the nation today, how often do you worry about each of the following?"

(Percent responding "often" or "sometimes")

	Class of 1984 (N=3,294)	Class of 1985 (N=3,286)	Class of 1986 (N=3,073)	Class of 1987 (N=3,370)	Class of 1988 (N=3,326)	Class of 1989 (N=2,849)	Class of 1990 (N=2,595)	Class of 1991 (N=2,595)	Class of 1992 (N=2,736)	Class of 1993 (N=2,807)	Class of 1994 (N=2,664)	Class of 1995 (N=2,646)	Class of 1996 (N=2,502)
Chance of nuclear war	69.4%	64.5%	69.1%	58.3%	57.3%	52.4%	45.1%	41.5%	33.4%	28.8%	27.9%	20.0%	21.6%
Population growth	25.3	25.7	24.1	26.6	27.5	29.6	33.0	30.6	35.2	38.9	35.4	34.9	37.4
Crime and violence	83.9	82.3	79.4	81.9	83.9	86.3	88.8	88.1	91.6	90.8	92.7	90.2	90.1
Pollution	49.1	46.9	44.2	45.2	45.5	55.9	67.2	72.1	71.9	72.8	66.5	63.6	62.9
Energy shortages	40.4	33.7	28.7	28.1	25.1	27.9	32.6	38.2	35.2	29.8	23.8	17.9	19.2
Race relations	43.1	43.4	43.4	44.2	53.3	53.6	57.1	59.4	68.7	75.4	71.6	68.9	70.7
Hunger and poverty	58.3	69.7	65.9	62.2	64.2	64.1	65.9	66.4	68.1	71.1	65.7	62.3	62.6
Using open land for housing or industry	30.0	30.4	26.8	30.5	29.4	30.8	33.9	33.8	34.7	32.9	32.7	28.9	32.6
Urban decay	18.0	17.9	17.0	18.5	19.9	19.8	20.4	21.7	25.8	25.3	25.6	23.0	25.1
Economic problems	66.2	60.4	60.6	55.6	56.2	57.6	56.8	63.9	70.6	71.8	62.6	55.7	57.9
Drug abuse	68.4	69.1	69.2	75.4	78.6	79.5	82.6	79.5	77.8	75.5	76.7	72.6	71.0

Note: These data are from a series of nationwide surveys of high school seniors conducted by the Monitoring the Future Project at the University of Michigan's Institute for Social Research from 1975 through 1996. The survey design is a multistage random sample of high school seniors in public and private schools throughout the continental United States. All percentages reported are based on weighted cases, the N's that are shown in the tables refer to the number of weighted cases.

Response categories were "never," "seldom," "sometimes," and "often." Readers interested in responses to this question for 1975 through 1983 should consult previous editions of SOURCEBOOK.

Source: Lloyd D. Johnston, Jerald G. Bachman, and Patrick M. O'Malley, Monitoring the Future 1985, pp. 174, 175; 1987, pp. 180, 181; 1989, pp. 180, 181; 1991, pp. 188, 189; 1993, pp. 190, 191; 1995, pp. 191, 192; (Ann Arbor, MI: Institute for Social Research, University of Michigan); Jerald G. Bachman, Lloyd D. Johnston, and Patrick M. O'Malley, Monitoring the Future 1984, pp. 174, 175; 1986, pp. 176, 177; 1988, pp. 180, 181; 1990, pp. 186, 187; 1992, pp. 189, 190; 1994, pp. 189, 190 (Ann Arbor, MI: Institute for Social Research, University of Michigan); and data provided by the Monitoring the Future Project, Survey Research Center; Lloyd D. Johnston, Jerald G. Bachman, and Patrick M. O'Malley, Principal Investigators. Table adapted by SOURCEBOOK staff. Reprinted by permission.

Source: Sourcebook of Criminal Justice Statistics 1996. Washington, DC: U.S. Government Printing Office, 1997, p. 181.

- Adults who make statements and act in ways damaging to a child's self-image
- Parents who expect their children to be young adults before they can be

Anderson asserts: "These are just some of the possible areas of adolescent stress. As parents or teachers it would be helpful to identify stress in our children's lives, and the place to start would be to ask the children."

Adolescents do communicate messages about their disturbances in growth and development. However, adults often do not listen, regardless of social position, class or status.

Adolescents in lower socioeconomic classes often must struggle to succeed academically and financially. Without scholarship assistance, college may be unaffordable. The need to balance education with earning an income can be exhausting and disheartening. Adolescents who are affluent commonly face pressure to gain admission to the highest-ranked colleges possible. If they don't get into Harvard, Yale or the like, they may be considered failures, especially if their parents attended such schools.

Life for some adolescents is often lonely and depressing. Parents are involved in demanding careers, travel a lot and leave child care to paid help or the extended family. They seldom do things as a family. When young people become bored with the happenings around them or with life in general, they often turn to antisocial or unlawful activity or to self-destruction.

Ruby Takanishi (1994, p. 11), executive director of the Carnegie Council on Adolescent Development, stresses that good health is critical not only to physical but also to psychological development: "If you have a toothache or a stomachache, or are worried about staying alive in a violence-prone neighborhood, even the most wonderful education won't get you very far." She cites the following statistics about American adolescents:

> Over a quarter of 10- to 18-year-olds live in poor or near-poor families. . . . The rates of physical, sexual, and emotional abuse have risen swiftly. Pregnancy rates and births outside of marriage are the highest among industrialized nations.
>
> About 20 percent of people with AIDS are 20- to 29-year-olds, many infected during adolescence. More kids are experimenting with drugs earlier. Suicide rates are sharply higher. And up to 33 percent of adolescents suffer some form of depression.

Although it is sometimes thought that youths with problems exist primarily in the inner city, this is simply not the case. According to Hawkins (1985, p. 51), thousands of middle-class youths are "wasting their formative years . . . killing time in discos, video parlors, shopping centers, and other hangouts." Hawkins explains: "Upset with their parents and tired of school, many of these teens band together, substituting peers for family. Police describe the activity as 'rat packing.' "

When this same phenomenon occurs in urban areas, the result would be called a *gang* rather than a rat pack. Hawkins (p. 54) notes that authorities fear that these rat packers "will become tomorrow's criminals or consign themselves to aimless lives. Ill-prepared for a complex society, they may pass on a confused legacy to their children," resulting in an even less desirable next generation.

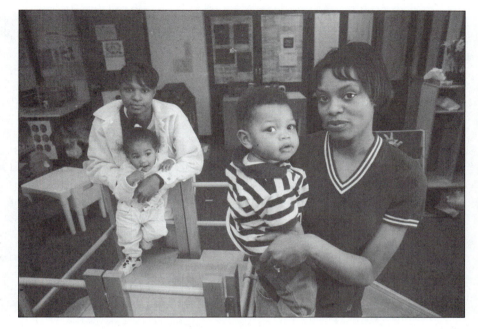

Two young mothers spend time with their children in a county-funded day care program nursery in a Minneapolis high school. They are 2 of 28 students who drop off their toddlers while they attend classes, making it easier for teenage mothers to finish school.

Youths Who Are on Drugs

The tremendous impact of drug use on the growth and development of our youths is vividly stated by Moore (p. 1): "One of the worst aspects of drug use may be its attraction to youths in urban ghettos, for it robs many of their chance for upward mobility. With that, some of the promise and justice of a democratic society is lost."

In a speech to the Child Welfare League of America, former Surgeon General Joycelyn Elders said children are "out in an ocean surrounded by the sharks—drugs, alcohol, homicide, suicide . . . and we've been sitting on the beach sipping from our fountains of 'just say no.' " She said it is easier for many children to find drugs than it is to find hugs ("Quiet Crisis . . . ," 1994). Lundgren (1997, p. 23) likewise warns:

> America's youth are rushing headlong into a plague which threatens lives and destroys families. The plague is drug and alcohol abuse by our youth, and it is on the rise. . . . In just four years, drug use has increased by 30% to 50% among all grade levels. Now, more than one out of every four 7th graders has experimented with drugs, more than 40% of 9th grade students and almost half of 11th grade students have done so, all in just the past six months.

Teen Pregnancy

One important change within our culture has been a more open attitude toward sex and at least a tolerance of sexual intimacy outside of marriage. In many instances, marriage is no longer a requirement to live together. According to polls, the majority of teenage males and females have engaged in sexual intercourse by age 19 (Caldas, 1994, p. 405). The result is a large increase in teenage pregnancy.

A study sponsored by the Robin Hood Foundation, a New York City charity, has found ("Public Cost of Teen . . .," 1996, p. A4): "As a group, girls under 18 give birth to 175,000 children each year." Furthermore, "taxpayers will spend nearly $7 billion [in 1996] to deal with social problems resulting from recent births to girls under age 18 . . . $2.2 billion annually in welfare and food stamp benefits, $1.5 billion in medical costs, $900 million in increased foster-care expenses and $1 billion for additional prison construction."

When teenagers become pregnant, not only is their own growth and development affected, the situation into which they bring their newborn children often is unsuited for the healthy growth and development of these children. Teenage pregnancy has created an "underclass" of poor young women with small children. These women have no training and limited resources.

Caldas (p. 403) reports that 60 percent of teen families live in poverty. Even more devastating, however, is "strong evidence for the intergenerational transfer of poverty to the children of single-parent families."

Some seldom-mentioned facts about teen pregnancy are set forth by Males (1994, pp. 408–409):

- The large majority of all "teenage" pregnancies are caused by adults. Men older than high school age account for 77% of all births among girls of high school age (ages 16–18) and for 51% of births among girls of junior high school age (15 and younger). Men over age 25 father twice as many "teenage" births as do boys under age 18.

- A large majority of all pregnant teenagers have histories of rape, sexual abuse, and physical abuse.

- Poverty is the key indicator of early pregnancy.

Males notes that adults model one behavior and preach a different behavior. He suggests (p. 408): "Attempting to contrive and preach 'values' that contradict the values adults practice is an exercise in futility." He concludes: "The problem is not that teenagers are confused or that they reject the values of adults around them, but that they copy them only too well." According to former Surgeon General Joycelyn Elders: "[T]he children of adolescent parents are more likely to become adolescent parents themselves, perpetuating the cycle" ("Teen Moms . . . ," 1994, p. A7).

The Fading of the American Dream

As youths develop and approach adulthood, they need to have feelings of self-worth and hope for their future. Our society places great pressure on people to be "successful." As noted by Eitzen (p. 566):

The highly valued individual in American society is the self-made person—that is, one who has achieved money, position, and privilege through his or her own efforts in a highly competitive system. Economic success, as evidenced by material possessions, is the most common indicator of who is and who is not successful. Moreover, economic success has come to be the common measure of self-worth.

Competition is pervasive in American society, and we glorify the winners. . . . What about the losers in that competition? How do they respond to failure? How do we respond to them? How do they respond to ridicule? How do they react to the shame of being poor? . . . They may respond by working harder to succeed, which is the great American myth. Alternatively, they may become apathetic, drop out, tune out with drugs, join others who are also "failures" in a fight against the system that has rejected them, or engage in various forms of social deviance to obtain the material manifestations of success.

Vietnamese-American Boy Scouts gather at a cultural fair in Fountain Valley, California. Their outlook on the future is optimistic because scouting provides an avenue for acquiring skills as well as values important in a democratic society.

Eitzen (p. 584) notes: "Some young people act in antisocial ways because they have lost their dreams." He compares a person's economic situation with a boat, noting that it is assumed that just as "a rising tide lifts all boats," a rising economy will elevate the financial status of everyone. This was generally true from 1950 to 1973, when the average standard of living rose steadily. In the past 20 years, however, this has not been true. As noted by Eitzen: "Since 1973 the water level was not the same for all boats, some boats leaked severely, and some people had no boat at all."

The American Dream is fading for many youths.

Homes, college education, things formerly taken for granted are now out of reach for millions of Americans. In addition, says Eitzen (p. 587): "Children, so dependent on peer approval, often find the increasing gap in material differences between themselves and their peers intolerable. This may explain why some try to become 'somebody' by acting tough, joining a gang, rejecting authority, experimenting with drugs and sex, or running away from home."

Smith (1993, p. 10) stresses that: "[O]ptimal growth cannot occur when young people do not regard their future as worthwhile." He suggests that many young people lack faith in the future because "the traditional ladder of success has uneven, broken, and even missing rungs." Youths who have no faith in the future are less likely to fear the consequences of using illegal means to obtain what appears to be out of reach through legal means. The dire result is described by Canada (1995, p. x):

> . . . we are all approaching one of the most dangerous periods in our history since the Civil War. Rising unemployment, shifting economic priorities, hundreds of thousands of people growing up poor and with no chance of employment, never having held a legal job. A whole generation who serve no useful role in America now and see no hope of a future role for themselves. A new generation, the handgun generation. War as a child, war as an adolescent, war as an adult.

On a more positive note, however, many U.S. teens reportedly believe their futures are bright regarding employment ("Survey: . . .," p. A10): "Nearly 71 percent of the respondents believe there will be many available opportunities after they graduate—72 percent for whites and 63 percent for black teenagers."

A large part of the responsibility for assuring that our youths feel that they have a promising future and a stake in our society rests with the family, the school and the community, the focus of the next chapter.

Summary

The juvenile justice system exists to serve the children and adolescents of our country. Eighteen is the most common age at which individuals are legally considered adults, no longer under the jurisdiction of the juvenile court. Until that time it is expected that the state will assure the healthy growth and development of its children.

The period from birth to age three is the most formative time of a child's life. The age at which humans are most aggressive is age two. For children to learn, they need drive, a cue, a response and reinforcement. Praise is usually better than punishment when teaching children. The positive needs to be accentuated.

Great care must be taken when using labels with children. Self-fulfilling prophecies occur when people live up to the labels they are given. Children and adolescents in particular incorporate labels as part of their self-image. Labeling theorists state that when a deviant label is attached to individuals, they become stigmatized and have little opportunity to be rewarded for conformist behavior. The label becomes a self-fulfilling prophecy.

Nearly one-fourth of our children live in poverty. Two of the most serious consequences of poverty for children are homelessness and an increased risk of lead poisoning.

Children with special needs include those who are emotionally/behaviorally disturbed, who have learning disabilities, who have an attention deficit disorder or who have behavior problems resulting from prenatal exposure to drugs, including alcohol, or to HIV.

Adolescence refers to the period from ages 12 to 19 or 20. Adolescence brings biological, psychological, emotional and social changes that often result in stress. It may also bring a fading of the American Dream for many youths.

Discussion Questions

1. What is meant by the quote that appears at the beginning of this chapter?
2. The adult world stresses material and financial gain, social status and winning at any cost. Can children adjust to or understand this attitude? What values should we communicate to children about these attitudes?
3. What are some common labels for youths used in local high schools—e.g., nerd? How can the labels hurt youths?
4. Can labels be beneficial? What might be some positive effects of labeling?
5. Does your community have any ghettos or areas where poverty exists? What are some of the visible signs of such conditions?
6. How does your community handle homeless people, particularly youths? Are there any special programs for homeless families with children?

7. At what age do people become adults in your state?
8. Do you know any children who have special needs or who may be at risk for not developing "normally"? If so, have they managed to overcome their particular problem?
9. Do you recall your adolescent period? How would you characterize it? What were stressors for you?
10. Do you believe the American Dream is attainable for those who are willing to sacrifice and to work hard?

References

Anderson, Daniel J. "Stress in Children Is Overlooked." (Minneapolis/St. Paul) *Star Tribune,* March 24, 1986, p. C5.

Armstrong, Thomas. "ADD: Does It Really Exist?" *Phi Delta Kappan,* February 1996, pp. 424–428.

Association for Children with Learning Disabilities. "Taking the First Step to Solving Learning Problems." Pittsburgh, PA: Association for Children with Learning Disabilities, pamphlet, n.d.

"Attention Deficit Disorder Study Finds Differences in the Brain." (Minneapolis/St. Paul) *Star Tribune,* July 16, 1996, p. A11.

Brazelton, T. Berry. *Identifying the Needs of Drug-Affected Children: 1990 Issue Forum.* Washington, DC: Office for Substance Abuse Prevention, U.S. Department of Health and Human Services, 1990.

Burgess, Donna M. and Streissguth, Ann P. "Fetal Alcohol Syndrome and Fetal Alcohol Effects: Principles for Educators." *Phi Delta Kappan,* September 1992, pp. 24–30.

Caldas, Stephen J. "Teen Pregnancy: Why It Remains a Serious Social, Economic, and Educational Problem in the U.S." *Phi Delta Kappan,* January 1994, pp. 402–405.

Canada, Geoffrey. *Fist, Stick, Knife, Gun.* Boston: Beacon, 1995.

Canning, Miles, ed. "Both Sides of Adolescence." Richfield, MN: Storefront/Youth Action, 1992.

Caticchio, John A. *Putting Humpty Back Together.* Wayzata, MN: Vivere Publications, 1990.

Cowley, Geoffrey. "Children in Peril." *Newsweek Special Issue,* Summer 1991, pp. 18–21.

"Developmental Risk Called High for U.S. Children: Study Raises Fears They Won't Be Responsible Adults." (Minneapolis/St. Paul) *Star Tribune,* April 12, 1994, p. A1.

Downing, David. "Coming Soon to a Classroom Near You: 'Crack Kids.'" *Advocate,* October 5, 1990, p. 9.

Dupaul, Gary J. and Stoner, George. *ADHD in Schools: Assessment and Intervention Strategies.* New York: Guilford Press, 1994.

Eitzen, Stanley. "Problem Students: The Sociocultural Roots." *Phi Delta Kappan,* April 1992, pp. 584–590.

Gelman, David. "The Miracle of Resiliency." *Newsweek Special Edition,* Summer 1991, pp. 44–47.

Glick, Barry. "Kids in Adult Correctional Systems." *Corrections Today,* August 1998, pp. 96–99.

Golden, Renny. *Disposable Children: America's Child Welfare System.* Belmont, CA: Wadsworth Publishing Company, 1997.

Griffith, Dan R. "Prenatal Exposure to Cocaine and Other Drugs: Developmental and Educational Prognoses." *Phi Delta Kappan,* September 1992, pp. 30–34.

Hall, Elizabeth; Lamb, Michael E.; and Perlmutter, Marion. *Child Psychology Today,* 2nd ed. New York: Random House, 1986.

Hawkins, Steve L. " 'Rat Pack' Youth: Teenage Rebels in Suburbia." *U.S. News & World Report,* March 11, 1985, pp. 51–54.

Hodgkinson, Harold. "Reform versus Reality." *Phi Delta Kappan,* September 1991, pp. 9–16.

Kaplan, George. "Suppose They Gave an Intergenerational Conflict and Nobody Came." *Phi Delta Kappan Special Report,* May 1991.

Katz, Michael. *Improving Poor People: The Welfare State, the "Underclass," the Urban Schools as History.* New Jersey: Princeton University Press, 1995.

Lemert, Edwin. *Social Pathology.* New York: McGraw-Hill, 1951.

Linehan, Michelle Fryt. "Children Who Are Homeless: Educational Strategies for School Personnel." *Phi Delta Kappan,* September 1992, pp. 61–66.

Louv, Richard. *Children's Future.* Boston: Houghton Mifflin, 1990.

Lundgren, Daniel E. "Youth Drug Use Climbing." *Law Enforcement Quarterly,* November 1996–January 1997, p. 23.

Males, Mike. "Poverty, Rape, Adult/Teen Sex: Why 'Pregnancy Prevention' Programs Don't Work." *Phi Delta Kappan,* January 1994, pp. 407–410.

Moore, Mark. *Drug Trafficking.* Washington, DC: National Institute of Justice, n.d.

"More Pregnant Women Are Drinking, CDC Says." (Minneapolis/St. Paul) *Star Tribune,* August 12, 1998, p. E5.

Needleman, Herbert L. "Childhood Exposure to Lead: A Common Cause of School Failure." *Phi Delta Kappan,* September 1992, pp. 35–37.

"Number of Children in Poverty Is Up 12 Percent, Study Says." (Minneapolis/St. Paul) *Star Tribune,* July 10, 1998, p. A6.

"Public Cost of Teen Pregnancy Put At Nearly $7 Billion This Year." (Minneapolis/St. Paul) *Star Tribune,* June 13, 1996, p. A4.

"Quiet Crisis—Half of Tots Face Problems." Reported by Associated Press. [Cited April 13, 1994.] Available from Prodigy Interactive Services Co., White Plains, NY.

Ruben, David. "What Makes a Child Violent?" *Parenting,* August 1998, pp. 96–102.

Samenow, Stanton E. *Before It's Too Late: Why Some Kids Get into Trouble—and What Parents Can Do About It.* New York: Times Books, 1989.

Sautter, R. Craig. "Crack: Healing the Children." *Phi Delta Kappan Special Report,* November 1992, pp. K1–K12.

Seidel, John F. "Children with HIV-Related Developmental Difficulties." *Phi Delta Kappan,* September 1992, pp. 38–56.

Smelter, Richard W.; Rasch, Bradley W.; Fleming, Jan; Nazos, Pat; and Baranowski, Sharon. "Is Attention Deficit Disorder Becoming a Desired Diagnosis?" *Phi Delta Kappan,* February 1996, pp. 429–432.

Smetanka, Mary Jane. "New Hope for 'At-Risk' Children: Schools Learning to Help Kids Build on Inborn Resilience." (Minneapolis/St. Paul) *Star Tribune,* November 1, 1993, pp. A1, A16.

Smith, Robert L. "In the Service of Youth: A Common Denominator." *Juvenile Justice,* Vol. 1, No.2, Fall/Winter 1993, pp. 16–22.

Stevens, Linda J. and Price, Marianne. "Meeting the Challenge of Educating Children at Risk," *Phi Delta Kappan,* September 1992, pp. 18–23.

"Survey: Girls At the Head of the Class." (Minneapolis/St. Paul) *Star Tribune,* August 12, 1998, p. A10.

Takanishi, Ruby. "Young Lives in the Balance: Participant Interview." *The Participant.* New York: TIAA/CREF, April 1994, pp. 10–11.

The Task Force Report on Juvenile Justice and Delinquency Prevention. *Juvenile Justice and Delinquency Prevention.* Washington, DC:U.S. Government Printing Office, 1977.

"Teen Moms Are Found to Feed Cycle of Welfare." (Minneapolis/St. Paul) *Star Tribune,* June 3, 1994, p. A7.

Thompson, Anna M. "Attention Deficit Hyperactivity Disorder: A Parent's Perspective." *Phi Delta Kappan,* February 1996, pp. 433–436.

Wilson, John J. "A National Agenda for Children: On the Front Lines with Attorney General Janet Reno." *Juvenile Justice,* Vol. 1, No. 2, Fall/Winter 1993, pp. 2–8.

<table>
<tr><td rowspan="4" style="font-size:large">Chapter</td><td rowspan="4" style="font-size:xx-large">4</td><td>The Family, the School</td></tr>
<tr><td>and the Community:</td></tr>
<tr><td>Powerful Influences</td></tr>
<tr><td>on Youths' Development</td></tr>
</table>

Chapter 4

The Family, the School and the Community: Powerful Influences on Youths' Development

What you live, you learn. What you learn, you practice. What you practice, you become. What you become is a pattern. Patterns create consequences.

—Author unknown

Do You Know

- Why the structure and interaction patterns of the home are important?
- What are characteristics of a healthy family?
- What *adult supremacy* refers to?
- What common values might be passed on to our youths?
- Which children may be at risk as they grow and develop?
- What the principle of *in loco parentis* is?
- How negative norms and behaviors might be offset?
- What is the likely result of succeeding in school?
- Whose approval is often most important during adolescence?
- What educational practices may encourage failure?
- How students might respond to failure in school?
- Whether failure in school and delinquency are linked?
- What have been identified as the biggest problems facing local public schools?
- How many children are born at risk of being educationally disadvantaged?
- What rights students have within the school?
- What standard has been set by the Supreme Court for cases involving students' rights?
- What effect community associations have on child development?

Can You Define

adult supremacy, caring, educare, *in loco parentis,* Norman Rockwell family, radial concept

INTRODUCTION

Powerful influences on the growth and development of our youths are the family, the school and the community, all of which have undergone tremendous changes in the past few decades. The preceding chapter on how children and adolescents develop should have made obvious the importance of these institutions.

Growth and development do not occur in isolation. They involve a complex interacting of family, school and community, with the family being the first and most vital influence. As children grow, the school becomes an important influence, be it preschool, kindergarten, public or private school. As youths approach adolescence, the influence of parents and teachers wanes and that of peers becomes stronger. All of this occurs within the broader community within which children live. This **radial concept** of the influences on growth and development is illustrated in Figure 4.1.

Chaskin and Rauner (1995) report on research into **caring** as the conceptual foundation for youths development. They explain (p. 671): "Fundamentally, caring as we used the term in our project involves the ways in which individuals and institutions protect young people and invest in their ongoing development." They contend that the family, school and community are integrally related in developing a caring environment (pp. 671, 673): "The family is the most common context in which a new human being learns about care and nurturing. . . . Schools have been identified as primary arenas for the nurture and promotion of caring. . . . Community institutions can also serve as sources of caring for young people and as venues for promoting caring behavior." They echo a theme presented in Chapter 3 on the devastating effects of poverty (p. 668):

> Of the many factors that can impede the development of caring, the researchers assert that poverty is the most pervasive, persistent, and devastating threat to caring in children and young people. Other problems that often accompany poverty—dangerous and depleted neighborhoods; crowded, unhealthy living conditions; inadequate schools; limited access to health care and other services; and single and/or teen parenthood—all bring stress to the family and increase the risk that affected children will not develop caring behaviors.

This chapter takes an in-depth look at the family, at practices such as spanking, at values that might be instilled in our youth and at how the disintegration of the family is affecting society as a whole, including the juvenile justice system. The second major influence, the school, has also undergone significant changes and is facing new challenges, including increased crime and violence and increasing numbers of children entering school not ready to learn. This chapter looks at common educational practices that might promote failure, how students might react to that failure and what link this has with delinquent behavior. It then discusses what steps schools have taken and what more might be done to enhance learning and success. Next is a brief discussion of students' constitutional rights within the school setting. The chapter concludes with a discussion of the third major influence in child development, the community.

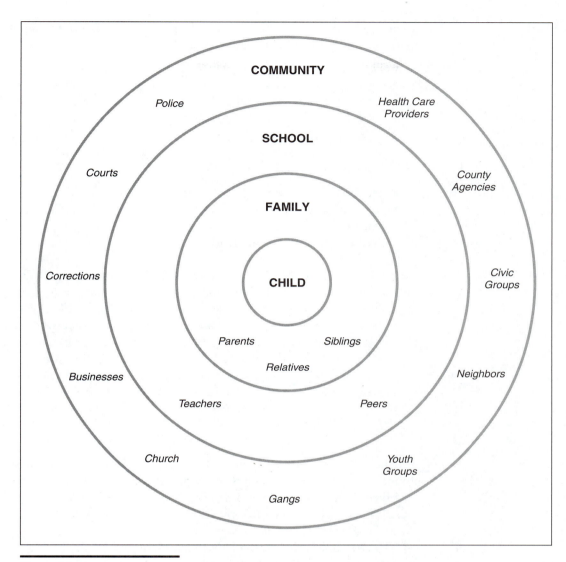

Figure 4.1
**The Radial Influences on
Growth and Development**

The Importance
of Family

The preceding discussion on growth and development highlights the vital role the family has in healthy growth and development. The *OJJDP Annual Report, 1990* (p. vi) notes: "Strong families are the foundation of a sound society. America is blessed with many. They teach the moral values that develop respect for one's own responsibilities and for the rights of others."

In November 1989, the General Assembly of the United Nations adopted several articles outlining the "rights of the child" (United Nations, 1989). The importance of the family was stressed in the preamble to this declaration of rights. The United Nations recognized that:

- The family, as the fundamental group of society and the natural environment for the growth and well-being of all its members and particularly children, should receive the protection and assistance that it needs to fully assume its responsibilities within the community.

- The child, for the full and harmonious development of his or her personality, should grow up in a family environment, in an atmosphere of happiness, love and understanding.

- The child should be fully prepared to live an individual life in society, and be brought up in the spirit of the ideals proclaimed in the Charter of the United Nations, and in particular in the spirit of peace, dignity, tolerance, freedom, equality, and solidarity.

These powerful statements convey not only the importance of the family, but also the values that the family is to instill in children as it nurtures them and teaches them to be individuals as well as contributing members of society.

The family is a significant force in the growth and development of children. The National Council of Juvenile and Family Court Judges dedicated its Metropolitan Court Judges Committee Report on Deprived Children (1986, p. 2) to:

. . . the goal of preserving and strengthening American families. Only by securing stable and nurturing family structures—with capable and caring parents and safeguarded and well-cared-for children—can our nation hope to surmount the tragedies of millions of children who are deprived primarily because of family failure.

The efforts of skilled and committed judges, legislators, law enforcement officers, health and child care workers, doctors, teachers, attorneys, volunteers and others involved in the lives of deprived children can do little without a rekindled national awareness that the family is the foundation for the protection, care and training of our children.

The closing statement of the Judges Committee report (pp. 41–42) makes amply clear the critical role of the family:

Both parents—natural, adopted or foster parents or parent substitutes—must actively demonstrate the love, trust, care, control and discipline which result in secure, emotionally happy and healthy children. It is the role of society to engender within its citizens the awareness of what it is to be a good parent. No public or private agency, child care, social worker, teacher or friend can replace the parents in the child's mind. To the extent that family life is damaged or failing, our children, their children and the nation will suffer. The high calling of "parenthood" must be more adequately recognized, respected and honored by our society. Therein lies the future of our nation.

The structure and interaction patterns of the home influence whether children learn social or delinquent behavior.

The family is, for most children, the strongest socializing force in their lives. To thrive, children need the love and support of their parents. Here a father helps his daughter with her homework.

In general, the family can have a positive impact on insulating children from antisocial and criminal patterns, providing it can control rewards and effectively maintain positive relationships within itself. Delinquency is highest when family interaction and controls are weak.

Family relationships are much more complex than relationships between two people. A family of five, for example, has 10 one-to-one relationships, 10 three-person relationships, and 5 four-person relationships for a total of 25 separate relationships. Parker et al. (1989, p. 109) noted that the larger the family becomes, the more complicated the relationships become. A family with eight children has a total of 1,011 different relationships.

The Family as the First Teacher

The family is usually the first teacher or model for behavior and misbehavior. It is the first social institution to affect children's behavior and to provide knowledge of and access to the goals and expectations of society. However, if the integration process between parents and children is deficient, the children may fail to learn appropriate behaviors. In the learning process, children should develop a sense of right and wrong. The home becomes their first classroom, and parents are their first educators. Canning (1992) emphasizes that:

- We need to find out what it is our children want and need; not what they don't like (p. 10).
- All of us have a life-long need for acceptance and positive strokes from others (p. 11).

- Our children face a world we don't fully understand and a future that we know will be different from our past (p. 15).
- Natural, normal development is characterized by the individual seeking independence from parents, finding an identity separate from the family, and making decisions based upon a developing sense of autonomy (p. 18).

Some psychologists who study families see the role of the family as *peoplemaking*. In this process, four main areas of learning are important (Parker et al., p. 110):

- Feelings of self-worth
- Communication patterns
- Rules about how people should feel and act
- Link to society—the ways members relate to other people and institutions

Children need to feel wanted and loved. They need to be able to communicate openly and clearly with others. They need to know what is expected of them and what to expect of others. And they need a sense of belonging to their family, their community and the broader society.

In healthy families, self-esteem is high, communication is direct and honest, rules are flexible and reasonable and members' attitudes toward the outside world are trusting and optimistic.

According to Parker et al. (p. 110):

Conversely, troubled families promote feelings of low self-worth, have distorted patterns of communication, have rigid, non-negotiable rules, and promote a blaming or fearful view of society.

Effective communication involves much more than simply talking and listening. It involves not only factual statements but also feelings and attitudes. It may require reviewing and adjusting beliefs; it may involve identifying problems and searching for solutions. Figure 4.2 illustrates this process.

Aggressive Behavior

Recall that children are most aggressive at age two. According to Ruben (1998, p. 99): "Most researchers agree that one of the most important factors affecting aggressive behavior—for better or worse—is a child's family. Not because of their genes (though some researchers feel there is a biological basis for some kids' aggression), but because of their social influence."

Psychologist Alan Kazdin, Ph.D., director of the Yale Child Conduct Clinic, says: "There are too many parents who, if their child comes home with a black eye, will respond, 'Go back and do the same to the kid who gave it to you'—or even, 'Beat that kid up or I'll beat you up.' . . . Children may be more or less prone to aggressiveness, but I don't think they're born to hurt other people. They have to learn it. So kids must be actively discouraged from violence—they must be taught by word and by example that it simply is not acceptable" (Ruben, p. 99).

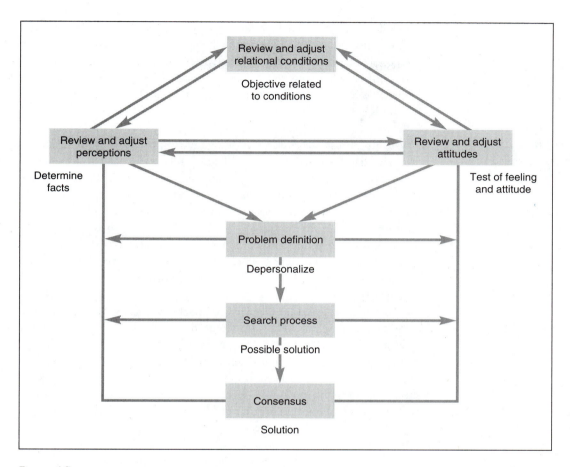

Figure 4.2
The Communication Process

According to a three-year study by the University of California, Santa Barbara, over 60 percent of all television programs contain violence (Ruben, p. 101). According to Dorothy Singer, co-director of the Yale University Family Television Research and Consultation Center, a clear correlation exists between heavy viewing of violent television (defined as more than four hours per day) and aggressive behavior in children (Ruben, p. 101). Singer adds, however, that parents who thoroughly discuss such "bad programs" with their children are often able to pull something positive from the show and get their values "out on the table."

The Centers for Disease Control (CDC) reports that violence is an epidemic—the leading cause of death in the United States is not heart disease, not cancer, but violence (Bonneville, 1995, p. 3). According to Harry Hoberman, assistant professor of psychiatry and adjunct professor of child development and psychology at the University of Minnesota: "Antisocial behavior is, in the short term, very functional and very reinforcing" (Bonneville, p. 4). For example, a child wants a toy from a sibling and grabs it. Hoberman continues: "But then kids get older and they get bigger. Because we haven't stamped out or effectively controlled antisocial behavior, kids as they reach adolescence become more intimidating. We tolerate far too much aggressive and antisocial behavior in preschool and younger children than we should. If we were very emphatic about our unwillingness to tolerate that kind of behavior early on, we would be better off. . . . We don't hold parents accountable. We don't necessarily hold kids accountable."

American Child-Rearing Rights and Practices

Physically punishing children is generally supported in the United States. The familiar adage, "Spare the rod, and spoil the child," attests to the traditional American view that it is parents' responsibility to teach their children right from wrong. Before children can reason, physical measures may be relied upon. The question becomes not so much whether such physical coercion is appropriate, but rather what *degree* of physical coercion is appropriate. In other words, when does punishment become abuse? Is a slap on the hand the same as a slap to the face? Is a "paddling" through clothing with a bare hand the same as a beating with a belt on a bare bottom? Or is physical coercion ever justified?

In 1994 an American teenager, Michael Fay, was found guilty of vandalizing some cars in Singapore. He was sentenced to serve time in jail as well as to receive six blows with a cane. Despite pleas for clemency from President Clinton, many, many American citizens supported the punishment. According to a Prodigy on-line poll, 75 percent of the 60,000 members responding said Fay should be flogged. Another 57 percent said U.S. courts should use flogging. In an article applauding the flogging of Michael Fay, a student at New York University (Wu, 1994, p. A25) wrote:

> [T]here is something simplistic and powerful about using whacks on the behind as corporal punishment, a back-to-the-basics method that may be the answer to the growing violence in this country.
> Too many 18-year-olds are running wild, waving guns, pointing them at people. Too many young people are bad and, most dangerously, too many are fearless. They roll their eyes at lectures, laugh at teachers when suspended and think of a night in jail as an adventure. They brag about their badness and bravery to friends. To the average 18-year-old, everything is like a TV sitcom. . . . at eighteen you live in a world without consequences.
> So, here's to Michael Fay from one 18-year-old to another. "Take it like a man, sonny. You've done something bad, so face up to your consequences. Remember the pain, the humiliation and fear. Let's hope you've learned your lesson."

Such reasoning is often used by parents in justifying the use of spanking to discipline their children.

The Spanking Controversy

A three-year violence prevention project conducted in Minnesota by Murray Straus, head of the Family Research Laboratory at the University of New Hampshire, suggests that parents seldom accomplish the positive results they hope for by spanking. In addition, the study found that spanking may have much less desirable impacts (Walsh, 1994, p. B1): "Children who are spanked are much more likely to be aggressive with other children. . . . They are also more likely to grow up to be aggressive adults." Walsh (p. B8) reports on other negative effects spanking may have:

> Straus said that spanking has been shown to be related to lower income and occupational achievement for children who go on to graduate from college and that it may inhibit the development of self-confidence. "Spanking," said Straus, "leaves children feeling powerless and depressed."

Straus also conducted the second National Family Violence Survey, funded by the National Institute of Mental Health. The findings of this and other studies are described in his book, *Beating the Devil Out of Them: Corporal Punishment in American Families.* In another article, West (1994, p. 13) reports that Straus confirms the harmful effects of spanking:

> Children who are spanked a lot are from two to five times more likely to be physically aggressive as children, to become juvenile delinquents as adolescents and, as adults, to suffer from depression, according to Straus. "The only people we allow to be hit are children," he says. "If you hit your neighbor, that would be a physical assault. That's a crime."

Despite such findings, spanking remains an issue. And, according to Straus's research, 90 percent of parents spank their toddlers (West, p. 13). Supporting the *reasonable* use of spanking, Dr. Den A. Trumbull, an Alabama pediatrician and authority on parental discipline, says spanking is a useful, harmless tool if used properly, especially for children ages two to six who are openly defiant of their parents. Dr. Trumbull also stresses using praise liberally for good behavior.

West (p. 14) notes that researchers say: "Most studies conducted on corporal punishment provide more heat than light. The research generally is loaded with more editorial comment than original data and more study is needed." West also notes that researchers generally accept two statements regarding parenting as true: (1) Most people tend to raise their children the way they were raised, good or bad; and (2) extreme levels of physical punishment are bad.

Adult Supremacy

Force and violence toward children, including physical punishment, has been characterized as **adult supremacy.** In this relationship, power is sanctioned by legal rules with the effect being to subordinate one person—within limits—to the arbitrary authority of another person.

Adult supremacy subordinates children to the absolute and arbitrary authority of parents.

The dangers of adult supremacy were noted over 90 years ago by Ledlie (1907, p. 449):

> The right of control based on family law produces subordination, not a mere obligation. It represents a power over free persons and a power which curtails the freedom of those subject to it, because the person in whom power vests is entitled to exercise it, up to a certain point, in his own interests alone, to exercise it, in a word, as he chooses.

Adults have a legally protected right to bodily integrity, free from assault, but children do not, except in extreme circumstances. Parents are authorized to use force against their children because society believes adults are older and presumably wiser, and because the right to rear one's child as one chooses is held to be fundamental.

Courts give parents wide latitude in disciplining their children so they learn to respect authority. Another explanation for adult supremacy, including violence and force against children, is given by Foster (1974, p. 4), who feels it is inherited from "a common law concept of status derived from a feudal order which denied children legal identity and treated them as objects or things, rather than persons." He notes that in the United States up until about 1900, the only person in the family who had any legal rights was the father. The status of children today is akin to the status of women and blacks before their emancipation. When issues arise regarding children's moral and legal rights, "there is a conflict between the principles of subordination and equality which are characteristics of a society that traces its origins to a patriarchal culture" (p. 6). This conflict indicates "paternalistic measures may be more protective of ancient paternal prerogatives than of the best interest of minors" (p. 55).

The power vested in parents brings to mind Acton's maxim that power tends to corrupt and absolute power corrupts absolutely—a thought-provoking idea, considering that children are the most powerless group in the world, both physically and politically.

Socialization

Children should learn in the home that others have rights that they must respect. They should learn about social and moral values; to be considerate of others' property, possessions and individual selves; to manage their own affairs and to take responsibility for their actions.

The family, in the socialization process, is also concerned with ways to suppress or eliminate undesirable behavior. Behavior that does not conform to social standards is disturbing to group members and is seen as a threat to the cohesiveness and psychological integrity of the group. When children display unacceptable behavior, the family corrects them to get rid of that behavior. It would be far more effective to teach them socially acceptable patterns, such as honesty and fair play.

It is partly because of the failure of families to teach children basic conformity to social values and standards that children look for alternative groups. This search for alternatives can produce the subculture group, or gang, and misbehavior.

Children develop their sense of being worthwhile, capable, important and unique from the attention and love given to them by their parents. They can develop a sense of worthlessness, incapability, unimportance and facelessness from a lack of attention and love, or from physical or sexual abuse. The development of social cognition as perceived by psychologists is outlined in Table 4.1.

Note that the development begins during the end of the critical first three years and ends for most children during adolescence. One important aspect of socialization is passing on the values of society. As noted by Pace (1991, p. 108):

Table 4.1
Development of Social Cognition

	Understanding Self	Understanding Others	Understanding Friends	Understanding Social Roles	Understanding Society
Preoperational Period (About age 2–7)	Understands concrete attributes Understands major emotions, but relies on situation	Understands concrete attributes, including stability of behavior	One-way assistance (age 4–9)	Can generalize role (age 4) Understands person can change role and remain same person	Feels no need to explain system (age 5–6)
Concrete Operational Period (About age 7–12)	Understands personal qualities Relies on inner feelings as guide to emotions Understands shame and pride	Understands personal qualities	Fairweather cooperation (age 6–12)	Understands that people can occupy two roles simultaneously	Understands social functions observed or experienced (age 7–8) Provides fanciful explanations of distant functions (age 9–10) Has acquired concrete knowledge of society
Formal Operational Period (After about age 12)	Capable of complex, flexible, precise description Understands abstract traits Establishes identity	Capable of complex, flexible, precise description	Intimate sharing (age 9–15)		Can deal with abstract conception of society, government, and politics (by age 15)

Source: Elizabeth Hall, Michael E. Lamb and Marion Perlmutter. *Child Psychology Today*, 2nd ed. New York: Random House, 1986, p. 562. Reprinted with permission of McGraw-Hill.

"The future of this nation depends upon the values they [our youths] are forming. They obviously will be the future decision-makers of our society."

Values

Values are extremely important in any society. Values reflect the nature of the society, indicate what is most important and describe how people are expected to behave. Throughout the ages societies have embraced certain values, taught these values to their children and punished those who did not adhere to them. When youths do not accept the values of society, conflict is inevitable.

Families need to examine their values and, if they are "good," teach them to their children. Canning (p. 36) suggests the following as common values:

- Equality: All people have the same rights.
- Honesty: Telling the truth; meaning what you say.
- Promise-Keeping: Keeping your promises; keeping your word.
- Respect: Treating everyone, including yourself, with dignity.
- Responsibility: Carrying out your obligations or duties and answering for your own actions.

- Self-Control: Being able to control your own actions.
- Social Justice: Being fair to all people.

Common values that might be passed on to children include equality, honesty, promise-keeping, respect, responsibility, self-control and social justice.

Unfortunately, in many families, no values or negative values, such as the use of violence to resolve disputes, are passed on. This is one focus of the next chapter.

Criminologist James Q. Wilson said in a speech about fighting crime that the approach must be to regain our "moral sense": "Obviously criminals are not inclined to follow the golden rule. . . . The question is not what our values ought to be. Every reasonable person knows what they ought to be. But what is the best way to inculcate them?" (von Sternberg, 1994, p. B9).

Causes of this lack of a moral sense in many of our youths include an increase in the number of children exposed to family-related risk factors and the disintegration of the traditional family.

Family-Related Risk Factors and the Disintegration of the Traditional Family

According to a recent report from the Bureau of the Census: "More than 10 percent of children experience three or more factors that place them at risk for problems later in life and 25 percent experience at least one" (National Criminal Justice Association, 1997, p. 10). The Census Bureau, which analyzes population data to reach its conclusions, has identified the following six parameters as indicators of risk to children's welfare:

- poverty
- welfare dependence
- absent parents
- one-parent families
- unwed mothers
- parents who have not completed high school

Eitzen (1992, p. 588) notes the changes that have occurred in American families: "These trends indicate widespread family instability in American society—and that instability has increased dramatically in a single generation." Unquestionably, the family has undergone great changes over the years. What began as an extended family, with two or three generations of a family living together, gradually became a nuclear family consisting of parents and their children. When the children grew up, they moved out and started their own families. Changes that have occurred in contemporary American society have been more problematic, including more single-parent families, blended families, adoptive families and dysfunctional families.

Children who may be at risk as they grow and develop are children of immigrants, those who are adopted, those whose parents are divorced, and those whose mothers or fathers are incarcerated.

Immigrants' Children

For immigrants there are many problems in addition to language barriers. Families are disrupted when some members emigrate while others are left behind. Role reversal commonly occurs as children more readily learn English and become translators for their parents, in effect, gaining control over them. Further, native customs and values may differ greatly from what is accepted in the United States. For example, Day (1992, p. 15) reports: "More than one Southeast Asian family has been investigated for child abuse after health professionals noted the skin lesions caused by traditional coin rubbing treatment." (*Coining*, thought to have healing powers, consists of rubbing warm oil and coins across the skin, and sometimes produces long, red bruises.) Finally, immigrants may also be subjected to prejudice and discrimination.

Children Who Are Adopted

Studies have shown that adopted children are more likely than others to become involved with the social service and juvenile justice systems. A study in Minnesota, for example, showed that although only 1 or 2 percent of children in Minnesota are adopted, 10 percent are in state juvenile residential treatment centers and 7 percent are in the county's petty offender program (Hopfensperger, 1988, p. A1).

Psychologists suggest that part of the reason for such statistics may be an intensification of the identity crisis so common during adolescence. This seems to be particularly problematic with children who are of a different racial background than their adoptive parents.

Children Whose Parents Are Divorced

More than 60 percent of all children born in the 1990s will spend at least some time in a single-parent household before reaching age 18. The magnitude of the collapse of family structure is historically unprecedented and is at the root of many social and economic problems. Hodgkinson (1991, p. 10) reports that: "The **Norman Rockwell family**—a working father, a housewife mother and two children of school age—constitutes only 6 percent of U.S. households" (bold added).

According to the Census Bureau: "In 1996, 4 percent of children lived with neither parent and 28 percent lived in one-parent families; in 1970, 3 percent of children lived with neither parent and 12 percent lived in one-parent families" (National Criminal Justice Association, 1997, p. 11).

A major study of children from one-parent families, conducted by the National Association of Elementary School Principals, found that 30 percent of the two-parent elementary school students were ranked as high achievers, compared with only 17 percent of the one-parent children. At the other end of the scale, 23 percent of the two-parent children were low achievers versus 38 percent of the one-parent children. One-parent students had more clinic visits and a higher rate of absence from school. One-parent students were consistently more likely to be late, truant and subject to disciplinary action. One-parent children were found to be more than twice as likely to drop out of school altogether.

One study (Wallerstein and Corbin, 1986) of father-child relationships after divorce looked at the amount of financial child support provided and its relationship to educational opportunity. This 10-year longitudinal study of 60 largely white, middle-class Northern California families included 131 children between the ages of 2 and 18 at the time of the divorce. This study found that not only did child support payments seldom increase, even as the cost of living increased, it also found that such payments often stopped immediately when the legal obligation was fulfilled, usually when the youth became 18. Unfortunately, it is at this age that youths aspiring to further education need the most financial support. The study concluded (p. 124): "It is surely tragic that the economic and psychological burdens of divorce not only fall upon children during their growing up years, but may affect them detrimentally throughout their entire adult lives."

Divorce has a shattering effect on families with young children, particularly if the mother has limited education or job skills. According to Hodgkinson (p. 10), some 15 million children are being reared by single mothers—whether divorced or never married. In addition, when mothers go back to work to support the family, the children may be left unsupervised: "At least two million school-age children have no adult supervision at all after school. Two million are being reared by *neither* parent" (Hodgkinson).

The Census Bureau found in the 1990s that two-thirds of all people in female-headed families with children under 18 get benefits from a welfare program. Further, of all never-married mothers, more than 80 percent receive some kind of government check. The federal government spends more than 100 billion dollars every year on assistance to families. But this aid does not come close to providing households with the security most intact families enjoy.

The leading item on Attorney General Janet Reno's "National Agenda for Children" is families:

> First, we need to develop family preservation programs that offer support to families *before* they are in a crisis situation so they are much more likely to stay together through life's difficulties. We've got to make sure that our parents are old enough, wise enough, and financially able to take care of their children. We've got to make a major effort against teen pregnancy in America. And we've got to offer parenting skill courses in every school so that children who have been raised without quality support from parents learn how to give it to their own children (Wilson, 1993, p. 2).

Children Whose Mothers or Fathers Are Incarcerated

A study by the National Council on Crime and Delinquency (NCCD), conducted in 1992 (National Criminal Justice Association, 1993), found that more than half of those women who were in jails and prisons had not seen their children while incarcerated. Typically, the women had histories of physical and sexual abuse and were drug users. Over one-third were serving sentences for drug offenses.

Eighteen percent of the women reported their children having learning or school-related problems; 16 percent reported their children having behavior

An inmate in the North Carolina Correctional Center for Women in Raleigh reads to her daughter in the MATCH center during her daughter's visit. The center was designed to allow female inmates to step out of their cells and into their roles as mothers for a short time.

problems. The study also found that these women tended to underestimate the severity of their children's problems. Further, children whose mothers have been incarcerated seem to be more likely to be incarcerated themselves if the relationship with their mother is damaged (National Criminal Justice Association, pp. 1–2, 4).

Another study found that one child in 50 under age 15 may have a parent in jail. The researchers reported that: "Possible medical consequences to children of inmates include exposure to tuberculosis, hepatitis, the AIDS virus or other infections acquired by the parent while incarcerated. . . . Besides poverty, one of the strongest risk factors for juvenile delinquency is a parent who has a criminal history" ("1 in 50 Under Age 15 . . . ," 1993, p. A1).

A study by the Child Welfare League has found a strong correlation between having an incarcerated parent and the probability that a child will at some point be arrested for a crime. "This finding has serious implications for the future, researchers said, considering that 1.5 million people—who have an estimated 1.6 million children—are currently imprisoned in the United States" ("Study Amplifies Crime's Link . . . ," 1997, p. 15).

The impact of family relationships on children necessarily has a vital influence on whether children thrive in school and are able to learn the skills they need to succeed in society. Unfortunately, for too many students, the level of success they achieve in school is often hampered by the "baggage" they bring with them from home—the result of improper socialization, inadequate parenting skills, divorce, poor nutrition, domestic violence, child abuse and neglect.

The Role of the School

Schools have a responsibility for the students who attend under the principle of *in loco parentis.*

The principle of in *loco parentis,* meaning "in place of parents," gives certain social and legal institutions the authority to act as a parent might in situations requiring discipline or need.

The school is one such institution. A dozen or more years in school has a huge impact on students, not only academically but also socially.

Origins of Our Public Schools

Following the American Revolution, the leaders of the newly created United States proposed a system of publicly funded schools to educate poor and rich children alike. These early advocates of public schools believed American citizens had a fundamental responsibility to educate all children in order to reach the following democratic goals ("Do We Still Need . . .," 1996, pp. 6–8):

- *To prepare people to become responsible citizens*—The founders believed that the success of American democracy depended on the development of an educated citizenry that would vote wisely, protect its rights and freedoms, root out political corruption, and keep the nation secure from internal and external threats to democracy.
- *To improve social conditions*—Pennsylvania physician and statesman Benjamin Rush said in 1786: "Fewer pillories and whipping posts and smaller gaols [jails] . . . will be necessary when our youth are properly educated, than at present."
- *To promote cultural unity*—The author Mary Antin wrote in 1912: "The public school has done its best for us foreigners, and for the country, when it has made us into good Americans."
- *To help people become economically self-sufficient*—Giving all Americans the basic literacy and arithmetic skills that they needed to succeed in the workplace of the new nation, thereby reducing poverty and its consequences.
- *To enhance individual happiness and enrich individual lives*—Benjamin Franklin said in 1749: "The good education of youth has been esteemed by wise men in all ages as the surest foundation of the happiness of both private families and of commonwealths."
- *To dispel inequities in education*—The civil rights leader and educator W. E. B. DuBois wrote in 1903: "Education and work are the levers to uplift a people. Work alone will not do it unless inspired by the right ideals and guided by intelligence. Education must not simply teach work—it must teach life."
- *To ensure a basic level of quality among schools*—Government funding and policies would overcome local stinginess and reconcile wide variations among curricula, attendance policies, length of the school year, and teacher qualifications.

These reasons for public schools are still valid today.

Children who experience success in school are likely to also experience success in life; those who experience failure in school are likely to also experience failure in life.

The Current Focus of Schools

The UN Convention on the Rights of the Child said of schools that "education should be directed at developing the child's personality and talents, preparing the child for active life as an adult, fostering respect for basic human rights and developing respect for the child's own cultural and national values and those of others" (United Nations, Article 29, p. 9).

Schools tend to stress academic learning, yet a decade ago a leading psychologist, Howard Gardner, set forth his theory of multiple intelligences. Gardner (1983, p. 69) warned, however:

> There is a universal human temptation to give credence to a word to which we have become attached, perhaps because it has helped us to understand a situation better. . . . [I]ntelligence is such a word; we use it so often that we have come to believe in its existence, as a genuine tangible, measurable entity, rather than as a convenient way of labeling some phenomena that may (but may well not) exist.

Gardner believes that each individual may have several different "intelligences": linguistic, musical, logical-mathematical, spatial, bodily-kinesthetic and personal. Not all intelligences are equally developed in any single person, but the potential in each area exists. The challenge to educators is to discover which "intelligences" are most developed in each student and to capitalize on these strengths. Being able to praise children for nonacademic accomplishments strengthens the teacher-student relationship and should promote learning and understanding.

Values and the School

Educators have long felt that the school should be a place where children not only studied academic subjects but were also taught basic values. In 1938, William Carr wrote a book entitled *The Purposes of Education in American Democracy*, in which he called for "education aimed at economic literacy, respect for law, acceptance of civic duties, and above all, loyalty to democratic ideals" (p. 1). Carr continued:

> Educational objectives depend upon a scale of values. Every statement of educational purposes, including this one, depends upon the judgment of some person or group as to what is true and what is false, what is ugly and what is beautiful, what is valuable and what is worthless, in the conduct of human affairs. Objectives are, essentially, a statement of preferences, choices, values. These preferences are exercised, these choices made, these values arranged in a variety of ways.

A contemporary examination of core values and the schools revealed that little has changed since the publication of Carr's book. According to Frymier et al. (1996, p. 3):

> The values that teachers think are important for children to learn today are remarkably similar to values that educators thought young people should learn 60 years ago. For example:
>
> - Democracy is right. Authoritarianism is wrong.
> - Honesty is right. Dishonesty is wrong.
> - Responsibility is right. Irresponsibility is wrong.
> - Freedom of speech is right. Restricting freedom of speech is wrong.
> - Courtesy is right. Discourtesy is wrong.
> - Tolerance is right. Intolerance is wrong.
> - Freedom of worship is right. Restricting freedom of worship is wrong.
> - Respecting the law is right. Violating the law is wrong.
> - Integrating schools is right. Segregating schools is wrong.
>
> Second, educators and non-educators alike think that the home is the primary agency for developing values in the young, but school and church both have an important role to play. Further, educators and non-educators agree that the rise in crime during the past 30 years is primarily the fault of the home. . . . [Finally,] schools are not doing nearly as well in teaching values as most of the educators who responded thought they should be doing.

The Need for Positive Values

The Thomas Jefferson Research Center, a nonprofit institution studying America's social problems, reports that in 1775 religion and morals accounted for more than 90 percent of the content in school texts. By 1926 it was 6 percent. In the 1980s it was almost nonexistent. A study of third-grade reading books showed that references to obedience, thoughtfulness and honesty began to disappear after 1930 (U.S. Congress, p. 11).

The findings of the Jefferson Research Center are reiterated by former Chief Justice Warren Burger (1981, p. 2): "Possibly some of our problem of behavior stems from the fact that we virtually eliminated from public schools and higher education any effort to teach values of integrity, truth, personal accountability and respect for others' rights."

One of the most effective ways to offset negative norms and behavior is to promote positive values in our schools.

Promoting positive values in the schools is difficult in a pluralistic society. A necessary first step is increasing the use of materials that promote both incentives and resources for confronting problems of moral commitment and choice. As noted by the National School Safety Center (1988, p. 3):

> While schools cannot be expected to shoulder the full responsibility for socializing thus-far unsocialized youth, the educational system is, nonetheless, an anchor around which the family, community, church, and public and private social service agencies can build a cooperative network to reduce and eventually eliminate negative gang activity.

Although the Center is referring to gang activity, this concept applies to the role of the educational system in building a cooperative network to reduce and eventually eliminate other forms of negative juvenile behavior as well.

Hope for the Future

Three of Attorney General Reno's seven items on the "National Agenda for Children" focus on education (Wilson, 1993, pp. 2–3). She recommends **educare** programs that she defines as: "safe, constructive child care for all children." Such programs should be linked with "expanded and improved Head Start programs" so that children can begin the learning process during the critical first three-year period. Reno also supports conflict resolution programs in the schools, freeing up teachers' time to teach, and developing truancy prevention programs in all elementary schools.

Another way to enhance and support the schools' efforts is to involve parents. Most teachers agree that children are much more likely to do well in school if parents become actively involved in their children's education. A National PTA survey, reported by Elam et al. (1993, p. 149), indicated that over 95 percent of the parents surveyed favored parental involvement in the school. Also encouraging is the focus on the schools by the Clinton administration. Six goals were proposed for attainment by the year 2000. The National PTA asked respondents to prioritize the goals. The results are summarized in Table 4.2.

The Importance of Success in School

The importance of succeeding in school was emphasized by noted educator William Glasser (1969, p. 5) in his classic work *Schools Without Failure:* "I believe that if a child, no matter what his background, can succeed in school, he has an excellent chance for success in life. If he fails at any stage of his educational career—elementary school, junior high, high school, or college—his chances for success in life are greatly diminished."

Children who succeed in school have a greater probability of succeeding in other areas of their lives.

A serious obstacle to achieving academically is an anti-achievement ethic in many schools. What is perceived as "cool" is skipping school, misbehaving in class, smarting off to teachers and others in authority. What is "uncool" is to get good grades. In a senior high school in a crime-infested ward of Washington, DC, according to Suskind (1994): "Teachers call what goes on here the 'crab bucket syndrome.' When one crab tries to climb from a bucket, the others pull

Table 4.2
**National Educational
Goals for the Year 2000**

Question: "How high a priority do you think each goal should have for the remainder of the decade?"

	Priority Assigned					National Totals	
						Very High	
	Very High	High	Low	Very Low	Don't Know	1993	1990
By the year 2000, all children in America will start school ready to learn.	41%	48%	8%	1%	2%	41%	44%
By the year 2000, the high school graduation rate will increase to at least 90%.	54	38	6	1	1	54	45
By the year 2000, American students will leave grades 4, 8, and 12 having demonstrated competency in challenging subject matter, including English, mathematics, science, history, and geography. In addition, every school will ensure that all students will learn to use their minds well so that they may be prepared for responsible citizenship, further learning, and productive employment in a modern economy.	59	33	6	1	1	59	46
By the year 2000, American students will be first in the world in science and mathematics achievement.	45	43	9	2	1	45	34
By the year 2000, every adult American will be literate and will possess the knowledge and skills necessary to compete in a global economy and to exercise the rights and responsibilities of citizenship.	54	37	7	1	1	54	45
By the year 2000, every school in America will be free of drugs and violence and will offer a disciplined environment conducive to learning.	71	19	7	2	1	71	55

Source: National PTA survey reported in Stanley M. Elam, Lowell C. Rose and Alec M. Gallup. "The 25th Annual Phi Delta Kappa/Gallup Poll of the Public's Attitudes Toward the Public Schools." *Phi Delta Kappan*, October 1993, p. 140. © 1993 *Phi Delta Kappa*.

it back down." Students are often torn between wanting to be accepted by their peers and wanting to succeed in school. Academic success in many schools assures social ostracism.

Peer approval and acceptance is often more important to adolescents than the approval of parents or teachers.

One reason children do poorly in school is because they see nothing of relevance to them, as Father John Culkin (1966, p. 51) noted:

> The schools are no longer dealing with the student of 1900 whose sources of information were limited to the home, church, school, and neighborhood gang. Today's student comes equipped with a vast reservoir of facts and vicarious experiences gleaned from the news media. All the analogies comparing the mind to a blank page or an empty bucket died with Edison. The teacher is now in competition with a host of rival communicators, most of them are smarter, richer, and considerably more efficient. Relevance and competence are educational tactics against which students have not devised a defense.

And that was over 30 years ago. Consider how much the media have advanced and what teachers now have to compete against. In addition to sometimes lacking relevance, several school practices actually encourage failure.

How Schools Promote Failure

Glasser notes (p. 59): "Probably the school practice that most produces failure in students is *grading*. If there is one sacred part of education, revered throughout almost the entire United States as utilitarian and necessary, it is A-B-C-D-F grading." He continues (p. 60):

> Today, grades are the be-all and end-all of education. The only acceptable grades are good ones, and these good grades divide the school successes from the school failures. Grades are so important that they have become a substitute for education itself. Ask your own small child what is most important in school and he will tell you, "Grades." . . . Grades have become moral equivalents. A good grade is correlated with good behavior, a bad grade with bad behavior, a correlation that unfortunately is very high.

In many schools what Glasser condemned 30 years ago continues to be standard practice.

A second educational practice Glasser says helps to produce failure is *objective testing*. Such testing is usually based on the memorization of facts, many of which students see as irrelevant. Only the "successful" student will continue to memorize these often irrelevant facts to continue to receive good grades.

Closely related to objective testing is the common educational practice of *grading on a normal curve*. By definition, in this system, 50 percent of the students must be below average!

According to Glasser (p. 72): "The fourth poor educational practice, closed-book examinations, is based on the *fallacy that knowledge remembered is better than knowledge looked up*." In the information age, it is critical that students learn to use references, not to simply memorize often irrelevant facts.

Another common school practice contributing to student failure is *tracking*, grouping students either by ability level or achievement and often labeling the high achieving group the "college-bound" or "college preparatory" group. Such tracking may have all of the negative consequences associated with labeling: stigma, self-fulfilling prophecy and lack of motivation to succeed. In addition, as evidenced in the study of second graders described in Chapter 3, teachers may not have high expectations for lower-track students or expend as much energy on teaching them as they do on the "high achievers." They may also tend to give lower grades because they do not assign the low achievers as much work and, further, such students do not need good grades because, unlike the high achievers, they are not expected to be college-bound.

Educational practices that may encourage failure include the A-B-C-D-F grading system, objective testing, grading on a curve, giving closed-book tests and tracking students.

Dill (1998, p. 30) describes yet another situation leading to school failure:

> In some cities, it is common practice to transfer students with behavior disorders to other schools, which often euphemistically is termed the "dance of the lemons." The school that ejects the students may then claim it has a zero suspension and expulsion rate, because mandatory transfers do not "count. . . ."
>
> The schools that receive these students often do not know why the student was transferred. Mandatory record disclosure laws vary from state to state; and the students' records, including parole conditions or police records, may not be accessible. The practice creates an absolute danger for the receiving school.

The educational practices discussed are not an indictment of the schools, but a partial explanation of why so many students fail in school and how this failure affects not only their school performance but also their behavior in other areas.

Poverty and Failure

School failure may also be associated with poverty. For example, in the United States, differences among eighth-grade mathematics achievement have been correlated with levels of school funding and rates of child poverty. According to Biddle (1997, p. 11):

> . . . poor children . . . are uniquely handicapped for education because of their poverty. The homes of poor children provide little access to the books, writing materials, computers, and other supports for education that are normally present in middle-class or affluent homes in America. Impoverished students are also distracted by chronic pain and disease; have poorer nourishment; tend to live in communities that are afflicted by physical decay, serious crime, gangs, and drugs; and must face problems in their personal lives because their parents or older siblings have left home, died, been incarcerated, or lead seriously disturbed lives. All of this means that poor children have a much harder time in school than their more affluent peers.

Student Response to Failure

When students fail to meet the expectations of teachers or parents, they may become involved in delinquent groups of youths who share similar experiences of abuse or failure. The group provides the needed outlet for frustration and anger. Some students skip school or drop out completely. Other youths run away. Some seek escape in alcohol and other drugs or attempt suicide.

Students' responses to failure include skipping school, joining gangs, dropping out of school, drinking, doing drugs, performing delinquent acts and even suicide.

Truancy—
The Dropout

Skipping class is something many students do at some point, usually just for a day or two, here and there. The results are often fairly innocuous—perhaps some late homework or a lecture from a parent. When such absences become habitual, however, it becomes a more serious issue. Garry (1996, p. 1) notes: "Today, truancy has become a major problem in this country that negatively influences the future of our youth and costs taxpayers thousands of dollars. With daily absentee rates as high as 30 percent in some cities, it is not surprising that truancy is rated among the major problems facing schools." Garry continues on the dangers of truancy: "Truancy may be the beginning of a lifetime of problems for students who routinely skip school. . . . Truancy is a stepping stone to delinquent and criminal activity. . . . Truant students are at higher risk of being drawn into behavior involving drugs, alcohol, or violence." And truant students are not the only ones who lose out. According to Garry (p. 2):

> Truancy is costly. It costs students an education, resulting in reduced earning capacity. It costs school districts hundreds of thousands of dollars each year in lost Federal and State funds that are based on daily attendance figures. It costs businesses, which must pay to train uneducated workers. It costs taxpayers, who must pay higher taxes for law enforcement and welfare costs for dropouts who end up on welfare rolls or underemployed.

The National Center for Education Statistics reported that in 1992, 4.5 percent of all high school students dropped out of grades 10, 11 and 12 (Cantelon and LeBoeuf, 1997, p. 1). Furthermore, approximately 11 percent of all persons aged 16 to 24 in the United States had not finished high school and were not currently enrolled. Cantelon and LeBoeuf state (p. 1):

> Four in ten dropouts said they left high school because they were failing or they did not like school, and just as many males as females reported they were leaving school because of personality conflicts with teachers. More males than females dropped out because of school suspension or expulsion.
>   . . . Although most dropouts reported school-related reasons for leaving school, most female dropouts reported family-related reasons. Twenty-one percent of females and 8 percent of males dropped out because they became parents.

The underlying reasons for dropping out are often more complex than simply not liking school or poor grades. As Bilchik (1997) notes: "Many children come to school as composites of the broken pieces of their lives—divorce, homelessness, learning disabilities, and mental illness—and from homes in which they must become self-sufficient at an early age. Some must deal with crime, drugs, and gangs in their neighborhoods; suffer abuse and neglect from adults; or become parents while still children themselves."

The Link between
Delinquency and
the Schools

Hodgkinson (p. 10) notes: "Today, more than 80% of America's one million prisoners are high school dropouts (costing taxpayers upwards of $20,000 each per year)." He concludes (p. 16): "America's children are truly an 'endangered species.' "

The link between failure in school and delinquency is strong.

Just as the family sometimes fails to provide a nurturing, caring environment or to control children, the school is sometimes nonsupportive and lacking in discipline and control.

Problems Facing Schools

How can our schools deal with students who are disruptive, incorrigible, thieving and violent? Why have teachers and students been viciously beaten, raped, stabbed and shot? And why do so many school programs focus on problems such as delinquency, truancy, alcoholism and drugs?

Many schools face serious problems with crime. And many schools do not provide realistic programs for underachievers and marginal students. They lack personal counseling, teachers who reach out to students and adequate evening and weekend activities for students.

The Gallup organization collaborated with Phi Delta Kappa, a professional education organization, in producing "The 30th Annual Phi Delta Kappa/Gallup Poll of the Public's Attitudes Toward the Public Schools." According to the poll (Rose and Gallup, 1998, p. 51): "Concern about fighting/violence/gangs (mentioned by 15%) replaces lack of discipline/more control and lack of financial support/funding/money at the top of the list of biggest problems mentioned [facing local schools] . . . Use of drugs is mentioned by 10%."

The 30th Gallup poll of attitudes toward public schools identified "fighting/violence/gangs" as the biggest problems facing local public schools.

According to past poll results, discipline was the number one problem every year from 1969 to 1985, except 1971. Then in 1986 the drug problem claimed the number one spot and ranked first among local school problems seven times, tying once with lack of proper financial support. In 1998 drugs dropped to fourth. This poll clearly reflects the public's rising concern over the amount of crime and violence in our nation's public schools.

Crime and Violence in the Schools

Research suggests that if left unchecked, disruptive behavior in the playgrounds, parking lots, halls and classrooms of our schools breeds violence. McConaghy (1994, p. 655) cautions: "Just as conditions in rundown and disorderly neighborhoods in urban centers invite a criminal invasion . . ., allowing disorderly behavior in schools leads to bullying, sexual assault, and verbal abuse of teachers." Citing numerous studies on childhood aggression, Ruben notes (pp. 98–99):

> More than half of all boys who turn into hard-core delinquents by age 13 could have been identified by their behavior in kindergarten. Other research shows similar findings: A long-term Norwegian study at the University of Bergen found that 60 percent of boys who were named as bullies in grades six to nine racked up at least one court conviction by age 24. And an ongoing study at the University of Michigan, following more than 500 children for 40 years, found that the kids tabbed by their peers as most aggressive at age 8 have gone on to commit more crimes, suffer more alcoholism, require more mental-health services, even compile more driving offenses than their less volatile counterparts.
>
> "Persistent childhood aggression often becomes a life-long issue for the individual, his victims, and ultimately for all of society," says psychologist Leonard Eron, Ph.D., a director of the Michigan study.

A study by Lockwood (1997) of violence among middle and high school students analyzed not only the types and frequency of violent incidents but also their dynamics—"the locations, the 'opening moves,' the relationship between disputants, the goals and justifications of the aggressor, the role of third parties, and other factors" (p. 1). In his study, Lockwood defined violence as "an act carried out with the intention, or perceived intention, of physically injuring another person" (p. 3), and he noted the following types and frequencies of violent acts among selected public high school students (p. 4):

- Kicked/bit/hit with a fist   67 percent of all violent incidents involved this action
- Pushed, grabbed, shoved   55 percent
- Beat up   21 percent
- Slapped   17 percent
- Threw something   14 percent
- Hit with something   14 percent
- Threatened with gun   10 percent
- Threatened with knife   8 percent
- Used gun   5 percent
- Used knife   2 percent

Note: the percentages total more than 100 percent because multiple types of actions may have occurred during any given violent incident.

As Lockwood explains (p. 4), a violent incident begins with an "opening move," which he defines as: "The action of the student, the student antagonist, or third party that initiates the violent incident." The most common types of opening moves noted (p. 5) were unprovoked offensive touching (throws, pushes, grabs, shoves, slaps, kicks, or hits) in 13 percent of incidents and interference with possessions (something owned or being used), also in 13 percent of incidents. Other opening moves noted were requests to do something (10 percent), backbiting/putting someone down (9 percent), verbal teasing or rough physical play (9 percent), insults (7 percent), crimes (theft and armed/unarmed robbery) (5 percent), accusations of wrongdoing (5 percent), defense of others (4 percent), physical challenges (3 percent), threats of physical harm (3 percent), advances to boyfriend/girlfriend of actor (3 percent), told authority figure of bad behavior of actor (1 percent), and other behavior perceived as offensive (11 percent).

The location of the opening move (p. 6) was most frequently on school grounds (45 percent). Of incidents originating on school property, most opening moves (39 percent) occurred in the classroom, followed by hall and stairway incidents (21 percent) and gym/locker room/playing field incidents (11 percent). Opening moves taking place on school buses (11 percent) were also considered to have occurred on school grounds. Other locations for opening moves were home locations (23 percent), public areas such as sidewalks, streets, malls and parks (30 percent), and other locations such as churches and summer camps (2 percent).

Several goals were commonly cited by students regarding their violent behavior (pp. 4–5):

- Retribution—punishing the antagonist for something he or she did (40 percent of all goals).
- Compliance—convincing the antagonist to desist from an offensive course of action (22 percent).
- Defense of one's self or others (21 percent).
- Promotion of one's image—by saving face, defending one's honor, or enhancing or maintaining one's reputation (8 percent).

In his study Lockwood asked students to explain their violent behavior and then separated these explanations into two categories (p. 5):

- Justifications—where students accept responsibility for their violent actions but deny the actions were wrong (84 percent of all explanations).
- Excuses—where students admit the act was wrong but deny responsibility (16 percent).

Examples of justifications are (p. 7): retaliation for harmful behavior, finding an antagonist's behavior offensive, acting in self-defense, helping a stranger who is being beaten and promoting one's image. Examples of excuses include (p. 7): free will being impaired by anger (fit of rage, heat of passion), free will being impaired by alcohol, reluctance or being pushed into action by the antagonist, and acting unintentionally.

Among his conclusions, Lockwood states (p. 8): "A preference for violent retaliation over other forms of redress, a strong belief in punishment, and a sensitivity to perceived injustice and mistreatment are core values at the heart of these students' violent responses. . . . If any belief warrants change, it is retribution, as this was the primary justification for violence."

A survey conducted by the U.S. Department of Education has found that nearly 20 percent of all middle and high schools report at least one serious crime, such as rape or robbery, each year, with most of the reported serious crime occurring in large urban schools ("Fed Survey . . .," 1998, p. 6). "Extrapolating results on the basis of a 1,200-school sample, survey analysts estimated that about 10 percent of public schools nationwide experienced more than 11,000 fights in which weapons were used, 4,000 rapes and other sexual assaults and 7,000 robberies during the 1996–97 school year" (p. 6).

According to the results of a study funded by the National Institute of Justice (Sheley et al., 1995), 20 percent of inner-city students surveyed reported being shot at, stabbed, or otherwise injured with a weapon while in school or on the way to or from school over the past few years. Other findings of this study included:

- 66 percent of students personally knew someone who carried a weapon to school.
- 25 percent reported carrying weapons themselves while in school.

- 66 percent personally knew someone who had been shot at, stabbed, or otherwise assaulted while in school.

- 33 percent agreed or strongly agreed that there was a lot of violence in their school.

As McEnery (1996) notes, teenage boys today are more likely to die from gunshot wounds than from all natural causes combined.

The first nationwide investigation of school-associated violent deaths revealed a total of 105 such deaths during a two-year period, leading researchers to conclude that school-associated violent deaths were more common than previously estimated (Kachur et al., 1996, p. 1729). The results of the study are presented in Table 4.3.

The National School Safety Center reported that during the 1997–1998 school year, 18 deaths involving multiple killings occurred at seven schools across the country—11 deaths at five high schools, five deaths at a middle school and two deaths at an elementary school (Partington, 1998, p. 6). Most of these incidents were widely publicized, and the youthful perpetrators received enormous attention *after* the event, yet many contend we need to pay better attention to students and situations *before* they turn deadly. Partington (p. 6) notes: "It has been reported that the Thurston High School perpetrator boasted of plans to kill and was caught with a stolen weapon shortly before the May 21 incident, yet no actions were taken. But in the week following the Springfield [Oregon] tragedy, schools were listening. Classes in the rural community of McLouth, Kan., were cancelled after a middle school student threatened to bring a gun to school, according to news service reports."

Behavioral psychologist Stephen Thomas suggests screening children for the effects of exposure to violence before they enter middle school, since Thomas views "exposure to everyday violence in the real world, as opposed to movies, television, and video games, as the root of the problem" (Partington, p. 6). Deborah Prothrow-Stith, assistant dean at Harvard's School of Public Health and a national leader in youth violence prevention, states: "Witnessing and experiencing violence are robust factors that predict violence. Hurt children hurt other children" (Gillis, 1998, p. 16).

While recent media coverage of slayings at our nation's schools might seem to indicate a rising level of school violence across the country, recent surveys of both students and school principals do not support such a trend. A study by the U.S. Departments of Education and Justice ("School Crime Not Increasing . . .," 1998, p. 2) has found: "Students in 1995 were more likely than those in 1989 to report they had experienced violent victimization, could obtain drugs, and were aware of the presence of street gangs at school. . . . However, the percent of children who report any kind of victimization at school did not change much from 1989 to 1995." According to this report (p. 2):

> There was a small increase—from 3.4 percent in 1989 to 4.2 percent in 1995—in the percent of these students who said they had experienced violent victimization. . . . The largest change was in the percent of students who reported the presence of street gangs in their schools, which almost doubled from 15.3 percent in 1989 to 28.4 percent in 1995.

Table 4.3
Characteristics of School-Associated Violent Deaths, 1992–1994 (N = 105)

	No.	(%)
Type of fatality		
Interpersonal (homicide)	85	(81.0)
Self-inflicted (suicide)	20	(19.0)
Time of fatal injury		
During school activities	46	(43.8)
Classes	23	(21.9)
Break period	11	(10.5)
After-school activities	12	(11.4)
Before or after official activities	46	(43.8)
Day with no classes or activities	8	(7.6)
Unknown or other	5	(4.8)
Location of fatal injury		
Elementary school	31	(29.5)
Secondary school	74	(70.5)
On campus	68	(64.8)
Classroom	10	(9.5)
Hallway	9	(8.6)
Other indoor location	12	(11.4)
Parking area	11	(10.5)
Other outdoor location	26	(24.8)
Off campus	37	(35.2)
Street/sidewalk	20	(19.0)
In vehicle	13	(12.4)
Private property	4	(3.8)
Type of community		
Urban	63	(60.0)
Suburban	32	(30.5)
Rural	10	(9.5)
Method of injury		
Firearm	81	(77.1)
Knife or other blade	18	(17.1)
Rope	5	(4.8)
No weapon	1	(1.0)
Motive (more than one may apply)		
Interpersonal dispute	35	(33.3)
Gang-related activities	33	(31.4)
Random victim event	19	(18.1)
Suicide	19	(18.1)
Dispute over romantic relationship	12	(11.4)
Robbery or attempted robbery	10	(9.5)
Dispute over money or property	7	(6.7)
Drug-related activities	6	(5.7)
Unintentional	5	(4.8)

Source: S. Patrick Kachur et al. "School-Associated Violent Deaths in the United States, 1992 to 1994." *Journal of the American Medical Association*, Vol. 275, No. 22, June 12, 1996, pp. 1729–1733.

Another study that surveyed public school principals about violence and discipline problems also suggests crime is not increasing in schools. . . .

The percent of public schools reporting that certain problems, such as physical conflicts among students, robbery or theft, vandalism, or student possession of weapons, were serious or moderate problems in their schools did not change drastically, and in some cases decreased slightly in 1996–97 from the percent of public schools that reported in 1990–91.

The National Crime Victimization Survey, School Crime Supplement, has found that within school, various types of problems tend to coexist (Chandler et al., 1998, p. 12):

> For instance, student reports of drug availability, street gang presence, and gun presence at school were all related to student reports of having experienced violent victimization at school. Reports of having experienced violent victimization were higher among students who reported that drugs were available than among students who reported that they were not. In addition, students who reported that street gangs were present were more likely than students who reported that they were not present to say that they had been violently victimized. Finally, students who reported seeing another student with a gun were more likely to say that they had experienced violent victimization than students who had not seen another student with a gun.

Of concern is that administrators across the country do not perceive drugs, gangs, weapons in the schools and the like as much of a problem. The National Center for Education Statistics (NCES) surveyed 1,234 school principals and administrators from elementary through high school. The report *Violence and Discipline Problems in U.S. Public Schools 1996–1997* identified the most serious issue as being student tardiness (40 percent identified this as a moderate or serious issue), followed by absenteeism/class cutting (25 percent). Drug use was identified by only 9 percent and gangs by only 5 percent (Skiba and Peterson, 1999, p. 374).

Fear and Its Effects

Shay Bilchik, administrator of the Office of Juvenile Justice and Delinquency Prevention, states (1998, p. 1):

> For many school-age children, . . . fear is a realistic response to conditions in and around their schools. The adverse effects of this fear are far reaching and often long lasting. When fear keeps children out of the classroom, it can limit their prospects and their potential contributions to society.
>
> America was founded on the promise of opportunity. Every child in our Nation deserves the chance to live the American dream, and education is the pathway to that dream and to a fulfilling and productive life. We must not allow fears engendered by bullying, gangs, weapons, and substance abuse to disrupt children's journey toward a better tomorrow.

Gillis (p. 12) notes that communities are now taking action against such fear:

> Increasingly, they're demanding that schools not only provide a safe space, but that they teach students the life skills to deal with violence on and off campus. New courses deal with anger management, conflict resolution, date rape, sexual harassment and abuse, domestic violence, and other topics far removed from the traditional curriculum. . . .
>
> "There's a big debate in education about losing academic time by doing these [violence prevention and sexual harassment] programs," says Freddie Landry, whose state anti-violence initiatives in Jefferson Parish, Louisiana, receive federal funding through the Safe and Drug Free School program. "But there are students who won't learn without them. . . . We have to go back to satisfying the basic need to feel safe."

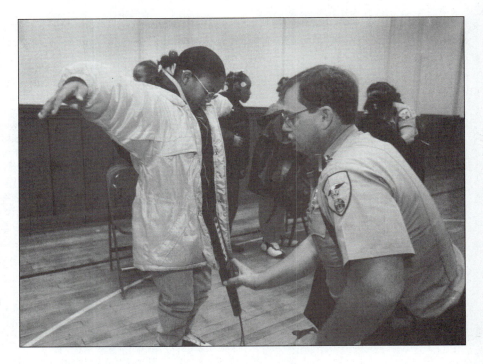

An Indianapolis police sergeant checks a seven year old with a metal detector. School administrators have begun checking even the school system's youngest students for weapons in response to arrests of three children who brought handguns to school.

In Defense of the Schools

Martin (1994, p. 39) describes some measures schools have taken, including having drive-by shooting drills, fencing in their campuses, adding metal detectors, conducting locker searches, banning the wearing of overcoats and backpacks that could conceal weapons and adding uniformed and armed security guards or police officers. Martin suggests that such measures are merely treating symptoms rather than focusing on the causes, and she notes (p. 40): "Since the causes of increased teen violence are societal—hopelessness, family breakdown, media violence, the drug culture, demographics—treating them requires nothing less than curing American society."

Partington (p. 6) states: "Although security equipment can be part of the solution, few believe it is the answer. Some schools are using security equipment such as closed-circuit television surveillance and metal detectors, but the limitations of such measures are all too evident. The Jonesboro, Ark., attack, in which two boys ages 11 and 13 were charged with killing five, occurred outside the school, which would have rendered metal detectors at school entrances ineffective." Quoting behavioral psychologist Stephen Thomas, Partington concludes: " 'It's not the gun; it's the hand on the gun. If we take back our kids, the streets will take care of themselves.'"

Frymier (1992, p. 32) claims: "Problems that most children face lie outside the school rather than inside, on the street rather than on the playground, and in the living room rather than in the classroom." In a similar vein, McClellan (1994, p. 4) cites statistics from the Center for the Study of Social Policy that indicate that of 1.7 million families begun in 1990, "45 percent are at risk because the mother was in her teens, the parents were unmarried, or the mother had not completed high school."

Approximately 45 percent of children being born are at risk of being educationally disadvantaged.

Adds McClellan: "Many of the factors that disadvantaged children face—poverty, family composition—are beyond the schools' realm of influence."

This is not to say that schools are powerless, however, in the battle against violence. Notes Evans (1996, p. 1): "Susan Colonna has been educating first- and second-graders at Thurston Elementary School in Springfield, Oregon, for 10 of her 15 years as a teacher. She decided to tackle the ugly issue of violence by teaching her second-grade students to look critically at the content of their favorite television shows." Colonna asked her students to share their views on violence, which resulted in a chart titled "What Violence Is." On the chart, children listed "acts such as stabbing; ripping out body parts in video games; shooting guns to hurt or kill; using bad words to hurt others' feelings; punching, pushing, scratching; kicking and punching; and using swords and weapons in TV shows" (p. 2). Then Colonna had her second-graders watch a 30-minute children's cartoon program of their choice and tally the incidents of violence. The results: out of 12 hours of programming, a total of 649 incidents of violence were noted by the children (p. 3).

Evans states (p. 4): "When the students decided to stop watching the programs they surveyed, they came up with a list of alternative activities, such as inviting a friend over to play, going fishing, jumping on the trampoline, or playing with the dog." Finally, as part of the project, Colonna had her students compose a "Declaration of Independence from Violence," which stated in part (p. 3):

> We, the second-grade students in Room 7 at Thurston Elementary School, Springfield, Oregon, declare that the world must have less violence so that we may live safe and happy lives.

Students' Rights within the School

Another area of concern to the juvenile justice system is protecting students' rights within the school. Until the past decade, the landmark case in student rights was *Tinker v. Des Moines Independent Community School District* (1969), which established the fact that students have constitutional rights that must be protected in the school.

Students have full constitutional rights within the school, including freedom of speech as well as the right to be free from illegal search and seizure.

Under *Tinker,* students' rights could not be removed unless exercising them would "substantially interfere with the work of the school or impinge upon the rights of other students." This standard changed in 1985. According to Rose (1988, p. 589), the Supreme Court set a new standard for cases involving student rights, a standard of reasonableness: "The change has increased the discretion of school officials in such areas as search and seizure, student publications, and student expression. In establishing the new standard, the Court seems to be giving school officials broad latitude in structuring an environment in which students can both learn and develop 'socially appropriate behavior.'"

The Court requires only that schools' actions in restricting students' constitutional rights be "reasonably related to legitimate pedagogical concerns."

This standard puts great responsibility on school administrators; it will probably reduce the likelihood that courts will intervene in school-related matters. The standard is based on three cases: *New Jersey v. T.L.O.* (1985), *Bethel School District #403 v. Fraser* (1986) and *Hazelwood School District v. Kuhlmeier* (1988). In all three cases, students claimed their constitutional rights were violated.

In *New Jersey v. T.L.O.,* a teacher observed two girls, one of whom was T.L.O., smoking cigarettes in a girl's rest room in violation of the school's rules. The girls were accompanied to the school administrator's office, where T.L.O. denied smoking at all. The administrator requested T.L.O.'s purse, inspected it, found cigarettes, marijuana and marijuana paraphernalia. Further examination disclosed money and change amounting to $40.98 and a letter from T.L.O. to a friend asking for her help to sell marijuana in school. The administrator contacted the police, who referred the matter to the juvenile court. The court ruled there was a violation of search and seizure. Upon appeal, the Supreme Court overturned the ruling, saying that schools can make rules for the administration of the school, and there was no violation of Fourth Amendment protection. As stated by Hoffman (1995, p. 80): "If the search is reasonable and not overly intrusive, then that search should be permitted."

In *Bethel School District #403 v. Fraser,* a student was suspended from school for three days and had his name removed from a list of candidates for graduation speaker because he used sexually explicit language in his campaign speech. The student brought suit, claiming his First Amendment right to free speech had been violated, but the Court said it was constitutional for a school "to prohibit the use of vulgar and offensive terms in public discourse," and it left the determination of this with the school board.

In *Hazelwood School District v. Kuhlmeier,* a principal prohibited the publication of two pages of a student newspaper because he felt the articles were inappropriate. One article was on student pregnancies, written from the point of view of three pregnant students; each gave a positive account of the experience. The other article was on the impact of divorce on students and included comments attributed to specific individuals; the principal considered this to be inappropriate. The Court upheld the prohibition as constitutional.

These three cases set the standard that governs a school's restriction of students' constitutional rights.

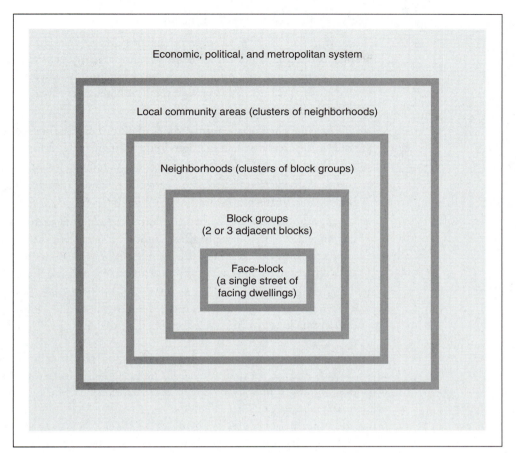

Economic, political, and metropolitan system

Local community areas (clusters of neighborhoods)

Neighborhoods (clusters of block groups)

Block groups
(2 or 3 adjacent blocks)

Face-block
(a single street of
facing dwellings)

Figure 4.3
A Community Viewed
as Nested Boxes

Source: Felton J. Earls and Albert J. Reiss, Jr. *Breaking the Cycle: Predicting and Preventing Crime.* Washington, DC: National Institute of Justice, 1994, p. 10.

Another area involving students' rights is random drug testing of student athletes. At the end of its 1995 session, the Supreme Court upheld the constitutionality of random drug testing for student athletes (*Vernonia School District 47J v. Acton*), stating that such screening does not violate Fourth Amendment protections against unreasonable search and seizure ("High Court Upholds . . .," 1995, p. 1).

**The Duty
of the Community**

Earls and Reiss (1994, pp. 10–11) note (Figure 4.3):

Painting a portrait of the community takes far more than a thousand words. Communities exist on many levels, from small ones that include a few neighboring families to large ones that cover a square mile or more.

These communities are nested like Russian boxes, each one fitting tightly inside a larger one. Because an individual's notion of community changes with age—a 3-year-old's may be a few houses while a teenager's may be measured in square miles—each level must be carefully defined.

Earls and Reiss (p. 11) explain the impacts that various levels of community may have on child development:

- The *face-block* includes apartments or houses facing each other on a single street. This small area often defines "the universe" for very young children. Consequently, information about the face-block may reveal patterns that influence early development.

- *Block groups* encompass normal zones of adult neighborliness and are usually the area in which children build their first friendships.

- *Neighborhoods* are traditionally small, socially homogeneous areas defined by social interaction patterns and geographic landmarks (main streets, parks, railroad tracks).

- *Local community areas* may provide correlates and data such as variations in prenatal care that directly affect human development. For example, local communities with high infant mortality rates and low-birthweight children also have high rates of murder and suicide.

- The *economic, political and metropolitan system* affects such factors as the availability of public transportation, the distance to good jobs, and the overall quality of basic services provided by the city.

These interwoven levels of community shape different people in different ways. As Earls and Reiss explain (p. 9): "The local community touches a person's development in many ways. At its most basic, it provides the physical environment that shapes one's health and sense of well-being. It also provides both formal and informal networks for being with others. These networks include neighbors, school, businesses, boys and girls clubs, drug treatment programs, and a host of other groups and organizations." Wilson (1987) comments that these multiple associations help to structure individual lives by modeling "how things ought to be done."

The web of community associations is a powerful element of everyday life and a defining factor in childhood development, serving to either help or hinder the learning of socially acceptable conduct.

Golden (1997, p. 195) states: "Community is not so much a description of people's closeness to one another as it is about their collective commitment to self-determination. . . . Citizenship without a commitment to grassroots democracy is inevitably undemocratic and elitist because it trades belief in people's ability to solve their own problems for the authority of experts."

Earls and Reiss (p. 9) note: "Every city has neighborhoods where crime and violence seem woven into the fabric of everyday life. New York has the Bronx, Chicago its West Side, Los Angeles its South Central L.A." They then ask: "Are such neighborhoods radically different from relatively crime-free communities? Do communities themselves plant and harvest the seeds of crime?" Reiss and Tonry (1986) answer these questions by pointing to decades of research that supports the idea that certain areas and neighborhoods *do* generate and transmit criminal behavior despite the characteristics of the population living there. As Golden (p.194) claims: "Poverty does not lead to violence, crime, and maltreatment of children. The shredding of community does." Golden continues:

> Without a connection to a community of support, people give up hope. Yet the despair, rage, and isolation of the poor are invisible. Michael Harrington argued, over twenty years ago, that the poor are invisible because suburbanization separated the middle class from seeing the problems of the urban poor. The majority don't see the elderly poor's desperate struggle to pay rent and live alone in a studio or one-room apartment. Poor people in America aren't "recognizable" because "it is much easier in the United States to be decently dressed than to be decently fed, housed or doctored."

Maggie Dexheimer Pharris, a sexual assault nurse clinician writing her doctoral dissertation on the public health epidemic of violence, says the United States must re-create a sense of community within its neighborhoods (Bonneville, p. 7). She looks to the past and a time when schools and churches were the focal points of a neighborhood for children, when neighbors knew neighbors and adults looked out for everyone else's kids. "Now, kids don't have that sense, that glue. [We must] reweave our social fabric" (p. 7).

Earls and Reiss (p. 10) present a scenario of how individuals, families and communities interact to produce crime:

> Antisocial or aggressive behavior, as well as the attitudes that steer people away from crime, develop as individuals and their families interact within a community and its organizations. . . .
>
> Suppose a young man suddenly loses his job.

> - An area with few economic opportunities or support networks may encourage him to slide toward crime or at least not actively prevent him from engaging in it.
> - An area with economic opportunities and support networks may discourage crime by encouraging employment and providing incentives for it.

> In this scenario, a particularly impulsive individual might be easily swayed by criminal opportunities. However, that same person might continue to be law-abiding if he lives in an area with career options and opportunities.

Getting communities and the public at large involved in preventing childhood violence must be a priority throughout this nation. As Greenbaum (1997, p. 8) notes: "Researchers have found that long-term public education campaigns on violence prevention, family education, alcohol and drug prevention, and gun safety curriculums in schools are effective in helping to reduce delinquency. . . . The public and private sectors, including the media, also can play significant roles in program design and implementation." Attorney General Janet Reno concludes (Coordinating Council, 1996): "More and more of our Nation's children are killing and dying. The only way we can break the cycle of violence is through a truly national effort implemented one community at a time. Everyone has a role—businesses, schools, universities, and especially parents. Every community and every citizen can find practical steps in the *Action Plan* to do something now about youth violence."

Summary

The family, the school and the community are powerful influences on children's development. The structure and interaction patterns of the home influence whether children learn socially acceptable or delinquent behavior. In healthy families, self-esteem is high, communication is direct and honest, rules are flexible and reasonable and members' attitudes toward the outside world are trusting and optimistic.

In some families, the concept of adult supremacy may threaten sound relationships. Adult supremacy subordinates children to the absolute and arbitrary authority of parents. Common values that might be passed on to our youth include equality, honesty, promise-keeping, respect, responsibility, self-control and social justice.

The schools also play a vital role in the development of our youths. They are given this responsibility through the principle of *in loco parentis,* meaning "in place of parents." This principle gives certain social and legal institutions, including the schools, the authority to act as a parent might in situations requiring discipline or need. It is similar to *parens patriae,* only at the local level.

One positive way to offset negative norms and behavior is to promote positive values in our schools. Children who succeed in school have a greater probability of succeeding in other areas of their lives. However, several common educational practices may encourage failure, including the A-B-C-D-F grading system, objective testing, grading on a curve, closed-book tests and tracking students. Students' responses to failure may include skipping school, joining gangs, dropping out of school, drinking, doing drugs, performing delinquent acts and even suicide. The link between failure in school and delinquency is strong.

Our schools face many problems, but according to a Gallup poll of attitudes about public schools, fighting, violence and gangs are currently the biggest problems facing local public schools. Also problematic is the number of children coming to school not ready to learn. Approximately 45 percent of children from families begun in 1990 were at risk of being educationally disadvantaged.

If students are to be taught respect for others, their own constitutional rights should be respected within the school. Students do have full constitutional rights, including freedom of speech as well as the right to be free from illegal search and seizure. However, the Supreme Court requires only that schools' actions in restricting students' constitutional rights be "reasonably related to legitimate pedagogical concerns."

The community plays a pivotal role in the healthy development of youths. Community associations are a powerful element of everyday life and a defining factor in childhood development, serving to either help or hinder the learning of socially acceptable conduct.

Discussion Questions

1. Do you believe controlled spanking in certain cases is justified? Were you spanked as a child?
2. What values do you feel should be passed on to the next generation?
3. Do you have personal experiences with an educational practice that promoted failure rather than success?

4. Did you ever skip school when you were young? If you did, do you remember why? Why do youths become truants? Is truancy the responsibility of the school, parents or youths?

5. Why should an individual be forced to get an education? Is refusing to go to school a delinquent act? Why or why not?

6. Should schools be forced into continually having to accept disruptive and incorrigible students? What are some alternatives? Do you think this matter is best resolved in the juvenile court? If not, where?

7. Do schools contribute to the problem of youths who are disruptive, antisocial, incorrigible and truant? How?

8. What were teachers like in your school? Did you ever feel like rebelling or staying away from school? Why? What could be changed?

9. Do schools expect too much from youths who display unacceptable behavior? How can such behavior be adjusted? Should the youths be put into the juvenile justice system?

10. Are there neighborhoods in your community where violence seems more tolerated than in others? If so, what factors contribute to this tolerance?

References

Biddle, Bruce J. "Foolishness, Dangerous Nonsense, and Real Correlates of State Differences in Achievement." *Phi Delta Kappan,* September 1997, pp. 9–13.

Bilchik, Shay. "From the Administrator." In Arnette, June L. and Walsleben, Marjorie C. *Combating Fear and Restoring Safety in Schools.* OJJDP Juvenile Justice Bulletin, April 1998, p. 1. (NCJ-167888)

Bilchik, Shay. "From the Administrator." In Cantelon, Sharon and LeBoeuf, Donni. *Keeping Young People in School: Community Programs That Work.* OJJDP Juvenile Justice Bulletin, June 1997, p. 1. (NCJ-162783)

Bonneville, Gayle. "Diagnosis: Violence." *Health Sciences,* University of Minnesota. Spring 1995, pp. 2–7.

Burger, Warren E. "Annual Report to the American Bar Association." Houston: February 8, 1981, p. 2.

Canning, Miles, ed. "Both Sides of Adolescence." Richfield, MN: Storefront/Youth Action, 1992.

Cantelon, Sharon and LeBoeuf, Donni. *Keeping Young People in School: Community Programs that Work.* OJJDP Juvenile Justice Bulletin, June 1997. (NCJ-162783)

Carr, William. *The Purposes of Education in American Democracy.* Washington, DC: Educational Policies Commission, 1938.

Chandler, Kathryn A.; Chapman, Christopher D.; Rand, Michael R.; and Taylor, Bruce M. *Students' Reports of School Crime: 1989 and 1995.* 1989 and 1995 School Crime Supplement to the National Crime Victimization Survey. Washington, DC: National Center for Education Statistics and the Bureau of Justice Statistics, March 1998. (NCJ-169607)

Chaskin, Robert J. and Rauner, Diana Mendley. "Youth and Caring: An Introduction." *Phi Delta Kappan,* May 1995, pp. 667–674.

Coordinating Council on Juvenile Justice and Delinquency Prevention. *Combating Violence and Delinquency: The National Juvenile Justice Action Plan.* Washington, DC: Office of Juvenile Justice and Delinquency Prevention, March 1996.

Culkin, Father John. "I Was a Teenage Movie Teacher." *Saturday Review,* July 16, 1966, p. 51.

Day, Thomas W. "Cross-Cultural Medicine at Home." *Minnesota Medicine,* March 1992, pp. 15–17.

Dill, Vicky Schreiber. *A Peaceable School.* Bloomington, IN: Phi Delta Kappa Educational Foundation, 1998.

"Do We Still Need Public Schools?" Bloomington, IN: Phi Delta Kappa, 1996.

Earls, Felton J. and Reiss, Albert J., Jr. *Breaking the Cycle: Predicting and Preventing Crime.* Washington, DC: National Institute of Justice, 1994. (NCJ-140541)

Eitzen, Stanley. "Problem Students: The Sociocultural Roots." *Phi Delta Kappan,* April 1992, pp. 584–590.

Elam, Stanley M.; Rose, Lowell C.; and Gallup, Alec M. "The 25th Annual Phi Delta Kappa/Gallup Poll of the Public's Attitudes Toward the Public Schools." *Phi Delta Kappan,* October 1993, pp. 137–152.

Evans, Alice. *Addressing TV Violence in the Classroom.* Phi Delta Kappa Research Bulletin, No.16, May 1996.

"Fed Survey Paints School-Crime Picture." *Law Enforcement News,* March 31, 1998, p. 6.

Foster, H. "A 'Bill of Rights' for Children." In *Child Abuse and Neglect,* 1974.

Frymier, Jack. *Growing Up Is Risky Business, and Schools Are Not to Blame.* Bloomington, IN: Phi Delta Kappa, 1992.

Frymier, Jack; Cunningham, Luvern; Duckett, Willard; Gansneder, Bruce; Link, Frances; Rimmer, June; and Scholz, James. *Values and the Schools: Sixty Years Ago and Now.* Bloomington, IN: Phi Delta Kappa Research Bulletin, No. 17, September 1996, pp. 1–4.

Gardner, Howard. *Frames of Mind: The Theory of Multiple Intelligences.* New York: Basic Books, 1983.

Garry, Eileen M. *Truancy: First Step to a Lifetime of Problems.* OJJDP Juvenile Justice Bulletin, October 1996. (NCJ-161958)

Gillis, Anna Maria. "School Violence: Fighting the Code of Silence." *AAUW Outlook,* Spring 1998, pp. 12–17.

Glasser, William. *Schools Without Failure.* New York: Harper & Row, 1969.

Golden, Renny. *Disposable Children: America's Child Welfare System.* Belmont, CA: Wadsworth Publishing Company, 1997.

Greenbaum, Stuart. "Kids and Guns: From Playgrounds to Battlegrounds." *Juvenile Justice,* Journal of the OJJDP, Vol. 3, No.2, September 1997, pp. 3–10. (NCJ-165925)

"High Court Upholds Random Drug Tests for Student Athletes." *NCJA Justice Bulletin,* Vol.15, No. 6, June 1995, pp. 1–2.

Hodgkinson, Harold. "Reform versus Reality." *Phi Delta Kappan,* September 1991, pp. 9–16.

Hoffman, Terrance W. "Student Searches in School." *Law and Order,* July 1995, pp. 80, 84–89.

Hopfensperger, Jean. "New Wave of Adopted Children Confronting Special Problems." (Minneapolis/St. Paul) *Star Tribune,* November 7, 1988, pp. A1, A9.

Kachur, S. Patrick; Stennies, Gail M.; Powell, Kenneth E.; Modzeleski, William; Stephens, Ronald; Murphy, Rosemary; Kresnow, Marcie-Jo; Sleet, David; and Lowry, Richard. "School-Associated Violent Deaths in the United States, 1992–1994." *Journal of the American Medical Association,* Vol. 275, No. 22, June 12, 1996, pp. 1729–1733.

Ledlie, J. *Sohm's Institute of Roman Law.* 1907. Out of print.

Lockwood, Daniel. *Violence Among Middle School and High School Students: Analysis and Implications for Prevention.* National Institute of Justice Research in Brief, October 1997. (NCJ-166363)

Martin, Deirdre. "Teen Violence: Why It's on the Rise and How to Stem Its Tide." *Law Enforcement Technology,* January 1994, pp. 36–42.

McClellan, Mary. "Why Blame Schools?" *Research Bulletin of the Center for Evaluation, Development, and Research,* No. 12. Bloomington, IN: Phi Delta Kappa, March 1994.

McConaghy, Tom. "School Violence: Not Just in the U.S." *Phi Delta Kappan,* April 1994, pp. 654–655.

McEnery, R. "Today's Schoolyard Bully Just Might Be Armed." *Asbury Park Press,* February 28, 1996.

National Council of Juvenile and Family Court Judges Metropolitan Court Judges Committee Report. *Deprived Children: A Judicial Response.* Washington, DC: U.S. Government Printing Office, 1986.

National Criminal Justice Association. "Adverse Teen Outcomes Linked to Risk Factors, According to Census." *NCJA Justice Bulletin,* December 1997, pp. 10–11.

National Criminal Justice Association. "Many Mothers Serving Time Never See Their Children, Says NCCD Report." *Juvenile Justice,* July 1993, pp. 1–2, 4.

National School Safety Center. *Gangs in Schools: Breaking Up Is Hard to Do.* Malibu, CA: Pepperdine University Press, 1988.

OJJDP Annual Report, 1990. Washington, DC: Office of Juvenile Justice and Delinquency Prevention, 1990.

"1 in 50 Under Age 15 May Have a Jailed Parent." (Minneapolis/St. Paul) *Star Tribune,* August 10, 1993, p. A1.

Pace, Denny F. *Community Relations Concept.* Incline Village, NV: Copperhouse Publishing, 1991.

Parker, L. Craig, Jr.; Meier, Robert D.; and Monahan, Lynn Hunt. *Interpersonal Psychology for Criminal Justice.* St. Paul, MN: West Publishing Company, 1989.

Partington, George. "Looking for Answers to Problem of Violent Attacks at Schools." *Access Control and Security Systems Integration,* June 1998, p. 6.

Reiss, Albert J., Jr. and Tonry, Michael, eds. "Communities and Crime." *Crime and Justice: Review of Research.* Vol. 8. Chicago: University of Chicago Press, 1986.

Rose, Lowell C. "'Reasonableness'—The High Court's New Standard for Cases Involving Student Rights." *Phi Delta Kappan,* April 1988, pp. 589–592.

Rose, Lowell C. and Gallup, Alec M. "The 30th Annual Phi Delta Kappa/Gallup Poll of the Public's Attitudes Toward the Public Schools." *Phi Delta Kappan,* September 1998, pp. 41–56.

Ruben, David. "What Makes a Child Violent?" *Parenting,* August 1998, pp. 96–102.

"School Crime Not Increasing, According to Surveys." *NCJA Justice Bulletin,* Vol. 18, No. 4, April 1998, pp. 1–5.

Sheley, Joseph F.; McGee, Zina T.; and Wright, James D. *Weapon-Related Victimization in Selected Inner-City High School Samples.* Washington, DC: National Institute of Justice, 1995. (NCJ-151526)

Skiba, Russ and Peterson, Reece. "The Dark Side of Zero Tolerance: Can Punishment Lead to Safe Schools?" *Phi Delta Kappan,* January 1999, pp. 372–382.

"Study Amplifies Crime's Link to Child Abuse and Neglect." *Law Enforcement News,* July/August 1997, p. 15.

Suskind, Ron. "Tormented for Learning." *The Wall Street Journal,* May 26, 1994.

United Nations. *Convention on the Rights of the Child.* Adopted by the General Assembly of the United Nations, November 20, 1989.

U.S. Congress, House Committee on Education and Labor. *Hearing Before Subcommittee on Elementary, Secondary, and Vocational Education on H.R. 123.* 96 Congress, 1st Session, April 24, 1979.

von Sternberg, Bob. "Expert: 'Moral Sense' Must Be Regained to End Crime." (Minneapolis/St. Paul) *Star Tribune,* April 28, 1994, p. B9.

Wallerstein, Judith S. and Corbin, Shauna B. "Father-Child Relationships After Divorce: Child Support and Educational Opportunity." *Family Law Quarterly,* Vol. 20, No. 2, Summer 1986, pp. 109–128.

Walsh, James. "To Hit Is to Harm, Anti-Spanking Project Stresses." (Minneapolis/St. Paul) *Star Tribune,* April 12, 1994, pp. B1, B8.

West, Nancy. "Should a Child Be Spanked?" *Parade Magazine,* April 17, 1994, pp. 12–14.

Wilson, John J. "A National Agenda for Children: On the Front Lines with Attorney General Janet Reno." *Juvenile Justice,* Vol. 1, No. 2, Fall/Winter 1993, pp. 2–8.

Wilson, W. J. *The Truly Disadvantaged: The Inner City, the Underclass, and Public Policy.* Chicago: University of Chicago Press, 1987.

Wu, Amy. "Flogging May Be Cure for Teenage Violence." (Minneapolis/St. Paul) *Star Tribune,* April 17, 1994, p. A25.

Cases

Bethel School District #403 v. Fraser, 478 U.S. 675, 106 S.Ct. 3159, 92 L.Ed.2d 549 (1986).

Hazelwood School District v. Kuhlmeier, 484 U.S. 260, 108 S.Ct. 562, 98 L.Ed.2d 592 (1988).

New Jersey v. T.L.O., 469 U.S. 325, 105 S.Ct. 733, 83 L.Ed.2d 720 (1985).

Tinker v. Des Moines Independent Community School District, 393 U.S. 503, 89 S.Ct. 733, 21 L.Ed.2d 731 (1969).

Vernonia School District 47J v. Acton, ___ U.S. ___, 115 S.Ct. 2386, 132 L.Ed.2d 564 (1995).

Chapter 5

Youths Who Are Victims

The cycle of abused and neglected children who have become abusing and neglecting parents with their children in turn being abused, neglected, running away, acting out and often ending up before the courts has not been broken.

—Metropolitan Court Judges Committee

Do You Know

- What often characterizes the homes of neglected children?
- What is required for human brains to develop properly?
- What are believed to be the two leading causes of child abuse?
- What the major cause of death of young children is?
- What the three levels of abuse are?
- How many states have banned corporal punishment for children?
- Which age group has the highest victimization rate?
- What the likely result of violence is for children?
- What five categories of missing children were identified in the NISMART study?
- What two federal agencies have concurrent jurisdiction for missing and exploited children?
- What the leading cause of suicide is?

Can You Define

child abuse, collective abuse, emotional abuse, extrafamilial sexual abuse, individual abuse, institutional abuse, intrafamilial sexual abuse, maximalist alarmist perspective, minimalist skeptical perspective, neglect, physical abuse, runaways, seesaw model, thrownaways

INTRODUCTION

Maltreatment of youths occurs in many ways. As noted by Bilchik (1997, p. 1): "The victimization of the weak by the strong—in this case, of children by adults—is one of the most shameful constants in human history. Unfortunately, contemporary American society is not immune from this repugnant behavior. The National Committee to Prevent Child Abuse [NCPCA] estimates that 1 million children suffered maltreatment in the United States in 1995 alone."

Statistics indicate a rising trend in the number of children known to be maltreated. Sickmund et al. (1997, p. 6) state: "The number of children identified as abused or neglected almost doubled between 1986 and 1993." In 1995, the NCPCA estimated that:

- There were 3,111,000 children reported to Child Protective Services as alleged victims of maltreatment.
- Reports have steadily risen over the past decade, with a 49 percent increase from 1986 to 1995.
- Approximately one million children were found to be victims of maltreatment each year from 1992 to 1995.
- During the past 10 years, more than three children died each day as a result of parental maltreatment.
- Abuse is the most common cause of death (48 percent), followed by neglect (37 percent) and a combination of abuse and neglect (15 percent).
- The majority of victims (85 percent) are under age five, and nearly half (45 percent) of the victims never reach their first birthday. (Kelley et al., 1997, p. 2)

These authors conclude that having a history of childhood maltreatment "increases the likelihood of problems during adolescent development" (p. 11). Such maltreated youths are at an increased risk for each of the following:

- Engaging in serious and violent delinquency
- Using drugs
- Performing poorly in school
- Displaying symptoms of mental illness
- For girls, becoming pregnant

A study conducted by the National Institute of Justice (Widom, 1992, p. 5) concluded: "Childhood victimization represents a widespread, serious social problem that increases the likelihood of delinquency, adult criminality, and violent criminal behavior. Poor educational performance, health problems, and generally low levels of achievement also characterize the victims of early childhood abuse and neglect." In addition, child victimization may follow the radial pattern discussed in Chapter 3, with victimization occurring not only within the family, but in the school and community as well.

Kelley et al. (p. 4) describe the subtypes of child maltreatment and rate their severity in Table 5.1.

Table 5.1
**Defining Child
Maltreatment and Rating
Its Severity**

Subtype of Maltreatment	Brief Definition	Examples of Least and Most Severe Cases
Physical Abuse	A caregiver inflicts a physical injury upon a child by other than accidental means.	*Least*—Spanking results in minor bruises on arm. *Most*—Injuries require hospitalization, cause permanent disfigurement, or lead to a fatality.
Sexual Abuse	Any sexual contact or attempt at sexual contact that occurs between a caretaker or responsible adult and a child for the purposes of the caretaker's sexual gratification or financial benefit.	*Least*—A child is exposed to pornographic materials. *Most*—A caretaker uses force to make a child engage in sexual relations or prostitution.
Physical Neglect	A caretaker fails to exercise a minimum degree of care in meeting a child's physical needs.	*Least*—Food is not available for regular meals, clothing is too small, child is not kept clean. *Most*—A child suffers from severe malnutrition or severe dehydration due to gross inattention to his or her medical needs.
Lack of Supervision	A caretaker does not take adequate precautions (given a child's particular emotional and developmental needs) to ensure his or her safety in and out of the home.	*Least*—An 8-year-old is left alone for short periods of time (i.e., less than 3 hours) with no immediate source of danger in the environment. *Most*—A child is placed in a life-threatening situation without adequate supervision.
Emotional Maltreatment	Persistent or extreme thwarting of a child's basic emotional needs (such as the need to feel safe and accepted).	*Least*—A caretaker often belittles or ridicules a child. *Most*—A caretaker uses extremely restrictive methods to bind a child or places a child in close confinement such as a closet or trunk for 2 or more hours.
Educational Maltreatment	A caretaker fails to ensure that a child receives adequate education.	*Least*—A caretaker allows a child to miss school up to 15% of the time (when he or she is not ill and there is no family emergency). *Most*—A caretaker does not enroll a child in school or provide any educational instruction.
Moral-Legal Maltreatment	A caretaker exposes or involves a child in illegal or other activities that may foster delinquency or antisocial behavior.	*Least*—A child is permitted to be present for adult activities, such as drunken parties. *Most*—A caretaker causes a child to participate in felonies such as armed robbery.

Source: Adapted from Barnett et al. (1993).

This chapter begins with a discussion of child neglect and abuse, including sexual abuse. This is followed by a discussion of children as victims of violence outside the home and as victims of crime. The chapter concludes with a description of the results of victimization, including youths who are delinquents, runaways, thrownaways, missing and even suicidal.

Children Who Are Neglected

Broadly defined, child **neglect** is inattention to the basic needs of a child, such as appropriate supervision, adequate clothing and proper nutrition (Johnson, 1998, p. 77). Often, the families from which neglected children come are poor and disorganized. They have no set routine for family activity. The children roam the streets at all hours. They are continually being petitioned to juvenile court for loitering and curfew violations. The family unit is often fragmented by death, divorce or the desertion of parents.

Broken homes often deprive children of affection, recognition and a sense of belonging unless there is a strong parent to overcome these responses and provide direction. If a child's protective shield is shattered, the child may lose respect for moral and ethical standards. The broken home, in and of itself, does not cause delinquency. But it can nullify or even destroy the resources that youths need in order to handle emotional problems constructively. Children from broken homes may suffer serious damage to their personalities. They may develop aggressive attitudes and strike out. They may feel that punishment is better than no recognition. Even when marriages are intact, both parents often work. Consequently, many parents spend little time in the home interacting with their children.

Some children are stunted in their growth by being raised in a moral vacuum in which parents ignore them. Even more problematic are parents who do not adhere to moral and ethical standards or who have different values than the dominant moral order; they set poor examples for their children. Such parents cannot ignore the probability that their children may model their actions.

The homes of neglected children often are disorganized, with parents who ignore the children or who set a bad example for them.

Some parents deliberately refrain from discipline in the mistaken belief that authoritative restrictions inhibit children's self-expression or unbalance their delicate emotional systems. At the other extreme are parents who discipline their children injudiciously, excessively and often, weighing neither transgression nor punishment. Parents' warped ideas, selfish attitudes and twisted values can lead to their children becoming delinquents. Family policies that are inconsistent, or that emphasize too much leniency or excessive punishment, may produce in children a form of retaliation that is directed at society in general.

Children's behavior develops from what they see and understand to be happening around them. If children are exposed to excessive drinking, the use of drugs, illicit sex, gambling and related vices by parents or adult role models, they may repeat these behaviors.

Neglected children often lack the food, clothing, shelter, medical care, supervision, education, protection or emotional support they need to ensure physical, mental and emotional health. They may also suffer emotional harm through disrespect and denial of self-worth, unreasonable or chronic rejection and failure to receive necessary affection, protection and a sense of family belonging.

Other victims of neglect are described by Cowley (1991, p. 18); these include the thousands who die from preventable accidents, the millions who go unvaccinated against common childhood diseases and the millions more poisoned by cigarette smoke or household lead. He concludes that: "American children remain the most neglected in the developed world." Cowley (p. 20) cautions: "Cigarette smoke not only poisons developing fetuses—causing a quarter of all low birth weights and a tenth of all infant deaths—but disables children who breathe it growing up."

Another large contributor to neglect is crack cocaine. Will (1994, p. A25) reports on the tremendous increase in cases of child abuse and neglect handled by the Legal Aid Society in New York as the direct result of crack, stating that

60 percent of all abuse and neglect cases involve drug allegations. Even more devastating, however, are the traumatic accidents that maim or kill children: "No disease, drug or environmental hazard rivals traumatic injuries as a killer of children. Every year mishaps claim the lives of 8,000 American youngsters and permanently disable 50,000" (Cowley, p. 20). Some of these mishaps result from safety hazards in the home. An estimated 90 percent of permanent childhood injuries could have been prevented by adequate supervision. Often the lack of supervision is the direct result of a parent being high on drugs or alcohol.

Certainly not all neglect is intentional. It may be the result of parental immaturity or a lack of parenting skills. It may also be the result of a parent's physical, psychological or mental deficiencies. Other parents who neglect their children may do so because they cannot tolerate stress, they cannot adequately express anger or they have no sense of responsibility.

Indicators of Neglect

Among the *physical indicators* of child neglect are frequent hunger, poor hygiene, inappropriate dress, consistent lack of supervision (especially in dangerous activities or for long time periods), unattended physical problems or medical needs and abandonment. The *behavioral indicators* of neglect may include begging, stealing food, extending school days by arriving early or leaving late, constant fatigue, listlessness or falling asleep in school, alcohol or drug abuse, delinquency, stealing and reporting that no one is at home to care for them (Bennett and Hess, 1998, p. 375).

Consequences of Neglect

As noted by Springer (1986, p. 75):

> It is generally accepted that maternal deprivation and infant neglect can result in neurological maldevelopment. Even given fulfillment of all chemical needs, mammalian nervous systems fail to develop properly absent appropriate sensory and emotional stimulations. Surrogate mothers in the form of colored television sets tending to [hold] captive infants in cages called playpens can result in the same kind of crippling that results from deprivation of chemical nutrients.
>
> The human brain is undeveloped at birth. For it to develop properly the infant must be fondled, touched, picked up, rocked, and carried. . . .
>
> Unloved children do not develop properly and are higher-risk candidates for entry into the justice system.

For human brains to develop properly, children need handling and love.

Springer (p. 75) cites the testimony of James W. Prescott before the Standing Senate Committee on Health, Welfare and Science:

> Human infants and animals who are deprived of sensory stimulation during the formal period of brain development develop a biological system of brain functioning and structure which predisposes these organisms—these animals, these children—to pathologically violent behavior.

A study by the National Institute of Justice (Widom, 1992, p. 1) suggests that neglect can lead to future violent behavior and that "far more attention needs to be devoted to the families of children whose 'beatings' are forms of abandonment and severe malnutrition."

Other children need assistance because the "beatings" are physical and violent.

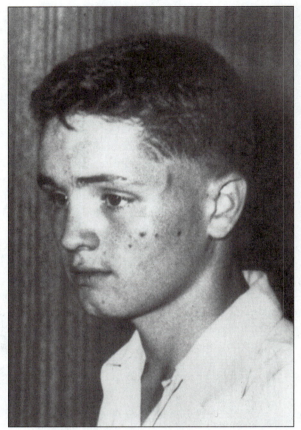

Charles Manson was subjected to severe emotional abuse as a child. Here, at age 14, he has just been released from a juvenile home. He later became the leader of a hippie ''family'' that murdered actress Sharon Tate. He is serving a life sentence.

Children Who Are Physically or Emotionally Abused

The problem of **child abuse** is a serious one. According to Johnson (p. 77): "Some studies suggest that as many as 60 million Americans are victims." Such abuse may be physical or emotional.

Strandberg (1997, p. 38) notes: "Physical child abuse is difficult to categorize because there is a wide spectrum of abuse. In some cases, child abuse is construed as discipline, just maybe gone a little too far." Indeed, great debate exists among child development scholars and parents about where the line between discipline and abuse should be drawn, and many parents who cause physical harm to their children while administering disciplinary measures claim they never *intended* to injure their children. The definition of **physical abuse,** however, leaves less room for interpretation and addresses the issue of intent, stating it is the *nonaccidental,* or intentional, physical injury of a child caused by the child's caretaker (Johnson, p. 77).

Injury to a child need not be limited to physical attacks and external wounds. Children may also be hurt on the inside through **emotional abuse,** the chronic failure of a child's caretaker to provide affection and support (Johnson, p. 78). Emotional abuse includes any treatment that seriously damages a child's emotional development. As an example Johnson (p. 78) states: "Charles Manson was raised by an uncle who subjected him to severe emotional maltreatment by constantly calling him derogatory names and sending him to school dressed in girl's clothes."

Unfortunately the physical and emotional abuse of children is nothing new to humankind. In fact, there were many times throughout history when such abuse was widely and openly practiced.

Historical Roots of Abuse

Throughout history children have been subjected to physical violence. Infants have been killed as a form of birth control, to avoid the dishonor of illegitimacy, as a means of power, as a method of disposing of retarded or deformed children and as a way of protecting financial security.

In ancient Greece a child was the absolute property of the father, and property was divided among the male children. The father would raise the first son and expose subsequent children to the elements. Under Roman law the father had the power of life and death (*patria potestas*) over his children and could kill, mutilate, sell or offer them as a sacrifice.

In the industrial, urban and machine age the exploitation of child labor was common. Children of all ages worked 16 hours a day, usually with irons and chains on their ankles to keep them from running away. They were starved, beaten and dehumanized, with many dying from exposure in the workplace, from occupational diseases or from suicide.

Karmen (1996, p. 220) notes: "For centuries, parents were permitted to beat their children in the name of imposing discipline. Religious and legal traditions legitimized parental violence toward youngsters as a necessary, even essential technique of child rearing (unless permanent injury or death resulted; then the problem was labeled 'cruelty to children')."

Before the creation of the first juvenile court in the United States, the Society for the Prevention of Cruelty to Children was formed in 1871 as a result of church workers removing a severely beaten and neglected child, Mary Ellen, from her home under the law that protected animals. The first Child Protection Service was founded in 1875. Some 50 years later the Social Security Act authorized public funds for child welfare.

In the 1940s advances in diagnostic X ray technology allowed physicians to detect the patterns of healed fractures in their young patients. In 1946 Dr. John Caffey, a pediatric radiologist, made the novel suggestion that the multiple fractures in the long bones of infants had "traumatic origin," perhaps willfully inflicted by parents. Two decades later Dr. C. H. Kempe and his associates coined the phrase *battered child syndrome* based on clinical evidence of maltreatment. Karmen (p. 221) notes: "In the typical case, the victim was younger than three years old and suffered traumatic injuries to the head and to long bones; and the parents claimed that the wounds were caused by an accident and not a beating." In 1964 individual states began enacting mandatory child abuse laws using Dr. Kempe's definition of a battered child, and by 1966 all 50 states had enacted such legislation.

*Child Abuse
and Neglect Laws*

Laws regarding child abuse and neglect have been passed at both the federal and the state levels. Typically child abuse/neglect laws have three components:

1. Criminal definitions and penalties
2. A mandate to report suspected cases
3. Civil process for removing the child from the abusive or neglectful environment

Federal Legislation

In 1974 the federal government passed P. L. 93-247, the Federal Child Abuse Prevention and Treatment Act. It was amended in 1978 under P. L. 95-266. The law states in part that any of the following elements constitutes a crime:

> The physical or mental injury, sexual abuse or exploitation, negligent treatment, or maltreatment of a child under the age of eighteen, by a person who is responsible for the child's welfare under circumstances which indicate the child's health or welfare is harmed or threatened.

Nonetheless federal courts have also ruled that parents are free to strike children because "the custody, care and nurture of the child resides first in the parents" (*Prince v. Massachusetts* [1944]) and is a fundamental liberty interest of the parents. This fundamental right to "nurture" has been supplanted by the U.S. Supreme Court with the "care, custody and management" of one's child (*Santosky v. Kramer* [1982]). This shift from "nurture" to "management" could herald a return to older laws, such as that expressed in *People v. Green* (1909): "The parent is the sole judge of the necessity for the exercise of disciplinary right and of the nature of the correction to be given." The court need only determine if "the punishment inflicted went beyond the legitimate exercise of parental authority."

Up to the present, the courts' role has been to decide what, when and to what degree physical punishment steps beyond "the legitimate exercise of parental authority" or what is "excessive punishment." The courts always begin with the presumption that parents have a legal right to use force and violence against their own children. In *Green,* 70 marks from a whipping was held to be excessive and unreasonable, even though the parent claimed he was not criminally liable because there was no permanent injury and he had acted in good faith. But the assumption remained that the parent had an unquestionable right "to administer such reasonable and timely punishment as may be necessary to correct growing faults in young children."

Current laws protect parents, and convictions for child abuse are difficult to obtain because of the circumstantial evidence, the lack of witnesses, the husband-wife privilege and the fact that an adult's testimony often is enough to establish a reasonable doubt. All too often the court determines the punishment to be reasonable, never reexamining the age-old presumption that hitting children is permissible.

A determination of "reasonableness" was made in *Ingram v. Wright* (1977) regarding the use of physical punishment of children by teachers. The Florida statute specified that the punishment was not to be "degrading or unduly severe." One student was beaten by 20 strokes with a wooden paddle; another was beaten by 50 strokes.

State Laws

Since the 1960s every state has enacted child abuse and neglect laws. On the whole, states offer a bit more protection to children by statute than does the federal government.

Legal definitions vary from state to state. California, for example, declares it illegal for anyone to willfully cause or permit any child to suffer or for any person to inflict unjustifiable physical or mental suffering on a child or to cause the child to "be placed in such situations that its person or health is endangered" (California Penal Codes, Sec. 273A).

Alaska defines abuse broadly: "The infliction, by other than accidental means, of physical harm upon the body of a child." Other state statutes are much less broad. For example Maryland's statute states that a person is not guilty of child abuse if the defendant's intentions were good, but his or her judgment was bad. The defendant in *Worthen v. State* (1979) admitted he had punished his two-year-old stepdaughter because she was throwing a temper tantrum, "but sought to explain as not having exceeded the bounds of parental propriety." The jury found him guilty of assault and battery for the multiple contusions about the girl's face, ribs, buttocks and legs, but the appellate court ordered a new trial because the trial court in its jury instructions had omitted the defense of good intentions and also the defense that the defendant had not exceeded the bounds of parental authority. What is "reasonable" varies from state to state, from one judge or court to another and from jury to jury.

Another category of our young who are victimized are children who are missing and exploited, often by choice because of intolerable conditions in the home, including abuse and violence.

The Causes of Abuse

Most emotional and physical child abuse is committed by parents or those caring for children. The causes of such abuse often center on a cycle of abuse passed from one generation to the next. Karmen (p. 222) states:

> Research into the backgrounds of physically abused children indicates the beatings are more likely to occur in dysfunctional families racked by a combination of symptoms of marital discord: where the two parents fight viciously; one or both of the parents are substance abusers; the mother was raised by a substance-abusing parent; and the mother was often beaten while she was growing up.

Other characteristics that correlate with child abuse include low income, social isolation and parental expectations that exceed the child's abilities.

The two leading causes of child abuse are believed to be violence between husbands and wives and poverty.

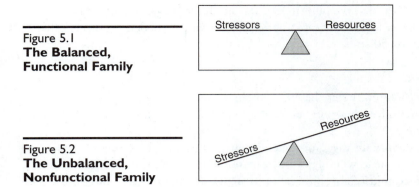

Figure 5.1
The Balanced, Functional Family

Figure 5.2
The Unbalanced, Nonfunctional Family

Further causes of child abuse include racial discrimination and the desensitization to violence by frequent viewing of brutality on television and in the movies.

A **seesaw model** to conceptualize the causes of child abuse has been developed by Ostbloom and Crase (1980). This model illustrates both functional and nonfunctional families and two critical factors: stress and resources. In the functional family, the resources are available to cope with daily stressors, resulting in a "balanced" family, as illustrated in Figure 5.1.

In the nonfunctional family, resources are insufficient to deal with the stresses and they become overpowering, as illustrated in Figure 5.2. To bring such families back into balance, stressors must be removed, or resources to cope with the stressors must be increased—or both.

The American Medical Association (1985, p. 797) has identified characteristics of children that increase their risk of being abused:

- Premature birth
- Birth of a child to adolescent parents
- Colic, which renders infants difficult to soothe
- Congenital deficiencies or abnormalities
- Hospitalization of the neonate [newborn], resulting in a lack of parental contact
- Presence of any condition that interferes with parent-child bonding

Indicators of Physical Abuse

Among the *physical indicators* of physical abuse are unexplained bruises or welts, burns, fractures, lacerations and abrasions. Such physical injuries may be in various stages of healing. Among the *behavioral indicators* of physical abuse are being wary of adults, being apprehensive when other children cry, showing extreme aggressiveness or extreme withdrawal, being frightened of parents and being afraid to go home (Bennett and Hess, p. 375).

Parents' behavior can also provide clues to physical abuse. This can include contradictory explanations for a child's injury; attempts to conceal a child's injury or to protect the identity of the person responsible; the routine use of harsh, unreasonable discipline inappropriate to the child's age or behavior and poor impulse control (Bennett and Hess, p. 376).

The North Dakota attorney general looks over some of the 700 pairs of children's shoes on display in the great hall of the state capitol in Bismarck to promote awareness of child abuse. Each pair of shoes represents a case of abuse or neglect where services were needed in just the first two months of the year.

Indicators of Emotional Abuse

Physical indicators of emotional abuse may include speech disorders, lags in physical development and a general failure to thrive. *Behavioral indicators* of emotional abuse may include such habit disorders as sucking, biting and rocking back and forth, as well as conduct disorders such as antisocial, destructive behavior. Other possible indicators are sleep disorders, inhibitions in play, obsessions, compulsions, phobias, hypochondria, behavioral extremes and attempted suicide (Bennett and Hess, p. 375).

The Seriousness of the Problem

Experts disagree on just how serious the problem of child abuse is. Karmen (p. 226) describes two conflicting views: the maximalist alarmist and minimalist skeptical perspectives. The **maximalist alarmist perspective** "contends that the time has come to reject the reluctance of earlier generations to face the facts and to recognize the enormity of the developing crisis. Parents are abusing and neglecting their children in record numbers, and exploitive adolescents, pedophiles (child molesters), and other abusers are preying upon youngsters with impunity." From the **minimalist skeptical perspective,** "huge numbers of honestly mistaken and maliciously false allegations are mixed in with true disclosures, making the problem seem worse than it really is and fueling the impression that it is spiraling out of control."

Abused children often suffer severe physical and emotional damage from family violence, unreasonable corporal punishment, verbal harassment, alcoholic and substance abuse and sexual or other exploitation.

Child abuse has been identified as the biggest single cause of death of young children.

A report on a symposium, "Joint Investigations of Child Abuse" (1993, p. 2), notes: "In 1991 at least four children a day died at the hands of their caretakers. Physical abuse accounted for most of the fatalities—60 percent—and neglect for 36 percent. . . . Almost half the known deaths involved children who were previous or current clients [of the child welfare system]." The abuse is sometimes inflicted by those outside the family, but more tragically and commonly it is inflicted in the homes by a child's natural parents or members of the immediate family.

Children who need foster care often suffer deprivation. Children who are habitually truant, or who have run away from home or who are homeless or chemically dependent are also at risk of being exploited for prostitution, pornography, theft or drug trafficking. Chronically incorrigible children—those who are found to be so unreasonably disobedient to the proper guidance or protection of parents or guardians that custodial supervision is called for—must also be considered to be at risk.

Three Levels of Abuse

Thus far in the discussion, child abuse has been discussed primarily as an act between individuals. In reality, however, three separate levels of abuse exist.

The three levels of abuse are collective, institutional and individual.

Collective Abuse

Collective abuse is seen in the poverty and other forms of social injustice previously discussed. As has been noted, millions of children live in poverty in our country. Children are eating and drinking contaminated food and water. Many are exploited for child pornography. Constant violence blares forth from television sets across the country. Child care is often grossly inadequate, and the physical punishment of children is widely sanctioned. The collective attitude in America ignores the natural and legal rights of children.

Americans also tend to ignore the problem of illegal child labor. For example, reporters from the Associated Press discovered 165 children working illegally in 16 states. Foster and Kramer (1997, p. A31) state: "From the packing plants of Washington to the sweatshops of New York City, poor and vulnerable children—especially those of migrant workers and illegal immigrants—are working long hours for low pay and being robbed of their childhood. A study estimates that 290,200 children were employed unlawfully in the United States [in 1996]. Among them were 59,600 children younger than 14."

Shoplifting is a common form of delinquent behavior. Some youths shoplift because they have no money to purchase wanted items. Others shoplift for the thrill of it.

Institutional Abuse

Institutional abuse of children includes the approved use of force and violence against children in the schools and the neglect and denial of children's due process rights in government institutions. However, the use of corporal punishment in schools has been declining, with "paddling" decreasing since the early 1980s (Benshoff, 1993, p. 4B).

Corporal punishment for children has been banned in 26 states.

Individual Abuse

Individual abuse is what we normally think of when child abuse is discussed. This is one or more people emotionally or physically abusing a child. Individual abuse includes child sexual abuse. A graphic example of such abuse was demonstrated by a Chicago couple who allegedly raped, drugged, and fed fried rats and boiled cockroaches to their four children over a period of at least four years ("Chicago Couple," 1996, p. A8).

Child Abuse and the Link with Delinquency

Child abuse has been directly linked with delinquency. When delinquent behavior occurs, it may bring about further abuse, resulting in a vicious cycle and ever worsening behavior, as illustrated in Figure 5.3.

Children and adolescents who have a pattern of delinquency that emanates from the home are imitating the behavior of parents or other family members. In extreme cases, children have been taught how to commit crimes. Because children do not receive the same penalties as adults, some parents actually teach their children to be pickpockets or pimps and to commit associated crimes.

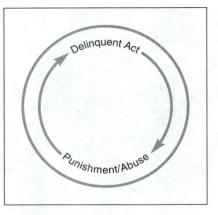

Figure 5.3
The Delinquency/
Abuse Cycle

In a classic work, *Unraveling Juvenile Delinquency,* the Gluecks (1950) reported that 85 percent of the delinquents released from a Massachusetts correctional institution were from families in which other members were delinquent. The research was conducted in the late 1940s and early 1950s, when families were less fragmented than families are now. In 45 percent of the delinquent cases, the mother of the offender had a criminal record; in 66 percent the father had a criminal record.

A survey by the National Institute of Justice of convicted male felons revealed that two-thirds of the inmates suffered some form of abuse or neglect as children ("Two-Thirds of Prisoners," 1998, p. 7):

- 35 percent reported severe physical abuse
- 14 percent reported some type of sexual abuse
- 26 percent of sex offenders reported sexual abuse
- 20 percent reported being neglected

Other studies have amplified the link between child abuse and criminal behavior. A study by the Child Welfare League found ("Study Amplifies," 1997, p. 15): "Abused or neglected children are 67 times more likely to be arrested between the ages of 9 and 12 than those who aren't. . . . The study also found a strong correlation between having an incarcerated parent and the likelihood that a child will later be arrested for a crime."

Many criminal justice professionals who deal on the front lines daily with juvenile delinquents contend the war on crime will be won only when the focus shifts from building more prison cells to investing more in children—through early childhood programs such as health care for children and pregnant women, Head Start for infants and toddlers, parenting training for high-risk families, programs aimed at preventing child abuse, recreational programs, after-school programs and mentoring programs. In fact, a survey of some of the nation's leading police chiefs ("Study Amplifies," p. 15) presented the following statement: "If America fails to pay for greater investments in programs to help youth and children now, we will all pay more later in crime, welfare and other costs." The results: nearly 90 percent of the chiefs surveyed agreed with the statement.

Children Who Are Sexually Abused

Every year roughly 100,000 cases of child sexual abuse are reported. Couple this with experts' estimates that more than 90 percent of child molestations are *not* reported to the criminal justice system (Holmes et al., 1993, p. 77), and the magnitude of the problem is apparent. Some experts feel that as many as 50 percent of young women have been sexually abused before their eighteenth birthday.

Sexual abuse is often classified as intrafamilial or extrafamilial. **Intrafamilial sexual abuse** is sexual abuse by a parent or other family member. **Extrafamilial sexual abuse** involves a friend or stranger. According to Duvall (1991, p. 109): "The sad, ugly truth in today's society is: with 85 to 90% of all the sexually abused children, the offender is someone the child knows, loves or trusts. The place most people remember as a safe haven is most likely the very place children are being raped; anally, orally, and vaginally; by someone they know, love or trust."

Indicators of Sexual Abuse

Rarely are the *physical indicators* of sexual abuse seen. Two possible indicators, especially in preteens, are venereal disease and pregnancy.

Among the possible *behavioral indicators* of sexual abuse are being unwilling to change clothes for or to participate in physical education classes; withdrawal, fantasy or infantile behavior; bizarre sexual behavior; sexual sophistication beyond one's age or unusual behavior or knowledge of sex; poor peer relationships; delinquent or runaway behavior; and reports of being sexually assaulted (Bennett and Hess, p. 376).

As with physical abuse, the behavior of parents may also provide indicators of sexual abuse. Such behaviors may include jealousy and being overprotective of a child. A parent may hesitate to report a spouse who is sexually abusing their child for fear of destroying the marriage or for fear of retaliation. Intrafamilial sex may be preferred to extramarital sex (Bennett and Hess, p. 401).

The Consequences of Being Sexually Abused

Sexual abuse can have many adverse affects on its young victims. Karmen (p. 222) notes a variety of effects from such abuse: "Affective problems were evidenced by guilt, shame, anxiety, fear, depression, anger, low self-esteem, concerns about secrecy, feelings of helplessness, and an inordinate need to please others. . . . Cognitive effects took the form of shortened attention spans and troubles concentrating."

Other studies have found that sexual and physical abuse of adolescent girls increases their risk of adopting certain problem behaviors ("Studies Identify Risks," 1997, pp. 7–8):

> Victims of sexual abuse more often than nonvictims reported a lack of parental supervision and a history of physical abuse. They also reported higher levels of school absenteeism, less involvement in extracurricular activities, and lower grades. . . .
>
> The findings also indicated associations between a history of sexual abuse and substance use, thoughts or attempts of suicide, and risky sexual behaviors.

*Sexual Abuse
and the Internet*

Experts estimate more than 10 million children currently go online and, by 2002, a total of 45 million children will do so ("Internet Crimes," 1998, p. 3). Parents are cautioned, however:

> In cyberspace, children are a mouse click away from exploring the world's greatest museums, libraries, and universities. Unfortunately, they are also a mouse click away from sexual exploitation and victimization.
>   . . . The Internet has become the new schoolyard for predators seeking children to victimize. Cloaked in the anonymity of cyberspace, sex offenders can capitalize on the natural curiosity of children, seeking victims with little risk of detection. Sex offenders who prey on children no longer need to lurk in parks and malls. Instead, they can roam from chat room to chat room trolling for children susceptible to victimization.

As Dees explains (1994, p. 53): "Adults with a sexual fascination for children, called pedophiles or chickenhawks, use these chat lines and member profiles to locate potential victims. Often, the chickenhawk will pose as another youth in order to establish a bond."

Armagh (1998, p. 11) likewise notes: "The stark truth about the Internet is that it can expose children to vile and degrading materials in the sanctuary of their homes and open the door to dangerous child sexual predators." Armagh adds (p. 10): "Today, the virtual playground of cyberspace affords these child sexual predators the opportunity to engage children in anonymous exchanges that often lead to personal questions designed to assess whether the child can be lured into sexual conversations and sexual contact."

The House of Representatives passed the Child Protection and Sexual Predator Punishment Act, imposing tougher penalties for sex crimes against children, particularly those facilitated by the use of the Internet. McCollum, the chairman of the House Subcommittee on Crime and the chief sponsor of the legislation, notes: "Children are rarely supervised while they are on the Internet. Unfortunately, that is exactly what cyber-predators look for. We are seeing numerous accounts in which pedophiles have used the Internet to seduce or persuade children to meet them to engage in sexual activities. Children who have been persuaded to meet their new on-line friend face to face have been kidnapped, raped, photographed for child pornography, and worse. Some children have never been heard from again" ("House Passes Measure," 1998, p. 5).

*Cultural Values
and Sexual Abuse*

Cultural values play a role in determining what constitutes abuse. Some practices regarded as normal and acceptable within one culture may be considered sexual abuse by mainstream society or by those from other cultures. For example in Somalia and other parts of Africa, female circumcision or female genital mutilation (FGM) is a rite of passage performed on infants and young girls. In the United States, however, this practice is considered abuse and is illegal, a situation that causes significant conflict for Somali women who have immigrated to this country. Miller (1998, p. A1) relates the story of one such woman:

> Hawa was 6 months old when she was "cut" for the first time. A village woman who had circumcised hundreds of girls cut out the Somali girl's sexual organs, scraped the sides of her labia, then sewed them together.

As Hawa grew, she realized that the tiny vaginal opening the old woman had left was too big by cultural standards. When the time came for Hawa to marry, what decent man would have her? So, at age 7—old enough to foresee her future, but too young to comprehend the pain she would face—Hawa asked to be cut again.

"Even now I can remember people holding my legs and the pain, because you don't have any medication or painkillers," said Hawa, now 28. "Then I wish they wouldn't have done it. But it was too late."

Today, Hawa—not her real name—is married, a mother, a full-time worker within her Somali community, and a Minneapolis resident who wants to see the centuries-old custom end.

According to the U.S. Department of Health and Human Resources, an estimated 160,000 girls and women in the U.S. immigrant community have submitted to FGM. Miller notes (p. A10):

> Every day, . . . women like Hawa struggle with the conflicting demands of two cultures. Somali tradition requires female circumcision, believing that it ensures a woman's virginity, enhances men's sexual pleasure and promotes marital fidelity. For these women and their daughters, it's connected to their body image, their self-image, their futures as wives. But their new American culture considers the practice child abuse and outlaws it. In Minnesota, parents, as well as practitioners, can be prosecuted.

Some contend it is hypocritical of the United States to censure another culture for doing to its young girls what America routinely does to its boys. Nonetheless, female circumcision remains illegal in this country, and it appears many of the younger Somali women living in the United States are choosing *not* to perpetuate the custom of FGM with their own daughters (Miller, p. A10).

Another example of how different cultures regard the issue of sexual abuse is seen in the practice of polygamy. Within certain areas of the United States, most notably in Utah, polygamy is an acceptable religious practice, accompanied by the cultural value that very young girls, some as young as 10, may be forced into arranged marriages. According to Cart (1998, p. A3): "One academic study a generation ago estimated the number of people living in polygamy in Utah at 30,000; those fighting the practice today believe the number is two or three times that." Cart also notes: "Former polygamy wives say they've seen rampant incest and child abuse." Cart tells the story of one girl subjected to such abuse (p. A3):

> The bedraggled girl walked 6 dusty miles to a gas station pay phone and punched 911. Then she did what she was taught never to do: She told. Help me, she said to the sheriff. My father beat me when I ran away from an arranged marriage with my uncle. I was his 15th wife.
>
> With one phone call to an outside world she scarcely knew, the battered 16-year-old gave voice to silent women who live within the secretive constraints of polygamy. Her tale of child abuse, incest and intermarriage has been the catalyst for the recent arrests of two patriarchs of the largest polygamous clan in the state [of Utah] and sparked unusually open debate about what one former polygamous wife calls "Utah's dirty little secret."

Other secretive communities within the United States, such as the elusive group known as the Travelers, also condone arranged marriages involving very young girls.

The Issue of Credibility

Because physical indicators of sexual abuse are often not present, allegations of sexual abuse can be difficult to prove. Investigators must also weed out false accusations. Goldstein and Tyler (1998, p. 1) state: "Sometimes, allegations of child sexual abuse arise in the context of divorce and custody cases. A study of 9,000 families embroiled in contested divorce proceedings found that 1 to 8 percent involved allegations of child sexual abuse. Unfortunately, the warlike atmosphere inherent in divorce often discredits valid claims. Though rare, false allegations of abuse do occur. Another study revealed that out of 169 cases of alleged child sexual abuse arising in marital relations courts, only 14 percent were deliberate, false allegations." Karmen (p. 230) notes:

> When allegations surface during the height of a divorce and tug-of-war over a child, two camps quickly emerge. People on one side argue that since there are no outsiders who witness violations of the incest taboo within the home, these "family secrets" usually are not exposed unless the parents break up. People on the other side contend that baseless allegations are being taken too seriously, and the resulting investigations ruin the lives of innocent parents, usually fathers.
>
> In the mid-1980s, an organization was formed to provide support to adults who insisted they were falsely accused. They nicknamed their predicament as the "SAID syndrome": sexual allegations in divorce. Their contention is that in most of these cases, a spiteful mother has pressured her daughter to echo a totally fictitious story about molestation that never occurred.

Coercing a child to lie about abuse that never occurred is a form of abuse all its own. Unfortunately, many youths become victims of this type of abuse when they are caught in the middle of custody battles. As parents fight to prove they are better equipped to raise the children, they unwittingly inflict a great deal of emotional and psychological damage on the very people they say they are trying to protect.

Children and Youths as Victims of Crime and Violence

One of the most obvious ways youths are victimized is by becoming a victim of crime. Chapter 4 discussed the amount of victimization that occurs in our nation's schools. The pervasiveness of violence in the United States, not only toward children, but also among adults, might, in part, be explained by our country's historical reliance upon force and violence in its international relations. In addition, American history is rooted in the genocide of native Americans, the slavery of African-Americans and in white male supremacy. These historical roots may, in part, explain the prevalence of violence.

According to Ringel (1997, p. 5): "Persons between ages 12 and 15 and between 16 and 19 had higher rates of violent crime victimization than those 25 or older. Persons age 12–19 were twice as likely as those age 25–34 and 3 times as likely as those age 35–49 to be victims of violent crimes. Persons age 12–19 had a violent crime victimization rate 20 times higher than those age 65 or older. For the crime of aggravated assault, individuals between ages 16 and 19 had a significantly higher rate of victimization than any other age group." Figure 5.4 shows the rate of violent victimization by age group.

Youths are victims of crime twice as often as those over age 25.

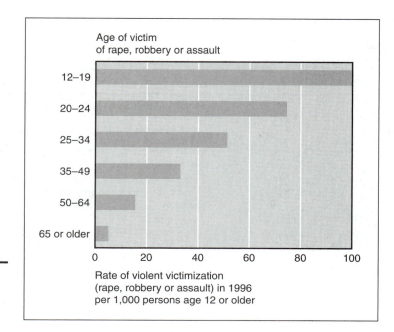

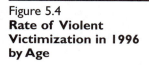

Figure 5.4
**Rate of Violent
Victimization in 1996
by Age**

Sickmund et al. (p. 1) state: "Between 1985 and 1995 nearly 25,000 juveniles were murdered in the United States—2,600 in 1995." They note (p. 1) that juvenile murder rates were highest for juveniles at both ends of the age spectrum and lowest for those in the middle; 17-year-olds had the highest murder rate (18.3 per 100,000 U.S. juveniles), followed by 16- and 15-year-olds (13.4 and 7.7, respectively) and those under the age of one (7.0). The murder rate of one-year-olds was 4.5. Furthermore (p. 1):

> In 1995, 72% of murdered juveniles were male, 49% were black, and 47% were white. Twenty-two percent of juvenile murder victims were murdered by family members, 37% by acquaintances, and 13% by strangers; in 28% of juvenile murders in 1995, the offender was unknown. Sixty-one percent of all juveniles murdered in 1995 were killed with a firearm.

Sadly, as the Centers for Disease Control and Prevention note, the United States ranks number one among the world's 26 wealthiest nations in the number of homicide, suicide and gun-related deaths involving children ("Which Is the Most-Violent," 1997, pp. A1, A10).

> Dr. Etienne Krug, the medical epidemiologist who conducted the study, said some researchers have suggested that the high rate of violent death among U.S. children may be associated with the low level of funding for social programs in the United States. Other theories, he said, blame the prevalence of U.S. violence on high numbers of working women, high divorce rates and social acceptability of violence in the United States.

According to Craig (1992, p. 67): "For some children, family violence is so severe that it results in intervention by public authorities. For many other youngsters, it remains a secret destroyer that slowly permeates the fabric of self and distorts the content of all relationships."

Table 5.2
Matrix for Organizing Risk Factors for Violent Behavior

Units of Observation and Explanation	Proximity to Violent Events and Their Consequences		
	Predisposing	Situational	Activating
Social Macrosocial	Concentration of poverty Opportunity structures Decline of social capital Oppositional cultures Sex role socialization	Physical structure Routine activities Access: weapons, emergency medical services	Catalytic social event
Microsocial	Community organizations Illegal markets Gangs Family disorganization Preexisting structures	Proximity of responsible monitors Participants' social relationships Bystanders' activities Temporary communication impairments Weapons: carrying, displaying	Participants' communication exchange
Individual Psychosocial	Temperament Learned social responses Perceptions of rewards/penalties for violence Violent deviant sexual preferences Social, communication skills Self-identification in social hierarchy	Accumulated emotion Alcohol/drug consumption Sexual arousal Premeditation	Impulse Opportunity recognition
Biological	Neurobehavioral* "traits" Genetically mediated traits Chronic use of psychoactive substances or exposure to neurotoxins	Transient neurobehavioral* "states" Acute effects of psychoactive substances	Sensory signal processing errors

*Includes neuroanatomical, neurophysiological, neurochemical, and neuroendocrine. "Traits" describe capacity as determined by status at birth, trauma, and aging processes such as puberty. "States" describe temporary conditions associated with emotions, external stressors, etc.

Source: Jeffrey A. Roth. *Understanding and Preventing Violence*. National Institute of Justice, Research in Brief. Washington, DC: February 1994, p. 7. Adapted from Albert Reiss, Jr., and Jeff A. Roth eds., *Understanding and Preventing Violence*, Washington, DC: National Academy Press, 1993, p. 297. Reprinted by permission

Roth (1994, p. 1) notes: "The level of violent crime in this country has reached high, though not unprecedented levels. . . . Violence falls most heavily on ethnic minority males and occurs most often in urban areas." Roth has developed a matrix that organizes the risk factors that underlie violent behavior (see Table 5.2).

Roth (pp. 5–6) presents two illustrations of how violence resulted in the death of a child and then shows how the matrix helps to explain what happened.

The first illustration involved Dave, Evelyn and their 10-month-old son Jason. Evelyn had just turned 20 when Jason was born, and Dave had just lost his job. The family was struggling, and Dave became moody and argumentative. During some of the arguments over money, Dave would slap Evelyn, but always begged forgiveness. He also began to resent Jason. Evelyn, hoping to help the situation, went back to work as a waitress. Her first day back at work Dave "hit bottom," overwhelmed by feelings of humiliation and rejection with his new role as babysitter. Jason's crying made it worse. And nothing Dave did could stop the crying. When Jason wet on Dave, Dave lost control, filled the bathtub with scalding water and held Jason in the tub by his arm and leg, causing third-degree burns over 35 percent of his body, according to the medical examiner's report.

The second illustration involves a beer bash in a "tough blue-collar suburb" involving two friends, Andy and Bob, who had begun drinking heavily as teenagers. In this tough town, Bob was known as one of the toughest, almost always winning his fights. He had recently lost his job for missing work and had recently spent time in jail following a bar brawl. At this particular beer bash, Bob began making passes at Andy's sister, who resisted the passes and finally slapped him. Several partygoers began laughing at Bob. Andy, wanting to protect his sister, came at Bob. As they began to fight, Andy's older brother told them to "take it outside," which they did. The crowd followed, cheering them on. Bob got a tire iron out of his car's trunk and knocked Andy out, then proceeded to get in his car and drive over him two times. Andy died in the hospital four hours later from massive internal injuries.

Roth uses these two examples to demonstrate the risk factors in operation, as shown in Table 5.3.

Violence and the Media

The influence of violence in the media is often blamed for the amount of violence in society. The American Medical Association (AMA) has urged advertisers to boycott programs that show violence. Dr. Robert McAfee, AMA president-elect, stated during hearings on violence in the media: "Violence in general is clearly an enormous and at least partially avoidable public health problem in this country today. . . . [P]articularly alarming is the prevalent depiction of violent behavior on television, especially in terms of its 'role-modeling' capacity to potentially promote 'real-world violence'" ("AMA Calls," 1993, p. 3).

The Convention on the Rights of the Child also stresses the important role played by the media in "disseminating information to children that is consistent with moral well-being and knowledge and understanding among peoples, and respects the child's cultural background" (United Nations, Article 17, p. 5). The media glamorizes "materialism, violence, drug and alcohol use, hedonistic lifestyles, and easy sex" (Eitzen, 1992, p. 588).

An article by Witkin, "Kids Who Kill" (1992, p. 181), reports: "Today's kids are desensitized to violence as never before, surrounded by gunfire and stuffed with media images of Rambos who kill at will." The article notes another significant change: "By far the biggest difference in today's atmosphere is that the no-problem availability of guns in every nook of the nation has turned record numbers of everyday encounters into deadly ones."

Surveys of violence on television generally conclude that too much violence is shown and that it adversely affects children. In one survey, three-fourths of the people responding felt that television had more influence on children than their

Table 5.3
Examples of Possible Risk Factors in Two Murders

Units of Observation and Explanation	Proximity to Violent Events and Their Consequences		
	Predisposing	Situational	Activating
Social Macrosocial	1. Low neighborhood social interaction.	1. No child care providers in neighborhood.	
	2. Neighborhood culture values fighting, drinking, sexual prowess.	2. No local emergency medical services.	
Microsocial	1. Dave began hitting Evelyn months ago.	1. Baby cries. Dave unable to cope.	1. Baby wets Dave.
	2. Widespread expectations of wild drinking parties at Andy's house.	2. Charlene humiliates Bob by resisting his advances.	2. Older brother says "take it outside," crowd goes outside to watch and cheer.
Individual Psychosocial	1. Dave has low self-esteem.	1. Dave humiliated by Evelyn's new job, his own lack of parenting skills.	
	2. Bob develops adolescent pattern of drinking and violent behavior.	2. Threats to Andy's family status, Bob's personal status.	
Biological	2. Possible familial traits of alcoholism and antisocial behavior in Bob's family.	2. Andy, Bob, and bystanders under alcohol influence.	
	Murder 1: 10-month-old baby scalded to death by father; no witnesses.	*Murder 2:* 20-year-old male beaten and intentionally run over by automobile; many witnesses.	

Source: Jeffrey A. Roth. *Understanding and Preventing Violence.* National Institute of Justice, Research in Brief, Washington, DC: February 1994, p. 8. Adapted from Albert Reiss, Jr., and Jeff A. Roth, eds., *Understanding and Preventing Violence*, Washington, DC: National Academy Press, 1993, p. 297. Reprinted by permission.

parents had (Milavsky, p. 1). Further, the American Psychological Association asserts that children see, on the average, 8,000 murders and 100,000 other violent acts on television before they finish elementary school (Martin, 1994, p. 38).

Others contend there is not enough data to correlate violence on television with violence in society. Milavsky (p. 3), for example, states:

> We cannot be sure that our common belief in television's impact on violence is correct. However, since an effect cannot entirely be ruled out, both those who produce television programs, and those who watch them, must be alert to the possibility of a causal link between violent television and violent behavior.

The American Psychological Association Commission on Violence and Youth takes a stronger position, stating (p. 33): "Children's exposure to violence in the mass media, particularly at young ages, can have harmful lifelong consequences." The Commission noted:

> Aggressive habits learned early in life are the foundation for later behavior. . . .
> A longitudinal study of boys found a significant relation between exposure to

television violence at 8 years of age and antisocial acts—including serious, violent criminal offenses and spouse abuse—22 years later.

The Cycle of Violence

Paisner (1991, p. 35) warns:

> Violence is learned behavior. Children who have witnessed abuse or have been abused themselves are *1,000* times more likely to abuse a spouse or child when they become adults than are children raised in a home without violence.

Violence is self-perpetuating. When adults teach children by example that those who are bigger and stronger can use violence to force their wishes on others who are smaller, the lesson is remembered. Children who witness domestic abuse learn:

- Anger is the same as violence.
- It's okay to hurt the people you care about most.
- Intimacy involves violence.
- Do NOT ask for what they need.
- Do NOT trust.
- Relationships hurt.
- It's okay to use violence to get what you want (*Community Cares*, 1998, p.7).

In addition, family violence has been directly linked with delinquency, especially violent offenses, a connection that is discussed in Chapter 6. The cycle of violence is illustrated in Figure 5.5.

Karmen (p. 7) also described a cycle of violence in which a victim is transformed into a victimizer over time:

> For example, a group of picked-on children may band together to beat up a bully; a physically abused child may grow up to parent his sons in the same punitive way he was raised; or a battered wife may launch a vengeful surprise attack against her brutal husband. In one study that tracked the fortunes and fates of about 900 abused children over a follow-up period of from fifteen to twenty years, researchers estimated that being victimized increased their odds of future delinquency and criminality by 40 percent.

Halvorsen (1993, p. A7) notes that: "Many American homes are not safe havens for children, but instead are training grounds for criminals. . . . Children are harmed by the sights and sounds of violence—and not just by physical blows that might rain down on them." Thornberry (1994) states that children exposed to multiple forms of family violence demonstrate twice the rate of youth violence as children from nonviolent families. Further, a survey of convicted criminals (Widom, 1995, p. 1) revealed "that a childhood history of physical abuse predisposes the survivor to violence in later years, and that victims of neglect are more likely to engage in later violent criminal behavior as well."

Violence often leads to more violence. Children who are abused are more likely to be delinquents and violent themselves.

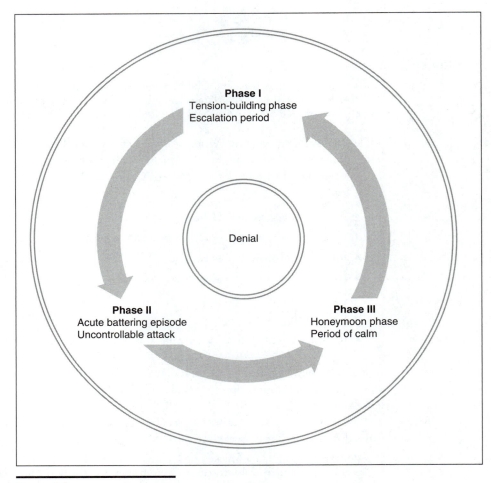

Figure 5.5
The Cycle of Violence

The connection between children's histories of neglect or abuse and subsequent delinquency, crime and other problems has been largely ignored by our juvenile justice and social service systems. This is difficult to understand, given that those who experience violent, abusive childhoods are more likely to become child or spouse abusers than those who have not.

Although child abuse is more prevalent among families in lower socioeconomic groups, family violence, abuse and neglect can be found in families of all social and economic backgrounds. Children are lied to and lied about, mutilated, shot, stabbed, burned, beaten, bitten, sodomized, raped and hanged. Figure 5.6 illustrates a model of intrafamily violence, the variables affecting it, individual characteristics of family members, precipitating factors, social variables and the consequences for the child, the family and society.

As Figure 5.6 shows, many familial variables and family member characteristics affect intrafamily violence. Furthermore, conditions in the society within which the family lives also affect familial violence. Such violence may have a multitude of consequences, not only for the child but also for the family and society at large.

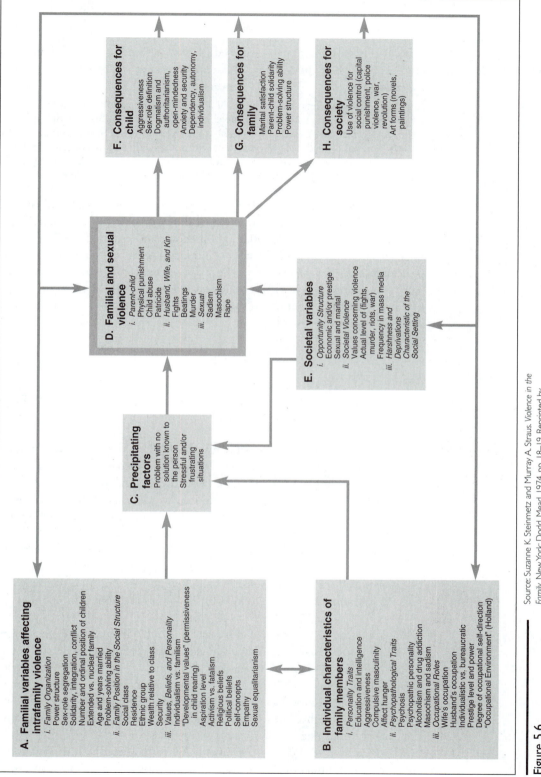

Figure 5.6
Model of Intrafamily Violence

Source: Suzanne K. Steinmetz and Murray A. Straus. *Violence in the Family.* New York: Dodd, Mead, 1974, pp. 18–19. Reprinted by permission.

Missing and Exploited Children

The Missing Children's Act was passed in 1982 and the Missing Children's Assistance Act in 1984. The Missing Children's Assistance Act of 1984 defines a *missing child* as:

> Any individual, less than 18 years of age, whose whereabouts are unknown to such individual's legal custodian—if the circumstances surrounding the disappearance indicate that (the child) may possibly have been removed by another person from the control of his/her legal custodian without the custodian's consent; or the circumstances of the case strongly indicate that (the child) is likely to be abused or sexually exploited (*Annual Report on Missing Children, 1990,* p. ix).

During the period 1985–1990, the National Incidence Studies of Missing, Abducted, Runaway, and Thrownaway Children in America (NISMART) conducted a telephone survey of 30,000 households and analyzed the FBI's data, police records and residential facilities and institutions, as well as community and professional services, to determine the scope of the missing children problem. The first findings of NISMART were released in May 1990. Among the key findings was that: "What has in the past been called the missing children problem is in reality a set of at least five very different, distinct problems" (Finkelhor et al., 1990, p. 4).

The five categories of missing children included in the NISMART study are runaways; thrownaways; nonfamily abducted children; family abducted children; and lost, injured or otherwise missing children.

A major conclusion of the study was that: "Many of the children in at least four of these categories were not literally missing. Caretakers did know where they were. The problem was in recovering them" (Finkelhor et al., p. 4).

NISMART used two types of definitions within each of the five distinct problem areas: *broad scope* and *policy focal* definitions. Broad scope definitions are more general, defining the problem the way a family might define it. Policy focal definitions, on the other hand, define the problem from the point of view of the police or other social agencies, being restricted to more serious episodes in which children truly are at risk and need immediate intervention. All broad scope and policy focal definitions in the following discussions are from this report.

Runaways

When adolescents cannot cope with a relationship in a family, they may perceive their only recourse to be running away. Historically, running away has been considered a behavioral manifestation of psychopathology. In fact, the American Psychiatric Association has classified the "runaway reaction" as a specific disorder.

Broad scope **runaways** were children who left home without permission and stayed away overnight. The policy focal definition of runaway added the condition that the youth had no familiar or secure place to stay.

Benalcazar (1982) cites many investigations that describe runaways as insecure, depressed, unhappy and impulsive, with emotional problems, low self-esteem and an unmanageable personal life. Running away may compound their problems. Many become streetwise and turn to drugs, crime, prostitution or

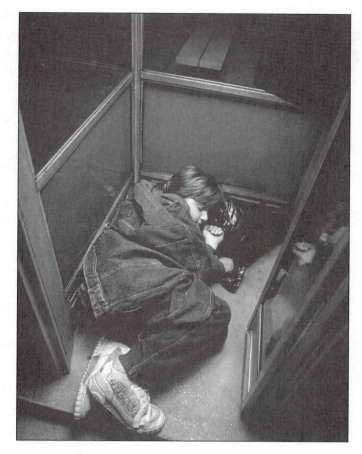

Running away from home is seen by many youths as a solution to problems at home or school.

other illegal activities. Typical runaways report conflict with parents, alienation from them, rejection and hostile control, lack of warmth, affection and parental support.

Runaways have a distinct age pattern. The police estimate that both male and female youngsters start runaway activity at approximately age 12 and reach a peak at age 14 or 15. At 16 a change usually occurs. The number of males who leave home declines sharply, while the number of females rises. The decline continues for males at 17, but the trend continues to climb for females. This decline in males and climb in females correlates significantly with maturity.

When males are absent from the home at age 12, the absence is usually one day or less. This is also true of females. Females, however, are more prone to recidivism and usually stay away longer. The older the runaways are, the longer they tend to stay away. Because females mature faster and can become self-sufficient faster, they stay away longer.

The NISMART project's researchers observe: "Today, we know that when many children run, it is often to escape from a protracted and painful family conflict or from physical, sexual or psychological abuse. We also know what may lie in wait for the long-term runaway: homelessness, drugs, crime, sexual exploitation, and suicide" (Sweet, 1990b, p. 17).

Problems reported by youths seeking services from runaway and homeless youth centers included such family problems as emotional conflict at home, parents who were too strict and physical abuse and neglect. The National Council of Juvenile and Family Court Judges has stated: "We know that many [youths] who are on the streets are there as a result of sound rational choices they have made for their own safety and welfare, such as avoiding physical abuse, sexual abuse, or extreme neglect at home." Other problems reported included parental drug and/or alcohol abuse, mental health problems within the family and domestic violence between the parents.

The two most frequently mentioned personal problems were a poor self-image and depression. Other problems included issues at school such as truancy, poor grades and not getting along with teachers; drug and/or alcohol abuse; and being in trouble with the justice system. As noted by Sweet (1990a, p. 1):

> Of all the youth at risk, runaways pose one of the most serious dilemmas for the juvenile justice system. Although not all runaways come to the attention of the system, juvenile justice professionals are responsible for protecting and intervening on their behalf. As the risks for victimization, illegal drug use, and delinquency continue to rise for runaway youth, the need remains crucial for the juvenile justice system to play its part in ensuring their safety.

In 1995, 249,500 youths were arrested for running away (*Sourcebook,* 1997, p. 368).

Thrownaways

Broad scope **thrownaways** face one of four situations:

1. They were told to leave.
2. They were not allowed back after having left.
3. No effort was made to recover the runaway.
4. They were abandoned or deserted.

Policy focal thrownaways were youths without a secure and familiar place to stay during some portion of the episode. All abandoned children were considered to fall within this category.

Nonfamily Abduction

NISMART used both legal and stereotypical definitions in this area. The legal definition of *nonfamily abduction* was the coerced, unauthorized *taking* of a child into a building, a vehicle or a distance of more than 20 feet; *detaining* a child for more than one hour; or *luring* a child for the purpose of committing another crime.

The stereotypical kidnapping required one of five circumstances: (1) gone overnight, (2) transported 50 or more miles, (3) ransom, (4) intent to keep, and (5) killed.

Researchers who study missing children have estimated that the number of children kidnapped and murdered by strangers is between 52 and 158 a year (Speirs, 1989, p. 1). The highest rate of missing children is among teenagers between ages 14 and 17. This is quite different from the estimates that thousands of children face this fate each year. Researchers have also found that girls are at greater risk than boys, as are racial minorities.

Family Abduction

The broad scope definition of *family abduction* is a situation in which a family member (1) took a child in violation of a custody agreement or decree or (2) in violation of a custody agreement or decree failed to return a child at the end of a legal or agreed-upon visit, with the child being away at least overnight. The policy focal definition of abduction involved one of three additional aggravating conditions: concealment, transportation out of state or intent to permanently alter custody. Parental kidnapping—the unlawful taking of a child by one parent from the legal custody of the other—is a troubling, intractable problem. Not only is parental kidnapping illegal, it can result in the abducted child becoming a bargaining chip to reduce support obligations or even to extort a reconciliation.

Although often the parent/kidnapper truly has the child's best interests at heart, the risks to the kidnapped child are great:

> Factors that are proven contributing causes to child abuse and neglect—such as financial difficulties, stress, worry, and isolation—are often present in abduction scenarios. Fearing discovery, for example, many abducting parents move from job to job and are reluctant to place their children with babysitters, relatives, or daycare centers or even to enroll them in school. Even if there is little risk of abuse or neglect, parental kidnapping is almost certain to intensify and prolong the psychological trauma and stress to a child caused by the divorce or separation of his or her parents (*Missing and Exploited Children*, 1988, pp. 39–40).

Lost, Injured or Otherwise Missing

The broad scope definition of *lost, injured or otherwise missing* children varied with the child's age, whether the child had any disabilities and the amount of time missing. Policy focal cases were broad scope incidents that were serious enough that the police were called.

Responsibility for Investigating Missing and Exploited Children

The primary responsibility for investigating missing and exploited children falls at the local and state levels, but the federal government is also involved. Two government agencies in particular have responsibilities in the area and come at the problem from very different perspectives.

> The Department of Health and Human Services through its Administration for Children, Youth and Families (ACYF) and the Justice Department through its Office of Juvenile Justice and Delinquency Prevention (OJJDP) have concurrent jurisdiction for missing and exploited children.

Both these agencies' authority comes from the 1974 Juvenile Justice and Delinquency Prevention (JJDP) Act, amended in 1978 by the Runaway and Homeless Youth (RHY) Act. The RHY Act took a "social welfare, emergency care" approach to the problem of runaways, playing down the law enforcement solutions. This approach is the focus of the ACYF:

> ACYF's approaches to locating, detaining, and returning runaway children do not involve law enforcement or juvenile justice authorities. Instead, they focus on such activities as having shelter staff encourage runaways to contact home; using "runaway switchboards" to exchange messages between runaways and their families; and utilizing mental health programs to provide crisis counseling (and, in some cases, longer term counseling) to assist reunification efforts (*Missing and Exploited Children*, p. 23).

The OJJDP approach is very different, focusing on the challenges that runaways present to law enforcement and the juvenile justice system. It is hampered by the OJJDP's emphasis on deinstitutionalization:

> However well motivated the thinking behind this policy [deinstitutionalization], the fact remains that secure custodial care has often been the only practical, effective means for protecting runaways themselves, and for protecting communities from the problems of juvenile prostitution, drug abuse, theft, and other criminal acts committed by runaway youngsters seeking to support a day-to-day, hand-to-mouth existence (*Missing and Exploited Children*, p. 25).

Clearly, these two approaches are often at odds with each other. Therefore, coordination between the two agencies is vital if the runaway problem is to be effectively addressed.

Youths and Suicide

As noted by suicidologist Wrobleski (1989, p. 29): "Teenager suicides are the lowest of any age group but get the most attention because it seems more tragic when a young person's life is cut short." According to Sickmund et al. (p. 3): "For every two youth (ages 0–19) murdered in 1994, one youth committed suicide." Furthermore: "Overall, suicides increased 14% between 1979 and 1994. For youth younger than age 15, the increase was 112%." Approximately 15 percent of high schools students report having suicidal thoughts, as summarized in Table 5.4.

The leading cause of suicide is untreated depression.

Sometimes depression may not be readily apparent. The person may try to cover it up with overactivity, preoccupation with trivia or acting-out behavior, such as delinquency, the use of drugs or sexual promiscuity.

The Role of Government

The saying goes: "It takes an entire village to raise a single child." The role of the community and, in particular, the lawmaking government, has become an issue in the quest for how to best raise "our" children. Karmen (p. 242) states:

> People are sharply divided over the proper role of government in the balance between social nurturance and social control. In reply to the question "Whose children are they?" one long-standing answer is that children belong to, or are the property of, their parents. But another way of looking at youngsters is to see them as "junior" citizens: Parents have custody of them, but the larger community has "visiting rights." In extreme cases, the community might even assert "joint custody" and violate the privacy of the family and the rights of the parents. Government agencies step in as parents-of-last-resort when a clear and present danger to the child is evident.

Many argue that government intervention is really interference in private family matters and that actions taken by child protection agencies and family courts should be kept to a minimum for the sake of family preservation. Edmonds (1994) warns, however, that the price for such inaction or minimal reaction may be a child's life. An analysis of case files revealed that, in 1993, of the nearly

Table 5.4
Students Reporting
Problem Behaviors

	Never	Seldom	Sometimes	Often	A lot
Have you thought about committing suicide?	70.0	14.4	8.8	3.2	3.6
Grades 6 to 8	74.6	11.8	7.2	2.8	3.6
Grades 9 to 12	65.8	16.9	10.2	3.5	3.6
12th grade	66.4	18.2	9.9	2.8	2.7

Note: These data are from a survey of 6th through 12th grade students conducted between September 1996 and June 1997 by PRIDE, Inc. Participating schools are sent the PRIDE questionnaire with explicit instructions for administering the anonymous, self-report survey. Schools that administer the PRIDE questionnaire do so voluntarily or in compliance with a school district or State request. For the 1996–97 academic year, survey results are based on students from 28 States. The following States participated in the 1996–97 PRIDE survey: Arizona, Arkansas, California, Colorado, Connecticut, Florida, Georgia, Illinois, Kentucky, Maine, Massachussets, Michigan, Missouri, Mississippi, New Hampshire, New Jersey, New York, North Dakota, Ohio, Oklahoma, Pennsylvania, Tennessee, Texas, Virginia, Washington, West Virginia and Wyoming. To prevent any one State from having a disproportionate influence on the summary results, random samples of students were drawn from those States where disproportionately large numbers of students were surveyed. Therefore, no one State comprises more than 10% of the sample. The results presented are based on a sample consisting of 141,077 students drawn from the total number of students who completed the PRIDE questionnaire.

[a]Percents may not add to 100 because of rounding.

Source: PRIDE, Inc., "1996–97 National Summary, Grades 6 through 12," Atlanta, GA: PRIDE, Inc., 1997. Table adapted by SOURCEBOOK staff. Reprinted by permission of PRIDE, Inc.

Sourcebook of Criminal Justice Statistics 1997, p. 226.

1,300 children who died from physical abuse or neglect, 42 percent were living with families who had been investigated for maltreating them (p. 2A).

Summary

Youths are victimized in many ways. Two of the most common types of victimization are neglect and abuse. Child neglect is inattention to the basic needs of a child. The homes of neglected children often are disorganized and broken and have parents who ignore the children or who set a bad example for them. Neglect can damage children's development, because children need handling and love for their brains to develop properly.

Child abuse is another way youths are victimized. The two leading causes of child abuse are believed to be violence between husbands and wives and poverty. Child abuse is the biggest single cause of death of young children. The three levels of abuse are collective, institutional and individual. Certain types and degrees of punishment may be considered abusive. Corporal punishment for children has been banned in 26 states.

Youths are also victimized by crime and violence twice as often as those over age 25. Violence often leads to more violence. Children who are abused are more likely to be delinquent and violent themselves. They are also more likely to run away, becoming part of the "missing and exploited children" problem. The five categories of missing children included in the NISMART study are runaways, thrownaways, nonfamily abducted children, family abducted children, and lost, injured or otherwise missing children.

The Department of Health and Human Services through its Administration for Children, Youth and Families (ACYF) and the Justice Department through OJJDP have concurrent jurisdiction for missing and exploited children. Children and youths who do not receive appropriate assistance may become suicidal. The leading cause of suicide is untreated depression.

Discussion Questions

1. What causes parents or custodians of children to abuse them?
2. Do your state laws against child abuse and neglect contain two or more of the following components: nonaccidental physical injury, physical neglect, emotional abuse or neglect, sexual abuse, abandonment?
3. Of all abuses, which one has the most lasting effect? Why?
4. How can society cope with abuse and strive to control it?
5. What protection does a child have against abuse? Should the courts remove parental rights in abuse cases?
6. Do courts act in the best interests of children when they allow abused children to remain with the family?
7. How does abuse differ with socioeconomic status?
8. Are the definitions of *child abuse* and *child neglect* the key elements in determining the volume of child abuse cases in various jurisdictions? How is the volume of cases determined?
9. In your area, how are children protected from abuse? Can the system be improved? How?
10. Why did the NISMART project have two different definitions for each of the five categories of missing children? Did you find these two definitions helpful or confusing?

References

"AMA Calls for Measures to Shield Children from TV Violence." *Juvenile Justice,* July 1993, pp. 3–4.

American Medical Association. "AMA Diagnostic and Treatment Guidelines Concerning Child Abuse and Neglect." *Journal of the American Medical Association,* Vol. 254, No. 6, 1985, pp. 796–800.

American Psychological Association. *Violence & Youth: Psychology's Response, Vol. 1. Summary Report of the American Psychological Association Commission on Violence and Youth.* n.d.

Annual Report on Missing Children, 1990. Washington, DC: Office of Juvenile Justice and Delinquency Prevention.

Armagh, Daniel. "A Safety Net for the Internet: Protecting Our Children." *Juvenile Justice,* Vol. 5, No. 1, May 1998, pp. 9–15.

Benalcazar, B. "Study of Fifteen Runaway Patients." *Adolescence,* Vol. 17, Fall 1982, pp. 553–566.

Bennett, Wayne M. and Hess, Kären M. *Criminal Investigation,* 5th ed. Belmont, CA: West/Wadsworth Publishing Company, 1998.

Benshoff, Anastasia. "Schools to Shelve Paddles." *The Rockford Register Star,* October 16, 1993, p. 4B.

Bilchik, Shay. "From the Administrator." In Kelley, Barbara Tatem; Thornberry, Terence P.; and Smith, Carolyn A. *In the Wake of Childhood Maltreatment.* OJJDP Juvenile Justice Bulletin, August 1997, p. 1. (NCJ-165257)

Cart, Julie. "'Utah's Dirty Little Secret.'" (Minneapolis/St. Paul) *Star Tribune,* August 24, 1998, p. A3.

"Chicago Couple Face Multiple Charges of Long-Term Abuse of Four Children." (Minneapolis/St. Paul) *Star Tribune,* February 7, 1996, p. A8.

Community Cares: Domestic Abuse Awareness, Lakeville, MN: Community Action Council, Inc., Fall 1998.

Cowley, Geoffrey. "Children in Peril." *Newsweek Special Issue,* Summer 1991, pp. 18–21.

Craig, Susan E. "The Educational Needs of Children Living with Violence." *Phi Delta Kappan,* September 1992, pp. 67–71.

Dees, Timothy M. "Cyberhip Chickenhawks: A Mix of Kids, Computers and Pedophiles." *Law Enforcement Technology,* October 1994, pp. 52–55.

Duvall, Ed, Jr. "What Is Happening to Our Children?" *Law and Order,* November 1991, p. 109.

Edmonds, P. "One Million Young Victims and Counting." *USA Today,* April 7, 1994, p. 2A.

Eitzen, Stanley. "Problem Students: The Sociocultural Roots." *Phi Delta Kappan,* April 1992, pp. 584–590.

Finkelhor, David; Hotaling, Gerald; and Sedlak, Andrea. *Missing, Abducted, Runaway, and Thrownaway Children in America. First Report: Numbers and Characteristics, National Incidence Studies, Executive Summary.* Washington, DC: Office of Juvenile Justice and Delinquency Prevention, May 1990.

Foster, David and Kramer, Farrell. "Illegal Child Labor Not Just a Foreign Problem." (Minneapolis/St. Paul) *Star Tribune,* December 19, 1997, pp. A31, A38.

Glueck, Sheldon and Glueck, Eleanor. *Unraveling Juvenile Delinquency.* Cambridge, MA: Harvard University Press, 1950.

Goldstein, Seth L. and Tyler, R. P. "Frustrations of Inquiry: Child Sexual Abuse Allegations in Divorce and Custody Cases." *FBI Law Enforcement Bulletin,* July 1998, pp. 1–6.

Halvorsen, Donna. "Children Who Witness Abuse Bear Scars, Experts Say," (Minneapolis/ St. Paul) *Star Tribune,* November 8, 1993, p. A7.

Holmes, Ronald M.; Holmes, Stephen T.; and Unholz, Jerrie. "Female Pedophilia: A Hidden Abuse." *Law and Order,* August 1993, pp. 77–79.

"House Passes Measure to Bar Child Abuse Through the Internet." *Criminal Justice Newsletter,* Vol. 29, No. 10, May 15, 1998, p. 5.

"Internet Crimes Against Children Program." *Missing and Exploited Children's Program.* Washington, DC: Office of Juvenile Justice and Delinquency Prevention, 1998.

Johnson, Richard R. "A Patrol Officer's Guide to Identifying Child Abuse." *Law and Order,* April 1998, pp. 77–79.

"Joint Investigations of Child Abuse: Report of a Symposium." U.S. Department of Justice and U.S. Department of Health and Human Services, July 1993.

Karmen, Andrew. *Crime Victims: An Introduction to Victimology.* 3rd ed. Belmont, CA: Wadsworth Publishing Company, 1996.

Kelley, Barbara Tatem; Thornberry, Terence P.; and Smith, Carolyn A. *In the Wake of Childhood Maltreatment.* OJJDP Juvenile Justice Bulletin, August 1997. (NCJ-165257)

Martin, Deirdre. "Teen Violence: Why It's on the Rise and How to Stem Its Tide." *Law Enforcement Technology,* January 1994, pp. 36–42.

Milavsky, J. Ronald. *TV and Violence.* National Institute of Justice, Crime File Study Guide. n.d.

Miller, Kay. "Circumcision Ritual Creates Cultural Conflict for Somali Women." (Minneapolis/St. Paul) *Star Tribune,* May 24, 1998, pp. A1, A10.

Missing and Exploited Children: The Challenge Continues. Washington, DC: U.S. Attorney General's Advisory Board on Missing Children, December 1988. National Criminal Justice Association.

Ostbloom, Norman and Crase, Sedahlia Jasper. "A Model for Conceptualizing Child Abuse Causation and Intervention." *Social Case Work: The Journal of Contemporary Social Work,* March 1980, pp. 164–172.

Paisner, Susan R. "Domestic Violence: Breaking the Cycle." *The Police Chief,* February 1991, pp. 35–38.

Ringel, Cheryl. *Criminal Victimization 1996: Changes 1995–96 with Trends 1993–96.* Washington DC: Bureau of Justice Statistics, National Crime Victimization Survey, November 1997. (NCJ-165812)

Roth, Jeffrey A. *Understanding and Preventing Violence.* National Institute of Justice, Research in Brief, February 1994.

Sickmund, Melissa; Snyder, Howard N.; and Poe-Yamagata, Eileen. *Juvenile Offenders and Victims: 1997 Update on Violence.* Washington, DC: Office of Juvenile Justice and Delinquency Prevention, National Center for Juvenile Justice, August 1997.

Sourcebook of Criminal Justice Statistics 1996. Washington, DC: Bureau of Justice Statistics, 1997. (NCJ-165361)

Speirs, Verne L. *Preliminary Estimates Developed on Stranger Abduction Homicides of Children.* OJJDP, Juvenile Justice Bulletin, January 1989.

Springer, Charles E. *Justice for Juveniles.* Washington, DC: U.S. Department of Justice, Office of Juvenile Justice and Delinquency Prevention, 1986.

Strandberg, Keith W. "Attacking Child Abuse." *Law Enforcement Technology,* May 1997, pp. 38–41.

"Studies Identify Risks to Adolescents' Safety, Health." *NCJA Justice Bulletin,* October 1997, pp. 7–12.

"Study Amplifies Crime's Link to Child Abuse and Neglect." *Law Enforcement News,* July/August 1997, p. 15.

Sweet, Robert W., Jr. "From the Administrator." OJJDP, Update on Statistics, November 1990a, p. 1.

Sweet, Robert W., Jr. "Missing Children: Found Facts." *National Institute of Justice, Reports,* November/December 1990b, pp. 15–18.

Thornberry, T. *Violent Families and Youth Violence.* Program of Research on Cause and Correlates of Delinquency. Washington, DC: Office of Juvenile Justice and Delinquency Prevention, 1994.

"Two-Thirds of Prisoners Were Abused as Children, Study Finds." *Criminal Justice Newsletter,* April 15, 1998, pp. 7–8.

United Nations, Article 17, p. 5.

"Which Is the Most-Violent Nation for Children? It's U.S." (Minneapolis/St. Paul) *Star Tribune,* February 7, 1997, pp. A1, A17.

Widom, Cathy Spatz. *The Cycle of Violence.* National Institute of Justice, Research in Brief, October 1992.

Widom, Cathy Spatz. *Victims of Childhood Sexual Abuse—Later Criminal Consequences.* National Institute of Justice, Research in Brief, March 1995.

Will, George F. "Child Abuse and Neglect Cases Soared with Advent of Crack." (Minneapolis/St. Paul) *Star Tribune,* May 1, 1994, p. A25.

Witkin, Gordon. "Kids Who Kill." *U.S. News and World Report,* April 8, 1991, pp. 26–32. Reprinted in *Annual Editions: Criminal Justice 92/93,* 16th ed., edited by John J. Sullivan and Joseph L. Victor. Guilford, CT: Dushkin Publishing Group, Inc. 1992, pp. 181–185.

Wrobleski, Adina. *Suicide: Why? 89 Questions and Answers About Suicide.* Minneapolis: Afterwords, 1989.

Cases

Ingram v. Wright, 430 U.S. 651, 97 S.Ct. 1401, 51 L.Ed.2d 711 (1977).

People v. Green, 155 Mich. 524, 532, 119 N.W. 1087 (1909).

Prince v. Massachusetts, 321 U.S. 158, 166, 64 S.Ct. 438, 442, 88 L.Ed. 645 (1944).

Santosky v. Kramer, 455 U.S. 745, 753, 102 S.Ct. 1388, 71 L.Ed.2d 599 (1982).

Worthen v. State, 42 Md.App. 20, 399 A.2d 272 (1979)—The International Year of the Child.

6

Chapter

Youths Who Break the Law and Those Who Victimize

The greatest future predictor of violent
behavior is a previous history of violence.
Without systematic and effective intervention,
early aggression commonly will escalate into
later violence and broaden into other
antisocial behavior.

—American Psychological Association Commission on Violence and Youth

Do You Know

- How researchers measure the nature and extent of youthful offenses?
- How prevalent delinquency is according to self-reports?
- What acts are classified as status offenses in most states?
- What delinquency offenses result in the highest number of juvenile arrests?
- The major theories of the causes of juvenile delinquency and the main thesis of each?
- What is a major characteristic of juvenile delinquency?
- What a psychopath is?
- How the public health model views violence in the United States and what should be done about it?

Can You Define

acting out, antisocial personality disorder, at-risk youths, broken-window theory, chronic juvenile offender, conduct disorder, contagion, delinquent, ephebiphobia, Index crimes, psychopathic behavior, serious juvenile offender, sociopathic behavior, Uniform Crime Report, violent juvenile offender

INTRODUCTION

Some actions discussed in Chapter 5, such as running away from home, not only place youngsters at risk of being victimized, they also violate the law and, therefore, put the youngsters at risk of being arrested. Sharp (1998, p. 109) warns: "If juvenile crime rates are not curbed—and soon—society may suffer needlessly." Among law enforcement agencies who took part in a poll on the subject of juvenile crime, 93 percent of respondents indicated that their jurisdictions are currently experiencing an increase in juvenile crime, with particular concern over the increase among 13- to 17-year-old teenagers (Sharp, p. 110). Furthermore: "Contrary to what a lot of people think, [poll respondents] do not see drugs as a major factor in juvenile crimes. Only 53% said they think drugs are involved."

This chapter looks at the sources of information about the ways in which youths break the law as well as the range of offenses that are committed by juveniles. This range goes from minor status offenses, such as violating a curfew law, to major violent crimes, such as rape and murder. The chapter also returns to the widespread problem of violence in our society and the effect it is having on our youths. The chapter concludes with a discussion of violence as a public health problem.

Measuring the Number of Juvenile Offenses Committed

Just how serious is the problem of youths breaking the law in the United States?

Researchers use three methods to measure the nature and extent of unlawful acts by juveniles: official data, self-report data and victim surveys.

Official Data

Official data is information and statistics collected by the police, courts and corrections agencies on the local, regional and national levels. One widely used official source of delinquency statistics is the Uniform Crime Report collected by the FBI. The FBI surveys over 15,000 police agencies every year.

The **Uniform Crime Report** (UCR) divides crimes into Part I and Part II. Part I, also called **Index crimes,** includes the eight major crimes: homicide and non-negligent manslaughter, forcible rape, robbery, aggravated assault, burglary, larceny, arson and motor vehicle theft.

The UCR's statistics on number of crimes reported and number of arrests illustrate the extent of the delinquency problem. The statistics must be interpreted cautiously, however. The data represent only youths who have been arrested. Many are never caught. It has been estimated that between 80 and 90 percent of our children under 18 commit some offense for which they could be arrested, but only about 3 percent of them are. In addition, multiple arrests of the same youth for different crimes are counted separately. The total number of arrests does not equal the number of youths who have been arrested, because chronic offenders have multiple arrests.

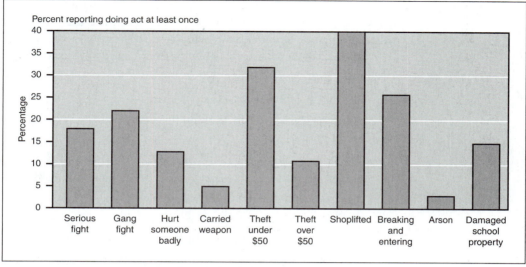

Source: Institute for Social Research. *Monitoring the Future, 1994.* Ann Arbor, MI: ISR, 1995.

Figure 6.1
Self-Reported
Delinquent Acts

Other sources of official statistics are the Bureau of Justice Statistics (BJS), the Office of Juvenile Justice and Delinquency Prevention (OJJDP) and the National Institute of Justice (NIJ).

Official statistics have several problems, such as how the data is collected, variations in interpretation and police bias in arrest decisions. Official statistics also do not provide information about the personality, attitudes and behavior of delinquents. This comes from self-reports.

Self-Reports

Self-report studies let youths personally reveal information about their violations of the law. Self-report formats include one-to-one interviews, surveys and anonymous questionnaires. According to Siegel and Senna (1997, p. 48): "When truancy, alcohol consumption, petty theft, and recreational drug use are included in self-report scales, delinquency appears almost universal."

According to self-report studies, delinquency is almost universal.

The University of Michigan's Institute for Social Research (ISR) has conducted surveys of thousands of high school seniors regarding delinquent activities, the self-reported results of which appear in Figure 6.1.

Victimization Data

A third source of information about the extent of the delinquency problem is victimization data. The Bureau of Justice Statistics of the U.S. Department of Justice, working with the U.S. Census Bureau, conducts annual house-to-house surveys of crime victims. The National Crime Victimization Survey (NCVS) involves interviews with about 50,000 people age 12 and older, twice a year, to gather information about crimes, including those not reported to police. Perkins (1997, p. 1) cites the following highlights from recently obtained NCVS data:

- Persons ages 12 to 24 comprised:

    22 percent of the population,

    35 percent of murder victims, and

    49 percent of serious violent crime victims.

- Persons ages 18 to 21 were the most likely to experience a serious violent crime, and blacks in that age group were the most vulnerable:

    72 victimizations per 1,000 blacks,

    50 victimizations per 1,000 Hispanics, and

    46 victimizations per 1,000 whites.

- Serious violent crime rates for persons ages 18 to 21 were 17 times higher than for persons age 65 or older.

Status Offenders

Status offenses are based solely on the offender's age and are unique to juveniles. The age limit for status offenses ranges from 16 to 19, but in most states it is 18. Anyone above the legal age who engaged in the same behaviors would not be committing an offense.

> Status offenses include actions such as violating curfew, habitual truancy, running away, incorrigibility, ungovernable conduct, being beyond the control of parents, being wayward, using tobacco and drugs and drinking alcohol.

The runaway problem was discussed in Chapter 5. However running away is a status offense in most communities, so the juvenile justice system has jurisdiction in the matter and can act "in the best interest of the child." In 1996 an estimated 195,700 youths were arrested for running away. Chesney-Lind and Shelden (1998, p. 43) note:

> Status offenses have always been closely identified with female delinquency. Running away from home and being unmanageable or incorrigible have long been seen as typical female offenses. . . . Clearly, though, an obvious gender bias is suggested in comparisons of referrals to juvenile court with self-report studies that show that boys and girls are about equally as likely to commit these types of offenses. . . . Running away very often leads girls to commit a variety of crimes in order to survive, among them engaging in prostitution.

A problem closely related to running away is truancy. Several approaches to this problem have been tried. Suburban Houston's Spring Branch Independent School District, for example, holds parents responsible for their absent teenagers. After phone calls and visits to the families of truants, the district files charges. Both parents can be fined up to $100 per day for a child's chronic truancy. But even monetary penalties haven't ended the problem. The school district averages four to six court cases per month to enforce attendance rules.

Truancy is the most frequent offense for those under age 15, probably because after that age those who would be truant have simply dropped out of school. The most frequent offense for those 16 or older is liquor violations.

In 1974 the federal government enacted a law that urged the decriminalization of incorrigible offenses such as truancy and running away. To ensure the continued flow of federal funds for youth programs, states changed their laws to prevent the prolonged incarceration of noncriminal minors.

One of the most common status offenses is curfew violation. Curfew laws are enacted so that police officers can maintain control over youths during the night-time when they are more likely to be getting into trouble. Youths who violate curfews often receive only a warning. At other times they are held at the police station until their parents come for them. Fines are used by some departments. In 1996 an estimated 185,100 youths were arrested for curfew violations and loitering. Curfew ordinances have been challenged in several communities as being unconstitutional because they discriminate against those who are not yet legally adults.

Vandalism

Vandalism is usually a mischievous, destructive act done to get attention, to get revenge or to vent hostility. Philip Zimbardo, a Stanford psychologist, reported in 1969 on some experiments that tested human behavior and vandalism. He arranged to have two comparable automobiles without license plates parked with their hoods up on a street in the Bronx, New York, and on a street in Palo Alto, California. The car in the Bronx was attacked by "vandals" within 10 minutes of its "abandonment."

The first people to arrive at the Bronx car were a family—father, mother and young son—who removed the radiator and battery. Within 24 hours virtually everything of value had been removed. Then random destruction began. Windows were smashed, parts torn off, upholstery ripped. Children began to use the car as a playground. Most of the adult "vandals" were well-dressed, clean-cut whites.

The car in Palo Alto sat untouched for more than a week. Then Zimbardo smashed part of it with a sledgehammer. Soon passersby were joining in. Within a few hours, the car had been turned upside down and utterly destroyed. Again, the "vandals" appeared to be primarily white adults. Commenting on this research in their classic work describing the **broken-window theory,** Wilson and Kelling (1982, pp. 29–38) state:

> Untended property becomes fair game for people out for fun or plunder, and even for people who ordinarily would not dream of doing such things and who probably consider themselves law-abiding. Because of the nature of community life in the Bronx—its anonymity, the frequency with which cars are abandoned and things are stolen or broken, the past experience of "no one caring"— vandalism begins much more quickly than it does in staid Palo Alto, where people have come to believe that private possessions are cared for, and that mischievous behavior is costly. But vandalism can occur anywhere once communal barriers— the sense of mutual regard and the obligations of civility—are lowered by actions that seem to signal that "no one cares."

This vandalized car in the South Bronx depicts graphically the broken-window theory: "Untended property becomes fair game for people out for fun or plunder." If it appears that no one cares—if broken windows go unfixed—vandalism and crime will flourish.

Rowdy children sometimes send a message of personal problems by vandalism. Destructive behavior can occur because children lack ways of communicating a need for help. In 1996, 141,600 juveniles were arrested for vandalism.

At-Risk Behaviors

Many of the status offenses are also a means to identify **at-risk youths.** Doyle (1996, p. 90) defines at-risk as "the potential and willingness of a young person to take unnecessary risks or chances outside of socially-accepted norms and mores, for the purpose of self-gratification, aggrandizement, and peer acceptance. At-risk behaviors include habitual truancy, incorrigibility, gang activity, drug abuse, alcoholism, suicide, promiscuity, criminal activity, tattooing or self-mutilating behaviors, vandalism, possession and use of weapons. And, in more and more cases, there is a propensity for using violence against others as a means of gaining personal power."

Underage Drinking

A 1997 Harvard study of college students' binge drinking found little change in behavior from 1993. The study, based on data from 14,521 students at 116 schools in 39 states, found that the number of binge drinkers and occasional drinkers was split equally, with 44 percent in each group. The remaining students said they abstained from drinking. Of more importance to the juvenile justice system, however, is that approximately 36 percent said they drove after drinking ("Harvard Study," 1998, p. 13).

In 1998 the OJJDP created the Combating Underage Drinking program to help states investigate and prosecute businesses that sell alcohol to minors and to combat underage drinking. The OJJDP has also released *Combating Underage Drinking—A Compendium of Resources,* a compilation of statistics concerning underage drinking trends and descriptions of existing programs that address the problem of alcohol and youths. It includes an annotated bibliography of books and journals addressing the issue. This compendium is available on the Internet at http://www.ncjrs.org/ojjhome.htm.

A Key Issue

Should the term *juvenile delinquency* encompass both those youths who commit serious, violent crimes and those who commit status offenses? Incorporating crimes and status offenses is a key issue in juvenile justice.

Juvenile Delinquents

A juvenile **delinquent** is a youth who commits an act that would be a crime were it to be committed by an adult. The term is intended to avoid stigmatizing youths as criminals. The term *delinquent* should not be applied to status offenders.

As noted previously, just who qualifies as a youth varies from state to state. No single nationally recognized age places youths into the juvenile justice system. Some states consider juveniles to be age 16 or under, others 19 or under. Most states, however, have established age 18, as was seen in Table 3.1.

Definitions

The National Coalition of State Juvenile Justice Advisory Groups, in its 1992 annual report to the President, the Congress and the Office of Juvenile Justice and Delinquency Prevention (pp. 13–14), includes the following definitions:

- **Serious juvenile offender**—A juvenile who has been convicted of a Part I offense as defined by the FBI Uniform Crime Report, excluding auto theft or distribution of a controlled dangerous substance, and who was 14, 15, 16, or 17 years old at the time of the offense.
- **Chronic juvenile offender**—A youth who has a record of five or more separate charges of delinquency, regardless of the gravity of the offenses.

The Coalition (p. 14) lists the following criteria as those most often mentioned as characterizing serious or chronic offenders:

- A delinquency adjudication prior to age 13
- Low family income
- Between the ages of 8 and 10 being rated troublesome by teachers and peers
- Poor school performance by age 10
- Psychomotor clumsiness
- Having a sibling convicted of a crime

Profile of Delinquency

No single type of personality is associated with delinquency. However, some characteristics are common among delinquents. Those who become delinquent are more likely to be socially assertive, defiant, ambivalent about authority, resentful, hostile, suspicious, destructive, impulsive and lacking in self-control.

Shea (1987) has suggested a profile of the delinquent as a male adolescent who has committed at least 50 felonies, who began crime at age five or six, and whose family is frustrated and exhausted. He typically is skipping school or has dropped out, and his friends have the same profile. The probability of chemical abuse is 75 percent. He is impulsive, irresponsible and unwilling to see or understand how his actions affect others.

Konopka's (1966, p. 112) classic in-depth study, *The Adolescent Girl in Conflict,* describes a 17-year-old girl who shows impulsive, irresponsible behavior:

> If we don't have money, we rob people. I helped. I knew the boy we robbed. I had gone with him. He was a show-off. He always talked about how much money he had.
>
> Did I think about whether he had worked for it? Oh, you don't think of that! You just think you need money. What did I want and need money for? Clothes . . . but I never bought clothes. I just drank. I used the money for drinking.

Sometimes the impulsiveness and irresponsibility goes even further, resulting in acting out or in psychopathic behavior, as will be discussed shortly.

Wolfgang's classic long-term study of delinquents in Philadelphia found that from 6 to 8 percent of male juveniles were responsible for over 60 percent of the serious juvenile offenses. His studies also showed that by the third arrest, a delinquent was almost guaranteed a life of crime.

Juvenile Arrest Statistics and Delinquency Rates

Table 6.1 shows the number of juvenile arrests in 1997. Property crimes continue to head the list.

The most frequent delinquency offenses are property crimes, with larceny-theft being the most common.

While these figures may seem alarmingly high, they actually represent a *decrease* in juvenile arrests for violent crimes. According to recent FBI statistics (*Crime in the United States,* 1997), the number of juveniles arrested in 1997 for violent crime Index offenses went down for the third straight year. Juvenile murder arrests dropped 39 percent in 1997 to their lowest level of the 1990s, yet remained 50 percent higher than they were a decade earlier.

Delinquency rates tend to increase dramatically as age increases, peaking in the later teenage years. According to Regnery (1991, p. 165): "Juveniles do commit crimes at a rate significantly higher than the rest of the population. In fact, 16-year-old boys commit crimes at a higher rate than any other single age group. These are criminals who happen to be young, not children who happen to commit crimes."

Arrest data show that the intensity of criminal behavior slackens after the teens and continues to decline with age. FBI arrest data (*Crime in the United States*) indicates that the peak age of arrest for property crimes is 16, for simple assault, 16 to 17, and for violent crimes, weapons and drug abuse violations, 18.

Burglary

Burglary is usually committed for quick financial gain, often to support a drug habit. It is the most accessible route to money for unemployed juveniles. In 1996, the juvenile arrest rate for burglary was approximately 440 per 100,000 juveniles ages 10 to 17. According to Snyder (1997, p. 7): "The juvenile arrest rate for burglary declined consistently between 1980 and 1996, with the 1996 rate 45% below that of 1980."

Table 6.1
Juvenile Arrests, 1997

Most Serious Offense	1997 Estimated Number of Juvenile Arrests	Percent of Total Juvenile Arrests		Percent Change		
		Female	Under Age 15	1988–97	1993–97	1996–97
Total	**2,838,300**	**26%**	**32%**	**35%**	**14%**	**–1%**
Crime Index Total	824,900	26	38	6	–4	–6
Violent Crime Index	123,400	16	30	49	–6	–4
Murder and non-negligent manslaughter	2,500	6	11	11	–39	–16
Forcible rape	5,500	2	38	6	–16	–2
Robbery	39,500	9	26	56	–2	–8
Aggravated assault	75,900	21	33	51	–5	–2
Property Crime Index	701,500	28	40	1	–3	–6
Burglary	131,000	10	38	–15	–9	–6
Larceny-theft	493,900	34	42	9	4	–4
Motor vehicle theft	66,600	16	26	–17	–30	–14
Arson	10,000	11	67	22	–2	–4
Nonindex						
Other assaults	241,800	29	41	84	17	0
Forgery and counterfeiting	8,500	39	12	2	3	–2
Fraud	11,300	35	16	58	3	–6
Embezzlement	1,400	45	5	6	74	0
Stolen property (buying, receiving, possessing)	39,500	13	27	–8	–15	–10
Vandalism	136,500	12	45	20	–12	–6
Weapons (carrying, possessing, etc.)	52,200	9	31	44	–23	–4
Prostitution and commercialized vice	1,400	56	15	–28	11	–8
Sex offense (except forcible rape and prostitution)	18,500	9	51	11	–13	4
Drug abuse violations	220,700	13	16	125	82	2
Gambling	2,600	3	13	166	–7	–6
Offenses against the family and children	10,200	37	35	150	73	8
Driving under the influence	19,600	17	2	–21	35	4
Liquor law violations	158,500	30	11	1	33	1
Drunkenness	24,100	17	13	–9	31	–5
Disorderly conduct	215,100	26	34	86	31	0
Vagrancy	3,100	15	24	–7	2	1
All other offenses (except traffic)	468,000	24	28	55	29	4
Suspicion	1,600	23	22	–38	–9	–26
Curfew and loitering	182,700	31	28	190	87	3
Runaways	196,100	58	41	19	–2	–4

- Between 1993 and 1997, juvenile arrests for murder declined 39 percent; during the same period, juvenile arrests for a weapons law violation dropped 23 percent.
- In about 15 percent of all juvenile arrests in 1997, the most serious charge was a drug abuse violation, a liquor law violation, drunkenness, or driving under the influence.
- The proportion of juvenile arrests involving younger juveniles (under age 15) was highest for the offense of arson (67 percent), followed by sex offenses (51 percent), vandalism (45 percent), larceny-theft (42 percent), other (simple) assaults (41 percent), and runaways (41 percent).
- 12 percent of juveniles arrested for vandalism were female and 45 percent were age 14 or younger.

Source: *Crime in the United States 1997*. Washington, DC: U.S. Government Printing Office, 1998, tables 29, 32, 34, 36, and 38. Arrest estimates were developed by the National Center for Juvenile Justice.

Arson

Arson, like vandalism, sends a message through a delinquent act. For many children setting fires is a symbolic act, often a symptom of underlying emotional or physical stress. Children who do not abandon normal childhood experiments with fire often are crying for help, using fire as an expression of their stress, anxiety and anger. What turns these troubled youths into repeat firesetters is positive reinforcement for their incendiary activities. Firesetting provides a sense of power and control. Juvenile firesetters often take out their hostility on school property.

Snyder (p. 7) notes: "Compared with other property crimes, the number of juveniles arrested for arson is very small. . . . Between 1990 and 1994, the rate of juvenile arson arrests increased from 26 to 34 per 100,000 juveniles ages 10 through 17. The juvenile arson arrest rate then declined in 1995 and 1996, falling back to the 1992 level." In 1996 the juvenile arrest rate for arson was approximately 30 per 100,000 juveniles ages 10 to 17.

Larceny-Theft

As mentioned, larceny-theft is the most frequent offense for which juveniles are arrested. In 1996 the juvenile arrest rate for larceny-theft was approximately 1,650 per 100,000 juveniles ages 10 to 17. According to Snyder (p. 7): "Compared with other property offenses, the juvenile arrest rate for larceny-theft remained relatively constant between 1980 and 1996. Over this period the juvenile arrest rate for larceny-theft gradually increased, so that the 1996 rate was 10% above the rate in 1980."

Motor Vehicle Theft

As with burglary and arson, the juvenile arrest rate for motor vehicle theft has declined in recent years. Snyder (p. 7) notes: "Juvenile arrest rates for motor vehicle theft soared between 1983 and 1990, with the rate up nearly 140% over this period." However: "Between 1990 and 1996, the juvenile arrest rate for motor vehicle theft declined substantially, returning to the 1987 level." In 1996 the juvenile arrest rate for motor vehicle theft was approximately 250 per 100,000 juveniles ages 10 to 17.

A Brief Recap on the Causes of Delinquency

Delinquency is a focal point for the juvenile justice system. More energy and effort are spent by those within the system on delinquency than on any other responsibility. The United States generates more after-care programs than any other country. But delinquency, its causes and effects are usually examined *after the fact,* with research on preventing delinquency getting little attention, which leaves us with the question: What leads youths to become delinquent?

Do children often grow up to be like their parents because they have inherited something from them, or because of the way their parents have raised them? This question is especially relevant for children who become delinquents. Many researchers have tried to answer the question "Why do youths become delinquent?" The vast array of theories that have resulted range from the very conservative to what some may consider outlandish. Modern research on the causes of crime and delinquency centers on such areas as biology, sociology and psychology.

Theories about the causes of juvenile delinquency include biological, behavioral, sociological and psychological theories.

The following theories provide a base to understand juvenile behavior and related offenses. They were discussed in greater depth in Chapter 2.

Biological Theories

Biological theorists contend that criminals are born, not made. The classic studies of Lombroso (1913) and Garofalo (1915) support a hereditary, genetic causation for deviant behavior. Some researchers feel that a genetic mishap may cause one member of a family to deviate from the norm. For example, Richard Speck, who murdered eight Chicago nurses, showed an unusual genetic structure—he had one extra male chromosome. Speck is not the only convicted criminal to display such a genetic abnormality.

Modern biological theorists possess scientific rigor, and they look to biochemical relationships, endocrine imbalances, chromosomal complements, brain wave activity and other biological determinants of behavior. Violence and aggression have been associated with the presence or absence of certain chemicals in the brain. The fact that biological explanations are supported by research cannot be ignored in looking at the causes of delinquent and antisocial behavior.

Behavioral Theories

A counter position to biological theory is behavioral theory, which contends that criminals are made, not born. Behavioral theorists argue that people become who they are because of their life experiences.

As children grow and develop, they learn from their families the rules that govern their conduct. Any wrongdoing or mischief reflects what was learned and manipulated for whatever gain might be desired, without taking into account the risk or punishment that might result. If children who misbehave are corrected by their parents, they are likely to conform to society's expectations; if they are not corrected, they are likely to ignore society's rules.

Sociological Theories

Sociological theorists take the behavioral position one step further. Socialization provides children with accepted behavior repertoires and endows them with the basic values of their social milieu. In the socialization process, children may also learn antisocial values, if such values are important in their social and cultural environment. In such instances socialization actually contributes to delinquent behavior.

Although delinquency often begins when children first enter schools, its most serious manifestations usually occur in adolescence. Most youths at one time or another test the limits, shoplift, steal from their mother's purse or engage in similar petty thefts. Such behavior is usually outgrown without intervention from the juvenile justice system if the parents administer appropriate discipline. Unfortunately not all youths outgrow these tendencies to misbehave. As Eitzen (1992, p. 585) states: "Some children are angry, alienated, and apathetic. A few are uncooperative, rude, abrasive, threatening, and even violent. Some abuse drugs. Some are sexually promiscuous. Some belong to gangs. Some are sociopaths." Eitzen goes on to state: "My strong conviction is that children are *not* born with sociopathic tendencies; problem children are socially created."

The Gluecks (1950) also favor a sociological causation for delinquency. Their extensive studies of delinquent boys enabled them to create a *predictive index.* The accuracy of this index was tested in the 1950s, and of 220 predictions, 209 were accurate. The social factors in their index included how children were disciplined and supervised, how much affection was shown in the home and family cohesiveness.

According to Sprinthall and Collins (1984, p. 344), the Gluecks' study had and continues to have important implications about the causes of serious delinquent behavior by teenagers:

- Delinquent behavior starts prior to adolescence. During adolescence the antisocial acts increase in seriousness and frequency.
- The home environment—especially the quality of the mother-son relationship—is a major causative factor.
- The economic status of delinquency-prone families is lower than that of nondelinquent families, even though there is no difference in the level of parental employment.
- There is virtually a 100 percent rate of school dropout for the delinquents.
- Follow-up studies indicate that in adulthood almost one-third of the delinquents engage in serious crimes.

Psychological Approaches

Many delinquent youths have to deal with poor home lives and destructive relationships. Such an environment can lead to a disturbed personality structure marked by negative, antisocial behavior. While many delinquents do not show significant psychological disturbances, enough do suffer from problems to allow psychological factors to be considered in the theory of delinquency.

According to psychoanalytical perspectives, violence is an expression of tension or psychic energy that builds up as a result of faulty emotional development and the absence of appropriate outlets for the pressure. This pressure is particularly apparent in adolescents. Adolescence is normally a time of inner tensions, excessive energy and ambiguity. It is a time when the individual is neither child nor adult. Youths still have childish needs and a desire for dependency, though they have adult expectations imposed by themselves or others. If the emotional foundation is weak, the result can be catastrophic.

A major characteristic of juvenile delinquents is that they act out their inner conflicts.

In **acting out,** youths freely express their impulses, particularly hostile ones. Acting out is the free, deliberate, often malicious indulgence of impulse, which often leads to aggression as well as other manifestations of delinquency, such as vandalism, cruelty to animals and sometimes even murder. Acting out essentially reflects an absence of self-control and a desire for immediate gratification.

Such a lack of self-control may result from an early history of severe parental rejection or deprivation, or from witnessing or being the victim of severe physical abuse and violence. Children strike back against a world they perceive as hostile. Acting out may also give adolescents a sense of importance, a way to overcome feelings of inadequacy and inferiority.

Adolescents who act out come from all socioeconomic levels and are not psychopathic according to conventional classifications. They may have a clear sense of conscience and be capable of strong feelings of loyalty to a gang. But their impulses are stronger than their consciences. The acting out may be a form of defense against feelings of anxiety produced by an awareness of guilt.

Other Factors

Other factors commonly cited as contributing directly to delinquency include poverty, unemployment, the breakdown of religion, the breakdown of the family, effects of the media (TV, movies, music), peer pressure and, most importantly, being abused as children, as was discussed in Chapter 5. According to Doyle (pp. 91–92), several factors contribute to the risk of a youth becoming delinquent:

- Divorce—the common denominator in about 90 percent of the juvenile cases handled by the Upland, California, Police Department
- Single-parent households
- Alcohol- and/or drug-abusing parent(s)
- Two-income households with diminished supervision of children
- Familial criminal history
- Transient patterns—frequent family moves or shuffling between relatives
- Special education needs or attention deficit disorder (ADD)

All of the theories ask the same basic question: "Are delinquents made or born?" The answer is both: Delinquency is caused by a *combination* of predisposing genetic traits influenced by social circumstances and life experiences. As explained by Wilson (1983, p. 86):

> We now have available an impressive number of studies that, taken together, support the following view: Some combination of constitutional traits and early family experiences account for more of the variation among young persons in their serious criminality than any other factors, and serious misconduct that appears relatively early in life tends to persist into adulthood. What happens on the street corner, in the school, or in the job market can still make a difference, but it will not be as influential as what has gone before.

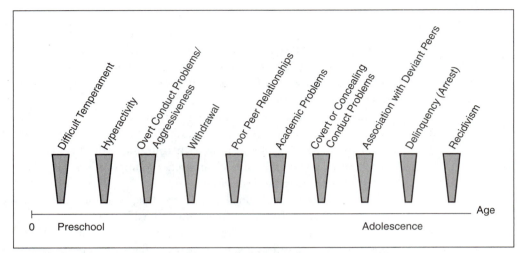

Figure 6.2
Approximate Ordering of the Different Manifestations of Disruptive and Antisocial Behaviors in Childhood and Adolescence

Source: Barbara Tatem Kelley et al. *Developmental Pathways in Boys' Disruptive and Delinquent Behavior.* OJJDP Juvenile Justice Bulletin, December 1997, p. 4. (NCJ-165692)

Also of great importance is how serious, chronic offenders are treated by the juvenile justice system. According to Crowe (1991, pp. 26, 27):

> It is a basic fact that many serious habitual juvenile offenders are not placed in pretrial detention or sentenced to institutional programs because they are too difficult to handle. This poses two serious issues:
>
> ■ Protection of the public from the progressively violent offender.
> ■ Protection of the public and property from the habitual who commits an estimated 10–20 offenses for every time he or she is caught.

These troubled, problem or delinquent children are officially invisible until they commit an extremely serious crime. Often, however, they can be identified much earlier.

Developmental Pathways

Longitudinal research from the Pittsburgh Youth Study, a component of the OJJDP's Program of Research on the Causes and Correlates of Delinquency, has revealed that the development of disruptive and delinquent behavior in boys typically occurs in an orderly, progressive manner. Kelley et al. (1997b, p. 2) have documented "three developmental pathways that display progressively more serious problem behaviors among boys in three conceptually similar domains: authority conflict (defiance and running away), covert actions (lying and stealing), and overt actions (aggression and violent behavior)." As these researchers explain (1997b, p. 2): "A pathway is identified when a group of individuals experience a behavioral development that is distinct from the behavioral development of other groups of individuals. In a developmental pathway, stages of behavior unfold over time in an orderly fashion." These pathways are illustrated in Figure 6.2.

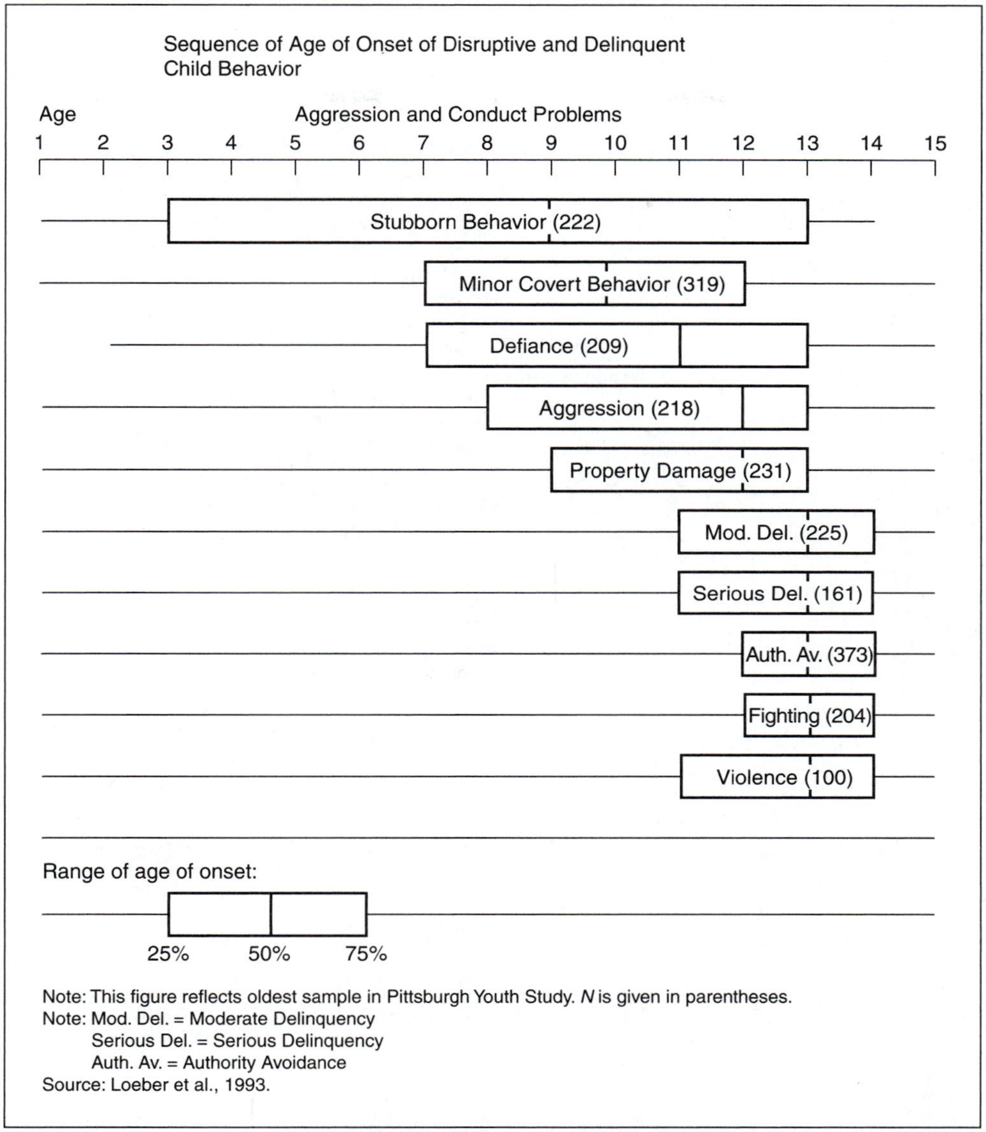

Figure 6.3
**Sequence of Age
of Onset of Disruptive
and Delinquent Child
Behavior**

Source: Barbara Tatem Kelley et al. *Developmental Pathways in Boys'
Disruptive and Delinquent Behavior.* OJJDP Juvenile Justice Bulletin,
December 1997, p. 8. (NCJ-165692)

Kelley et al. (1997b, p. 4) have identified an approximate ordering of the different manifestations of disruptive and antisocial behaviors (Figure 6.3). As indicated, a difficult temperament is generally the earliest problem noted in infants, with hyperactivity becoming more apparent once a child begins to walk, and so on. Figure 6.4 shows a similar ordering of prosocial developmental tasks that counterbalance the antisocial behaviors identified in Figure 6.3. Kelley et al. (1997b, p. 4) see "children's failures to master these developmental tasks and to acquire other prosocial skills

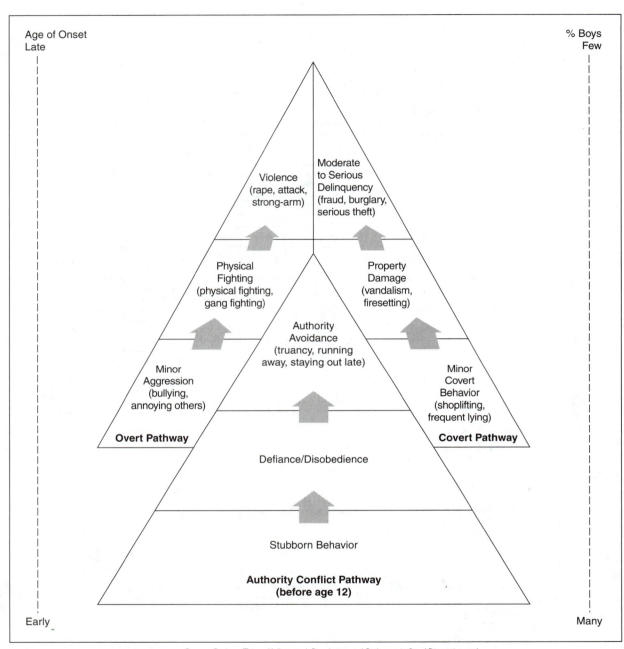

Figure 6.4
**Three Pathways to Boys'
Disruptive Behavior
and Delinquency**

Source: Barbara Tatem Kelley et al. *Developmental Pathways in Boys' Disruptive and Delinquent Behavior.* OJJDP Juvenile Justice Bulletin, December 1997, p. 9. (NCJ-165692)

Table 6.2
Items Used to Generate 10 Sets of Behaviors (Middle and Oldest Samples)

Stages	Component Behaviors	Instrument Used	
		Retrospective	Prospective
Authority conflict			
Stubbornness	Stubbornness	DISC	MCBC, YSR
Defiance	Doing things own way	DISC	MCBC
	Refusing to do things	DISC	MCBC
	Disobedience	DISC	MCBC
Authority avoidance	Staying out late	DISC	MCBC, YSR
	Truancy	DISC	MCBC, YSR, SRD
	Running away	DISC	MCBC, YSR, SRD
Covert behavior			
Minor covert behavior	Lying	DISC	MCB, YSR
	Shoplifting	SRD	MCBC, SRD
Property damage	Setting fires	SRD	MCBC, SRD
	Damaging property	SRD	SRD
Moderately serious delinquency	Joyriding	SRD	SRD, MCBC
	Pickpocketing	SRD	SRD
	Stealing from car	SRD	SRD
	Fencing stolen goods	SRD	SRD
	Writing illegal checks	SRD	SRD
	Using illegal credit cards	SRD	SRD
Serious delinquency	Stealing a car	SRD	SRD
	Selling drugs	SRD	SRD, MCBC
	Breaking and entering	SRD	SRD
Overt behavior			
Aggression	Annoying others	DISC	MCBC
	Bullying	DISC	MCBC
Fighting	Physical fighting	DISC	MCBC, YSR
	Gang fighting	SRD	SRD, MCBC
Violence	Attacking someone	SRD	SRD
	Strong-arming	SRD	SRD
	Forcing sex	SRD	SRD

Note: DISC = Diagnostic Interview Schedule for Children—Parent Version
  MCBC = Maternal Child Behavior Checklist
  SRD = Youth Self-Reported Delinquency Scale
  YSR = Youth Self-Report

Note: Most of the measures were also used in the youngest sample, but some measures for the boys were adapted because of their young age.

Source: Barbara Tatem Kelley et al. *Development Pathways in Boys' Disruptive and Delinquent Behavior*. OJJDP Juvenile Justice Bulletin, December 1997, p 7. (NCJ-165692)

reflected in these tasks as breeding grounds for the development of disruptive and delinquent behavior. Therefore, many youths who eventually become seriously and chronically delinquent somewhere during childhood and adolescence probably missed opportunities to learn one or more key prosocial behaviors."

Earlier research (Loeber et al., 1993) sequenced the age of onset for disruptive and delinquent child behavior, shown in Table 6.2. Conduct such as stubborn behavior "tended to occur earliest at median age 9, with a wide range of onset—the 25th percentile at age 3 and the 75th percentile at age 13. This was followed by minor covert acts, such as lying and shoplifting, at median age 10. Defiance, which involves doing tasks in one's own way, refusing to follow directions, and disobeying, emerged next at median age 11. Aggressive behaviors, such as bullying and annoying others, followed at age 12, along with property damage, such as vandalism and firesetting. More seriously aggressive acts, such as physical fighting and violence, came last at median age of 13" (Kelley et al., 1997b, p. 6).

Violent Juvenile Offenders

The National Coalition of State Juvenile Justice Advisory Groups, in its 1992 annual report (pp. 13–14), includes the following definition:

> **Violent juvenile offender**—A youth who has been convicted of a violent Part I offense, one against a person rather than property and who has a prior adjudication of such an offense, or a youth who has been convicted of murder.

The Coalition (pp. 15–16) notes that violent offenders showed "an exceptionally high incidence of head injuries and a history of serious physical or sexual abuse." In fact, many violent offenders come from family environments so abusive they must be removed from their homes and placed in foster homes. Lamberg (1996, p. 1712) states: "In California, 65% of children going into the adult criminal system come from the foster care system."

Bilchik (1997, p. 1) states: "Over the past decade, juvenile violence has spread like an epidemic among a small, but nonetheless significant, segment of America's young people." According to Kelley et al. (1997a, p. 1): "By the early 1990's, rates of criminal violence, including youth violence, reached unparalleled levels in American society. Compared to adolescents in other countries, American teenagers exhibit alarmingly high rates of violence. For example, an American 17-year-old is 10 times more likely to commit murder than his or her Canadian counterpart." Sickmund et al. (1997, p. 24) note an important distinction, however: "Today's juvenile doesn't commit more acts of violence than a generation ago, but more juveniles are violent." Figure 6.5 illustrates how violent juvenile offenders "fit" into the larger picture of delinquent youths.

The scene pictured in "Kids Who Kill" (Witkin, 1991, pp. 181–182) graphically portrays the deadliness of some youths:

> The datelines change daily, but the stories are chillingly similar. In Washington, DC, 15-year-old Jermaine Daniel is shot to death by his best friend. In New Haven, Conn., Markiest Alexander, 14, is killed in a drive-by shooting. In St. Louis, Leo Wilson, 16, is robbed of his tennis shoes and Raiders jacket and then shot dead. In New York, a 14-year-old boy opens up with a semiautomatic pistol in a Bronx schoolyard, wounding one youngster and narrowly missing another, apparently in a dispute over a girl. . . .
>
> During every 100 hours on our streets we lose more young men than were killed in 100 hours of ground war in the Persian Gulf. . . . Where are the yellow ribbons of hope and remembrance for our youth dying in the streets?

Newspaper headlines herald the frightening situation regarding violent youths:

- Cops seize gas can [from a car driven by a 13-year-old suspect] in St. Paul arson that killed 5 kids—(Minneapolis/St. Paul) *Star Tribune,* March 12, 1994.

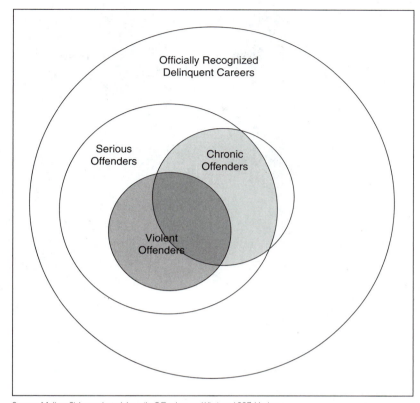

Figure 6.5
Types of Delinquency

Source: Melissa Sickmund et al. *Juvenile Offenders and Victims: 1997 Update on Violence.* Office of Juvenile Justice and Delinquency Prevention, August 1997, p. 25. (NCJ-165703)

- Kids [6-year-old boy and 8-year-old twin boys] charged in infant's beating—(Minneapolis/St. Paul) *Star Tribune,* April 26, 1996.

- Boy [11 years old] is found guilty in death of neighbor—(Minneapolis/ St. Paul) *Star Tribune,* August 11, 1998.

In another case: "A 6-year-old Richmond, Calif., boy has been charged with attempted murder after allegedly dumping a neighbor's newborn baby out of its bassinet, pummeling it, kicking it, and perhaps beating it with a stick. The incident in April left the baby with a fractured skull, brain-damaged, and on life support" (Lamberg, p. 1712).

Many believe juvenile violence will be an unavoidable part of life in American society unless significant changes are made in how such youths are identified *before* they become seriously delinquent. Minneapolis Police Chief Robert Olson, whose department is bracing for the prospect of continued violence by juveniles in upcoming years, states: "We ain't seen nothin' yet. If we don't get a grip on this generation, there's going to be the devil to pay. They have no conscience, no morals, and they're living for today. They're hardened criminals by age 16 or 17" ("What They are Saying," 1996, p. 1).

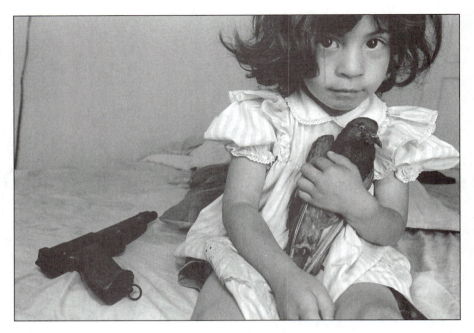

A three-year-old Los Angeles girl plays with a BB gun. She knows how to load and fire it. Guns are a natural part of the lives of many children who, like this girl, live in the Watts area of Los Angeles.

Reasons for the increase in the seriousness of the offenses and the decrease in the age of the offenders range from the problems of increasing gang activity and drug use in the elementary schools to the heightened level of violence in society in general and to increasing stress on families, especially in economically deprived areas. Martin (1994, p. 36) suggests two other primary reasons for the rise in teen violence: "A shift in adolescent attitudes toward the value of life and the ready availability of handguns."

Guns and Juveniles

A survey of 63 juvenile offenders in Atlanta, Georgia, ages 13 through 18, found that 84 percent of the youths had owned a gun, and that 84 percent of gun carriers acquired their first gun before the age of 15 (Ash et al., 1996, p. 1754). When asked about carrying a gun, one 17-year-old female offender stated: "You feel safer. You can protect yourself. If you don't have [a gun] you'll be paranoid and always watching your back. You feel more authoritative when you have a gun and have fun instead of being paranoid" (Ash et al., p. 1756). Indeed, 40 percent of the youths surveyed said they felt safer and more energized, excited or powerful when they carried a gun, and most indicated that guns were readily available (Ash et al., p. 1754).

In many cases youths obtain weapons not by buying them but as gifts from parents or other relatives. In Springfield, Oregon, a 15-year-old boy apparently murdered his parents and then opened fire on his high school campus—killing four and wounding 22—with a semiautomatic rifle given to him by his father. In this case Hall (1998, p. 6) notes: "His father bought him the semiauto rifle used in the crime and several handguns in order to 'defuse' the kid's unusual interest in weapons, according to published news reports on the incident that quoted family friends. Was that appropriate?"

Many think it is wholly inappropriate for parents or legal guardians to supply children with weapons and that such adults should be held liable, under parental-responsibility laws, for any crimes the youths commit with those weapons. Unfortunately, as Barry Krisberg, president of the National Council on Crime and Delinquency in San Francisco, notes (Faltermayer, 1998, p. 36): "Parental-responsibility law is a gray area. It's a toothless tiger. We have no research on the laws' effectiveness at all." Child access prevention (CAP) laws also hold adults accountable when underage youths are allowed access to guns and, according to Faltermayer, are much harder to dismiss than parental-responsibility laws (p. 37):

> Shannan Wilber, attorney at the Youth Law Center in San Francisco, says that unlike parent-responsibility laws, CAP laws draw a direct causal relationship between adults and the crimes committed by juveniles. "Where there is a clear connection," she says, "such as a parent's possession of firearms and failure to keep them away from their kids, it's easier to connect that to a subsequent criminal act by the child. It's more concrete." Florida passed the first CAP law in 1989, and 14 other states have enacted similar legislation.
>
> . . . Joe Sudbay, director of state legislation at Handgun Control Inc. in Washington, says . . .: "The whole point of these laws is not to punish. The point is to prevent." Do they? According to a study published in the *Journal of the American Medical Association* last October, unintentional deaths dropped 23% among children younger than 15 years old in the years covered by CAP laws.

In addressing the various ways America can prevent delinquency, Reno (1998, p. 81) advocates: "Most of all, we've got to get the guns out of the hands of our children. If you look at the figures and look at the rise in youth violence, one of the spikes is youth committing homicides against youth. The only comparable spike that matches it is youth in possession of guns."

Violent Adolescent Females

Girls have traditionally entered the juvenile justice system through their involvement in status offenses. Peters and Peters (1998, p. 28) note: "Females are still overrepresented in the juvenile system due to status offenses, but a shift toward violent crime is evident. . . . The most common violent offenses for which juvenile females are arrested are aggravated assault and robbery." They state that violence by adolescent girls is the result of "a complex combination of victimization, substance abuse, economic conditions and dysfunctional family systems" (p. 29). Furthermore:

> Researchers have linked the violence perpetuated against females to the increased involvement of females in violent crime. The suggestion is that females are becoming the perpetrators in response to their own victimization. For example, researchers suggest that abused adolescent females are at increased risk of becoming violent juvenile offenders and that female offenders have been victimized in up to 70 percent of cases.

Such research supports the theory that violence perpetuates violence.

The Link between Violence and Later Violent Criminality

According to the American Psychological Association (p. 6): "Social forces such as prejudice, economic inequality, and attitudes toward violence in the mainstream American culture interact with the influences of early childhood to foster the expression of violence." The Association describes several developmental experiences that violent youths frequently share (p. 21):

> Youth at greatest risk of becoming extremely aggressive and violent tend to share common experiences that appear to place them on a "trajectory toward violence." These youth tend to have experienced weak bonding to caretakers in infancy and ineffective parenting techniques, including lack of supervision, inconsistent discipline, highly punitive or abusive treatment, and failure to reinforce positive, prosocial behavior. These developmental deficits, in turn, appear to lead to poor peer relations and high levels of aggressiveness.
>
> Additionally, these youth have learned attitudes accepting aggressive behavior as normative and as an effective way to solve interpersonal problems. Aggressive children tend to be rejected by their more conforming peers and do poorly in school, including a history of problems such as poor school attendance and numerous suspensions. These children often band together with others like themselves, forming deviant peer groups that reinforce antisocial behaviors. The more such children are exposed to violence in their homes, in their neighborhoods, and in the media, the greater their risk for aggressive and violent behaviors.

Conduct Disorder

A term that appears often in discussions about youth problems is **conduct disorder**—a "nice term for the anger exploding among more and more teenagers" (Hallinan, 1994, p. A9). The American Psychiatric Association states that this disorder is characterized by prolonged antisocial behavior and can range from truancy to fistfights. Hallinan cites formal surveys indicating that from 2 to 6 percent of American youths—between 1.3 and 3.8 million—have such a conduct disorder. As noted by Hallinan (p. A9): "Two influential studies—one in 1988 and one in 1991—concluded that conduct disorder is a lifelong disability for which there currently is no cure."

The American Psychiatric Association (1987, pp. 344–346) has also defined **antisocial personality disorder** as a disorder that exists in individuals age 18 or older, who show evidence of a conduct disorder before age 15 as well as a pattern of irresponsible and antisocial behavior since the age of 15. It occurs in about 3 percent of American males and less than 1 percent of American females. Table 6.3 lists the behaviors indicative of conduct disorders and irresponsible, antisocial behavior.

The Association asserts (p. 343): "In early adolescence these people characteristically use tobacco, alcohol, and other drugs and engage in voluntary sexual intercourse unusually early for their peer group. . . . Almost invariably there is a markedly impaired capacity to sustain lasting, close, warm, and responsible relationships with family, friends, or sexual partners." The Association lists the following predisposing factors:

- Attention deficit hyperactivity disorder and conduct disorder during prepuberty
- Absence of consistent parental discipline
- Abuse as a child
- Removal from the home
- Growing up without parental figures of both sexes

Table 6.3
Antisocial Personality
Disorder

A. Current age at least 18.

B. Evidence of conduct disorder with onset before age 15, as indicated by a history of *three* or more of the following:
    (1) was often truant
    (2) ran away from home overnight at least twice while living in parental or parental surrogate home (or once without returning)
    (3) often initiated physical fights
    (4) used a weapon in more than one fight
    (5) forced someone into sexual activity with him or her
    (6) was physically cruel to animals
    (7) was physically cruel to other people
    (8) deliberately destroyed others' property (other than by fire-setting)
    (9) deliberately engaged in fire-setting
    (10) often lied (other than to avoid physical or sexual abuse)
    (11) has stolen without confrontation of a victim on more than one occasion (including forgery)
    (12) has stolen with confrontation of a victim (e.g., mugging, purse-snatching, extortion, armed robbery)

C. A pattern of irresponsible and antisocial behavior since the age of 15, as indicated by at least *four* of the following:
    (1) is unable to sustain consistent work behavior, as indicated by any of the following (including similar behavior in academic setting if the person is a student):
        (a) significant unemployment for six months or more within five years
        (b) repeated absences from work unexplained by illness in self or family
        (c) abandonment of several jobs without realistic plans for others
    (2) fails to conform to social norms with respect to lawful behavior, as indicated by repeatedly performing antisocial acts that are grounds for arrest (whether arrested or not), e.g., destroying property, harassing others, stealing, pursuing an illegal occupation
    (3) is irritable and aggressive, as indicated by repeated physical fights or assaults (not required by one's job or to defend someone or oneself), including spouse- or child-beating
    (4) repeatedly fails to honor financial obligations, as indicated by defaulting on debts or failing to provide child support or support for other dependents on a regular basis
    (5) fails to plan ahead, or is impulsive, as indicated by one or both of the following:
        (a) traveling from place to place without a prearranged job or clear goal for the period of travel or clear idea about when the travel will terminate
        (b) lack of a fixed address for a month or more
    (6) has no regard for the truth, as indicated by repeated lying, use of aliases, or "conning" others for personal profit or pleasure
    (7) is reckless regarding his or her own or others' personal safety, as indicated by driving while intoxicated, or recurrent speeding
    (8) if a parent or guardian lacks ability to function as a responsible parent, as indicated by one or more of the following:
        (a) malnutrition of child
        (b) child's illness resulting from lack of minimal hygiene
        (c) failure to obtain medical care for a seriously ill child
        (d) child's dependence on neighbors or nonresident relatives for food or shelter
        (e) failure to arrange for a caretaker for young child when parent is away from home
        (f) repeated squandering, on personal items, of money required for household necessities
    (9) has never sustained a totally monogamous relationship for more than one year
    (10) lacks remorse (feels justified in having hurt, mistreated, or stolen from another)

D. Occurrence of antisocial behavior not exclusively during the course of schizophrenia or manic episodes

Source: American Psychiatric Association. *Diagnostic and Statistical Manual of Mental Disorders*, 4th ed. (Copyright 1994 American Psychiatric Association), pp. 344–346. Reprinted with permission.

Psychopathic or Sociopathic Behavior

Psychopathic or **sociopathic behavior** refers to chronic asocial behavior that is rooted in severe deficiencies in the development of a conscience.

The failure to develop feelings of guilt is usually attributed to the absence or neglect of a strong identification with stable parental figures, or to having parents who have problems with social values. The failure to develop a conscience begins with the use or exploitation of children by parents. The children are encouraged to carry out the parents' own forbidden impulses and wishes. This encourages children in their own antisocial behavior. Such patterns of behavior usually originate with an overly dominant mother and a child who believes in acting out maternal wishes. Psychopaths are remarkable for emotional blandness, particularly about actions that profoundly shock normal people.

> Psychopaths are virtually lacking in conscience. They do not know right from wrong.

They may, however, profess to recognize and speak smoothly about devotion to accepted values, and they can be charming in casual personal contacts. Psychopaths often make glib promises and resolutions. Meanwhile, they may be stealing from the person or company they work for, or from the person they are talking to at a particular time. They are profoundly egocentric and never see their own responsibility for anything that goes wrong. Although most psychopaths have normal intelligence, their thinking is essentially superficial. Despite an ability to learn, they do not profit by the lessons of their own experience, so their behavior is out of step with what they abstractly know. In fact they not only seem indifferent to the consequences for other people of what they do, but they do not seem concerned about the almost certain unfortunate consequences for themselves. They are incurably, unrealistically optimistic.

The Public Health Model and the Law Enforcement Perspective

One innovative approach to violence is to view it not just as a problem to be dealt with by the criminal justice system, but as a threat to our national health. When violence is viewed in this way, it makes sense to adopt the approach used in our public health system. A basic principle of the public health response to problems is to focus resources on the areas of greatest need.

> In viewing violence as a public health problem, practitioners have targeted "adolescent and young black males who live in the neighborhoods with the highest levels of violence" (Rosenfeld and Decker, 1993, p. 37).

All too often, however, as noted by Astroth (1994, p. 411):

> It is common today to hear that almost half of all young people between the ages of 10 and 17 are at risk of school failure, substance abuse, delinquency, and teenage pregnancy. Today's mythology that most or all youths are "at risk" scatters valuable resources and dilutes efforts to help the minority of youths who are genuinely troubled.

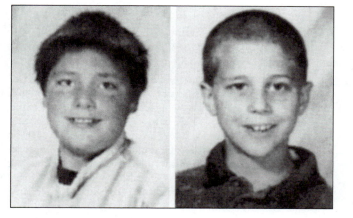

On March 24, 1998, 13-year-old Mitchell Johnson (left) and his 11-year-old cousin, Andrew Golden, allegedly lured their classmates outside their middle school in Jonesboro with a fire alarm and then began gunning them down. Four students and a teacher were killed and ten others were wounded.

Astroth argues: "U.S. teenagers today are, by nearly every important measure, *healthier, better educated, and more responsible* than teens of the past." They are, in fact, for the most part much healthier than the adults who label them "at risk." Astroth suggests that American adults are suffering from **ephebiphobia**—"a fear and loathing of adolescence" (p. 412). He notes that throughout history, adults have felt that youths were getting out of control. As far back as Socrates' day, adults bemoaned the behavior of their youths:

> The children now love luxury. They have bad manners, contempt for authority, they show disrespect for elders, love chatter in place of exercise. They no longer rise when their elders enter the room. They contradict their parents, chatter before company, gobble up their dainties at the table, cross their legs, and tyrannize over their teachers.—Socrates (500 B.C.)

Astroth (p. 412) concludes: "Unfortunately, the notion of 'youth at risk' has become a lens through which we view *all* young people, so that today adolescence is seen as some incurable social disease."

Another contribution from the public health model is the metaphor of **contagion** as a way to explain the spread of violence. As noted by Rosenfeld and Decker (p. 46):

> Violence is a "contagious" social process. Acts of violence tend, under certain circumstances, to spread rapidly within high-risk areas and groups. . . . Some analyses locate the source of high rates of violence in subcultures of violence that encourage people—young males in particular—to use physical force as a way of commanding respect and settling conflicts. Others view violence as spread through cycles of revenge and retaliation among perpetrators and victims linked to one another in "social and moral networks."

This second explanation of the rapid spread of violence as a kind of retaliation or self-help can be viewed as an indication that those who engage in violence have no faith in the system. They perceive that justice is not to be obtained through the system. This was vividly illustrated in the public's rush to buy guns following the Los Angeles riots resulting from the Rodney King verdict in 1992. A further consideration when discussing a public health approach to violence is how law enforcement views violence. According to Rosenfeld and Decker (pp. 45–46): "From the perspective of law enforcement, the single most important fact about the social reality of violence in our society: the persons at highest risk for violence—and therefore with the greatest need for prevention—are criminal offenders." They note the challenges facing those who try to deal with the violence problem:

> It is inherently difficult in our society, with its heavily armed population, traditions of self-protection, a popular culture saturated with violent images and examples—and a criminal justice system that institutionalizes violent retribution in the form of capital punishment—to shape sensible and effective anti-violence policies and programs. These barriers confront both public health and law enforcement responses to violence. An additional policy barrier, however, derives from the distinct intellectual traditions of the two approaches. Law enforcement is part of the classical tradition that conceives of human action as a product of rational and moral choice. Public health is rooted in positivist conceptions of human behavior as "caused" by external forces that, in principle, are subject to modification.

How these conflicting philosophies translate into programming for the prevention and treatment of delinquency is discussed in Section Four.

No matter what the influences are, the need to be proactive is apparent. Some, like Hall, advocate a hard-line approach (p. 6): "And what should be done with teen-aged criminals once they've acted? You noticed I said, 'criminals.' Not 'troubled youth,' 'wayward teens,' 'juvenile delinquents' or any other trendy, politically correct, sensitive euphemism of the moment." In answer to his own question, Hall replies: "[The] murder of four in Oregon [serves as] a reminder: continue treating young murderers and violent felons as adults." Others, like Reno, are more humanitarian (pp. 75–76): "People are beginning to understand the terrible, terrible problem we face. The youth population has been on its way down in the last several years and, at the same time, youth violence has been up. We are talking not only about saving children from going to jail but about saving their lives. . . . The youth population is going up in the next 10 to 15 years, and if we don't get a handle on the rise in youth violence now, we are in deep trouble."

The Coordinating Council on Juvenile Justice and Delinquency Prevention has drafted an *Action Plan,* which sets forth eight specific objectives for community action that are "designed to address and reduce the impact of juvenile violence and delinquency" (*Combating Violence*, 1996, pp. 2–13):

1. Provide immediate intervention and appropriate sanctions and treatment for delinquent juveniles.

2. Prosecute certain serious, violent, and chronic juvenile offenders in criminal court.

3. Reduce youth involvement with guns, drugs, and gangs.

4. Provide opportunities for children and youth.

5. Break the cycle of violence by addressing youth victimization, abuse, and neglect.

6. Strengthen and mobilize communities.

7. Support the development of innovative approaches to research and evaluation.

8. Implement an aggressive public outreach campaign on effective strategies to combat juvenile violence.

The Council's "Urgent Call to Action" is a fitting conclusion for this chapter, underscoring again the importance of family, school and community in addressing the problem of juvenile violence in collaboration with the juvenile justice system (p. 1):

> This Nation must take immediate and decisive action to intervene in the problem of juvenile violence that threatens the safety and security of communities—and the future of our children—across the country. Demographic experts predict that juvenile arrests for violent crimes will more than double by the year 2010, given population growth projections and trends in juvenile arrests over the past several decades.
>
> There is, however, reason for hope. . . . We can interrupt this escalation of violence based on identified positive and negative characteristics—protective and risk factors—that are present or lacking in communities, families, schools, peer groups, and individuals. These factors either equip a child with the capacity to become a healthy, productive individual or expose that child to potential involvement in crime and violence. Of equal importance, communities are learning that they can make dramatic changes in delinquency levels by taking steps that successfully reduce the risk factors and strengthen the protective factors in children's lives.

Summary

Researchers use three methods to measure the nature and extent of unlawful acts by juveniles: official data, self-report data and victim surveys. According to self-report studies, delinquency is almost universal. One reason is that status offenses are often included as acts of delinquency. Status offenses include actions such as violating curfew, habitual truancy, running away, incorrigibility, ungovernable conduct, being beyond the control of parents, being wayward, using tobacco and drugs and drinking alcohol. The most frequent delinquency offenses are property crimes, with larceny-theft being the most common.

Theories of the causes of juvenile delinquency include biological, behavioral, sociological and psychological theories. A major characteristic of juvenile delinquents is that they act out their inner conflicts. Some delinquency is rooted in psychopathic behavior. Psychopaths are virtually lacking in conscience and do not know right from wrong.

The public health model stresses targeting those most in need of help, specifically adolescent and young black males living in violent neighborhoods.

Discussion Questions

1. What are the most common status offenses in your community?
2. Were you ever stopped (or arrested) for a status offense when you were a juvenile? Did you know anyone who was? How did you feel?
3. Do other countries have status offenses?
4. Have there been any instances of youths involved in serious, violent crime in your community in the past year?
5. Do you believe that status offenders should be treated the same as youths involved in serious, violent crime?
6. When you think of juvenile delinquency and serious, violent crime, what comes to mind?
7. At what age does a juvenile become an adult in your state? Do you think the age is appropriate?

8. Is human development fixed more by biological inheritance or by life experiences?
9. Should parents and guardians be held legally responsible when a juvenile commits a violent crime? Why or why not?
10. For serious, violent crimes, such as armed robbery and murder, should the age of the offender even be an issue?

References

American Psychiatric Association. *Diagnostic and Statistical Manual of Mental Disorders,* 3rd ed. Washington, DC: American Psychiatric Association, 1987.

American Psychological Association. *Violence & Youth: Psychology's Response.* n.d.

Ash, Peter; Kellermann, Arthur L.; Fuqua-Whitley, Dawna; and Johnson, Amri. "Gun Acquisition and Use by Juvenile Offenders." *Journal of the American Medical Association,* Vol. 275, No. 22, June 12, 1996, pp. 1754–1758.

Astroth, Kirk A. "Beyond Ephebiphobia: Problem Adults or Problem Youths?" *Phi Delta Kappan,* January 1994, pp. 411–413.

Bilchik, Shay. "From the Administrator." In Barbara Tatem Kelley; David Huizinga; Terence P. Thornberry; and Rolf Loeber. *Epidemiology of Serious Violence.* OJJDP, Juvenile Justice Bulletin, June 1997, p. 1. (NCJ-165152)

Chesney-Lind, Meda and Shelden, Randall G. *Girls, Delinquency and Juvenile Justice,* 2nd ed. Belmont, CA: Wadsworth Publishing Company, 1998.

Combating Violence and Delinquency: The National Juvenile Justice Action Plan. Washington, DC: Coordinating Council on Juvenile Justice and Delinquency Prevention, March 1996. (NCJ-157105)

Crime in the United States 1996. Washington, DC: U.S. Department of Justice, Federal Bureau of Investigation, November 1997. (NCJ-167578)

Crowe, Timothy D. *Habitual Juvenile Offenders: Guidelines for Citizen Action and Public Responses.* Washington, DC: Office of Juvenile Justice and Delinquency Prevention, October 1991.

Doyle, Greg. "Juvenile Violence: Identifying the At-Risk Teenager." *Law and Order,* June 1996, pp. 90–92.

Eitzen, Stanley. "Problem Students: The Sociocultural Roots." *Phi Delta Kappan,* April 1992, pp. 584–590.

Faltermayer, Charlotte. "What Is Justice for a Sixth-Grade Killer?" *Time,* April 6, 1998, pp. 36–37.

Glueck, Sheldon and Glueck, Eleanor. *Unraveling Juvenile Delinquency.* Cambridge, MA: Harvard University Press, 1950.

Hall, Dennis. "Another Teen Killer Strikes; Time to Get Serious, America." *Police,* July 1998, p. 6.

Hallinan, Joe. "The Age of Rage." (Minneapolis/St. Paul) *Star Tribune,* May 9, 1994, p. A9.

"Harvard Study Reports No Change in Extent and Nature of College Students' Binge Drinking." *NCJA Justice Bulletin,* Vol. 18, No. 9, September 1998, pp. 13–14.

Kelley, Barbara Tatem; Huizinga, David; Thornberry, Terence P.; and Loeber, Rolf. *Epidemiology of Serious Violence.* OJJDP Juvenile Justice Bulletin, June 1997a. (NCJ-165152)

Kelley, Barbara Tatem; Loeber, Rolf; Keenan, Kate; and DeLamatre, Mary. *Developmental Pathways in Boys' Disruptive and Delinquent Behavior.* OJJDP Juvenile Justice Bulletin, December 1997b. (NCJ-165692)

Konopka, Gisela. *The Adolescent Girl in Conflict.* Englewood Cliffs, NJ: Prentice Hall, 1966.

Lamberg, Lynne. "Kids Who Kill: Nature Plus (Lack of) Nurture." *Journal of the American Medical Association,* Vol. 275, No. 22, June 12, 1996, pp. 1712–1713.

Loeber, R.; Wung, P.; Keenan, K.; Giroux, B.; Stouthamer-Loeber, M.; Van Kammen, W. B.; and Maughan, B. "Developmental Pathways in Disruptive Child Behavior." *Development and Psychopathology,* Vol. 5, 1993, pp. 103–133.

Martin, Deirdre. "Teen Violence: Why It's on the Rise and How to Stem Its Tide." *Law Enforcement Technology,* January 1994, pp. 36–42.

National Coalition of State Juvenile Justice Advisory Groups. *Myths and Realities: Meeting the Challenge of Serious, Violent, and Chronic Juvenile Offenders, 1992 Annual Report.* Washington, DC, 1993.

Perkins, Craig A. *Age Patterns of Victims of Serious Violent Crime.* Washington, DC: Bureau of Justice Statistics Special Report, September 1997. (NCJ-162031)

Peters, Sheila R. and Peters, Sharon D. "Violent Adolescent Females." *Corrections Today,* June 1998, pp. 28–29.

Regnery, Alfred S. "Getting Away with Murder: Why the Juvenile Justice System Needs an Overhaul." In *Taking Sides: Clashing Views on Controversial Issues in Crime and Criminology,* 2nd rev. ed., edited by Richard C. Monk. Guilford, CT: Dushkin Publishing Group, Inc., 1991, pp. 164–170.

Reno, Janet. "Taking America Back for Our Children." *Crime and Delinquency,* Vol. 44, No. 1, January 1998, pp. 75–82.

Rosenfeld, Richard and Decker, Scott. "Where Public Health and Law Enforcement Meet: Monitoring and Preventing Youth Violence." *American Journal of Police,* Vol. 12, No. 3, 1993, pp. 11–57.

Sharp, Arthur G. "Juvenile Crime." *Law and Order,* March 1998, pp. 109–116.

Shea, Cay. "A Current Look at the Chronic/Serious Juvenile Offender in Minnesota." Seminar presented at Minneapolis, MN, October 1987.

Sickmund, Melissa; Snyder, Howard N.; and Poe-Yamagata, Eileen. *Juvenile Offenders and Victims: 1997 Update on Violence.* Washington, DC: Office of Juvenile Justice and Delinquency Prevention, August 1997. (NCJ-165703)

Siegel, Larry J. and Senna, Joseph J. *Juvenile Delinquency,* 6th ed. St. Paul, MN: West Publishing Company, 1997.

Snyder, Howard N. *Juvenile Arrests 1996.* OJJDP, Juvenile Justice Bulletin, November 1997. (NCJ-167578)

Sprinthall, Norman A. and Collins, W. Andrew. *Adolescent Psychology: A Developmental View.* New York: Random House, 1984.

"What They are Saying." *Law Enforcement News,* September 15, 1996, p. 1.

Wilson, James Q. "Thinking about Crime." *The Atlantic Monthly,* September 1983, p. 86.

Wilson, James Q. and Kelling, George L. "The Police and Neighborhood Safety: Broken Windows." *The Atlantic Monthly,* March 1982, pp. 29–38.

Witkin, Gordon. "Kids Who Kill." *U.S. News and World Report,* April 8, 1991, pp. 26–32. Reprinted in *Annual Editions: Criminal Justice 92/93,* 16th ed., edited by John J. Sullivan and Joseph L. Victor. Guilford, CT: Dushkin Publishing Group, Inc., 1992, pp. 181–185.

Chapter

7

Youths Who Are Gang Members

Street gangs prey upon their neighborhood much like a malignant growth which continues to spread through its host until only a wasted shell remains.

—Los Angeles White Paper

Do You Know

- What the difference is between a gang, a street gang and a youth gang?
- What separates a gang from a club?
- Where street gangs may be found?
- How street gangs acquire their power?
- What basic functions are served by youth gangs?
- What are some causes of gangs?
- How contemporary gangs can be classified?
- What the most common gangs are?
- What two well-known black street gangs are called?
- What characteristics distinguish youth gangs?
- How gangs are typically structured?
- How gang members can be identified?
- How gang members communicate?
- What purpose is served by graffiti?
- What activities gangs typically engage in?
- What might indicate gang activity?

Can You Define

conflict gang, corporate gang, crew, criminal gang, expressive violence, gang, graffiti, hedonistic gang, instrumental gang, instrumental violence, moniker, predatory gang, representing, retreatist gang, scavenger gang, socialized delinquency, street gang, tagging, territorial gang, turf, youth gang

INTRODUCTION

Youth gangs are an increasing problem for the juvenile justice system. According to the Bureau of Justice Assistance (BJA) (*Addressing Community*, 1998, p. 3):

Contemporary gangs—variously known as youth, delinquent, street, or criminal gangs—have become a widespread threat to communities throughout the Nation. Once considered largely an urban phenomenon, gangs have increasingly emerged in smaller communities, presenting a challenge that severely strains local resources.

McCorkle and Miethe (1998, p. 41) note: "The past decade has witnessed increasing concern about street gangs and their role in violent crime and drug trafficking." McCort (1996, p. 33) adds: "Over the past 15 years, street gangs have undergone a swift and dramatic change that has had a significant impact upon America. The problem that was once restricted to large cities is now shared by small suburban and rural communities as well. These gangs have become a driving influence on violent crime, drug trafficking and community stability. All segments of American society are affected in terms of crime, safety, community image and quality of life." According to Wexler (1997, p. 28): "Thirty years ago, only 23 American cities reported gang activity. Today, the number has risen to more than 700 cities nationwide."

Surveys of criminal justice professionals across the country confirm that the problem of gangs is not an isolated one. A *Police* magazine survey of law enforcement administrators reports (Hall, 1998, p. 72): "Drugs—and the crime often associated with street narcotic activity—was cited more often as a 'problem' than anything else—in both small and medium-sized towns, cities and in the heartland. . . . Close behind drugs as a named problem and cited on a quarter of all surveys and in phone interviews were gangs and youth violence." Another national survey shows that over 80 percent of prosecutors in large cities affirm that gangs are a problem in their jurisdictions, that gang numbers are rising, and that the levels of "gang-related" violence are also increasing (Johnson et al., 1995).

This chapter examines the gang phenomenon, beginning with current definitions used regarding gangs. A brief history of gangs in the United States is presented, followed by a description of the current scope of the gang problem and a discussion of the theories about why youths join gangs. Next is a close-up look at gangs and gang membership, including the various types of gangs and the characteristics of the gang subculture. The chapter concludes with a look at the criminal activities of gangs, the relationship between gangs and drugs and some common myths about gangs.

Definitions

It has been noted that: "The media, the public, and community agencies use the term 'gang' more loosely than the law enforcement community. . . . The public's definition of a gang describes a group of individuals—mostly inner-city youth—who are highly organized, heavily involved in the drug trade, and very dangerous" (*Addressing Community*, p. 9). Clear (1997, p. xii) points out: "The subject of gangs . . . is complicated by social class, economics, ethnic loyalty, and political policy. The term gang cannot be taken to mean any one social phenomenon but instead refers to a multiplicity of experiences, motives, and patterns by which youth assemble and claim an identity."

According to a Los Angeles White Paper, the following definition is accepted by law enforcement: "A gang is any group gathered together on a continuing basis to commit antisocial behavior." Jackson and McBride (1985, p. 20) offer one of the most functional definitions of a **gang:**

> "A gang is a group of people that form an allegiance for a common purpose, and engage in unlawful or criminal activity."

The Minnesota statute defining a gang is typical of many states:

Criminal gang means any ongoing organization, association, or group of three or more persons, whether formal or informal, that:

- Has, as one of its primary activities, the commission of one or more of the offenses listed in section . . .
- Has a common name or common identifying sign or symbol; and
- Includes members who individually or collectively engage in or have engaged in a pattern of criminal activity.

The Minnesota statute also provides that if a gang member commits a felony, the sentence is to be three years longer than the statutory maximum for that crime.

> A **street gang** is a group of individuals who meet over time, have identifiable leadership, claim control over a specific territory in the community and engage in criminal behavior.

Dart (1992, p. 96) suggests that street gangs are associations of individuals with the following characteristics in varying degrees:

- A gang name and recognizable symbols
- A geographic territory
- A regular meeting pattern
- An organized, continuous course of criminality

> Criminal behavior is what separates a gang from a club such as the Boy Scouts.

Street gangs engage in criminal activity either individually or collectively. They create an atmosphere of fear and intimidation in a community. The term *street gang* is preferred by most local law enforcement agencies because it "includes juveniles and adults and designates the location of the gang and most of its criminal behavior."

> The **youth gang** is a subset of the street gang.

Huff (1993, p. 4) gives the following definition of a youth gang:

> A collectivity consisting primarily of adolescents and young adults who (a) interact frequently with one another; (b) are frequently and deliberately involved in illegal activities; (c) share a common collective identity that is usually, but not always, expressed through a gang name; and (d) typically express that identity by adopting certain symbols and/or claiming control over certain "turf" (persons, places, things, and/or economic markets).

Spergel et al. (1990, p. 3) suggest:

> The notion of *youth gang* incorporates two concepts: often a more amorphous "delinquent group" (e.g., a juvenile clique within a gang), and the better organized and sophisticated "criminal organization." The latter may be an independent group or clique of the gang and usually comprises older youth and young adults primarily engaged in criminal income-producing activity, most commonly drug trafficking.

An important distinction must be made between youth gangs and delinquent groups. In *Addressing Community Gang Problems,* the BJA (p. 10) states: "One way to distinguish between the two is to compare gang behavior with delinquent-group behavior. Research has shown that gang members engage in significantly more criminal behavior than members of delinquent groups; they have higher rates of police contact, more arrests, and more drug-related offenses. Moreover, gang membership tends to inhibit what is known as the 'maturational effect.' Most youth become less likely to engage in further criminal behavior as they grow older; this is not the case with gang members." The *Encyclopedia of Crime and Justice* (Kadish, 1983, p. 1673) states:

> Youth gangs are self-formed associations of youths distinguished from other types of youth groups by their routine participation in illegal activities. They differ from other types of law-violating youth groups by manifesting better-developed leadership, greater formalization, more clearly defined identification with localities or enterprises, and a greater degree of deliberate intent in the conduct of crimes.

A Brief History of Gangs in the United States

Gangs and gang violence are an integral part of American history. Organized groups for crime and antisocial behavior go back to colonial times when John Hancock (the largest signature on the Declaration of Independence) amassed a fortune as an entrepreneur smuggling goods with his organized group. As noted by Gates and Jackson (1990, p. 20): "Young people of similar ethnic or social interests have banded together into gangs since the birth of our nation."

Street gangs have operated in the United States since the 1820s. Irish Americans in New York City organized the Forty Thieves, which murdered, robbed and mugged. These gang members came from areas of overcrowded, substandard housing, poor or nonexistent health care, broken homes and few opportunities to improve their situation. The 1800s also had rural gangsters such as Jesse and Frank James. The 1920s and 1930s saw the rise of criminal syndicates, the Mafia or Cosa Nostra, and notorious gangsters such as John Dillinger, Machine Gun Kelly, Pretty Boy Floyd, Bonnie Parker and Clyde Barrow, George "Baby Face" Nelson and

Ma Barker and her son, Fred. These predecessors of today's gangs relied heavily on extortion, intimidation, robbery and violence to gain power and wealth.

Shelden et al. (1997, pp. 7–9) discuss the origin and evolution of certain gangs, such as Los Angeles gangs:

> The economic boom of the 1920s helped bring thousands of Mexican immigrants to the area. These Mexicans were primarily rural and poor and brought with them a tradition known as *palomilla* (in Spanish this means a covey of doves) in which a number of young men in a village would group together in a coming-of-age cohort. In the Los Angeles area these young men began to identify with a particular neighborhood or parish during the 1920s and 1930s. These groups . . . were to be the forerunners of the modern Chicano gangs of East Los Angeles. . . .
>
> In the Southern California area during the Depression thousands of Mexican immigrants were repatriated and deported. This process had a very negative effect on the Mexican-American population, with many feeling that they were unwanted. Racist policies and widespread discrimination set in, culminating with the famous Zoot Suit riots of 1943. About the same time a death at a party in East Los Angeles resulted in sensational press coverage (which included stereotypic descriptions of Chicano gangs). The police arrested 22 gang members for conspiracy to commit murder, resulting in 12 convictions. Also, police began to engage in periodic sweeps within gangs' areas. These two events, more than any others, helped bring youths closer together and transformed informal youth groupings . . . into gangs. . . .
>
> The origins of African-American gangs in Southern California are similar to those of the Chicano gangs, even though they emerged a generation later. The most popular of these gangs are the Bloods and the Crips and their various offshoots (called sets). Like their Mexican counterparts, African-Americans came from rural areas (mostly the rural South). . . . Their traditional way of life in the South was mostly church-based with close family ties. . . . By the late 1960s these African-American youths . . . "found themselves alienated from the old rural values that had sustained their parents. They were racially locked out of the dominant Anglo culture and, in most cases, economically locked out of the African-American middle class. . ." (Reiner, 1992:5).
>
> The Watts riots of 1965 did for African-American gangs roughly what the Zoot Suit riots did for Chicano gangs. One result of the Watts riots was that young African-Americans were seen in a more negative light by the media and by the rest of society. Also, African-American youth began to see themselves differently.

For nearly as long as gangs have existed, researchers have studied gangs in search of understanding and solutions on how to best handle them. The BJA states (p. 19): "The most influential study of gangs in the early part of this century was Thrasher's *The Gang*, published in 1927. Thrasher identified 1,313 different gangs in Chicago and provided the foundation for generations of researchers concerned with the gang phenomenon. Thrasher's study was the first truly sociological analysis that did more than simply describe the gang problem. He addressed some of the social-psychological issues that prompt individuals to join gangs, such as the quest for adventure." The reasons why youths join gangs are discussed in greater detail shortly.

Despite all the research on gangs, how and why they form, and ensuing attempts to prevent or break down such associations, youths today continue to join gangs, and the problems of gangs have spread to nearly every corner of the United States.

Table 7.1	State	Gang Members
Top Ten States in Terms of Gang Membership	California	254,618
	Illinois	75,226
	Texas	57,060
	Ohio	17,025
	Indiana	17,005
	New Mexico	16,910
	Arizona	16,291
	Florida	15,247
	Nevada	12,525
	Minnesota	12,382

Source: Al Valdez. "Gangs: Migration or Imitation?" *Police*, January 1998, p. 49. Reprinted by permission.

Current Scope of the Gang Problem

Street gangs now exist across the country. From their beginnings on the East Coast, they have flourished in California, particularly the Los Angeles area, Chicago and other major U.S. cities. Valdez (1998a, p. 49) notes that California leads the nation with 254,618 gang members. Table 7.1 ranks the top ten states in the country in gang membership.

Howell (1998, p. 1) notes a rapid proliferation of youth gangs in the United States from 1980 to the mid-1990s. In 1980 an estimated 286 jurisdictions reported a total of more than 2,000 gangs and almost 100,000 members (Miller, 1992). In 1996, however, nearly 4,800 jurisdictions reported the presence of more than 31,000 gangs and approximately 846,000 gang members (Moore and Terrett, in press). A survey by the OJJDP's National Youth Gang Center found that, of the more than 2,000 law enforcement agencies reporting gang activity in their jurisdictions, 49 percent described their gang activity as 'getting worse'" (Burch and Chemers, 1997, p. 1).

> Street gangs can be found throughout the United States, not only in large cities, but also in the suburbs, small towns and even rural areas.

The Los Angeles and Chicago gangs have invaded other previously untouched areas of the country. As noted by Taylor (1991, p. 103): "The increase and spread of youth gangs in today's United States constitute a movement that must be recognized and understood. Gangs can no longer be defined in traditional, preconceived terms. Social and economic factors have redefined them, and their imperialistic spread is a multidimensional movement."

Miller (1991, p. 263) suggests: "Youth gangs in the 1980s and 1990s are more numerous, more prevalent, and more violent than in the 1950s, probably more so than at any time in the country's history." They are no longer confined to the two coasts and Chicago, but can be found in most major cities in the United States as well as in small towns and even rural areas. Among the attractions of the smaller towns are less competition from other gangs for the drug market and less rivalry and violence from such competition, resulting in more money and more power. Often the police presence is less also. Valdez (1998a, pp. 48–49) notes: "Gangs move within a city or town, from city to city, from county to county and from state to state for a variety of reasons":

- Family
- Divorce and separation
- Parole and probation
- Drug sales
- Search for a better life
- School expulsion
- Forced relocation
- Gang alliances
- Military

According to Howell (1998, p. 2), the typical age range of youth gang members is 12 to 24, and the average age of gang members is between 17 and 18 years, although this average "tends to be older in cities in which gangs have been in existence longer, like Chicago and Los Angeles." Furthermore: "Although younger members are becoming more common, it is the older membership that has increased the most." Blacks and Hispanics together make up over 87 percent of the gang populations, far in excess of their representation in the general population (National Institute of Justice, 1992, p. 18). Many gangs are involved in serious crimes. The rate of violent offenses for gang members is three times as high as for nongang delinquents.

Owens and Wells (1993, p. 25) write that: "According to the FBI, the Crips and the Bloods have now spread to more than 100 cities and count more than 40,000 members." Further, according to Dart (p. 96):

> Violence perpetrated by street gangs is a principal—if not the major—social affliction affecting American communities today. In the last decade of the 20th century, gangs exist in virtually every community—suburban, as well as inner-city—in every metropolitan area. Rather than seeking socially acceptable means of achieving influence, gangs use violence, harassment, intimidation, extortion, and fear to control a neighborhood.

A report on the IACP Summit on violent crime in America describes the current gang problem as being partially responsible for the rise in violent crime (International Association of Chiefs of Police, 1993, p. 61):

> The rise of gangs has fueled much of the increase in violent crime. What were once loosely knit groups of juveniles and young adults involved in petty crimes have become powerful, organized gangs. There appear to be gangs intent on controlling lucrative drug trade through intimidation and murder, and also street gangs simply claiming "turf." Today, as never before, cities and neighborhoods, even those without long histories of youth gang activity, have been literally overrun by both types of gang violence. While gangs are not new, today's level of gang violence, organization, and sophistication is unprecedented.

The problem of gangs has escalated, in part, because of the easy availability of guns. Gates and Jackson (p. 20) suggest: "The knives, clubs and occasional firearms once used by gang members have given way to semi- and fully automatic assault rifles—with devastating results." They also note: "Gang members are attacking peace officers at an alarming rate." For example, in Minneapolis, on September 25, 1992, veteran patrol officer Jerome Haaf was shot in the back in an act attributed to a street gang (the Vice Lords) who wanted to assassinate a police officer.

Street gangs acquire their power in the community through their violent behavior.

Gang members are, in their own way, quite conservative, often believing in capital punishment. They know that if one of their gang members is killed, the likelihood of the killer being apprehended, let alone sufficiently punished, is very slim. Hence, they are likely to take vengeance into their own hands, resulting in the all-too-common gang shootings. Part of the reason for such violence is that gang members have little faith that "the system" will provide justice for the murdered gang member.

Law Enforcement News, in "Getting a Grip on Slippery Gang Problems" (1993, p. 13), states: "Today's gangs exhibit a propensity for committing violent acts without remorse or regard for innocent bystanders, who are blithely referred to as 'mushrooms' in gang parlance." Another way to view the seriousness of the problem is to see it through the words of a Los Angeles gang member (Shakur, 1993, pp. 69–70):

> I was six years old when the Crips were started. No one anticipated its sweep. The youth of South Central were being gobbled up by an alien power threatening to attach itself to a multitude of other problems already plaguing them. An almost "enemy" subculture had arisen, and no one knew from where it came. No one took its conception seriously. But slowly it crept, saturating entire households, city blocks, neighborhoods, and eventually the nation-state of California.
>
> Today, no school, library, institution, business, detention center, or church is exempt from being touched in some way by the gang activity in South Central. Per year, the gangs in South Central recruit more people than the four branches of the U.S. Armed Forces do. Crack dealers employ more people in South Central than AT&T, IBM, and Xerox combined. And South Central is under more aerial surveillance than Belfast, Ireland. Everyone is armed, frustrated, suppressed, and on the brink of explosion.

Causes of Gangs and Why Youths Join Them

Two separate yet very related questions are: (1) What causes gangs? and (2) Why do youths continue to join gangs? Myriad studies have identified causes for gangs and what attracts kids to join them. "In a gang," says Dart (p. 96), "troubled youths find the fellowship and sense of identity they lack; participation in gang activities leads to acceptance." This was also the conclusion of the National Coalition of State Juvenile Justice Advisory Groups (1993, p. 19): "Gangs seem to fill a desperate need on the part of many urban youths for stability, structure and a sense of belonging, and there is a major correlation between neighborhood poverty and social disorganization and gang activity."

Street gangs offer their members a feeling of belonging as well as protection from other youths. They may also provide financial power.

The National School Safety Center (1988, p. 2) notes:

> Youth gangs are not a new phenomenon in America. Philadelphians convened in 1791 to decide how to deal with bands of young people disrupting that city, and officials in New York City admitted to having gang problems as early as 1825. Over the years, many other urban areas have experienced the unrest resulting from gangs of young people banding together for a variety of reasons. Such youths may just want to occupy time, fill an emptiness in their lives or experience a sense of belonging. Whatever the reason, when a gang evolves, communities almost always suffer serious consequences.

Gangs form as the result of many personal, social and economic factors, including family structure and influences such as parental guidance and lack of responsibility, peer pressure and ego fulfillment, racism and cultural discord, socioeconomic factors and a phenomenon known as socialized delinquency. Table 7.2 summarizes the prevailing theories about why gangs exist.

Gangs may result from a variety of personal, social and economic factors, including family structure and influences such as parental guidance and lack of responsibility, peer pressure and ego fulfillment, racism and cultural discord, socioeconomic factors and socialized delinquency.

These combined factors may be pictured as spokes in a wheel. The more spokes, the stronger the wheel. The gang member's family unit is the hub of the wheel, supporting the rest.

Family Structure

Probably the most important factor in the formation of a gang member is family structure. Shelden et al. (p. 58) state:

> Nearly every criminologist agrees that the family is probably the most critical factor related to crime and delinquency. In fact, for over 50 years research has shown that three or four family-related factors best distinguish the habitual delinquent from the rest of his or her peers. These factors include the affection of the parents towards the child (the lower the level of affection, the higher the rate of delinquency), the kind of discipline the parents use (those who use consistently harsh and physical discipline will produce the most habitual and violent delinquent), the prolonged absence of one or both parents (those from single-parent households are more likely to become delinquent), and the degree of supervision provided by the parents (the lesser the amount of supervision, the higher the rate of delinquency).

Chapter 4 discussed the importance of families in developing children's feelings of belonging and self-worth. If youths do not get this support at home or at school, they will seek it elsewhere. The largest draw a gang has for its young members is a sense of belonging, of importance, of family.

Investigators have found certain common threads running through most families that have hard-core gang members. A family containing gang members is quite often a racial minority on some form of government assistance. It often lacks a male authority figure. If a male authority figure is present, he may be a criminal or drug addict, therefore representing a negative role model. Typically, adult family members lack more than an elementary school education. Children live with minimal adult supervision.

Table 7.2 **Theories of Why Gangs Exist**	Theory/Creator or Major Proponent	Premise
	Social Disorganization Theory/Thrasher	Industrialization, urbanization and immigration break down institutional, community-based controls in certain areas. Local institutions in these areas (schools, families, churches) are too weak to give the people living there a "sense of community." Consequently, within such environments, conventional values are replaced by a subculture of criminal values and traditions that persist over time, regardless of who moves into or out of the area.
	Strain Theory/Merton	The lack of integration between culturally defined goals (professional success, wealth and status) and the legitimate, institutionalized means of achieving these goals imposes a strain on people, who may, as a result, react with deviant, criminal behavior. Thus, people at an economic disadvantage are motivated to engage in illegitimate activities (perhaps because of the unavailability of jobs, lack of job skills, education, and other factors).
	Cultural-Deviance (Subcultural) Theory/Cohen	Working-class youth are ill-prepared for participation in middle-class institutions and thus become frustrated. This situation leads to reaction formation, which, in turn, fosters the development of a delinquent (gang) subculture, in which the values of middle-class society are turned upside down. These values enable youth to gain status and improved financial standing through non-utilitarian, malicious, negative behavior.
	Social Learning Theory/Sutherland	Youth become delinquent through association with other delinquents and also through contact with social values, beliefs and attitudes that support criminal/delinquent behavior.
	Social Bond (Control) Theory/Hirschi	Youths drift into gangs because of the limbo-like nature of adolescence—being suspended between childhood and adulthood, having greater expectations placed on them than when they were children, yet lacking the rights and privileges of adults. Proper socialization is essential at this critical juncture, which effectively "bonds" youth to society. What keeps people "in check" and away from deviant behavior is the social bond to society, especially the internalized norms of society.
	Social Development Theory	Integrates social learning theory with control/bonding theory. The major cause of delinquency is a lack of bonding to family, school and prosocial peer groups coupled with the reinforcement of delinquent behavior. Looks at 17 risk factors (societal/cultural and individual/interpersonal) present before the onset of delinquency to determine whether, and to what extent, one is likely to become involved in persistent delinquent activity.
	Labeling Perspective	Youths who are simply "hanging out" together may be referred to as a gang often enough that they come to feel as if they are a gang.
	Critical/Marxist Perspectives	The capitalist political and economic system produces inequality. Those oppressed by capitalism engage in various types of crimes related to accommodation and resistance (predatory crime, personal crime) in an attempt to adapt to their disadvantaged positions and to resist the problems created by capitalist institutions.

Source: Adapted from Randall G. Shelden et al. *Youth Gangs in American Society.* Belmont, CA: Wadsworth Publishing Company, 1997, pp. 28–49. Reprinted by permission.

Youths in Brooklyn, New York, play with toy guns as a prelude to becoming gang members, when real guns will replace these toys.

When a child first encounters law enforcement authorities, the dominant figure (usually the mother) makes excuses for the child, normally in the form of accusations against society. Thus children are taught early that they are not responsible for their actions and are shown how to transfer blame to society.

A second common type of family structure is one that may have two strong family leaders in a mother and father. Usually graduates from gangs themselves, they see little wrong with their children belonging to gangs. This attitude serves to perpetuate the traditional gang culture.

A third common family structure involves immigrant groups and parents who do not speak English. The children tend to adapt rapidly to the American way of life and, en route, lose respect for their parents and the "old ways" of their native culture. They quickly become experts at manipulating their parents, and the parents lose all control. This family structure is often seen with Asian gang members.

It is important to recognize that many of these family structures overlap.

Peer Pressure and Ego Fulfillment

A natural part of adolescence is a shift from seeking the approval and acceptance of parents and teachers to seeking the approval and acceptance of one's peers. When a child's family has never been a true source of approval or acceptance, as is the case with many gang-members-to-be, the need for acceptance by peers is that much stronger. Consequently, the lure of the gang may be nearly irresistible, and the transition into gang life may occur more readily for these youths.

For some kids the "prestige" and recognition that come with gang affiliation fulfill an egotistic need that they cannot achieve through other, more mainstream, associations. They may see themselves as rebels, "gangstas," who belong with the "bad boys," and the sense of danger and adventure inherent in gang activity satisfies a need to take risks. In fact biochemical research has shown that certain people thrive on the adrenaline rush that accompanies fear and risk-taking, and some postulate that youths who are drawn to gangs may have a biological/chemical makeup that drives them to seek dangerous liaisons.

*Racism and
Cultural Discord*

Racism played an early and important role in the formation of street gangs in California. The races did not mix. Black gangs were, and still are, totally black. White gangs tend to include whites only. Hispanic gangs may allow a sprinkling of blacks or whites to join.

Racism often results in a particular group banding together, lending support to one another and excluding all other groups, sometimes even seeking to harm members of other groups. Although racism is most often associated with white people showing prejudice against nonwhites, in reality racism refers to the belief that one's own ethnic group is superior to all others. Walker et al. (1996, p. 55) clarify the role of racism in gang formation: "Most gangs are racially and ethnically homogenous. . . . Although violent conflicts do occur between and within ethnic gangs, violence is seldom the reason for gang formation. Racism as a societal phenomenon that creates oppressive conditions can contribute to gang formation. However, individual racism explains very little in terms of the formation of gangs or the decision to join gangs." They also mention neo-Nazi, or skinhead, gangs as a notable exception, with gang formation almost exclusively a function of individual racism.

Typically when blacks or Hispanics move into a predominantly white neighborhood, the minority ethnic members will band together for support. As Walker et al. (p. 54) state: "Most ethnic gangs reflect a mixture of their members' culture of origin and the American 'host' culture; indeed, many gangs form as the result of clash between the two cultures." This happens not only in the cities, but also in the suburbs, and not only within neighborhoods, but within schools. As noted by Spergel (1990, p. 171): "Youth gangs tend to develop during times of rapid social change and political instability. They function as a residual social institution when other institutions fail and provide a certain degree of order and solidarity for their members." Spergel also suggests:

> Race or ethnicity and social isolation interact with poverty and community disorganization to account for much of the gang problem. The gang is an important social institution for low-income male youths and young adults from newcomer and residual populations because it often serves social, cultural, and economic functions no longer adequately performed by the family, the school and the labor market.

*Socioeconomic
Pressure*

To some members, the gang is all about money and power. According to Sgt. Jackson of the Los Angeles Police Department gang unit: "Their goal is money. That's the most important thing in the mind of a gang member. He wants power, prestige, a chance to get out of the ghetto—and this all revolves around money. For him, that means selling drugs" (McGarvey, 1991, p. 27).

Huff (1989, p. 527) states that poverty and unemployment are often equated with gang membership and notes that youth who do not have "legitimate options" for buying stylish clothes or flashy cars may see gangs, crime and selling drugs as attractive alternatives. Such a perspective is supported by both the strain and cultural-deviance theories described in Table 7.2.

Clear (p. xii) states: "Even though young people from every social class get together in thrill-seeking groups, it is poverty—often abject poverty—that can convert an ordinary part of growing up into a volatile social problem." Particularly vulnerable to such socioeconomic pressure and poverty are immigrant groups; this has been the case in the United States for many years. For example Mexicans immigrating to California in the early part of the twentieth century were looked on as a source of unskilled, cheap labor. They were relegated to barrios, neighborhoods comprised almost entirely of Hispanic populations and reinforced by a continuous flow of immigrants. Before long competition for jobs between the growing immigrant population and native Californians led to hatred and rivalries between the groups. Rivalries grew into neighborhood disputes. The same set of circumstances led to the formation of street gangs of African and Asian ancestry.

In a pioneering work on gangs—*The Gang: A Study of 1,313 Gangs in Chicago* (1927)—Thrasher concluded that gangs resulted from a breakdown in social controls, particularly among newly arriving immigrants who settled in Chicago's ganglands. Gangs created a social order where none existed. This can be a partial explanation for why so many Asian gangs are currently forming across the country.

Socialized Delinquency

Socialized delinquency is common among lower-class children who have been frustrated or hurt by a predominantly middle-class society. To youths socialized delinquency is not delinquency at all. It is delinquency only in terms of middle-class standards. When individuals behave in ways that are sanctioned by the culture they belong to—the gang—they feel no guilt for their unlawful activities. The gang, in effect, becomes a surrogate family. Within this family, violence toward others is common. One reason for this is that gang members were often neglected or abused as children.

A tragic example of socialized delinquency is that of Chicagoan Robert Sandifer, nicknamed "Yummy" because of his love of food. At age 11 he stood accused of killing a 14-year-old neighbor. It is speculated that because Yummy became the focus of an extensive manhunt, he was killed by his own gang members: "Neglected and abused by his family, bounced from group homes to squad cars, and killed, police say, by his own street gang, Robert was buried Wednesday, a symbol of the nation's most troubled children" ("Slain Boy," 1994, p. A7).

Other Reasons Why Gangs Form

Huff (1989, pp. 526–527) undertook a two-year study of youth gangs in Ohio (Cleveland and Columbus) and found that these gangs originated in three ways:

1. Breakdancing/"rappin" groups evolved into gangs as a result of intergroup conflict involving dancing, skating, and/or "rappin" competition.

2. Street corner groups similarly evolved into gangs as a result of conflicts with other "corner groups."

3. Street gang leaders already experienced in gang life moved to Ohio from Chicago or Los Angeles. These more sophisticated leaders were often charismatic figures who were able to quickly recruit a following from among local youth.

Jankowski (1990) proposes that most gang members join gangs for one or more of the following reasons:

1. Material reasons—the gang is not only a steady source of income but also a financial security system for members' families.

2. Recreation—the gang provides a source of entertainment, as well as drugs and alcohol. However, most gangs frown on members becoming chemically dependent because it makes them less reliable to the organization.

3. A place of refuge and camouflage—provides cover from the law and the protection of group identity.

4. Physical protection—a "strength in numbers" philosophy. The gang provides protection from predators and other dangers that exist in low-income communities.

5. A time to resist—gives gang members the chance to resist becoming like their parents, who are often trapped in dead-end jobs or unemployed.

6. Commitment to community—a sort of local patriotism, prevalent in communities where gangs have existed for many generations. Often parents belonged, or still belong to, a community gang, and the children are carrying on the tradition.

Types of Gangs

Contemporary gangs can usually be classified as one of three types. The following description of these three types of gangs is adapted, in part, from Taylor (pp. 105–109).

Contemporary gangs may be classified as scavenger, territorial or corporate.

Scavenger Gangs

Members of a **scavenger gang** often have no common bond beyond their impulsive behavior and the need to belong. Leadership changes weekly, even daily sometimes. They are urban survivors who prey on the weak of the inner city. Their crimes are usually petty, senseless and spontaneous. They often commit acts of violence just for fun. They have no particular goals, no purpose and no substantial camaraderies. Generally scavenger gang members are characteristically low achievers and illiterates with short attention spans. They are prone to violent, erratic behavior, and most come from the lower class and the underclass.

Territorial Gangs

A **territorial gang, crew** or individual designates something, someplace or someone as belonging exclusively to the gang. The traditional designation of a gang's territory is better known as **turf.**

Once scavenger gangs get serious about organizing, they become territorial gangs. At this stage the gang defines itself and someone assumes leadership. Gangs defend their turf in order to protect their particular business. Mobility through financial power has greatly enhanced the traditional definition of territory and turf. Prior to the windfall of illegal drug profits, the concept of *territory* was confined to the immediate neighborhood. However, today, with the power of organized crime, technology and increased financial leverage, a gang's territory can be intrastate, interstate or even international.

Organized/Corporate Gangs

These well-organized groups are characterized by having very strong leaders or managers. The primary focus of a **corporate gang** is participation in illegal moneymaking operations. Discipline is akin to that of the military, and goals resemble those of Fortune 500 corporations.

These organized/corporate gangs may have ties throughout the country, and, according to Saccente (1993, p28): "Since street gangs accumulate large sums of money, they must utilize legitimate businesses, financial institutions, family members, lawyers and other professions to process and hide their assets." He notes that viewing gangs as criminal organizations allows law enforcement to use the antiracketeering laws found in RICO statutes.

RICO (Racketeer Influenced and Corrupt Organization Act) was an important measure of the Organized Crime Control Act passed in 1970. The act was designed to limit the activity of organized crime by defining racketeering to include conspiring to use racketeering as a means of making income, collecting loans or conducting business. Although aimed at organized crime, RICO statutes can also be applied to the illegal activities of gangs.

It is presumed that most gangs have not yet achieved this heightened level of criminal organization. Decker et al. (1998, p. 395) examined the extent to which street gangs are becoming like organized crime enterprises and found: "With the exception of the Gangster Disciples in Chicago, there is little evidence that gangs are assuming the attributes of organized crime groups."

Another way of classifying gangs has been proposed by Huff (1989, pp. 528–529).

Gangs may be classified as hedonistic, instrumental or predatory.

A **hedonistic gang** focuses on having a good time, usually by smoking pot, drinking beer and sometimes engaging in minor property crimes.

An **instrumental gang,** in contrast, focuses on money, committing property crimes for economic reasons rather than for the thrill. Although some may sell drugs, this is not their primary activity. Members may also smoke pot and drink beer. This categorization fits well with the distinction between **instrumental violence** and **expressive violence.** As Bell noted during a hearing before the House Select Committee on Children, Youth and Families (1989, p. 79):

Instrumental violence is where, if I don't have a watch and you have one, I'm going to use violence as an instrument to get your watch. That's a criminal justice kind of issue.

Expressive violence has absolutely nothing to do with what I'm going to gain. It's, you know, you step on my toe, I'm in a bad mood, I've had a head injury, have been in a family where there's violence. I've been violent all my life, I've been violent in schools, no one has ever said anything to me about it. I'm socializable, but I still pop off every so often. And then somebody commits a murder. That is the majority of the homicides in the country. Most of the violence in this country is expressive. It is not instrumental. You are not going to have solutions for expressive violence by addressing instrumental violence issues. It's just not going to happen.

A **predatory gang** commits more violent crimes against persons, including robberies and street muggings. These gangs are likely to use hard drugs such as crack cocaine, which contributes to their volatile, aggressive behavior.

Yet another way to classify gangs is provided by Cloward and Ohlin (1960)—criminal, conflict or retreatist. These typologies are based on the concept of differential opportunity: people in all socioeconomic levels share the same basic goals, but those in the lower class have limited means by which to achieve them. Such a disadvantage may lead some to join a gang as an alternative way to reach their goals.

Gangs may also be classified as criminal, conflict or retreatist, based on the concept of differential opportunity.

According to Cloward and Ohlin, the **criminal gang** tends to develop in stable, low-income areas where adolescents may have close relationships with adult criminals. The gang is very organized, well-managed, often very lucrative and teaches youths the ways of the criminal business world. They use business savvy and financial acumen to achieve status, not having to rely very heavily on violence. Examples of such criminal gangs may be seen in many Chinese gangs, who are closely associated with the legitimate economic and social institutions within their communities. Organized crime operations also fit within this typology.

The **conflict gang** usually exists in dilapidated areas with transient populations. Poverty is a defining element of their communities, and status is achieved not through the use of business connections but with violence. The Bloods and the Crips, to be discussed shortly, are examples of conflict gangs.

The **retreatist gang** seeks status and success through both legitimate and illegitimate means, although it lacks the skills required to be a criminal gang and also lacks the risk-taking, violent edge needed to be a conflict gang. Their structure tends to be disorganized and their membership quite transitory. Cloward and Ohlin refer to such gangs as "double failures" who typically retreat to the fringes of society, withdrawing from regular social interaction and becoming immersed in heavy drug use. Examples of retreatist gangs are seen in the Vietnamese youth gangs, particularly in southern California, who avoid drug dealing because it is perceived as being too risky, yet whose members are heavy into drug use, especially cocaine.

The Los Angeles County Sheriff's Department *White Paper* (1992) refers to street gangs as traditional (having a long heritage) or nontraditional (formed more recently).

Street gangs are usually either traditional or nontraditional.

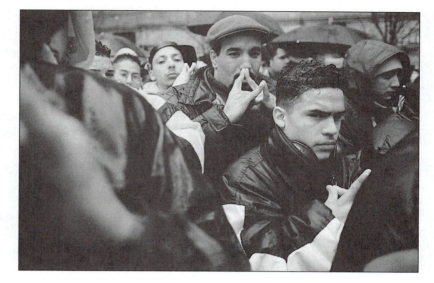

Latin King gang members gather outside the federal courthouse in support of a gang leader sentenced to life in prison. They communicate with each other by hand signals.

Traditional gangs are the typical Hispanic gangs found in barrios. Often members can trace the gang's heritage back to previous generations. An established system of traditional motivations has been formulated, and it is adhered to.

The nontraditional gang is also called a transitional gang. This type of gang has not been active long enough to have adopted long-standing traditions. Black street gangs of today still struggle with their gang identity.

Typically, gangs are structured around race or nationality.

_____

The most common gangs are Hispanic, black and Asian.

Hispanic Street Gangs

Hispanic gangs originated in Los Angeles, the valleys of California, New York (Puerto Rican), Miami (Mariel Cubans, Dominicans), Washington, DC and other urban barrios. The structure of Hispanic street gangs is similar throughout the western United States. Codes of conduct have been established. Leadership roles in Hispanic gangs are not formally recognized positions. Leadership positions are not usually assumed by any individual permanently, but by any member who demonstrates unique qualities of leadership needed at a particular moment.

These street gangs lack a solid chain of command. They cannot operate efficiently as a unit. They divide themselves, according to age, into groups called *cliques*. The gangs themselves usually adopt names that have some geographical significance in their neighborhood. Examples are "18th" (street) and "Lomas" (hills). A gang sees itself as the protector of its neighborhood. Gang wall writings or **graffiti** are used by gangs to identify the boundaries of their turf. The graffiti lettering of Hispanic gangs tends to be highly stylized. Gang members are loyal to the death. They are proud, even boastful, of their gang membership.

Black Street Gangs

Black street gangs have existed in the Los Angeles area for many years. Other places of origin for black gangs include Chicago, New York, Miami and other major urban ghettos. From the 1920s through the 1960s, black street gangs went virtually unnoticed. In the early 1970s, a group of high-school-aged "youths" began to terrorize local campuses and neighborhoods. This gang called itself the Crips. Members extorted money from other students and were involved in violence. This type of activity grew, and in a matter of a few years, many neighborhoods had their own gangs. The violence of the groups was directed not only at rival gang members, but often at innocent nongang victims.

In the mid-1970s, a change occurred. The Crips built a reputation for being the strongest force among the black street gangs. Soon other gangs started renaming themselves, incorporating the word Crip into their new names. Although these gangs adopted the Crip name, they maintained their own leaders and membership and were independent.

Some of these rival gangs continued to fight among themselves, and a polarization of forces developed from these feuds. The black gangs divided themselves into Crips and non-Crips. In gang terminology, the factions were called Bloods (non-Crips) and Cuz (Crips).

The Crips and the Bloods are rival black street gangs.

In addition to the Crips and the Bloods, the Players, Untouchables and Vice Lords are other prominent black gangs. According to Valdez (1998c, p. 47): "Some experts believe the largest street gang in America is the Black Gangster Disciples, a Folk Nation gang with an estimated 50,000 members."

Black gang activity is no longer isolated in gang neighborhoods. The activities of such groups are not restricted to gang feuds but include crimes of various sorts in many areas of the country.

Asian Gangs

Asian gangs have their origins among recent emigrees from Viet Nam, Hong Kong and the Philippines. Their gang activity has centered in New York; New Orleans; Los Angeles and Orange County; California, Portland, Oregon; Seattle; San Francisco; and Houston.

In the early 1900s, the Tongs (secret fraternal organizations) used boys as lookouts for the adult Tong members. These boys were called Wah Ching. After a period of time, and as the Tongs became more legitimate, the need for the Wah Chings declined, but the Wah Chings themselves did not disband. They still operate, largely taking up where the Tongs left off.

Even though the Tongs now are primarily benevolent societies, they will, when they deem it necessary, carry out violence through the agency of the Wah Chings. Eventually, because of excessive violence, the Chinese community itself spoke out against the Wah Chings. As differences of opinion developed within the Wah Chings, the group split into two factions. The older members became known as Yu Li, while the younger gang members retained the name Wah Ching.

Originally a member of the Yu Li, Joe Fong became disenchanted with the Yu Li and further fragmented the gang by forming the Joe Fong gang or

Joe Boys. The 1967 massacre at the Golden Dragon restaurant in San Francisco's Chinatown was a result of the Joe Fong gang attacking the Wah Ching gang. All three gangs (Yu Li, Joe Boys and Wah Chings) exist today and have spread to most major cities of the United States and Canada.

The Home Invaders are young Asian males who work in groups, moving about the country brutalizing and robbing other Asian families. Valdez (1997b, p. 50) notes: "Well-armed and well-organized, these groups specialize in home robberies." According to Burke (1990, p. 23): "The robberies are normally committed during the evening hours when confrontation is ensured. They rely upon intimidation and fear of retaliation to gain valuables." These gangs tend to focus their crimes on their own Southeast Asian communities because these refugees hold philosophies that make them easy targets: (1) they distrust police and, therefore, are highly unlikely to report the crime and (2) they distrust commercial banks and, as a result, tend to keep money and valuables in their homes (Valdez, 1997b, p. 50).

Vietnamese gangs are also proliferating and posing a serious problem in that they are highly mobile and are especially vicious in their crimes against fellow Vietnamese.

Unlike other groups, Chinese gang members do not have a particular dress code, so their identity as gang members is difficult to establish on sight. Another difficulty in dealing with Asian gangs is that most western police officers do not know how to translate names into English, making accurate record keeping and tracking of gang members difficult (Harlan, 1993, p. 51).

Ima (1992, p. 22) notes that refugee families face many issues that may contribute to youths joining gangs, including:

- Disrupted families—loss of a parent or family members.
- Role reversal—children become translators for their parents and, consequently, gain control over them.
- Disagreement on values and norms—youths accept American customs more rapidly than their parents.

Ima (p. 26) also notes several factors that contribute to academic failure, which is also linked with gang membership: family instability, early marriage and childbearing, lack of access to jobs, language barriers and racism. Youths with dysfunctional families who are not succeeding in school are prime candidates for gangs.

Native American Gangs

As with other racial minorities in the United States, Native American youths have been drawn into gangs in reaction to cultural discord, poverty and other social pressures. As noted by Valdez (1998c, p. 47): "Today, due to a number of social factors, the gang lifestyle has an ideal target recruitment group in young Native Americans, males and females alike, especially those who live on the reservations." Valdez also reports: "Unfortunately, Native American gang members have adopted the same types of criminal gang activities and gang-motivated violent attacks we see throughout the United States. . . . With below-poverty living conditions and lack of parent or guardian awareness, drug sales offer an easy way to survive."

Other Ethnic Gangs

Filipino neighborhood street gangs are similar in structure and operation to Hispanic groups. As a result Filipino gangs gravitate toward Mexican gangs in their associations and friendships. The most common Filipino gangs are the Santanas, the Tabooes and Temple Street.

The Korean community also has very active gangs. The foremost is called the Korean Killers. It is unique in that it is primarily a theft-oriented gang.

Jamaican Posses consist of immigrant Jamaicans in the United States with roots in their native Jamaica. Groups have been identified in New York; Boston; Philadelphia; Washington, DC; Houston; Atlanta; Detroit; Seattle; and Anchorage, among other locations.

Pacific Islander gangs consist primarily of Samoans who have migrated to western urban areas, such as Los Angeles, San Francisco and Portland.

White Gangs

The Justice Department estimates that three-quarters of the nation's known gangs are made up of minorities, primarily blacks and Hispanics, but the number of white youths in gangs is increasing. "Getting a Grip on Slippery Gang Problems" (p. 13) notes: "A number of jurisdictions report that youths from predominantly white, affluent suburbs are banding together in gangs, whose criminal activities are gradually escalating from graffiti and vandalism to beatings and drive-by shootings. In upper middle-class Westchester County, N.Y., . . . authorities estimate that 1,500 youths belong to as many as 70 gangs."

Specific types of gangs consisting primarily or entirely of Caucasians are White Stoner gangs, biker gangs and neo-Nazi (skinhead) gangs.

Stoner Gangs

Stoner gangs consist of middle-class, typically Caucasian, youths involved in drugs, alcohol, and heavy metal and punk rock music (their name is derived from the fact they are "stoned" much of the time). Although not as likely to engage in violent crimes, they are often involved in Satanism, posing a unique problem to law enforcement and the juvenile justice system. They may mutilate animals, rob graves and desecrate human remains and churches. Stoners tend to wear colorful T-shirts, jeans and tennis shoes and to have long hair.

Biker Gangs

Outlaw motorcycle or biker gangs are predominantly Caucasians, and most are branches of the Hells Angels and other notorious motorcycle groups. They tend to be heavily involved with the manufacture and sale of methamphetamine. Trethewy and Katz (1998, p. 53) state: "Once considered nothing more than rowdy toughs on two-wheelers, motorcycle gangs have evolved into crime units that are sufficiently well-oiled and well-organized to rival the Mafia. . . . They have written constitutions, bylaws and a hierarchical leadership structure. Members pay dues and attend regular meetings to confirm loyalty to the gang leadership. . . . If members break rules or bylaws, their misdeeds are punished with penalties ranging from fines to murder."

Neo-Nazi gang members, or skinheads, who find themselves in prison seek out other members of their gang, usually successfully. While in prison these white male supremacist inmates may recruit others into the gang.

Biker gangs have become increasingly sophisticated (Trethewy and Katz, p. 56): "Computers keep club records, fax machines bring out-of-country chapters closer together, cellular phones and pagers make communication easier for gang members to conduct business, and even Internet web sites are common among motorcycle gangs in the '90s." Furthermore (p. 55): "Many of today's biker gang members and associates are earning college-level degrees in computer science, finance, business, criminal justice and law. These curricula improve the gang's expertise in highly profitable criminal enterprises."

While the majority of motorcycle gang membership consists of adults, gang interaction with youths is certainly possible. Trethewy and Katz state (p. 53): "Categorizing this counterculture is complicated because of the interrelationships and networking not only with other motorcycle gangs, but also with prison gangs, street gangs, racist groups, drug groups and traditional organized crime families." Thus exposure of youths to these sophisticated motorcycle gangs may foster a strong desire to "jump in" and may lead to early recruitment.

Neo-Nazi Gangs

Neo-Nazi gangs tend to articulate white supremacy, racism and Nazi symbols. Some call themselves skinheads and sport close-cut hair or shaved heads.

Prison Gangs

The influence of the gang is also felt within the corrections portion of the juvenile justice system. The Youth Authority in Stockton, California, estimates that about 65 percent of its inmates belong to gangs (Rushing, 1993, p. 12):

> Far removed from the battlefields of the "hood," gangsters in the California Youth Authority spill blood for the same things—rivalries, revenge, respect.
> Towering cyclone fences topped with razor wire surround the most serious criminals in the juvenile justice system, but they can't keep out the gang hatred that has cost so many lives on the street.

Those not affiliated with gangs prior to their confinement find that not belonging to a gang can be dangerous. As one 18-year-old said (Rushing, p. 13): "If you're claiming nothing [no gang affiliation], they'll be messing with you every day. They know you're not going to be doing nothing back, you know what I'm saying, because you got no backup to help you."

Females in Gangs

In 1993 Esbensen and Huizinga estimated that 10 to 25 percent of all gang members were female. More recent data by Esbensen, however, shows a rise in this percentage: "With our finding that 38 percent of gang members in our sample are female, this study contributes to the growing body of research reporting greater rates of female participation in gangs than was previously acknowledged" (Esbensen and Winfree, 1998, p. 520).

Female involvement and status in gangs may be (1) as auxiliary members of male gangs, (2) as full-fledged members of coed gangs or (3) as members of all-female gangs. Several all-female gangs exist in New York City, including The Sandman Ladies (Puerto Rican females with a biker image) and The Sex Girls (African-American and Hispanic females who deal drugs). According to Laflin (1996, p. 87): "Female gangs are usually structured identically to male gangs, with initiation rites, meetings, and other characteristics of a formal organization. These women oftentimes grew up together and trust and depend upon each other to survive."

Ross (1993, pp. 8–9) notes that while the numbers of females in gangs is still relatively small, it is growing, and the girls tend to be more violent. She includes the statement of a former female gang member: "You want to be where the men are, because that's where the power is. It's not enough anymore to just have dinner made. Now you have to go out and have a gun battle and go rip off a few cars, and come home and have dinner ready."

Esbensen and Winfree (p. 521) report: "Our findings do not support the notion that gang girls are mere sex objects with no involvement in the violent acts that the gang boys commit. The gang girls commit the same variety of offenses as the boys, but at a slightly lower frequency. Further, the gang girls are two to five times more delinquent than the nongang boys." Laflin (p. 87) states: "Gangs consisting of female members, whether it be auxiliary branches of male gangs or fully autonomous female organizations, are fully capable and disposed to commit as many crimes as any male gang." And, like juveniles, females arouse less suspicion than male adults. Females are used by gangs in a variety of ways:

- To serve as lookouts for crimes in progress
- To conceal stolen property or tools used in committing crimes
- To carry weapons for males who don't want to be caught with them
- To carry information into and out of prison
- To provide sexual favors (they are often drug dependent and are physically abused)
- To commit actual crimes

Some gangs, such as the Tiny Rascals pictured here, have both male and female members. Also depicted are two symbols of gang life: hand signals and guns.

In addition to the three basic types of gangs in which females are found, Valdez (1997a, p. 41) notes involvement in another type—the "party gangs":

> Today, females are active in criminal street gangs as well as self-reported nongang groups such as party crews, clubs, posses and cliques. Females play an active role in these highly social gangs. Many members, especially females indicate the groups are a better alternative to street gangs. The emphasis of these groups is to party, dance, drink and have sex. "Keep the peace" is the motto.
>
> A closer examination will reveal that these groups fit the general definition of a street gang. The crimes they are most often involved in are misdemeanor level and do not get a lot of law enforcement or media attention. "Huffing" nitrous oxide (laughing gas), underage drinking, marijuana smoking and trespassing are the most common crimes. Nevertheless, these groups are street gangs.

Valdez (1997a, p. 41) cautions: "There is no doubt that female gangsters can be just as aggressive and volatile as male gang members. Many female gangsters believe that male law enforcement officials are afraid to frisk them and they take advantage of that."

Characteristics of the Youth Gang Subculture

According to Miller (1983, p. 1671), youth gangs can be distinguished from other forms of law-violating youth groups on the basis of five characteristics.

Five characteristics that distinguish youth gangs are leadership, organization, associational patterns, domain identification and illegal activity.

Gang Structure— Leadership and Organization

Compared to other types of law-violating youth groups, gangs usually have a more formalized structure and may include the common organizational elements of internal differentiation, hierarchical authority and advanced planning. Varying levels of involvement can be found in most gangs.

Most gangs contain leaders, hard-core members, regular members and fringe members or wannabes.

Gang leadership tends to be better defined and more clearly identifiable than leadership in other types of delinquent groups. The leaders are usually the oldest members of the gang and have extensive criminal records. They may surround themselves with hard-core members, giving orders and expecting unquestioned obedience.

The hard-core members usually commit the crimes and are the most violent. They have usually had to earn the right to become true gang members through some sort of initiation ("turning" or "jumping in"). Kody Scott is a prime example of a hard-core member. He explains the actions that led to his being accepted into a Los Angeles Crip gang (Shakur, p. 13):

> In 1977, when I was thirteen, while robbing a man I turned my head and was hit in the face. The man tried to run, but was tripped by Tray Ball, who then held him for me. I stomped him for twenty minutes before leaving him unconscious in an alley. Later that night, I learned that the man had lapsed into a coma and was disfigured from my stomping. The police told bystanders that the person responsible for this was a "monster." The name stuck, and I took that as a moniker over my birth name.

"Monster" also describes the effect of being accepted into the gang (p. 69):

> My life was totally consumed by all aspects of gang life. I had turned my bedroom into a virtual command post, launching attacks from my house with escalating frequency. My clothes, walk, talk, and attitude all reflected my love for and allegiance to my set. Nobody was more important than my homeboys—nobody. In fact, the only reason my little brother and I stayed close is because he joined the set. Anybody else I had nothing in common with.

On the fringes of most gangs are youths who aspire to become gang members, called *wannabes*. They dress and talk like the hard-core members, but they have not yet been formally accepted into the gang. Their progression from high-risk youth to wannabe to hard-core gang member is illustrated in Table 7.3.

Another group of youths could be described as "potentials" or "could be's." Figure 7.1 also shows the relationship of these youths to the gang. Many of these youths are what Dr. Cline (1979) would describe as "character-disturbed." His profile of a character-disturbed child is contained in Table 7.4.

These characteristics are very similar to those outlined in Chapter 6 for people with behavior disorders, antisocial individuals and even psychopaths.

Associational Patterns

Compared to other types of law-violating youth groups, gangs tend to have closer relational bonds and more continuous affiliation between members. Gangs usually adopt specific criteria for membership eligibility, and many gangs

Table 7.3	Ages	Risk Indicators
The Development and Path of a High-Risk Youth	8	Youth plays outdoors a lot and is difficult to bring into the house.
	9	Youth gets into mischief and neighborhood disputes.
	10	Youth has first contact with police for petty thefts, vandalism, firesetting and animal abuse.
	11	Youth engages in malicious and mischievous play; enters into delinquent networking (gang) activity; engages in stealing and destroying property.
	12	Youth develops conflict with societal norms and values, resulting in further peer and older youth criminal networking activity; experiments with drugs and alcohol; bullies younger children; is truant and unruly.
	13–14	Youth's gang identity emerges as a result of community's failure to integrate youth into adult law-abiding society; commits residential burglaries and bicycle thefts; deals with stolen property; becomes runner for drug entrepreneur.
	15–16	Youth's behavior characterized by loyalty to the gang; gang becomes family and provides education and experience. Youth commits burglaries and other thefts to finance drugs and alcohol; sells drugs; engages in auto theft and fraud. Youth's high truancy results in underachieving, leading to school dropout; becomes a social thrownaway; comes to the attention of the police.
	16–17	Gang member: Youth, because of behavior, becomes institutionalized for violent acts: murder, rape, assault; is heavy drug and alcohol user.
		Gang nonmember or loner: Youth is highly socially dysfunctional; turns on family to vent frustration over inability to be socially stable; considers and may fulfill self-destruction.
	18–20	Gang member: Youth goes from delinquent to more criminal associates; is intravenous drug abuser; commits crimes to satisfy addiction; is highly volatile; commits crimes against women and, if married, abuses spouse and children.
		Gang nonmember: Youth, if no criminal record or a gang dropout and from a highly dysfunctional family, has tendency to commit violent acts against women and children.

Table 7.4	
Profile of Character-Disturbed Child	1. Lack of ability to give and receive affection
	2. Self-destructive behavior
	3. Cruelty to others
	4. Phoniness
	5. Severe problems with stealing, hoarding and gorging on food
	6. Speech pathology
	7. Marked control problems
	8. Lack of long-term friends
	9. Abnormalities in eye contact
	10. Parents appear angry and hostile
	11. Preoccupation with fire, blood or gore
	12. Superficial attractiveness and friendliness with strangers
	13. Various types of learning disorders
	14. A particular pathological type of lying—"primary process lying"

Source: Foster Cline, M.D. *Understanding and Treating the Severely Disturbed Child*. 1979, p. 128. Evergreen Consultants, P.O. Box 2380, Evergreen, CO 80439. Reprinted with permission.

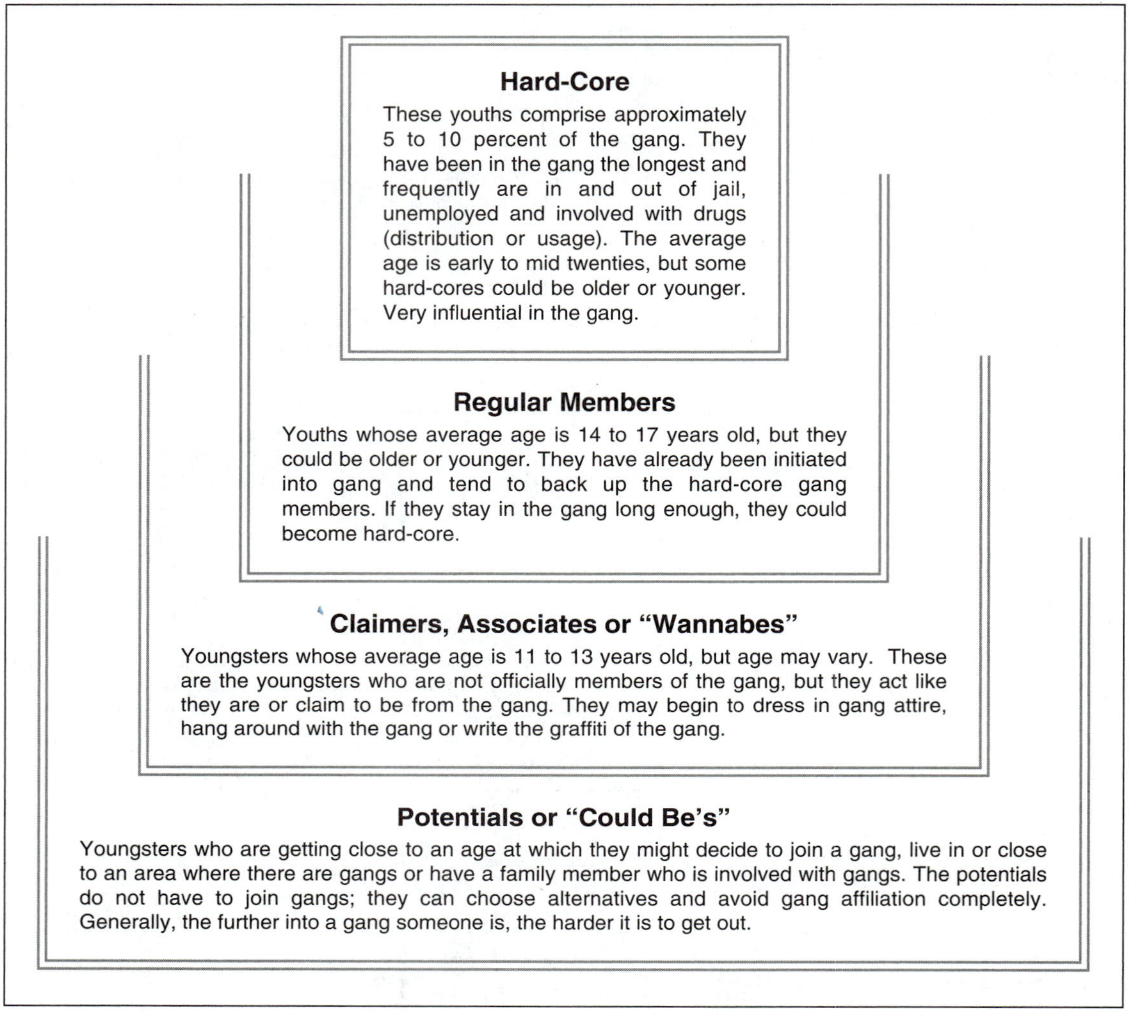

Hard-Core

These youths comprise approximately 5 to 10 percent of the gang. They have been in the gang the longest and frequently are in and out of jail, unemployed and involved with drugs (distribution or usage). The average age is early to mid twenties, but some hard-cores could be older or younger. Very influential in the gang.

Regular Members

Youths whose average age is 14 to 17 years old, but they could be older or younger. They have already been initiated into gang and tend to back up the hard-core gang members. If they stay in the gang long enough, they could become hard-core.

Claimers, Associates or "Wannabes"

Youngsters whose average age is 11 to 13 years old, but age may vary. These are the youngsters who are not officially members of the gang, but they act like they are or claim to be from the gang. They may begin to dress in gang attire, hang around with the gang or write the graffiti of the gang.

Potentials or "Could Be's"

Youngsters who are getting close to an age at which they might decide to join a gang, live in or close to an area where there are gangs or have a family member who is involved with gangs. The potentials do not have to join gangs; they can choose alternatives and avoid gang affiliation completely. Generally, the further into a gang someone is, the harder it is to get out.

Figure 7.1
Gang Organizational Chart

employ initiation rituals, often involving one or more criminal acts, as a prerequisite to membership. Gang members also demonstrate associational patterns and bonds through certain identifying characteristics such as their names, symbols and communication styles.

Gang Recruitment

Transforming a youth into a gang member involves a slow assimilation. Once youths reach an age at which they can prove themselves with peer leaders within the gang, they may perform some sort of rite of passage or ceremony called "turning," "quoting" or "jumping in." Or they may be "courted in," simply accepted into the gang without having to prove themselves in any particular way. Female gang members are sometimes "sexed in" to male or coed gangs.

According to Shelden et al. (p. 101): "Most youth are informally socialized into the gang subculture from a very early age so that they do not so much join a gang, but rather evolve into the gang naturally. Actually turning or being jumped is little more than a rite of passage."

Identifying Gang Members

Law enforcement officers can deal more effectively with youths if they can identify those who are likely to be gang members.

Gang members may be identified by their names, symbols (including clothing and tattoos) and communication styles, including sign language and graffiti.

Gang Names Gang names vary from colorful and imaginative to straightforward. They commonly refer to localities, rebellion, animals, royalty and religion. Localities are typically streets (for example, the Seventeenth Streeters), cities or towns (the Center City Boys), neighborhoods (the Westsiders) and housing projects (the Tiburon Courts). Names denoting rebellion, revolution or lawlessness include the Gangsters, Outlaws, Hustlers, Savages, Warlords and Assassins. Common animal names include the Tigers, Cougars, Panthers, Cobras, Ravens and Eagles. Royal titles include the Kings, Emperors, Lords, Imperials, Knights, Dukes and even Royals. Religious names include the Popes and Disciples. Gangs may also be designated by the leader's name such as "Garcia's Boys." Often, a locality is coupled with another category, for example, the South Side Savages.

Within a gang, a member may adopt a **moniker** to be used in place of the given name. According to Wilson (1997, p. 14): "Several different styles of monikers exist. Many reflect a distinctive aspect of a gang member's personality, physical characteristics, reputation, or other trait. Some convey boldness or devotion to the gang lifestyle. Others reinforce the gang member's ego." The BJA notes (*Addressing Community*, p. 44): "Black gang members use colorful monikers such as 'Mad Bear,' 'Super Fly' and 'Killer.'"

Gang Symbols Gangs use symbols or logos to identify themselves. Many times these symbols are taken from professional or college sports teams (for example, the Latin Kings use the L.A. Kings logo as an identifying symbol), religion and the occult (crosses and pentagrams and other universally recognized symbols, including the Playboy bunny).

Clothing It is important for gang members to reinforce their sense of belonging by adopting a gang style of dress. As noted by Wrobleski and Hess (2000, p. 302): "Gang symbols are common. Clothing, in particular, can distinguish a particular gang. Perhaps best known is the typical attire of an outlaw motorcycle gang member: tattered Levis, scuffed boots, leather vests and jackets with their own unique emblems. Sometimes 'colors' are used to distinguish a gang." Gang members also use jerseys, hats and jackets with emblems.

Gang clothing is of two basic types. The first shows that the person belongs to a gang without specifically identifying which one. *Color* is often significant, as certain color combinations are frequently associated with specific gangs. The second type specifically identifies a gang. Such gang clothing may include jackets or sweatshirts with the gang name.

Representing also signifies gang allegiance. Representing is a manner of dressing that uses an imaginary line drawn vertically through the body. Anything to the left of the line is representing left, anything to the right is representing right: for example, a hat cocked to the right, right pant leg rolled up, and a cloth or bandana tied around the right arm.

Other important symbols may include certain hairstyles, gold jewelry in gang symbols and certain cars. The following list itemizes some identifying symbols of some better known gangs:

- *Black Gangster Disciples* wear blue and black colors, represent to the right, and have as symbols a six-point star, flaming heart and crossed pitchfork.
- *Vice Lords* wear red and black colors, represent to the left and have as symbols a five-point star, a circle surrounded by fire, a half-crescent moon, a pyramid, top hat, cane, white gloves and martini glass.
- *Latin Kings* wear gold and black colors, represent to the left and have as a symbol a three- or five-point star.
- *Asian gangs* usually wear no colors and show no representation. They are often deadly and violent.
- *Skinheads* wear black boots and leather jackets and have as a symbol the swastika. Their heads are bald or very nearly bald.

Tattoos Some gangs, particularly outlaw motorcycle gangs and Hispanic gangs, use tattoos as a method of communication and identification. The traditional Hispanic gang uses tattoos extensively, usually visible on arms, hands or shoulders. By contrast, black gang members are not enthusiastic about using tattoos to identify their members. Branding, however, is becoming somewhat popular among black and Asian gangs. Commenting on the Southeast Asian gang community trend of burning and scarring their arms and hands, Valdez (1996, p. 20) states:

> Displaying these body modifications or inflicting them in the presence of other gang members gives the wearer instant respect among his or her peers. The marks also serve as a kind of silent advertisement to the rest of the population. Without saying a word, a person wearing these marks or tattoos can walk into a cafe or restaurant and intimidate the owner into providing free food or paying for protection.

Gang Communication Styles Street gangs communicate primarily through their actions. Youth gangs need and seek recognition, not only from their community, but also from rival gangs. A variety of verbal and nonverbal gang communication is ever-present. Clothing, tattoos and symbols can be powerful and effective communication tools. Other avenues of gang communication include slang, hand signals and graffiti.

Gang members communicate through clothing, tattoos, symbols, slang, hand signals and graffiti.

Gang Slang Following is a list of terms commonly used by gang members[1]:

- bent—drunk
- cap—a verbal comeback
- crab—derogatory name for a Crip
- Cuz—alternate name for a Crip, often used in greeting
- down—to meet expectations
- five-O—the police
- gat—gun
- head up—to fight one-on-one
- hemmed up—to be hassled or arrested by the authorities
- homeboy—someone from the same neighborhood or gang. Also called a homie
- hood—short for neighborhood. Also called turf
- hoo ride—drive-by-shooting
- jacket—reputation
- jet—to leave
- jumped in—being initiated into a gang, sometimes by getting beaten up
- kickin' it—hanging out with the gang
- peel—kill
- rifa—to rule
- smoke—kill

Hand Signals Another method of gang communication is that of flashing gang signs or hand signals. The purpose of these hand signals is to identify the user with a specific gang. Hand signs communicate allegiance or opposition to another group. Most hand signs duplicate or modify signing used by the deaf and hearing impaired. Figure 7.2 shows some ways various gangs identify themselves with hand signs.

Graffiti Certainly the most observable gang communication is wall writings or graffiti, an important part of the Hispanic and black gang traditions. It proclaims to the world the status of the gang, delineates the boundaries of their turf and offers a challenge to rivals. Graffiti may show opposition for rival gangs by displaying a rival gang's symbols upside down, backwards or crossed out—a serious insult to the rival.

Graffiti is a method of communication commonly used to mark a street gang's turf.

Police can gain much valuable information from gang graffiti. For instance, one may be able to determine what gang is in control of a specific area by noting the frequency of the unchallenged graffiti. Throwing a *placa* on a wall

---

[1]Many of these terms are from "'Gangster' Rap Terminology," *Criminal Organizations,* Vol. 8, No. 2, 1993, p. 10.

The signs shown on these pages are an important part of the sign language of the gangs. The letters and numbers represent affiliation with the particular gang. It is important and advisable not to imitate any of the signs being shown. To do so could represent affiliation or identification with a specific gang and could lead to unfortunate consequences.

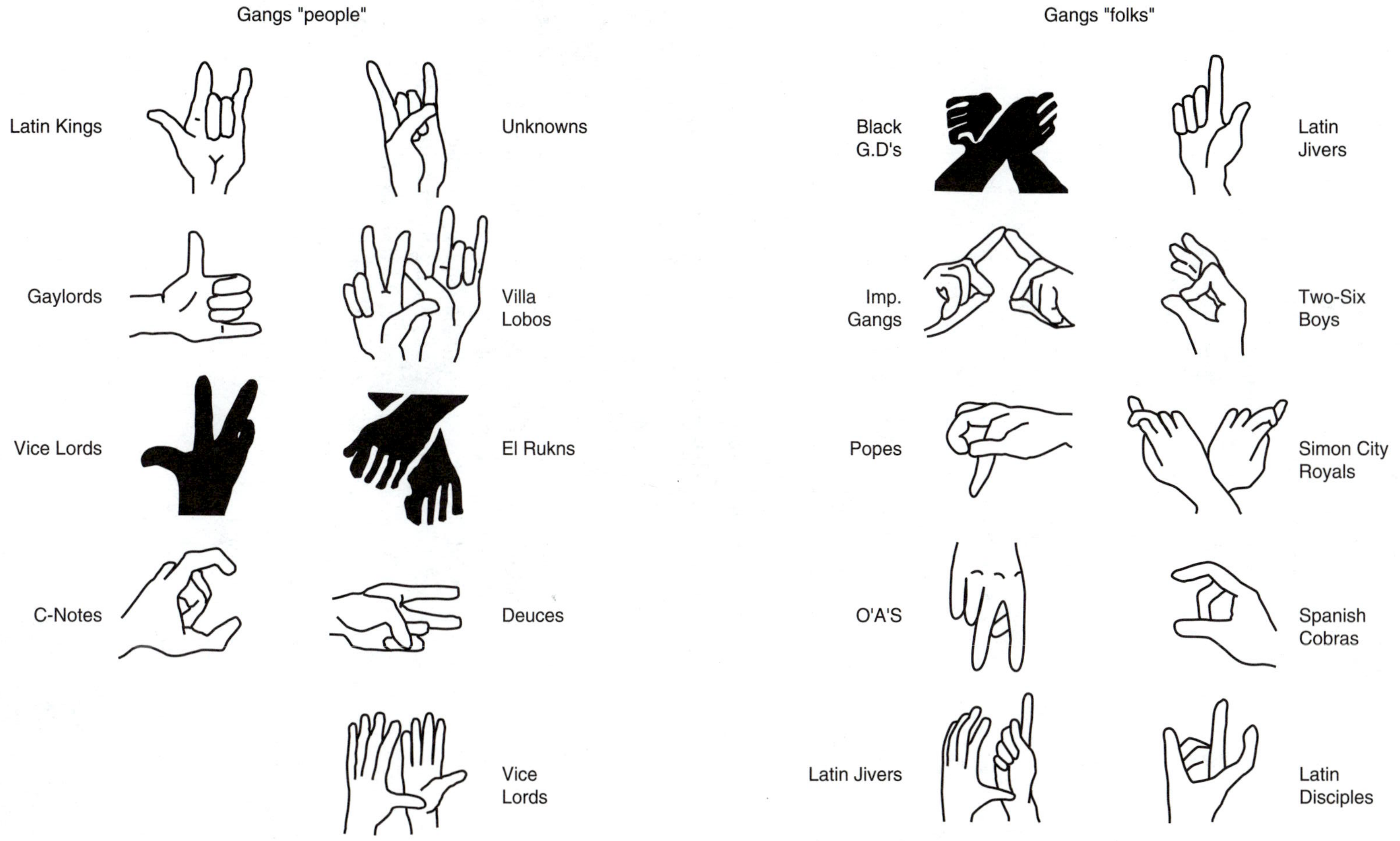

Gangs "folks"

Latin Jivers

Two-Six Boys

Simon City Royals

Spanish Cobras

Latin Disciples

Black G.D's

Imp. Gangs

Popes

O'A'S

Latin Jivers

Gangs "people"

Unknowns

Villa Lobos

El Rukns

Deuces

Vice Lords

Latin Kings

Gaylords

Vice Lords

C-Notes

Source: "Gang Awareness," City of Chicago, Department of Human Services, The Youth Development Services Division, in cooperation with the Gang Crime Unit of the Chicago Police Department and the Chicago Crime Commission, no date, pages 4–5. Reprinted by permission.

Figure 7.2
Gang Signs

Graffiti has been called the "newspaper of the street" for gangs. Often abbreviations such as R.I.P. (rest in peace) are found as in the upper left corner of this graffiti.

corresponds to claiming a territory. Writing left unchanged reaffirms the gang's control. As one moves away from the center or core area of a gang's power and territory, more rival graffiti and cross-outs are observed.

Valdez (1998b, p. 39) notes: "Graffiti can serve several functions for the street gangsters. Among other things, it can be used to mark off turf boundaries, be a way to give insults to rival gangs, act as a warning of impending death, list fallen comrades, announce the presence of a gang in a certain area of the city or show gang alliances." The BJS adds (*Addressing Community*, p. 37): "Gang graffiti can become dialogue between gangs and eventually a record of gang wars—from initial territorial claims, to challenges to individuals and gangs, to records of individual deaths."

The black and Hispanic styles of wall writings differ vastly. Black gang graffiti lacks the flair and attention to detail evidenced by Hispanic gang graffiti. Much of the black gang wall writing is loaded with profanity and expressions not found in the Hispanic graffiti.

Gang symbols in the form of graffiti usually appear throughout the turf and define boundaries. Such graffiti usually includes the gang name and the writer's name. It may also assert the gang's power by such words as *rifa,* meaning "to rule," or *P/V* meaning "por vida" (for life). In other words, the gang rules this neighborhood for life. The number 13 has traditionally meant that the writer used marijuana, but now it also can mean that the gang is from Southern California. Valdez (1998b, p. 47) cautions: "A common way to miss the valuable information within graffiti is to not consider it as the written form of the gang language. Each type of gang may select a few phrases, words, numbers or symbols to represent its gang. . . . The written language takes on a particular personality, just as the gang does."

Slahor (1993, p. 55) describes another type of graffiti, called **tagging,** which mimics gang graffiti, but often those doing the tagging are not members of gangs or involved in criminal activity (other than vandalism). According to Gross and

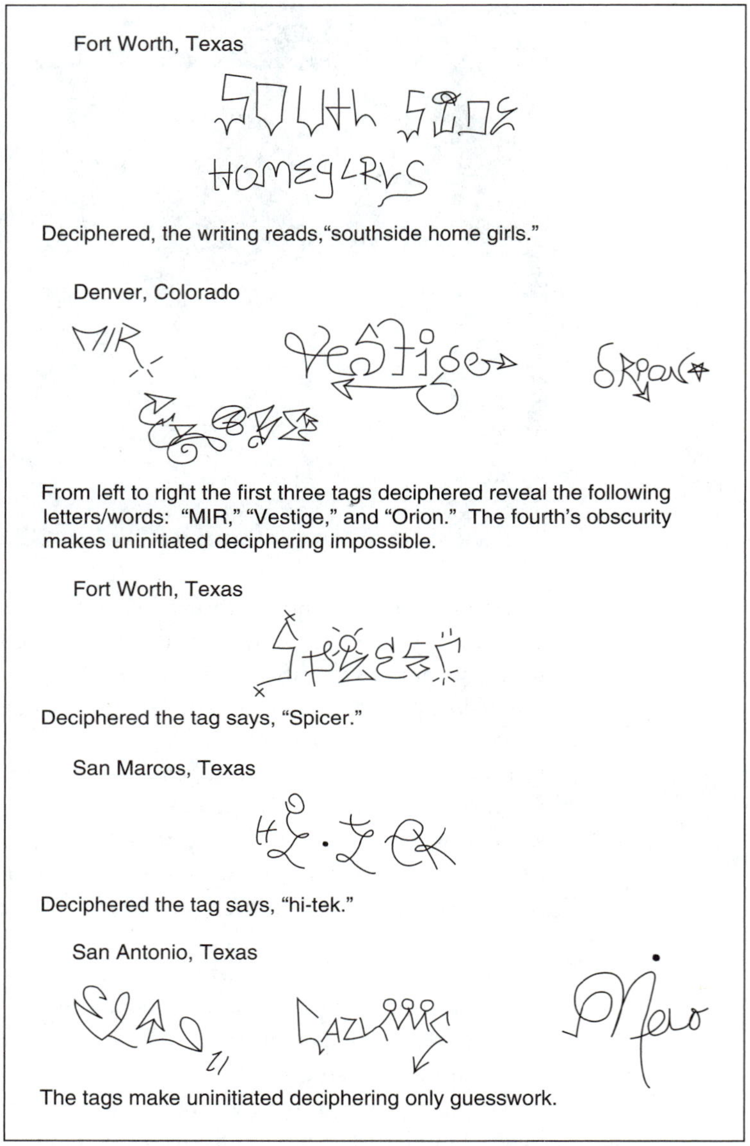

Fort Worth, Texas

Deciphered, the writing reads, "southside home girls."

Denver, Colorado

From left to right the first three tags deciphered reveal the following letters/words: "MIR," "Vestige," and "Orion." The fourth's obscurity makes uninitiated deciphering impossible.

Fort Worth, Texas

Deciphered the tag says, "Spicer."

San Marcos, Texas

Deciphered the tag says, "hi-tek."

San Antonio, Texas

The tags make uninitiated deciphering only guesswork.

Figure 7.3
Examples of Tagging

Source: Daniel D. Gross and Timothy D. Gross. "Tagging: Changing Visual Patterns and the Rhetorical Implications of a New Form of Graffiti." *Et cetera,* Fall, 1993, pp. 259–262. Reprinted from *ETC: A Review of General Semantics,* Fall 1993, with permission of the International Society for General Semantics.

Gross (1993, p. 258), tagging as a new form of graffiti has appeared in the last 25 years. They note: "The dominant visual impression of this phase includes words, though the graffiti only leaves a hint of words. . . . The words both reveal and conceal their identity. They reveal themselves to the insider or initiated but conceal themselves from the uninitiated." Gross and Gross identify two types of tagging: "Individual tagging or extended tagging called 'gang writing.'" They note: "These two types of graffiti decorate the walls of modern civilization worldwide." They provide the tagging examples in Figure 7.3. The differences between tagger and gang graffiti are listed in Table 7.5.

Table 7.5
**Differences between
Tagger and Gang Graffiti**

Tagger Graffiti	Gang Graffiti
Communication secondary, if present at all	Intent made to communicate
Artistic effort a major consideration	Artistic effort secondary, if present at all
Territorial claims infrequent	Territorial claims prominent
Explicit threats rare	Explicit threats made
Explicit boasts about tagger common	Explicit boasts made about gang
Pictures and symbols dominant, letters and numbers secondary	Letters, numbers, and symbols dominant
Police intelligence value limited	Intelligence to police provided

Source: *Addressing Community Gang Problems: A Practical Guide*. Washington, DC: Bureau of Justice Assistance, May 1998, p. 37. (NCJ-164273)

In some instances taggers band together into a crew. Sometimes the tagging becomes very serious and may even turn deadly. Ayres (1994, p. 4A) quotes a 17-year-old tagger: "I mean, like you tag this wall with spray real fast—sizzzzt! sizzzzt!—and nobody catches you and then another crew sees what you've done and tries to tag over you and you have to go after them—hey, like I say, it's a rush." Ayres notes: "Many taggers now refer to themselves as 'tag bangers,' carrying guns, knives and clubs along with their marker pens and cans of spray paint." What were once friendly neighborhood rivalries have turned into warfare over "tagger turf." At the time this was written, the Los Angeles police were looking for one tagger they believed was responsible for three murders.

Regardless of the method of communication, gang messages are clear. Gang members are telling the world that their gangs or barrios are number one, the best. They also are expressing their commitment to turf and gang.

Domain Identification

Youth gangs characteristically claim identification with and control over specific domains—geographic locations, facilities or enterprises. The best-known manifestation of gang domain identification is the "turf" phenomenon. Gangs establish turf, territorial boundaries, within which they operate and which they protect at all costs from invasion by rival gangs. Solidarity and neighborhood cohesiveness are intense. In fact, the query, "Where are you from?" is the challenge of the street. An inappropriate response may bring a severe beating or even death.

Illegal Activity

The primary characteristic distinguishing gangs from lawful groups is illegal activity. Gang members commit a full range of street crimes, although the most distinctive form of gang offense is gang fighting, in which two or more gangs engage in violent combat. Occasionally, innocent bystanders are caught in the crossfire, yet as Shelden et al. (p. 128) note: "The major victims of gang violence are other gang members. Innocent bystanders are rarely the victims, despite claims of law enforcement and other officials to the contrary."

Gang activity ranges from property crimes to violent crimes against persons and includes graffiti painting, vandalism, arson, student extortion, teacher intimidation, drug dealing, rape, stabbings and shootings.

Gang activity, when viewed from a juvenile justice perspective, is a study in violent crime. A perpetual cycle of violence by gang rivalries can date back many years. Gang members often do not know why they came to be rivals. One gang member stated, "I don't know why we fight them. We've fought 'em since my father's time."

Often gang members have minimal financial or worldly assets. Their most important possession becomes their reputation. A "hard look" or minor insult directed at a gang member by a rival gang member must be avenged, an attitude that results in the bloodbaths often seen on urban streets. In fact, a gang's reputation is often enhanced by engaging in vicious, violent crimes. For example, as one individual said of the gangs in his community (McGarvey, p. 25): "You want to know about our gangs? Last week they killed a 21 year old. They cut off his head, put his body in a car and set fire to it. He was buried yesterday without his head."

Drive-by shootings receive much media attention, particularly when stray bullets hit an innocent child or adult. Sometimes the shooters hit their mark and realize after the fact that it was a case of mistaken identity. Howell (1997, p. 11) states: "Gang-related drive-by shootings have increased in certain cities. Interestingly, killing is a secondary intent; promoting fear and intimidation among rival gangs is the primary motive."

Gang members many also engage in acts of violence as part of their initiation process. Gustafson (1998, p. B1) reports: "The Asian Crips went on a 12-day rampage earlier this spring, repeatedly raping at least seven young Hmong girls as part of a gang initiation ritual."

Often the activities of gangs are glamorized when, in fact, the members are just "hanging out" or acting like most teenagers do. As noted by Huff (1989, p. 530):

> Gang members actually spend most of their time engaging in exaggerated versions of typical adolescent behavior (rebelling against authority by skipping school, refusing to do homework, and disobeying parents; wearing clothing and listening to music that sets them apart from most adults; and having a primary allegiance to their peer group instead of their parents or other adults). They appear to "drift" into and out of illegal behavior. . . .
>
> [Illegal] activities committed by youth gangs during the course of this study [of Ohio gangs] include theft, auto theft, intimidation and assault in school and on the street, robbery, burglary, rape, group rape, drug use, drug sales, and even murder. . . . As one gang member said during his interview: "People may say there's no gangs 'cause they don't see no colors, but if they be robbin' people, shootin' people, and killin' people, they still a gang."

Thornberry and Burch (1997) report on a study conducted to determine what portion of delinquency in American society is attributable to gang members. Among the findings (p. 2) were that gang membership made up 30 percent of the youth population, yet 65 percent of the delinquent acts were committed by gang members: "The data . . . indicate that gang members' delinquencies are not proportionate to their representation in the larger population." Furthermore: "The disproportionate contribution of gang members to delinquency is greater for the more serious crimes. The general results of the study are presented in Figure 7.4.

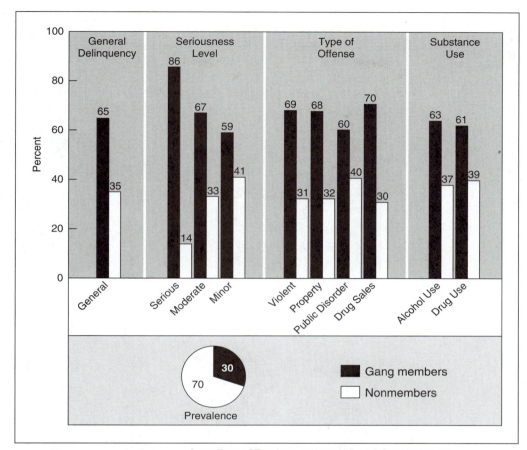

Figure 7.4
**Percent of Delinquent
Acts Attributable
to Gang Members
and Prevalence
of Gang Membership**

Source: Terence P. Thornberry and James H. Burch II. *Gang Members and Delinquent Behavior.* OJJDP Juvenile Justice Bulletin, June 1997, p. 3.

Huff (1998, p. 1), reporting on an NIJ study, also reports that: "Criminal behavior committed by gang members is extensive and significantly exceeds that committed by comparably at-risk but nongang youth." The study found that gang members were much more likely to commit certain crimes: auto theft; theft; assaulting rivals; carrying concealed weapons in school; using, selling and stealing drugs; intimidating or assaulting victims and witnesses; and participating in drive-by shootings and homicides than nongang members, as shown in Table 7.6.

Established law enforcement techniques work much better with black gang members than with Hispanics, since black gang members' personal freedom is often more important to them than their gangs. They may be more likely to deal or inform on their "homeboys" than Hispanic gang members are.

Table 7.6
Comparison of Gang and Nongang Criminal Behavior (Cleveland)

Crime (p[1])	Gang N=47	Nongang N=49
Auto Theft (***)	44.7%	4.1%
Assault Rivals (***)	72.3	16.3
Assault Own Members (*)	30.4	10.2
Assault Police (n.s.)	10.6	14.3
Assault Teachers (n.s.)	14.9	18.4
Assault Students (n.s.)	51.1	34.7
Mug People (n.s.)	10.6	4.1
Assault in Streets (*)	29.8	10.2
Theft-Other (***)	51.1	14.3
Intim/Assault Vict/Wit (***)	34.0	0.0
Intim/Assault Shoppers (*)	23.4	6.1
Drive-by Shooting (***)	40.4	2.0
Homicide (**)	15.2	0.0
Sell Stolen Goods (*)	29.8	10.2
Guns in School (***)	40.4	10.2
Knives in School (***)	38.3	4.2
Concealed Weapons (***)	78.7	22.4
Drug Use (**)	27.7	4.1
Drug Sales (School) (n.s.)	19.1	8.2
Drug Sales (Other) (***)	61.7	16.7
Drug Theft (***)	21.3	0.0
Bribe Police (n.s.)	10.6	2.0
Burglary (Unoccupied) (*)	8.5	0.0
Burglary (Occupied) (n.s.)	2.1	2.0
Shoplifting (n.s. [0.58])	30.4	14.3
Check Forgery (n.s.)	2.1	0.0
Credit Card Theft (n.s.)	6.4	0.0
Arson (*)	8.5	0.0
Kidnapping (n.s.)	4.3	0.0
Sexual Assault/Molest (n.s.)	2.1	0.0
Rape (n.s.)	2.1	0.0
Robbery (*)	17.0	2.0

Level of statistical significance: *p<.05, **p<.01, ***p<.001; n.s. = no significant difference.

Source: Ronald C. Huff. *Comparing the Criminal Behavior of Youth Gangs and At-Risk Youths.* National Institute of Justice Research in Brief, October 1998, p. 4. (NCJ-172851)

Indicators of Gang Activity

The telltale signs of gang activity will show up in a variety of ways.

Indicators of gang activity include graffiti, intimidation assaults, open sale of drugs, drive-by shootings and murders.

Gang affiliation might be verified in the following ways:

- Self-admission
- Body tattoos of gang symbols
- Jewelry or apparel associated with gangs
- Written communications such as doodling on notebooks
- Hand-signing
- Vocabulary and use of monikers
- Group photos that include known gang members
- Known gang associates
- Reliable informants

Other signs that an individual may be involved in a gang include abrupt changes in personality and behavior, newly acquired and unexplained money or, conversely, requests to borrow money, and "hanging around" behavior.

Clay and Aquila (1994, pp. 66) caution against overreacting to what appear to be the "trappings" of a gang. They cite a seminar on how to recognize gang graffiti and the facilitator's description of a new gang sign that was showing up in suburban school yards. A probation officer in attendance had the following discussion with the facilitator:

> "Is this [sign] usually painted in white on a brick wall?" The facilitator said that it usually was. The probation officer continued, "Is it usually on a wall where there are no windows?" The facilitator agreed again and asked whether the probation officer knew anything about this new gang. The officer didn't answer but continued his own line of questioning: "Is it usually about three feet off the ground, with white rectangles on either side of it on the ground?" At this point one of the other task force members chimed in with, "Yeah, I've seen that, too." Undaunted, the probation officer went on, "If you go about 20 yards away from the wall, I bet you will find a white stripe painted on the ground."
>
> All eyes were now riveted on the probation officer. "It's a strike zone!" he said. "It's used for wall ball. Kids throw a tennis ball against the wall, and it acts as your backstop."

Clay and Aquila conclude (p. 68): "When you set out to find signs of gang activity, an innocent drawing can become the symbol of some strange new gang."

Gangs' Influence on the Schools

Schools are a prime recruiting ground for gangs. They are also a market for illicit drugs and for extorting money from other students. Often gangs will stake out certain areas of a school as their turf. The Los Angeles *White Paper* (1992, p. 11) notes:

> Gang activity on school campuses is evidenced by various symptoms. Acts of vandalism, arson and graffiti painting, although secretive in nature, are often considered gang involved. Stabbings and shootings between rival gangs take a toll of innocent students and teachers. Student extortion and teacher intimidation are also present. The presence of a sufficient number of gang members in a class effectively renders the teacher powerless to enforce discipline or to teach.

Dill (1998, p22) lists the following "more obvious indications" of gangs operating in a school:

- Gangs have been present in the community in the past.
- Groups of students congregate by racial identity, occasionally calling their group a name that would solidify their identity ("The Red Rozes," "The Perfect Perils," etc.).
- There is an increasing number of violent, racially based incidents.
- The rate of absenteeism is increasing, and crimes in the community increasingly are committed by truants.
- Graffiti and crossed-out graffiti are visible on or near the school.
- Colors are worn symbolically by various groups who also employ hand signals and wear unique symbols on T-shirts or in jewelry.
- Students carry beepers, cell phones, or pages, suggesting that drugs are available in or around the school.

A nationwide survey conducted by the Bureau of Justice Statistics and the National Center for Education Statistics revealed that the number of students reporting gang activity and violent crime increased significantly from 1989 to 1995 ("Gangs, Violence, 1998, p. A5). Forgione, U.S. commissioner of education statistics, noted that "the gang increase came in every type of community. In central cities, students reporting street gangs rose 24.8 to 40.7 percent; in suburbs, from 14.0 to 26.3 percent, and in nonmetropolitan areas, from 7.8 to 19.9 percent" (p. A5).

A key impediment to dealing with youth gang members is the inability to share information, since the records of juveniles are often sealed.

Drugs and Gangs

It is well known that many gang members abuse certain drugs, such as alcohol, marijuana, phencyclidine (PCP) and cocaine. The BJS notes (*Addressing Community*, p. 21): "In some gangs, using drugs is an important means of gaining social status. In others, drug use is forbidden, especially if the gang is involved in selling them." A relatively recent phenomenon is the increasing number of gang members who sell narcotics for monetary gain. Authorities say that members of the Crips and the Bloods have infiltrated cities from Alaska to Washington, DC, selling cocaine and its derivative, crack. And other gangs are engaging in this lucrative business opportunity as well. As Sgt. Jackson, Los Angeles Police Department, observes: "How can you tell a kid who's making $500 a week guarding a rock house that he really ought to be in school or that he ought to be getting up at 4 a.m. every day to ride his bicycle around the neighborhood to deliver the morning papers?"

Yet differing views exist as to the true extent of drug trafficking within gangs. Howell (1997, p. 11) states: "Although youth gangs appear to be increasing their involvement in drug trafficking, empirical research has not documented extensive networks of drug trafficking as an organized activity managed by youth gangs. The consensus among the most experienced gang researchers is that the

Table 7.7 **Common Differences between Street Gangs and Drug Gangs**	Characteristic	Street Gangs	Drug Gangs
	Crime focus	Versatile ("cafeteria-style")	Drug business exclusively
	Structure	Larger organizations	Smaller organizations
	Level of cohesion	Less cohesive	More cohesive
	Leadership	Looser	More centralized
	Roles	Ill-defined	Market-defined
	Nature of loyalty	Code of loyalty	Requirement of loyalty
	Territories	Residential	Sales market
	Degree of drug selling	Members may sell	Members do sell
	Rivalries	Intergang	Competition controlled
	Age of members	Younger on average, but wider age range	Older on average, but narrower age range

Source: Adapted from M. W. Klein. *The American Street Gang.* New York: Oxford University Press, 1995, p. 132. Reprinted by permission.

organizational structure of the typical gang is not particularly suited to the drug-trafficking business." In other words, the typical street gang lacks the skills needed to organize and manage a successful drug trafficking operation. However, other gang researchers contend that gangs are "formal, rational organizations with established leadership structures, roles, rules, and the kind of control over members that would enable gangs to organize and manage drug trafficking operations" (Howell, 1997, p. 9). Certainly this description may apply to a few gangs, but not to as many as some would have us think. Shelden et al. (p. 154) note: "Drug dealing on the part of gang members is significant, but not to the extent that is portrayed by the media." Klein (1995, p. 132) identifies some common differences between street gangs and drug gangs (Table 7.7).

It is generally agreed that gangs organize along one of two basic lines: violence-oriented gangs who exist to fight or entrepreneurially focused gangs structured to make money. Among those gangs for whom drug trafficking is a primary activity, however, violence may accompany their entrepreneurial activities. "Studies also document youth gang drug wars. Two ongoing youth gang wars over drug markets in Chicago accounted for more than 100 homicides during 1987–1994," a total representing 11 percent of all gang-related killings in the city for that time span (Howell, 1997, p. 10).

Gang Myths

This chapter has contained many generalizations about gangs and gang members from many sources. A fitting conclusion is to consider the following myths about gangs[2]:

- **Myth**—*The majority of street gang members are juveniles.*

  Fact—Juveniles, those who are 18 years or younger, actually compose a minority of gang membership. In Los Angeles County, juveniles represent

---

[2]Courtesy of Lorne Kramer, Chief of Police, Colorado Springs, Colorado.

only about 20 percent of gang members. Across the nation, the tenure of gang membership is increasing from age 9 or 10 years up to more than 40 years. Money, drugs and lax juvenile laws each are key factors in this transition to attract kids to gangs at younger ages.

- **Myth**—*All street gangs are turf-oriented.*

  Fact—Some gangs may not claim any specific turf, while other gangs may operate in multiple locations or even in very unsuspecting small cities. One Asian gang that operated crime rings from Florida to California had its headquarters in a small Pennsylvania town of fewer than 4,500 residents.

- **Myth**—*Gang weapons usually consist of chains, knives and tire irons.*

  Fact—Perhaps brass knuckles, knives and chains were the key weapons in the gangs of yesteryear, but today Uzis, AK-47s and semiautomatic firepower are the weapons of choice.

- **Myth**—*All gangs have one leader and are tightly structured.*

  Fact—Most gangs are loosely knit groups and likely will have several leaders. If one member is killed, other potential gang leaders seem to be waiting in the wings.

- **Myth**—*One way to cure gang membership is by locking the gang member away.*

  Fact—Incarceration and rehabilitation of hard-core gang members has not proven to be effective. Changing criminal behavior patterns is difficult. Prisons often serve as command centers and institutions of higher learning for ongoing gang-related crime. Often prisoners are forced to take sides with one group or another simply for protection.

- **Myth**—*Gangs are a law enforcement problem.*

  Fact—Gangs are a problem for everyone. Communities need to develop systemwide programs to effectively address the gang problem in their areas.

Not merely a school problem either, gangs are a community problem and a national challenge. Responding to gangs requires a systematic, comprehensive and collaborative approach that incorporates prevention, intervention and suppression strategies. While each strategy has a specific vision and a pressing mandate, the greatest hope is on the side of prevention, for only by keeping children from joining gangs in the first place will the rising tide of terror and violence that gangs represent be halted.

Summary

A gang is a group of people who form an allegiance for a common purpose and engage in unlawful or criminal activity. A street gang is a group of individuals who meet over time, have identifiable leadership, claim control over a specific territory in the community and engage in criminal behavior. Criminal behavior is what separates a gang from a club such as the Boy Scouts. The youth gang, for criminal justice policy purposes, is a subset of the street gang.

Street gangs can be found throughout the United States, not only in large cities, but in the suburbs, small towns and even rural areas. They acquire their power in the community through their violent behavior. Street gangs provide their members a feeling of belonging as well as protection from other youths. They may also provide financial power. Gang membership may result from a variety of personal, social and economic factors, including family structure and influences such as parental guidance and lack of responsibility, peer pressure and ego fulfillment, racism and cultural discord, socioeconomic factors and socialized delinquency.

Contemporary gangs may be classified as scavenger, territorial or corporate. They may also be classified as hedonistic, instrumental or predatory, or as criminal, conflict or retreatist, based on the concept of differential opportunity. Further, they may be classified as traditional or nontraditional. The most common gangs are Hispanic, black and Asian. Two well-known rival black street gangs are the Crips and the Bloods.

Five characteristics that distinguish youth gangs are leadership, organization, associational patterns, domain identification and illegal activity. Most gangs contain leaders, hard-core members, regular members and fringe members or wannabes.

Gang members may be identified by their names, symbols (including clothing and tattoos) and communication styles, including sign language and graffiti. Gang members communicate through clothing, tattoos, symbols, hand signals and graffiti. Graffiti is a method of communication commonly used to mark a street gang's "turf." Gang activity ranges from property crimes to violent crimes against persons and includes graffiti painting, vandalism, arson, student extortion, teacher intimidation, drug dealing, rape, stabbings and shootings.

Indicators of gang activity include graffiti, intimidation assaults, the open sale of drugs, drive-by shootings and murders.

Discussion Questions

1. Are there gangs in your community? If so, do they cause problems for the police?
2. Have you seen any movies or TV programs about gangs? How are gang activities depicted?
3. What do you think are the main reasons people join gangs?
4. How does a youth gang differ from a group such as a Boy Scout troop or a school club?
5. How does a youth gang member differ from other juvenile delinquents?
6. Should convicted youth gang members be treated like other juvenile delinquents, including status offenders?
7. What might influence you to become a gang member? To not become a gang member?
8. Do you believe the juvenile justice system should support gang summits that claim to be working toward peaceful, lawful ways to improve the situation of gang members?
9. How much, if any, do gangs today differ from those of the 1960s and 1970s?
10. Do you think the gang problem will increase or decrease?

References

Addressing Community Gang Problems: A Practical Guide. Washington, DC: Bureau of Justice Assistance, May 1998. (NCJ-164273)

Ayres, B. Drummand, Jr. "The Addictive Art of Graffiti Tagging." (Minneapolis/St. Paul) *Star Tribune,* March 16, 1994, p. A4.

Bell. *Down These Mean Streets: Violence By and Against America's Children.* Hearings before U.S. House of Representatives, Committee on Children, Youth and Families. 101st Congress, 1st Session, May 16, 1989, p. 79.

Burch, James H., II and Chemers, Betty M. *A Comprehensive Response to America's Youth Gang Problem.* Washington, DC: Office of Juvenile Justice and Delinquency Prevention, Fact Sheet #40, March 1997. (FS-9640)

Burke, Tod W. "Home Invaders: Gangs of the Future." *The Police Chief,* November 1990, pp. 23–25.

Clay, Douglas A. and Aquila, Frank D. "Gangs and America's Schools." *Phi Delta Kappan,* September 1994, pp. 65–68.

Clear, Todd R. Foreword. In Randall G. Shelden, Sharon K. Tracy and William B. Brown, *Youth Gangs in American Society.* Belmont, CA: Wadsworth Publishing Company, 1997, pp. xi–xiii.

Cline, Foster. *Understanding and Treating the Severely Disturbed Child.* Evergreen, CO: Evergreen Consultants, 1979.

Cloward, R. and Ohlin, L. *Delinquency and Opportunity.* Glencoe, IL: Free Press, 1960.

Dart, Robert W. "Chicago's 'Flying Squad' Tackles Street Gangs." *The Police Chief,* October 1992, pp. 96–104.

Decker, Scott H.; Bynum, Tim; and Weisel, Deborah. "A Tale of Two Cities: Gangs as Organized Crime Groups." *Justice Quarterly,* Vol. 15, No. 3, September 1998, pp. 395–425.

Dill, Vicky Schreiber. *A Peaceable School: Cultivating a Culture of Nonviolence.* Bloomington, IN: Phi Delta Kappa Educational Foundation, 1998.

Esbensen, Finn-Aage and Huizinga, David. "Gangs, Drugs and Delinquency." *Criminology,* Vol. 31, 1993, pp. 565–590.

Esbensen, Finn-Aage and Winfree, L. Thomas. "Race and Gender Differences Between Gang and Nongang Youth: Results from a Multisite Survey." *Justice Quarterly,* Vol. 15, No. 3, September 1998, pp. 505–525.

"Gangs, Violence on the Rise in U.S. Schools." (Minneapolis/ St. Paul) *Star Tribune,* April 13, 1998, p. A5.

Gates, Daryl F. and Jackson, Robert K. "Gang Violence in L.A." *The Police Chief,* November 1990, pp. 20–22.

"Getting a Grip on Slippery Gang Problems." *Law Enforcement News,* December 31, 1993, p. 13.

Gross, Daniel D. and Gross, Timothy D. "Tagging: Changing Visual Patterns and the Rhetorical Implications of a New Form of Graffiti." *Et cetera,* Fall 1993, pp. 251–264.

Gustafson, Paul. "Authorities Crack Down on Asian Gang Accused of Raping Hmong Girls." (Minneapolis/St. Paul) *Star Tribune,* June 7, 1998, pp. B1, B9.

Hall, Dennis. "Chiefs' Survey: Drugs, Gangs, Domestic Violence Top List." *Police,* August 1998, pp. 72–76.

Harlan, Alan. "Battling Organized Asian Crime Gangs." *Law and Order,* February 1993, pp. 51–54.

Howell, James C. "Youth Gang Drug Trafficking and Homicide: Policy and Program Implications." *Juvenile Justice,* Vol. 4, No. 2, December 1997, pp. 9–20.

Howell, James C. *Youth Gangs: An Overview.* OJJDP, Juvenile Justice Bulletin, August 1998. (NCJ-167249)

Huff, C. Ronald. "Youth Gangs and Public Policy." *Crime & Delinquency,* Vol. 35, No. 4, October 1989, pp. 524–537.

Huff, C. Ronald. "Gangs in the United States." In A. P. Goldstein and C. Ronald Huff, *The Gang Intervention Handbook,* 1993.

Huff, C. Ronald. *Comparing the Criminal Behavior of Youth Gangs and At-Risk Youths.* National Institute of Justice Research in Brief, October 1998. (NCJ-172851)

Ima, Kenji. *A Handbook for Professionals Working with Southeast Asian Delinquent and At-Risk Youth*. San Diego, CA: Southeast Asian Youth Diversion Project, June 1992.

International Association of Chiefs of Police. "Violent Crime in America: Recommendations of the IACP Summit." *The Police Chief*, June 1993, pp. 59–60.

Jackson, Robert K. and McBride, Wesley D. *Understanding Street Gangs*. Sacramento, CA: Custom Publishing, 1985.

Jankowski, M. S. *Islands in the Street: Gangs and American Urban Society*. Berkeley, CA: University of California Press, 1990.

Johnson, C.; Webster, B.; and Connors, E. *Prosecuting Gangs: A National Assessment*. Washington, DC: U.S. Government Printing Office, 1995.

Kadish, Sanford H., ed. *Encyclopedia of Crime and Justice*. New York: Free Press, 1983.

Klein, M. W. *The American Street Gang*. New York: Oxford University Press, 1995, p. 132.

Laflin, Melanie. "Girl Gangs." *Law and Order*, March 1996, pp. 87–89.

Los Angeles County Sheriff's Department, Operation Safe Streets Gang Unit. *Street Gangs of Los Angeles County: A White Paper*. Revised February 1, 1992.

McCorkle, Richard C. and Miethe, Terance D. "The Political and Organizational Response to Gangs: An Examination of a 'Moral Panic' in Nevada." *Justice Quarterly*, Vol. 15, No. 1, March 1998, pp. 41–64.

McCort, Michael C. "The Evolution of Street Gangs: A Shift Toward Organized Crime." *The Police Chief*, June 1996, pp. 33–38, 51–52.

McGarvey, Robert. "Gangland: L.A. Super Gangs Target America." *American Legion Magazine*, February 1991, pp. 25–27, 60–61.

Miller, Walter B. "Youth Gangs and Groups." In *Encyclopedia of Crime and Justice*. Vol. 4, edited by Sanford H. Kadish. New York: Free Press, 1983, pp. 1671–1679.

Miller, Walter B. "Why the United States Has Failed to Solve Its Youth Gang Problem." In *Gangs in America*, edited by C. Ronald Huff. Newbury Park, CA: Sage Publications, 1991, pp. 263–287.

Miller, Walter B. *Crime by Youth Gangs and Groups in the United States*. Washington, DC: Office of Juvenile Justice and Delinquency Prevention, 1992. (NCJ-156221)

Moore, J. P. and Terrett, C. P. *Highlights of the 1996 National Youth Gang Survey*. Washington, DC: Office of Juvenile Justice and Delinquency Prevention, Fact Sheet, in press.

National Coalition of State Juvenile Justice Advisory Groups. *Myths and Realities: Meeting the Challenge of Serious, Violent, and Chronic Juvenile Offenders, 1992 Annual Report*. Washington, DC: 1993.

National Institute of Justice. *Research and Evaluation Plan, 1992*. April 1992.

National School Safety Center. *Gangs in Schools: Breaking Up Is Hard to Do*. Malibu, CA: Pepperdine University Press, 1988.

Owens, Robert P. and Wells, Donna K. "One City's Response to Gangs." *The Police Chief*, February 1993, pp. 25–27.

Ross, Martha. "Woman Warriors." *The Times/Bleeding Colors*, Special Edition, September 26, 1993, pp. 8–9.

Rushing, Rocky, ed. *The Times/Bleeding Colors*. Special Edition, September 26, 1993, pp. 12–13.

Saccente, D. D. "RAP to Street Gang Activity." *The Police Chief*, February 1993, pp. 28–31.

Shakur, Sanyika. *Monster: The Autobiography of an L.A. Gang Member*. New York: Penguin Books, 1993.

Shelden, Randall G.; Tracy, Sharon K.; and Brown, William B. *Youth Gangs in American Society*. Belmont, CA: Wadsworth Publishing Company, 1997.

Slahor, Stephenie. "Nipping in the Bud: The Task Force Approach to Gangs." *Law and Order*, May 1993, p. 55.

"Slain Boy, 11, Is Buried, a Sad Symbol for Nation." (Minneapolis/St. Paul) *Star Tribune*, September 8, 1994, pp. A7, A10.

Spergel, Irving A. "Youth Gangs: Continuity and Change." *Crime and Justice*, Vol. 12, 1990, pp. 171–275.

Spergel, Irving A.; Chance, Ronald L.; and Curry, G. David. *National Youth Gang Suppression and Intervention Program.* OJJDP, Juvenile Justice Bulletin, June 1990.

Taylor, Carl S. "Gang Imperialism." In *Gangs in America,* edited by C. Ronald Huff. Newbury Park, CA: Sage Publications, 1991, pp. 103–115.

Thornberry, Terence P. and Burch, James H., II. *Gang Members and Delinquent Behavior.* OJJDP, Juvenile Justice Bulletin, June 1997. (NCJ-165154)

Thrasher, Frederic M. *The Gang: A Study of 1,313 Gangs in Chicago.* Chicago: University of Chicago Press, 1927.

Trethewy, Steve and Katz, Terry. "Motorcycle Gangs or Motorcycle Mafia?" *The Police Chief,* April 1998, pp. 53–60.

Valdez, Al. "A New Gang Threat Rears Its Ugly Head." *Police,* July 1996, pp. 20–21.

Valdez, Al. "Girls in the Hood: Dangerous Liaisons." *Police,* September 1997a, pp. 40–41.

Valdez, Al. "Southeast Asian Gangs." *Police,* April 1997b, pp. 50–51.

Valdez, Al. "Gangs: Migration or Imitation?" *Police,* January 1998a, pp. 48–49.

Valdez, Al. "Interpreting That Writing on the Wall." *Police,* April 1998b, pp. 39–40.

Valdez, Al. "Native American Gangs Spreading." *Police,* February 1998c, p. 47.

Walker, Samuel; Spohn, Cassia; and DeLone, Miriam. *The Color of Justice: Race, Ethnicity, and Crime in America.* Belmont, CA: Wadsworth Publishing Company, 1996.

Wexler, Sanford. "Gangbusters." *Law Enforcement Technology,* March 1997, pp. 28–35.

Wilson, Craig R. "What's In a Name? Gang Monikers." *FBI Law Enforcement Bulletin,* May 1997, pp. 14–17.

Wrobleski, Henry M. and Hess, Kären M. *Introduction to Law Enforcement and Criminal Justice,* 6th ed. St. Paul, MN: West/Wadsworth Publishing Company, 2000.

8 The Role of Law Enforcement

Children spend up to 25 percent of their waking hours in school. It has been estimated that 18 percent of their time is spent with their peers—other children. Another 18 percent of their waking hours may be spent in front of the television. Police are the only other significant parental type, albeit surrogate, in contact with our children.

—Timothy D. Crowe

Do You Know

- What factors affect how police officers resolve juvenile delinquency problems?
- What street justice is?
- Whether the police have discretionary power when dealing with juveniles?
- What action police usually take when confronting juveniles?
- What the five primary objectives of juvenile law enforcement are?
- What the fundamental nature of the juvenile justice system is?
- What "window of opportunity" exists with youths who are in detention?
- What primary responsibility officers assigned a child abuse or neglect case have?
- What the majority of police dispositions involve?
- What predelinquent indicator often goes unnoticed?
- What seems to be the most visible indicator of a future victim or offender?
- How prevention methods have changed over the years and why?
- What the focus of the TOP program is? Project DARE?
- What professionals are very important in delinquency prevention programs?
- What greatly influences youths' attitudes towards law and law enforcement?
- What paradigm shift affects how law enforcement deals with youths?

Can You Define

community policing, community relations, detention, deterrence, funnel effect, paradigm, police-school liaison program, SHOCAP, station adjustment, street justice, window of opportunity

INTRODUCTION

As noted by Pace (1991, pp. 108–109): "Of all minority groups, the most important one is the young. Their importance is emphasized because they represent all segments of society. The future of this nation depends upon the values they are forming. They obviously will be the future decision-makers of our society." Juvenile justice is basically concerned with three distinct types of youths: those who are victims of neglect and/or abuse, those who commit minor (status) offenses and those who commit serious crimes (delinquents). The police are charged with protecting youths, both victims and offenders, and dealing fairly with them. Questions of what is in the best interest of the youth must be balanced with what is best for the community. Also, the crime-fighting philosophy must be balanced with the service ideal.

This chapter begins with a discussion of the contemporary juvenile justice system within which law enforcement functions. Next is a discussion of the various dispositions police officers can make when dealing with youths, be they victims or offenders. It discusses police discretion and whether the system is too lenient. The law enforcement portion of the juvenile justice system is examined from the time of taking into custody (arrest), to detention, to intake and, finally, to prosecution.

The issue of the overrepresentation of minorities being processed by the system is then discussed, followed by a more in-depth look at how law enforcement interacts with the various types of children and juveniles within its jurisdiction: neglected and abused children, status offenders, serious habitual offenders and gang members. Next prevention efforts undertaken by law enforcement are briefly reviewed, including such well-known programs as the DARE program. The chapter ends with a look at how law enforcement is changing and the challenges this is presenting.

The Contemporary Juvenile Justice System

In the first section of this text you were introduced to how the juvenile justice system evolved and became distinct from the adult system. The juvenile system has retained, however, the three basic components of the adult system: law enforcement or the police, courts and corrections. The process usually begins with the police, who may turn the youth over to the juvenile court, who in turn may turn the youth over to the correctional component of the system. At any point in this process, youths may be diverted—one of the goals of the system. Figure 8.1 illustrates not only the more complex flow of the system but also how it correlates to the adult system.

According to Crowe (1991, p. 36): "The system is designed intentionally to let juvenile offenders 'drop through the cracks'." He suggests that this is probably all right because children naturally get into trouble and most deserve a "second chance." This results in what is often called the **funnel effect;** that is, at each point in the system fewer and fewer youths pass through.

Crowe suggests that since the police arrest only 100 out of every 1,000, or only 10 percent of the youths with whom they come into contact, the police are really more a part of the community than of the system. The system appears to

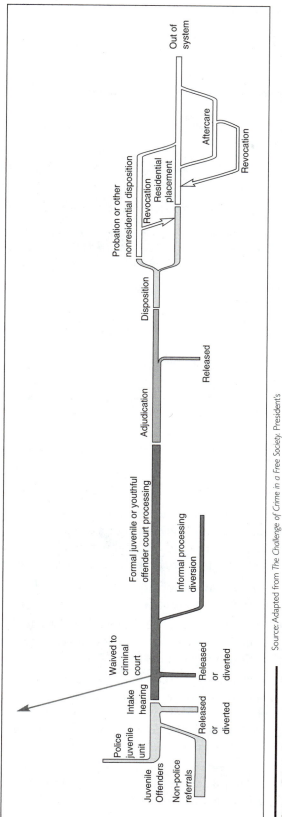

Figure 8.1
Progression through the Juvenile Justice System

Source: Adapted from *The Challenge of Crime in a Free Society.* President's Commission on Law Enforcement and Administration of Justice, 1967. This revision, a result of the Symposium on the 30th Anniversary of the President's Commission, was prepared by the Bureau of Justice Statistics in 1997. *What Is the Sequence of Events through the Criminal Justice System?* Washington, DC: Bureau of Justice Statistics, January 1998 (Chart). (NIJ-167894)

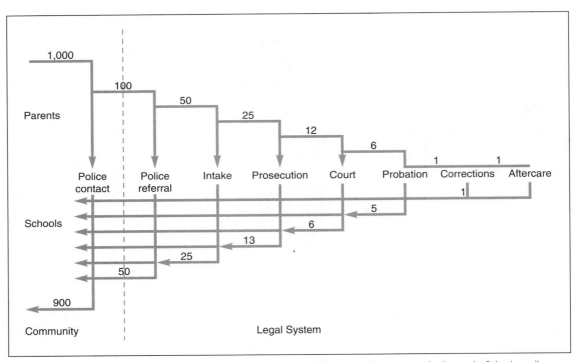

Figure 8.2
The Funnel Fallacy—
Processing and Dropout
Rates of the Juvenile
Justice System

Police really are primary participants in the community, instead of the juvenile justice system, since 90 percent of their contacts do not result in arrest.
Source: Timothy D. Crowe. *Habitual Juvenile Offenders: Guidelines for Citizen Action and Public Responses.* Serious Habitual Offender Comprehensive Action Program (SHOCAP) Washington, DC: Office of Juvenile Justice and Delinquency Prevention, October 1991, p. 36.

work for most juveniles, but where it breaks down is in its ineffectiveness with the serious juvenile offender, as illustrated in Figure 8.2.

Research projects and informal surveys suggest the following breakdown of what actually happens in the juvenile justice system (Crowe, 1991, pp. 34–35):

- *Police contact*—For every 1,000 young persons in contact with police, 10 percent or *100* are arrested.

- *Police referral*—Police commonly drop charges or reprimand and release about 50 percent of all juveniles who are arrested. Therefore, only *50* cases are filed with court intake.

- *Intake screening and referral*—Of the 50 cases formally presented to the court intake, which is usually a detention counselor or state probation official, only about 50 percent or *25* are sent forward. The remainder are counseled and released or put on informal supervision. Few are actually placed in pretrial detention.

- *Prosecution screening*—Unless a young offender has been arrested before or the immediate offense is serious, fewer than 50 percent of the cases, or *12* juveniles, will be referred to the court. The rest have charges dropped or are placed on deferred prosecution while attending treatment programs, as a condition of dropping charges.

- *Court trials*—Fewer than 50 percent of cases presented result in the adjudication of delinquent status. This means only six accused delinquents are found guilty and sentenced.
- *Court disposition*—Most (five out of six) sentences are for probation with some sort of supervision, which may include counseling or treatment. *One* juvenile is incarcerated in a state reform school or a residential treatment program.
- *Probation*—The five juveniles placed on probation generally see the probation counselor weekly or monthly and follow a set of rules that restrict the delinquent from certain locations, associations, or activities.
- *State corrections*—The *one* juvenile from the original 1,000 contacted by the police serves a sentence in a state program.
- *After-care*—The *one* juvenile sentenced to a state program is probably released eventually on parole, euphemistically referred to as after-care.

Says Crowe (1991, pp. 36–37):

The "funnel fallacy" teaches us a number of crucial lessons:

- *First*—The conventional conception of the role of the schools and police is not accurate.
- *Second*—Schools and police are fundamental to the community control of delinquency.
- *Third*—School and police officials have more contact with our children than does anyone else, except parents.
- *Fourth*—The juvenile justice system is irrelevant to the prevention and diversion of delinquency, because the schools and the police are not a significant part of the system. They are at the opening of the "funnel" and have been mistakenly excluded from the concept of the community's responsibility for controlling delinquency.
- *Fifth*—Parents, school officials and police are the primary actors in the basic function of "parenting" in contemporary society.
- *Sixth*—The contact and information that *could* be shared between parents, schools and police are the *key* to the effective functioning of the juvenile justice system. They are the filter to the end of the "funnel" that feeds the legal system that has only one purpose—effective control of individuals whom the community is unable to control!

Many government agencies are involved directly and indirectly with juveniles. Most are under the U.S. Department of Justice through its Office of Justice Programs. The Office of Justice Programs coordinates the activities of these program offices and bureaus: The Bureau of Justice Statistics (BJS), the National Institute of Justice (NIJ), the Bureau of Justice Assistance (BJA), the Office of Juvenile Justice and Delinquency Prevention (OJJDP) and the Office for Victims of Crime (OVC). (See Figure 8.3.) These offices often conduct joint efforts and programs.

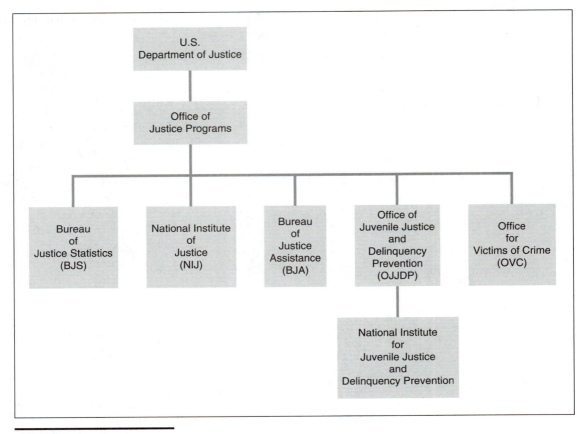

Figure 8.3
**Agencies of the
U.S. Department
of Justice Coordinated
by the Office of Justice
Programs**

Police Dispositions

Police dispositions involve all contacts officers make concerning children's health, safety and welfare. The dispositions range from taking no action to referring the children to social service agencies or to the juvenile court. Police also deal with a wide range of youths, from those who need protection from abuse or neglect to those who have committed status offenses to those who have committed violent criminal acts. For status offenses the police have many alternatives that are guided by the community, the local juvenile justice system and individual officer discretion. The dispositions police make in cases of violent criminal behavior are a different matter, however. The reporting, investigation and disposition in these cases follow a direct criminal justice scheme, and the police have limited alternatives and limited discretion.

In the disposition of matters related to children, how police resolve matters depends on the officers' discretion and the specific incident.

Whether the police actually arrest a juvenile usually depends on several factors, the most important being the seriousness of the offense. Other factors affecting the decision include:

- Character
- Age
- Gender
- Race
- Prior record
- Family situation
- Attitude

In investigating how a juvenile suspect's race, gender, socioeconomic status (SES) and offense type influence police officers' arrest decisions, Sealock and Simpson (1998, p. 427) discovered: "When other variables are controlled, females are less likely to be arrested than their male counterparts and . . . race and SES also significantly affect the arrest decision." Furthermore: "Within gender-type offense categories, we found evidence that officers consider offense seriousness and, most notably, the number of prior police contacts in arrest decisions."

When the offense is relatively minor, however, females tend to become the predominant juvenile justice client. Herz (1998, pp. 184–185) notes: "Female status offenders continue to be institutionalized at higher rates than male status offenders, particularly in private facilities." Herz's research also found (p. 185): "Female status offenders may be more likely to receive diagnostic services than are their male counterparts," which may result in harsher dispositional outcomes for such female offenders. As Herz explains (p. 185): "Overall, diagnostic services surfaced as a strong predictor of disposition outcomes in all cases. Instead of viewing diagnostic services as a rehabilitative alternative to additional intervention, court officials seemed to interpret diagnostic services as an indicator of problem behavior relative to who initiates the complaint as well as to the expectations of appropriate punishment."

The decision may also be influenced by public opinion, the media, available referral agencies and the officer's experience. Officers' actions usually reflect community interests. For example, conflict may occur between the public's demand for order and a group of young people wanting to "hang around." How police respond to such hanging around is influenced by the officer's attitude and the standards of the neighborhood or community, rather than rules of the state. Each neighborhood or community and the officer's own feelings dictate how the police perform in such matters.

Some localities may handle a delinquent act very differently from others. For example, police investigating an auto theft in the suburbs and finding a youth responsible will often simply send the youth home for parental discipline. The youth will receive a notice of when to appear in court. In contrast, urban juveniles—especially minority youths—caught stealing an automobile are often detained in a locked facility. Sometimes, however, urban youths are at an advantage. What rural law enforcement officers may perceive as criminal behavior is often viewed as a prank by that officer's urban counterpart. Clearly, justice for juveniles is not a neatly structured, impartial decision-making process by which the rule of law always prevails and each person is treated fairly and impartially.

Sometimes police may "roust" and "hassle" youths who engage in undesirable social conduct, but they probably will not report the incident; in this case, **street justice** is the police disposition.

Street justice occurs when police decide to deal with a status offense in their own way—usually by ignoring it.

Police Discretion and the Initial Contact

Between 80 and 90 percent of youths commit some offense for which they could be arrested, yet only about 3 percent of them are. This is in large part because they do not get caught. Further, those who are caught have usually engaged in some minor status offense that can be better handled by counseling and releasing in many instances. Although the "counsel and dismiss" alternative may be criticized as being "soft" on juveniles, this approach is often all that is needed to turn a youth around.

Decades ago the Task Force on Juvenile Delinquency and Youth Crime, part of the President's Commission on Law Enforcement and the Administration of Justice, highlighted the wide range of police discretion and the lack of guidelines for them to use (1967, p. 14):

> The range of police dispositions is considerable, and the criteria for selection of a disposition are seldom set forth, explicitly, ordered in priority, or regularly reviewed for administrative purposes. Inservice training designed to assist police in exercising their discretionary functions is unusual.

Police officers have considerable discretionary power when dealing with juveniles.

Law enforcement officers have a range of alternatives to take:

- Release the child, with or without a warning, but without making an official record or taking further action.
- Release the child, but write up a brief contact or field report to juvenile authorities, describing the contact.
- Release the child, but file a more formal report referring the matter to a juvenile bureau or an intake unit, for possible action.
- Turn the youth over to juvenile authorities immediately.
- Refer the case directly to the court, through the district or county attorney.

In some instances youths engaging in delinquent acts are simply counseled. In other instances they are returned to their families, who are expected to deal with their child's deviant behavior. Sometimes they are referred to social services agencies for help. And sometimes they are charged and processed by the juvenile justice system.

Positive face-to-face contacts between police officers and children can help promote the idea of the police officer as a friend and helper.

The most common procedure is to release the child, with or without a warning, but without making an official record or taking further action.

Figure 8.1 illustrates the flow of the juvenile justice system. Parents, schools and the police are the main sources for the referral of youths into the juvenile justice system. Of these three sources, the police are, by far, the most common source of referrals.

In a few jurisdictions, if the child is not released without official record, he or she is automatically turned over to the juvenile authorities, who make all further decisions in the matter. If the child is referred to court, another decision is whether police personnel should release or detain the child.

Objectives in Handling Juveniles

Police officers usually follow a set of objectives in handling juveniles. In most jurisdictions the law specifies that the first objective is to protect the juvenile. Second, officers are to investigate. Third, they are to determine the causes of the victimization or delinquency. These causes are usually exposed in a dialogue between the youth and authority. Fourth, every effort is made to prevent further victimization or delinquency. And fifth, the officers seek a proper disposition of the case.

The objectives of police officers handling juvenile cases are (1) to protect the juvenile, (2) to investigate, (3) to determine the causes of the victimization or delinquency, (4) to prevent further victimization or delinquency and (5) to properly dispose of the case.

Officers try to dispose of juvenile cases in a way that considers the best interests of both the juvenile and the community. The intake process of the juvenile justice system requires the development of employee screening practices, certification standards and caseload guidelines. Caseworkers should be certified to practice on the basis of education, training and experience.

Taken into Custody

Police contact with children may result either from a complaint received or from observing questionable behavior. In their initial contact with juveniles, the police are indirectly guided by the language of the Juvenile Court Act, which states that juveniles are "taken into custody," not arrested. This is interpreted to mean the police's role is to salvage and rehabilitate youth, a role indirectly sanctioned by many judges who condone or encourage settling disputes and complaints without referral to the court.

When a juvenile is taken into custody, this is technically not considered an arrest. The law enforcement process for arrest is modified in most jurisdictions when juveniles are apprehended. Police officers should be concerned about the mental health of juveniles. They should be good listeners and try to discover the problem or the reason for the juveniles' behavior.

It is paramount in administering juvenile justice that youths be protected by all sociolegal requirements. All actions must be in the best interest of the child. This is important whether the child involved is an offender or a victim.

The fundamental nature of the juvenile justice system is rehabilitative rather than punitive.

Most states' juvenile justice systems reflect this basic rehabilitative philosophy. In addition the Supreme Court has emphasized the full constitutional rights of persons under legal age. The protection, critical to the juvenile offender, is twofold:

1. At no point in any criminal investigation may the rights of the juvenile be infringed upon.
2. A crime by a juvenile must be proven beyond a reasonable doubt, and all subsequent efforts by a state should be directed toward correlating and eliminating the cause of the crime rather than punishing the individual for having committed it.

Juveniles must be treated with consideration in order to build their respect for authority. Officers must be firm but fair, and they must show genuine interest. They must try to understand the juveniles' reasoning. In handling juveniles, if officers resort to vulgarity or profanity, lose their tempers, display prejudicial behavior or label juveniles as "liars" or "no good," this is counterproductive. Such actions are often followed by further disruptive conduct by the juvenile or by a lack of cooperation in any attempt to divert juvenile conduct.

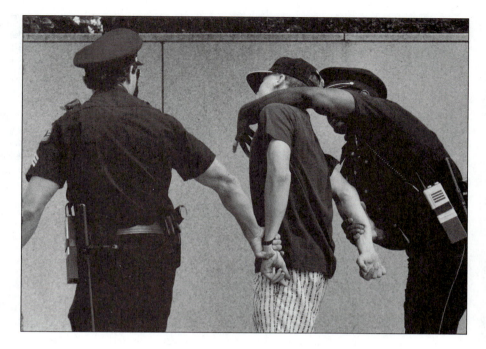

Youths are not arrested; they are "taken into custody." Here a 15-year-old is taken into custody for trying to start a riot in Dallas, Texas. Because he is a minor, he was turned over to his parents.

According to Crowe (1991, p. 20) it now takes up to three times longer to detain (arrest) a juvenile than an adult because of public policy establishing so many safeguards for juveniles. Crowe also states that a detained juvenile is much less likely than an adult to receive official sanction. Given this situation Crowe argues: "No wonder that uniformed police officers, who have 90 percent of the contact with juveniles, are more likely to exercise their discretion 'to do nothing' than to bother with a youngster who is just going to be released anyway."

If a youth is detained, the officers must remember that juveniles have the same constitutional rights as adults, including the right to remain silent, the right to counsel, the right to know the specific charge and the right to confront witnesses. As noted by the Minnesota POST (Police Officer Standards and Training) Board (1992, p. 72): "Although certain procedures of the juvenile justice system may differ from those of the adult system, peace officer duties and responsibilities for ensuring the rights of juveniles and thoroughly investigating the elements of juvenile criminal offenses is as great as or greater than their responsibilities of carrying out the same duties pertaining to adults."

Given the *parens patriae* philosophy underlying the juvenile justice system, it might be expected that the police would exercise extra care in dealing with youths. Krisberg and Austin (1993, p. 85) suggest the opposite is occurring: "Evidence suggests that youths are treated as harshly as their adult counterparts and with less respect for their constitutional rights. . . . Critics of police handling of juveniles attribute the tendency of police to ignore the civil rights of youths to the conflict of controlling crime while attempting to maintain a benevolent treatment approach."

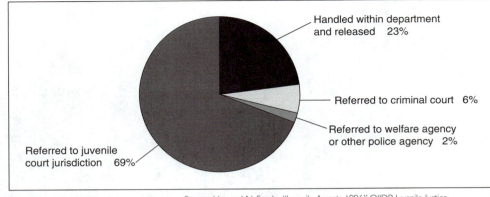

Figure 8.4
**Police Dispositions
of Juvenile Offenders
Taken into Custody, 1996**

Source: Howard N. Snyder. "Juvenile Arrests 1996." OJJDP Juvenile Justice Bulletin, November 1997, p. 6.

Of the juvenile offenders taken into custody in 1996, over two-thirds (69 percent) were referred to juvenile court jurisdiction. Slightly fewer than one-fourth (23 percent) were handled within the department and released—called **station adjustment.** Figure 8.4 shows the police dispositions of juvenile offenders taken into custody in 1996.

One problem of referral for juvenile authorities and the court, especially in a metropolitan area, is that it may be difficult to determine by appearance alone if a person is a juvenile. Youths may lie about or try to manipulate their age for practical reasons. For example, a youth detained on a status offense may claim to be over the age limit and, consequently, *not* an offender. Or youths taken into custody for minor offenses such as disorderly conduct or prostitution often claim to be over the age limit, reasoning that if treated as adults they will simply be forced to spend a night in jail, hear a lecture by a judge and accept whatever penalty is disposed. If they identify themselves as juveniles, their detention usually is extended, and interference with their freedom and liberty may well be more substantial.

In small towns and in rural areas, the procedure for the prereferral process is to release the youths to their custodians, allowing the custodians to dispense justice and relieve the workload of the court.

Detention

Krisberg and Austin (p. 73) define **detention** as: "The period in which a wayward youth is taken into custody by police and probation prior to a petition being filed and an adjudication hearing by the juvenile court." Detention is governed by two requirements of the JJDP Act: (1) removing all juveniles from adult jails and lockups and (2) separating juvenile and adult offenders. The act states:

Provide that juveniles alleged to be or found to be delinquent and youths within the purview of paragraph (12) (i.e., status offenders and nonoffenders) shall not be detained or confined in any institution in which they have regular contact with adult persons incarcerated because they have been convicted of a crime or are awaiting trial on criminal charges.

In addition state laws and department policies may affect who is detained and under what conditions. Most state statutes governing the detention of juveniles are quite general. Among the common criteria used by states are (Krisberg and Austin, p. 73):

- For the juvenile's protection, or for the protection of the person or property of others
- No parental care available for the juvenile
- To ensure a juvenile's presence at the juvenile court hearing
- The seriousness of the offense and the juvenile's record

Release vs. Detention

Juvenile court statutes often require that once children have been taken into custody, they may be released only to their parents, guardians or custodians. Where such a law exists, a decision to detain automatically follows if the parents, guardians or custodians cannot be found. The child is placed in detention and must be referred to court. Thus the police are removed from the referral process.

In most states police may take a child into custody for the child's own protection until appropriate placement can be made. Standards to guide police personnel in the decision whether to release or detain may be formally prepared in written instructions by police administrators and court authorities. In some states *mandatory referral* to juvenile authorities or even directly to court may be required for all crimes of violence, felonies and serious misdemeanors. Similarly all juveniles on parole or probation may be referred. Some jurisdictions refer if the juvenile has had previous contact with the police. Figure 8.5 summarizes the federal jail removal and separation requirements for juveniles.

Stewart (1990, p. 1) suggests that during detention, police have "a **window of opportunity** . . . an opportunity to be an agency for change for youngsters who have by law come under its control. Drug testing can be used diagnostically to identify high-risk youth before they become established in the cycle of illicit drug use and crime" (boldface added).

The strong link between illicit drug use and crime has been well established by research in the past decade. Bilchik (1998, p. iii) notes: "Juvenile drug use . . . has risen significantly over the past several years, with one of two high school seniors in 1996 reporting having used illicit drugs. While this problem is of concern in itself, the clear correlation between substance abuse and other forms of delinquency gives further reason for concern." (See Table 8.1.) Crowe (1998, p. 1) adds:

> Drug testing can be used as an intervention tool to help youth overcome denial of substance abuse problems, hold them accountable for their behavior, and underscore a consistent message to all youth about striving to live drug free. Such interventions will enhance the lives of individual youth and their families, protect citizens in the community, and preserve the resources of the juvenile justice system currently being consumed to address juvenile crime related to substance abuse.

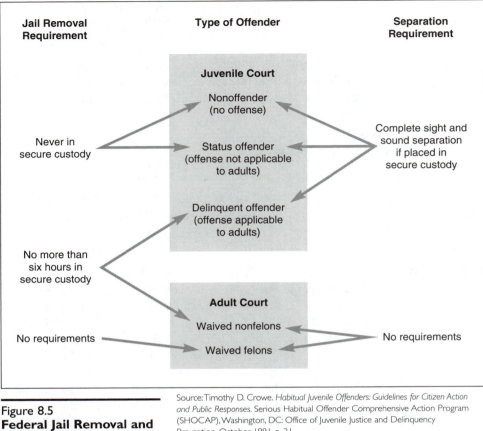

Figure 8.5
Federal Jail Removal and Separation Requirements for Juveniles

Source: Timothy D. Crowe. *Habitual Juvenile Offenders: Guidelines for Citizen Action and Public Responses.* Serious Habitual Offender Comprehensive Action Program (SHOCAP), Washington, DC: Office of Juvenile Justice and Delinquency Prevention, October 1991, p. 21.

Table 8.1
Association between Threatening or Delinquent Activities and Use of Alcohol or Other Drugs by 6th through 12th Graders

Type of Substance Used	Percentage of Students Who:			
	Carried a Gun to School	Participated in Gang Activities	Threatened to Harm Another	Got into Trouble with the Police
Liquor	76.4	68.4	51.7	65.3
Marijuana	71.1	59.7	36.7	54.2
Inhalants	38.2	26.9	13.8	18.1
Cocaine	37.2	19.4	7.8	12.8

Source: National Parents' Resource Institute for Drug Education, 1997. *PRIDE Questionnaire Report: 1996–97 National Summary Grades 6 through 12.* Atlanta, GA: National Parents' Resource Institute for Drug Education. Reprinted by permission.

During detention, a window of opportunity exists to identify youths on drugs and, therefore, at risk of becoming repeat offenders. Such youths can be put into drug-treatment programs, hopefully averting the drug-crime-drug cycle.

Other windows of opportunity are discussed in Chapter 12.

The Serious Habitual Offender Comprehensive Action Program (**SHOCAP**) of the Office of Juvenile Justice and Delinquency Prevention suggests the following action steps at detention (Crowe, 1991, p. 48):

- Establish a policy of separate and secure holding of all designated habitual offenders
- Provide a special close custody classification for all designated habituals to protect staff and other correctional clients
- Monitor and record all activities and transactions of designated habitual offenders

Intake

The intake officer decides if a case should move ahead for court processing. This officer may release the juvenile to the parents with a warning or reprimand. Or the officer may release the youth on the condition that he or she enroll in a community diversion program or be placed on probation and be under the supervision of a juvenile court officer. Youths released at intake with no further processing should be followed up after any referral to a community agency by either the police or the intake unit. Such follow-up promotes closer cooperation between the agencies involved.

For habitual offenders SHOCAP suggests the following action steps at intake (Crowe, 1991, p. 48):

- Mandatory holding of all designated habituals brought in on new charges
- Immediate notification of prosecutor of the intake
- Special follow-up and records preparation for the detention hearings

If the intake officer determines that the case should move ahead for court processing, the officer will recommend that a petition (charge) be filed and will refer the case to the juvenile court prosecutor. In addition, if a petition is recommended, the intake officer determines if the youth is to be detained until further court action is taken or be released to the custody of the parents pending the hearing. When juveniles are detained, this decision is reviewed by a judge or court administrator at a detention hearing.

Prosecution

When the prosecutor receives the recommendation for petition by the intake officer, at least three options are available: dismiss the case, file the petition or determine that the charges are so serious that the case should be heard in adult court, waiving jurisdiction. If a petition is filed, this begins the formal adjudication process. Based on police reports, the county attorney may refer a juvenile to the screening unit of the juvenile court.

Circumstances may vary depending on the age and experience of the officer making the disposition. This exercise of individual authority, or street justice, may be repeated by court personnel, probation officers and correction workers. The rhetoric is the same for all within the system.

For the prosecution of habitual offenders, SHOCAP recommends these action steps (Crowe, 1991, pp. 48–49):

- File petition (charges) with the court based upon the highest provable offense.
- Resist any pretrial release
- Seek a guilty plea on all offenses charged
- Vertically prosecute all cases (assign only one deputy district attorney to each case)
- Provide immediate response to police and detention officials upon notification of the arrest
- Participate in interagency working groups and on individual case management teams
- Share appropriate information with the crime analyst or official designated to develop and maintain profiles on habitual offenders
- Establish a formal policy of seeking the maximum penalty for each conviction or adjudication

Children involved in juvenile justice system proceedings may be fingerprinted or photographed under specific conditions. Section 56 of the Uniform Juvenile Court Act specifies that law enforcement officers may take and file fingerprints of children age 14 and older who are involved in the crimes of murder, non-negligent manslaughter, forcible rape, robbery, aggravated assault, burglary, housebreaking, purse snatching and automobile theft. Children's fingerprint files should be kept separate from adult files and should be kept locally—not sent to a central state or federal depository unless in the interest of national security. The fingerprints should be removed from the file and destroyed if the child is adjudicated not to be delinquent or if the child reaches age 21 and has not committed a criminal offense after reaching age 16. If latent fingerprints are found during an offense and law enforcement officers have probable cause to believe they are the prints of a particular child, they may fingerprint the child, regardless of age or the offense. If the comparison of the latent and inked prints is negative, the fingerprint card is to be immediately destroyed.

Section 56 also specifies that, without a judge's consent, children should not be photographed after being taken into custody unless the case is transferred to another court for prosecution.

Overrepresentation Issues

The National Coalition of State Juvenile Justice Advisory Groups (1993, p. 35) notes: "Research confirms that from arrest through sentencing and incarceration, disproportionate representation and differential treatment are evident along the entire system continuum." The Coalition sets forth two points of view that may explain the disproportionate representation of minority juveniles in the system:

One [view] urges that the problem rests with the system which employs, unintentionally or not, a "selection bias" that results in a disproportionate number of minority youth in the system. In other words, minority youth do not commit more crimes than any other youth; they merely get treated differently and more harshly at various points in the system. The other view posits that the nature and volume of offenses committed by minority youth are the real issue. In other words, minority youth commit more offenses, and more serious offenses, than other youth because of the social and economic conditions in which they are forced to live.

The Tofflers (1990, p. 3) suggest that it is "simple-minded" to blame poverty for the crime problem. They note that numerous societies throughout the world with extreme poverty do not have the crime problem anywhere approaching the magnitude of crime in the United States. They also note, however: "It is equally witless to assume that millions of poor, jobless young people—not part of the work-world culture and bursting with energy and anger—are going to stay off the streets and join knitting clubs."

Next turn your attention to a closer view of those who find themselves being processed by the system.

Neglected and Abused Children

Nationwide more than one million children are neglected or abused each year (Bilchik, 1997, p. 1). Another two million youths are vulnerable as runaways or missing. Bennett and Hess (1998, pp. 360, 367) note:

> Law enforcement agencies are charged with investigating all crimes, but their responsibility is especially great where crimes against children are involved. Children need the protection of the law to a greater degree than other members of society because they are so vulnerable, especially if the offense is committed by one or both parents. Even after the offense is committed, the child may still be in danger of further victimization. . . .
>
> In most states, action must be taken on a report within a specified time, frequently three days. If in the judgment of the person receiving the report it is necessary to remove the child from present custody, this is discussed with the responsible agency such as the welfare department or the juvenile court. If the situation is deemed life-threatening, the police may temporarily remove the child.
>
> No matter who receives the report or whether the child must be removed from the situation, it is the responsibility of the law enforcement agency to investigate the charge. . . .
>
> An officer may take a child into temporary custody, without a warrant if there is an emergency or if the officer has reason to believe that leaving the child in the present situation would subject him or her to further abuse or harm.

The primary responsibility of police officers assigned to child neglect or abuse cases is the immediate protection of the child.

Police officers must also balance the rights of children against those of the children's parents.

Among the service providers mandated to report incidents of suspected child abuse or neglect are child care providers, the clergy, educators, hospital administrators, nurses, physicians, psychologists and those in the social services. The following conditions might lead an officer to place a child in protective custody:

- Maltreatment in the home that might cause the child permanent physical or emotional damage
- A parent's refusal to provide needed medical or psychiatric care for a child
- The child is physically or mentally incapable of self-protection
- The home's physical environment poses an immediate threat
- The parents cannot or will not provide for the child's basic needs
- The parents abandon the child

The National Institute of Justice (NIJ) undertook a study of the police response to abused children. The research first looked at the statutory framework for police actions in cases of child abuse and neglect. This was followed by a telephone survey conducted by the Police Foundation in the spring of 1988. The third portion of the study was site visits by Police Foundation staff for in-depth examinations of four agencies. The major findings of this study were as follows (Martin and Besharov, 1991, pp. 5–7):

- The vast majority of police agencies routinely report abuse and neglect to their local child protective service agencies.
- Over three-quarters of police agencies believe that child protective service agencies inform the police of all cases of sexual abuse brought to their attention; a smaller proportion believe they are being notified of all cases of physical abuse and neglect.
- Police and sheriff's departments conduct a large number of investigations of child abuse and neglect. A rough estimate, based on data from 59 urban agencies, suggests that they are informed of and investigate more than 200,000 cases annually.
- Of those cases closed by the police, nearly 40 percent of the sexual abuse cases and about a quarter of physical abuse and neglect cases result in the arrest of a suspected perpetrator. (Additional numbers of cases are investigated but not closed.)
- Nearly two-thirds of the police agencies surveyed have child abuse policies, about half of which recently had been adopted or updated.
- The vast majority of police agencies provide at least some training on identifying child abuse cases to all new recruits, and provide training on the handling of investigations to new child abuse investigators.
- About half of the police agencies with more than 250 officers have a squad of investigators who have received specialized training and work full time on investigating child abuse cases.
- In more than three-quarters of the police agencies, a specialized investigator is either on duty or on call 24 hours a day.
- The presence of a specialized child abuse squad, but not its organizational location, affects case dispositions. For example, agencies having a

specialized sexual abuse squad close significantly more sexual abuse cases than do those without such a squad (but with a lower arrest rate).

- Eighty-one percent of the responding departments have interagency agreements regarding child abuse investigations. Fifty percent of agencies have written agreements with at least one other agency; 31 percent of agencies have informal agreements.

- Virtually all interagency agreements involve child protective services and the police; prosecutors and other law enforcement agencies are included in about two-thirds of the agreements; and about one-half involve the medical community. Participation by school, juvenile court, mental health and private community service agencies is less widespread.

- Police practices across disparate jurisdictions are similar despite the variations in statutory provisions.

The findings suggest that police agencies should consider a variety of ways to improve their response to child abuse, including:

- A strong commitment by high-level administrators to improving the agency's response to child abuse

- A written, agencywide child abuse policy

- Written interagency protocols

- Interagency teams to handle child abuse investigations

- Immediate telephone notification of the police by protective service agency workers regarding all sexual abuse cases and all cases of serious physical injury or danger

- Initial interviews conducted jointly with child protective agency workers, particularly in sexual abuse cases

- Patrol officers who are trained in the identification of abuse

- Specialized investigators, rather than patrol officers, to handle all cases

- Expertise in child exploitation and pornography investigations within the unit handling child abuse

- Child abuse specialists, skilled as investigators and comfortable interviewing young children

- Sexual, ethnic, and language diversity within the unit

- Child-friendly interview settings

- Limited and selective use of videotaping and anatomical dolls by properly trained individuals

- Victim advocates available throughout the legal process, particularly in sexual abuse cases

The study found that written policies dealing with the police response to child abuse increased departmental capabilities. About half (67 of the 122 agencies responding) had written policies.

Youths Who Are Sexually Abused

Peters (1991, p. 21) urges that police departments have specialists in dealing with children who are sexually abused:

> Neither police academies nor law schools cover such topics as understanding the psychological needs of victims as well as the dynamics of incest, recognizing the frequently vague symptoms of abuse and knowing how to elicit sensitive information about sexual behavior from youngsters. The typical officer and the average prosecutor do not have an understanding of the child pornography underworld, juvenile prostitution, sex rings or ritualistic abuse.

Considering the probability that a sexually abused child will become a child abuser or engage in violent crimes, the importance of reducing this probability by effectively dealing with sexually abused children cannot be underestimated. Peters (p. 23) stresses that law enforcement should treat child abuse as a significant issue: "Failure to assign high priority and competent professionals to child abuse cases, however, guarantees grim consequences, both in terms of current individual tragedies and future social implications."

Missing Children

The National Center for Missing and Exploited Children's (NCMEC) Investigator's Guide (Patterson, 1987, p. vii) notes:

> Missing child cases often involve a violation of the law and always involve the need to provide protection for the child. Even those youths who voluntarily leave home run the risk of becoming involved in criminal activity or exploitation through involvement in prostitution, child pornography, or with pedophile "protectors." Studies show that 85 percent of exploited children are missing when exploitation occurs.

The NCMEC provides two services to law enforcement agencies investigating missing children cases. The first is an age progression program that creates photographs of a child that approximate what the child would look like at the present time. The greatest age difference they have created is from age 6 to age 31. Out of the 200 cases they have handled so far, 28 living children have been located (Strandberg, 1994, p. 47). In addition, they have identified several dead children.

The second service is called Project KidCare, provided in collaboration with Polaroid Corporation. This service consists of an educational packet and a high-quality photo in a form the NCMEC and law enforcement consider ideal.

Status Offenders

The majority of police dispositions involve status offenses.

Approximately 90 percent of police dispositions involve status offenders, according to the Uniform Crime Report.

The status offenders with whom the police make contact are often from middle socioeconomic families. This is especially true for runaways, incorrigibles and truants.

In making dispositions on juvenile matters, the police have found that the parents are often so absorbed with their own desires and problems that they have little time to consider their children's needs. They tend to rely on church, school or civic groups to guide their children. They often pursue a policy of appeasement in the home rather than maintaining family discipline. In effect these parents want society to be their babysitters. The increasing reliance on community services and the parental emphasis on individual rights rather than responsibilities in the training and education of their children has, to a large extent, weakened the family and contributed to the growing delinquency problem, as was discussed in Chapter 4. Partly as a result of this lack of parental guidance, law enforcement agencies are faced with the constant problem of making arrests on such charges as curfew violations, loitering, vagrancy and running away.

Curfew Violations and Loitering

When youths' behavior is such that the community wants them off the streets at night, a curfew is established for the public good. According to Ruefle and Reynolds (1996, p. 64): "The origins of curfew ordinances are murky, but most sources trace them back to a public safety regulation imposed by Alfred the Great (849–899) that required the residents of Oxford, England to retire and cover their fires when an evening bell was rung." Ruefle and Reynolds also note (p. 81): "In the case of juvenile curfew ordinances, criminal justice policy tends to repeat itself. The 1990s popularity of curfews as a city-level response to youth crime is simply the most recent revival of a delinquency control measure that has waxed and waned across urban America several times during the last century. . . . One survey documented the fact that, as of March 1995, 146 (73 percent) of the 200 largest American cities had curfews." A 1997 survey of 347 cities found that more than 90 percent of them reported nighttime curfews as a useful tool for police officers and a good use of police officers' time ("Cities Find Youth," 1997, p. 10).

When youths hang around corners, walkways, alleys, streets and places of business without any purpose, their loitering must be controlled for the safety and security of the public. Both curfew violations and loitering can be offenses for those under legal age. (Loitering is also an adult offense in some states.) Cruising and hanging out or loitering are frequent activities of juveniles. Such activities are not always harmless, however, as noted by Revering (1993, p. 39):

> The tragic death of a young Minnesota soldier who was beaten by a teenage mob recently in Colorado Springs, Colorado, is a glaring example of the violence that seethes beneath unchecked cruising and loitering problems. In each community where cruising and loitering have been allowed to escalate, youth gangs began to infiltrate and vandalism and violence became the norm.

In one community a study of the citations issued for cruising and loitering revealed that 85 to 90 percent of the offenders were from outside the community (Revering, p. 40). Some communities combat this problem by antiloitering and anticruising ordinances. They also establish curfews targeted at juveniles to combat the problem during the evening hours.

In March 1994 Orlando, Florida, passed an anticruising measure allowing Orlando police to write citations to any driver passing through downtown four times within two hours. They also passed a curfew law. The American Civil Liberties Union (ACLU) has threatened to sue Orlando, contending that such a law constitutes nightly house arrest and deprives parents of their right to set hours for their children.

The ACLU was successful in getting a similar curfew lifted in March 1994, in Dade County. Circuit Judge Norman Gerstein wrote in his nine-page order halting the enforcement of the one-month-old curfew: "Juveniles, like adults, have constitutional rights under the Florida Constitution" (Yanez, 1994, p. 7B).

Addressing challenges of unconstitutionality, Morrison (1997, p. 44) points out that a curfew must pass a "two-pronged test of demonstrating a compelling state interest and being narrow in interpretation" in order to meet constitutional standards. He mentions as "an excellent example of an ordinance which meets these standards," the nighttime curfew imposed in Dallas, Texas (pp. 44–45):

> Specifically, the curfew applies to juveniles under 17 years of age and only between the hours of 11 p.m. to 6 a.m., Sunday through Thursday, and midnight to 6 a.m. on Friday and Saturday. The exemptions include juveniles who are accompanied by an adult, traveling to or from work, responding to an emergency, married, or attending a supervised activity.

Morrison also notes that such curfews often face resistance from police officers, who see curfews as "baby-sitting detail and an infringement upon real crime fighting efforts" (p. 45). Furthermore: "The problems many agencies face include a lack of adequate personnel resources to fully enforce a curfew law. If an officer picks up a child and transports him or her to the station, waits for a parent and does the necessary paperwork, it could take several hours. Taking a street officer off the beat, even for an hour, requires shifting units to cover the officer's beat. Coverage as well as street protection is reduced." Nonetheless many officers do see curfews as a way to curtail youth crime. Deputy William M. Harris of the Bay County, Florida, Sheriff's Department believes: "After midnight, there's nothing for a juvenile to do on the streets except get into trouble. . . . If the parents won't take the initiative on their own, perhaps a [law-enforced] curfew will do it for them" (Morrison, p. 45).

Runaways

The police are interested in runaways because of public concern for the youths' safety and welfare, not because they have committed crimes. Youthful runaway behavior often is a precursor of future delinquent behavior and is usually—in most law enforcement agencies—the least investigated status offense.

Technically runaways are individuals under the statutory age of an adult who leave home without authorized consent and who are reported to the police as missing. The object of the police search is to locate such youths and return them to their families. Generally no police investigation, social service inquiry or school inquiry is conducted to determine why these children left home, why they were truant because of this absence or why they continue to run away.

Running away is a predelinquent indicator, but its value often is not recognized by the parents, police, school, social agencies or the courts.

If the danger signal is ignored, society loses another battle in controlling antisocial behavior or criminal activity. Runaways may become violent, even killing others for survival, or they may turn to robbery, burglary, drug abuse and prostitution to meet their needs.

Because children run away for many reasons, police must be sensitive in their treatment of runaways. Police must treat runaways differently to account for their age, sex, family social order, paternal makeup (original, adopted or foster) or who represents control.

When the police take an initial complaint report on a runaway, the responsible adults seldom can give a reason for the youths leaving home. In middle-class families, with few exceptions, parents do not know why their child left home. They firmly believe their son or daughter was the victim of something evil, was under the influence of neighborhood children or that the fault lies with the school system.

Police experience has shown, without too much inquiry, that these so-called sinister happenings that parents fear seldom occur. They are a screen to the real problem. In most instances police do not investigate why a child left home, nor do court services personnel, unless the matter is disposed of in juvenile court and requires a final disposition of aftercare. This may be the result of priorities in personnel allocation, a lack of court support or a lack of support from state agencies.

If police dispositions are to be effective, the family must recognize the early signs of maladjustment in children. Running away is the most visible indicator of a possible future victim (assaulted, murdered) or involvement in criminal activity to support individual needs (prostitution, pornography, burglary, theft, robbery).

In its early stages, running away can often be corrected by cooperative law enforcement policies and parents. The parents must constantly be informed of the consequences of running away and advised about available assistance. Police officers can take a professional approach in their association with children and youths who get into minor offenses by being available and helping to meet their needs. Officers know that children and youths want the opportunity to talk openly and freely about themselves and their lives to someone who will listen without judging and who will be interested in them as individuals rather than as problems to be solved or disposed of in some manner.

When officers have handled matters directly with the youth and the family without going through a formal process, it has totally remade the lives and personalities of a number of seemingly hopeless youths who could have become delinquents.

Truants

Recall from Chapter 4 the vital role of the school in preparing children for productive adult lives and developing their respect for human rights and national values through education. When children skip school habitually, they miss some very valuable lessons, not only academically but socially. They also tend to engage in delinquent or criminal activity while on these unsanctioned hiatuses. For these reasons truancy is a major problem in many school districts.

Antitruancy ordinances enacted in some cities have met with varied success. In examining the effectiveness of such an ordinance in Los Angeles, Parks and Gonzales (1998, pp. 45–46) found:

> Strong anti-truancy enforcement has had a significant impact on those crimes more frequently committed by juveniles, with decreases in every category and an overall decrease in reported daytime crimes of 27.1 percent. In essence, there were 8,710 fewer victims in 1996–97 than during the same period in 1994–95. It is significant that this reduction was accomplished while patrol officers remained available to handle their normal workload of high priority calls.

Underage Drinking

As with curfews, some officers see underage drinking as a low priority for law enforcement. A study by Wagenaar and Wolfson (1995) of police personnel revealed that many officers rank enforcement activity against teenage alcohol use near the bottom of all police responsibilities. A related study (Wolfson et al., 1995) found many reasons why officers placed underage drinking so low on the priority list:

- Perceived legal obstacles in processing juveniles
- Unpleasant, tedious paperwork
- Special detention procedures required for minors
- Lack of juvenile detention facilities or centers already above capacity
- Lack of significant punishment for underage drinking
- Personal disagreements regarding underage drinking laws, particularly as they apply to persons age 18 to 20

Despite the many objections officers give, serious and valid reasons exist for making the enforcement of underage drinking laws a higher priority. As Little and Bishop (1998, p. 2) state: "In short, the loss of life, property damage, economic costs, and negative health effects associated with underage drinking, as well as public outcry for police attention, provide sufficient reasons to make the illegal use of alcohol by teens a greater concern among police agencies."

Statistics regarding the blood alcohol concentration levels of motor vehicle drivers involved in fatal crashes are shown in Table 8.2. Of interest is the decrease from 1985 to 1995 in the percentage of minors who were under the influence of alcohol at the time of their accidents. Perhaps efforts to stop underage drinking and driving are having a positive impact.

Little and Bishop (pp. 2–4) list several tactics available to law enforcement agencies in tackling teen drinking:

- *Undercover stings*—aimed at stopping the sale of alcohol to teens. A minor operative is sent into a licensed establishment, such as a bar, restaurant or convenience store, to buy alcohol.
- *Cops 'n Shops*—differs from undercover stings in that the focus is on the violator rather than the alcoholic beverage retail industry. Officers pose as employees and arrest any minor who tries to buy alcohol.

Table 8.2
Blood Alcohol Concentration Level of Motor Vehicle Drivers Involved in Fatal Crashes

By age, United States, 1985–95

Blood Alcohol Concentration	1985	1986	1987	1988	1989	1990	1991	1992	1993	1994	1995
Ages 15 and younger											
Some and impaired (0.01% to 0.09%)	15.5%	15.3	15.8	13.6	10.8	12.4	14.0	11.9	9.7	10.3	10.0
Intoxicated (0.10% or more)	8.8%	8.1	7.9	6.0	6.0	5.9	5.4	4.4	3.6	6.5	4.4
Total number	479	504	469	448	402	409	364	350	383	397	415
Ages 16 to 20											
Some and impaired (0.01% to 0.09%)	35.5%	36.5	33.3	32.3	29.9	31.7	29.8	26.8	24.5	22.6	20.6
Intoxicated (0.10% or more)	23.9%	23.7	21.0	20.7	19.5	21.1	20.0	17.6	16.1	14.1	12.7
Total number	9,386	10,163	9,910	10,171	9,442	8,821	8,002	7,192	7,256	7,723	7,738

Source: U.S. Department of Transportation, National Highway Traffic Safety Administration. *Traffic Safety Facts 1995.* Washington DC: U.S. Department of Transportation, 1996, p. 36. Table adapted by SOURCEBOOK staff, p. 286.

- *Party patrols*—a way to make a large number of arrests for underage drinking. Police receive a tip on a party planned by minors and go to the site.
- *Walk-throughs*—an officer enters an alcoholic beverage retail outlet, such as a restaurant or bar, and observes the activity of patrons and employees to detect underage drinking and the service of alcohol to minors.

The Police as Mentors to Troubled Youths

Police committed to a mentoring relationship have an enormous impact on youths who are at risk of becoming chronic offenders. Carefully selected and trained police personnel can be the conduit to restoring youthful lives to productive relationships with families, schools and the community.

In dealing with troubled youths who are at risk of becoming juvenile offenders, mentoring is especially effective, because it strikes directly at the individual's alienated condition. The youth's isolation and sense of meaninglessness is often dissolved over time through a long-term relationship characterized by respect. The youth's sense of powerlessness is eroded through a relationship with someone who helps to clarify their choices and who empowers them to make responsible decisions.

Police mentoring is the most effective means available for optimizing meaningful contact between society and alienated youth. As the youth begins to bond with a mentor, a new world view crystallizes, opening up a new range of perceived choices that reflects the values of the mentor and the community. Mentoring remains the best hope for reclaiming our troubled youths, our families, communities and society as a whole.

An opposite view of dealing with status offenders was set forth in the ninth recommendation to the President of the United States by former Attorney General William Barr (1992, p. 27):

> With respect to the larger group of juveniles, excessive leniency wastes the opportunity to salvage the youth and instead encourages them to become career criminals. As to the group of chronic offenders, excessive leniency fails to adequately protect society from these violent criminals. Tough, smart sanctions tailored to the particular offender will both reduce the number of juveniles who become chronic offenders and better protect society from those who do.
> *Recommendation 9*
> Establish a range of tough juvenile sanctions that emphasize discipline and responsibility to deter nonviolent first-time offenders from further crimes.
> One of the key challenges for a State juvenile justice system is to deter the youthful offender from further transgressions. For the vast majority of juveniles, this should be possible if we are smart in imposing sanctions. To this end, States should develop a range of tough but fair sanctions for nonviolent first-time juvenile offenders, where the emphasis is on instilling values of discipline and responsibility. These sanctions should include the option of institutional settings.

Barr also writes (p. 25):

> To a large extent, the success or failure of the criminal justice system will depend upon its effectiveness in handling youthful offenders—ensuring that for the vast majority of juvenile offenders their first brush with the law is the last, and ensuring that the small group of chronic hardened youthful offenders are incapacitated for extended periods.

This "get tough" attitude has been criticized by some, however, such as Brodt and Smith (1991, p. 176), who suggest:

> In practice, getting tough means "let's get tough" with the following groups: (1) blacks; (2) Chicanos; (3) the poor; (4) the uneducated; (5) youth from single parent families; (6) the unemployed; (7) illegitimate youth; (8) welfare families and (9) abused children.

Serious, Habitual Offenders

It is well documented that a large number of crimes are committed by a small number of repeat offenders. Oftentimes these recidivists are also violent. Offenses classified by the FBI as violent crimes include homicide, forcible rape, aggravated assault and robbery. Juvenile arrests for violent crimes make up less than 1 percent of the total number of almost 10 million arrests for violent crimes. Nonetheless the problem is serious. In 1995, 2,548 persons under age 18 were arrested for murder and non-negligent manslaughter, and 4,190 persons under age 18 were arrested for forcible rape (*Sourcebook,* 1997, pp. 372–375). However, chronic, serious juvenile offenders often "fall through the cracks" of the juvenile justice system because efforts are not coordinated.

As noted by Kline (1993, p. 32): "Looking the other way in the face of juvenile delinquency has spawned a generation of career offenders whose activities are far more vicious and sophisticated than the joy-riders and hubcap thieves of happier days." In response to rising numbers of habitually violent youths, the Colorado Springs Police Department instituted a Serious Habitual Offender/

Directed Intervention (SHO/DI) Program aimed at this group of juvenile offenders. The goal of the program was threefold:

- To develop trust and cooperation between agencies serving juveniles
- To identify and overcome real and perceived legal obstacles to cooperative efforts
- To build a credible interagency information process to identify and track habitual juvenile offenders

Says Kline: "The ultimate goal was to 'incapacitate' the repeat offender, whether through detention, incarceration, probation or other means, so that for some period of time, his crimes would stop, and efforts could be made to change his ways."

One important component of the program was a court order signed by a juvenile judge allowing the police department to share information with the other agencies in the juvenile justice system. Another important outcome of the program was a change in how the juvenile portion of the justice system was viewed. Traditionally juvenile matters received low priority. "Kiddy Court" was not taken seriously, and beginning lawyers were assigned to prosecute juveniles. This practice was changed with the institution of the SHO/DI Program.

SHOCAP, introduced earlier in the chapter, is aimed at juveniles who are a chronic, serious threat to a community's safety. As noted by Owens and Wells (1993, p. 26):

Through SHOCAP, the police department works with other juvenile-related agencies, including prosecutors, courts, corrections, the schools and human resources, to ensure a comprehensive and cooperative information and case management process that results in informed sentencing disposition. SHOCAP enables the juvenile and criminal justice system to focus additional attention on juveniles who repeatedly commit serious crimes, yet may somehow "fall through the cracks" of the system.

SHOCAP suggests the following action steps for the management of habitual offenders for the police, including municipal and county law enforcement agencies (Crowe, 1991, p. 47):

- Develop special crime analysis and habitual offender files
- Coordinate interagency activities and services for designated habitual offenders
- Prepare profiles of habitual offenders
- Conduct instantaneous radio checks of a juvenile's prior police contacts for patrol officers
- Use field interrogation cards or juvenile citations to document reprimands and non-arrest situations
- Institute directed patrol assignments to increase field contacts, assist in community control of probationers, and follow up on habitual truancy cases

- Provide daily transmittal of all field interrogation or juvenile citation cards to probation authorities
- Supply regularly updated lists of designated habitual offenders to all police officers

The importance of such action steps is stressed by Barr (p. 24):

> The criminal justice system must recognize that some youthful offenders are simply criminals who happen to be young. Every experienced law enforcement officer has encountered 15- or 16-year-olds who are as mature and as criminally hardened as any adult offender. Although this group represents only a small fraction of our youth, they commit a large percentage of all violent crimes. As painful as this fact may be, public safety demands that law enforcement recognize and respond to this criminal element. The challenge for a State's juvenile justice system is to identify this group of hard-core offenders and to treat them as adults.

He recommends (p. 31):

- Increase the ability of the juvenile justice system to treat the small group of chronic violent juvenile offenders as adults
- Provide for use of juvenile offense records in adult sentencing

Dealing with Gangs and Gang Members

The director of the Bureau of Alcohol, Tobacco and Firearms, Stephen Higgins (1993, p. 46), stresses: "Despite the dedication of thousands of law enforcement officers nationwide, the gang epidemic shows no sign of abating; on the contrary it is increasing." He notes (p. 47): "On January 9, 1992, then-Attorney General William P. Barr officially recognized street gangs as meeting the definition of organized crime and committed the investigative resources of both ATF and the FBI to augment the state and local authorities already battling this national crisis."

Gang activity is a chief concern for law enforcement and of vital interest to the general public. Police are determined to do something about gangs to satisfy the public need for peace and order. Though the police can make arrests whenever gang members break the law, a gang has the advantage. Gangs can congregate and recruit without breaking the law. Only a small fraction of gang-related crimes can be solved by arrest. Thus if an arrest is the only recourse, police soon feel helpless, and the public believes the police are doing nothing.

When this situation exists, the police do chase gang members away from where they congregate. Citizens and communities reinforce the police in this "no report activity," a use of informal social control. This type of police conduct is condoned by the public when the final disposition is looking out for the needs of the average citizen.

As early as the 1970s, the Los Angeles Police Department saw the need for specialized units to deal with the gang problem. Their first such program was called Community Resources Against Street Hoodlums (CRASH). CRASH consisted of several specially trained units of patrol officers and detectives organized on a bureau or area level. CRASH put tremendous pressure on the Los Angeles gangs and resulted in many gang members being arrested. In 1988 the department instituted another program to focus specifically on the problem of narcotics and black street gangs. This program was called Gang-Related Active Trafficker Suppression (GRATS). As noted by Gates and Jackson (1990, p. 21): "The GRATS program targets street gangs involved in drug manufacturing, distribution and street sales."

The Anaheim Police Department has instituted a program to combat the graffiti problem using a computerized system called GREAT (General Reporting, Evaluating and Tracking). The department considers a tagging crew to be nothing short of a gang (Molloy and Labahn, 1993, p. 122): "The members of a crew associate with one another constantly; they share a common sign, symbol and name; and they have a common purpose of criminal anti-social behavior. They are a gang." The criteria the Anaheim police have established for a person to be a crew member includes the following:

- Self-admitted member
- Information from an untested informant corroborated by independent information
- Resides in or frequents the crew's area, wears common dress, uses or has common signs, symbols and/or tattoos, and associates with known members
- Has several arrests in the company of known members with offenses consistent with membership
- Maintains a close relationship with a member

The Anaheim Police Department has also instituted an undercover school operation, "Operation GETUP" (Graffiti Enforcement Through Undercover Programs). This program resulted in 37 criminal cases filed against 17 suspects.

Another program also has the acronym GREAT—the Gang Resistance Education and Training program—developed by the Bureau of Alcohol, Tobacco and Firearms, the Federal Law Enforcement Training Center and the Phoenix Police Department. This program, similar to the DARE program, helps students say no, but in this case to gangs. The audience is older; GREAT focuses on seventh graders. Students are taught to set goals, resolve conflicts nonviolently, resist peer pressures and understand the negative impact gangs can have on their lives and on their community.

In 1987 the OJJDP established a research and development program to study the gang problem. As part of this program they conducted a national survey of youth gang problems and programs. This survey identified five strategies being used by organizations and cities to deal with the gang problem (Spergel et al., 1990, p. 2):

- *Suppression,* including such tactics as prevention, arrest, imprisonment, supervision and surveillance (Most frequently employed—used by 44 percent)
- *Social intervention,* including crisis intervention, treatment for youths and their families, outreach, and referral to social services (Used by 31.5 percent)

- *Social opportunities,* including the provision of basic or remedial education, training, work incentives, and jobs (4.8 percent)
- *Community mobilization,* including improved communication and joint policy and program development among justice, community-based, and grassroots organizations (8.9 percent)
- *Organizational development or change,* including special police units, vertical prosecution, vertical probation case management, and special youth agency crisis programs. The organizational development strategy modified the other four strategies (10.9 percent)

Owens and Wells (p. 27) describe a developing OJJDP program component for SHOCAP called the Gang Offender Comprehensive Action Program, or GO-CAP:

> Like SHOCAP, GO-CAP uses case management activity to pursue vigorous prosecution of all gang offenders via the Street Terrorism Act. . . .
>
> As a developmental component of SHOCAP, GO-CAP not only strengthens the city's Community-Oriented Problem-Solving Program, but shows promising applicability for most jurisdictions in the United States.

Saccente (1993, p. 31) urges law enforcement to view street gangs as criminal organizations and to capitalize on laws against organized crime: "RICO, money-laundering and asset forfeiture laws, although different, have a common thread: they complement each other in their efforts to arrest and prosecute gang members and ultimately weaken the street gang structure." A study on street gangs (Conly, 1993, pp. 48, 49) suggests the following:

> In many urban communities there are tensions between police forces and the communities they serve. Law enforcement departments often feel hard pressed to find the staff time to meet the challenges in these communities, while residents are anxious for increased attention to their needs by law enforcement. Added to this problem is racial tension between members of law enforcement departments and minority communities.
>
> In communities where gangs exist, residents have often retreated in fear, leaving the police and the gangs to battle each other. Nevertheless, the residents are not disinterested: they want the police to understand their problems while keeping the streets safe. In this regard, David Fattah, co-director of the House of Umoja in Philadelphia, observed that the role of the police in communities where there are gangs should be to show dignity and firmness without abuse. In his view, many law enforcement departments appear as military outposts in the community. If they were more approachable, "kids would go to them instead of some other group, like a gang."
>
> *Typical Law Enforcement Approaches to Gangs.* Most law enforcement efforts are aimed primarily at crime control: gathering information; developing information systems; making arrests; and sharing information with others in the law enforcement community. Increasingly, they also include prevention activities:
>
> - Participating in community awareness campaigns (e.g., developing public service announcements and poster campaigns)
> - Contacting parents of peripheral gang members (through the mail or in personal visits) to alert them that their children are involved with a gang
> - Sponsoring gang hotlines to gather information and facilitate a quick response to gang-related issues

- Organizing athletic events with teams of law enforcement officers and gang members
- Establishing working relationships with local social service agencies
- Making presentations on gangs in schools and community groups as a combined effort at prevention and information gathering
- Sponsoring school-based gang and drug prevention programs (e.g., DARE)
- Serving as a referral for jobs and other community services

Kennedy (1998) advocates **deterrence** as a possible method of handling gangs, in which future criminal activity is prevented by showing offenders that the consequences of committing crime outweigh any benefits gained. This requires law enforcement to take a hard-line approach. For example in Minneapolis, Minnesota, in June 1997:

> A dozen members of the Bogus Boyz, a street gang composed of members ejected from other gangs and notorious for street violence, are arrested on Federal weapons charges after a short, intensive investigation spearheaded by the Minneapolis Police Department's gang unit, in cooperation with Federal authorities. At the same time, teams of police and probation officers hit the streets to visit some 250 individuals identified by the gang unit as the city's most chronic gang offenders. The teams tell the gang members:
>
> > The Bogus Boyz arrests were no accident. The Bogus Boyz were violent, and their violence won them this treatment. This is how the city is doing things from now on. We've got a dozen agencies, from probation to the Feds, meeting regularly and focusing on gang violence. Where we find it, we're going to act.
>
> Gang officers visit injured gang members—victims of assaults by other gangs—in the hospital and say to them:
>
> > This is a terrible thing that's happened to you. But understand, we're going to deal with it. Retaliation will not be tolerated. Remember the Bogus Boyz. (Kennedy, p. 3)

Ivie (1997, p. 54) discusses the youth intervention and education initiatives developed by the Mesquite (Texas) Police Department to deal with their youth gang situation: "In response to the growing gang problem, the city took another approach, bringing together the city manager, the superintendent of schools and then-Chief Travis Hass to address current and anticipated gang-related issues. [This led to the] formation of a Youth Services Advisory Committee, composed of representatives of the city, the school district, the ministerial alliance, the business community and the community at large." Ivie (pp. 55–56) lists some of the programs included in Mesquite's package:

- Slama Bama Jama—designed to convey an anti-gang, anti-violence message to the students through music, athletic demonstrations and dramatic skits

- Ropes Challenge Adventure Course—designed to provide an opportunity for at-risk young people to enhance their self-esteem and interact with positive youth and adult role models

- Evening Out with a Cop—an afternoon and evening session with a careful balance of selected at-risk youth, student leader/role-model youth, police officers and municipal officials

- School Resource Officers—a full-time officer is assigned to each of the four high schools as a role model, mentor, counselor, confidant, and educational resource
- Law Enforcement Teaching Students (LETS)—officers conduct a six-week, 12-lesson program in each fifth-grade classroom in all elementary schools, focusing on avoiding drugs and developing positive self-esteem and decision-making skills

Such programs have a positive impact not only on youths but also on the officers involved. As Ivie concludes (p. 56): "Exposed to role-model young people in unprecedented numbers, officers who might otherwise tend to become jaded or cynical about today's young people instead are encouraged. They realize most young people are good kids who make the right choices in life."

Prevention Strategies

Common sense suggests that it is better to prevent youths from becoming victims or victimizers. FBI Director Louis J. Freeh states: "Crime prevention is like health prevention: if we don't inoculate children against diseases, we have epidemics that take a terrible toll. Prevention is one of the most valuable tools in the anti-crime arsenal, and we must use it to help reduce the pandemic of crime that now exists" ("Youth Programs," 1997, p. 28).

The thrust of **community policing** is toward proactive, problem-oriented policing, seeking causes to crime and allocating resources to attack those causes. Among the many preventive strategies available, one that costs nothing is fair and just treatment of juveniles during all contacts, whether the juvenile is a victim, a status offender, a delinquent or a gang member. Peace officers can serve as role models for personal responsibility and accountability and expect the same from the youths with whom they come in contact.

Other preventive efforts commonly engaged in by police departments include educational programs, recreation programs, crime prevention programs and diversion programs. However juvenile delinquency prevention programs conducted by law enforcement agencies reflect public policy and public attitudes. They often result from a reaction to a specific incident rather than from long-range preventive goals.

Early Efforts at Delinquency Prevention

When law enforcement first formally recognized the importance of actively promoting positive community relations, the approach selected was the best one possible under the existing conditions. In an effort to "get the boys off the streets" and control gang activity, the New York police started the Police Athletic League (PAL) over 50 years ago. Youngsters, mostly males, were given instruction in boxing (for Golden Glove competition), basketball and baseball. Police sponsored athletic games and tournaments.

Law enforcement also promoted programs about subjects of interest to children and their parents, including a variety of safety programs:

bicycle, auto, household (poisons and related household hazards), guns and outdoor water.

_____

Initially law enforcement sought to build a positive image rather than to develop constructive, lasting delinquency prevention programs.

Many law enforcement agencies continue to provide one-time and seasonal programs designed to address a particular problem rather than carefully planned, long-range programs.

Evolution of Prevention Programs

In the 1930s and 1940s, aside from PAL, law enforcement directed its energies toward school safety patrol programs. These programs were started with the assistance of civic and community groups for pedestrian safety. When conditions changed in the 1950s and 1960s, and mass busing of children to schools became the norm, the programs began to dissipate.

Delinquency prevention programs promoted by the police often focused on matters common to children and of concern to parents, with no eye to the future. For example in the 1960s cough medicine containing codeine, a morphine derivative, was being sold faster than druggists could stock the shelves. When law enforcement and parents became aware that such over-the-counter drugs could be purchased without a prescription, and that children of all ages were buying them, prevention programs pushed to stop future purchases. Eventually legislation restricted the purchases of such cough medicine.

Police-School Liaison Programs

A much publicized delinquency prevention plan was developed in 1958 in Flint, Michigan, with the cooperation of school authorities, parents, social agencies, the juvenile court officials, businesses and the police department. The foundation for the **police-school liaison program** was established many years before its inception, when people living in the community identified with different political, social, ethnic, economic and regional sections of large communities. A workable relationship through the public school system began.

Police-school liaison officers do not enforce school regulations, which are left to the school superintendent and staff. Instead school liaison officers work with students, parents and school authorities to apply preventive techniques to problems created by antisocial youths who have not or will not conform to the community's laws and ordinances.

The techniques used by school liaison officers involve counseling children and their parents, referring them to social agencies to treat the root problems, referring them to drug and alcohol abuse agencies and being in daily contact in the school to check their progress. Often school liaison officers deal with predelinquent and early delinquent youths with whom law enforcement would not have been involved under traditional programs.

The police-school liaison program exemplifies those programs designed to alleviate problems encountered by the community through the cooperative efforts of all citizens. However, budget reductions in many communities have adversely affected the police-school liaison program.

The Flint Program

The goals of the Flint Police-School Liaison Program are as follows:

- To reduce crime incidents involving school-age youths
- To improve the attitudes of school-age youths and the police toward one another
- To suppress by enforcement of the law any and all illegal threats that endanger the child's educational environment

In the Flint program, the liaison officers' home base is the middle or senior high school because these schools are centralized and accessible. Also the bulk of investigations and contacts with juveniles are at this level. Liaison officers become acquainted with the building directors at the various schools and reassure them that they are available should they be needed. They check the club activities at the schools and periodically appear at various club affairs to become familiar with their rules and procedures. At the same time, they check for any loitering in and around the schools during these events and take steps to correct any matters that conflict with city ordinances. As a rule school personnel supervise the social events. The officers do not become involved in matters pertaining to school policy, but they are available to give advice and help.

Liaison officers frequently patrol the elementary school areas until school starts in the morning, and also during the noon hour and after school. They watch for any suspicious people or automobiles and for infractions of safety rules regarding routes to and from school. They also check the middle school areas for anyone loitering around the building or grounds trying to pick up students in the area. Appendix B provides a detailed job description for a police-school liaison officer.

Many aspects of the police-school liaison program benefit students, the school and the community. The communication developed between the law enforcement agencies and school personnel provides information to guide young people. Respect for law enforcement agencies is built up in the minds of the youths. The police-school liaison officer becomes their friend. The effective preventive work of the police-school liaison program may be a considerable part of the answer to the problem of juvenile antisocial behavior.

The Albuquerque Program

Lesce (1996, p. 66) reports on how one public school system uses unarmed officers to confront problems: "The Albuquerque Public School System, comprising 118 grade, middle, and high schools, has 27 commissioned officers to oversee the safety of its 90,000 students and almost 11,000 employees, including 6,000 teachers." School police cooperate closely with school administrators to tackle such problems as gangs and tagging, drug and alcohol abuse by students

Police-school liaison officers are a very visible reminder of the need for law and order. They stress positive interactions with students who do not misbehave as well as dealing with those who are delinquent.

and even workplace violence by school staff. The ultimate priority is to provide a safe environment in which students can learn. Lesce concludes (p. 70): "Albuquerque parents rarely worry about the safety of their schoolchildren, partly because of the efforts of Albuquerque's unarmed school officers, who patrol the schools 24 hours a day."

Goals of Liaison Programs

The goals of the police-school liaison program fall into two general categories: preventing juvenile delinquency and improving community relations.

Preventing Juvenile Delinquency

In seeking to prevent juvenile delinquency, police-school liaison programs focus on both preventive actions and the official investigation of criminal activity, apprehension and court referral. Officers assigned to school liaison programs approach delinquency prevention through a variety of activities:

- Officers *act as instructors* before various school groups and classes.
- Officers *act as counselors* to students, separately or with school personnel.
- Officers *maintain contacts with parents or guardians* of students who exhibit antisocial behavior.
- Officers *make public appearances*.
- Officers *maintain files* of information on students contacted.
- Officers *investigate complaints of criminal activity* occurring within the school complex and the surrounding area.
- Officers *maintain close contact with other police agencies*.

Improving Community Relations

The second general goal of police-school liaison programs focuses on **community relations,** projecting and maintaining an image of the police as serving the community, rather than simply enforcing laws. Enhancing community relations is accomplished in several ways.

Public appearances are a key technique. Officers speak and present films or slide programs before many types of groups, such as PTAs, service groups, church fellowships, civic gatherings, youth clubs and civil rights groups. There is usually an interplay of ideas at such gatherings, and the officers sell the ideal of community service.

Another focus is *parent contacts.* Behavioral problems are often apparent in the school before they develop into more serious delinquent activity. Officers in the school know about such problems and can contact parents. They can work together with the parents to avoid any progression into serious delinquent behavior. Most parents take an interest in their children. This dissipates the age-old contest of parent versus school in the control of children. Likewise, it affects their attitude toward anyone else in authority disciplining their children.

Possibly the most effective community relations technique at the officers' disposal is *individual contact.* Officers have contact with many young people at every age level. In projecting an image of the "good guys," they influence the attitudes not only of those students counseled, but also of their friends and families. Many popular myths about laws and law enforcement officers are dispelled through this type of interaction.

Another important area is *liaison work with other interested agencies,* including juvenile courts, social agencies, mental health agencies, other schools and private organizations. Officers gain operational knowledge of each and learn to coordinate their efforts with these other agencies to better treat children.

Displaying interest indicates to these agencies that police are concerned with more than simply apprehension and detention in dealing with juvenile delinquency. Undoubtedly teachers have a definite effect on their students' attitudes. Officers who help teachers with problem students improve teachers' image of the police. This, along with personally knowing a police officer, does much in long-range police-community relations and, as any preventive program must be, this preventive program is long range.

Finally, *recreational participation* is a type of interaction with youths that breaks down many walls of resentment. Officers who participate in organized athletics with youngsters build a rapport that is carried over into their other contacts with those youths.

Other Programs

One program in Illinois, the Police and Children Together (PACT) camp project, "was designed to bring youth and law enforcement personnel together in a cooperative setting that would strengthen bonds between youth and police, and enable positive teamwork among all of the participants" (Koertge and Hill, 1996, p. 26). As one planning committee member stated: "If one kid who comes to the camp finds himself or herself being coerced into joining a gang or doing something bad—if that kid can pick up the phone and call a police officer for help, I will feel that we have succeeded."

Another program in Minnesota tries to fight crime by helping children learn to read. As Ramsey County Sheriff Bob Fletcher explains (Smith, 1996, p. B3): "If you can't read, then you do poorly in school. These kids get behind; they lose self-esteem, and then they look for other ways to position themselves. They become young bullies. . . . And by age 8, they're being arrested for vandalism, assault and theft." So for two hours every Tuesday afternoon, employees and deputies from the sheriff's department, St. Paul police officers and members of the Holy Childhood Parish volunteer as tutors and mentors to 30 to 40 neighborhood kids. Still, Fletcher realizes their efforts may be lost on some kids: "The odds are against us. There's a lot of competition out there for their hearts and their souls. There's the violence on TV and at home, and there's poverty. . . . But you have to try. You have to take risks."

Other well-known programs found throughout the country include the Officer Friendly program and the police dog McGruff ("Taking a bite out of crime") program. The McGruff program goes beyond delinquency prevention and seeks to help youths contribute positively to the community. Sometimes the McGruff crime dog also promotes safety. For example at Halloween, many police departments distribute trick or treat bags to children. These bags feature McGruff and list some tips for a safe Halloween.

Explorer posts are also popular. These posts are an advanced unit of the Boy Scouts of America; they include high school students between ages 14 and 18. Explorers wear uniforms similar to those of law enforcement officers and are taught several skills used in law enforcement, such as firearms safety, first aid, fingerprinting and the like.

Another successful police-community prevention effort is that of the Rochester (New York) Police Department.

Rochester's Teens on Patrol (TOP) program uses youths to patrol the city's parks and recreational areas in the summer.

Each summer about 100 youths are hired to keep order in the parks. At the same time, they learn about police work. Many TOP participants have gone on to become police officers.

DARE

Probably the best known school-based drug prevention program is the Drug Abuse Resistance Education (DARE) Program developed in 1983 by the Los Angeles Police Department and the Los Angeles Unified School District. As noted by the Bureau of Justice Assistance (1991, p. i), the DARE program has several noteworthy features, including the following:

- DARE targets elementary school children.
- DARE offers a highly structured, intensive fifth and sixth grade curriculum.

The Drug Abuse Resistance Education (DARE) program is designed to teach elementary-age school children to say "No" to drugs. Experienced police officers teach the 17 classroom sessions. Although highly popular, the effectiveness of the program has not been demonstrated.

- DARE uses uniformed law enforcement officers to conduct the class.
- DARE represents a long-term solution to a problem that has developed over many years.

The Los Angeles Police Department and the Los Angeles Unified School District jointly sponsor the Drug Abuse Resistance Education (DARE) program.

The program is designed for elementary school children and consists of 17 classroom sessions taught by experienced police officers. The focus is on teaching elementary-age youths to say "no" to drugs, to resist peer pressure and to find alternatives to drug abuse by:

- Providing the skills for recognizing and resisting social pressures to experiment with tobacco, alcohol and drugs
- Helping enhance self-esteem
- Teaching positive alternatives to substance use
- Developing skills in risk assessment and decision making
- Building interpersonal and communications skills

In 1996 approximately 25,000 DARE officers taught the program in more than 70 percent of school districts in all 50 states, reaching 25 million school children in the United States and another 8 million students in 30 other countries (Abshire, 1996, p. 29). Furthermore a Gallup poll found that over 90 percent of students who participated said DARE had taught them the skills to avoid drugs and alcohol (Abshire, p. 52).

Over the years many proponents and critics of the DARE program have surfaced, with numerous arguments presented to support the differing views. As a positive benefit, a study by Sigler and Talley (1995, p. 118) found: "The DARE program is successful in providing information. DARE students are more likely to have attitudes favorable to avoidance of drug use. DARE students have stronger anti-drug attitudes than the control group at the end of the training and appear to have retained aspects of this perspective one year later." Charlie J. Parsons, executive director of DARE America, states:

> One of the byproducts of the DARE program, which I find very important, is the relationship that it helps build. This is the students' first encounter with anyone from law enforcement, and they see that the officers are human beings. Long term, this is going to pay a lot of dividends for society. Very much in vogue is community-based policing, and DARE is the essence of community-based policing (Strandberg, 1998, p. 49).

Gruber (1998, p. 52) echoes: "I do believe that the [DARE] program's success can be measured in terms of the positive relationships it offers between the police department and the children we serve and, in turn, their families, the next generation of young adults and, of course, our whole community."

Opponents point out, however, that DARE is an awareness program, not a prevention program (Hough, 1998, p. 49). A six-year study by Rosenbaum at the University of Illinois at Chicago found "that DARE had little effect on preventing future drug use as the students got older, and in some cases, may have contributed to the likelihood of their involvement in drugs and alcohol" ("Truth, DARE," 1998, p. 1). Rosenbaum concluded: "DARE is a good program in the short run, but it does not have the effects that parents, teachers or police think it's having" (p. 10).

Many DARE opponents within the law enforcement community are hesitant to publicly criticize the program because their chiefs and sheriffs have invested significant time, money and political capital into it (Sharp, 1998, p. 47). Some, however, are not at all reluctant to censure "the mother of all feel-good crime-prevention programs." As Dolnick (1998, p. 8) denounces: "Our ability to do something about drug abuse is being killed by chiefs and sheriffs who measure DARE's success by the number of T-shirts they see at DARE 'graduation ceremonies.'" He adds: "The fact is that smiling kids *do not* denote success. A program that drains millions of dollars of funding and diverts personnel into schools *is not* worthwhile if it doesn't work. A program that displaces other, more effective programs *is harmful.*"

Despite the many criticisms of DARE, Sharp (p. 45) notes that it remains "immensely popular among law enforcement; 95 percent of the departments that responded [to a recent poll] sponsor their own programs," believing them to be highly effective.

The National DARE Parent Program
A new addition to the DARE program is the DARE Parent Program (DPP), created to stimulate interest from the community and to motivate families to actively participate in preventing substance abuse. The program consists of a

This canine officer and his partner "Books" have just completed a demonstration at an open house of a crime prevention association. Such contacts can do much to build good relationships between the police and the citizens they serve, including our youths.

series of meetings at which parents learn about the DARE program their children are participating in, as well as how to recognize signs of drug use, how to use local program resources and how to communicate effectively with their children (Bureau of Justice Assistance, 1993).

The Importance of Teachers in Delinquency Prevention Programs

Since most delinquency prevention programs are based in schools or, at least, focus on school-age populations, it is critical that teachers be included in any delinquency prevention programs.

Teachers are of vital importance to the success of any delinquency prevention program.

Teachers from all grade levels might be taken on ride-alongs so they can see the consequences for those who drop out of or fail in school.

The Officer on the Street and Youths' Attitudes

The importance of the officer on the street cannot be overlooked. Every law enforcement officer, no matter at what level, has an opportunity to be a positive influence on youths. Ultimately youths' perceptions about the law and law enforcement will be based on one-on-one interactions with law enforcement officers.

Youths' attitudes toward law and law enforcement are tremendously influenced by personal contacts with law enforcement officers. Positive interactions are critical to delinquency prevention.

Positive interactions, however, may not come automatically or easily, particularly with certain segments of the population. Leiber et al. (1998, p. 169) note: "[Juveniles'] attitudes toward the police do not develop simply as a function of actual contacts with the police. . . . Minority youth consistently expressed more negative views of the police than did whites, and race/ethnicity was the strongest predictor of perceptions of police fairness and police discrimination. Greater commitment to delinquent norms consistently predicted negative attitudes toward the police." These researchers conclude: "The imposition of legal authority and social control in certain neighborhoods engenders a pervasive resentment and resistance, and . . . youthful residents of those neighborhoods harbor a general disrespect for the law itself."

Such an "imposition of legal authority" is part of the nature of the "get tough on crime" trend.

The "Get Tough" Trend

In recent years many police departments have applied the prevention technique of "getting tough with juveniles." Unfortunately the effect of this technique often is to make the police the villain or enemy, and it may alienate youths. Children no longer see law enforcement officers as "jolly cops." Instead the police are more often viewed as enemies who are ignorant of the present and have no vision of the future. This negative view of the police is explained by Pace (p. 109):

> The law, to a young person, is often considered a "necessary evil." They do not understand the law, nor do they usually wish to learn about it. Rebellion against most laws, and especially those concerning the control of traffic, generates much hostility and animosity among the young.
>
> This hostility to law is naturally projected to police officers because they represent the negative forces that impose impossible sanctions. It is often said that the young do not like the police and the feeling is often mutual.

Coordination of Efforts and Community Policing

The need for cooperative efforts when dealing with juveniles has been stressed in preceding chapters. Law enforcement needs to draw upon the expertise of psychologists, psychiatrists and social workers. They also need the assistance of parents, schools, churches, community organizations and businesses. Such collaboration is at the heart of a paradigm shift occurring within law enforcement—community policing.

A **paradigm** is a model or way of viewing things. Traditionally law enforcement has been *separate* from the community and *reactive,* responding to incidents as they occur. Over the past few years, however, the emphasis has shifted to viewing law enforcement—indeed, the entire juvenile justice system—as part of the community, reliant upon collaborative efforts to deal with our nation's youths.

The paradigm shift to community policing directly affects law enforcement as well as the juvenile courts and corrections.

According to Johnson (1996, p. 1), community policing is America's best chance to end youth violence:

> In America, the relationship between police and youths can be described on a continuum of positive to very negative—even deadly. Some common problems between police and youth have been a lack of trust, little or no contact between line officers and youths except in negative contexts, high levels of anger and emotions, and racial and cultural differences. There is almost a natural adversarial relationship between police, who must control behaviors, and youths, who are anxious to experience new behaviors.

Johnson proposes youth-focused community policing as a way to:

- Increase positive contacts and confidence levels between police departments and youths
- Give youths and other community leaders the opportunity to have a voice in setting local priorities and improving the quality of life in their neighborhoods
- Address crime reduction, crime prevention and problem solving

Police officers need to be aware of the referral resources available in the community, including not only the names of the resource agencies but also addresses, phone numbers and contact persons. Among the possible referral resources for the juvenile justice system are the following:

- Child welfare and child protection services
- Church youth programs
- Crisis centers
- Detox centers
- Drop-in centers or shelters for youths
- Guardian *ad litem* programs
- Human services councils
- Juvenile probation services
- School resources, including chemical dependency counselors, general counselors, nurses, school psychologists and social workers
- Support groups such as AlAnon, Emotions Anonymous and Suicide Help Line
- Victim/witness services
- YMCA or YWCA programs
- Youth Service Bureaus

Ideally police officers would serve on community boards and task forces that promote services for youths. A good example of law enforcement's alliance with the community is seen in the efforts of the Adams County Sheriff's Department in Brighton, Colorado, in how they handled the problems of the Goat Hill neighborhood. Deputy Bob Fuller, one of the founders of the Goat Hill initiative, states: "We looked at everything, and we got as many people involved as we could. They went first to the schools and got the administration and teachers on board. From there, the community was contacted and invited to participate in the project. Along the way, sports figures, business leaders and anyone else who could be affected was invited to participate. Out of this, many programs were developed" (Siska and Shipley, 1997, p. 30).

Responding to a Changing Society

Policing today is at a critical point. People of different races, cultures and languages are coming into closer contact with each other, and enormous demands are being made on their understanding and tolerance. There are widening class divisions, more broken families and homelessness, a growing anger on the part of the disadvantaged and a rise in violence.

These are the signs of a society in transition, but they are also the seeds of social unrest. Like migration, social disorder is cyclical. What happens in the present can be a reenactment of the past of social conflict that pitted different races and different generations against each other.

Policing is also cyclical. To be prepared for the future requires a strategic plan that anticipates changes likely to occur in the future. The police must be in partnership with the community. Policing must be proactive, identifying local crime and disorder problems. Problem-oriented policing means getting at root causes, analyzing the needs of the community and recognizing those factors that endanger the physical, mental and moral well-being of the citizen. But making the transition from a reactive, incident-driven style of policing to a more proactive, problem-directed style, community-oriented policing, requires a comprehensive strategy directed to the officer on the street, who intervenes one-on-one in efforts to make the community safe.

To identify and solve problems, the police must be able to associate with the youths of a community, especially those who misbehave and are on the brink of criminal activity. Officers in the community understand its "trouble areas" and the environmental factors that have contributed to the personalities and behaviors of young offenders.

Summary

Law enforcement is the initial contact in the juvenile justice system. In the disposition of matters related to children, how police resolve matters depends on the officers' discretion and the specific incident. Street justice occurs when police decide to deal with a status offense in their own way—usually by ignoring it. Police officers have considerable discretionary power when dealing with juveniles. The most common procedure is to release the child, with or without a warning, but without making an official record or taking further action.

The objectives of police officers handling juvenile cases are (1) to protect the child or youth, (2) to investigate, (3) to determine the causes of the victimization or delinquency, (4) to prevent further victimization or delinquency and (5) to properly dispose of the case.

The fundamental nature of the juvenile justice system is rehabilitative rather than punitive. During detention a window of opportunity exists to identify youths who are on drugs and, therefore, at risk of becoming repeat offenders. Such youths can be put into drug treatment programs, hopefully averting the drug-crime-drug cycle.

The primary responsibility of police officers assigned to child neglect or abuse cases is the immediate protection of the child. Approximately 90 percent of police dispositions involve status offenders, according to the Uniform Crime Report. Running away is a predelinquent indicator, but its value often is not recognized by the parents, police, schools, social agencies or the courts. If police dispositions are to be effective, the family must recognize the early signs of maladjustment. Running away is the most visible indicator of possible victimization (assault, murder) or involvement in criminal activity to support individual needs (prostitution, pornography, burglary, theft, robbery).

Initially law enforcement sought to build a positive image rather than develop constructive, lasting delinquency prevention programs. Examples of the latter include Rochester's Teens on Patrol (TOP) program, which uses youths to patrol the city's parks and recreational areas in the summer. The Los Angeles Police Department and the Los Angeles Unified School District jointly sponsor the Drug Abuse Resistance Education (DARE) program. Teachers are of vital importance to the success of any delinquency prevention program.

Youths' attitudes toward law and law enforcement are tremendously influenced by personal contacts with law enforcement officers. Positive interactions are critical to any delinquency prevention attempts. The paradigm shift to community policing directly affects law enforcement as well as the juvenile courts and corrections.

Discussion Questions

1. How are referrals handled in your state? Do police contribute the greatest percentage of referrals?
2. Do you believe that police should make unofficial referrals, such as to community service agencies? What problems would police face when referring youths to community service agencies?
3. Do the police display a helping attitude toward youths when they make their referrals?
4. Do you believe the social standing, race and age of juveniles influence the referral procedure?
5. Should acts of violence by a juvenile automatically require that the youth be referred to a detention facility?
6. Which do you think is more effective, "street justice" by police or processing juveniles through the court system? Why?
7. Should the police be in the schools as a crime prevention method? Why or why not?
8. What police delinquency prevention programs are available in your area? Do they work? Why or why not?
9. Joe, a 13-year-old white male, has been apprehended by a police officer for stealing a bicycle. Joe took the bicycle from the school grounds shortly after a program at the school by the police on "Bicycle Theft Prevention." Joe admits to

taking the bicycle, but says he only intended to "go for a ride" and was going to return the bicycle later that day. Joe has no prior police contacts that the officer is aware of. The bicycle has been missing for only an hour and is unharmed. What should the officer do in handling the incident? Do you think the bicycle theft prevention program is worthwhile? Why or why not?

10. Do you have any personal experiences with delinquency prevention programs and police?

References

Abshire, Richard. "DARE: 'Warm and Fuzzy' or Solid Success?" *Law Enforcement Technology,* May 1996, pp. 28–33, 52.

Barr, William P. *Combating Violent Crime: 24 Recommendations to Strengthen Criminal Justice.* Washington, DC: U.S. Department of Justice, July 28, 1992.

Bennett, Wayne and Hess, Kären M. *Criminal Investigation,* 5th ed. Belmont, CA: West/Wadsworth Publishing Company, 1998.

Bilchik, Shay. Foreword. In Ann H. Crowe, *Drug Identification and Testing in the Juvenile Justice System.* Washington, DC: Office of Juvenile Justice and Delinquency Prevention, May 1998.

Bilchik, Shay. Foreword. In Mercedes Lawry, *Court Appointed Special Advocates: A Voice for Abused and Neglected Children in Court.* OJJDP, Juvenile Justice Bulletin, March 1997. (NCJ-164512)

Brodt, Stephen J. and Smith, J. Steve. "Public Policy and the Serious Juvenile Offender." In *Taking Sides: Clashing Views on Controversial Issues in Crime and Criminology,* 2nd rev. ed., edited by Richard C. Monk. Guilford, CT: Dushkin Publishing Group, Inc., 1991, pp. 171–180.

Bureau of Justice Assistance. *An Introduction to DARE: Drug Abuse Resistance Education,* 2nd ed. Washington, DC, October 1991.

Bureau of Justice Assistance. *An Introduction to the National DARE Parent Program.* Washington, DC, June 1993.

"Cities Find Youth Curfews to be Effective, According to Mayors' Survey." *NCJA Justice Bulletin,* December 1997, p. 10.

Conly, Catherine H. *Street Gangs: Current Knowledge and Strategies.* Washington, DC: National Institute of Justice, August 1993.

Crowe, Ann H. *Drug Identification and Testing in the Juvenile Justice System.* Washington, DC: Office of Juvenile Justice and Delinquency Prevention, May 1998.

Crowe, Timothy D. *Habitual Juvenile Offenders: Guidelines for Citizen Action and Public Responses.* Serious Habitual Offender Comprehensive Action Program (SHOCAP). Washington, DC: Office of Juvenile Justice and Delinquency Prevention, October 1991.

Dolnick, Jed M. "Painful Truth about the DARE Program." *Law Enforcement News,* September 15, 1998, p. 8.

Gates, Daryl F. and Jackson, Robert K. "Gang Violence in L.A." *The Police Chief,* November 1990, pp. 20–22.

Gruber, Charles A. "A Positive Evaluation of DARE." *Law and Order,* April 1998, p. 52.

Herz, Denise. "The Differential Effects of Informal and Formal Social Controls on the Processing of Status Offenders." *Journal of Contemporary Criminal Justice,* Vol. 14, No. 2, May 1998, pp. 173–192.

Higgins, Stephen E. "Interjurisdictional Coordination of Major Gang Investigations." *The Police Chief,* June 1993, pp. 46–47.

Hough, John W. "DARE: An Opponent's View." *Law and Order,* April 1998, pp. 48–50.

Ivie, Harmon. "Youth Intervention and Education Initiatives." *The Police Chief,* September 1997, pp. 54–56.

Johnson, Tim. "Community Policing: America's Best Chance to End Youth Violence." *Community Policing Exchange,* January/February 1996, p. 1.

Kennedy, David. "Pulling Levers: Getting Deterrence Right." *National Institute of Justice Journal,* July 1998, pp. 2–8.

Kline, E. M. "Colorado Springs SHO/DI: Working Smarter with Juvenile Offenders." *The Police Chief,* April 1993, pp. 32–37.

Koertge, George F. and Hill, Janice R. "PACT: Bringing Police and Children Together." *The Police Chief,* August 1996, pp. 26–34.

Krisberg, Barry and Austin, James F. *Reinventing Juvenile Justice.* Newbury Park, CA: Sage Publications, 1993.

Leiber, Michael J.; Nalla, Mahesh K.; and Farnworth, Margaret. "Explaining Juveniles' Attitudes Toward the Police." *Justice Quarterly,* Vol. 15, No. 1, March 1998, pp. 151–174.

Lesce, Tony. "Policing Public Schools." *Law and Order,* October 1996, pp. 66–70.

Little, Bobby and Bishop, Mike. "Minor Drinkers/Major Consequences: Enforcement Strategies for Underage Alcoholic Beverage Law Violators." *FBI Law Enforcement Bulletin,* June 1998, pp. 1–4.

Martin, Susan E. and Besharov, Douglas J. *Police and Child Abuse: New Policies for Expanded Responsibilities.* Washington, DC: Office of Justice Programs, National Institute of Justice, June 1991.

Minnesota POST Board. *Learning Objectives.* St. Paul, MN: 1992.

Molloy, Joseph T. and Labahn, Ted. " 'Operation GETUP' Targets Taggers to Curb Gang-Related Graffiti." *The Police Chief,* October 1993, pp. 120–125.

Morrison, Richard D. "Curfews—The Latest Crime Prevention Tool/Fad." *Law Enforcement Technology,* April 1997, pp. 44–46.

National Coalition of State Juvenile Justice Advisory Groups. *Myths and Realities: Meeting the Challenge of Serious, Violent, and Chronic Juvenile Offenders, 1992 Annual Report.* Washington, DC, 1993.

Owens, Robert P. and Wells, Donna K. "One City's Response to Gangs." *The Police Chief,* February 1993, pp. 25–27.

Pace, Denny F. *Community Relations Concepts.* Incline Village, NV: Copperhouse Publishing Company, 1991.

Parks, Bernard C. and Gonzalez, Ben. "Truancy Citations and Crime Reduction." *The Police Chief,* August 1998, pp. 42–46.

Patterson, John C. *Investigator's Guide to Missing Child Cases: For Law-Enforcement Officers Locating Missing Children,* 2nd ed. National Center for Missing and Exploited Children. October 1987.

Peters, James M. "Specialists a Definite Advantage in Child Sexual Abuse Cases." *The Police Chief,* February 1991, pp. 21–23.

President's Commission on Law Enforcement and the Administration of Justice. *The Challenge of Crime in a Free Society.* Washington, DC: U.S. Government Printing Office, 1967.

Revering, Andrew C. "Cruising and Loitering: Preludes to Serious Crime." *The Police Chief,* April 1993, pp. 39–40.

Ruefle, William and Reynolds, Kenneth Mike. "Keep Them at Home: Juvenile Curfew Ordinances in 200 American Cities." *American Journal of Police,* Vol. 15, No. 1, 1996, pp. 63–84.

Saccente, D. D. "RAP to Street Gang Activity." *The Police Chief,* February 1993, pp. 28–31.

Sealock, Mirian D. and Simpson, Sally S. "Unraveling Bias in Arrest Decisions: The Role of Juvenile Offender Type-Scripts." *Justice Quarterly,* Vol. 15, No. 3, September 1998, pp. 427–457.

Sharp, Arthur G. "Is DARE a Sacred Lamb?" *Law and Order,* April 1998, pp. 42–47.

Sigler, Robert T. and Talley, Gregory B. "Drug Abuse Resistance Education Program Effectiveness." *American Journal of Police,* Vol. 14, No. 3/4, 1995, pp. 111–121.

Siska, Paul and Shipley, David. "The Law Enforcement Alliance with the Community: Reaching Out to Youth." *The Police Chief,* February 1997, pp. 30–33.

Smith, Mary Lynn. "Reading Program Aims to Fight Crime." (Minneapolis/St. Paul) *Star Tribune,* February 8, 1996, p. B3.

Sourcebook of Criminal Justice Statistics 1996. Washington, DC: Bureau of Justice Statistics, 1997. (NCJ-165361)

Spergel, Irving A.; Chance, Ronald L.; and Curry, G. David. "National Youth Gang Suppression and Intervention Program." OJJDP, Juvenile Justice Bulletin, June 1990.

Stewart, James K. "From the Director." In "Urine Testing of Detained Juveniles to Identify High-Risk Youth" by Richard Dembo et al. NIJ, Research in Brief, May 1990.

Strandberg, Keith W. "Age Progression and Kidcare." *Law Enforcement Technology,* February 1994, pp. 46–49.

Strandberg, Keith W. "DARE and Other Youth Programs." *Law Enforcement Technology,* May 1998, pp. 48–60.

Toffler, Alvin and Toffler, Heidi. "The Future of Law Enforcement: Dangerous and Different." *FBI Law Enforcement Bulletin,* January 1990, pp. 2–5.

"Truth, DARE and Consequences." *Law Enforcement News,* April 15, 1998, pp. 1, 10.

Wagenaar, A. C. and Wolfson, Mark. "Deterring Sales and Provision of Alcohol to Minors: A Study of Enforcement in 295 Counties in Four States." *Public Health Reports,* Vol. 110, No. 4, 1995, pp. 419–427.

Wolfson, Mark; Wagenaar, A. C.; and Hornseth, Gary. "Law Officers' Views on Enforcement of the Legal Drinking Age: A Four-State Study." *Public Health Reports,* Vol. 110, No. 4, 1995, pp. 428–437.

Yanez, Luisa. "Judge Lifts Curfew for Dade Teen-Agers." (Ft. Lauderdale) *Sun-Sentinel,* March 17, 1994, p. 7B.

"Youth Programs That Work." *The Police Chief,* February 1997, pp. 26–28.

Chapter **9**

The Role
of the Juvenile Court

There is evidence in fact, that there may be
grounds for concern that the child receives
the worst of two possible worlds; that he gets
neither the protections accorded adults nor
the solicitous care and regenerative treatment
postulated for children.

—Justice Abe Fortas, *In re Gault*

Do You Know

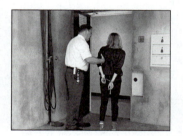

- If the juvenile court is primarily civil or criminal?
- What three classifications of children are under juvenile court jurisdiction?
- What two factors determine if the juvenile court has jurisdiction?
- What the three types of juvenile courts are?
- What two actions juvenile courts may take on behalf of children in need?
- Who can certify a juvenile as an adult?
- What three phases occur when filing a petition?
- What rights children involved in the juvenile justice system have?
- How Supreme Court decisions have changed juvenile court procedure?
- What the trend is in the disposition of juvenile cases?
- What factors are considered in a juvenile sentencing law?
- What types of intervention are available for deprived children?
- What dilemmas the juvenile courts face?

Can You Define

adjudicate, adjudicatory hearing, CASA, certification, concurrent, disposition, dispositional hearing, guardian *ad litem*, hearing, jurisdiction, mechanical jurisprudence, petition, preliminary hearing, referee, restitution, reverse certification, summons, waiver

INTRODUCTION

In the United States, justice for juveniles is administered by a separate system with its own specific court. In 1995 courts with juvenile jurisdiction processed an estimated 1,714,300 delinquency cases (Sickmund et al., 1998, p. 5). The juvenile justice court system enforces and administers a blend of civil and criminal law, but theoretically the system is a civil system. A civil system was adopted by early juvenile courts to avoid inflicting the stigma of a criminal conviction on youths processed by the courts.

The juvenile justice system is basically a civil system.

Juvenile court is bound more by the rules of the court, generally, than statutes. It covers a much broader variety of legal matters, and it is vastly more extensive than the adult criminal system. And at no point in history has the challenge been greater for the juvenile court. As Judge Glenda Hatchett states (1998, p. 83):

> This country has responded to juvenile crime by creating "get tough" and "three strikes" legislation that focuses on children who have already penetrated the system so deeply that it has become easy for people to no longer claim them as their own. The juvenile court has a unique opportunity to divert children from crime and delinquency and to reframe the discussion so that we are focused on what we do before strike one. In the new millennium, the juvenile court must focus on early intervention and prevention-based programming to effectively address the needs of America's children. . . . We only get one chance to get it right for this generation of children while they are still our children.

This chapter examines the basic philosophy of the juvenile court, its jurisdiction, the types of juvenile courts and the characteristics exhibited in most such courts. This is followed by a discussion of the juvenile court process from intake through adjudication to the final disposition. The issue of waiver and certification to adult court is examined, including the criticisms of some who feel that such waivers are used too extensively. The roles of guardian *ad litem,* CASA and court referees are also discussed.

Next the discussion focuses on the youths as they are being served by juvenile court, including those who are abused and neglected, the status offenders and the delinquents. The chapter concludes with a discussion of the issue of juvenile records, the dilemma facing juvenile courts and the criticisms that have been made of the juvenile courts.

Basic Philosophy of Juvenile Court

Bilchik (1996, p. iii) states:

> The philosophy of the juvenile court as an agent of reform is the foundation of our juvenile justice system. Serving as the crux of society's response to delinquency, the court plays a critical role in the lives of children. Juvenile courts mandate appropriate sanctions to ensure accountability and establish treatment plans in order to strengthen offenders' sense of responsibility and to protect the public. Clearly, the court is on the front line of the fight against violence.

Another philosophy underlying the juvenile court is that of *parens patriae,* a concept previously discussed. These fundamental philosophies led to a distinc-

Table 9.1
The Language of Juvenile and Adult Courts

Juvenile Court Term	Adult Court Term
Adjudication: decision by the judge that a child has committed delinquent acts.	Conviction of guilt
Adjudicatory hearing: a hearing to determine whether the allegations of a petition are supported by the evidence beyond a reasonable doubt.	Trial
Adjustment: the settling of a matter so that parties agree without official intervention by the court.	Plea bargaining
Aftercare: the supervision given to a child for a limited period of time after he or she is released from training school but while he or she is still under the control of the juvenile court.	Parole
Commitment: a decision by the judge to send a child to training school.	Sentence to imprisonment
Delinquent act: an act that if committed by an adult would be called a crime. The term does not include such ambiguities and noncrimes as "being ungovernable," "truancy," "incorrigibility," and "disobedience."	Crime
Delinquent child: a child who is found to have committed an act that would be considered a crime if committed by an adult.	Criminal
Detention: temporary care of an allegedly delinquent child who requires secure custody in physically restricting facilities pending court disposition or execution of a court order.	Holding in jail
Dispositional hearing: a hearing held subsequent to the adjudicatory hearing to determine what order of disposition should be made for a child adjudicated as delinquent.	Sentencing hearing
Hearing: the presentation of evidence to the juvenile court judge, his or her consideration of it, and his or her decision on disposition of the case.	Trial
Juvenile court: the court that has jurisdiction over children who are alleged to be or found to be delinquent. Juvenile delinquency procedures should not be used for neglected children or for those who need supervision.	Court of record
Petition: an application for a court order or some other judicial action. Hence, a "delinquency petition" is an application for the court to act in a matter involving a juvenile apprehended for a delinquent act.	Accusation or indictment
Probation: the supervision of a delinquent child after the court hearing but without commitment to training school.	Probation (with the same meaning as the juvenile court term)
Residential child care facility: a dwelling (other than a detention or shelter care facility) that is licensed to provide living accommodations, care, treatment, and maintenance for children and youths. Such facilities include foster homes, group homes, and halfway houses.	Halfway house
Shelter: temporary care of a child in physically unrestricting facilities pending court disposition or execution of a court order for placement. Shelter care is used for dependent and neglected children and minors in need of supervision. Separate shelter care facilities are also used for children apprehended for delinquency who need temporary shelter but not secure detention.	Jail
Take into custody: the act of the police in securing the physical custody of a child engaged in delinquency. The term is used to avoid the stigma of the word "arrest."	Arrest

Source: From *Crime and Justice in America: A Human Perspective*, by Harold J. Vetter and Leonard Territo. Copyright © 1984 by West Publishing Co. Reprinted by permission of Wadsworth Publishing Co.

tion between juvenile and adult criminal courts that is reflected in the different terminology used by each court system (Table 9.1).

The aim of the first juvenile court was to offer youths and adolescent offenders individualized justice and treatment rather than punishment. Just as the terminology used in the juvenile justice system differs from that used in

Table 9.2
Comparison of Juvenile Court and Adult Criminal Court

Characteristic Feature	Juvenile Court	Adult Court
Purpose	Protect/treat	Punish
Jurisdiction	Based mainly on age	Based on offense
Responsible noncriminal acts	Yes (status offense)	No
Court proceedings	Less formal/private	Formal/public
Proceedings considered to be criminal	No	Yes
Release of identifying information to press	No	Yes
Parental involvement	Usually possible	No
Release to parental custody	Frequently	Occasionally
Plea bargaining	Less frequently; open admission of guilt more common	Frequently
Right to jury trial	No (*McKeiver* case)	Yes
Right to treatment	Yes	No
Sealing/expungement of record	Usually possible	No

the adult system, several characteristic features of the systems also differ, as summarized in Table 9.2.

Jurisdiction of the Juvenile Court

The **jurisdiction** of the juvenile court refers to the types of cases it is empowered to hear. In almost every state, the juvenile court's jurisdiction extends to three classifications of children: (1) those who are neglected, dependent or abused because those charged with their custody and control mistreat them or fail to provide proper care; (2) those who are incorrigible, ungovernable, wayward or truant and (3) those who violate laws, ordinances and codes classified as penal or criminal.

> The jurisdiction of the juvenile court includes children who are in poverty, neglected or abused; who are unruly or commit status offenses and who are charged with committing serious crimes.

All 50 states have jurisdiction over the first and third categories. Only Idaho does not expressly provide for jurisdiction over children who are beyond the control of their parents or guardians. According to Springer (1986, p. 44):

The general purpose of the juvenile court is to do justice. Among the special purposes of the court are the following:
　　To settle civil controversies that relate to the protection, care, and custody of abused, neglected, and endangered children. . . .
　　To protect abused, neglected, and endangered minors by means of placement and protective orders.

Springer notes as a failing of the juvenile court system its "one-pot" jurisdictional approach, in which deprived children, status offenders and youths who commit serious crimes are put into the same "pot." Springer also notes that historically (p. 45):

> All three kinds of children were thought to be the products or victims of bad family and social environments; consequently, it was thought, they should be subject, as wards of the court, to the same kind of solicitous, helpful care.

The common declaration of status was that of wardship.

Springer (pp. 62–63) describes a proposed change in legislation that would remove deprived children from the delinquency jurisdiction of the court and make them subject to civil sanctions only. The legislation would also remove status offenders and those children whose parents could not control them from the delinquency jurisdiction of the court. Under the proposed legislation, delinquent jurisdiction is reserved for juveniles who commit criminal offenses.

The proposed disposition of juveniles falling within the civil jurisdiction of the juvenile court are as follows (pp. 63–64):

- In all cases in which minors are adjudicated to be within the court's civil jurisdiction, the court should within a reasonable time conduct a dispositional hearing to determine what actions to take. Minors within civil jurisdiction are entitled to care, guidance, and control within their own homes unless their best interests require otherwise.

- If minors are removed from their homes or from their parents' control, the care should be as equivalent to that given in their homes as possible.

- Except for emergency protection detention, minors within civil jurisdiction should not be detained except for violating probation or by direct court order. No minor under civil jurisdiction should be placed in any penal institution for youth or any reformatory, training center, general penal institution, or any secure residential facility to house or punish criminal offenders or delinquents.

The importance of differentiating between criminal and noncriminal conduct committed by juveniles and the limitation on the state's power under *parens patriae* was established over a hundred years ago in *People ex rel. O'Connell v. Turner* (1870). In this case Daniel O'Connell was committed to the Chicago Reform School by an Illinois law that permitted the confinement of "misfortunate youngsters." The Illinois Supreme Court's decision was that the state's power of *parens patriae* could not exceed that of the parents except to punish crime. The court ordered Daniel to be released from the reform school.

Factors Determining Jurisdiction

In most states two factors determine the jurisdiction of the court.

Jurisdiction of the juvenile court is determined by the offender's age and conduct.

The limit for the exercise of the juvenile court's jurisdiction is determined by establishing a maximum *age* below which children are deemed subject to the improvement process of the court. A "child" is generally defined as a person under the maximum age that establishes the court's jurisdiction. Age 18 is accepted in two-thirds of the states and in the District of Columbia.

However some states are currently lowering their juvenile court age cap in response to acts of violence committed by children younger than the established jurisdictional age. For example a bill has been proposed in Texas to reduce from 14 to 10 the age at which youths can be tried in adult criminal court, and to allow juveniles as young as 11 to be charged with capital crimes ("Texas Lawmaker," 1998, p. 4). The bill's sponsor, Rep. Jim Pitts, was motivated by the school shooting in Jonesboro, Arkansas, in which four students and a teacher were killed by two boys, ages 11 and 13. Says Pitts: "Legislators who created the current juvenile laws could not have anticipated violent crimes being committed by children this young. . . . Texas must not allow a similar incident to occur and not be prepared to deal with it."

The jurisdictional age, generally, is the same for all children and all forms of conduct. Some states, however, differentiate between delinquent and deprived. Connecticut, for example, has a jurisdictional age of 16 in cases of children alleged to be delinquent or "defective" and age 18 in cases of children alleged to be abused, dependent, neglected or "uncared for." Georgia has a jurisdictional age of 17 for delinquent or unruly children and 18 for deprived children.

The issue of jurisdiction and age was first questioned in 1905 by the Pennsylvania Supreme Court. Frank Fisher was adjudicated a delinquent in the Philadelphia Juvenile Court. On appeal his lawyer challenged the constitutionality of the legislation establishing the court, urging in particular that Fisher was denied due process in the manner in which he was taken into custody and that he was denied his constitutional right to a jury trial for a felony. The Pennsylvania Supreme Court upheld a lower court's sanction. The court found that due process, or lack of it, simply was not at issue, since its guarantee applied only to *criminal* cases. The state could, on the other hand, place a child within its protection without any process at all if it saw fit to do so. Recall that in *Commonwealth v. Fisher* (1905) the court stated: "To save a child . . . the legislature surely may provide for the salvation of such a child . . . by bringing it into the courts of the state without any process at all, for the purpose of subjecting it to the state's guardianship and protection." The court further stated:

> The natural parent needs no process to temporarily deprive his child of its liberty by confining it to his own home, to save it and to shield it from the consequences of persistence in a career of waywardness; nor is the state, when compelled as *parens patriae,* to take the place of the father for the same purpose, required to adopt any process as a means of placing its hands upon a child to lead it into one of its courts.

Similarly, the court argued, a jury trial could hardly be necessary to determine whether a child deserved to be saved. The court had the jurisdiction and the responsibility of age and conduct, not due process.

Besides the jurisdictional age, *conduct* determines the juvenile court's jurisdiction. Although the definition of delinquency varies from state to state, the violation of a state law or local ordinance (an act that would be a crime if committed by an adult) is the main category. Youths who violate federal laws or laws from other states, who are wayward, incorrigible or habitually truant or who associate with immoral people are all considered delinquent and subject to the jurisdiction of the juvenile court.

Other Cases within Juvenile Court Jurisdiction

In addition to having jurisdiction over children who are in need of protection, who commit status offenses or who commit serious crimes, some juvenile courts have authority to handle other issues, such as adoptions, illegitimacy and guardianship.

The jurisdiction of the court is further extended by provisions in many states that it may exercise its authority over adults in certain cases involving children. Thus in many states the juvenile court may require a parent to contribute to child support, or it may charge and try adults with contributing to the delinquency, neglect, abuse or dependency of a child.

The state is the "higher or ultimate parent" of all the children within its borders. The rights of the child's own parents are always subject to the control of the state when in the opinion of the court the best interests of the child demand it. If the state has to intervene in the case of any child, it exercises its power of guardianship over the child and provides him or her with the protection, care and guidance needed.

Although the substantive justice system for juveniles is administered by a specialized court, a great deal of variation exists in the juvenile law between different jurisdictions. Before a court with juvenile jurisdiction may declare a youth a ward of the state, it must be convinced that a basis for that wardship exists. The possible bases for a declaration of wardship include demonstrations that the child is abused or neglected, or has committed a status offense or a criminal act.

Offenses Excluded from Juvenile Court Jurisdiction

Not all offenses committed by young people are within the jurisdiction of the juvenile court. There are no firm assurances that a case will be heard in the juvenile court. The juvenile judge is given discretion to waive jurisdiction in a case and to transfer it to a criminal court if the circumstances and conduct dictate, as will be discussed later.

In some states delinquency is not exclusively within the scope of the juvenile court. Jurisdiction in juvenile court may be **concurrent** with criminal court jurisdiction—that is, it happens at the same time or may occur in either. Often this concurrent jurisdiction is limited by law to cases being handled by either court. Furthermore, certain offenses, such as murder, manslaughter or rape, may be entirely excluded from juvenile court jurisdiction. In states with such laws, children charged with these offenses are automatically tried in criminal court. Several states have excluded specified offenses from juvenile court jurisdiction. Colorado statutes, for example, state:

> Juvenile court does not have jurisdiction over: children 14 or older charged with crimes of violence classified as Class 1 felonies; children 16 or older who within the previous two years have been adjudicated delinquent for commission of a felony and are now charged with a Class 2 or Class 3 felony or any nonclassified felony punishable by death or life imprisonment.

Delaware excludes first-degree murder, rape and kidnapping, unless the case is transferred to juvenile court from criminal court. Hawaii excludes Class A felonies in certain cases if the child is 16 years or older. Illinois excludes murder, criminal sexual assault, armed robbery with a firearm and possession of a deadly weapon in a school committed by a child 15 or older. Several other states exclude youths who have had previous problems with the law.

Venue and Transfer

Usually proceedings take place in the county where the juvenile lives. If a proceeding involving a juvenile begins in a different county, the court may ask that the proceedings be transferred to the county where the juvenile lives. Likewise transfer can be made if the child's residence changes before proceedings begin.

Types of Juvenile Courts

The term *juvenile court* really is a misnomer. Only in isolated cases have completely separate courts for juveniles been established. Where they have been, it has been primarily in the larger cities. Boston, for example, has a specialized court for handling juvenile matters, but its jurisdiction is less than citywide. A few states (Connecticut, Rhode Island and Utah) have separate juvenile court systems. Elsewhere throughout the country, juvenile court jurisdiction resides in a variety of courts: municipal, county, district, superior or probate. Some are multiple-judge courts; others are served by a single judge.

A survey by the National Council on Crime and Delinquency identified the various types of courts throughout the country that handle cases involving juveniles. According to Dedel (1998, p. 512): "Fourteen states (32 percent) had more than one type of court that handled cases involving juveniles. Overall, 30 percent of responding states processed juveniles in family court, 75 percent used a juvenile court, 9 percent used probate court, 23 percent used criminal court, 2 percent used other courts, and 2 percent did not respond to the item."

Throughout their history, juvenile courts have been separated into three types: designated courts, independent and separate courts, and coordinated courts.

Designated courts are those in municipalities, counties, districts and circuits that are designated to hear children's cases and while so functioning are called juvenile courts. The great majority of juvenile courts are designated courts and usually preside in counties.

Independent and separate courts are those whose administration is entirely divorced from that of other courts. Many separate and independent courts are presided over by judges from other courts, however, so their separateness and independence is more in name than in reality.

The last type of court with jurisdiction involving children is *coordinated courts*. These courts are coordinated with other special courts, such as domestic relations or family courts.

Juvenile Drug Courts

As the juvenile court reaches its 100th anniversary, it has struggled with increasingly complex and difficult caseloads and diminishing resources. One approach to the crowded court dockets is the drug court. As noted by Kimbrough (1998, p. 11): "In an environment that is increasingly punitive, juvenile drug courts are emerging as a promising option for providing appropriate and meaningful treatment responses to juveniles and their families while ensuring accountability." As Kimbrough describes, a typical juvenile drug court offers delinquents who meet certain eligibility criteria the option of participating in the drug court rather than in a traditional case processing. The two most common criteria are having a substance abuse problem and not having committed a violent offense. The juvenile and his or her parents must participate in an intensive treatment regimen in addition to receiving sanctions ranging from community service to short-term detention.

As Kimbrough (p. 12) notes: "The heart of the juvenile drug court is the drug court team—the judge, prosecutor, public defender, treatment provider, probation officer, and others—which works together to encourage the juvenile's rehabilitation."

Teen Court

Another innovative alternative to the traditional juvenile court is the teen court, also called peer or youth court. According to Godwin (1996, p. 1):

> In a teen court, juvenile offenders are held accountable for substance use and other misdemeanor offenses and sentenced by a jury of their peers to community service, counseling, restitution, and/or an apology to the victim.
>   . . . Teen courts also present communities with opportunities to teach young people valuable life and coping skills and promote positive peer influence for youth who are defendants and for volunteer youth who play a variety of roles in the teen court process. These volunteers serve not only as jurors but also as defense or prosecuting attorneys, court clerks, bailiffs, and even—in some cases—judges. Teen court mobilizes a diverse mix of volunteer youth and adults for active and constructive involvement in addressing problems in their towns and cities.

Godwin notes that teen courts provide an effective intervention in jurisdictions where the enforcement of misdemeanor charges is given low priority due to heavy caseloads of more serious offenses. Furthermore: "Most teen courts require defendants to plead guilty prior to participation in the program; however, a small number of these courts are structured to determine guilt or innocence."

In contrast to the unique approach of teen courts in handling young misdemeanants, consider next the characteristics of traditional juvenile courts.

Characteristics of the Juvenile Court

The juvenile court has had an uneven development and has manifested a great diversity in its methods and procedures. However as early as 1920, Evelina Belden of the United States Children's Bureau listed the following as the essential characteristics of the juvenile court:

- Separate hearings for children's cases
- Informal or chancery procedure

- Regular probation service
- Separate detention of children
- Special court and probation records
- Provisions for mental and physical examinations

Unfortunately many juvenile courts lack these characteristics. Critics argue that such courts cannot claim to be juvenile courts.

In the United States, juvenile courts vary from one jurisdiction to another, manifesting all stages of the system's complex development. Its philosophy, structure and functions are still evolving. Rarely is the court distinct and highly specialized. In the more rural counties, it is largely rudimentary. Usually it is part of a court with more jurisdiction. In Minnesota, for example, it is a part of the probate court. Judges hold sessions for juveniles at irregular intervals or when the hearings can be held in clusters. Since there is great diversity, no simple description of U.S. juvenile courts can be given.

The Juvenile Court Process

Changes in the juvenile court interrelate with such factors as industrialization, urbanization, population shifts, the use of natural resources, the rapid acceleration of technology and the acceleration of transportation and communication. All have influenced the family and neighborhood, forcing communities to find new or additional sources of social control. This has given considerable impetus to taking a broader look at the juvenile court process, illustrated in Figure 9.1.

Custody and Detention

Juveniles typically enter the court system through some sort of interface with the police. Children can be taken into custody by court order, under the laws of arrest, or by a law enforcement officer if there are "reasonable grounds to believe that the child is suffering from illness or injury or is in immediate danger from his surroundings . . . or to believe that the child has run away." The Uniform Juvenile Court Act (UJCA) of 1968 notes: "The taking of a child into custody is not an arrest, except for the purpose of determining its validity under the constitution of this state or of the United States."

Section 14 of the UJCA deals with the detention of children:

A child taken into custody shall not be detained or placed in shelter care prior to the hearing on the petition unless his detention or care is required to protect the person or property of others or of the child or because the child may abscond or be removed from the jurisdiction of the court or because he has no parent, guardian, or custodian or other person able to provide supervision and care for him and return him to the court when required, or an order for his detention or shelter care has been made by the court pursuant to this Act.

The National Juvenile Detention Association provides the following definition: "Juvenile detention is the temporary and safe custody of juveniles who are accused of conduct subject to the jurisdiction of the court who require a restricted environment for their own or the community's protection while pending legal action" (*OJJDP Guide*, 1997, p. 33). Wordes and Jones (1998, p. 546)

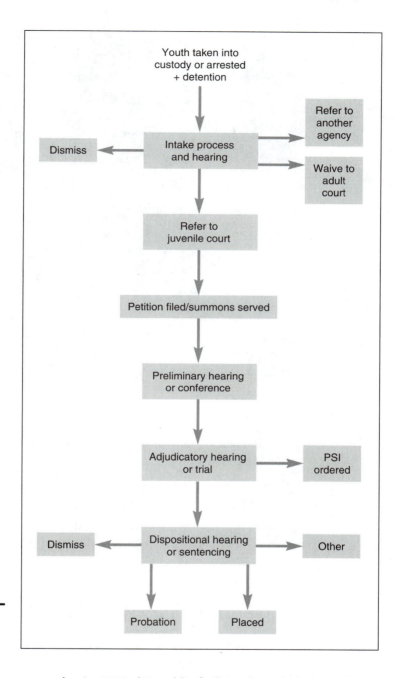

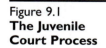

Figure 9.1
**The Juvenile
Court Process**

report that in 1995, 450 public facilities through the United States were qualified as juvenile detention facilities and held a daily population of approximately 23,000 youths.

Once children are taken into custody, they should either be released to their parents, guardians or custodians; brought before the court; or delivered to a detention or shelter care facility, or to a medical facility if needed. This is to be done "with all reasonable speed and without first taking the child elsewhere."

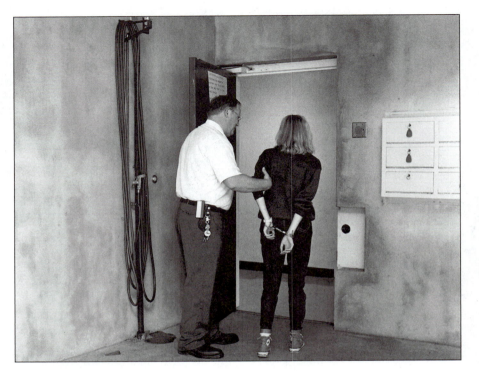

Officers on the street have great discretion, especially when dealing with juveniles. They may take a juvenile into custody, as shown here, or they may simply give them a warning, often referred to as street justice.

The parent, guardian or custodian and the court must be promptly given a written notice stating the reason the child was taken into custody. The UJCA provides in Section 16 that a delinquent can be detained only in:

- A licensed foster home or a home approved by the court
- A facility operated by a licensed child welfare agency
- A detention home or center for delinquent children that is under the direction or supervision of the court or other public authority, or of a private agency approved by the court
- Any other suitable place or facility, designated or operated by the court

The final omnibus or catchall clause in this provision of the UJCA weakens the effectiveness of the act.

Section 16 further specifies that delinquents may be kept in a jail or other adult detention facility only if the preceding are not available, the detention is in a room separate from adults and it appears that public safety and protection reasonably requires detention. The act requires that the person in charge of a jail inform the court immediately if a person under age 18 is received at the jail. The act further stipulates that deprived or unruly children "shall not be detained in a jail or other facility intended or used for the detention of adults charged with criminal offenses or of children alleged to be delinquent." The intent of this section is to protect children from the harm of exposing them to criminals and the "degrading effect of jails, lockups, and the like."

Section 17 states that if a child is brought before the court or delivered to a detention or shelter care facility, an investigation must be made immediately as to whether detention is needed. If the child is not released, a petition must be filed promptly with the court. In addition an informal detention hearing should be held within 72 hours to determine if detention is required. A written notice of the time, place and purpose of the hearing is given to the child and, if possible, to the parents or guardians. Before the hearing begins, the court must inform the people involved of their right to counsel—court appointed if they cannot afford to pay private counsel—and of the child's right to remain silent during the hearing.

Probation Services

Probation services are commonly sought for juveniles who are taken into custody and placed in detention. The UJCA describes how probation officers can be appointed and notes that:

> A competent probation staff is essential to achieving the objectives of the juvenile court system. The staff must be adequately trained, working loads must be limited, and conditions must be provided that permit the giving of the required time and attention called for by each individual case.
>
> A probation service may be established on either a local or a statewide basis. Competent authorities disagree on the relative merits of the two alternatives. The National Council of Juvenile Courts favors a local system, stressing the importance of having these services provided by court personnel responsible to and under the direction of the juvenile court judge, since he is responsible for the successful conduct of the juvenile program. Proponents of the statewide system stress the frequent inadequacy of local resources to provide the needed minimum service required and contend that better probation service is provided by a state system, and that the prospect of the judge successfully achieving the objectives of the court's program is therefore enhanced.

According to guidelines set forth in the UJCA, probation officers should:

- Make investigations, reports and recommendations to the juvenile court
- Receive and examine complaints and charges of delinquency, unruly conduct or deprivation of children
- Supervise and assist children placed on probation
- Make appropriate referrals to other private or public agencies if needed
- Take into custody and detain children who are under their supervision or care as delinquent, unruly or deprived children, if the children's health or safety is in danger
- Arrange to have children removed from the jurisdiction of the court

Probation officers do *not* have the powers of law enforcement officers. The act notes that: "The primary role of the probation officers is the care and protection of the child, and in delinquency cases, his treatment and rehabilitation as well. Incompatible roles such as the power of arrest, conducting the accusatory proceeding in juvenile court, representing the child in court, have been excluded."

Intake

Intake is the initial phase of the juvenile court process. In most jurisdictions the offender is referred immediately to juvenile authorities or to an "intake unit." At the intake stage of the referral, an intake officer decides to adjust, settle or terminate the matter. The intake officer also makes referrals to other interests out of concern for the health, welfare and the safety of the child. This process in most states is called the intake hearing. The purpose of these proceedings is not to adjudicate the affirmation (guilty) or denial (not guilty) of juveniles in the matter, but to determine if the matter requires the court's attention. The intake unit serves in an advisory capacity.

Another important function of the intake hearing is to provide an authoritarian setting in which a severe lecture or counsel may be administered to the youth so as to avoid future difficulties. Beyond a lecture several other options are available to intake officers:

- Write a reprimand
- Divert to another social agency
- Direct to the district/county attorney's office for a petition
- Dismiss the matter

Intake cases are screened in the referral process by an officer appointed by the juvenile court. This officer is usually a probation officer or designated court personnel, not a lawyer.

In matters handled by intake, the biggest disparity from state to state is in how abused, neglected and dependent children are helped, and in how the best interests of the child are defined. The amount and quality of social services available for implementing such help vary greatly. Two distinct kinds of court action may result.

Court action on behalf of neglected, abused or dependent children may be noncriminal or criminal.

The first action on behalf of neglected, abused or dependent children is *noncriminal.* It seeks to identify whether the child is in danger and, if so, what is needed for the child's protection. The parents may lose custody of the child, be required to pay child support or be ordered to make adjustments in care, custody and control. This type of action does not permit punitive sanctions against the parents, however.

A second option is *criminal* prosecution of the parents, on charges that they have committed a harmful act against the child or have failed to discharge their responsibility, thus placing the child in active danger. This action does not involve the status of the child. The scope of the court's position in these referrals is based on the juvenile court's responsibility for the welfare of the child under the philosophy of *in loco parentis.*

Referrals carry the same weight as a court process and are subject to rules of law and procedure to protect children. Referrals include the information that court personnel need to proceed in a directed course, such as diversion or channeling to the proper authority.

As noted in Figure 9.1, the intake hearing may lead to several outcomes, including dismissal of the case or referral to another agency. If the conclusion of the intake hearing is that the case should proceed to court, a determination must be made whether to try the case in juvenile or criminal court. Before discussing the referral to juvenile court, consider what happens when a juvenile is waived to adult (criminal) court.

Waiver and Certification

The juvenile court may waive jurisdiction and transfer a case to criminal court (**waiver**). DeFrances and Strom (1997, p. 1) report: "The percentage of petitioned cases judicially waived to criminal court has remained relatively constant at about 1.4% since 1985. In 1994, 12,300 juvenile cases were judicially waived." Some states have mandatory adult court requirements for 14-, 15- and 16-year-olds for certain serious, violent offenses. The prosecuting attorney may make the decisions in other major crime situations. When waiver occurs certain procedural guidelines apply. For example no statements made by the child before the transfer may be used against him or her in the criminal proceedings following the transfer.

Another possibility is that the court may decree that a juvenile should be certified as an adult (**certification**). Certification is of paramount importance, since it may result in far more severe consequences to the juvenile than would have occurred had the youth remained under the jurisdiction of the juvenile court.

While waiver and certification do not happen often, when either does occur, juveniles go through the same procedures and have the same constitutional rights as adults tried in a criminal court. Recall from Chapter 1 that the procedural requirements for waiver to criminal court were articulated by the Supreme Court in *Kent v. United States*.

Jurisdictions may consider the child's age, alleged offense or a combination of other factors when determining whether a juvenile is fit for transfer to adult court. The procedures differ from state to state, and, according to Deddeh and Amador (1996–1997, p. 26): "California is one of only 10 states relying solely on a judicial determination of unfitness before a minor can be sent to adult court. In 40 other states, minors are automatically sent to adult court if accused of certain serious crimes, or are sent there in serious cases if the DA thinks it appropriate."

In some states the court makes the decision to certify a juvenile as an adult. In other states this is done by the prosecutor.

Deddeh and Amador state (p. 26):

> In deciding whether to find a minor "fit" for treatment in the juvenile system or "unfit" for that system and properly tried as an adult, the court must determine if the minor would be amenable to the care, treatment and training program available through the facilities of the juvenile court.

Table 9.3
Attitudes toward Treating Juveniles as Adults if Charged with Serious Property Crime, Selling Drugs, or Serious Violent Crime, by Demographic Characteristics, United States, 1995

Question: "Please tell me for each of the following statements whether you strongly agree, agree, neither agree nor disagree, disagree, or strongly disagree."
(Percent responding "strongly agree" or "agree")

Respondents	A juvenile charged with a **serious property crime** should be tried as an adult.	A juvenile charged with **selling illegal drugs** should be tried as an adult.	A juvenile charged with a **serious violent crime** should be tried as an adult.
National	62.6%	69.1%	86.5%
Sex			
Male	68.3	69.6	87.8
Female	57.4	68.6	85.2
Race			
White	63.1	69.7	86.9
Black	57.7	65.4	81.7
Hispanic	66.2	66.7	86.3
Age			
18–29 years	60.2	68.0	86.1
30–39 years	60.4	67.5	86.0
40–59 years	64.0	68.8	87.7
60 years +	68.2	74.0	86.6
Community			
Urban	60.5	67.1	85.4
Suburban	60.1	66.9	87.5
Small city	62.8	67.6	86.2
Rural/small town	64.7	72.0	85.9

Source: Adapted from *Sourcebook of Criminal Justice Statistics 1996*.
Washington, DC: Bureau of Justice Statistics, 1997, p. 155. (NCJ-165361)

That decision is guided and shaped by an evaluation of the following five criteria:

- The degree of criminal sophistication exhibited by the minor
- Whether the minor can be rehabilitated prior to the expiration of the juvenile court's jurisdiction
- The minor's previous delinquent history
- Success of previous attempts by the juvenile court to rehabilitate the minor
- The circumstances and gravity of the offense alleged in the petition to have been committed by the minor

In serious cases, the court must find the minor "fit" under every criterion or an overall finding of fitness cannot be made.

According to Harris (1988, pp. 655–656): "Legislatively mandated waiver and reduced ages of majority encourage the handling of greater numbers of juveniles within the criminal justice system. Determinate sentencing provisions, such as mandatory terms of incarceration for certain offenders, mimic provisions adopted by the criminal justice system in previous years." Despite such sentencing reforms, however, many perceive that when juveniles are waived to adult court, they are treated leniently. Nonetheless most Americans favor the transfer of juveniles to criminal court when they are charged with serious crimes, as shown by the results of a survey conducted through the College of Criminal Justice at Sam Houston State University (Table 9.3).

The National Coalition of State Juvenile Justice Advisory Groups (1993, p. 26) reports: "Recent studies show that juveniles are now receiving more severe sanctions in the adult court than youths with similar charges received in the juvenile court." In addition, according to the coalition, violent youths required an average of 246 days to be transferred, convicted in and sentenced by the criminal court in comparison to an average of 98 days for juvenile court processing. DeFrances and Strom (p. 6) state: "For juvenile offenders convicted in criminal court, several sentencing options exist. In most States the criminal court imposes adult correctional sanctions. However, in some States the criminal court can impose a blended sentence, juvenile and/or adult correctional sanctions. . . . In several other States that criminal court can transfer the case back to juvenile court for sentencing."

Reverse Certification

In some states the criminal court has exclusive jurisdiction over juveniles who commit specified serious crimes, such as murder, but the court may transfer the case to juvenile court by a process known as **reverse certification.** For example New York statutes specify that juvenile court jurisdiction:

> Excludes children 13 or older charged with second degree murder and children 14 or older charged with second degree murder, felony murder, kidnapping in the first degree, arson in the first or second degree, assault in the first degree, manslaughter in the first degree, rape in the first degree, sodomy in the first degree, aggravated sexual abuse, burglary in the first or second degree, robbery in the first or second degree, attempted murder, or attempted kidnapping in the first degree, unless such case is transferred to the juvenile court from the criminal court.

Furthermore, according to the UJCA, if during a criminal proceeding it is learned that the defendant is under age 18 or was under age 18 at the time the offense occurred, the case may be transferred back to juvenile court.

If a case involving a youth is referred to juvenile court, a petition is filed and the case moves from intake into the adjudication phase.

Petition and Summons

The **petition** is a document similar to the complaint in the adult system, alleging that a juvenile is a delinquent, status offender or dependent and asking the court to assume jurisdiction. It sets forth:

- The facts that bring the child within the jurisdiction of the court, with a statement that it is in the best interest of the child and the public that the proceeding be brought and, if delinquency or unruly conduct is alleged, that the child is in need of treatment or rehabilitation
- The name, age and residence address, if any, of the child on whose behalf the petition is brought
- The names and residence addresses, if known to petitioner, of the parents, guardian or custodian of the child and of the child's spouse, if any
- Whether the child is in custody and, if so, the place of detention and the time it occurred

Any person, including a law enforcement officer, may make a petition, but it will not be filed until the court or someone authorized by the court determines and endorses that the filing of the petition is in the best interest of the public and the child.

Several states have separated the procedures for delinquency from those for status offenses and children in need of the court's protection. A delinquency petition may be issued. The same procedure is used with children in need of protection or services (CHIPS).

After the petition is filed, the court fixes a time for a hearing. If the youth is in detention, the hearing must be within 10 days of the filing of the petition. When the hearing date is set, a **summons** is issued to the child, if 14 years or older, the parents, guardians or custodians, and to any other people to appear before the court. The summons accompanies the petition and clearly states that the person is entitled to a lawyer.

The summons should be served at least 24 hours before the hearing for persons within the state at a known address, or sent by registered or certified mail at least five days before the hearing if the address is not known or the person lives out of state. Sometimes the court elects to issue a Notice in Lieu of Summons to send with the petition to the parents or guardians. This is a somewhat less formal, less intimidating process.

Following the filing of a petition and the service of a summons, the case enters into a series of three hearings.

The three phases following the filing of a petition are (1) the preliminary hearing or conference, (2) the adjudicatory hearing or trial and (3) the dispositional hearing or sentencing.

Preliminary Hearing

The *preliminary hearing* or conference satisfies those matters that must be dealt with before the case can proceed further. At this first hearing, the judge informs the parties involved of the charges in the petition and of their rights in the proceeding. The hearing may also be used to determine whether an alleged delinquent should remain in detention or in the custody of juvenile authorities.

In the matter of detention, if the judge, with the assistance of a probation officer, determines that the child's behavior is a threat to the public, is a danger to himself and others or that the child will not return to court voluntarily, the judge can order the child to remain in custody. Dependent, neglected or abused children, as well as status offenders, may be placed in foster care or a residential shelter. If the case involves an abused, neglected or dependent child, a guardian is usually appointed to act as an advocate for the child. This person is often a representative of a social service or welfare agency.

Guardian *Ad Litem*

A **guardian** *ad litem* (GAL) is a representative of a juvenile, appointed by the juvenile court judge solely for the best interest of the child and to represent that interest on his or her behalf. The Child Abuse Prevention and Treatment Act of

At the preliminary hearing a judge explains the charges to the youth as well as his rights.

1974 required the provision of a GAL to all youths whose cases were heard in family court.

While most often an attorney, the guardian *ad litem* can be anyone the juvenile court judge determines will accept that responsibility and act in the child's best interest. The guardian *ad litem* fulfills this responsibility in all matters involving juveniles, whether they are neglected, abused, dependent or delinquent. Karmen (1996, p. 236) notes: "In criminal proceedings against an abuser, the GAL is supposed to serve as a counselor, interpreter, defender against system-induced trauma (insensitive handling), monitor, coordinator, advocate (of rights to privacy, protection from harassment), and spokesperson (about wishes, fears, and needs)."

CASAs

Most states have volunteer guardian *ad litem* programs called **CASA**—Court Appointed Special Advocate for Children. (Casa means *home* in Spanish.) As of October 1998, 678 CASA programs were operating within the United States. One of the primary functions of a CASA is to conduct investigations as to the best placement in foster homes for children. CASA founder David W. Soukup states (Lawry, 1997, p. 2): "As a judge, I had to make tough decisions. I had to decide whether to take a child from the only home he's ever known, or leave him someplace where he might possibly be abused. I needed someone who could tell me what was best for that child—from the child's viewpoint. That's what CASA does."

According to Lawry (p. 3): "CASA volunteers are the eyes and ears of the court, making objective assessments of a child's needs." They are the safety net that keeps many children from falling through the cracks of the child welfare system by aiding in permanency planning efforts and helping thousands of children to find safe, nurturing homes. As Salvadore T. Mule, past president of the

National Council of Juvenile and Family Court Judges, puts it (Lawry, p. 3): "Abused and neglected children need someone to speak up for them. No one does this more effectively and with more dedication than the CASA volunteer. As a judge, I rely heavily on the CASA's insight and recommendation to the court. CASA does work."

CASAs work primarily in cases of child neglect, physical abuse, psychological abuse, sexual abuse, abandonment or when parents are unwilling or unable to care for their children. As explained by Lawry (pp. 2–3):

> CASA volunteers investigate, evaluate and recommend to the court what is in the child's immediate and long-term interests. In that capacity they serve as:
>
> - Investigators—to determine relevant facts through personal interviews and a review of records, documents, and clinical data.
> - Advocates—to present an accurate portrait of the child before the court at hearings through written reports and direct testimony to make sure that the judge, social service staff, and legal counsel fulfill their obligations.
> - Monitors—to ensure compliance with court orders by all parties and to bring to the court's attention any changes in circumstances that require modification of a court order; to ensure that the child remains safe until a permanent resolution is reached.

Referees

In many states the law provides for the juvenile judge to appoint a full- or part-time court **referee,** an individual to act as a hearing officer, to reduce testimony to findings of fact and to make recommendations on disposition. The powers of the referee are limited by law. In some states that have referees, the referee is not empowered to make a final order, but acts as an advisor to the court. The referee's recommendation may be approved, modified or rejected by the juvenile judge, but when approved or modified it becomes a court order.

Juvenile court referees are a valuable asset to the court, particularly when a judge's caseload is more than can be effectively handled, since referees allow judges more time to focus attention on difficult cases. Referees automatically hear specific cases (often routine, simple cases) and automatically follow guidelines. Judges normally would hear cases in which child custody is in question, as well as serious delinquency cases in which violence occurred. Referees also are not involved in matters where the jurisdiction of the court is in question, such as the transfer or certification of a juvenile to a criminal court. The referee's role, therefore, is to assist the juvenile court judge, rather than to replace or become the judge. Before hearing a case, however, the referee must inform the parties involved that they are entitled to have the matter heard by the judge. If they want a judge, they get one.

Adjudication

To **adjudicate** is to judge. The *adjudicatory hearing* or trial is to determine if the allegations of the petition are supported by a preponderance of evidence (for status offenses) or by evidence that proves beyond a reasonable doubt that a delinquent act occurred. Oran (1985, p. 11) defines an adjudication as "the formal giving, pronouncing, or recording of a judgment for one side in a lawsuit." *Adjudicative facts* are "The 'who, what, where, etc.,' facts about persons having a dispute before an *administrative agency.*" In terms of the

The adjudicatory hearing is similar to an adult trial. Youths are entitled to a lawyer at this stage as well as at all stages of the juvenile court proceedings.

juvenile court, adjudication refers to the judge's determination (decision) that a youth is a status offender, a delinquent or neither.

At this stage the child makes a plea, either an admission or denial of the allegations in the petition. If the allegations are sustained, the judge makes a finding of fact (that the child is delinquent, abused, neglected or otherwise in need of supervision), sets a date for a dispositional hearing and orders a social investigation or presentence investigation (PSI) or a predisposition report.

The Predisposition Report

The probation officer who conducts the investigation and completes the report seeks the best available information. The probation officer's report includes the sociocultural and psychodynamic factors that influenced the juvenile's behavior and provides a social history that the judge can use to determine a disposition for the case. Judges' decisions can be greatly influenced by such reports.

The reports must be factual and objective—professional statements about a child's family, social and educational history, and any previous involvement with private or public agencies. The report also indicates the child's physical and mental health as reported by a court psychologist or psychiatrist.

A report typically includes (1) interviews with the child; (2) interviews with family members; (3) psychological and psychiatric examinations of the child and family members (usually just parents or custodians) and the results of tests and exams; (4) interviews with employers, youth workers and clergy when appropriate; (5) interviews with the complainant; (6) interviews with the police, their reports and any witnesses; (7) interviews with teachers and school officials; (8) a review of police, school and court records and (9) a recommendation of which treatment alternatives should be available in the case.

The National Advisory Committee (NAC) for Juvenile Justice and Delinquency Prevention recommends that probation departments prepare three-part predisposition reports (JPOI Working Group, 1993, p. 42):

1. Information concerning the nature and circumstances of the offense, and the juvenile's role, age and prior contacts.
2. Summary of information concerning:

   - The home environment and family relationships;
   - The juvenile's educational and employment status;
   - The juvenile's interests and activities;
   - The parents' interests; and
   - The results of medical or psychiatric evaluations.

3. Evaluation of the above, a summary of the dispositional alternatives available and the probation officer's recommendation.

The probation officer must present the findings with supporting statements about the situation found in the investigation and a recommendation. The recommendation occasionally is not transcribed, but given orally to the judge. The completed report should be comprehensive enough to help the judge make the best disposition available, based on the merits of the case and the service needs of the youth.

The Child's Rights

Children have specific rights during a hearing. Children are entitled to have a lawyer present at all stages of any proceedings under the UJCA and, if unable to afford private counsel, to have the court provide counsel. The due process requirement of the appointment of counsel for needy children charged with delinquency was established by *Kent v. United States* and *In re Gault*, discussed in Chapter 1.

Children have the same rights as adults, except trial by jury and, in some states, the right to bail. Children have the right to an attorney at all stages of the proceedings, the right to introduce evidence and tell their side of the story, the right to cross-examine witnesses and the right to remain silent during the hearing.

Children are also entitled to introduce evidence and to tell their side of the story, as well as the right to cross-examine adverse witnesses. Children charged with delinquency need not be witnesses against themselves. According to Section 27: "A confession validly made by a child out of court is insufficient to support an adjudication of delinquency unless it is corroborated in whole or in part by other evidence."

Nature of the Hearing

According to Section 24 of the UJCA: "Hearings under this Act shall be conducted by the court without a jury, in an informal but orderly manner, and separate from other proceedings." The prosecuting attorney presents the evidence supporting the petition. The **hearing** may be recorded electronically or minutes may be kept. The child may be excluded from the hearing while the charges are being made.

Traditionally hearings in juvenile court matters have been closed to the public. A Supreme Court ruling, however, has allowed states to open such proceedings on an experimental, pilot basis. According to Walsh (1998, p. B2), seventeen states currently allow open court hearings in child protection cases. Some public defenders argue that the Court's ruling has introduced a major conflict into juvenile court procedure, that open hearings violate federal confidentiality rules and, as a result, place states in jeopardy of losing millions of dollars in federal money for child protection, foster care and adoption services. Trial judges, however, contend they are bound by the Court's decision and are refusing to close juvenile hearings, while others point out that some states, such as Michigan, have had open courts for nearly a decade and haven't lost any federal funding. Nonetheless the practice of open courts in juvenile cases has upset many and raised concerns that the welfare of juvenile court clients is in jeopardy.

Toward a More Adversarial Court

In 1967 the U.S. Supreme Court decided a landmark juvenile justice case. For the first time in the history of the United States, the basic philosophy and practices of the juvenile court were reviewed. The Court concluded (*In re Gault*):

> While there can be no doubt of the original laudable purpose of the juvenile courts, studies and critiques in recent years raise serious questions as to whether actual performance measures well enough against theoretical purpose to make tolerable the immunity of the process from the constitutional guarantees applicable to adults.

A series of Supreme Court decisions has changed the juvenile court's procedures into a more adversarial approach.

A brief review of these landmark cases is provided in Table 9.4. These Supreme Court decisions had a major impact on the adjudication process of the juvenile justice system and the procedural rights afforded to juveniles. Some constitutional requirements have been applied to those parts of the states' juvenile proceedings that are adjudicative. In many cases these changes have reflected a move toward a more adversarial system in the juvenile courts. Another result of these decisions was an overall criminalization of the juvenile court (Feld, 1993). One safeguard, however, against a full adversarial system in juvenile court is the provision of guardian *ad litems* and CASAs.

Disposition

The final stage of the juvenile court process is the sentencing stage, or disposition. At the ***dispositional hearing*** the judge states what will happen to the youth. Springer (p. 50) says: "**Disposition,** called the 'heartbeat of the juvenile

	Case	Year	Holding
Table 9.4 Landmark Juvenile Supreme Court Cases	*In re Gault*	1967	Required that the due process clause of the Fourteenth Amendment apply to proceedings in state juvenile courts including the right of notice, the right to counsel, the right against self-incrimination and the right to confront witnesses.
	In re Winship	1970	Established proof beyond a reasonable doubt as the standard for juvenile adjudication proceedings, eliminating lesser standards such as a preponderance of the evidence, clear and convincing proof and reasonable proof.
	McKeiver v. Pennsylvania	1971	Established that a jury trial is not a required part of due process in the adjudication of a youth as a delinquent by a juvenile court.
	Breed v. Jones	1975	Established that a juvenile cannot be adjudicated in juvenile court and then tried for the same offense in an adult court (double jeopardy).
	Schall v. Martin	1980	Established that preventive detention fulfills a legitimate state interest of protecting society and juveniles by detaining those who might be dangerous to society or to themselves.

court,' is the euphemism used in juvenile court parlance to describe what is to be done for or to a child, once the child's status as poor, naughty, or criminal has been adjudicated by the court." The court has several options. It can:

- Dismiss the case with no charges at all
- Refer the youth to a social service agency
- Order that the youth make restitution
- Put the youth on probation
- Sentence the youth to a correctional facility
- In some states order the death penalty

For more than two decades, the Juvenile Justice and Delinquency Prevention (JJDP) Act of 1974 has guided juvenile courts in the disposition of youthful offenders. During this time the JJDP Act's central mandate has been the deinstitutionalization of status offenders (DSO). However, as Holden and Kapler (1995, p. 3) note: "Citizens and lawmakers are calling for more punitive measures against juvenile offenders, especially those who commit serious or violent felonies." According to Raley (1995, p. 15): "During the 1980s, the Federal focus shifted from delinquency prevention to criminal justice, emphasizing:

- Prosecution of serious juvenile offenders
- The plight of missing children
- Mandatory and tougher sentencing laws
- Programs to prevent school violence"

Raley continues (p. 15): "The 1992 amendments to the JJDP Act . . . added constructive initiatives addressing juvenile gangs, youth development, mentoring, and prevention." Yet, despite 20 years of amendments, Raley notes "the JJDP Act endures" (p. 16).

The trend in juvenile dispositions remains the deinstitutionalization of youths.

If the court finds from clear, convincing evidence that a child is deprived or in need of treatment or rehabilitation, the court decides on the proper disposition of the case. *Deprived children* may be permitted to remain with their parents or guardians subject to specific conditions and limitations. Temporary legal custody may be given to any individual the court finds qualified to receive and care for the child. Children may be placed in an agency or other private organization licensed or authorized to receive and provide care for children, such as the Child Welfare Department.

If a court finds on proof beyond a reasonable doubt that the child is delinquent or unruly, it proceeds immediately or at a postponed hearing to hear evidence as to whether the child is in need of treatment or rehabilitation. A child found to be *delinquent* may be placed on probation or placed in an institution, camp or other facility for delinquent children. A child found to be *unruly* may receive any disposition authorized for a delinquent child except commitment to the state institution to which commitment of delinquent children is made. The order of disposition committing a delinquent or unruly child to an institution is in effect for two years or until the child is discharged.

A delinquent or unruly child thought to be suffering from *mental retardation* or *mental illness* may be committed for a period not exceeding 60 days to an appropriate institution, agency or individual for study. If the child is determined to be committable under state laws, the court may order the child detained. If the child is not committable, the court proceeds with the disposition of the child as appropriate.

If a child is or is about to become a *nonresident* of the state, the court may defer hearing on the need for treatment or rehabilitation and ask that the juvenile court of the child's new or prospective residence accept jurisdiction over the child. Likewise the *resident child received from another state* should be accepted by the child's new or prospective residence. These provisions facilitate cooperative action between the courts of the two states involved.

It is important to recognize that an order of disposition or other adjudication in a juvenile court is *not* a conviction of a crime. Section 33 of the UJCA states that: "A child shall not be committed or transferred to a penal institution or other facility used primarily for the execution of sentences of persons convicted of a crime." The Comment regarding this section states:

> Although several states permit commitment or transfer of a delinquent child to a penal institution, its constitutionality is in serious doubt since it permits confinement in a penal institution as a product of a non-criminal proceeding. Such legislation has been held invalid in a number of states. See *In re Rich,* 125 Vt. 373, 216 A.2d 266 (1966).

Restitution

An increasingly popular disposition of the juvenile court is **restitution,** that is, personally righting a wrong, or restoring property or a right to a person unjustly deprived of the property or right. As victims' rights movements gain momentum, more attention is being paid to this group. One way this is happening is through restitution programs.

Closely related to restitution is the victim-offender mediation program, modeled after the Victim Offender Reconciliation Program (VORP) that originated in Canada in the mid-1970s. As noted by Hughes and Schneider (1990, p. 1), the purposes of the original VORP project were:

- To provide an alternative method of dealing with crime
- To allow victim and offender an opportunity to reconcile and mutually agree on restitution
- To use a third party to mediate and facilitate reconciliation
- To deal with crime as a conflict to be resolved

Crowley (1998, p. 10) identifies the "three faces of restitution" seen in victim-offender mediation:

- Monetary restitution—a specific dollar amount is agreed to that the offender will pay to the victim through scheduled payments.
- Community service—commonly arranged through a probation agency, whereby a juvenile performs unpaid labor for the community or a specific neighborhood or institution. A hoped-for by-product of community service is that the juvenile develops useful life skills and learns responsibility.
- Direct service agreements—holding juveniles accountable by having them work directly with and for their victim(s). For example a 13-year-old boy who admitted to burglarizing the vehicles of elderly mobile home residents was made to mow their lawns, rake their leaves and sweep their driveways.

Hughes and Schneider (p. 9) report on a nationwide survey of 240 organizations involved in juvenile justice and known to be using mediation. Their response rate was greater than 70 percent. One noteworthy result was that, although the perceived effectiveness of dispositional alternatives varied, all respondents rated restitution as the most effective way to reduce recidivism, rehabilitate offenders, increase victim satisfaction, hold offenders accountable and be fair to both offenders and victims. Mediation was rated second most effective in most instances. However incarceration was seen as equally effective, if not slightly more so, than mediation in increasing victim satisfaction. (See Figure 9.2.)

Support for mediation programs was highest among juvenile court judges, followed by family members and alternative juvenile program providers. Least supportive were state legislators, although they, too, were on the positive side, as shown in Figure 9.3.

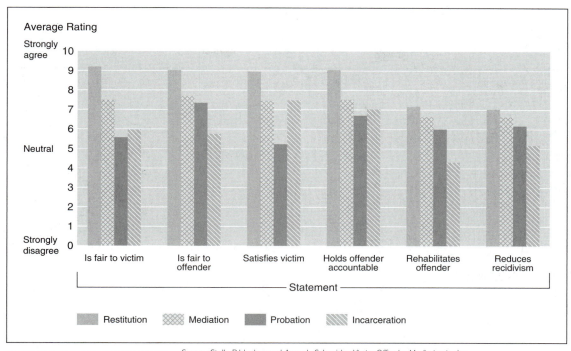

Figure 9.2
Perceived Effectiveness of Dispositional Alternatives

Source: Stella P. Hughes and Anne L. Schneider. *Victim-Offender Mediation in the Juvenile Justice System.* Restitution Education, Specialized Training & Technical Assistance Program (RESTTA). September 1990, p. 9.

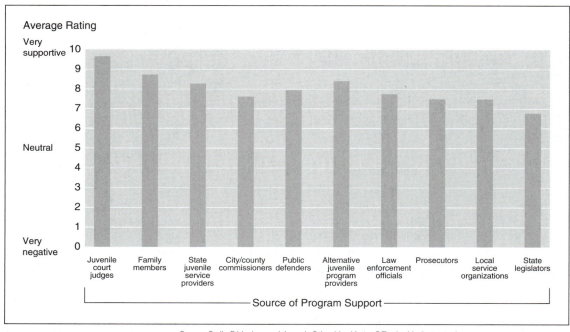

Figure 9.3
Amount of Support from Various Sources

Source: Stella P. Hughes and Anne L. Schneider. *Victim-Offender Mediation in the Juvenile Justice System.* Restitution Education, Specialized Training & Technical Assistance Program (RESTTA). September 1990, p. 7.

Table 9.5
Method of Execution,
by State, 1996

Lethal Injection		Electrocution	Lethal Gas	Hanging	Firing Squad
Arizona[a,b]	New Hampshire[a]	Alabama	Arizona[a,b]	Delaware[a,c]	Idaho[a]
Arkansas[a,d]	New Jersey	Arkansas[a,d]	California[a]	Montana[a]	Oklahoma[a,e]
California[a]	New Mexico	Florida	Maryland[f]	New Hampshire[a,g]	Utah[a]
Colorado	New York	Georgia	Mississippi[a,h]	Washington[a]	
Connecticut	North Carolina[a]	Kentucky	Missouri[a]		
Delaware[a,c]	Ohio[a]	Nebraska	North Carolina[a]		
Idaho[a]	Oklahoma[a]	Ohio[a]	Wyoming[a,i]		
Illinois	Oregon	Oklahoma[a,e]			
Indiana	Pennsylvania	South Carolina[a]			
Kansas	South Carolina[a]	Tennessee			
Louisiana	South Dakota	Virginia[a]			
Maryland[f]	Texas				
Mississippi[a,h]	Utah[a]				
Missouri[a]	Virginia[a]				
Montana[a]	Washington[a]				
Nevada	Wyoming[a]				

Note: The method of execution of Federal prisoners is lethal injection, pursuant to 28 CFR, part 26. For offenses under the Violent Crime Control and Law Enforcement Act of 1994, the method is that of the State in which the conviction took place, pursuant to 18 USC 3569.

[a] Authorizes two methods of execution.

[b] Arizona authorizes lethal injection for persons sentenced after 11/15/92; those sentenced before that date may select lethal injection or lethal gas.

[c] Delaware authorizes lethal injection for those whose capital offense occurred after 6/13/86; those who committed the offense before that date may select lethal injection or hanging.

[d] Arkansas authorizes lethal injection for persons committing a capital offense on or after 7/4/83; those who committed the offense before that date may select lethal injection or electrocution.

[e] Oklahoma authorizes electrocution if lethal injection is ever held to be unconstitutional and firing squad if both lethal injection and electrocution are held unconstitutional.

[f] Maryland authorizes lethal injection for all inmates, as of 3/25/94. One inmate, convicted prior to that date, has selected lethal gas for method of execution.

[g] New Hampshire authorizes hanging only if lethal injection cannot be given.

[h] Mississippi authorizes lethal injection for those convicted after 7/1/84 and lethal gas for those convicted earlier.

[i] Wyoming authorizes lethal gas if lethal injection is ever held to be unconstitutional.

Source: Tracy L. Snell. *Capital Punishment 1996*. Washington, DC: Bureau of Justice Statistics Bulletin. December 1997, p. 5. (NCJ-167031)

Feinman (1990, p. 3) stresses that any restitution program that places youths in paid or unpaid positions also assumes responsibility for their safety and their behavior. Restitution programs must consider:

- Injuries sustained by the juvenile in a court-ordered placement
- Injuries or harm done by the juvenile at the worksite
- Loss or damages caused by the youth as the result of a crime committed at the workplace

Capital Punishment

The United States is one of only three countries in the world that allows people who committed crimes while they were children to be executed. This practice has been disapproved by the United Nations Convention on the Rights of the

Child. On June 26, 1989, the Supreme Court ruled that the death penalty for 16- and 17-year-olds is not necessarily "cruel and unusual punishment" and that juveniles may be executed. The decision of whether to apply the death penalty to juveniles is now in the hands of the individual states (*Stanford v. Kentucky* and *Wilkins v. Missouri*).

According to Snell (1997, p. 9), at year-end 1996, 64 of the 2,849 prisoners on death row (2.2 percent) had been 17 or younger at the time of their arrest. Streib (1998) notes that from January 1, 1973 through December 31, 1997, a total of nine men were executed in the United States for crimes they committed as juveniles. Every offender was age 17 at the time of the offense, five were white, three were black and one was Latino, and their ages at execution ranged from 24 to 33.

Snell (p. 5) reports that at the end of 1996, 14 states and the federal system authorized age 18 as the minimum age for capital punishment, and 18 states authorized a minimum age for capital punishment *less* than 18 (Table 9.5).

To better understand the dispositions handed to juveniles, consider the nature of juvenile sentencing laws.

Juvenile Sentencing Laws

The state of Washington passed a Juvenile Justice Act in 1977, creating a mandatory sentencing policy that required juveniles ages 8 to 17 adjudicated delinquent to be confined in an institution for a minimum term. As noted in the act:

> It is the intent of the legislature that a system be developed capable of having primary responsibility for being accountable for and responding to the needs of youthful offenders. It is the further intent of the legislature that youth, in turn, be held accountable for their offenses and that both communities and juvenile courts carry out their function consistent with this intent. (Section 13.40.010[2] Supp.1978)

To accomplish its goal, the act includes a formal scoring sheet to determine how long an adjudicated youth must spend in confinement.

The mandatory sentencing policy in Washington is based on the juvenile's age, the current offense and the criminal history of the offender.

Similar in concept to adult sentencing guideline grids, the score under the Washington system is computed by plotting the type of offense along the vertical axis of a table and the juvenile's age along the horizontal axis. A numeric score is reached, which is then multiplied by a weighting factor based on the youth's prior criminal record. This final number is then plotted on another grid to determine the sentence. Systems such as these help to guide judges in their sentencing and tend to make sentencing more equitable from one case to the next.

As with adult criminal sentencing, juvenile sentencing has had its share of criticism, reform attempts and alternative remedies. Mears (1998, p. 446) notes that during the 1960s, "sentencing philosophy toward juveniles shifted from rehabilitation to retribution and from offender- to offense-based sanctioning." Regarding the trend to toughen up juvenile sentencing, Mears (p. 443) states: "In recent years, sentencing reforms in state and federal systems have been driven largely by a desire to 'get tough on crime' as well as to reduce the inconsistency and disparities that can result from judicial discretion. However, research on these reforms has revealed many intended consequences that result from conflicting goals, organizational context, and prosecutorial discretion and that threaten to offset any putative gains made through these reforms."

Some states have attempted legislation making parents responsible for the delinquency of their children. According to Dundes (1994, p. 113): "A 1988 amendment to California's Penal Code Section 272 criminalizes any act or omission of a parent which 'causes or tends to cause or encourage' juvenile delinquency." Dundes notes that California's legislators resorted to such a parental responsibility law in a desperate effort to prevent gang crime. However while such "punish-the-parent" legislation is not new, it has not proved to be very effective and seems to stem "from a recurring distrust of those who are both poor and different" (p. 127). Furthermore, such laws tend to burden police officers with difficult, subjective decision making regarding what constitutes "adequate parenting" (p. 114).

Whatever the sentence and however the court arrives there, it should be individualized. Mechanical jurisprudence should be avoided in the juvenile justice system.

Mechanical Jurisprudence

Legal philosopher H. L. A. Hart (1965, p. 125) expresses an underlying assumption in any government of laws:

> It is a feature of human predicament . . . whenever we seek to regulate, unambiguously and in advance, some sphere of conduct by means of general standards to be used without further official direction on particular occasions. . . . If the world in which we live were characterized only by the finite number of features, and these together with all the modes in which they could be made in advance for every possibility, we could make rules, the applications of which to particular cases never called for a further choice. Everything could be known, and for everything since it could be known, something could be done and specified in advance by rule. This could be a world for "mechanical jurisprudence."

Mechanical jurisprudence suggests that everything is known and that, therefore, laws can be made in advance to cover every situation. Unfortunately the concept of mechanical jurisprudence is often applied to juvenile conduct and behavior, as illustrated in the following example from a report entitled "Karen's Kids" (1987) on the CBS television program *60 Minutes*.

The program reported a case of a mother found by the court to be mentally unstable, who had her five children removed from home by a court order. The woman was hospitalized for mental illness and her children placed in a foster home until she recovered. The arrangement with the foster parents was to be short term, but it lasted for two years. During that time the foster parents petitioned the court to adopt the children. The hospitalized mother was asked to forfeit her parental rights so the adoption could proceed. The mother refused and wanted the children removed from the foster home. The social service agency proceeded to do so. The foster parents obtained a restraining order to ensure that the children would stay together. The children provided a deposition that they were very happy with the foster parents and that they did not want to return to their natural mother because she and her male friends physically abused them. The mother confirmed abusing the children, but denied knowing if any male friends had done so.

The two older girls, ages 11 and 13, were vehemently opposed to being removed from the foster parents and attempted suicide and running away. Despite this the state social service agency's director ordered the children removed. The order was executed by uniformed sheriff's deputies, who removed the children despite pleas to the state agency by friends and neighbors. They also submitted pleas and requests to various bureaucrats and politicians with no success. The children were placed in five separate foster homes, the mother lost parental rights and the foster parents were discharged from the foster parent program. The two girls continued to run away from their new foster parents and attempted suicide twice. It would appear in this instance that the court's inflexibility was *not* in the best interest of the children involved.

Mechanical jurisprudence is inappropriate in our justice system because everything cannot be known about any offense. Further since delinquency includes a wide variety of different behaviors, there is no single common problem of delinquency but, instead, a series of separable problems each with its unique psychodynamic and social orientation.

Youths Who Come before the Court

By this point you are well aware of the three types of children and youths served in the one-pot juvenile justice system.

Those Who Are Neglected or Abused

Participants at a conference of the National Committee for Prevention of Child Abuse discussed two kinds of intervention for deprived children: coercive and therapeutic.

Coercive intervention is out-of-home placement, detainment or mandated therapy or counseling. Therapeutic intervention is a recommendation of an appropriate treatment program.

Participants were in agreement that coercive intervention should be used with children only when necessary, either to protect society or to impose an effective treatment plan for the children. Several policy recommendations came out of the conference, including the following:

- *Therapeutic intervention for all abused children who come to the attention of the court exhibiting problem behavior, regardless of the disposition of the case.* The present drift toward stricter delinquency statutes in some States, in which community protection is foremost and the best interest of the child standard is secondary, is based on an erroneous assumption. Protection of the community and rehabilitation of the child are not conflicting goals. . . . Among this group of abused children, there are two subgroups in particular in need of attention: the child exhibiting violent behavior and the sexually abused child.

- *Specific and different treatment within the correctional system of the young person who was abused.* . . . Much of our Nation's delinquent population is in a debilitated condition—physically (neurologically), developmentally, and psychologically. . . . We know, for instance, that treatment for the abused child will have to take place over a long term. We know that corporal punishment, physical coercion, and violent or belittling language are inappropriate therapeutic tools; they add institutional abuse to the existing familial abuse.
- *Early intervention.* The optimal point of intervention with an abused delinquent would be before the abuse occurred. The earliest treatment intervention we can offer the young abused child would be aimed at keeping him from becoming a delinquent as a later reaction to the earlier abuse. The next opportunity for early intervention occurs when the young person comes to the attention of the court, before he becomes delinquent. Youth who enter the court as Minors ("Persons" or "Children" in different States) in Need of Supervision could be recognized as the abused children they often are and helped in such a way as to preclude further delinquent activity.
- *Attractive, benign, broad-based intervention styles and services.* Services are needed that do not identify the clients as abusive, abused, or delinquent. Efforts to strengthen families, particularly the development and provision of services that could be called parent education, are recommended.

Status Offenders

Children and their families who are brought before the court for status offenses occupy a great share of the court's workload. Status offenders can try the patience of the court because such children often are considered to simply be "in need of supervision," resulting in a group of acronyms: CHINS (children in need of supervision), FINS (families in need of supervision), JINS (juveniles in need of supervision) and PINS (persons in need of supervision).

The juvenile courts in some states have dispensed justice that is harsher for status offenders than for criminal law violators because status offenses are annoyances. There has always been a need to distinguish status offenses from delinquent acts. Often status offenses fall into a separate classification for the court to consider in its dispensing of justice. Recall that according to the American Bar Association, juvenile delinquency liability should include only such conduct as would be designated a crime if committed by an adult.

The referral of status offenses to juvenile court has been viewed by many as an ineffective waste of valuable court resources. Critics believe that resources would best be used for the more serious recidivist delinquents the court has to deal with. Whether the court is dealing with status offenders or youths who have committed violent crimes or protecting abused or neglected children, it no longer has free reign. The juvenile court must grant many aspects of due process to the youths who come under its jurisdiction.

In 1995 U.S. juvenile courts formally disposed an estimated 146,400 status offense cases (Sickmund et al., p. 33). Forty-three percent of the petitioned sta-

Table 9.6
Petitioned Status Offense Case Rates, by Age at Referral and Offense, 1995

Case Rate = Cases per 1,000 youth in age group.

	Data Table			
Age	Runaway	Truancy	Ungovernable	Liquor
10	0.0	0.1	0.0	0.0
11	0.1	0.2	0.1	0.0
12	0.2	0.6	0.3	0.1
13	0.6	1.3	0.7	0.2
14	1.4	2.3	1.1	0.7
15	1.8	2.8	1.2	1.5
16	1.8	1.6	1.1	3.6
17	1.2	1.5	0.7	6.6

Source: Melissa Sickmund; Anne L. Stahl; Terrence A. Finnegan; Howard Snyder; Rowen S. Poole; and Jeffrey A. Butts. *Juvenile Court Statistics 1995.* Washington, DC: Office of Juvenile Justice and Delinquency Prevention, U.S. Department of Justice, May 1998, p. 39. Reprinted by permission of the National Center for Juvenile Justice. (NCJ-170607)

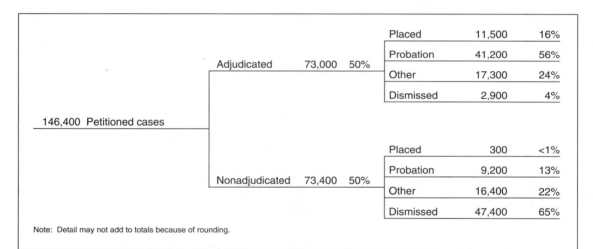

Note: Detail may not add to totals because of rounding.

Figure 9.4
Juvenile Court Processing of Petitioned Status Offense Cases, 1995

Source: Melissa Sickmund; Anne L. Stahl; Terrence A. Finnegan; Howard Snyder; Rowen S. Poole; and Jeffrey A. Butts. *Juvenile Court Statistics 1995.* Washington, DC: Office of Juvenile Justice and Delinquency Prevention, U.S. Department of Justice, May 1998, p. 35. Reprinted by permission of the National Center for Juvenile Justice. (NCJ-170607)

tus offense cases were referred to juvenile court by law enforcement agencies (p. 34). Truancy and liquor law violations each accounted for slightly more than a quarter (26 percent) of these cases. Table 9.6 summarizes the status offenses by age at referral. As might be expected, the truancy rate drops as juveniles become older, but the liquor violations rise. Figure 9.4 shows the processing of petitioned status offense cases in 1995.

Table 9.7
Delinquency Cases, by Most Serious Offense, 1995

Most Serious Offense	Number of Cases	Percent Change		
		1986–95	1991–95	1994–95
Total	**1,714,300**	**45%**	**21%**	**7%**
Person Offense	**377,300**	**98**	**36**	**8**
Criminal homicide	2,800	84	20	−6
Forcible rape	6,800	47	19	4
Robbery	39,600	53	27	6
Aggravated assault	93,200	137	33	6
Simple assault	205,500	103	47	12
Other violent sex offense	9,300	50	9	−3
Other person offense	20,100	72	−2	−4
Property Offense	**871,700**	**23**	**3**	**3**
Burglary	139,900	−2	−9	−2
Larceny-theft	418,800	28	10	10
Motor vehicle theft	53,400	23	−26	−13
Arson	10,400	78	42	10
Vandalism	121,700	40	9	−2
Trespassing	64,400	18	9	1
Stolen property offense	33,100	10	9	2
Other property offense	29,900	46	−5	6
Drug Law Violation	**159,100**	**120**	**145**	**28**
Public Order Offense	**306,300**	**48**	**37**	**6**
Obstruction of justice	110,100	53	45	8
Disorderly conduct	85,100	82	46	9
Weapons offense	47,000	132	38	−9
Liquor law violation	12,200	−39	−1	2
Nonviolent sex offense	10,500	−21	−8	−4
Other public order	41,300	19	31	17
Violent Crime Index*	**142,400**	**99**	**30**	**5**
*Property Crime Index***	622,500	20	1	5

*Violent Crime Index includes criminal homicide, forcible rape, robbery, and aggravated assault.

**Property Crime Index includes burglary, larceny-theft, motor vehicle theft, and arson.

Note: Detail may not add to totals because of rounding. Percent change calculations are based on unrounded numbers.

Source: Melissa Sickmund; Anne L. Stahl; Terrence A. Finnegan; Howard Snyder; Rowen S. Poole; and Jeffery A. Butts. *Juvenile Court Statistics 1995.* Washington, DC: Office of Juvenile Justice and Delinquency Prevention, U.S. Department of Justice, May 1998, p. 5. Reprinted by permission of the National Center for Juvenile Justice. (NCJ-170607)

Over half of the nonadjudicated cases were dismissed, fewer than 1 percent were placed, and 13 percent received probation. In contrast, of those that were adjudicated, only 4 percent were dismissed, 16 percent were placed, and more than half were put on probation.

Delinquent Offenders   In 1995 juvenile courts handled 1,714,300 delinquency cases, a 7 percent increase over the 1994 caseload and a 45 percent increase from 1986 (Sickmund

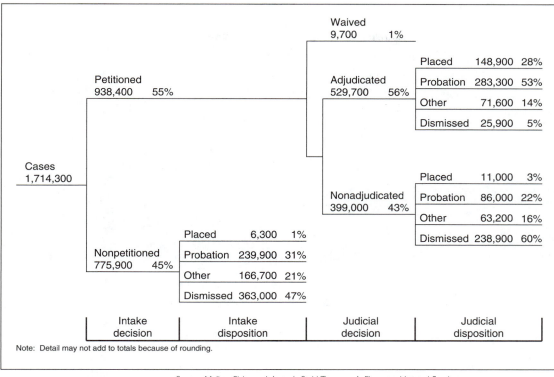

Source: Melissa Sickmund; Anne L. Stahl; Terrence A. Finnegan; Howard Snyder; Rowen S. Poole; and Jeffrey A. Butts. *Juvenile Court Statistics 1995*. Washington, DC: Office of Juvenile Justice and Delinquency Prevention, U.S. Department of Justice, May 1998, p. 9. Reprinted by permission of the National Center for Juvenile Justice. (NCJ-170607)

Figure 9.5
Juvenile Court Processing of Delinquency Cases, 1995

et al., p. 5). Eighty-six percent of the delinquency referrals were made by law enforcement (p. 7). In 22 percent of the cases, the most serious charge was a person offense, 51 percent were property offenses, 18 percent public order offenses and 9 percent drug offenses. The juvenile courts waived 1 percent of all petitioned delinquency cases to criminal court (p. 13). Table 9.7 shows the number of delinquency cases handled by juvenile courts in 1995, by most serious offense. The processing of these delinquency cases is summarized in Figure 9.5. Compared to the processing of status offense cases, the percentage adjudicated and nonadjudicated are strikingly similar, as were the other judicial dispositions, especially the nonadjudicated cases.

Property cases were a major part of the juvenile court load, with larceny-theft the most common offense. Figure 9.6 shows the 1995 delinquency case rates of male and female offenders by age at referral.

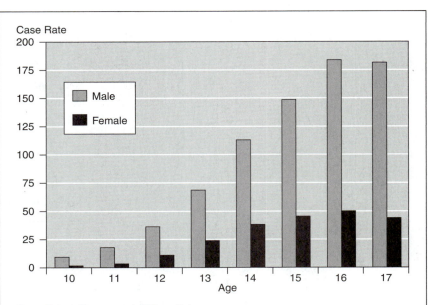

Case Rate = Cases per 1,000 youth in age group.

Data Table		
Age	Male	Female
10	9.7	1.9
11	18.3	4.4
12	36.7	11.8
13	69.7	24.7
14	113.2	39.0
15	149.0	46.3
16	183.6	50.7
17	181.7	44.3

Figure 9.6
Delinquency Case Rates,
by Sex and Age
at Referral, 1995

Source: Melissa Sickmund; Anne L. Stahl; Terrence A. Finnegan; Howard Snyder; Rowen S. Poole; and Jeffrey A. Butts. *Juvenile Court Statistics 1995.* Washington, DC: Office of Juvenile Justice and Delinquency Prevention, U.S. Department of Justice, May 1998, p. 23. Reprinted by permission of the National Center for Juvenile Justice. (NCJ-170607)

Issues Facing the Juvenile Court—Dilemmas and Criticisms

In the United States, legislators have tremendous interest in the handling of juveniles and the rights guaranteed them by their birth. The "child savers" are still present, and those who wish to get tough with juveniles are continually lobbying for severe measures in all phases of the juvenile process. The U.S. Supreme Court is prepared to protect children and their parents against the custom of informality within the system.

The juvenile court's current dilemma hinges on its dual roles as a court of law and as a social service agency.

The juvenile court must gain strength in its judicial role and retain and develop only that part of its social service role necessary to administer individualized justice. As a court, even in the administration of individualized justice, it must express and reinforce the values of society.

The facts of adjudication and disposition cannot be examined as if they are separate from each other. The juvenile court must be seen as a court—not as an administrative agency—designed in its adjudication to protect children from the traumatic experiences of a criminal trial and to balance the interests of the child and the community. It is not especially equipped to do welfare work. Whenever possible it should be divested of jurisdiction and adjudication over cases in which the child is simply in need of aid. It should be governed by simple, specific rules, so that while children are receiving guidance and protection, their rights and the security of the community are not neglected.

After they had been operating for half a century, criticism of the nation's juvenile courts began surfacing during the 1950s. In 1949 the lawyer-sociologist Paul Tappan published a volume on juvenile delinquency that drew together and raised for the first time a number of problems inherent in the work of the court:

- The persistence in some courts of punitive practices, in contrast to rehabilitative theory
- The abandonment of all semblance of regularized legal procedures or due process
- The jurisdictional accretions by the court in the context of a preventive rationale

The Fundamental Nature of Juvenile Court

The juvenile court has been criticized for its fundamental system. What most critics or people unfamiliar with the jurisdiction of the court fail to understand is that the scope of the court is varied and that criminal law, or law that refers to antisocial conduct, is only one part of the court's responsibility.

All courts within the juvenile justice jurisdiction exercise the principles of civil procedures, which emphasize notice and opportunity to defend. They also emphasize due process factors that protect juveniles who come under their authority, making dispositions for the child's best interest.

In effect the juvenile court is less a law enforcement agency and more a social agency, handling truants, orphans, runaways and other misguided youths. It is, however, also responsible for youthful gang members, robbers, rapists and murderers. The court is seen as being inadequate to satisfy the community's need to express its disapproval of antisocial conduct.

Attacks on the juvenile court's jurisdiction and procedures have been continually repelled, however. While shortcomings have been acknowledged, they have been characterized as the usual shortcomings one might expect in any novel and untried enterprise, which faith, time and money surely would cure. For a century, therefore, the juvenile courts have been permitted to develop and mature, nurtured by judicial support and large doses of faith, if not money.

Criminalization of Juvenile Court

Both the IACP and the National Council of Juvenile Court Judges have expressed concern that the juvenile courts are becoming too formalized and are beginning to resemble the adult courts. This concern was expressed by Chief Justice Warren Burger in his dissenting opinion in *In re Winship* (1970):

> My hope is that today's decision will not spell the end of a generously conceived program of compassionate treatment intended to mitigate the rigors and trauma of exposing youthful offenders to a traditional criminal court; each step we take turns the clock back to the pre-juvenile court era. I cannot regard it as a manifestation of progress to transform juvenile courts into criminal courts, which is what we are well on the way toward accomplishing.

Quality of Representation

A report by the American Bar Association's (ABA) Juvenile Justice Center suggests that juveniles are not receiving adequate legal representation in delinquency proceedings and that juvenile courts are not meeting the requirements established in *In re Gault* ("Juveniles' Legal," 1996, p. 13). The ABA's assessment report identified high caseloads as the "single most important barrier to effective representation," with the average annual caseloads of some public defenders exceeding 500 cases, more than 300 of which were in juvenile court. Other barriers to adequate legal representation were found to be high turnover rates in juvenile defender positions, a lack of professional support, the unavailability of computerized legal research, lack of bilingual staff and a shortage of client meeting space (p. 13). Puritz and Wan Long Shang (1998, p. 2) note:

> The impact of inadequate representation on youth—and their lawyers—is devastating. Children represented by overworked attorneys frequently do not understand what is happening in court and come away with the impression that their attorneys do not care about them. Similarly, burnout, job dissatisfaction, and anxiety over never having enough time to do a complete job are serious problems for many caring juvenile defense attorneys.

They further suggest:

> While substantial deficiencies in access to counsel and the quality of representation exist in juvenile court, it would be incorrect to conclude that effective representation of young people cannot and does not exist. High-quality defender-based programs that deliver first-rate legal services to juveniles usually have one or more of the following characteristics:

- Ability to limit or control caseloads
- Support for entering cases early and the flexibility to represent, or refer, clients in related collateral matters such as special education
- Comprehensive initial and ongoing training and available resource materials
- Adequate nonlawyer support and resources
- Hands-on supervision of attorneys
- Work environments that value and nurture juvenile court practice

Racism and Discrimination

Many have criticized the juvenile justice system for perpetuating the unequal treatment of minority youths. Hatchett (p. 85) asserts: "The criminal and juvenile justice systems are not immune from the 'isms' that plague most institutions of America. Systematic racism, classism, and discrimination in the adjudication of juvenile cases have led to the overrepresentation of minority youths in the juvenile and criminal justice systems. Black youth only make up 15% of all young people in this nation, but they occupy 65% of all bed space in detention facilities. . . . Native American youth make up 60% of the children prosecuted in the adult federal system."

Others agree that racism is a problem but that it's not always against ethnic and racial minorities. According to Secret and Johnson (1997, p. 445): "Research suggests that America's juvenile justice systems have not escaped the negative effects of racism . . . black youth are usually more likely to receive harsher treatment than whites in regard to prehearing detention and final penalty. With regard to judging an accused youth to be delinquent or a status offender, the analysis reveals a reversal of this relationship between race and harshness of outcomes: Whites are more likely to be found delinquent." In other words, blacks receive harsher treatment at intake and disposition, while whites endure harsher treatment during adjudication.

Other factors contributing to racial discrimination at the various stages of the juvenile justice process, such as court location and family status, have been documented by DeJong and Jackson (1998, p. 489):

> Juveniles living in urban counties are more likely to be referred to juvenile court, and . . . juveniles living in a single-mother household are more likely than juveniles living with both parents to be referred to court and to receive secure placement. Race-specific models indicate that black youths are likely to receive harsh treatments in urban courts; yet white youths are not treated differently on the basis of court location. In addition, living in a single-mother household is a disadvantage for white youths when they are referred and sentenced, but family status is not a determinant for black youth.

Gang Membership—"Master Status"

It has been theorized that certain types of offenders receive biased treatment by the justice system because of their social affiliations or "master status." Gang members have been identified as one such group. Miethe and McCorkle (1997, p. 420) contend: "Gang membership [has] a significant net effect on both charging and sentencing decisions." More specifically (p. 425):

> There is a gap between actual practices and the formal organizational structure and policies. In the present context, the "get tough" political rhetoric on gangs is thwarted by the legal obstacles involved in gang prosecution.
>
> Second, the formal labeling of a suspect as a gang member has mixed consequences. This designation may stimulate greater social control efforts by police (e.g., unfounded arrests, harassment) against known gang members or other individuals whose social profile fits this label. Alternatively, however, . . . this label may impede successful prosecution because the stereotypical imagery surrounding these offenders (e.g., dangerous, revenge-seeking, impulsive youth) may further amplify victims' and witnesses' fears of retaliation. Thus, . . . our results suggest that gang membership may remain one of the few master statuses that benefits offenders in charging and sentencing decisions.

Court Files and Records

Juvenile records are open to inspection only by the judge, officers and professional staff of the court; the parties to the proceedings and their counsel and representatives; a public or private agency or institution providing supervision or having custody of the child under court order; a court and its probation and other officials or professional staff and the attorney for the defendant.

Section 55 of the UJCA states that: "Law enforcement records and files concerning a child shall be kept separate from the records and files of adults. Unless a charge of delinquency is transferred for criminal prosecution, the interest of national security requires, or the court otherwise orders in the interest of the child, the records and files shall not be open to public inspection or their contents disclosed to the public." Juvenile records may be sealed if:

1. [Two] years have elapsed since the final discharge of the person.
2. Since the final discharge the person has not been convicted of a felony, or of a misdemeanor involving moral turpitude, or adjudicated a delinquent or unruly child and no proceeding is pending seeking conviction or adjudication.
3. The person has been rehabilitated. This is to protect a "rehabilitated youth from the harmful effects of a continuing record of the adjudication of delinquency."

In October 1997 the Senate Judiciary Committee approved S. 10, essentially a juvenile justice overhaul bill. Among the items covered in the bill was legislation to merge juvenile offense records into the adult criminal records system, "ending a system in which juvenile arrest records have been kept secret, even from courts and other criminal justice agencies" ("SEARCH Says," 1998, p. 4). According to this bill, juvenile records would have to be retained for the same length of time as adult records and would have to be made available to schools, law enforcement and the courts. Robert Belair, general counsel to SEARCH, notes that 44 states have already amended their laws to extend adult criminal court jurisdiction and adult system recordkeeping to juveniles at a younger age and for a greater range and number of offenses. He states: "The era of two-track justice where a juvenile could have an active, serious, and violent criminal career and then begin again at age 18 or 19 as an adult first offender is largely over."

A national conference cosponsored by the Bureau of Justice Statistics and SEARCH addressed the topic of merging juvenile and adult records (*Juvenile and Adult Records,* 1990) and revealed a wide range of opinions. Representative statements from these various viewpoints follow.

In Favor of One Record

Marvin E. Wolfgang, Sellin Center for Studies in Criminology and Criminal Law: "The dual system of juvenile and criminal justice that prevents the sharing of information and permits a serious, chronic violent juvenile to become a virgin offender after his 19th birthday is a strange cultural invention. . . . However, . . . highly selective sharing of a juvenile record should be used only to inform" (p. 18).

Reggie B. Walton, Deputy Presiding Judge of the DC Superior Court: "Judicial officers, strapped with the difficult responsibility of deciding whether an offender should be released or detained, must be put in the position to make the most informed decision possible" (p. 44).

Ken Moses, Inspector, Crime Scene Investigation Unit, San Francisco P.D.: "Some jurisdictions keep juvenile prints out of the AFIS database, which, in my mind, is a major catastrophe. Any exclusion of criminal fingerprints from such a file is counterproductive, not only to society but also to the interests of juvenile justice" (p. 51).

Ronald D. Castille, Philadelphia D.A.: "We ought to have liberal access to all records to make informed decisions about the disposition of both juvenile and adult cases" (p. 58).

Opposing One Record

Mark H. Moore, Professor of Criminal Justice at Harvard University: "The proposal for 'one record, one system' would make a hash of either one or the other systems, and perhaps both of them, because they are founded on different philosophies" (p. 47).

Romae T. Powell, Georgia Juvenile Court Judge: "The juvenile justice system's goal is to use their records to rehabilitate, treat, supervise, protect and change children. . . . One record, one system, then, in my opinion, will destroy this mandate . . ." (p. 38).

Howard N. Snyder, Director of Systems Research, National Center for Juvenile Justice, cautions: "The considerations in merging juvenile and adult legal records are both technical and philosophical. The technical problems are easily addressed; the philosophical ones require us to take a careful look at why this nation has established a separate juvenile justice system" (p. 54).

Proposed Changes

The saying "desperate times call for desperate measures" has recently been applied to the juvenile court, with some suggesting that the country do away with these distressed forums altogether. According to Butterfield (1997, p. A1): "The nation's juvenile courts, long a troubled backwater of the criminal justice system, have been so overwhelmed by the increase in violent teen-age crime and the breakdown of the family that judges and politicians are debating a solution that was once unthinkable: abolishing the system and trying most minors as adults." Butterfield also notes (pp. A1, A13):

> In interviews around the country, judges, probation officers, prosecutors and defense lawyers described a juvenile court system in perhaps the worst chaos of its history.
>
> In Chicago, where the first juvenile court was created in 1899, judges today preside over assembly-line justice, hearing an average of 60 cases a day, about six minutes per case. In New Orleans, public defenders have to represent their poor clients with no office, no telephone, no court records and little chance to discuss the case before trial. . . .
>
> Almost everywhere, with juvenile courts starved for money, record-keeping is so primitive that often the judge, the prosecutor and the defense attorney have different records on the same defendant, making an accurate assessment of the case impossible.

While the juvenile court has withstood much criticism from those who claim it is damaged beyond repair, many believe it can still work, and some constructive proposals for improvement have been put forth. Krisberg and Austin (1993, p. 184) suggest two changes that might improve our juvenile courts:

Closed hearings have not been particularly successful in shielding youngsters from adverse publicity in high profile cases. Moreover, the seemingly hidden juvenile court operations have contributed to the public perception that the court is overly lenient. When open hearings have been tried there have been few negative consequences.

A corollary issue involves the quality of juvenile court judges. In many jurisdictions, assignment to the juvenile court is not a highly sought after judicial appointment. The juvenile court too often is a dead-end along the judicial career track. Even deeply committed judges may seek rotation out of juvenile court to assist their legal careers. Similar observations can be made about attorneys who practice in juvenile court. There are serious questions about the adequacy of legal training and the competence of lawyers in many juvenile courts.

SHOCAP believes that the judiciary offers only passive support for the "habitual juvenile offender" designation, but that the chief judge of a court may support the program by authorizing the sharing of information. Strategies that might be used include the following (Crowe, 1991, p. 49):

- Authorize the inspection of records of the juvenile court, probation, protective services, prosecutor, school and police by the crime analyst or official designated to monitor the habitual offender
- Place limits on "deferred adjudication," especially for designated habitual offenders, who may also claim to have drug problems

The National School Safety Center suggested a way to accomplish the first strategy described by SHOCAP. This center focuses national attention on cooperative solutions to problems that disrupt education. It emphasizes efforts to rid schools of crime, violence and drugs, and encourages programs to improve student discipline, attendance and achievement. The center offers publications, visual aids and other resources to law enforcement officers, school personnel, court personnel and legislators. Table 9.8 presents the National School Safety Center's proposed "Model Interagency Juvenile Record Statute."

Summary

The juvenile justice system is basically a civil system, but it has evolved into the adversarial form typical of our adult criminal system. Juvenile court jurisdiction includes children who are in poverty, neglected or abused, who are unruly or commit status offenses and who are charged with committing serious crimes. This jurisdiction is determined by the offender's age and conduct.

Throughout their history juvenile courts have been separated into three types: designated courts, independent and separate courts and coordinated courts. Court action on behalf of neglected, abused or dependent children may be noncriminal or criminal.

In some states the court makes the decision to certify a juvenile as an adult. In other states this is done by the prosecutor. If court action is to be taken and a petition is filed in juvenile court, the case goes through three phases: (1) the preliminary hearing or conference, (2) the adjudicatory hearing or trial and (3) the dispositional hearing or sentencing.

Table 9.8
Model Interagency
Juvenile Record Statute

A. The following records are confidential and shall not be released to the general public except as permitted by this statute:
1. Juvenile court records, which include both legal and social records (legal records include petitions, dockets, motions, findings, orders and other papers filed with the court other than social records. Social records include social studies and medical, psychological, clinical or other treatment reports or studies filed with the court);
2. Juvenile social service, child protective service agency or multidisciplinary team records, whether contained in court files or in agency files (this includes all records made by any public or private agency or institution that now has or has had the child or the child's family under its custody, care or supervision);
3. Juvenile probation agency records, whether contained in court files or in probation agency files;
4. Juvenile parole agency records, whether contained in court files or in parole agency files;
5. Juvenile prosecutor, state attorney, district attorney or county attorney records relating to juvenile cases;
6. Juvenile law enforcement records, including fingerprints and photographs; and
7. School records that are maintained by school employees on all students, including but not limited to, academic, attendance, behavior and discipline records.

B. Access to the records listed in Section A is permitted without court order for official use to the following:
1. All courts;
2. All probation or parole agencies;
3. All attorneys general, prosecutors, state attorneys, district attorneys, county attorneys;
4. All social service or protective service agencies or multidisciplinary teams;
5. All law enforcement agencies;
6. All schools attended by the minor; and
7. All persons, agencies or institutions that have responsibility for the custody, care, control or treatment of the minor.

C. The juvenile court may issue an order releasing juvenile records to any person, agency or institution asserting a legitimate interest in a case or in the proceedings of the juvenile court.

D. Juvenile records may be sent to a central repository, which may be computerized. The central repository may be accessed by all agencies and organizations listed in Section B above.

E. The juvenile, the juvenile's parents and guardians and the juvenile's attorney may have access to the legal records maintained on the juvenile that are in the possession of the juvenile court without court order. The juvenile's attorney may have access to the social records maintained on the juvenile that are in the possession of the juvenile court and to the records listed in Section A above for use in the legal representation of the juvenile. The juvenile on whom records are maintained may petition the court to correct any information that is incorrect.

The National School Safety Center [1988] has proposed this model juvenile record-sharing statute for the stated purpose of "foster[ing] the sharing of information among those organizations and agencies that need information from juvenile records to adequately perform their jobs as they work in an official capacity with youths and their families." The focus of the statute is restricted to the sharing of records among child-serving agencies and does not concern itself with the broader issue of public access to juvenile records.

Source: Used with permission from *The Need to Know: Juvenile Record Sharing.* Copyright 1989 by the National School Safety Center.

Children have the same rights as adults, except trial by jury and, in some states, the right to bail. Children have the right to an attorney at all stages of the proceedings, the right to introduce evidence and tell their side of the story, the right to cross-examine witnesses and the right to remain silent during the hearing.

A series of Supreme Court decisions has caused the juvenile courts to make their procedures more adversarial, yet the trend in juvenile dispositions remains the deinstitutionalization of youths. The mandatory sentencing policy in the state of Washington is based on the juvenile's age, the current offense and the criminal history of the offender.

Coercive intervention includes out-of-home placement, detainment or mandated therapy or counseling. Therapeutic intervention is the recommendation of an appropriate treatment program.

The juvenile court's current dilemma stems from its dual roles as a court of law and as a social service agency. Solving this dilemma is a great challenge facing our juvenile courts.

Discussion Questions

1. If to adjudicate is to hear and decide a case, why is this terminology used for criminal matters in juvenile court? Should the juvenile court have two separate courts for civil and criminal matters?
2. What changes to the adjudication process should be considered in your state? What would be the advantages or disadvantages of these changes?
3. Should a guardian *ad litem* be provided in addition to a defense counsel in all juvenile proceedings? Why or why not?
4. Are there inconsistencies in the justice dispensed by the juvenile courts in your area?
5. Should there be a separate justice system for juveniles, or should all juveniles be dealt with in the adult system?
6. What types of behavior should the juvenile court deal with?
7. What criteria are used in decisions to waive juvenile court jurisdiction?
8. What are the major decision points in the adjudication process in juvenile court in your state? Are these decisions mechanical or determined by individual judges based on specific cases?
9. Does the public have the right to know which juveniles are committing crimes by publishing their names with the offense? Why or why not?
10. Should delinquency proceedings be secret?

References

Bilchik, Shay. Foreword. In Jeffrey A. Butts; Howard N. Snyder; Terrence A. Finnegan; Anne L. Aughenbaugh; and Rowen S. Poole. *Juvenile Court Statistics 1994.* Washington, DC: Office of Juvenile Justice and Delinquency Prevention, 1996. (NCJ-163709)

Butterfield, Fox. "With Juvenile Courts in Chaos, Some Propose Scrapping Them." *The New York Times,* July 21, 1997, pp. A1, A13–A15.

Crowe, Timothy D. *Habitual Juvenile Offenders: Guidelines for Citizen Action and Public Response.* Serious Habitual Offender Comprehensive Action Program (SHOCAP). Washington, DC: Office of Juvenile Justice and Delinquency Prevention, October 1991.

Crowley, Jim. "Victim-Offender Mediation: Paradigm Shift or Old-Fashioned Accountability?" *Community Links,* Spring 1998, p. 10.

Deddeh, Peter C. and Amador, Robert O. "Trying Violent Juveniles as Adults." *Law Enforcement Quarterly,* November 1996–January 1997, pp. 25–29.

Dedel, Kelly. "National Profile of the Organization of State Juvenile Corrections Systems." *Crime and Delinquency,* Vol. 44, No. 4, October 1998, pp. 507–525.

DeFrances, Carol J. and Strom, Kevin J. *Juveniles Prosecuted in State Criminal Courts.* Washington, DC: Bureau of Justice Statistics and the Office of Juvenile Justice and Delinquency Prevention, March 1997. (NCJ-164265)

DeJong, Christina and Jackson, Kenneth C. "Putting Race into Context: Race, Juvenile Justice Processing, and Urbanization." *Justice Quarterly,* Vol. 15, No. 3, September 1998, pp. 487–504.

Dundes, Lauren. "Punishing Parents to Deter Delinquency: A Realistic Remedy?" *American Journal of Police,* Vol. 13, No. 4, 1994, pp. 113–133.

Feinman, Howard. *Liability and Legal Issues in Juvenile Restitution.* Restitution Education, Specialized Training and Technical Assistance Program (RESTTA), May 1990.

Feld, Barry C. "Criminalizing the American Juvenile Court." In *Crime and Justice: A Review of Research,* Vol. 17, edited by Michael Tonry. Chicago: University of Chicago Press, 1993, pp. 197–280.

Godwin, Tracy M. *A Guide for Implementing Teen Court Programs.* Fact Sheet #45. Washington, DC: Office of Juvenile Justice and Delinquency Prevention, August 1996. (FS-9645)

Harris, Patricia M. "Juvenile Sentence Reform and Its Evaluation: A Demonstration of the Need for More Precise Measures of Offense Seriousness in Juvenile Justice Research." *Evaluation Review,* Vol. 12, No. 6, December 1988, pp. 655–666.

Hart, H. L. A. *The Concept of Law.* Oxford: Oxford University Press, 1965.

Hatchett, Glenda. "Why We Can't Wait: The Juvenile Court in the New Millennium." *Crime and Delinquency,* Vol. 44, No. 1, January 1998, pp. 83–88.

Holden, Gwen A. and Kapler, Robert A. "Deinstitutionalizing Status Offenders: A Record of Progress." *Juvenile Justice,* Vol. 2, No. 2, Fall/Winter 1995, pp. 3–10.

Hughes, Stella P. and Schneider, Anne L. *Victim-Offender Mediation in the Juvenile Justice System.* Restitution Education, Specialized Training and Technical Assistance Program (RESTTA), September 1990.

Juvenile and Adult Records: One System, One Record? Proceedings of a BJS/SEARCH Conference conducted June 28–29, 1988. January 1990.

Juvenile Probation Officer Initiative (JPOI) Working Group. *Desktop Guide to Good Juvenile Probation Practice.* Washington, DC: Office of Juvenile Justice and Delinquency Prevention, May 1993.

"Juveniles' Legal Counsel Sorely Lacking, ABA Says." *NCJA Justice Bulletin,* March 1996, pp. 13–14.

"Karen's Kids." *60 Minutes,* CBS. Aired December 1987.

Karmen, Andrew. *Crime Victims: An Introduction to Victimology.* Belmont, CA: Wadsworth Publishing Company, 1996.

Kimbrough, Robin J. "Treating Juvenile Substance Abuse: The Promise of Juvenile Drug Courts." *Juvenile Justice,* Vol. V, No. 2, December 1998, pp. 11–19.

Krisberg, Barry and Austin, James F. *Reinventing Juvenile Justice.* Newbury Park, CA: Sage Publications, 1993.

Lawry, Mercedes. *Court Appointed Special Advocates: A Voice for Abused and Neglected Children in Court.* OJJDP, Juvenile Justice Bulletin, March 1997. (NCJ-164512)

Mears, Daniel P. "Evaluation Issues Confronting Juvenile Justice Sentencing Reforms: A Case Study of Texas." *Crime and Delinquency,* Vol. 44, No. 3, July 1998, pp. 443–463.

Miethe, Terance D. and McCorkle, Richard C. "Gang Membership and Criminal Processing: A Test of the 'Master Status' Concept." *Justice Quarterly,* Vol. 14, No. 3, September 1997, pp. 407–426.

National Coalition of State Juvenile Justice Advisory Groups. *Myths and Realities: Meeting the Challenge of Serious, Violent, and Chronic Juvenile Offenders, 1992 Annual Report,* 1993.

OJJDP Guide to Good Juvenile Detention Practice. Washington, DC: U.S. Government Printing Office, 1997.

Oran, Daniel. *Law Dictionary for Nonlawyers,* 2nd ed. St. Paul, MN: West Publishing Company, 1985.

Puritz, Patricia and Wan Long Shang, Wendy. *Innovative Approaches to Juvenile Indigent Defense.* Washington, DC: Juvenile Justice Bulletin, December 1998. (NCJ-171151)

Raley, Gordon A. "The JJDP Act: A Second Look." *Juvenile Justice,* Vol. 2, No. 2, Fall/Winter 1995, pp. 11–18.

"SEARCH Says States Could Meet Juvenile Records Mandate in S. 10." *Criminal Justice Newsletter,* Vol. 29, No. 4, February 17, 1998, p. 4.

Secret, Philip E. and Johnson, James B. "The Effects of Race on Juvenile Justice Decision Making in Nebraska: Detention, Adjudication, and Disposition." *Justice Quarterly,* Vol. 14, No. 3, September 1997, pp. 445–478.

Sickmund, Melissa; Stahl, Anne L.; Finnegan, Terrence A.; Snyder, Howard N.; Poole, Rowen S.; and Butts, Jeffrey A. *Juvenile Court Statistics 1995.* Washington, DC: Office of Juvenile Justice and Delinquency Prevention, May 1998. (NCJ-170607)

Snell, Tracy L. *Capital Punishment 1996.* Bureau of Justice Statistics Bulletin, December 1997. (NCJ-167031)

Springer, Charles E. *Justice for Juveniles.* Washington, DC: U.S. Department of Justice, Office of Juvenile Justice and Delinquency Prevention, 1986.

Streib, Victor L. *The Juvenile Death Penalty Today: Death Sentences and Executions for Juvenile Crimes Over the Last Quarter Century, 1973–1997.* Ada, OH: Ohio Northern University, 1998.

Tappan, Paul. *Juvenile Delinquency.* New York: McGraw-Hill, 1949.

"Texas Lawmaker Urges Executions for Crime Committed at Age 11." *Criminal Justice Newsletter*, Vol. 29, No. 6, March 17, 1998, p. 4.

Walsh, James. "Judges Refuse to Close Juvenile Hearings." (Minneapolis/St. Paul) *Star Tribune*, July 17, 1998, pp. B1, B2.

Wordes, Madeline and Jones, Sharon M. "Trends in Juvenile Detention and Steps Toward Reform." *Crime and Delinquency*, Vol. 44, No. 4, October 1998, pp. 544–560.

Cases

Commonwealth v. Fisher, 213 Pa. 48, 62 A. 198, 199, 200 (1905).

In re Gault, 387 U.S. 1, 19–21, 26–28, 87 S.Ct. 1428, 1439–1440, 1442–1444, 18 L.Ed.2d 527 (1967).

Kent v. United States, 383 U.S. 541, 86 S.Ct. 1045, 16 L.Ed.2d 84 (1966).

People ex rel. O'Connell v. Turner, 55 Ill. 280, 8 Am.Rep. 645 (1870).

In re Rich, 125 Vt. 373, 216 A.2d 266 (1966).

Stanford v. Kentucky, 492 U.S. 361, 109 S.Ct. 2969, 106 L.Ed.2d 306 (1989).

Wilkins v. Missouri, 492 U.S. 361, 109 S.Ct. 2969, 106 L.Ed.2d 306 (1989).

In re Winship, 397 U.S. 358, 90 S.Ct. 1068, 25 L.Ed.2d 368 (1970).

Chapter 10 The Role of Corrections

It is in the juvenile justice system that we will succeed or fail in reducing corrections populations . . . If we do not address juvenile corrections fully, these children will end up as tomorrow's clients in the adult system.

—John J. Wilson

Do You Know

- Whether juveniles have a right to treatment?
- How the conservative and liberal approaches treat juveniles?
- Who the first probation officer was?
- What the most common disposition from the juvenile court is?
- What the formal goal of probation is?
- What the essence of juvenile probation is? Its three common goals?
- What the two main functions of a probation officer traditionally have been?
- What the single greatest pressure on probation officers is?
- What the effect of isolating offenders from the community might be?
- What kinds of nonresidential programs have been implemented?
- What the five major categories of residential community-based corrections are?
- What the most frequently used intermediate sanctions are?
- What three justifications are given for putting juveniles in locked facilities?
- What incarcerated groups are overrepresented?
- How public and private correctional institutions differ?
- If juvenile institutions model adult institutions in social organization? Culture?
- How prison gangs differ from street gangs?

Can You Define

aftercare, boot camp, foster group home, foster home, group home, intensive supervision, ombudsman, parole, probation, probation officer, shelter, shock incarceration, training schools

INTRODUCTION

Corrections serves several functions, with one of the most obvious being to protect the public by removing juvenile offenders from the community. Corrections has a dual function with these offenders, holding them accountable for their behavior and providing them with the educational, vocational, personal and social skills needed to successfully return to the community. The complexities of juvenile corrections are summarized by Madruga (1996–1997, p. 15):

> Even as the law gets tougher with juveniles who commit serious, often violent crimes, the juvenile justice system still struggles to counsel and correct erring youth.
>   . . . We struggle daily to find a balance between the ages-old goal of nurturing the errant kid and the vital goal of protecting the public from pubescent predators.

Dedel, in examining the national profile of the organization of state juvenile corrections systems, found (1998, p. 509):

> The states varied considerably in terms of the organization of the state's juvenile correctional agency within the state government. Thirty-two percent of state juvenile correctional agencies functioned as a subdivision of a children, youth, and family agency; 30 percent were freestanding agencies with cabinet-level status reporting directly to the chief executive; and 18 percent functioned as a subdivision of the Department of Corrections. Twenty-one percent indicated that their state's organization did not fall into the above categories. Most typically, these states functioned as a subdivision of their state's Department of Health and Human Services.

Also noted was a lack of consistency in the types of state-operated and state-administered juvenile facilities across the country (p. 509):

- 100 percent of states had at least one training school
- 40 percent had at least one ranch, camp or farm
- 40 percent had at least one group home
- 36 percent had at least one detention facility
- 36 percent had at least one diagnostic facility
- 32 percent had at least one residential facility
- 27 percent had at least one community supervision program
- 14 percent had at least one foster care facility

This chapter focuses on the correctional portion of the contemporary juvenile justice system. Corrections includes an array of choices existing along a continuum, from least restrictive and intensive to most restrictive and intensive supervision. This chapter begins by looking at the right to treatment and the most common, least restrictive disposition of the juvenile/family court—probation. This is followed by a discussion of several community-based correctional alternatives, including day treatment alternatives and residential programs such as shelters, group homes, foster homes and camps. Next, further along the continuum of increasing restriction, intermediate sanctions are explored, including intensive supervision, electronic monitoring and boot camps. The chapter concludes with a discussion of youths who are institutionalized—who they are and the conditions under which they are confined.

The Right to Treatment

The U.S. Supreme Court has apparently based the right to treatment on the principle that the restriction of fundamental liberties through involuntary confinement must follow the "least restrictive alternative" available. This principle was stated by the Supreme Court in *Shelton v. Tucker* (1960):

> In a series of decisions this Court has held that, even though the governmental purpose be legitimate and substantial, that purpose cannot be pursued by means that broadly stifle fundamental personal liberties when the end can be more narrowly achieved. The breadth of legislative abridgement must be viewed in the light of less drastic means for achieving the same basic purpose.

Under this rationale, the state violates a person's constitutional rights if it fails to confine and provide treatment in the least restrictive setting possible.

The U.S. Supreme Court has never definitively ruled on whether there is a constitutionally based right to treatment. The state does violate the individual's rights if it fails to confine and provide treatment in the least restrictive setting possible.

Two opposing views exist as to just what this treatment should consist of.

Conservative and Liberal Philosophies of Corrections

The conservative attitude is to "get tough," "stop babying these kids" and "get them off the streets." Such conservative philosophies accept retribution as grounds for punishment and believe in imprisonment to control crime and antisocial behavior. Rehabilitative programs may be provided during incarceration, but it is imprisonment itself, with its attendant deprivations, that must be primarily relied on to prevent crime, delinquency and recidivism. Correctional treatment is not necessary.

The conservative philosophy of juvenile justice is to "get tough" on juveniles— to punish and imprison them.

This "law and order" reaction typifies conservatism, a trend that first affected adult offenders and now extends into juvenile justice. As Ohlin (1998, p. 147) notes:

> In many states we see increasing incarceration even as delinquency rates decline. Juvenile reform legislation now calls for more mandatory sentencing and more determinate sentences for juveniles, lowering of the upper age of juvenile jurisdiction, greater ease in obtaining waivers to adult court for juvenile prosecution, and greater access to juvenile records.
> There is also a greater preoccupation with chronic, violent offenders that has led to a redirection of resources for their confinement. In the absence of reliable criteria for identifying such offenders, this preoccupation tends to stereotype all delinquents and is likely to raise the level of precautionary confinements. It is also likely that due process reforms, which make the juvenile system look much like the adult system, will also lead to the same result.

Many, however, sharply criticize this "get tough" approach and all its trappings, such as the need to build more prisons to hold the rising number of incarcerated youths. To express this senselessness, Judge David B. Mitchell quotes a Duval County (Florida) state attorney (1998, p. 24): "'Those who advocate increased prisons as a solution to youth crime are equal to those who advocate increasing the number of grave sites as a treatment for cancer.' It is simply mindless and a perversion." At the opposite end of the spectrum from this conservative, "get tough" philosophy is the liberal view of juvenile justice.

The liberal philosophy of juvenile justice advocates "treatment, not punishment" for youths who are antisocial and wayward. Liberal ideologies tend to favor community corrections because, as Sutherland and Cressey note (1966, p. 51):

> The person or personality is . . . a part of the kinds of social relationships and values in which he participates; he obtains his essence from rituals, values, norms, rules, schedules, customs, and regulations of various kinds which surround him; he is not separable from the social relationships in which he lives.

The liberal philosophy of juvenile justice stresses treatment and rehabilitation, including community-based programs.

Probation

Probation allows youths adjudicated delinquent to serve their sentences in the community under supervision. Probation originated with John Augustus (1784–1859), a prosperous Boston shoemaker. One August morning in 1841 he was in court when a wretched-looking man was brought into court and charged with being a drunkard. Augustus spoke briefly with the man and then provided the man's bail on the provision he sign a pledge to never drink spirits again and to return to court at a set time as a reformed man.

For the next 18 years, Augustus spent much time visiting the courts, showing an interest in prisoners and bailing out misdemeanants who could not pay the fines themselves. He would help offenders to find work or a place to live. His own home was filled with people he bailed out. When Augustus and a defendant returned to court, he would report on the progress of the defendant's rehabilitation and recommend a disposition in the case. These recommendations were usually accepted by the court.

John Augustus was the first probation officer.

During the first year of his work, Augustus assisted 10 drunkards, who because of his help received only small fines instead of imprisonment. Augustus later assisted other types of offenders, young and old, men and women. As he continued his work, he was able to report that out of 2,000 cases, only 10 failed to appear and jumped bail or probation.

Several aspects of the system used by Augustus remain a basic part of modern probation. He thoroughly investigated each person he considered helping. He considered the character of the person, his or her age and likely future influences. Augustus not only supervised each defendant but also kept a careful case record, which he submitted to the court.

Probation is now the most widely used disposition of the juvenile or family court. During 1995 the majority (59 percent) of juveniles adjudicated delinquent were placed on probation (Scalia, 1997, p. 1).

Probation is the most common disposition of the juvenile court.

Probation is a guidance program to help juveniles overcome problems that may lead to further delinquency and to supervise them. It functions as an alternative to a correctional facility and operates much like adult probation.

The formal goal of probation is to improve the delinquent's behavior—in short, rehabilitation.

Probation's goal of rehabilitation is sometimes short-circuited by the public's preoccupation with *control*. Probation may reflect public demands that the court "do something" about recurrent misconduct. It may be organized to keep the delinquent in line, to prevent any further trouble, and so the ultimate goal of reforming the delinquent's personality and conduct becomes subordinated to the exigencies of maintaining immediate control. Probationary supervision, consequently, takes on a decidedly short-term and negative character. Probation becomes a disciplinary regime to inhibit troublesome conduct.

Supervision

Supervision is the essence of probation.

As noted in the JPOI *Desktop Guide to Good Juvenile Probation Practice* (1993, p. 79):

> The common thread that runs through all approaches to supervision is utility; that is, that juvenile justice intervention *must* be designed to guide and correct the naturally changing behavior patterns of youth. Unlike adult probation, juvenile supervision views a young offender as a developing person, as one who has not yet achieved a firm commitment to a particular set of values, goals, behavior patterns or lifestyle. As such, juvenile justice supervision is in the hopeful position of influencing that development and thereby reducing criminal behavior. . . .
>
> Probation departments [should] consider the converging interests of the juvenile offender, the victim, and the community at large in developing individualized case plans for probation. This approach to policy and practice resolves the habitual conflicts between rehabilitation vs. punishment, treatment vs. control, the community vs. the offender, and public safety vs. youth development. Probation must endeavor to not only protect the public and hold the juvenile offender accountable, it must also attempt to meet his needs.

Other common goals of probation are (1) to protect the community from delinquency, (2) to impose accountability for offenses committed and (3) to equip juvenile offenders with the competencies they need to live productively and responsibly in the community.

Often, by the time a juvenile is placed on probation, he or she has a record of previous run-ins with the juvenile justice system, usually the police. The police regard probation as something juveniles "get away with" or "get off with." Many juveniles who receive probation instead of being sentenced to a correctional facility view it the same way. Some youths have stated, "I never see my P.O. [probation officer]. It's a joke! Don't ask me to tell you what he looks like, I can't remember. When I get done with this beef, I'll be cool, so I don't get hassled again."

The Probation Officer

The role of the **probation officer** was first introduced in Chapter 9 (Juvenile Court). Probation officers are in the unique position of serving both the court and the correctional areas of juvenile justice. While technically considered a correctional employee, a probation officer is an officer of the court first and foremost. As noted by Hurst (1990, p. 19):

> Courts of juvenile and family jurisdiction remain institutions of hope, and juvenile probation is still a primary means by which that optimism is actualized. The court is a forum which assumes that children are capable of growing, developing, and changing, and that this growth and development can be directed toward social conformance by well-trained juvenile probation officers.

The probation officer has traditionally been responsible for two key functions: (1) personally counseling youths who are on probation and (2) serving as a link to other community services.

While counseling skills are considered important, the role of probation officers has shifted to that of social service "brokers." In many jurisdictions the probation officer links "clients" with available resources within the community, such as vocational rehabilitation centers, vocational schools, mental health centers, employment services, church groups and other community groups like Girl Scouts, Boy Scouts and Explorers. This broad use of community resources has some inherent risks. Linking youths to such groups may actually amplify a small problem into a much larger one. Overattendance by a youth in one or more of these groups may become an attention-getting device. The overprescription of community group participation may also reinforce the youth's or the community's perception of the problem as serious. In either case further delinquency may well result.

In 1987 the National Center for Juvenile Justice (NCJJ) established the Juvenile Probation Officer Initiative (JPOI) to increase professionalism in juvenile probation. Thomas (1991, p. 62) notes: "The JPOI's fundamental principle is that it is not enough for officers to muddle through as best they can. In juvenile probation, proactive is better than reactive, dynamic is better than static, and science is better than art." The JPOI provides technical assistance when requested.

In addition the JPOI has developed *The Desktop Guide to Good Juvenile Probation Practices,* a reference book written by and for juvenile probation officers. The *Guide,* representing the collective experience of over 40 probation professionals, was sent to officers around the country. The following information (pp. 384–390) is a condensation and adaptation of this guide.

The mission of juvenile probation is "to assist young people to avoid delinquent behavior and to grow into mature adults and to do so without endangering the community" (p. 3). Effective probation officers have the following characteristics:

- Strong, sustained commitment to people—viewing each probationer as an individual and conveying to them that they are cared about
- Family involvement
- Involvement with community agencies
- Informal community involvement—enlisting the support of community members to assist probationers
- Opportunistic supervision—picking the right time for intervention

A national survey of juvenile probation professionals found that they regard basic interviewing techniques to be the most important skill for juvenile probation officers to possess upon hiring or to acquire early in their careers. Two other vital skills are information gathering and report preparation.

The Current Role of Probation Officers

In many states probation officers determine whether the juvenile court has jurisdiction, especially at the intake stage of contact with a child. The probation representative also determines, to some degree, whether a formal or an informal hearing is called for.

Informal hearings have critics, because informal processing requires an explicit or tacit admission of guilt. The substantial advantages that accrue from this admission (the avoidance of court action) also act as an incentive to confess. This casts doubt on the voluntary nature and truthfulness of admissions of guilt. The process results in informal probation.

Informal probation can be a critical time in the life of a juvenile. If it succeeds, the youngster may avoid further juvenile court processing and its potentially serious consequences. If informal probation efforts fail, the usual recourse is for the probation officer to request that a petition be filed to make the case official. This could result in the youth being confined in a locked or controlled facility for disciplinary action.

Filing Petitions and Court Hearings

Recall from Chapter 9 the three phases of the system that a youth usually goes through after a petition is filed. The probation officer may play an important role in each of these phases.

During the first phase, the preliminary hearing, the judge may determine with the assistance of a probation officer whether a child's behavior is a threat to the public or to himself. If so, the judge will order preventive detention of the youth.

During the second phase, the adjudication hearing, the judge will usually order a social investigation, presentence investigation (PSI), or predisposition report. The probation officer is responsible for investigating and assessing the child's home, school, physical and psychological situation. The *predisposition* or *presentence investigation report* has the objective of satisfying the goal of the juvenile court, which is to provide services.

Other Services

In addition to assessing the needs of probationers, devising a case plan or contract and supervising compliance with that contract, probation officers can also serve as mature role models. They can provide family counseling, crisis intervention and mediation. Mediation can be used in diverting cases at intake, settlement of cases by community groups or by the probation officer and settling disputes between a juvenile and the school or family.

Crogan (1996–1997, p. 17) notes: "Probation officers play a unique role . . . By statute, they are officers of the court who make recommendations on dispositions for both adult and juvenile cases. They also manage the cases of adults and juveniles on probation, attempting to keep them drug-free, out of trouble, and doing the things they need to do to lead more normal and productive lives." The demanding, challenging, multifaceted role of the juvenile probation officer is illustrated in Table 10.1.

Problems with Probation

Courts often attribute juveniles' troubles to something that is wrong with the youths or with their social milieu. The courts seldom sense that a juvenile's problems may be due to the court's program for guidance and control. In many cases probation officers simply do not have the training, skills or resources to provide probationers with the kinds of assistance they might require.

Another factor is time. Even if probation officers possessed the skills necessary to do psychotherapy, vocational guidance and school counseling with diverse types of youths, caseloads dictate that they would not have the time to exercise these skills.

Excessive caseloads are probably the single greatest pressure on probation officers.

In most probation offices, especially in large urban areas, certain characteristics pervade the personality of the office. Juveniles are viewed by their records, in terms of the trouble they have caused or gotten into. Records are not regarded as formulations assembled by various people in the juvenile justice system. That is to say, a juvenile's record is treated as a set of relevant facts instead of as a social product created by an organization.

	Role	Description
Table 10.1 **The Multifaceted Role of the Juvenile Probation Officer**	Cop	Enforces judge's orders
	Prosecutor	Assists D.A., conducts revocations
	Father confessor	Establishes helpful, trustful relationship with juvenile
	Rat	Informs court of juvenile's behavior/circumstances
	Teacher	Develops skills in juvenile
	Friend	Develops positive relations with juvenile
	Surrogate parent	Admonishes, scolds juvenile
	Counselor	Addresses needs
	Ambassador	Intervenes on behalf of juvenile
	Problem solver	Helps juvenile deal with court and community issues
	Crisis manager	Deals with juvenile's precipitated crises (usually at 2 A.M.)
	Hand holder	Consoles juvenile
	Public speaker	Educates public re: tasks
	P.R. person	Wins friends, influences people on behalf of probation
	Community resource specialist	Service broker
	Transportation officer	Gets juvenile to where he has to go in a pinch
	Recreational therapist	Gets juvenile to use leisure time well
	Employment counselor	Gets kid a job
	Judge's advisor	Court service officer
	Financial advisor	Monitors payment, sets pay plan
	Paper pusher	Fills out myriad forms
	Sounding board	Listens to irate parents, kids, police, teachers, etc.
	Punching bag	Person to blame when anything goes wrong, kid commits new crime
	Expert clinician	Offers or refers to appropriate treatment
	Family counselor/marriage therapist	Keeps peace in juvenile's family
	Psychiatrist	Answers question: why does the kid do it?
	Banker	Juvenile needs car fare money
	Tracker	Finds kid
	Truant officer	Gets kid to school
	Lawyer	Tells defense lawyer/prosecutor what juvenile law says
	Sex educator	Facts of life, AIDS, and child support (Dr. Ruth)
	Emergency foster parent	In a pinch
	Family wrecker	Files petitions for abuse/neglect
	Bureaucrat	Helps juvenile justice system function
	Lobbyist	For juvenile, for department
	Program developer	For kid, for department
	Grant writer	For kid, for department
	Board member	Serves on myriad committees
	Agency liaison	With community groups
	Trainer	For volunteer, students
	Public information officer	"Tell me what you know about probation"
	Court officer/bailiff	In a pinch
	Custodian	Keeps office clean
	Victim advocate	Deals with juvenile's victim

Source: Adapted from: Juvenile Probation Officer Initiative (JPOI) Working Group, *Desktop Guide to Good Juvenile Probation Practice.* Washington, DC: Office of Juvenile Justice and Delinquency Prevention, May 1993, pp. 119–120.

Privatizing Juvenile Probation Services

Problems such as illegal drug use, street gangs, school violence, and abused, homeless and runaway youths have strained the resources of the juvenile justice system. Given that probation departments are the single largest component of juvenile corrections, these departments especially feel the strain. One proposed solution is privatization. To investigate this option, the OJJDP funded a three-year project called the Private Sector Probation Initiative. OJJDP chose the National Office for Social Responsibility (NOSR) to carry out the project. The Private Sector Probation Initiative Project developed seven steps for agencies to follow to transfer services from public to private sector operation (Donahue, 1989, p. 2):

Step 1. Prepare a comprehensive, realistic plan for accomplishing the transfer.

Step 2. Enlist the help of the business and professional communities and form a public-private partnership.

Step 3. Assess the agency's existing organizational structure, procedures, and services.

Step 4. Identify the juvenile probation functions most suited to privatization, and adjust or redesign probation components as needed.

Step 5. Write clear, concise solicitations or Requests for Proposals. Select a contractor to carry out the privatized function.

Step 6. Implement the conversion of the probation function to contractor operation.

Step 7. Establish a monitoring process to track the contractor's performance and evaluate the quality of services provided.

The demonstration sites showed that juvenile probation departments can successfully improve some functions by transferring them to the private sector.

Probation as a Disposition

A problem commonly encountered at the dispositional stage is a lack of options for helping or treating a youngster. Inexperienced or uninformed probation officers may recommend treatment that is simply not available. Often a youngster is placed on or continued on probation because of a lack of viable alternatives.

After the dispositional hearing, if the court orders that a youngster be placed on probation, certain procedures and commitments must be satisfied. An order must give the probation officer authority for controlled supervision within the community. The terms of the probation are described in the order.

An important responsibility of the probation officer is helping the court to establish the conditions for probation. Two kinds of probationary conditions are usually established: mandatory and discretionary. Most mandatory conditions specify that probationers (1) may not commit a new delinquent act, (2) must report, as directed, to their probation officer and (3) must obey all court orders.

The discretionary conditions are more extensive, as illustrated by the discretionary conditions set forth in New Jersey Juvenile Statutes:

- Pay a fine
- Make restitution
- Perform community service
- Participate in a work program
- Participate in programs emphasizing self-reliance, such as intensive outdoor programs that teach survival skills, including but not limited to camping, hiking and other appropriate activities
- Participate in a program of academic or vocational education or counseling, which may require attendance after school, evenings and weekends
- Be placed in a suitable residential or nonresidential program for the treatment of alcohol or narcotic abuse
- Be placed in a nonresidential program, operated by a public or private agency that provides intensive services to juveniles for specified hours, which may include education, counseling to the juvenile and the juvenile's family if appropriate, vocational counseling, work or other services
- Be placed with any private group home (with which the Department of Correction has entered into a purchase of service contract)

The New Jersey statute also allows the court to set conditions for the probationer's parents and to revoke the juvenile's driving license as a condition of probation. Conditions may include such matters as the following:

- Cooperating with the program of supervision
- Meeting family responsibilities
- Maintaining steady employment or engaging in or refraining from engaging in a specific employment or occupation
- Pursuing prescribed educational or vocational training
- Undergoing medical or psychiatric treatment
- Maintaining residence in a prescribed area or in a prescribed facility
- Refraining from consorting with certain types of people or frequenting certain types of places
- Making restitution or reparation
- Paying fines
- Submitting to search and seizure
- Submitting to drug tests

A study conducted in Utah showed that for cases involving robbery, assault, burglary, theft, auto theft and vandalism, recidivism rates are lowered when juveniles agree or are ordered to pay restitution to their victims either directly or through money earned from community service (Butts and Snyder, 1992, p. 1).

Several constraints govern the setting of conditions. The conditions must be do-able, must not unreasonably restrict constitutional rights, must be consistent with law and public policy and must be specific and understandable. If the conditions are *not* met, probation can be revoked. This is normally accomplished by the probation officer reporting the violation of conditions to the juvenile court. A violation of probation starts the judicial process over, beginning with a revocation hearing, where evidence and supportive information are presented before a juvenile judge. (Such hearings are also called *surrender hearings* or *violation hearings*.) If the court decides to revoke the probation, the youth can be institutionalized.

Community-Based Corrections Programs

The community corrections philosophy follows the juvenile justice rhetoric of treatment and restoration instead of punishment and decay. McCarthy and McCarthy (1997, p. 330) state: "The juvenile justice system uses community-based correctional programs to a significantly greater degree than the adult criminal justice system because juveniles, more often than adults, have significant family and community ties that reintegration programs can enhance and reinforce. The widely held belief that most juveniles deserve a second or third chance to remain in the community also facilitates the use of community programs for juveniles."

Isolating offenders from their normal social environment may encourage the development of a delinquent orientation and, thus, further delinquent behavior.

Community-based correctional programs, such as probation, foster care and group homes, try to normalize social contacts, reduce the stigma of being institutionalized and provide opportunities for jobs and schooling. Community-based programs might include involving young people in community activities; training and employing youths as subprofessional aides; establishing Youth Services Bureaus to provide programs for young people; increasing the involvement of religious institutions, private social agencies, fraternal groups and other community organizations in youth programs; and providing community residential centers.

Programs such as work release enable delinquents to leave institutions to work in the community. Similar programs may provide release to delinquents for education. Under these programs youths receive conditional releases to halfway houses, prerelease centers and residential treatment facilities. Living within the community, youths go to work or school under some supervision and counseling.

Nonresidential corrections programs include community supervision, family crisis counseling, proctor programs, and service-oriented programs, including recreational programs, counseling, alternative schools, employment training programs, and homemaking and financial planning classes.

Nonresidential Day Treatment Alternatives

Many state and local governments are turning to day treatment for delinquent juveniles because it appears to be effective and is less costly than residential care. Alternatives might include evening and weekend reporting centers, school programs and specialized treatment facilities. Such programs can provide education, tutoring, counseling, community service, vocational training and social/recreational events.

Day treatment programs tend to succeed because they can focus on the family unit and the youth's behavior in the family and the community. They are also effective from a legal standpoint in those states that require that youths be treated in the least restrictive environment possible.

Community-based corrections has supplemented, not replaced, institutionalization. The community also sometimes provides residential, nonsecure facilities with accompanying programs.

Nonsecure Residential Programs

Residential programs are divided into five major categories.

The five major categories of residential programs are shelters, group homes, foster homes, foster group homes and other types of nonsecure facilities.

Shelters

A **shelter** is a nonsecure residential facility where juveniles may be temporarily assigned, often in place of detention or returning home, after they are taken into custody or after adjudication while they wait for more permanent placement. Shelters usually house status offenders and are not intended for treatment or punishment.

Group Homes

The **group home** is a nonsecure facility with a professional corrections staff that provides counseling, education, job training and family-style living. The staff is small because the residence generally holds a maximum of 12 to 15 youths. Group home living provides support and some structure in a basically nonrestrictive setting, with the opportunity for a close, but controlled, interaction with the staff. The youths in the home attend a school in the community and participate in community activities. The objective of the home is to facilitate reintegrating young offenders into society.

Group homes are used extensively in almost all states. Some are operated by private agencies under contract to the juvenile court. Others are operated directly by probation departments or some other governmental unit.

Some, called boarding homes, deserve special mention. Since these homes often accommodate as few as three or four youths, they can be found in an apartment or flat in an urban setting. They are sometimes called "Mom and Pop" operations because the adults serve as parent substitutes. The adults are usually paraprofessionals whose strengths are personal warmth and an ability to relate to young people.

An example of a community-based residential treatment program is the program developed for Rutgers Medical School. Middlefield, in North

Brunswick, New Jersey, is located in an old farmhouse on common grounds with a juvenile detention facility and a county jail for adults. In early 1980 Harriet Hollander developed a program for the Middlefield facility. At the time, the facility had 12 residents, all males. Criteria for admission to the program included being capable of social participation—that is, showing the capacity to organize thoughts, possessing minimal language skills to communicate ideas, and having the potential to internalize behavior.

Unacceptable to the program were juveniles who had violent or aggressive behavior or drug or alcohol addiction. The Middlefield program stressed juvenile development; it was somewhat different from most group homes because of its focus on the individual rather than on the group. The program was designed to "build responsibility in terms of actions; to help develop within the individual a good sense of values; and to give the boys direction in life" (Hollander, 1981). It emphasized offering both academic and vocational education with various community activities and trips. It also used Rutgers' Community Health Center and Alcoholics Anonymous for individual, group and family counseling.

Hollander stated that the program was "a community-based treatment program built on a mental health model." This description places Middlefield in the category of programs that presume some psychological disturbance or disorder to be the cause of delinquency. It therefore used psychological and mental health correctional strategies. Perhaps because of its focus on the individual and special blend of treatment approaches, the program has not produced the results desired for a group home setting.

Foster Homes

A **foster home** is intended to be family-like, as much as possible a substitute for a natural family setting. Small and nonsecure, foster homes are used at any of several stages in the juvenile justice process. In jurisdictions where a juvenile shelter is not available, foster homes may be used when law enforcement authorities take a juvenile into custody.

Foster care is used less for misbehaving and delinquent children than it is for children whose parents have neglected, abused or abandoned them. Social service agencies usually handle the placement in and funding of foster care programs. The police and courts coordinate their efforts through these agencies.

Foster Group Homes

A **foster group home** is a blend of group home and foster home. Foster group homes provide a "real family" concept and are run by single families, not professional staffs. They are nonsecure facilities usually acceptable to neighborhood environments that can give troubled youths a neighborhood-family type relationship. Foster group homes can be found in various parts of the United States.

Other Nonsecure Facilities

Correctional farms, ranches and camps for youths are usually located in rural areas. These facilities are an alternative to confinement or regimented programs. The programs with an outdoor or rural setting encourage self-development,

Students at Texas Youth Commission's state school correctional facility in San Saba, Texas, play basketball behind the fences and razor wire surrounding the facility. The San Saba unit, which specifically houses violent offenders, is one of 13 TYC facilities in the state.

provide opportunities for reform and secure classification and placement of juveniles according to their capabilities. Close contact with staff and residents instills good work habits.

According to the National Advisory Committee (1980, p. 431): "The camps and ranches . . . require a programmatic emphasis on outside activity, basic self-discipline and the development of vocational and interpersonal skills. . . . The camp provides a setting for juveniles to develop good work habits, learn to work, and develop skills. Further, residents perform useful and necessary work that benefits the community in general."

The Dilemma of Community Programs

Court dispositions are often compromises among deterrence, incapacitation, retribution and rehabilitation. Community-based programs do not permit the freedom of dismissal or of suspended judgments, but neither do they isolate offenders from the community as institutions do. Community programs are sometimes perceived as being easy on youngsters, and thus as not providing enough supervision to ensure deterrence, incapacitation and retribution. Nonetheless commitment to such programs represents a considerable degree of restriction and punishment when compared to dismissal, suspended judgment or informal processing out of the system at an early stage.

Intermediate Sanctions

Intermediate sanctions include intensive supervision, house arrest with electronic monitoring and shock incarceration or boot camps. Such sanctions provide swift, certain punishment, while avoiding the expense and the negative effects of institutionalization.

Three common forms of intermediate sanctions are intensive supervision, electronic monitoring and boot camps.

Intensive Supervision

Intensive supervision is highly structured probation. It usually includes the following features (JPOI, p. 87):

- A greater reliance placed on unannounced spot checks; these may occur in a variety of settings including home, school, known hangouts and job sites.
- Considerable attention directed at increasing the number and kinds of collateral contacts made by corrections staff with family members, friends, staff from other agencies and concerned residents in the community.
- Greater use of curfew, including both more rigid enforcement and lowering the hour at which curfew goes into effect. (Other measures for imposing control include home detention and electronic monitoring.)
- Surveillance expanded to ensure seven-day-a-week, 24-hour-a-day coverage.

Other components of intensive supervision are clear, graduated sanctions with immediate consequences for violations; restitution and community service; parent involvement; youth skill development, and individualized and offense-specific treatment.

To determine if a probationer needs intensive supervision, the probation officer should have a classification procedure. Since intensive supervision is extremely time-consuming, it should be reserved for those probationers at greatest risk of violating their probation. The National Institute of Corrections (NIC) Classification Project has been adopted by many juvenile court jurisdictions. NIC research suggests that an assessment of the following variables appears to be universally predictive of future delinquent behavior (JPOI, p. 81):

- Age at first adjudication
- Prior delinquent behavior (combined measure of number and severity of priors)
- Number of prior commitments to juvenile facilities
- Drug/chemical abuse
- Alcohol abuse
- Family relationships
- School problems
- Peer relationships

The NIC calls for a reassessment every six months. After the assessment is completed, a case plan must arrange services so that the youth, the family and the community are all served. The National Council on Crime and Delinquency (NCCD) has a case planning strategy that involves the following components (JPOI, p. 83):

1. Analysis:
   a. Identification of problem.
   b. Identification of strengths and resources.
2. Problem prioritization based upon:
   a. Strength—Is the problem an important force in the juvenile delinquent's problems?
   b. Alterability—Can the problem be modified or circumvented?
   c. Speed—Can the changes be achieved rapidly?
   d. Interdependence—Will solving the problem help resolve other problems?

This case plan is next reduced to a contract between the probation department, the juvenile offender and the family. The probation officer must then present this contract to the juvenile and the parents and get them to agree to it. The probation officer then monitors compliance with the contract.

Electronic Monitoring

Electronic monitoring (EM), sometimes referred to as *house arrest,* has been tried with some success in several jurisdictions. In fact it is sometimes a key component in intensive probation and parole programs. According to the Bureau of Justice Assistance monograph, *Electronic Monitoring in Intensive Probation and Parole Programs* (1989), electronic monitoring can be used to impose curfew, home detention (more restrictive than curfew, the offender must be home except when at work or at treatment) or home incarceration (the offender must be at home at almost all times). The use of EM has grown considerably.

The monograph (p. 3) suggests that electronic monitoring provides a "supervision tool that can satisfy punishment, public safety and treatment objectives." It can:

- Provide a cost-effective community supervision tool for offenders selected according to specific program criteria.
- Administer sanctions appropriate to the seriousness of the offense.
- Promote public safety by providing surveillance and risk control strategies indicated by the risk and needs of the offender.
- Increase the confidence of legislative, judicial and releasing authorities in Intensive Supervision Probation or Parole Program designs as a viable sentencing option.

Figure 10.1 illustrates the key decision points where EM can be used.

Boot Camps

Juvenile boot camps are fundamentally the same as those for adults, and their use as an intermediate sanction has been growing. Over half the states and the

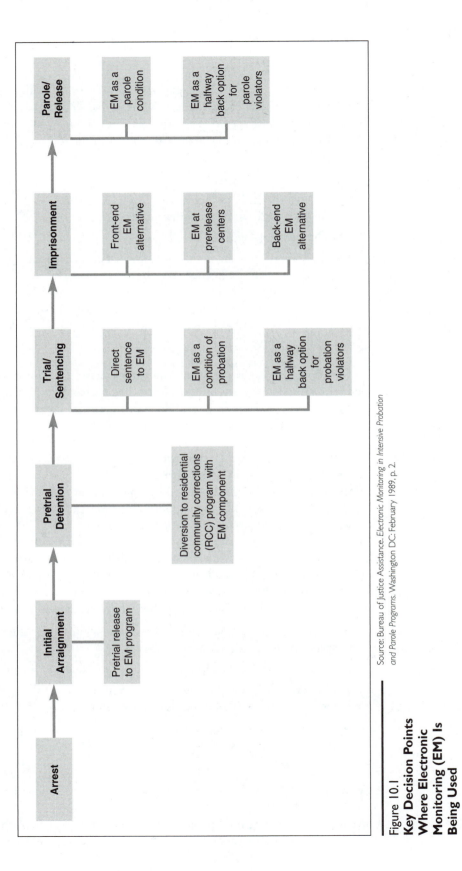

Figure 10.1
Key Decision Points Where Electronic Monitoring (EM) Is Being Used

Source: Bureau of Justice Assistance. *Electronic Monitoring in Intensive Probation and Parole Programs.* Washington DC: February 1989, p. 2.

Standing at attention in the Lakeview Shock Camp, Brocton, New York, inmates must eat quickly and are not permitted to talk.

federal system currently operate at least one boot camp. Also known as **shock incarceration,** a **boot camp** stresses military discipline, physical fitness and strict obedience to orders, as well as educational and vocational training and drug treatment when appropriate. Most boot camps are designed for young, nonviolent, first-time offenders as a means of punishment and rehabilitation without long-term incarceration. Furthermore, offender consent is required for placement in shock incarceration.

Parent (1994, p. 8) notes: "Boot camps are in sync with calls for harsher punishment. They provide striking visual images that provoke visceral responses in members of the viewing public." MacKenzie (1993, pp. 22–23) describes some elements of a typical day in boot camp:

> Upon arrival at the boot camp prison, male inmates have their heads shaved (females may be permitted short haircuts) and are informed of the strict program rules. At all times they are required to address staff as "Sir" or "Ma'am," must request permission to speak, and must refer to themselves as "this inmate." Punishments for even minor rule violations are summary and certain, frequently involving physical exercise such as push-ups or running in place. A major rule violation can result in dismissal from the program.

Taylor (1992) stresses that boot camps must be tailored to fit juveniles' needs. He lists the following recommendations of the American Correctional Association for successful boot camps for juveniles (p. 124):

- It is important to focus on concrete feelings and self-concept, since both are strongly related to delinquent behavior. The more negative feelings a youth has, the lower his or her self-esteem. Counseling in the experiential context is powerful because it deals with daily activities in a real rather than artificial environment.

- It is important to provide discipline through physical conditioning. Physical conditioning improves health and boosts self-esteem, which helps reduce aggressive misbehavior.

- Structure, as well as discipline, is important since these juveniles tend to be manipulative and defensive.

- It is important to help the juveniles feel they have a sense of control over their lives, and to identify their strengths and channel them in positive directions. The experiential learning aspects of the program should help develop this sense of control.

- Successful programming involves literacy, academic and vocational education; intensive value clarification; and resocialization that makes participants aware of the long-term effects of their behavior.

- It is necessary for the juveniles to actively participate in the program for some time before they can begin drawing their own conclusions rather than having others do it for them.

Boot camps should be thought of as a foundation rather than as a cure, according to Hengesh (1991). He believes that most offenders entering the boot camps lack basic life skills, are in poor physical condition, have quit school and have had frequent encounters with the justice system. Their self-esteem is low, and they are seen as losers. Hengesh (p. 106) contends: "Young offenders have a false sense of pride and have built up resentment for authority. This must be stripped away before we can begin to make any change." This is one of the primary functions of the prison boot camp, just as it is in a military boot camp. The camps are intended to provide a "foundation of discipline, responsibility and self-esteem" to be built on. Hengesh (p. 108) stresses that: "The programming, physical conditioning and work programs must all be geared to showing offenders they can achieve, and that it feels good to achieve."

Several examples of successful boot camp operations have been noted around the country. Oklahoma's Regimented Inmate Discipline (RID) is one of the country's oldest boot camps, having opened in 1984. As noted by Frank (1991, p. 102): "The intense, highly structured program is designed to get offenders to the point where they can meet the challenges of daily life in the community." The boot camp is organized into a three-platoon system, with inmates entering at the third platoon and working their way up to the first platoon. According to Frank (p. 105): "The RID program works because it combines programming and discipline. Each is vitally important to the preparing of better educated, more confident and disciplined young men who can succeed as law-abiding, productive members of their communities."

Inmates who successfully complete boot camp in Willow River, Minnesota, can have as much as two years taken off their original sentence, but it is not an easy six months. As noted by deFiebre (1993, p. A1), the khaki-uniformed inmates spend "16-hour days full of military-style discipline and drill, strenuous physical training, manual labor, education and drug treatment."

Inmates in Butler Shock, New York, are sentenced to six months in what Waldron (1990, p. 145) calls "part of the newest fad in corrections—boot camp–style prisons." The superintendent there asserts: "We do break them down and then build them back up. Everything we do is done for a purpose." If the inmates make it through, they win parole, no matter how long the judge sentences them to serve. In a typical group, about half make it to graduation.

In Georgia boot camps are known as Special Alternative Incarceration (SAI). As noted by Bowen (1991, p. 100), Georgia's boot camps are unique in their five-tier approach that extends from least to most restrictive:

1. Probation detention centers (PDCs) to rehabilitate low-risk offenders. Beds turned over every 120 days.
2. Probation/SAI Boot Camps for offenders needing more severe attention. Beds rolled over every 90 days.
3. Inmate Boot Camps for potential parolees. Beds turned over every 90 days.
4. Intensive Discipline Program (IDP) units for severe offenders assigned to isolation because of misconduct. Beds turned over every 30 days.
5. Intensive follow-up. Following boot camp, those who are released into the community have intensive supervision for 90 days.

A relatively new site for boot camps is the jail. Austin et al. (1993, p. 5) suggest that to be effective, a jail boot camp must address several key issues:

- Relief of crowding
- Rehabilitation
- Improving jail operations and community relations

The possible goals for jail boot camps can vary greatly. Those most often stressed are reducing recidivism, providing general education and drug education and developing good work skills. Most successful programs also have an aftercare component.

Boot camps for juvenile offenders have received mixed reviews about how well they achieve their intended goals. Peters et al. (1997, p. 16) state: "The boot camp environment appears to create a setting that facilitates learning and academic education, even for such a troubled population. . . . A significant majority of youth improved at least one grade level in literacy and math skills in the equivalent of less than half an academic year, with many improving two grade levels or more."

While boot camps may have achieved a degree of success in educating offenders, they seem to have fallen short of other goals. Carlson et al. (1999, p. 345) note: "Similar to adult graduates of boot camps, juveniles completing boot camp still retain a high risk of recidivism, with estimates of rearrest rates ranging anywhere between 28 and 74 percent." Florida Senate Republican Leader Locke Burt (Kaczor, 1997, p. 6B) asserts: "If people were expecting a magic bullet, boot camps aren't it. But I think it does help some kids some of the time." According to Kaczor: "Teens at Bay County's camp in Panama City [Florida] don't need any studies to figure their odds for being arrested again. 'Sir, a 50-50 chance, sir,' said a thin 14-year-old boy. 'You just have to have enough will power to stay away from it, sir.' Does he have it? 'Sir, yes, sir.'"

Having looked at the nonsecure facilities such as ranches, shelters and camps, focus now on the facilities that serve most youths who are not placed on probation or diverted from the system.

Institutionalization

Juvenile offenders are placed in a variety of correctional institutions, often alongside adult offenders. According to Carlson et al. (p. 346): "Estimates place the number of facilities holding juveniles at over 11,000, of which only one-third are specifically designed for juveniles. The remainder are adult jails, police lockups and state correctional facilities."

Some of the most secure institutions are merely storage facilities for juvenile offenders. Here juvenile delinquents often simply "do their time," with release based on conditions of overcrowding and, amazingly, the inability of the system to "rehabilitate" the offender. Such nonconstructive time, when juveniles should be developing their values and planning their futures, can be devastating. Although lockups may be needed for a portion of the chronic, violent offenders, they serve as criminal training schools for other juveniles.

SHOCAP suggests the following for state correctional officers (Crowe, 1991, pp. 49–50):

> State juvenile corrections authorities are responsible for the housing and rehabilitation of adjudicated delinquents who are sentenced to either a definite or indefinite period of incarceration and/or treatment. Many state corrections agencies have had to classify custody levels and diagnose the treatment needs of juvenile offenders without the benefits of the detailed profiles that are being developed on serious habitual offenders. Therefore, some strategies are:
>
> - Provide all profile information to correctional authorities upon sentencing of a designated habitual offender
> - Share correctional case histories and diagnostic reports with the crime analyst or other officials designated to develop and maintain profiles of habitual offenders
> - Develop special classification and custody levels for designated habitual offenders
> - Limit placements of habituals to the most secure programs and keep them separate from juveniles of similar status
> - Conduct special diagnostic and program activities to control behavior while in institutional programs and to assist in the eventual return to the community

Juveniles Sentenced to Adult Institutions

Many correctional agencies are trying to successfully integrate young offenders into their adult prison populations, but the obstacles can be hard to overcome. Regarding the placement of youths in adult correctional systems, Glick (1998, p. 96) states: "Stories of young offenders challenging adult offenders, the unpredictable nature of these young people, and the inability of staff to predict with any consistency or reliability their behavior, are plentiful." Glick notes the following documented trends about violent youthful offenders (p. 96):

- Juveniles commit more violent offenses against persons than do adults.
- Imposing adult norms on juveniles can create hybrid inmates with more social, emotional and interpersonal problems.

Two youngsters share this cell in a youth detention facility. The mattress on the floor shows the overcrowded conditions.

- Young offenders' safety in adult facilities appears to be the major problem challenging officials in adult facilities.
- The boundaries of the adult as a "reasoning and responsible" individual are constantly being redrawn to encompass younger and younger persons (reducing the age of responsibility below the 14- to 16-year-old age category).

Ziedenberg and Schiraldi (1998, p. 26) take a closer look at some of the risks juveniles face when sentenced to adult facilities: "Whatever kind of threat you choose, be it rape, assault or suicide, prison is a most dangerous place for young offenders." Nonetheless all 50 states have laws allowing juveniles to be tried as adults, and 42 states have recently toughened those laws (p. 26). Addressing the risks, Ziedenberg and Schiraldi (p. 24) note one study that found "the suicide rate of juveniles in adult jails is 7.7 times higher than it is in juvenile detention centers." Regarding rape, the authors cite a study in which "nearly 10 percent of the youth interviewed reported that another inmate had attempted to sexually attack or rape them in adult prisons, while closer to 1 percent reported the same in juvenile institutions."

Detention Facilities

The nation's original training and industrial reform schools have survived to the present under new names—detention centers. They still function, however, under the same regimented format. Detention centers, unlike group homes and shelters, are secure, locked facilities. They hold juveniles prior to and following adjudication. (Detention was discussed from a law enforcement perspective in Chapter 8 and again as part of the court process in Chapter 9.)

In 1989 the National Juvenile Detention Association (NJDA) developed and ratified a comprehensive national definition of juvenile detention (Smith, 1991, p. 56):

Juvenile detention is the temporary and secure custody of children, accused or adjudicated of conduct subject to the jurisdiction of the family/juvenile court, who require a physically restricting environment for their own or the community's protection while pending legal action.

Further, juvenile detention provides and maintains a wide range of helpful services which include, but are not limited to, the following: education, visitation, private communications, counseling, continuous supervision, medical and health care, nutrition, recreation and reading.

In addition to advising the court on the proper course of action required to restore the child to a productive role in the community, detention also includes or provides a system for clinical observation and diagnosis, which complements the wide range of helpful services.

Formally only three purposes justify putting juveniles in a locked facility: (1) to secure their presence at court proceedings, (2) to hold those who cannot be sent home and (3) to prevent juveniles from harming themselves or others, or from disrupting juvenile court processes.

The NJDA clearly states that juvenile detention is to be reserved for juveniles who are violent and/or who pose a serious threat to community safety. Even with such restrictions, detention centers across the country are overflowing. Previte (1997, p. 76) states: "More than half a million youth per year pour into secure, publicly-operated juvenile detention centers. More than half of the youth detained in the United States now are served in crowded facilities. In 1996 the Camden County (N.J.) Youth Center reached almost triple capacity. Newark reached 250 percent of capacity; Oklahoma City, 202 percent; Las Vegas, 183 percent; Chicago, 168 percent; Miami, 152 percent; and Dallas, which expanded into a new building only 20 months ago, 116 percent."

This critical shortage of detention space for violent juvenile offenders has led to fervent debate between those who support and those who oppose housing juveniles in adult facilities. Backstrom (1998, p. 14), a proponent of such an approach, asserts: "We cannot overlook the fact that today's juvenile offenders often are sophisticated, gang-connected juveniles committing violent crimes, and there are fewer reasons to be concerned about segregating these hard-core juvenile offenders from adults. . . . In many cases, 15- to 25-year-old offenders commit offenses together." On the other side of the debate are opponents like Roush and Dunlap, who state (1998, p. 15):

There are significant differences between adults and children (person under 18 years old), and public safety is best served by correctional efforts that restore youth to healthy, law-abiding lifestyles. The mission of adult corrections, as defined by politicians, the public and the courts, is at odds with these principles. . . . Research indicates that juveniles are five times more likely to be sexually assaulted and two times more likely to be beaten in prison than in a juvenile institution. Placing them in adult prisons constitutes deliberate indifference to their well-being and dehumanizes them. In addition to being costly in terms of time and resources, it prevents reconciliation and healing.

Juvenile victimization, however, may also occur in detention centers where the offender populations consist entirely of youths. According to Smith (p. 58): "The weaker juvenile who is sentenced to a ten-day detention stay may be subject to violent acts, victimized by extortion and emotionally scarred." Smith (p. 60) concludes:

> Judges and probation officers who fall prey to the popular wisdom that espouses a get-tough policy on troublesome but non-dangerous teens are doing them a grave disservice. These youths need services, not time in detention centers. Detention is a preadjudicatory service for dangerous youths; to place chronic misdemeanants in that environment allows them to become victims of a system that should be their protector.

In some areas a detention center is incorporated in a jail. Finckenaur (1984, p. 132) visited an "all-purpose jail" in Tyler, Texas, and reported:

> On the upper floor of this jail (on a very humid day in late June, with the temperature soaring into triple figures) approximately a dozen juveniles were confined in a large bullpen cell. This cell was literally a "hot box," dark and without ventilation. Some of the juveniles were from out of state, and the average stay for most was somewhere around 45 days. Because these youths were confined in an adult facility, and because the sheriff was attempting to maintain physical separation of juveniles and adults, the youth had nowhere to go and nothing to do for just about the entire duration of their incarceration.

The National Advisory Commission on Corrections referred to the jailing of juveniles as a "disconcerting phenomenon." Because they are intended to be temporary holding facilities, jails and detention centers offer little or nothing in the way of correctional treatment.

Prior to adjudication juveniles may be detained for periods that range from a day to several weeks. This raises the question of whether detention is appropriate before a juvenile is adjudicated delinquent. One rationale for detention prior to adjudication is that it serves as an informal punishment, advocated by those who believe in "getting tough on juveniles."

Training Schools

Training schools exist in every state except Massachusetts, which abolished them in the 1970s. They vary greatly in size, staff, service programs, ages and types of residents. Some training schools resemble adult prisons, with the same distinguishing problems of gang-oriented activity, homosexual terrorism and victimization, which often leads to progressive difficulties or suicide.

Most legislation requires training schools to provide both safe custody and rehabilitative treatment. A 1983 federal court case, however, rejected the idea of a constitutional right to treatment and training: "We therefore agree . . . that, although rehabilitative training is no doubt desirable and sound as policy and perhaps of state law, plaintiffs have no constitutional right to rehabilitative training" (*Santana v. Collazo*, 1983).

Juveniles in Public Institutions

The number of youths detained in or committed to both short-term and long-term public facilities is increasing. For example according to Harlow (1998, p. 3): "An estimated 2.3% of jail inmates were under age 18 in 1996, up from 1.5% in 1989 and 1.3% in 1983." Survey estimates place the actual number of

Table 10.2
Percent of Juveniles in Custody on February 15, 1995

Race/ethnicity	All facilities	Public	Private
Total juveniles in custody	100%	100%	100%
White, non-Hispanic	37	32	53
Minorities	63	68	47
Black	40	43	34
Hispanic	19	21	10
Asian/Pacific Islander	2	3	1
Native American	2	1	2

Minorities were more than two-thirds of all juveniles in custody in public facilities and were just under half of juveniles in private facilities.

Source: Melissa Sickmund, Howard N. Snyder and Eileen Poe-Yamagata. *Juvenile Offenders and Victims: 1997 Update on Violence*. Washington, DC: Office of Juvenile Justice and Delinquency Prevention, August 1997, p. 42. (NCJ-165703)

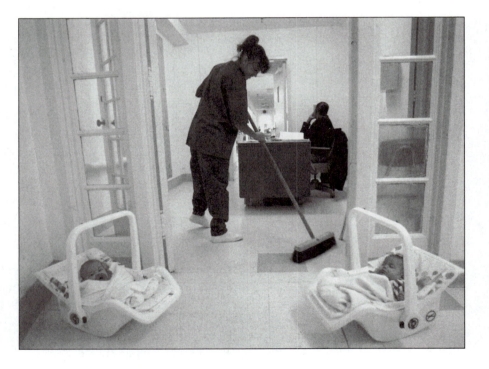

A 19-year-old inmate sweeps the nursery playroom floor at New York's maximum-security women's prison in Bedford Hills with her twin daughters nearby.

juvenile jail inmates nationwide between 9,100 and 11,780 (Gilliard and Beck, 1998, p. 6; Harlow, p. 3).

An investigation of the characteristics of inmates of public long-term juvenile institutions shows a pattern not unlike that of America's jails and prisons. The disadvantaged and the poor make up a large percentage of the population. In addition, disproportionate minority confinement (DMC) is common as shown in Table 10.2. Note that minority youth outnumber nonminority white youth in public custody facilities by more than two to one. In private facilities nonminority white youths slightly outnumber minority youth.

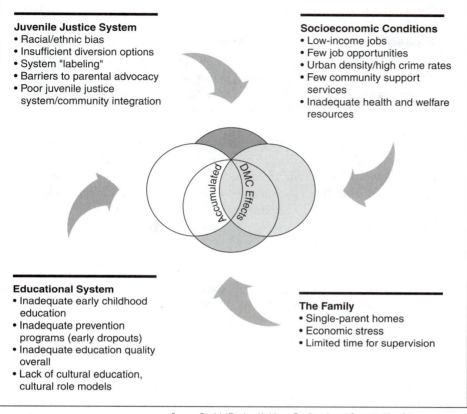

Juvenile Justice System
- Racial/ethnic bias
- Insufficient diversion options
- System "labeling"
- Barriers to parental advocacy
- Poor juvenile justice system/community integration

Socioeconomic Conditions
- Low-income jobs
- Few job opportunities
- Urban density/high crime rates
- Few community support services
- Inadequate health and welfare resources

Educational System
- Inadequate early childhood education
- Inadequate prevention programs (early dropouts)
- Inadequate education quality overall
- Lack of cultural education, cultural role models

The Family
- Single-parent homes
- Economic stress
- Limited time for supervision

Accumulated DMC Effects

Source: Patricia Devine, Kathleen Coolbaugh and Susan Jenkins. *Disproportionate Minority Confinement: Lessons Learned from Five States.* OJJDP Juvenile Justice Bulletin, December 1998, p. 8.

Figure 10.2
Underlying Factors That Contribute to Minority Overrepresentation

From previous chapters, underlying reasons for this overrepresentation of minority youths in public custody facilities should come to mind. Several are illustrated in Figure 10.2.

The percentage of minorities and males in juvenile institutions far exceeds their proportions in the general population.

Some of the imbalance of males and minorities in juvenile institutions is likely because they tend to commit more serious offenses than females and whites. Also minorities and males compile lengthier official records of delinquency than females and whites.

One project of an OJJDP and ACA partnership is a training curriculum in cultural differences for law enforcement and juvenile justice officials. The training curriculum is designed to reduce the overrepresentation of minority youths in the juvenile justice system.

Juveniles in Private Institutions

Whereas the private institutions of an earlier period were products of philanthropic or religious impulse, the newer ones result from a more pecuniary, entrepreneurial drive. From the earliest days, private institutions attracted more youths from more affluent backgrounds than did public institutions. Many of the newer private institutions have chosen to emphasize their mental health and drug treatment programs. In this way they can capitalize on young people from families who have medical insurance or who can pay the costs of their children's confinement and treatment.

In 1991 the ACA surveyed juvenile corrections agencies on their use of private sector contracts, including all 50 states and the District of Columbia. The response rate was 98 percent. All respondents indicated they had at least one private sector contract (Levinson and Taylor, 1991, p. 242). Private juvenile facilities include detention centers, shelters, reception centers, training schools, ranches, camps and halfway houses.

Compared to public correctional institutions, private correctional institutions confine more whites, more girls, more status offenders and more dependent and neglected youths. The inmates are younger, and their stay is usually much longer.

Several reasons may account for this disparity. First the population of private institutions probably includes a larger proportion of dependent and neglected children who have few family resources. For these youths the institution becomes a surrogate home placement, which may last for several years. Second, because confinement is a profit-making activity, the private institutions are reluctant to discharge youths as long as their families can pay the bills. As a final proposition, private institutions are not forced to discharge to make room for new admissions, as is often the case in the public institutions. Public institutions often consider bed space as a criterion for release.

Private institutions may offer greater diversity in programs and structures than public institutions. They also may have very strict rules. For example a private institution promoting itself as a placement option for girls describes in its brochure the following requirements:

1. No coffee, tea, magazines, TV, radios, cigarettes, newspapers will be brought in.
2. No dresses or skirts above the knee. No pants or pants suits allowed.
3. No eye shadow.
4. Only two letters are written out, and those only to relatives or guardians.
5. All bags and boxes will be inspected on entering and leaving.
6. All money sent will be kept by the Home and given as needed. No girl will be allowed to have money in her room.
7. If while at the Home any girl should run away, her bags, clothes, etc., will not be sent home—they will be the property of the Home.

8. If anyone brings pants, eye make-up, or any of the items listed as not allowed, they will be taken and destroyed.

9. No telephone calls will be made except in an emergency or of great importance.

10. Phone calls are permitted once a month from parents or guardians.

11. During June, July, and August, all phone calls will be received only between 9:30 A.M. and 4:00 P.M. Monday through Friday.

12. Calls will be limited to five minutes unless an emergency.

13. No visiting in the girl's room—all visiting must be in a reception room or one of the visiting rooms.

14. Any girl that leaves the dorm with parents must have permission from one of the staff when she leaves and report in when returning.

15. The Home will not be responsible for the girls' actions when they are with parents.

16. All medical, dental, and other personal bills will be mailed to the parent or guardian for payment.

Social Structure within Correctional Institutions

Correctional institutions—whether high or low security, locked or unlocked facilities, public or private, sexually integrated or segregated—often have an elaborate informal social organization and culture. The social organization includes a prestige hierarchy among inmates and a variety of inmate social roles. The inmate culture includes a complex of norms that indicate how inmates should relate to one another, to staff members and to the institutional regimen. As described by Brown (1983, pp. 126–127):

> The institutional setting, with its large number of aggressive boys confined in tight quarters, served to encourage fighting.
>
> Fights were a daily occurrence. Somebody was upset about something. The reason did not matter, only the result. A wrong word, a wrong look, or being at the wrong place at the wrong time could create a confrontation. There was little to be done about it; either fight or be considered a "punk."
>
> Sometimes it was possible to find another way out, but not always. Usually it came down to a winner and a loser. Fighting was more than a way to vent frustration. It was also a means of gaining status and self-respect. . . . To be considered a "bad ass" was the highest compliment and afforded the greatest respect. A "rep" meant power and power meant control over people and situations. The top-ranked boys on campus and in a cottage had the fewest hassles. Other boys usually left them alone, choosing boys of lower rank on whom to take out their frustrations. Nobody wanted to lose a fight; it was a bad reputation and rank. Nonetheless, the time inevitably came when a face-off with a boy of similar or higher rank could no longer be avoided. It was then that ranking often changed and the power that accompanied rank sometimes shifted.

The sociopolitical events in juvenile correctional institutions are the same as those found in adult institutions.

Upham, a juvenile correctional worker in Hennepin County's (Minnesota) juvenile jail, which houses the worst juvenile offenders, notes:

This is their environment, especially if they're here a long time. . . . They make a lot of contacts, they get a lot of reinforcement for their negative behavior, they tell their war stories. . . . They stop growing in a way. They don't have normal experiences. They have this siege mentality. . . . They're not working on their careers. They're already in their careers here. Their careers are being in the system. Detention for some of these kids is not so bad an option. They're safe. They get three meals a day. They get rest. They get attention. They say they don't like it, but they keep coming back" (Brandt, 1993, p. B7).

A log book listing of cases of in-house violence serious enough to be taken to court reveals another glimpse of how brutal the world of young inmates can be:

1/9—Danny attacks Jeffrey while he is watching TV, causing multiple fractures of the jaw which require a number of surgical procedures.

2/15—Jorge assaults Henry outside Evergreen Lodge with a sharpened flat metal bar with one end cut to be sharp. Henry had never had any problems with Jorge but became an enemy when he got in an argument with the head of Jorge's Southern Chicano Gang. The victim suffered lacerations on the skull and neck.

12/28—Stuart and Lee assault and injure Michael, an American Indian inmate, with an X-Acto knife, repeatedly slashing him and causing lacerations to his back, arms, thumbs, scalp and chest. Michael had allegedly made some racially derogatory remark.

Prison Gangs

Prison gangs are quite different from the street gangs described in Chapter 7. Jackson and McBride (1985, p. 55) say that prison gang members are "cold, calculating and purposeful," in contrast to street gang members, who operate "through pure emotion." Prison gangs also rely on anonymity, whereas street gangs thrive on notoriety. Street gang members are usually undisciplined and not sophisticated enough to fit into a prison gang until they have been through the entire juvenile justice system.

Prison gangs are better disciplined, more calculating and more sophisticated than street gangs. They also rely on anonymity.

According to Jackson and McBride (pp. 55–56):

The prison gang will wait until the youthful offender has progressed through the juvenile justice system—from probation camps, reform schools and finally to prison. At this point the recruit has become wise in the ways of penal institutions and has matured sufficiently to be recruited into the prison gang. In today's justice system, only the worst of a very bad lot are sentenced to state prison, and they are the types that the prison gang is seeking.

. . . A phenomenon which both youth authorities and prison officials have noticed recently is a rift between prison gangs and the street gang members, in that the latter seem to be achieving an independence from the prison gangs.

. . . Some prisons are reporting that a number of street gangs have so many members at a particular institution that they are a force in themselves.

Male/Female Compared

The world of institutionalization is not much different for females in a locked facility than for their male counterparts. Violence, role identity and establishing power are equally important for self-preservation. In the Youth Authority facility of Ventura, California, a staff member relates (Lerner, 1986, p. 41):

> Since judges are reluctant to send women to the Youth Authority except for the most serious crimes, those who do end up there are frequently in for violent offenses. The staff also consider many of them more dangerous than their male colleagues. As an example . . . a recent case of a young woman who tried to poison another female inmate by lacing her breakfast cereal with Ajax cleanser.
>
> As at other Youth Authority facilities, there is also homosexual activity at Ventura. Two young women had managed to elude the staff and bed down together for the night. Curiously, while male homosexuals are looked down upon by male inmates and seen as the bottom of the pecking order . . . among women this is reversed and the lesbians often have considerable status among their peers. Another difference between male and female society . . . is that while the male code requires that no inmate snitch on another, "the women will tell on each other in a minute."

The Impact of Incarceration

Despite the diverse ideologies and strategies pursued by correctional institutions, to a great extent they all generate an underlife that includes an informal social organization and an inmate code. While they are confined, youths are immersed in a culture that defines the institution, its staff and many of its programs in negative terms. This perspective does not lend itself to seeing the institution as benefiting the "best interests" of the youths.

Confinement that subjects inmates to assaults and threats of violence is considered cruel and unusual punishment by some states. Juveniles who are victims of assaults by other inmates may sue for violation of their right to be reasonably protected from violence in the facility.

Further if juveniles are kept in isolation (segregation) to protect them from assault, they may nevertheless suffer such sensory deprivation and psychological damage as to violate their constitutional rights. Confinement often leads to the ultimate self-destruction—suicide.

The impact of incarceration on juveniles often conflicts with the purpose of the juvenile justice system, which was created to remove children from the punitive forces of the criminal justice system. Exposing juveniles to coercive institutional conditions may jeopardize their emotional and physical well-being.

Recall that one provision of the JJDP Act was that status offenders and nonoffenders (youths who are abused or neglected) should be removed from juvenile detention and correctional facilities. It further mandated that when youths were detained in the same facilities as adults that they were to be completely segregated.

Conditions of Confinement

Conditions of Confinement: Juvenile Detention and Corrections Facilities was a study commissioned by the OJJDP in 1988. The study was "the most comprehensive nationwide research ever conducted on the juvenile detention and corrections field" (Wilson, 1994b, p. iii). The study included all 984 public and private juvenile detention centers, reception centers, training schools and ranches, camps and farms in the

United States. Excluded were youth halfway houses, shelters and group homes, police lockups, adult jails and prisons and psychiatric and drug treatment programs.

The study identified four areas with substantial deficiencies: living space, security, control of suicidal behavior and health care. Forty-seven percent of confined juveniles lived in crowded facilities (p. 7). The study also estimated that there were 18,000 incidents of suicidal behavior and 10 suicides. Further, juvenile and staff injury rates were higher in crowded facilities, and juvenile-on-juvenile violence rates were highest for juveniles housed in large dormitories.

Puritz and Scali (1998, p. xi) state: "Subjecting youth to abusive and unlawful conditions of confinement serves only to increase rates of violence and recidivism and to propel children into the adult criminal justice system. Well-documented deficiencies in living space, security, control of suicidal behavior, health care, education and treatment services, emergency preparedness, and access to legal counsel threaten not only the well-being of youth, but the community that will receive them after their release."

According to the OJJDP study, three areas in which conditions of confinement appeared adequate were (1) food, clothing and hygiene, (2) recreation and (3) living accommodations.

Improving Conditions

Puritz and Scali (p. 1) note: "A substantial body of law establishes the rights of detained and incarcerated youth and protects them from dangerous conditions and practices of confinement." In 1980 Congress enacted the Civil Rights of Institutionalized Persons Act (CRIPA) to help eradicate unlawful conditions of confinement for juveniles held in correctional facilities. Through CRIPA the Department of Justice is authorized to bring actions against state or local governments for violating the civil rights of any person institutionalized in a publicly operated facility. Puritz and Scali (p. 1) call CRIPA "an important tool in eliminating systemic violations of juveniles' statutory and constitutional rights in detention or correctional facilities."

Another way to improve confinement conditions and to protect the rights of youths in custody is to establish **ombudsman** programs. As Puritz and Scali (p. 9) explain: "Ombudsmen can monitor conditions, service delivery systems, investigate complaints, report findings, propose changes, advocate for improvements, access appropriate care, and help to expose and reduce unlawful deficiencies in juvenile detention and correctional facilities."

Parole

Parole is a planned, supervised early release from institutionalization that is authorized by the correctional facility. Parole is unlike probation in authority and concept. Probation can be granted only by the juvenile court subject to the court's stipulations. It provides the individual with freedom and continuity within the community. Parole is a release from confinement issued by the correctional facility or a board upon a recommendation by the correctional facility. Each state has its own procedures for parole, as do federal corrections.

In Minnesota the Department of Corrections parole agents supervise juveniles who have been sentenced to a correctional facility. The release of a juvenile from a correctional institution is the responsibility of a juvenile hearing officer. The juvenile hearing officer uses a scale that incorporates the severity of the offense and the delinquent history.

Following is an example of a point system that might be used to sentence juvenile offenders under a proposal prepared for the Justice Department. The higher the point score, the more severe the punishment (Shenon, 1986):

> John Doe, a troubled 13-year-old with one conviction in a burglary case, is convicted of another. Under the sentencing guidelines in his state, the sentence might be determined like this:
>
> - Under the point system, first-degree burglary is a 50-point crime.   50
> - John's previous conviction for burglary adds 20 points to the total.   +20
> - Because his previous conviction was within the last year (an indication that he may be a persistent lawbreaker), an extra 10 points are added.   +10
> - Because John is only 13, his punishment should be less severe than that for an older offender. The scores of 13-year-olds are therefore multiplied by one-half. (The score for a 17-year-old might be multiplied by 1.5, producing a larger point total and more serious punishment.)   x 0.5
>
> Total   40
>
> Under the sentencing guidelines, 40 points might correspond to a three-month sentence in a youth detention center.

Once back in the community, the youth is supervised by a parole officer, or by a probation officer who is given that responsibility. The youth is required to abide by a set of rules, which, if violated, can return the youngster to a locked or secure facility. The conditions under which a typical juvenile parole agreement is granted include obeying all federal, state and local laws and ordinances; obtaining approval before purchasing or using any motor vehicle, borrowing money, going into debt, doing any credit or installment buying, changing residence, changing employment, changing vocational or school programs or getting married; obtaining permission before leaving the state for any reason; keeping in close contact with the supervising agent; not possessing or using narcotics or other drugs except those prescribed by a physician; and not purchasing or otherwise obtaining any type of firearm or dangerous weapon.

The parole officer makes regular contacts and visits to the youth's residence, school or place of employment. One of the parole officer's objectives is to involve the family, school and community in helping the youth to rehabilitate and integrate back into the community. This is also the goal of probation officers.

Aftercare

Aftercare is the supervision of youths for a limited time after they are released from a correctional facility but while they are still under the control of the facility or the juvenile court. SHOCAP suggests the following for parole/aftercare efforts for habitual offenders (Crowe, p. 50):

> Many times the same agency handles intake, detention, probation, corrections, and after-care. After-care is a euphemism for parole which was intended to do more than guarantee good behavior on release. After-care counselors continue

the treatment process as the young person re-enters life in the community. Some strategies are:

- Provide special placements of designated habitual offenders in after-care programs that provide the maximum intensive supervision
- Share information regarding rules and case histories with school officials and police
- Adopt active community control including limited forms of house arrest
- Apply immediate sanctions for infractions of rules, including revocation where criminal offenses are committed

According to Snarr (1992, pp. 337–338):

In many jurisdictions, aftercare (parole) is an afterthought. It is the weakest link in the system and in great need of improvement. This could be done by thinking more in terms of providing continuing treatment. Many times little or no thought and planning are given to the transition when a youth is released from an institution or residential setting and faced with living back in the community.

Many juveniles being released from confinement and requiring aftercare come from dysfunctional or abusive homes and must be provided with alternative living arrangements. The types of aftercare that can help youths to transition back into the community include the following (Snarr, p. 338):

- Home visits prior to release
- Living arrangement prepared for the youth upon release
- A continuation of the treatment program and services within the community
- Identification of community support systems to include the family and social worker
- Availability of 24-hour supervision
- A contract to achieve specific goals
- A gradual phasing-out of services and supervision based on the youth's response, not on a predetermined schedule

The OJJDP funded a project to look at the aftercare needs of high-risk youths, which resulted in the project called Intensive Community-Based Aftercare Programs. The goal was to reduce recidivism rates. As a first step to identify high-risk recidivists, the project developed a framework based on five principles (Altschuler and Armstrong, 1990, p. 170):

- Preparing youths for gradually increased responsibility and freedom in the community
- Helping youths to become involved in the community and getting the community to interact with them
- Working with youths and their families, peers, schools and employers to identify the qualities necessary for success
- Developing new resources and supports where needed
- Monitoring and testing youths and the community on their abilities to interact

An Example of Effective Aftercare

The Allegheny Academy, Pennsylvania, was designed for repeat juvenile offenders who failed in traditional probation programs but were not in need of, or likely to be helped by, institutionalization. Costanzo (1990, pp. 114–116) describes how the program is run. Students are referred to the academy by the judge or by their probation officer. The academy is open daily and has a fleet of 15 passenger vans to provide safe, round-trip transportation for the juveniles. They come to the academy after school and leave between 8:00 P.M. and 9:00 P.M., with a 10:30 P.M. curfew. On the weekend most arrive around noon. The students sleep at home and, with good behavior, can sometimes spend entire weekends at home. While at the academy, students study traditional school subjects, learn trades and receive counseling. A sports program is also available.

Importance of Juvenile Corrections Partnerships

Juvenile corrections does not operate in a vacuum. Cooperation and partnerships with other elements of the justice system are necessary for corrections to achieve full effectiveness. Chunn (1994, p. 8) comments on the complexities and idiosyncrasies involved: "It is the nature of juvenile justice to be part social work, part custody, part education and part rehabilitation." All four of these roles fall within the realm of correctional responsibility, yet the diversity of correctional programs, approaches and philosophies that exists between and within the states, and the lack of communication and partnering that occurs, often works against correctional efforts. For example:

> In the United States, juvenile detention is the purview of the court in some states but not in others. Some states have no training schools but operate camps and ranches instead. Some systems prohibit treatment services while juveniles are in detention; others require it. Some states have a close working relationship with their Office of Juvenile Justice and Delinquency Prevention Program's state advisory group, but others are barely on speaking terms. Some agencies are part of the Department of Corrections; others are in the Department of Human Resources. Such diversity inhibits progress for the juvenile justice system as a whole (Chunn, p. 8).

The OJJDP has committed to partnering with juvenile corrections systems for three important reasons: (1) improving the juvenile justice system is a major purpose of the JJDP Act, (2) the study *Conditions of Confinement* shows the need for improvement and (3) the increase in juvenile violence must be addressed. At the center of the OJJDP commitment is its Comprehensive Strategy for Serious, Violent and Chronic Juvenile Offenders. The acting administrator of the OJJDP, John Wilson (1994a, p. 223), listed the following 10 goals for improvement:

- The cost of juvenile corrections must be reduced.
- Conditions of confinement must be improved.
- Detention facility and training school populations must be decreased to their designed capacity.
- Identification of treatment needs must be improved.
- A continuum of program options must be established and made available to meet the needs of each juvenile in the system.

- Inequality in the administration of juvenile justice must be eliminated.
- Disproportionate representation of minorities in secure confinement in the juvenile justice system must be erased.
- Ensuring due process and quality legal representation for juveniles must be addressed.
- Delinquency prevention must be a community priority.
- Effective aftercare programs must be developed.
- The use of alternatives to incarceration for nonviolent accused and adjudicated offenders must be increased.

Summary

Although the U.S. Supreme Court has never definitively ruled on whether there is a constitutionally based right to treatment, the state does violate the individual's constitutional rights if it fails to confine and provide treatment in the least restrictive setting possible. What this treatment consists of is a subject of controversy. The conservative philosophy of juvenile justice is to "get tough on juveniles"—to punish and imprison them. The liberal philosophy of juvenile justice stresses treatment and rehabilitation, including community-based programs.

John Augustus was the first probation officer, and today probation is the most common disposition of the juvenile court. Supervision is the essence of probation, and the formal goal of probation is to improve the delinquent's behavior—in short, rehabilitation. Other common goals of probation are (1) to protect the community from delinquency, (2) to impose accountability for offenses committed and (3) to equip juvenile offenders with the abilities they need to live productively and responsibly in the community.

The probation officer has traditionally been responsible for two key functions: (1) personally counseling youths who are on probation and (2) serving as a link to other community services. Excessive caseloads are probably the single greatest pressure on probation officers.

Isolating offenders from their normal social environments may encourage the development of a delinquent orientation and, thus, further delinquent behavior. Community-based corrections, therefore, should be considered seriously for juvenile offenders.

Nonresidential corrections programs include community supervision, family crisis counseling, proctor programs, and service-oriented programs, including recreational programs, counseling, alternative schools, employment training programs and homemaking and financial planning classes.

The five major categories of residential programs are shelters, group homes, foster homes, foster group homes and other types of nonsecure facilities. The National Advisory Committee for Juvenile Justice and Delinquency Prevention recommended foster homes for neglected juveniles and those charged with status offenses.

Three common forms of intermediate sanctions are intensive supervision, electronic monitoring and boot camps.

Formally only three purposes justify putting juveniles in a locked facility: (1) to secure their presence at court proceedings, (2) to hold those who cannot be sent home and (3) to prevent juveniles from harming themselves or others, or from disrupting juvenile court processes.

The percentages of minorities and males in juvenile institutions far exceed their proportions in the general population. Compared to public correctional institutions, private correctional institutions confine more whites, more girls, more status offenders, and more dependent and neglected youths. The inmates are younger and their stay is usually much longer.

The sociopolitical events that occur in correctional institutions for youths are the same as those found in adult institutions. Prison gangs are better disciplined, more calculating and more sophisticated than street gangs. They also rely on anonymity.

Discussion Questions

1. How effective is probation in juvenile justice? What, if any, changes should be made in the juvenile probation process?
2. Should a juvenile have close supervision while on probation? If not, describe how you would supervise a youth who had committed a violent crime and was placed on probation, or one who was a status offender.
3. Should parents, custodians or guardians of youths be actively involved in a youth's probation? Why or why not?
4. Do you favor a system of state or local probation? What does your state have?
5. Is community corrections worthwhile? Does it work? What would you do to improve it?
6. Is there a difference in attitude between a youth who has been confined and one who has been directed by programs in community corrections? What makes the difference?
7. Do community corrections give judges more options in sentencing youths? Is this an advantage or disadvantage?
8. Should violent offenders be subject to community corrections or directed to a secure facility? Why?
9. What are some potential alternatives to secure detention? What problems may be involved in expanding alternative programs?
10. Do you support a conservative or a liberal approach to treating juveniles? Why? Why do you think our society is now inclined to a "get tough on juveniles" attitude?

References

Altschuler, David M. and Armstrong, Troy L. "Designing an Intensive Aftercare Program for High-Risk Juveniles." *Corrections Today,* December 1990, pp. 170–171.

Austin, James; Jones, Michael; and Bolyard, Melissa. "The Growing Use of Jail Boot Camps: The Current State of the Art." NIJ, Research in Brief, October 1993.

Backstrom, James C. "Housing Juveniles in Adult Facilities: A Common-Sense Approach." *Point/Counterpoint: Correctional Issues.* Lanham, MD: American Correctional Association, 1998, p. 14.

Bowen, Andy. "In Georgia: Making Boot Camps Bigger and Better." *Corrections Today,* October 1991, pp. 98–101.

Brandt, Steve. "The In Crowd: Hennepin County's Jail for Juveniles Is Jammed." (Minneapolis/St. Paul) *Star Tribune,* April 11, 1993, pp. B1, B7.

Brown, W. K. *The Other Side of Delinquency.* New Brunswick, NJ: Rutgers University Press, 1983.

Butts, Jeffrey A. and Snyder, Howard N. "Restitution and Juvenile Recidivism." OJJDP, Update on Research, September 1992.

Carlson, Norman A.; Hess, Kären M.; and Orthmann, Christine M. H. *Corrections in the 21st Century: A Practical Approach.* Belmont, CA: West/Wadsworth Publishing Company, 1999.

Chunn, Gwendolyn C. "Setting the Course for the Future." *Corrections Today,* December 1994, p. 8.

Costanzo, Samuel A. "In Pennsylvania: Juvenile Academy Serves as Facility Without Walls." *Corrections Today,* December 1990, pp. 112–117.

Crogan, Alan M. "Probation's Role in Juvenile Rehabilitation." *Law Enforcement Quarterly,* November 1996–January 1997, pp. 17–18.

Crowe, Timothy D. *Habitual Offenders: Guidelines for Citizen Action and Public Response.* Serious Habitual Offender Comprehensive Action Program (SHOCAP). Washington, DC: Office of Juvenile Justice and Delinquency Prevention, October 1991.

Dedel, Kelly. "National Profile of the Organization of State Juvenile Corrections Systems." *Crime and Delinquency,* Vol. 44, No. 4, October 1998, pp. 507–525.

deFiebre, Conrad. "Hard Times, Happy Endings: 'Boot Camp' Inmates Give Their Best for Early Release." (Minneapolis/St. Paul) *Star Tribune,* April 26, 1993, pp. A1, A11.

Donahue, Terrence S. "Privatizing Juvenile Probation Services: Five Local Experiences." OJJDP, Update on Programs, November/December 1989.

Electronic Monitoring in Intensive Probation and Parole Programs. Washington, DC: Bureau of Justice Assistance, February 1989.

Finckenaur, James O. *Juvenile Delinquency and Corrections: The Gap Between Theory and Practice.* Orlando: Academic Press, 1984, p. 132.

Frank, Sue. "Oklahoma Camp Stresses Structure and Discipline." *Corrections Today,* October 1991, pp. 102–105.

Gilliard, Darrell K. and Beck, Allen J. *Prison and Jail Inmates at Midyear 1997.* Bureau of Justice Statistics Bulletin. January 1998. (NCJ-167247)

Glick, Barry. "Kids in Adult Correctional Systems." *Corrections Today,* August 1998, pp. 96–99.

Harlow, Caroline Wolf. *Profile of Jail Inmates 1996.* Bureau of Justice Statistics Special Report. April 1998, (NCJ-164620)

Hengesh, Donald J. "Think of Boot Camps as a Foundation for Change, Not an Instant Cure." *Corrections Today,* October 1991, pp. 106–108.

Hollander, Harriet. *Relationship of Characteristics of Incarcerated Juveniles to Issues of Program Development and Staff Training: A Psycho-Education Model.* A Report Prepared by the Project on Psycho-Education and Juvenile Delinquency, College of Medicine and Dentistry of New Jersey, Community Health Center. Piscataway, NJ: Rutgers Medical School, March 1981.

Hurst, Hunter. "Juvenile Probation in Retrospect." *Perspectives,* Winter 1990, pp. 16–19.

Jackson, Robert K. and McBride, Wesley D. *Understanding Street Gangs.* Sacramento, CA: Custom Publishing, 1985.

Juvenile Probation Officer Initiative (JPOI) Working Group. *Desktop Guide to Good Juvenile Probation Practice.* Washington, DC: Office of Juvenile Justice and Delinquency Prevention, May 1993.

Kaczor, Bill. "Juvenile Boot Camps Show High Rearrest Rates." (Ft. Lauderdale) *Sun-Sentinel,* June 22, 1997, p. 6B.

Lerner, Steve. *The California Youth Authority, Part Two: Bodily Harm.* Bolinas, CA: Common Knowledge Press, 1986.

Levinson, Robert B. and Taylor, William J. "ACA Studies Privatization in Juvenile Corrections." *Corrections Today,* August 1991, pp. 242, 248.

MacKenzie, Doris Layton. "Boot Camp Prisons in 1993." *National Institute of Justice Journal,* November 1993, pp. 21–28.

Madruga, Robert E. "The Goal is Rehabilitation." *Law Enforcement Quarterly,* November 1996–January 1997, pp. 15–16, 24, 38.

McCarthy, Belinda Rodgers and McCarthy, Bernard J., Jr. *Community-Based Corrections,* 3rd ed. Belmont, CA: Wadsworth Publishing Company, 1997.

Mitchell, David B. "Congress Needs to Consult Profession Before Enacting Juvenile Justice Reform." *Corrections Today,* October 1998, pp. 20–24.

National Advisory Committee for Juvenile Justice and Delinquency Prevention. *Standards for the Administration of Justice.* Washington, DC: U.S. Government Printing Office, July 1980, pp. 431–447.

Ohlin, Lloyd E. "The Future of Juvenile Justice Policy and Research." *Crime and Delinquency,* Vol. 44, No. 1, January 1998, pp. 143–153.

Parent, Dale G. "Boot Camps Failing to Achieve Goals." *Overcrowded Times,* August 1994, pp. 8–11.

Peters, Michael; Thomas, David; and Zamberlan, Christopher. *Boot Camps for Juvenile Offenders.* Office of Juvenile Justice Delinquency Prevention Program Summary. September 1997. (NCJ-164258)

Previte, Mary Taylor. "Preventing Security Crises at Youth Centers." *Corrections Today,* February 1997, pp. 76–79.

Puritz, Patricia and Scali, Mary Ann. *Beyond the Walls: Improving Conditions of Confinement for Youth in Custody.* Washington, DC: Office of Juvenile Justice and Delinquency Prevention, January 1998. (NCJ-164727)

Roush, David W. and Dunlap, Earl L. "Juveniles in Adult Prisons: A Very Bad Idea." *Point/Counterpoint: Correctional Issues.* Lanham, MD: American Correctional Association, 1998, p. 15

Scalia, John. *Juvenile Delinquents in the Federal Criminal Justice System.* Bureau of Justice Statistic Special Report. January 1997. (NCJ-163066)

Shenon, Philip. "Federal Study on Youth Urges Fixed Sentences." *New York Times,* August 29, 1986.

Smith, J. Steven. "A Lesson from Indiana: Detention Is an Invaluable Part of the System, But It's Not the Solution to All Youths' Problems." *Corrections Today,* February 1991, pp. 56–60.

Snarr, Richard W. *Introduction to Corrections,* 2nd ed. Dubuque, IA: Wm. C. Brown, 1992.

Sutherland, Edwin H. and Cressey, Donald R. *Principles of Criminology,* 7th ed. Philadelphia: J. B. Lippincott, 1966.

Taylor, William J. "Tailoring Boot Camps to Juveniles." *Corrections Today,* July 1992, pp. 122–124.

Thomas, Douglas W. "The Juvenile Probation Officer Initiative: Making a Tough Job a Little Easier." *Corrections Today,* February 1991, pp. 62–65.

Waldron, Thomas W. "Boot Camp Prison Offers Second Chance to Young Felons." *Corrections Today,* July 1990, pp. 144–169.

Wilson, John J. "Developing a Partnership with Juvenile Corrections." *Corrections Today,* April 1994a, pp. 74, 223–224.

Wilson, John J. Foreword. In Dale G. Parent, et al. *Conditions of Confinement: Juvenile Detention and Corrections Facilities: Research Summary.* Washington, DC: Office of Juvenile Justice and Delinquency Prevention, February 1994b, p. iii.

Ziedenberg, Jason and Schiraldi, Vincent. "The Risks Juveniles Face: Housing Juveniles in Adult Institutions Is Self-Destructive and Self-Defeating." *Corrections Today,* August 1998, pp. 22–28.

Cases

Santana v. Collazo, 714 F.2d 1172, 1177 (1st Cir. 1983).

Shelton v. Tucker, 364 U.S. 479, 488, 81 S.Ct. 247, 252, 5 L.Ed.2d 231 (1960).

11

The Role of the
Broader Community

Violence and crime have grown to an
intolerable level that detrimentally impacts
the lives of all citizens. This condition will
continue unless, and until, all segments of our
society assume their responsibilities and
respond in a coordinated fashion.

—IACP Summit on Violent Crime, 1993

Do You Know

- How to define community?
- What the broken-window phenomenon refers to?
- What community policing is?
- How social work has influenced juvenile justice policy?
- What parts of the juvenile justice system social work is involved in?
- What the current emphasis in social services for youths is?
- What type of intervention appears to hold the greatest promise?
- What basic skills should be taught in the schools in addition to reading, writing and math?
- What benefits are derived from using volunteers in community-based corrections?
- Why jobs are important to youths?

Can You Define

broken-window phenomenon, community, community policing, integrated community

INTRODUCTION

The importance of the family and the schools in the development of our youths was stressed in the second section of this book. The importance of the community in the form of community corrections was described in Chapter 10. Unfortunately for today's youth, many parents are too stressed, many schools are too impersonal and many communities are too disorganized to fulfill the basic need of children to belong. When children are estranged from family, friends, school and productive work, the seeds of discouragement and alienation are sown. The result, all too often, is antisocial behavior. Alienated youths often become angry, antisocial offenders.

The Office of Juvenile Justice and Delinquency Prevention *OJJDP Annual Report 1990* notes in its Foreword (p. v): "The answers to our problems [of delinquency] will not be found in Washington alone. If Pennsylvania Avenue and Capitol Hill are not joined by Main Street, U.S.A., the road ahead will be a dead end. But working together, we shall continue to take steps in the right direction." Criminologists Miller and Ohlin (1985) concur:

> Delinquency is a community problem. In the final analysis the means for its prevention and control must be built into the fabric of community life. This can only happen if the community accepts its share of responsibility for having generated and perpetuated paths of socialization that lead to sporadic criminal episodes for some youth and careers in crime for others.

This chapter focuses on the broader community and the role it plays in the juvenile justice system. It begins with defining *community* and looking at perceptions of the community and how they can be positive or negative influences on those growing up. Next you will examine the current trend toward a justice system that seeks to align itself more closely with the community. The most common evidence of this trend is the implementation of community policing in departments across the country.

This discussion is followed by an in-depth look at the role of social workers and social services. Just as probation officers were officers of the court as well as practitioners in corrections, so social workers may be an integral part of every aspect of the juvenile justice system, while at the same time being a part of the broader community.

Next you will consider the role of the schools, especially as it relates to dealing with the problems of violence and gangs. The chapter concludes with a discussion of how citizens, civic organizations and the community as a whole can contribute to solving the problems of crime and violence associated with our youths.

Community Defined

Community can have several meanings. It can refer to a specific geographic area, such as a small town or a suburb. It can be thought of as a group of people with common interests, such as a community of worshippers in a congregation. In the legal sense, it refers to the area over which the police and the courts have jurisdiction.

In a more philosophical sense, according to Manning (1991, p. 33): "Community represents a sense of integration that people wish, hope, and

Youths from Detroit and the city's Grosse Pointe suburbs work together to paint a mural on the wall of a building on the dividing line between their communities. The Detroit side of the border—economically devastated, mostly African-American—contrasts sharply to the Grosse Pointe side, which is wealthy and mostly white.

envision as being a central part of their collective lives." In such an **integrated community** they feel ownership and take pride in what is right, responsibility for what is wrong. They also share values and agree on what is acceptable and unacceptable behavior, and they expect conformity to those values. Without such integration, the justice system is greatly hindered, as noted by Mastrofski (1991, p. 49):

> A basis for police action requires that a group of people—say a neighborhood—shares a definition of what constitutes right order, threats to it, and appropriate methods for maintaining it. To the extent that community implies a basis for citizens to work collectively with police to restore and preserve order, it also requires a sense of group identity or attachment—a "we-ness" derived from shared experience and integration.

Klockars (1991, pp. 247–248) suggests a sociological definition of community: "Sociologically, the concept of community implies a group of people with a common history, common beliefs, and understandings, a sense of themselves as 'us' and outsiders as 'them' and often, but not always, a shared territory."

In this chapter **community** will be used in both the legal, geographic sense and the philosophical, sociological sense.

Community is not only the geographic area over which the justice system has jurisdiction; it also refers to a sense of integration, of shared values, and a sense of "we-ness."

Perceptions of Community

Children are very aware of their communities and how they feel about them. In an article describing what some Minnesota children think of their communities, Monaghan (1994, p. E1) states that the essays the children wrote on their neighborhoods and the community "are emphatically positive. What's needed, a majority say, is more of the same." Among the essays included in the article is the following:

Age 14, grade 8, St. James (a small town): The close bond between the people of my community is very special. We are a small community which keeps the relationships between people very close. We're like one giant family, working together to get things accomplished and enjoying together the things we have already accomplished.

The positive outward appearance of the community is important to this child, as are the friendliness and caring of the people in the neighborhood. Unfortunately, not all communities generate such positive feelings. In a classic article, "Broken Windows," Wilson and Kelling (1982, p. 31) describe how a run-down neighborhood can promote crime:

Social psychologists and police officers tend to agree that if a window in a building is broken *and is left unrepaired,* all the rest of the windows will soon be broken. This is as true in nice neighborhoods as in run-down ones. Window-breaking does not necessarily occur on a large scale because some areas are inhabited by determined window-breakers whereas others are populated by window-lovers; rather, one unrepaired broken window is a signal that no one cares, and so breaking more windows costs nothing. (It has always been fun.)

The **broken-window phenomenon** states that if it appears "no one cares," disorder and crime will thrive.

The article on Minnesota children's attitudes is not all positive, as Monaghan notes (p. E1):

Behind their applause and celebration, a thundering negative rumbles.
  It is crime.
  It hangs over the more than 7,000 student essays like an angry, darkening cloud. . . .
  Fear of gangs, rape, murder, kidnapping and shooting comes through clearly in essays from the country, the suburbs and the Twin Cities. For the city kids in the high-crime areas, though, the thunder about crime is the loudest and most frightening.

Monaghan shares part of an essay written by a 10-year-old Asian student from one of St. Paul's poorest areas: "The best thing about my neighborhood is that my school is near my house so if I get robbed on my way home I could just scream and my mom would hear me and come out."

The problems in our communities are enumerated by Inkster (1992, p. 28): "People of different races, cultures and languages are coming into closer contact with each other and enormous demands are being made on their understanding and tolerance . . . There are widening class divisions, more broken families and homelessness, growing anger on the part of the disadvantaged, and a rise in violent crime." This does not imply, however, that communities must simply accept crime and violence. Some youths can see the crime and violence but are able to make a positive from it—what was referred to as *resilience* earlier (Monaghan, p. E2). They see the community pulling together.

It is this sense of community values and the power of the community that has resulted in the awareness that the justice system cannot function alone, that it needs the support and *assistance* of the broader community.

The Community and the Juvenile Justice System

Chapter 4 described the influence of the community on youths' development. The community also plays a vital role in the juvenile justice system, helping to prevent crime and violence and to help rehabilitate youths involved in crime and violence. Bownes and Ingersoll (1997, p. 1) state:

> Effective reduction of youth violence and victimization requires a balance of strong policing, holding youth accountable for their behavior, and targeted prevention through community action. . . . Through Title V incentive grants for Local Delinquency Prevention Programs (Community Prevention Grants), OJJDP allocated $20 million in fiscal year 1997 to States to complement law enforcement and justice system efforts by helping local communities foster strong families and nurture law-abiding and healthy children.

Many other federally funded programs exist to help youths, as summarized in Appendix C.

Helping Communities Fight Crime (1997) stresses: "Crime prevention is community-based. It requires partnerships on the local level among mayors, police and prosecutors, probation officers, business leaders, social service and job training personnel, health care providers, religious leaders, community activists, housing officials, parents, teachers, mentors and youth."

Chaiken (1998, p. 43) asserts: "Partnerships that include a spectrum of community institutions and organizations promote comprehensiveness of services that endure over the long term." Furthermore: "The most comprehensive partnerships can have major payoffs, as shown in Spokane, where they have led to neighborhood revitalization and the development of youth as active community participants and leaders. The ultimate result should be a reduction in crime, as has already happened in Spokane's West Central neighborhood."

Ellis (1998, p. 102) stresses: "What seems clear is that there are effective strategies for combating juvenile delinquency. One person's vision can make a difference, but it truly does take a village to raise a child." Whether it is called a village, a neighborhood or a community, the trend is for the juvenile justice system to seek the support and assistance of the broader community. One way in which this is being done is through community policing.

Community Policing

Mastrofski et al. (1998, p. 1) state: "Community policing—a relatively recent addition to law enforcement—aims to increase interaction and cooperation between local police and the people and neighborhoods they serve. Its goals are to reduce and prevent crime and to increase feelings of safety among residents." *Helping Communities Fight Crime* (p. 30) provides the following description:

> Community policing is a philosophy that promotes community, government and police partnerships; proactive problem solving; and community engagement to address the causes of crime, fear of crime and other community issues. Both core components—community partnership and problem solving—suggest reevaluation of many aspects of how police organizations routinely operate. Community policing brings together police, government and community—those most interested in addressing crime and disorder problems—into a cooperative venture.

Joseph E. Brann, Director of the Office of Community Oriented Policing Services, states: "Community policing helps law enforcement get to the heart of preventing crime. This successful approach focuses attention right where it should be—on partnerships with the community, problem solving and prevention. We are now beginning to see its benefits as crime goes down and quality of life goes up" (*Helping Communities,* p. 18). Commander Michael J. Nila of the Aurora, Illinois, Police Department asserts:

> Through community policing we are reawakening the sense of responsibility in the community. They no longer think that their responsibility ends with picking up the phone and calling the police. In neighborhoods where community policing has taken hold, there is a real sense of community. We are seeing neighborhoods which are truly neighborhoods, and citizens becoming caretakers. They are living up to their responsibilities (Strandberg, 1997, p. 46).

Community policing takes many forms across the country. As noted by Miller and Hess (1998, p. xxii):

> Community policing offers one avenue for making neighborhoods safer. Community policing is not a program or a series of programs. It is a philosophy, a belief that working together, the police and the community can accomplish what neither can accomplish alone. The *synergy* that results from community policing can be powerful. It is like the power of a finely tuned athletic team, with each member contributing to the total effort. Occasionally heroes may emerge, but victory depends on a team effort.

Wilson and Kelling (1989, p. 49) describe the types of changes that occur in a police department that institutes community policing:

> Community-oriented policing means changing the daily work of the police to include investigating problems as well as incidents. It means defining as a problem whatever a significant body of public opinion regards as a threat to community order. It means working with the good guys and not just against the bad guys.

In other words community policing is proactive rather than reactive, and it is problem driven rather than incident driven. According to Swope (1998, p. 112): "Community policing has been defined as a philosophical characterization of a nontraditional approach to policing. It requires police to recognize differences in communities, provides customized services and necessitates the forming of partnerships and collaborating with other agencies in problem solving."

Community policing is a philosophy that embraces a proactive, problem-oriented approach to working with the community to make it safe.

Breci and Erickson (1998, p. 16) report that a Department of Justice survey of police departments in areas with populations exceeding 50,000 found that more than 50 percent of the agencies reporting have already implemented community policing, and another 20 percent plan to do so.

Although community policing makes sense to many within the justice system, it is sometimes difficult for administrators to change. As noted by Wilson and Kelling (1989, p. 49): "While the phrase 'community-oriented policing' comes easily to the lips of police administration, redefining the police mission is more difficult. To help the police become accustomed to fixing broken windows as well as arresting window breakers requires doing things that are very hard for many administrators to do."

Wilson and Kelling (1989, p. 52) note that implementing community policing may also cause dissention within the ranks. Officers with opposing views of the nature of police work face off, in what has been described as the conflict between the crime fighter function and the social service function: "In every department we visited, some of the incident-oriented officers spoke disparagingly of the problem-oriented officers as 'social workers,' and some of the latter responded by calling the former 'ghetto blasters'."

Yet another obstacle facing community policing, according to Wilson and Kelling (1989, p. 52), is lack of interagency cooperation:

> The problem of interagency cooperation may, in the long run, be the most difficult of all. The police can bring problems to the attention of other city agencies, but the system is not always organized to respond. In his book *Neighborhood Services,* John Mudd calls it the "rat problem": If a rat is found in an apartment, it is a housing inspection responsibility; if it runs into a restaurant, the health department has jurisdiction; if it goes outside and dies in an alley, public works takes over.

This lack of interagency cooperation is also stressed by Krisberg and Austin (1993, pp. 184–185): "The current organization of adolescent social and health services is characterized by rigidly drawn agency turfs and budgetary categories. This situation contributes to fragmented and often wasteful deployment of scarce public resources."

Among the most important "public resources" are social workers.

The Role of Social Workers and Social Services

Social workers are involved in community supervision programs for troubled youths and their families, in juvenile court-sponsored, community-based diversion programs and in school-based counseling programs. These programs are designed to help youths in conflict with their families as well as youths in conflict with the law.

The public interest in preventing delinquency and controlling youths and the interest in youth crime and rehabilitating youthful offenders are topics constantly discussed in communities and state legislatures across the country. Referral programs range from diversionary actions to socially designed programs in the "best interest of the child" and the best interest of the public safety.

Referring youths to adjustment and corrective programs under the guise of treatment is an issue of growing concern due to the increased demands for public and private services and the limited available resources. As a result legislators, policy makers and juvenile justice professionals are taking a hard look at the social services available and how they are being invested in youth referral programs. They are also asking if better ways exist to serve youths and to protect the public.

There is great interest in assessing and treating youths with emotional and behavioral problems. Many families experience child management problems at one time or another: incorrigibility, defiance, waywardness, temper tantrums, school disruptiveness, truancy and related problems. And many children experience neglect and abuse which, as already discussed, are often the prelude to delinquency.

Treatment philosophies are regularly debated. Many feel that the juvenile courts are too lenient. They advocate a "get tough" attitude, emphasizing responsibility of actions and a system of accountability rather than the rehabilitation and treatment that is the hallmark of most existing state codes.

The public is also concerned about the inability of social services to properly investigate and treat cases of child physical and sexual abuse.

Social workers have greatly influenced trends in juvenile justice policy in the areas of diversion, victim restitution, the decriminalization of status offenders and deinstitutionalization.

Social workers are among the few involved in the juvenile justice system who are willing to disregard the jargon of *treatment, control* or *punishment.* They work with both adjudicated and nonadjudicated juveniles, trying to find the best way to prevent the recurrence of mischievous or antisocial behavior. By teaming up with law enforcement and the courts, social workers can operate in all areas of juvenile justice. As a result innovative new programs and relationships have been developed, enhancing social work's role in the justice system and extending the reach of social justice, especially to minority and low-income youths.

Social work functions in all aspects of the juvenile justice system.

Usually a combination of approaches is most effective. Social work can provide a range of services that may include, but by no means be limited to, direct counseling with the juvenile. The broader role of social work within the context of juvenile facilities may include advocacy and brokerage on behalf of juveniles in their relations with family members, social agencies, school officials and potential employers. Social work tries by a variety of means to ease juveniles' passage through the most difficult stage of life and to prevent institutionalized youths from becoming brutal, embittered adults.

Needy, Neglected or Abused Children

Social work also addresses the needs of nondelinquent children and families. Since the passage of the Social Security Act in 1935, the federal government has supported many services for children and families, from programs commonly called "welfare" to foster care maintenance and a range of adoption services.

In 1961 Congress amended part of the Social Security Act to provide states with substantial federal reimbursement for the cost of providing foster care to poor children. State child welfare departments, in association with the court, assigned more and more children to foster care and group homes.

In 1975 parents and advocates pressed Congress to adopt the Education for All Handicapped Children Act, which grants all children the right to free and appropriate education in the least restrictive environment possible. This law discouraged removing handicapped children from public schools, and offered fiscal incentives to states in exchange for meeting federal standards.

In 1978 Congress passed the Indian Child Welfare Act, giving tribes greater control over the adoption and foster placement of their children and encouraging alternatives to placement by providing limited funds for services to Native American children and families.

After five years of testimony on foster care and adoption, in 1980 Congress passed the Adoption Assistance and Child Welfare Act, an important achievement for families at risk of extended or permanent separation. The act requires that reasonable efforts be made to bring children who have been taken from their families for over 12 months back to the juvenile court. The court then reviews each case and makes a disposition for the best interests of the children and their families. Thus children are no longer placed in limbo with no further review. The purpose of the act is to assure that children and their families no longer suffer extended separation from each other without at least an annual review.

Current Emphasis

The federal emphasis on diverting status and minor offenders from the juvenile justice system stimulated the development of services for delinquent and troubled youths. This philosophy emphasized the importance of a wide range of activities and programs, commonly referred to as community-based services.

The current emphasis in social services for youths is diversion to a wide range of community-based services and programs.

These services include residential treatment centers, youth service bureaus, group or foster homes, halfway houses and adolescent units in psychiatric hospitals. These facilities vary in such important considerations as the degree of security provided, whether they are residential or nonresidential, the extent and nature of treatment provided and size.

Studies suggest that family therapy is more effective in dealing with the problems of youths than is traditional juvenile justice intervention.

Social workers often use behavioral and structural techniques in intrafamilial communication. This positive attention paid to the child is generally more effective than probation.

Stern (1991) describes a Family Trouble Center in Memphis, Tennessee, that provides counseling and assistance for children who have been abused and for their abusers. The center offers anger management groups as well as support counseling for victims. It provides mediation through contracts and referral services to other agencies for protective shelter. In addition it provides alcohol and drug counseling and community outreach and education. One of its greatest strengths as a new resource, according to Stern (p. 73), "lies significantly in networking with existing agencies."

Another social service center is described by Snow (1992). This is the Child Advocacy Center in Marion County, Indiana. This center also serves as an advocate for abused children. Like the Family Trouble Center in Memphis, this center uses a multiagency approach. To make such an approach work those operating the Marion County Child Advocacy Center offer the following suggestions (Snow, p. 287):

- There should not be a "Director." Instead, consider having a "Coordinator." Workers often resist taking orders from a member of another agency.
- Agencies involved must keep their work force stable. Workers must get to know one another if they are to develop relationships of coordination and cooperation.
- Agencies must enter into the new relationship with open minds. Police, for example, often think of welfare workers as being "bleeding hearts," and of prosecutors as being unresponsive to police needs. To put such feelings aside takes strong leadership in each agency.
- Ensure that agencies don't attempt to take over each other's responsibilities once they learn each other's roles.

Another approach to providing services to youths that was proposed by the Clinton administration is a National Youth Service. This service would provide up to $10,000 to pay for college for young people who work a certain number of hours in their communities. Smith (1993, p. 13) poses this question: "Assume that Congress, in concert with the President, enacted a National Youth Service Program that, on the basis of freely selected work in public service, would entitle youth—all youth and not just special or disadvantaged youth—to various benefits." Among the benefits might be college scholarships, cash or a "myriad of other desirable rewards."

For social services the Serious Habitual Offender Comprehensive Action Program (SHOCAP) suggests the following action steps in dealing with habitual offenders (Crowe, 1991, pp. 47–48):

> Social Services . . . agencies will range from public to private, with sometimes erratic funding services. Occasionally, family and mental health services are combined with probation and parole agencies. Some actions are:
>
> - Identify or establish special service and placement opportunities for drug, alcohol, or behaviorally troubled habitual offenders;
> - Share case history or diagnostic information with appropriate officials and participate on case management teams formed to assist in the community control of habituals;
> - Request police patrol and crime analysis follow up on neglect, abuse, and other problem case areas;
> - Provide case support for obtaining civil commitments on troubled, problem, or delinquent youth who are designated as habituals.

The Role of the Schools

The role of the schools was first discussed in Chapter 4. Kirst (1991, p. 615) notes some of the risks facing children in schools in the 1990s:

> Johnny can't read because he needs glasses and breakfast and encouragement from his absent father; Maria doesn't pay attention in class because she can't understand English very well and she's worried about her mother's drinking and she's tired from trying to sleep in the car.

Other students are worried about their physical safety. "You can't be concerned with the issues of learning if you have to worry about your hide." Recall the worrisome statistics given in Chapter 4 regarding violence in the schools.

Kaufman et al. (1998) report that between 1989 and 1995, the percentage of students ages 12 through 19 who avoided one or more places at school for fear of their own safety increased, from 5 to 9 percent (p. viii). In 1996 students ages 12 through 18 were victims of about 255,000 incidents of nonfatal serious violent crime at school. Five percent of all 12th graders reported they had been injured with a weapon such as a knife, gun or club during the past 12 months while they were in school (p. vi). At the middle and high school levels, physical attack or fight without a weapon was the most commonly reported crime. In addition, over the five-year period from 1992–1996, teachers were victims of 1,581,000 nonfatal crimes at school including 619,000 violent crimes (rape or sexual assault, robbery, and aggravated and simple assault)(p. vii).

According to Kipper (1996, p. 26): "To address the rising problem of school-related violence, law enforcement officials must bring the community together on several basic issues. First, there must be understanding that school crime and violence are community issues—not just school problems. . . . The second issue that must be faced by both law enforcement and school officials is the concept that the school is the community and the community is the school."

The traditional subjects taught in our schools have been expanded by including interpersonal skills in mediation and conflict resolution. Recall that this was one of the recommendations made by Attorney General Janet Reno (Wilson, 1993, p. 3): "I support conflict resolution programs in our public schools to teach our children how to resolve conflicts peacefully." Hamburger (1993, p. A11) writes that Reno received the heartiest applause at a day-long conference on violence as she called for controlling guns in the hands of our youths:

> We've got to let young people know that there is no excuse for putting a gun up beside somebody's head and hurting them—not poverty, not broken homes, not any of the circumstances that people sometimes ascribe as causes of these crimes. . . .
>
> There are 2 million guns out there now and they're going to be in the hands of children, and we've got to teach children right now that you don't solve problems with guns and fists and knives. And teachers are leading the way.

Important basic skills that schools now teach are conflict resolution and mediation.

LeBoeuf and Delany-Shabazz (1997, p. 1) advocate: "By teaching young people how to manage conflict, conflict resolution education can reduce juvenile violence in juvenile facilities, schools, and communities, while providing lifelong decisionmaking skills."

Smith (1990) describes a school-based program in a New Mexico training school that teaches youths to use mediation to settle their differences peacefully. The program seeks to break the cycle of violence and abuse by teaching anger and conflict management skills. In mediation a neutral third party listens objectively to both sides in a dispute, then helps the disputants to identify the issues, explore solutions and agree on a satisfactory compromise to settling the problem. It is a confidential, voluntary process that is meeting with much success, not only in this institution but in schools throughout the country.

Research supports the finding that students who have a positive school experience not only learn better but have higher self-esteem and are better socialized. They are much more likely to become contributing members of society. Because of this, in 1984 then-President Ronald Reagan directed the Departments of Justice and Education to form the National School Safety Center (NSSC). This center is structured in five specialized sections: law enforcement, education, legal, research and communications. Together these five sections are to provide a comprehensive approach to school safety.

Another organization that is heavily involved in school safety is the National Crime Prevention Council. This organization, in conjunction with the National Institute for Citizen Education in the Law, has developed a program called Teens, Crime and the Community (TC&C), which combines education and student action to reduce crime and at the same time develop students' sense of mutual responsibility (Modglin, 1989, p. 9). Funded by the OJJDP, the TC&C curriculum includes information on how and why crimes occur, how community is defined and how individual and group action can help protect the community against crime. TC&C also includes information on 10 ways students can make their own schools safer (Modglin, p. 10):

1. School crime watches apply Neighborhood Watch concepts to the school.
2. Cross-age teaching provides a chance for middle and high school students to present prevention information to younger students.

3. Mediation programs, in which trained students act as a neutral third party, help resolve conflicts without violence.

4. Plays and prevention performances present information to the student body in appealing ways.

5. Student forums and discussions promote the use of research and resource persons to develop student insight into problems and possible solutions.

6. Surveys on crime and other issues collect facts, engage student interest and spread word of impending projects.

7. Crime prevention clubs teach students to watch out for and help overcome crime.

8. School crime prevention fairs or special observance days give students an opportunity to participate in workshops on prevention and safety.

9. Community service activities build students' self-esteem and school pride.

10. Student courts consider and dispose of student infractions.

SHOCAP states the following regarding the role of the schools in dealing with habitual juvenile offenders (Crowe, p. 47):

> School districts must have a legally acceptable code of conduct and set of disciplinary procedures. Once these are established, the school district may:
>
> - Identify the school assignment of students who have been classified as habituals by local authorities;
> - Share disciplinary code violations and other pertinent data with the police, crime analysts, or other officials designated responsible for profiling habitual delinquents;
> - Separate designated habituals by school assignments;
> - Establish procedures for notification of principals and teachers regarding the presence and special needs of habituals (care must be taken to protect staff and students, while avoiding unfair discrimination against the habitual).

Ingersoll and LeBoeuf (1997, p. 6) note:

> More than 500,000 delinquency cases disposed each year by juvenile courts result in court orders allowing the juvenile offender to remain in the community on probation—or return to the community following a residential placement—and continue normal activities such as school and work. Regular school attendance and community service often are conditions of these orders.
>
> For the vast majority of children on probation or in aftercare, educational success is critical to preventing recidivism and further involvement in the juvenile and criminal justice systems.

Gangs in the Schools

One important way that schools can be made safer is to address the problem of gangs in the school. This is the focus of a program called Gang Resistance Education and Training (GREAT), a program patterned after the nationally used antidrug program DARE. As noted by Lesce (1993, p. 49): "The eight-week program teaches students how to set goals for themselves, how to resist pressure, and understanding how gangs impact the quality of their life." In the promotional material for this program, the success of the program is attributed to the mutual commitment of law enforcement and educational agencies to unite in a common goal to:

- Provide children with accurate knowledge about gang involvement.
- Provide children with the skills necessary to combat the stresses that set the stage for gang involvement.
- Provide children with the skills to resist negative peer pressure.
- Provide children alternatives to gang involvement.

Moriarty and Fleming (1990, pp.15-16) offer the following 10-step plan for gang prevention in the schools:

1. Be honest. Admit to the potential for problems.
2. Get smart. Know the gang symbols and paraphernalia.
3. Identify your school's leaders and get them on your side.
4. Don't close the doors at 3:15. Keep students involved after school.
5. Work with the police.
6. Involve transfer students. Give new students activities and opportunities to fit in.
7. Educate the teaching staff.
8. Get parents on your side.
9. Find role models.
10. Provide career counseling for marginal students.

Daily preventive measures that can be taken in schools include being observant for signs of gang activity, allowing no unauthorized outsiders in the school, enforcing a policy of hall passes, practicing zero tolerance for infractions of school rules and enforcing such rules firmly, fairly and consistently.

The Role of Community Agencies, Businesses and Volunteers

Oregon passed legislation to comply with the mandates of the Juvenile Justice and Delinquency Prevention (JJDP) Act, giving communities the chance to address their own youth problems in ways that suited their unique needs. English (1990, p. 8) notes, using the JJDP Act as a model, that the Oregon Community Juvenile Services Act seeks to:

1. Establish statewide standards for juvenile services by creating a State Juvenile Services Commission.
2. Provide appropriate preventive, diversionary and dispositional alternatives for young people.
3. Encourage coordination of the various elements of the juvenile services system.
4. Promote local involvement in developing improved services for youth.

Specific goals for the program include the following:

- The family unit shall be preserved;

- Intervention shall be limited to those actions that are necessary and will utilize the least restrictive and most effective and appropriate resources;

- The family shall be encouraged to participate actively in whatever treatment is afforded a child;

- Treatment in the community, rather than commitment to a State juvenile training school, shall be provided whenever possible;

- Communities shall be encouraged and assisted in the development of alternatives to secure temporary custody for children not eligible for secure detention.

SHOCAP, as might be expected, also stresses community involvement and coordination. As noted by Crowe (p. 43): "Many of the agencies and officials have co-existed for years. Most are totally unaware of their ignorance of how other operations work, or of the problems and needs of other components of the system." SHOCAP has devised a community model for controlling habitual offenders and a functional model for a community habitual offender program, as shown in Figures 11.1 and 11.2.

Successful efforts do not have to be so formalized. They can be as informal as the mayor of a city calling for the removal of graffiti, as Minneapolis Mayor Sayles Belton did in her "Don't Deface My Space" campaign. Another practical, grass-roots approach is the "Neighborhood Tool Kit" series of stories about things that citizens are doing and can do to make their neighborhoods "friendlier, safer, more vital, more attractive places to live" (Iggers, 1994, p. E1). A lead-in to the column by Iggers quotes John McKnight, Center for Urban Affairs and Policy Research, of Northwestern University:

> There is a mistaken notion that our society has a problem in terms of effective human services. Our essential problem is weak communities. While we have reached the limits of institutional problem solving, we are only at the beginning of exploring the possibility of a new vision for community.

This newspaper column focuses on removing eyesores, creating jobs, cleaning up alleys, combating crime, starting block clubs and the like.

Community Involvement and Volunteers

Most community-based corrections programs' success is heightened by citizen involvement. Such community participation plays a crucial role in "normalizing" the environment and developing offenders' ties to the community, as well as in changing community attitudes toward offenders.

Community participation through volunteerism helps to improve programs, breaks down isolation and helps youthful offenders to explore possibilities for adjustment to the community.

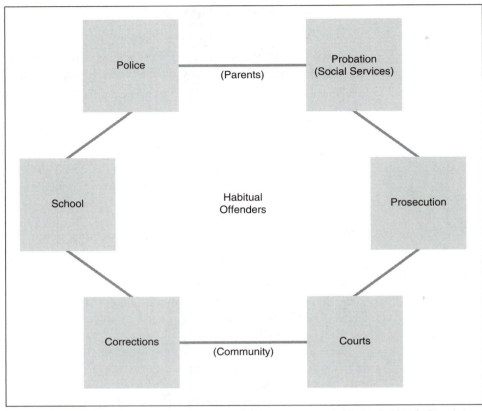

Figure 11.1
**A Community Model
for Controlling Habitual
Offenders**

Source: Timothy D. Crowe. *Habitual Juvenile Offenders: Guidelines for Citizen Action and Public Responses.* Serious Habitual Offender Comprehensive Action Program (SHOCAP). Washington, DC: Office of Juvenile Justice and Delinquency Prevention, October 1991, p. 44.

Volunteers are encouraged to assess needs and review all activities, programs and facilities to ensure their suitability in light of community standards and offender needs. Volunteers are used in some institutions and as aides to adjunct institutional programs, such as work release, that are carried out within the community. In some jurisdictions volunteers serve as assistants in probation, parole and other community-based alternatives to incarceration.

Volunteers have been an integral part of justice for centuries. Traditionally the role of volunteers in private endeavors has been to fill gaps between governmental social services and the actual need. In 1912 volunteers rallied for the child labor laws that were the result of the first White House Conference on Children in 1910. In the 1930s volunteers filled the gap in welfare and mental health programs until President Franklin Roosevelt made vast social changes. The rehabilitative powers of the local community and its volunteers were popularized during the late 1960s and the 1970s, and today volunteerism continues to increase.

Some programs use senior citizens as volunteers, working with high-risk juveniles. Briscoe (1990, p. 94) describes one such program in Jefferson County,

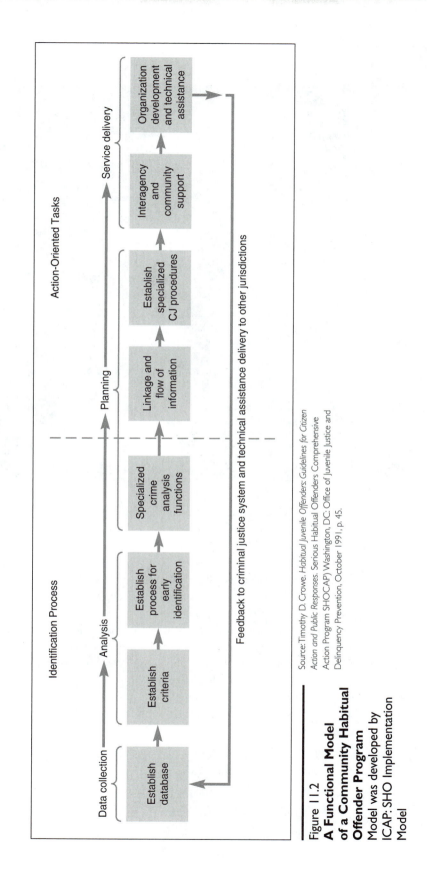

Figure 11.2
**A Functional Model
of a Community Habitual
Offender Program**
Model was developed by
ICAP: SHO Implementation
Model

Identification Process

Action-Oriented Tasks

Data collection → Analysis → Planning → Service delivery

Establish database

Establish criteria

Establish process for early identification

Specialized crime analysis functions

Linkage and flow of information

Establish specialized CJ procedures

Interagency and community support

Organization development and technical assistance

Feedback to criminal justice system and technical assistance delivery to other jurisdictions

Source: Timothy D. Crowe. *Habitual Juvenile Offenders: Guidelines for Citizen Action and Public Responses. Serious Habitual Offenders Comprehensive Action Program SHOCAP)* Washington, DC: Office of Juvenile Justice and Delinquency Prevention, October 1991, p. 45.

The Green Chair Project in Minneapolis hires inner-city youths to build chairs that are sold to citizens for $50. In 1994 the project created jobs for 18 youths who built 200 chairs.

Texas, which has a foster grandparent program in the county's juvenile detention center. She notes: "Even children who are sometimes hostile and aggressive work calmly and quietly in the presence of a foster grandparent."

Jobs and Restitution

Some community efforts focus on creating jobs for youths. As noted by Smith (1993, p. 14): "Work is important in defining who we are. It helps us measure our value both to ourselves and others."

Some dispositions of the juvenile court include restitution in the form of either work or pay. Providing jobs for youths who are required to make restitution helps them to fulfill their obligations. As noted by Bazemore (1989): "Among some 400 juvenile restitution programs, 34 percent indicated in a recent national survey that they arranged paid job slots for referrals." Reasons given for investing time and effort to develop jobs for offenders include the following (Bazemore, p. 1):

- Increasing the possibility that poor or hard-to-employ offenders can make monetary restitution to victims
- Avoiding lack of work as an excuse for nonpayment
- Improving the enforcement of restitution orders
- Increasing the certainty and timeliness of payments to victims
- Improving the program's efficiency in monitoring restitution

As part of their penalty, youths caught marking up public buses in San Francisco must spend time removing graffiti from the buses.

- Permitting the recommendation of realistic payment schedules to the court through program control over the source of earnings (Program managers can be assured that restitution is not being paid by parents or through theft.)
- Allowing for larger restitution orders and greater return to victims

Bazemore (p. 1) suggests that work is an important part of a balanced approach to juvenile justice: "From the accountability perspective, work can instill a sense of responsibility and an understanding of the value of goods and money. Work can be emphasized by those who argue that a major goal of juvenile justice should be to enhance offender competence, and advocates of treatment emphasize the therapeutic effects of employment." Bazemore also notes: "Instilling positive work values and habits fits well with the accountability and responsibility ethic of restitution programs."

Successful job programs share the following common characteristics (Bazemore, p. 9):

- "Sell" employers and the community on offender employment
- Build on existing community resources and support

- Develop a funding "package" adequate to provide ongoing support for the jobs component
- Select work placements and projects that have value to employers, offenders, and the community
- Establish and maintain high standards of youth supervision and positive employer relations
- Influence the priorities of the local juvenile justice system toward an emphasis on restitution and work

Many of these programs have an advisory board to assist them. The Erie Earn-It Program in Texas, for example, has an advisory board consisting of a businessperson, a chamber of commerce member, a media representative, an attorney, a public accountant, a private citizen and a juvenile probation officer (Bazemore, p. 15).

Jobs are important to youths not only for the money they can generate but for the feelings of self-worth that may accompany a job.

Two federal programs are important sources of jobs for young people. The first, the Job Corps, has 106 centers across the country with over 40,000 jobs filled at any given time. As noted by Conly (1993, p. 44): "About 30 percent of the residents complete vocational training; some complete their GEDs. . . . [Eighty-four] percent of its graduates are placed either in jobs (67 percent) or in school (17 percent)."

The second program is Youth Opportunities Unlimited (YOU). This is a multimillion-dollar demonstration project funded by the Department of Labor's Job Training Partnership. According to Conly (p. 44): "The program is grounded in the assumption that many social problems—gangs, drug addiction, juvenile delinquency—have a common source: poverty and a lack of economic and educational opportunities." The YOU program tries to address this problem by providing not only jobs but support programs in health care, housing, recreation and family services. The program is currently operating in seven communities of fewer than 25,000 people with poverty rates of 30 percent or higher. In San Diego the YOU demonstration project is involved in the following efforts (Conly, pp. 44–45):

- An alternative school will serve 50 "at-risk" ninth and tenth graders.
- Local Boys' and Girls' Clubs will provide expanded sports and recreational activities, giving young people an alternative to gangs.
- An Hispanic organization will operate a family learning center.
- Local labor unions will sponsor a pre-apprenticeship program to help youths learn about possible careers.
- A teen parenting center is being established.
- Two social workers will provide case management to youths.
- Various community and city agencies will open offices at the YOU center to serve the needs of youths and families in the target area.

The Importance of Coordination

Bownes and Ingersoll (p. 1) assert: "If this country is to reduce delinquency and resultant criminality, there must be a coordinated, substantial, and sustained public and private investment of financial and human resources in families, communities, and the systems that support and protect them." The critical importance of coordinating efforts is clearly stated by Prothrow-Stith (1991, p. 139):

> When a kid enters the emergency room with a gunshot wound to his thigh after having been shot in a dispute over a jacket, I want him to be as well treated for the "disease" of violence as he is for the traumatic injury he has sustained. When that young man is blanketed in therapeutic interventions that involve his parents, his pregnant girlfriend, the probation officer assigned to him on a previous case, the kid who shot him with whom perhaps he has had a long-standing feud, his school, which is about to expel him, and perhaps even his younger brother who has just started to act out violently—that's when we will start to make a difference.

McDonald and Howard (1998, p. 1) describe a program called Families and Schools Together (FAST) that also includes the community. They note that the program "addresses the urgent social problems of youth violence and chronic juvenile delinquency by building and enhancing youth's relationships with their families, peers, teachers, school staff, and other members of the community. These relationships form a social safety net of multifaceted protective factors.

Rosenfeld and Decker (1993, pp. 27–28) describe an Assault Crisis Team (ACT) that can provide such services. The team consists of medical, social service, educational and criminal justice professionals in addition to community residents with training in violence intervention. These teams operate in four settings: a hospital emergency room, a juvenile detention center, an adult jail and a high-risk neighborhood. According to Rosenfeld and Decker (p. 28): "The function of ACT is three-fold: *Monitoring* levels and patterns of violence, *mentoring* youth at risk for violence, and *mediating* disputes with a high potential for violence."

Another example of cooperative efforts is the Safe Policy program in Sarpy County, Nebraska. Safe Policy is an acronym for School Administrators for Effective Police, Prosecution Operations, Leading to Improved Children and Youth Services. An article in *Law Enforcement News* described the program as follows ("Network," 1994, p. 5):

> Safe Policy is a countywide network involving officials from schools, law enforcement, juvenile justice, social service, business and private agencies, who meet monthly to share information and ideas to prevent juveniles from getting into trouble with the law and to help those who have already had brushes with the criminal justice system. . . .
>
> The Safe Policy concept is an "open organizational theme" that urges agencies and institutions to overcome "organizational barriers" and identify the most pressing youth problems in the communities.

This is encouraging as the report of the American Psychological Association's Commission on Youth and Violence notes (p. 5):

> The Commission's work overwhelmingly affirms a message of hope: Our society can intervene effectively in the lives of children and youth to reduce or prevent their involvement in violence. Violence involving youth is not random, uncontrollable, or inevitable.

The report warns, however, that intervention may be less than successful if society continues to accept violence and aggression in certain circumstances. Among the societal factors that may limit successful intervention are the following (pp. 61–62):

- Corporal punishment of children, because harsh and continual punishment has been implicated as a contributor to child aggression;
- Violence on television and in other media, which is known to affect children's attitudes and behaviors in relation to violence; and
- Availability of firearms, especially to children and youth. Firearms are known to increase the lethality of violence and encourage its escalation.

The potential success of antiviolence interventions may be limited by the social and economic contexts in which some Americans spend their lives. These macrosocial considerations are beyond the scope of psychological interventions and require a society-wide effort to change. They include:

- Poverty, social and economic inequality, and the contextual factors that derive from these conditions (i.e., living in crowded housing and lack of opportunity to ameliorate one's life circumstances), which are significant risk factors for involvement in violence;
- Prejudice and racism, particularly because strongly prejudiced attitudes about particular social or cultural groups, or being a member of a group subjected to prejudice and discrimination, is a known risk factor for involvement in violence; and
- Misunderstanding of cultural differences, which must be addressed in intervention planning.

The commission remains hopeful about the future because most of these factors are "within our power to change" (p. 5).

Summary

The role of the broader community in assisting the juvenile justice system cannot be ignored. Community is not only the geographical area over which the justice system has jurisdiction, it is also a sense of integration, of shared values and a sense of "we-ness." Without such "we-ness," areas may experience the broken-window phenomenon—if it appears no one cares, disorder and crime will thrive.

The importance of community is recognized in areas that have implemented community policing. Community policing embraces a proactive, problem-oriented approach to working with the community to make it safe.

Another important community resource is social services. Social workers have greatly influenced trends in juvenile justice policy in the areas of diversion, victim restitution, the decriminalization of status offenders and deinstitutionalization. Social workers operate in all aspects of the juvenile justice system, although in the first juvenile courts social workers were probation officers. The current emphasis in social services for youths is diversion to a wide range of community-based services and programs.

Other emphases include family therapy and teaching conflict resolution and mediation skills. Studies suggest that family therapy is more effective in dealing with the problems of youths than is traditional juvenile justice intervention. Important basic skills that schools now teach are conflict resolution and mediation.

Community participation through volunteerism helps to improve programs, breaks down isolation and helps youthful offenders to explore possibilities for adjustment to the community. In addition, jobs are important to youths not only for the money they generate but for the feelings of self-worth that accompany a job.

Discussion Questions

1. Is there a sense of community where you live? Are there any instances of the broken-window phenomenon?
2. What are the advantages and disadvantages of community policing? Is it used in your community?
3. Why is there a need for social workers? How extensively should social workers be involved in juvenile justice?
4. Should social workers handle youths directly from courts or probation officers? Why or why not?
5. Do social workers seek the best ways to prevent recurrences of mischievous or antisocial juvenile behavior? What do they do?
6. Should social services provide education for disruptive youths who do not want to go to school? Why or why not?
7. A 15-year-old boy has been caught shoplifting food from a large supermarket. Security personnel call the police. While waiting for the police, the youth tells them that he has not eaten anything for a week. There is no food at his home. The police are advised of the youth's story. The police investigate, find the youth was telling the truth, and advise the supermarket. The supermarket manager does not want to make a formal complaint. Should this matter be handled by social services or the juvenile court? What would happen in your area?
8. What are the social service programs in your state? Do these programs serve the purpose they were designed for, or do they add to the array of referral programs in existence?
9. Should all juvenile incidents be referred to the juvenile court, or is there justification for referral to other agencies as long as the offense is not serious? Which do you support? What criteria would you use?
10. Should schools be able to refer a disruptive juvenile to an agency that might help the juvenile rather than involve the police? Why or why not?

References

American Psychological Association. *Violence & Youth: Psychology's Response* Vol. 1. *Summary Report of the American Psychological Association Commission on Violence and Youth.* n.d.

Bazemore, S. Gordon. *The Restitution Experience in Youth Employment.* Restitution Education, Specialized Training, and Technical Assistance (RESTTA) Program, September 1989.

Bownes, Donna and Ingersoll, Sarah. *Mobilizing Communities to Prevent Juvenile Crime.* OJJDP, Juvenile Justice Bulletin, July 1997. (NCJ-165928)

Breci, Michael G. and Erickson, Timothy E. "Community Policing: The Process of Transitional Change." *Law Enforcement Bulletin,* June 1998, pp. 16–21.

Briscoe, Judy Culpepper. "In Texas: Reaching Out to Help Troubled Youths." *Corrections Today,* October 1990, pp. 90–95.

Chaiken, Marcia R. *Kids, COPS, and Communities.* Washington, DC: National Institute of Justice, June 1998.

Conly, Catherine H. *Street Gangs: Current Knowledge and Strategies.* Washington, DC: National Institute of Justice, August 1993.

Crowe, Timothy D. *Habitual Juvenile Offenders: Guidelines for Citizen Action and Public Responses.* Serious Habitual Offender Comprehensive Action Program. Washington, DC: Office of Juvenile Justice and Delinquency Prevention, October 1991.

Ellis, Sheryl. "It *Does* Take a Village." *Corrections Today,* August 1998, pp. 100–102.

English, Tom. "Improving Juvenile Justice at the Local Level." *NIJ Reports,* March/April 1990, pp. 7–10.

Hamburger, Tom. "School Violence Common, Data Say." (Minneapolis/St. Paul) *Star Tribune,* December 17, 1993, pp. A1, A11.

Helping Communities Fight Crime: Comprehensive Planning Techniques, Models, Programs and Resources. The President's Crime Prevention Council Catalog, 1997.

Iggers, Jeremy. "The Solutions Have to Be on a Human Scale." (Minneapolis/St. Paul) *Star Tribune,* May 23, 1994, p. E1.

Ingersoll, Sarah and LeBoeuf, Donni. *Reaching Out to the Youth Out of the Education Mainstream.* Juvenile Justice Bulletin. OJJDP, February 1997. (NCJ-163920)

Inkster, Norman D. "The Essence of Community Policing." *The Police Chief,* March 1992, pp. 28–31.

Kaufman, Phillip; Chen, Xianglei; Choy, Susan P.; Chandler, Kathryn A.; Chapman, Christopher D.; Rand, Michael R.; and Ringel, Cheryl. *Indicators of School Crime and Safety, 1998.* Washington, DC: U.S. Department of Education and U.S. Department of Justice, October 1998. (NCJ-172215)

Kipper, Bobby. "Law Enforcement's Role in Addressing School Violence." *The Police Chief,* June 1996, pp. 26–31.

Kirst, Michael W. "Improving Children's Services: Overcoming Barriers, Creating New Opportunities." *Phi Delta Kappan,* April 1991, pp. 615–618.

Klockars, Carl B. "The Rhetoric of Community Policing." In *Community Policing: Rhetoric or Reality,* edited by Jack R. Greene and Stephen D. Mastrofski. New York: Praeger, 1991, pp. 239–258.

Krisberg, Barry and Austin, James F. *Reinventing Juvenile Justice.* Newbury Park, CA: Sage Publications, 1993.

LeBoeuf, Donni and Delany-Shabazz, Robin V. *Conflict Resolution.* OJJDP Fact Sheet #55. March 1997. (FS-9755)

Lesce, Tony. "Gang Resistance Education and Training (G.R.E.A.T.)." *Law and Order,* May 1993, pp. 47–50.

Manning, Peter K. "Community Policing as a Drama of Control." In *Community Policing: Rhetoric or Reality,* edited by Jack R. Greene and Stephen D. Mastrofski. New York: Praeger, 1991, pp. 27–45.

Mastrofski, Stephen D. "Community Policing as Reform: A Cautionary Tale." In *Community Policing: Rhetoric or Reality,* edited by Jack R. Greene and Stephen D. Mastrofski. New York: Praeger, 1991, pp. 48–67.

Mastrofski, Stephen D.; Parks, Roger B.; and Worden, Robert E. *Community Policing in Action: Lessons from an Observational Study.* National Institute of Justice Research Preview. June 1998. (FS-000199)

McDonald, Lynn and Howard, Deborah. "Families and Schools Together." OJJDP Fact Sheet #88, December 1998.

Miller, Alden and Ohlin, Lloyd. *Delinquency and Community.* Beverly Hills, CA: Sage Publications, 1985.

Miller, Linda S. and Hess, Kären M. *The Police in the Community: Strategies for the 21st Century,* 2nd ed. Belmont, CA: West/Wadsworth Publishing Company, 1998.

Modglin, Terry. "School Crime: Up Close and Personal." *School Safety,* Spring 1989, pp. 9–11.

Monaghan, George. "Kids Crave Community, Fear Crime." (Minneapolis/St. Paul) *Star Tribune,* January 4, 1994, pp. E1–E3.

Moriarty, Anthony and Fleming, Thomas W. "Mean Suburban Streets: Youth Gangs Aren't Just a Big-City Problem Anymore." *American School Board Journal,* July 1990, pp. 13–16.

"Network Steers Youth Away from Trouble." *Law Enforcement News,* February 14, 1994, p. 5.

OJJDP Annual Report, 1990. Washington DC: Office of Juvenile Justice Delinquency and
    Prevention, 1990.
Prothrow-Stith, D. *Deadly Consequences.* New York: Harper-Collins, 1991.
Rosenfeld, Richard and Decker, Scott. "Where Public Health and Law Enforcement Meet:
    Monitoring and Preventing Youth Violence." *American Journal of Police,* Vol. 12, No. 3,
    1993, pp. 11–57.
Smith, Melinda. "New Mexico Youths Use Mediation to Settle Their Problems Peacefully."
    Corrections Today, June 1990, pp. 112–114.
Smith, Robert L. "In the Service of Youth: A Common Denominator." *Juvenile Justice,* Vol. 1,
    No. 2, Fall/Winter 1993, pp. 9–15.
Snow, Robert. "Agencies Turned Advocate." *Law and Order,* January 1992, pp. 285–287.
Stern, Harriet W. "Family Trouble Center." *Law and Order,* March 1991, pp. 72–75.
Strandberg, Keith W. "The State of Community Policing." *Law Enforcement Technology,* October
    1997, pp. 42–46.
Swope, Ross E. "Creating Time for New Operations." *Law and Order,* August 1998,
    pp. 112–113.
Wilson, James Q. and Kelling, George L. "Broken Windows." *Atlantic Monthly,* March 1982,
    pp. 29–38.
Wilson, James Q. and Kelling, George L. "Making Neighborhoods Safe." *Atlantic Monthly,*
    February 1989, pp. 46–52.
Wilson, John J. "A National Agenda for Children: On the Front Lines with Attorney General
    Janet Reno." *Juvenile Justice,* Vol. 1, No. 2, Fall/Winter 1993, pp. 2–8.

12 Approaches to Prevention

The truism that an ounce of prevention is worth a pound of cure surely applies to delinquency. If we are to check . . . violent crime by juveniles, we must go beyond treating symptoms, however diligently, to examine causes. Nor must we be so preoccupied with what is wrong with a minority of our youth that our tunnel vision blinds us to what is right with the majority.

—OJJDP

Do You Know

- What approach to the delinquency problem emerged in the late sixties?
- What three approaches to prevention are?
- What the three general levels of prevention are?
- How the numerator and denominator approaches to prevention differ?
- What the two-pronged public health model for prevention consists of?
- What an effective prevention approach must address?
- What kinds of programs are recommended by the Metropolitan Court Judges Committee to help prevent child abuse and neglect?
- What the committee recommends for disabled families?
- What the committee recommends for children at risk?
- What the TARAD program does?
- What antigang programs can be implemented?

Can You Define

denominator approach, Gould-Wysinger Award, numerator approach, primary prevention, protective factors, risk factors, secondary prevention, tertiary prevention

INTRODUCTION

Common sense says that it is better to prevent a problem than to react to it once it arises. This is true for juvenile delinquency as well as for child neglect and abuse.

Traditionally our society's approach to youthful crime has been reactive. Juvenile courts and diversion programs have responded to crimes by juveniles with a wide range of services focused on punishment, control or rehabilitation.

In 1967 the President's Commission on Law Enforcement and the Administration of Justice advocated: "In the last analysis, the most promising and so the most important method of dealing with crime is by preventing it—by ameliorating the conditions of life that drive people to commit crime and that undermine the restraining rules and institutions erected by society against anti-social conduct."

In the late 1960s a new approach for dealing with delinquency emerged—a focus on the prevention of crime.

Subsequently this prevention emphasis was written into federal law in the Juvenile Delinquency Prevention Acts of 1972 and 1974, and the Juvenile Justice Amendments of 1977.

Attorney General Janet Reno also advocates prevention ("Reno Calls for," 1993): "America would rather build prisons than invest in a child and we've got to change that. Unless we invest in children, we will never have enough dollars to build all the prisons necessary to house people 15 and 20 years from now." Cullen et al. (1998, p. 197) suggest:

> As the United States turned into the twentieth century, progressive reformers called attention to the plight of children in urban areas and embarked on efforts, including the founding of the juvenile court, to save them. As we now ready ourselves for the next millennium, we perhaps are in another "Progressive Era" in which a child-saving movement will gain strength and create the space for policies that improve the lives of children.

Each municipality, county and state is unique in its particular crime problems. Each is also unique in how it approaches crime and how it disposes of those who engage in crime. What constitutes delinquency is subject to varied interpretations across places, times and social groupings. A youth's behavior may be viewed as "delinquent" by police, as "acting out" by mental health professionals, as "sin" by a member of the clergy and as "just plain mischief" by someone who views some misbehavior as a normal part of growing up.

This chapter begins with some theoretical considerations related to prevention, including prevention compared to control, the three levels of prevention, which youths should be targeted in prevention programs and prevention as an attack on causes. Next the discussion focuses on specific approaches to preventing child abuse, drug and alcohol abuse, delinquency, violence and gangs. The chapter concludes with descriptions of exemplary programs in each area.

Classification of Prevention Approaches

A program report by the National Criminal Justice Association (1997, p. 9) states: "Delinquency prevention efforts are broad based, and their impact sometimes is difficult to gauge precisely. They touch on almost every aspect of public policy that addresses children's issues, including programs traditionally associated with education, housing, law enforcement, or health and human services–related agencies."

Several approaches to classifying prevention efforts have been set forth. Following are two ways to look at and classify prevention efforts.

Prevention vs. Control

Technically prevention is a measure taken *before* a delinquent act occurs in order to forestall the act; control is a measure taken *after* a delinquent act occurs (Lejins, 1967). In this context, Lejins defines three kinds of prevention relevant for law enforcement.

Prevention can be corrective, punitive or mechanical.

- *Corrective prevention* focuses on eliminating conditions that lead to or cause criminal behavior.
- *Punitive prevention* relies on the threat of punishment to forestall criminal acts.
- *Mechanical prevention* is directed toward "target hardening," making it difficult or impossible to commit particular offenses. Locks on doors, bars on windows, alarms, security guards and many other options are available to protect possible targets of criminal acts.

Another way to classify prevention efforts is by level. These levels encompass the three methods just discussed.

Three Levels of Delinquency Prevention

The National Coalition of State Juvenile Justice Advisory Groups (1993, p. 21) notes:

The first line of defense against all forms of juvenile crime is still prevention, whether *primary,* directed at the population as a whole, or *secondary,* aimed at a specific at-risk population, or *tertiary,* targeted at an offending population in order to prevent repetition of the behaviors.

Tertiary prevention is referred to as *treatment* in this text and is discussed in the next chapter.

Prevention may be primary, secondary or tertiary.

Primary Prevention

Primary prevention is directed at modifying and changing crime-causing conditions in the overall physical and social conditions that lead to crime. Corrective and mechanical prevention fit into this level.

An example of primary prevention is the community crime prevention program in Seattle, Washington. This program focused on the prevention of residential burglaries. These were crimes of opportunity by juveniles who entered homes through unlocked doors and windows during the day when residents were away.

Prevention efforts were aimed at contributing environmental factors. Certain neighborhoods and types of housing were identified as being vulnerable to burglaries using demographics, criminal incidents and physical characteristics statistics. The community then gave citizens home security checklists. Citizens in target areas used these checklists to protect their homes against relatively easy entry by burglars.

This program was directed at making crime more difficult, rather than at attacking individual motivations to commit crime. Such deterrence programs effectively increase the risks of and decrease the opportunities for burglary. However, the National Coalition of State Juvenile Justice Advisory Groups (p. 37) urges:

> We need a society that is committed to primary prevention, one that acknowledges that the variety and quality of support systems for families, particularly at the poverty level, are the best possible formula for preventing crime. Adequate health care, including the delivery of prenatal services to pregnant women, sufficient housing, strong Head Start and other preschool enrichment programs for all eligible children, an effective system of day care to allow parents to work while still providing for their children, safe neighborhoods, and quality educational opportunities all are necessary components of a society committed to its children.

As noted by the American Psychological Association (APA) (pp. 55–56) in its discussion of primary prevention programs: "Prevention programs directed early in life can reduce factors that increase risk for antisocial behavior and clinical dysfunction in childhood and adolescence." Among the most promising primary prevention programs are those that include family counseling for pregnant women and for new mothers in the home, with continued visits during the first few years of the child's life. The American Psychological Association (p. 55) reports that in a 20-year follow-up of one "home visitor" program, positive effects were seen for both the at-risk child and the mother.

Preschool programs also hold promise if they include activities to develop intellectual, emotional and social skills and introduce children to responsible decision making. According to the APA (p. 56):

> Primary prevention programs of the type that promote social and cognitive skills seem to have the greatest impact on attitudes about violent behavior among children and youth. Skills that aid children in learning alternatives to violent behaviors include social perspective-taking, alternative solution generation, self-esteem enhancement, peer negotiation skills, problem-solving skills training, and anger management.

Secondary Prevention

Secondary prevention seeks early identification and intervention into the lives of individuals or groups that are found in crime-causing circumstances. It focuses on changing the behavior of those who are likely to become delinquent. Punitive prevention fits into this level.

One highly publicized program of this type was undertaken in Rahway, New Jersey. Eighty boys and girls identified as being delinquency-prone were divided into experimental and control groups. The experimental group was taken to an adult prison in Rahway. According to Sprinthall and Collins (1984, pp. 340-341):

> Hard-core adult lifers verbally confronted them with the error of their ways. The adult criminals yelled at, bullied, and threatened the delinquents. They related the unvarnished truth about prison life, such as the brutality, the homosexual rapes, the degradation, and the lack of personal freedom.
>
> A film was made of the program for national television. The publicity became enormous, especially after preliminary findings revealed that from 80 to 90% of the treated teenagers had reversed their behavior. . . .
>
> When the follow-up results were carefully and objectively examined, however, the mighty promise of the project was undone. In fact, the findings . . . indicated that the program was worse than no treatment at all. The control groups had fewer subsequent arrests than the treatment group.

Scaring the pants off youths as a way to prevent juvenile delinquency does not appear to work. The APA (p. 56) notes:

> Secondary prevention programs that focus on improving individual affective, cognitive, and behavioral skills or on modifying the learning conditions for aggression offer promise of interrupting the path toward violence for high-risk or predelinquent youth. . . .
>
> Programs that attempt to work with and modify the family system of a high-risk child have great potential to prevent development of aggressive and violent behavior.

Tertiary Prevention

Tertiary prevention, the third level, is aimed at preventing recidivism—that is, it focuses on preventing further delinquent acts by youths already identified as delinquent. Tertiary prevention, also called treatment or rehabilitation, is the focus of Chapter 13.

Which Youths to Target

Recall that the public health model (Chapter 6) called for focusing the scarce resources of the juvenile justice system on those at greatest risk—young black males living in areas of poverty with high crime rates and drug dealing. Using a mathematical analogy, if we were to look at the number of at-risk youths compared to the total number of youths, the at-risk youths would be the *numerator* and the total number of youths would be the *denominator.* Smith (1993, pp. 10–11) suggests that we should be dealing with the denominator for best results:

> Delinquency programs that focus solely on juvenile offenders will not reduce the prevalence of youth crime any more than employment programs that focus exclusively on the unemployed will lower unemployment rates.
>
> The medical and scientific model demonstrates the effectiveness of the denominator approach. For example, numerator approaches in polio, tuberculosis, and other infectious diseases have made little impact on prevalence; but denominator approaches, such as vaccination, screening, and the like, have virtually eradicated a number of these diseases. The results have been dramatic and lasting. Denominator approaches work because they deal with the general public health as well as specific symptoms.

Smith suggests that one reason the denominator approach is ignored is because it tends to generate "turf fights" and to require innovative approaches to problems that we have almost come to accept. Further, says Smith (p. 11): "The impulse [is] to do something now to relieve individual suffering rather than focus on a broader perspective that will prevent systemic suffering in the future."

The **numerator approach** focuses on individuals and symptoms, whereas the **denominator approach** focuses on the entire group and causes.

The denominator approach is consistent with the public health model.

Prevention and the Public Health Model

Effective crime prevention has recently been based on the public health model, using a two-pronged strategy involving risk factors and protective factors. As Hawkins explains (1995, pp. 10–11):

> Increasingly, the preventive approach used in public health is being recognized as appropriate for use as part of a criminal justice strategy. . . . Seeking to prevent cardiovascular disease, researchers in the field of public health first identified risk factors . . . [that] increased a person's chances of contracting the disease. . . . Equally important, they determined that certain protective factors . . . helped prevent the development of heart problems.
>
> These public health researchers were concerned with halting the onset of heart disease in order to avoid risky, invasive, and costly interventions . . . Their goal was to reduce or counter the identified risk factors for heart disease in the population at large . . . [and] promote those behaviors and attitudes that reduce risk of heart disease.

The public health model's two-pronged strategy reduces known risk factors and promotes protective factors.

Applying this strategy to juvenile crime prevention, Hawkins (pp. 11–13) identifies a plenitude of **risk factors** within the community, the family, the school and the individual that increase the probability that a young person will exhibit certain adolescent problem behaviors, including violence. For example five risk factors found within the community that are known to increase youths' violent behavior are the availability of guns, community laws and norms favorable to crime, media portrayals of violence, low neighborhood attachments and community disorganization, and extreme economic deprivation. Table 12.1 lists these risk factors and the associated adolescent behaviors.

Hawkins (p. 13) also identifies three categories of **protective factors** that "reduce the impact of negative risk factors by providing positive ways for an individual to respond to these risks":

- Individual characteristics—a resilient temperament and positive social orientation
- Bonding—positive relationships with family, teachers and other adults
- Healthy beliefs and clear standards

Table 12.1
Risk Factors for Health and Behavior Problems

Risk Factors	Substance Abuse	Delinquency	Teenage Pregnancy	School Dropout	Violence
Community					
Availability of drugs	√				
Availability of firearms		√			√
Community laws and norms favorable toward drug use, firearms, and crime	√	√			√
Media portrayals of violence					√
Transitions and mobility	√	√		√	
Low neighborhood attachment and community organization	√	√			√
Extreme economic deprivation	√	√	√	√	√
Family					
Family history of the problem behavior	√	√	√	√	
Family management problems	√	√	√	√	√
Family conflict	√	√	√	√	√
Favorable parental attitudes and involvement in the problem behavior	√	√			√
School					
Early and persistent antisocial behavior	√	√	√	√	√
Academic failure beginning in elementary school	√	√	√	√	√
Lack of commitment to school	√	√	√	√	
Individual/Peer					
Rebelliousness	√	√		√	
Friends who engage in the problem behavior	√	√	√	√	√
Favorable attitudes toward the problem behavior	√	√	√	√	
Early initiation of the problem behavior	√	√	√	√	√
Constitutional factors	√	√			√

Data Source: J. D. Hawkins and R. F. Catalano. *Risk-Focused Prevention: Using the Social Development Strategy.* Seattle: Developmental Research and Programs, Inc. 1998.

Source: J. C. Howell, ed. *Guide for Implementing the Comprehensive Strategy for Serious, Violent, and Chronic Juvenile Offenders.* Washington, DC: Office of Juvenile Justice and Delinquency Prevention, U.S. Department of Justice. 1995 (May).

Prevention as an Attack on Causes

Of the three levels of prevention, primary and secondary prevention most closely approach the essence of the term *prevention,* in that they seek to preclude delinquent acts *before* they occur. Tertiary prevention is really remediation aimed at forestalling future acts after an initial act has been committed and detected.

Primary and secondary prevention activities do not begin only after juveniles are arrested. These prevention approaches can be effective only if they address the underlying causes of delinquency. To prevent a behavior from occurring, those factors that stimulate the behavior must be removed. Conditions that stimulate delinquent acts and a lack of constraints to inhibit those acts are both potential causes of delinquency; therefore effective prevention must address both the conditions and the lack of constraints.

Effective prevention approaches must address the causes of delinquency.

An editorial in the Minneapolis/St. Paul *Star Tribune* quotes former Minneapolis Chief of Police, Tony Bouza: "We have to stop swatting at the mosquitoes and start looking to the swamps that produce them" ("Fighting Crime," 1994, p. A10). This editorial goes on to suggest:

> The best argument for betting on prevention is that nothing else seems to work. Punishment certainly doesn't. Since the mid-1970s sentences have gotten stiffer and the U.S. prison population has tripled—while the violent crime rate continues to inch upward. . . . A mountain of evidence links lawbreaking to poverty, abuse, school failure, joblessness and family chaos. . . .
>
> With crooks as with mosquitoes, it's far harder to get rid of this year's swarm than to prevent next year's from hatching. That takes foresight and forebearance— and an excruciating wait for the payoff. But the alternative to such patient, strategic crime-fighting is an onslaught that no amount of swatting will repel.

The National Center for the Assessment of Delinquent Behavior and Its Prevention (NCADBIP) has developed 12 strategies to distinguish among delinquency prevention approaches. Each strategy addresses a distinct presumed cause of delinquency and an accompanying approach, as summarized in Table 12.2.

Preserving Families to Prevent Delinquency

The importance of families has been stressed throughout this text. As noted in the dedication to *Deprived Children: A Judicial Response* (Metropolitan Court Judges Committee, 1986, p. 2):

> The efforts of skilled and committed judges, legislators, law enforcement officers, health and child care workers, doctors, teachers, attorneys, volunteers and others involved in the lives of deprived children can do little without a rekindled national awareness that the family is the foundation of the protection, care and training of our children.

In keeping with the requirements of the JJDP Act, the Office of Juvenile Justice and Delinquency Prevention's *Annual Report* features "'selected exemplary juvenile delinquency programs,' with emphasis on community-based programs 'that involve and assist families of juveniles'" (Sweet, 1992, p. 1). The report featured three such programs. One of the three, Court Appointed Special Advocates (CASA), was described in Chapter 9 under the discussion of the preliminary hearing. Recall that these volunteers were to ensure that the courts are familiar with the needs of any neglected or abused child and that such children are most appropriately placed in the child's best interest.

Table 12.2
Causes of Delinquency and Associated Strategies of Delinquency Prevention

Presumed Cause	Strategy	Goal of Strategy
Physical abnormality/illness	Biological-physiological (health promotion, nutrition, neurological, genetic)	Remove, diminish, control underlying physiological, biological or biopsychiatric conditions
Psychological disturbance or disorder	Psychological/mental health (epidemiological/early intervention, psychotherapeutic, behavioral)	Alter internal psychological states or conditions generating them
Weak attachments to others	Social network development (linkage, influence)	Increase interaction/involvement between youths and nondeviant others; increase influence of nondeviant others on potentially delinquent youths
Criminal influence	Criminal influence reduction (disengagement from criminal influence, redirection away from criminal norms)	Reduce the influence of delinquent norms and persons who directly or indirectly encourage youths to commit delinquent acts
Powerlessness	Power enhancement (informal influence, formal power)	Increase ability or power of youths to influence or control their environments, directly or indirectly
Lack of useful, worthwhile roles	Role development/role enhancement (service roles, production roles, student roles)	Create opportunities for youths to be involved in legitimate roles or activities that they perceive as useful, successful, competent
Unoccupied time	Activities/recreation	Involve youths in nondelinquent activities
Inadequate skills	Education/skill development (cognitive, affective, moral, informational)	Provide individuals with personal skills that prepare them to find patterns of behavior free from delinquent activities
Conflicting environmental demands	Clear and consistent social expectations	Increase consistency of expectations/messages from institutions, organizations, groups that affect youths
Economic necessity	Economic resources (resource maintenance, resource attainment)	Provide basic resources to preclude the need for delinquency
Low degree of risk/difficulty	Deterrence (target hardening/removal, anticipatory intervention)	Increase cost and decrease benefits of criminal acts
Exclusionary social responses	Abandonment of legal control/social tolerance (explicit jurisdictional abandonment, implicit jurisdictional abandonment, covert jurisdictional abandonment, environmental tolerance	Remove certain behaviors from control of the juvenile justice system; decrease the degree to which youths' behaviors are perceived, labeled, treated as delinquent

Source: Hawkins et al. Reports of the National Juvenile Justice Assessment Center. *A Topology of Caused-Focused Strategies of Delinquency Prevention.* Washington, DC: National Institute for Juvenile Justice and Delinquency Prevention, U.S. Government Printing Office, 1980.

High school youths in a program sponsored by Student Conservation Association, Inc. work on the Hulls Gulch trail in the Boise, Idaho, foothills. The New Hampshire based non-profit group organizes outings to introduce urban youths to the outdoors.

The next program, Permanent Families for Abused and Neglected Children, is a training and technical assistance project of the National Council of Juvenile and Family Court Judges (NCJFCJ). A focus of the program is the preservation of families that are suffering from drug abuse. When a drug-dependent infant is born and is placed outside its biological family, the court tries to learn if the mother is willing and able to undergo drug treatment, with the goal being eventual reunification of the family.

The third program, Targeted Outreach, is a delinquency intervention program sponsored by the Boys and Girls Clubs of America (BGCA). According to Sweet (p. 1): "Targeted Outreach is one of the latest developments in a series of progressive steps undertaken by Boys and Girls Clubs of America over the past 19 years to expand services to disadvantaged youth." Targeted Outreach provides positive alternatives for at-risk youths through a referral network that links the clubs with schools, courts, police and other community youth-service agencies. The core program activities are designed to promote a sense of belonging, competence, usefulness and power or influence.

These goals are very similar to those of the Boy Scouts of America, who also have much to offer high-risk youths, as noted by Helgemoe (1992, p. 157): "To build a stronger America and to bring juveniles at risk into society's mainstream, we must instill or reaffirm ethical standards and moral values. The Boy Scouts of America offers an excellent method for accomplishing this goal."

Another program that emphasizes the family is Des Moines, Iowa's, An In-Home Family Support Services, which views delinquency as resulting in some measure from an unstable home and family environment. In such situations family members often are not supportive of each other, and adults are hindered from socializing children positively. The program seeks to improve family communication and stability, bolster self-esteem and to teach effective parenting skills.

Parks and Lugo (1998) report on the efforts made in one Los Angeles region known as the Hollenbeck Area, a conglomerate of four communities spread over more than 15 square miles and including more than 195,000 residents and 50 known gangs comprised of nearly 10,000 validated gang members. In 1995 the Hollenbeck Area Parent Awareness Program was created to help local parents to identify and deal with drugs, gangs and other problematic behavior afflicting their children. The program taught parenting skills and how to control children at risk of becoming gang members, drug abusers or participants in other types of criminal activity. Commenting on the basic premise of the program, Parks and Lugo (p. 52) state: "If parents take a strong role in controlling their children, juvenile crime will be drastically reduced. Toward that end, Hollenbeck's schools, churches and police have joined forces to help educate area parents regarding their responsibilities and legal ability to discipline their children."

Farrington (1994, p. 221) observes: "It is clear that problem children tend to grow up into problem adults and that problem adults tend to produce more problem children. Major efforts to tackle the roots of crime are urgently needed, especially those focusing on early development." Cullen et al. (p. 189) concur: "Early intervention programs, which target high-risk children and high-risk families, have the potential to prevent considerable amounts of crime by stopping the development of children into juvenile and adult criminals. The generality of deviance—the tendency for those who go into crime to engage in other forms of misconduct—means that prevention programs may also have general preventative effects across a range of problem behaviors."

Preventing Child Neglect and Abuse

Given that a disproportionate number of neglected and abused children become delinquents, preventing child neglect and abuse serves a dual function. According to the National Committee for the Prevention of Child Abuse (NCPCA) (1986, p. 23):

> In general, it is agreed that the preventive strategies and programs aimed against child abuse would also prevent delinquency both indirectly, by preventing the abuse that leads to delinquency, and directly, by strengthening family and social supports for all individuals in the community.
>
> Preventive programs include: support programs for new parents; parent education; child care opportunities; treatment programs for abused children and young adults to prevent them from becoming abusing parents; life skills training for children and young adults; self-help groups and other neighborhood supports; and family support services.
>
> Generally, prevention should be offered early and without excessive intrusion. Prevention would most sensibly be aimed at reducing common causes or correlates of child abuse and delinquency, such as poor parenting skills, isolation from positive community supports, and family stress.

A student at Capital High School in Helena, Montana, holds the school's Baby Think It Over doll. The $250 infant simulator is used in child development classes to teach students how their lives will change if they become parents.

Another influential group to consider the problems of children who have been abused, deprived or neglected is the Metropolitan Court Judges Committee, a committee of the National Council of Juvenile and Family Court Judges. The National Council was founded in 1937 to improve the nation's complex juvenile justice system. Located at the University of Nevada, Reno, its training division, the National College of Juvenile Justice, has reached more than 65,000 juvenile justice professionals, an influence unparalleled by any judicial training organization in the country.

Recommendations of the Metropolitan Court Judges Committee

The Metropolitan Court Judges Committee also stresses the importance of preventive measures (pp. 35–40): "The response of society to the tragedy of deprived children has been after-the-fact and ineffective. . . . Prevention of child abuse and neglect requires the awareness and involvement of the entire community. Deprived children are everyone's business. Their social and economic costs affect all Americans now and in the future." Among the committee's recommendations are the following:

- *Priority for prevention.* Prevention and early intervention efforts must receive a high priority, with a greater emphasis placed on providing adequate services to prevent child abuse, neglect and family breakups through adequate education, early identification of those at risk, and family-based counseling and homemaker services.
- *Parenting education.* Continuing education in parenting and in understanding the physical and emotional needs of children and families should be widely available in schools, health care systems, religious organizations, and community centers.
- *Teenage parents.* Communities must provide special parenting education and services for pregnant teenagers as well as teenage parents, including counseling on relinquishment and adoption.

- *Child care facilities.* Adequate child care facilities and services, with training, licensing, and monitoring of the providers, should be available to all parents needing such services.
- *Employee assistance programs.* Employer-sponsored assistance and counseling programs for family violence and child abuse or neglect, such as those used for alcoholism and drug abuse, should be established.

Early prevention programs should include making prevention a priority and providing parenting education, programs for teenage parents, child care facilities and employee assistance programs.

- *Children's disabilities.* Identification and assessment of the physically, mentally, or emotionally disabled or learning disabled child must occur as early as possible.
- *Help for disabled.* Services and education must be designed for and provided to mentally ill, emotionally disturbed, and physically or developmentally disabled children and parents.

Services and education must be provided for children with disabilities, e.g., learning disabled, emotionally disturbed, mentally ill or physically or developmentally disabled.

- *Child support enforcement.* Judges must assure that child support orders are expedited and vigorously enforced and urge cooperation among all components of the child support enforcement process and all federal and state government agencies which may affect child support enforcement proceedings.
- *Exploited children.* Persons convicted of exploiting children through pornography, prostitution, or drug use or trafficking must be severely punished. High priorities also must be given to national efforts to curtail the availability to children of pornography and excessively violent materials.
- *Runaway and incorrigible children.* Courts and communities must provide services and courts must intervene, where necessary, to assist homeless, truant, runaway, and incorrigible children. Parents must be held personally and financially accountable for the conduct of their children.
- *Truancy and school dropouts.* Courts should cooperate with schools and other agencies to substantially reduce truancy and dropouts by coordinating and providing services and assistance to the habitual truant.
- *Security and custody.* The courts should have authority to detain, in a secure facility, for a limited period, a runaway, truant, or incorrigible child whose chronic behavior constitutes a clear and present danger to the child's own physical or emotional well-being, when the court determines there is no viable alternative.

All children at risk, including runaways, habitual truants, the chronically incorrigible and those not receiving any or inadequate child support, must be considered when providing prevention services.

OJJDP Exemplary Programs for Neglected and Abused Children

Most of the programs described in this chapter have been selected by the OJJDP as being exemplary. Three of these exemplary programs were discussed earlier in this chapter. Eleven programs described in this chapter have received the **Gould-Wysinger Award,** an award established in 1992 to give national recognition for local achievement in improving the juvenile justice system and helping our nation's youths. These programs' descriptions were written by Allen (1993), the director of special projects for the Coalition of Juvenile Justice and overseer for administration of the award solicitation process. These programs are designated GWA in the sections to come.

Kansas Children's Service League Juvenile Assessment and Intake Service

The Juvenile Assessment and Intake Service (JAIS), which serves Topeka and Shawnee Counties, protects children from unnecessary out-of-home placement and involvement with Social and Rehabilitation Services (SRS) and the juvenile court. The program advises SRS and the juvenile court about children who need special guidance, structure or protection; reduces the number of children classified as Children-in-Need-of-Care who may be placed unnecessarily in locked detention; and assists law enforcement officers with decisions involving the placement of children.

Law enforcement officers, who provide all referrals to JAIS, increasingly use the service, and the number of contacts for information or referral has grown steadily. The rate of unnecessary placement of Children-in-Need-of-Services in locked detention has significantly decreased. (GWA)

Home for the Prevention of Juvenile Delinquency, Puerto Rico

This program provides shelter and other support services to 28 girls, the majority of whom have been removed from their homes because of sexual abuse or abandonment. Most of the girls, who range in age from 4 to 18, have parents who are physically or mentally unable to care for them adequately. The program provides crisis intervention, counseling, tutoring, educational placement, community services, and recreational and social activities. (GWA)

Programs in the Schools

Prevention programs in Rhode Island and Oregon schools use alternative education programs to reach at-risk youths. Such programs are based on the belief that failure in school increases the likelihood that youths will commit delinquent acts. The school is considered an appropriate vehicle to help children meet their early developmental needs in six major roles in life: learner, individual, producer, citizen, consumer and family member. Helping children to recognize and prepare for these roles should prevent problems, including delinquency, in later life.

Included in other prevention programs are:

- *Job/career programs* that help youths to define their career interests, provide vocational training and teach youths how to look for a job and other employment services.
- *Advocacy programs* in which youths, their families and school staff members monitor and pressure for needed changes in youth services.

Cantelon and LeBoeuf (1997, p. 2) report on one collaboration at work for youths:

> The Communities In Schools (CIS) network is a web of local, state, and national partnerships working together to bring at-risk youth four basics every child needs and deserves:
>
> - A personal one-on-one relationship with a caring adult.
> - A safe place to learn and grow.
> - A marketable skill to use upon graduation.
> - A chance to give back to peers and community.
>
> CIS treats the student and his or her family in a holistic manner, bringing together in one place a support system of caring adults who ensure that the student has access to the resources that can help him or her build self-worth and the skills needed to embark on a more productive and constructive life.

Berger and Graham (1998, p. 7) discuss the problem of suspended students and how, instead of staying home under parental supervision during such suspensions, such students often tend to hang out at the mall, loiter at local convenience stores or engage in criminal activity such as breaking into homes and cars. To counter such unsupervised suspension, a North Miami Beach, Florida, community created the Alternative to Suspension Program (ASP), bringing together parents, schools and law enforcement in an effort to keep suspended students off the streets and away from criminal activity. Berger and Graham (pp. 7–8) note:

> The key to the alternative program is structure. Students serve their suspensions in a classroom setting away from the school. Their parents or guardians drop them off each day at 8:30 and pick them up at 3 p.m. . . . A part-time teacher provides instruction in reading and math, a school counselor holds group and individual behavior-modification sessions, and police officers from the department's community policing and crime prevention units discuss crime and criminal behavior.
>   . . . Topics of discussion include drug and alcohol abuse, burglary and robbery, gangs, sexual assault and date rape, vandalism, conflict resolution, and self-esteem issues. The methods used to convey these messages are as diverse as the students themselves. Officers use printed materials, audio and videotapes, and role-play scenarios, as well as more traditional discussions and lectures.
>   . . . By the end of the school year, 121 out of 165 students had successfully completed the program and returned to school.

Furthermore by the time their suspension was over, more than 90 percent of the students had improved their math skills (p. 8).

In another innovative program, instructors from the Salt Lake City Community College's (SLCC) criminal justice program provide classroom safety training to Salt Lake–area school district teachers (Slama, 1998, p. 38). Citing recent school shootings as an impetus for the program, coordinator Mike Miskinis states: "We're offering a comprehensive educational program that is designed to provide professional educators with the tools necessary to deal with the problems in schools. We want teachers to recognize potential problems and address them before they become reality. . . . People think the shooting in Arkansas doesn't happen in Utah, or won't happen in their classroom, but it can." Training courses offered include handling gangs and juvenile delinquency; hate, bias and ritualistic

In some programs, teachers work one-on-one with at-risk students to help them acquire basic skills such as reading, writing, and conflict resolution.

crimes; school and workplace violence; threat assessment; crisis management and negotiation; weapons; psychological profiling; self-defense; and community-oriented policing strategies.

To prevent weapons incidents in schools, Dorn (1998, pp. 33–34) advises: "The following countermeasures have proven effective in reducing weapons violations and assaults on campus and in school safety zones:

- The assignment of armed, sworn, carefully selected and specially trained police personnel to the middle school and high school settings
- Implementation of a well-designed dress code and code of conduct
- Classroom educational programs, periodic announcements over the school intercom system, posters, signs, student behavior contracts and video presentations
- Specific countermeasures [including] a variety of weapons screening efforts that help to deter violations by creating the perception among potential offenders that they will be caught and punished."

McGillis (1996, pp. 2–3) reports on New York City's School-Based Community Centers known as "Beacons of Hope":

> The Beacon Community Center Program ("the Beacons") offers an integrated strategy to help youths and their families. Developed in New York City in 1991, the Beacons program converts local school buildings into active community centers for use after school, on weekends, and during the summer. . . .
>
> A core concept of the Beacons is that efforts to prevent violence, drug abuse, and other social problems must simultaneously address a wide range of critical needs of at-risk groups rather than provide isolated intervention.

The Beacons program follows a public health model by incorporating services and activities that focus on important risk and protective factors, as shown in Table 12.3.

Table 12.3
Risk and Protective Factors

Category	Risk Factors	Protective Factors
Individual	Alienation, lack of bonding to society	Resilient temperament, positive attitudes
Family	Child abuse, family conflict, parental rejection	Bonding with prosocial family members, provision of clear standards for behavior by the family
School	Early academic failure, lack of commitment to school	Bonding with teachers, commitment to school
Peer Group	Friends involved in crime and violence	Healthy friendships with prosocial peers
Community	Poverty, high rates of drug abuse and crime	Clear standards for behavior and recognition of positive behavior

Source: Daniel McGillis. *Beacons of Hope: New York City's School-Based Community Centers.* National Institute of Justice Program Focus, January 1996, p. 3. (NCJ-157667)

OJJDP Exemplary Programs in the Schools[1]

Anger Management Program, North Dakota

Located in Bismarck, the Anger Management Program works with youths and their parents to help them control outbursts of angry, aggressive behavior. The 10-week training program reduces the frequency of aggressive or violent incidents by developing awareness of anger patterns and teaching new skills for handling anger-provoking situations. The curriculum includes separate groups for parents, junior and high school students, and fifth and sixth graders.

Young people enrolled in the program have reduced their involvement in aggressive and violent incidents. The program draws on the resources of virtually every youth-serving agency, public and private, that maintains a local staff. The State training school and a private residential facility have requested training in anger management so that they can incorporate a similar component in their programs. (GWA)

Bright Future Project, Tennessee

This juvenile delinquency prevention project provides academic and social support to African-American youths age 5 to 15. Bright Future provides study resources to help youths complete their homework assignments. Reading and comprehension testing and prescribed tutoring are available for a limited number of youths. Decision-making rap sessions, discussions, and practice sessions are also provided. Supervised opportunities allow youths to contribute to their community by participating in neighborhood improvement projects.

The program serves some 30 children per day. Teachers note that the quantity and quality of schoolwork of participants have improved. The program has gained the respect of the community, and the Neighborhood Association has become the center of community life largely as a result of this project. (GWA)

McAlester Alternative School Project, Oklahoma

The McAlester Alternative School Project was developed to provide education services to at-risk students in the McAlester Public School District. The school allows

[1] Program descriptions provided by Allen (1993).

students to learn at their own pace in a more relaxed setting. It provides onsite child care for teen parents and teaches fundamentals of child care. Class sizes are small, and a counselor is available throughout the day to provide personal, crisis, and career counseling. Attendance is voluntary. The school has helped meet the needs of a community experiencing serious socioeconomic problems. (GWA)

Griffin Alternative Learning Academy, Florida

Griffin Alternative Learning Academy (GALA) diverts students from failing in school, being suspended, needing court intervention, or dropping out of school. The program focuses on disruptive, unsuccessful, disinterested, and otherwise problematic students at Griffin Middle School in Leon County. The objective is to mainstream or promote 75 percent of the at-risk students back into regular classes by providing individualized academic assistance and business mentoring.

A project evaluation confirmed overall improvement in participants' grade-point averages, a decrease in the number of absences and suspensions, and a reduction in delinquency referrals. All participants were promoted to the next grade. Because of the success of the program, the Governor's JJDP Advisory Committee funded replications of the project in two other schools. (GWA)

General Delinquency Prevention Programs

Helping Communities Fight Crime (1997, Foreword) notes: "Concerning our nations' young people, it is crucial that we dedicate at least the same commitment to keeping our kids from falling into crime as to enforcing the law after it is violated. . . . Prevention and intervention are equally important in any effort to address adult crime." To that end Jane Alexander, Chair for the National Endowment for the Arts, states: "Give a child a paintbrush or a clarinet, and he is much less likely to pick up a gun or a needle. Give a child a chance to explore and express perceptions of the world, and you are encouraging positive behavior. This has everything to do with crime prevention" (*Helping Communities Fight Crime,* p. 4). Table 12.4 lists the myriad activities communities nationwide are using to achieve their crime prevention goals.

Several programs are aimed at the general concept of delinquency prevention. Five OJJDP exemplary projects described by Allen are general projects.

OJJDP Exemplary Programs

Project HELP, North Carolina

Project HELP (Helping Equip Little People) is an early intervention program that concentrates on delinquency prevention. The goals of the program are to promote wholesome values and moral living, impart work-readiness skills, develop social and cultural skills, give youths an opportunity to interact with positive adult role models and involve parents in all phases of the program.

The program serves youths ages 6 to 10 who have exhibited behaviors that make them at-risk of entering the juvenile justice system. Volunteers, who are matched with an appropriate youth, work with program staff, parents, and youths to develop individual programs and create opportunities for leadership development.

To date every parent of a child in the program has become involved, and three-quarters of the children have participated in the social and cultural enrich-

Table 12.4
Community Activities to Achieve Crime Prevention Goals

Academic enrichment	Enforcement of weapons laws	Probation and supervised release
After-school activities	Environmental work projects	Public education
Aftercare services	Family support services	Public-private partnerships
Apprenticeships	Gang intervention	Recognition
Building safety and security	Gun safety	Recreation
Child care	Health care access	Safe passages/corridors
Child protective services	Home visits	School antidrug/weapon policies
College scholarships	Housing placement	Self-defense training
Community mobilization	Housing renovation	Service integration
Community policing	Interagency coordination	Shelters
Community schools	Job creation	Sports leagues
Community service	Job placement	Stress management
Computer skills training	Job training	Summer jobs for youth
Conflict resolution	Leadership skills development	Substance abuse education
Counseling	Literacy	Substance abuse treatment
Cultural awareness	Media campaigns	Theater and the arts
Domestic violence awareness	Mental health screening	Transportation
Domestic violence shelters	Mentoring	Tutoring
Drug courts	Nutrition services	Victim restitution
Drug testing	Outreach	Youth involvement
Educational stipends	Parent education and training	Zoning
Employment skills	Parental involvement	
Enforcement of drug laws	Park and neighborhood clean-up	

Source: *Helping Communities Fight Crime: Comprehensive Planning Techniques, Models, Programs and Resources.* Washington, DC: The President's Crime Prevention Council Catalog, 1997, p. 4.

ment programs. Everyone has participated in community service activities either through the schools, local civic groups, or the housing authority. Not one participant has become involved with the juvenile justice system. (GWA)

"Graffiti Street," Virgin Islands
"Graffiti Street" is a teen talk show designed to prevent juvenile delinquency by improving communication and developing understanding between youths and adults. The format uses a teen panel, guest speakers, and guest performers. Participants represent a cross-section of the population. The show is very popular with youths and adults and has received a national public broadcasting award. (GWA)

Hollandale Temporary Holding Facility, Mississippi
The Hollandale Temporary Holding Facility was established to provide a separate facility that meets all federal and state standards for juveniles awaiting further action by a youth authority. Facility staff are on call 24 hours a day. Emergency care and crisis intervention include youth court counselors' services and referrals to a local community health service. The facility also provides supervised educational and recreational activities while youths are awaiting disposition or placement.

The facility holds juveniles who would otherwise have been placed in an adult jail or lockup—decreasing by 90 percent the number of juveniles held in adult jails and lockups in the six counties served. (GWA)

Regional Juvenile Justice Program Development, Washington State

The Regional Juvenile Justice Program Development program is an interagency approach to developing strategies for preventing and reducing juvenile delinquency in Snohomish County. The major goal of the program is to implement the Juvenile Justice and Delinquency Prevention Act. . . . Project staff develop and recommend procedures for the coordination of local juvenile justice activities and work to ensure that duplication and conflict between agencies are minimized, service gaps are identified, and systemwide problems are addressed. The program serves as a resource for the State Advisory Group (SAG) in identifying technical assistance and training needs, providing information and assistance to local agencies to help them develop proposals responsive to SAG priorities, and reviewing and prioritizing proposals for SAG funding.

Other program activities include collecting data for a needs assessment to identify local juvenile justice needs.

Rites of Passage, Iowa

Rites of Passage was developed to address minority overrepresentation by reducing the delinquency rate among middle school African-American males from high-risk situations. The project involves tutoring, mentoring, crisis intervention, individual and family counseling, and recreational activities. Development of participants' self-esteem and personal responsibility are emphasized. The project is so safe and supportive that participants come even when activities have not been scheduled. The project has built a community of trust among participants and their mentors. As a result participants' family lives and academic performance have significantly improved. (GWA)

Violence Prevention

The OJJDP report, "A Comprehensive Strategy for Serious, Violent, and Chronic Juvenile Offenders," calls for increasingly intensive treatment. The report identifies six principles for preventing delinquent conduct and reducing serious, violent and chronic delinquency ("OJJDP Strategy," 1993, p. 3):

- Strengthen families to instill moral values and provide guidance and support to children.
- Support core social institutions such as schools, religious institutions, and other community organizations to alleviate risk factors for youth.
- Promote delinquency prevention strategies that reduce the impact of risk factors and enhance the influence of protective factors for youth at the greatest risk of delinquency.

Table 12.5 **Strategies to Prevent Youth Violence**	Education	Legal/Regulatory Change	Environmental Modification
	Adult mentoring	Regulate the use of and access to weapons:	Modify the social environment:
	Conflict resolution		Home visitation
	Training in social skills	Weaponless schools	Preschool programs such as
	Firearm safety	Control of concealed weapons	Head Start
	Parenting centers	Restrictive licensing	Therapeutic activities
	Peer education	Appropriate sale of guns	Recreational activities
	Public information and education campaigns	Regulate the use of and access to alcohol:	Work/academic experiences
			Modify the physical environment:
		Appropriate sale of alcohol	Make risk areas visible
		Prohibition or control of alcohol sales at events	Increase use of an area
		Training of servers	Limit building entrances and exits
		Other types of regulations:	
		Appropriate punishment in schools	
		Dress codes	

Source: National Center for Injury Prevention and Control.

- Intervene immediately when delinquent behavior occurs.
- Institute a broad spectrum of graduated sanctions that provide accountability and a continuum of services to respond appropriately to the individual needs of an offender.
- Identify and control the small segment of serious, violent and chronic juvenile offenders.

In written testimony at a hearing on October 23, 1993, John J. Wilson, the acting director of OJJDP, wrote:

Most delinquency prevention efforts have been unsuccessful because of their negative approach—attempting to keep juveniles from misbehaving. Our . . . strategy recommends instead positive approaches that emphasize opportunities for healthy social, physical and mental development ("OJJDP Strategy," p. 3).

The National Center for Injury Prevention and Control has also established a set of strategies to prevent youth violence that involve education, legal/regulatory change and environmental modification, as shown in Table 12.5.

Drug Prevention Programs

Because of the known link between drug abuse and delinquency, many programs focus on drug abuse prevention.

DARE

DARE is perhaps the best-known and most recognized drug prevention program in the country. DARE and its spinoff project, the National DARE Parent Program, were discussed in detail in Chapter 8.

The National Commission on Drug-Free Schools

The report of the National Commission on Drug-Free Schools (1990, p. iv) includes the following remark by then-President George Bush in recognition of drug-free schools:

> Ultimately the most important weapons in the war on drugs are the least tangible ones; self-discipline, courage, support from the family, and faith in one's self. The answer is traditional values. And if we want to stop our kids from putting drugs in their bodies, we must first ensure that they have good ideas in their heads and moral character in their hearts.

The report (pp. 35–36) suggests that a comprehensive drug education and prevention program should have eight key elements:

- Student survey, school needs assessment, and resource identification.
- Leadership training of key school officials and staff with authority to develop policies and programs.
- School policies that are clear, consistent, and fair, with responses to violations that include alternatives to suspension.
- Training for the entire staff on the following:
  — The school's alcohol and drug policies and policy implementation throughout
  — Drug use, abuse, and dependency
  — Effects on family members and others
  — Intervention and referral of students
- Assistance programs/support for students from preschool through grade 12, including the following:
  — Tutoring, mentoring, and other academic activities
  — Support groups (e.g., Alcoholics Anonymous and Children of Alcoholics)
  — Peer counseling
  — Extracurricular activities (e.g., sports, drama, journalism)
  — Vocational programs (e.g., work-study and apprenticeship)
  — Social activities (including drug-free proms and graduation activities)
  — Alternative programs (e.g., Upward Bound and Outward Bound)
  — Community service projects
- Training for parents, including the following information:
  — The effects of drug use, abuse, and dependency on users, their families, and other people
  — Ways to identify drug problems and refer people for treatment
  — Available resources to diagnose and treat people with drug problems
  — Laws and school policies on drugs, including alcohol and tobacco
  — The influence of parents' attitudes and behavior toward drugs including alcohol and tobacco, and of parents' expectations of graduation and academic performance of their children

- — The importance of establishing appropriate family rules, monitoring behavior of children, imposing appropriate punishments, and reinforcing positive behavior
- — Ways to improve skills in communication and conflict management
- — The importance of networking with other parents and knowing their children's friends and their families

- Curriculum for preschool through grade 12, including the following subjects:[2]
  - — Information about all types of drugs, including medicines.
  - — The relationship of drugs to suicide, AIDS, drug-affected babies, pregnancy, violence, and other health and safety issues.
  - — The social consequences of drug abuse
  - — Respect for the laws and values of society, including discussions of right and wrong
  - — The importance of honesty, hard work, achievement, citizenship, compassion, patriotism and other civic and personal values
  - — Promotion of healthy, safe, and responsible attitudes and behavior
  - — Ways to build resistance to influences that encourage drug use, such as peer pressure, advertising, and other media appeals (refusal skills)
  - — Ways to develop critical thinking, problem-solving, decision-making, persuasion, and interpersonal skills
  - — Ways to develop active participation, cooperative learning, and consensus-building skills
  - — Ways to increase self-control and self-esteem based on achievement and to cope with stress, anger, and anxiety
  - — Strategies to get parents, family members, and the community involved in preventing drug use.
  - — Information on contacting responsible adults when young people need help and on intervention and referral services
  - — sensitivity to cultural differences in the school and community and to local drug problems
  - — Information about how advertising works

- Collaboration with community services to provide the following services:
  - — student assistance programs;
  - — employee assistance programs for school staff;

---

[2] Curriculum must be developmentally oriented, age-appropriate, up-to-date and accurate. Individual components work best as part of a comprehensive curriculum program. When presented in isolation, components such as information about drugs can exacerbate the problem.

— Latchkey child care

— Medical care, including treatment for alcohol and other drug abuse

— Nutrition information and counseling

— Mental health care

— Social welfare services

— Probation services

— Continuing education for dropouts and pushouts

— In-service training for teachers and counselors in intervention techniques and procedures

— programs for students at high risk of drug use

The report also includes a 24- by 28- inch chart detailing the roles and responsibilities for a drug-free school and community. Across the top are the specific groups involved: students, family, community organizations/parent groups, schools/colleges and universities, religious organizations, media, business/industry, health and social services, law enforcement/judicial and government. Down the left side are the functions to be undertaken: awareness/education, education/training, assessment, policy/legislation, prevention, intervention, treatment/aftercare, funding and research.

The National Crime Prevention Council's Programs

The National Crime Prevention Council (NCPC) has also focused efforts on drug abuse prevention. They identified three communities and highlighted their success in reducing drug abuse by using the talents of youths within the community. As noted in their foreword (National Crime Prevention Council, 1992, p. i):

> Too many of us, when we look at young people, see problems or potential problems. What we could and should be seeing are enormous resources—talented, enthusiastic, able people who want to do good and want to be part of the community.
>
> Faced with a drug problem that (though modestly diminished) is still pernicious, we cavil against the shortage of resources but overlook millions of young people who can counsel, educate, organize, and otherwise prevent drug abuse and crime on behalf of their communities.
>
> NCPC believes strongly that young people can and want to be part of the solution to the drug problem. We believe that young people can design and carry out projects that will help reduce the demand for drugs in their communities, using modest fiscal resources combined with intelligence, dedication, and energy to effect remarkable changes. Moreover, youth working to prevent drug abuse deliver a far stronger and more effective message to peers than does adult carping and lecturing.

The NCPC lists the following reasons to use youths in the local drug wars (p. 1):

■ The act of taking on responsibility, far from confounding adolescents, sustains them.

■ Experience-based learning is a highly effective means of teaching a variety of skills and disciplines.

- Service to our communities is part of the dues all of us should expect to pay as members of a free, democratic society.

- Youths need to feel that they, as individuals, have a place and a stake in their communities, that they are needed and their contributions valued.

- Youths by working in partnership with adults gain important exposure to the adult world, exposure that is too often in short supply in modern communities.

- The value of reinforcing positive behaviors has long been known, but our social structures tend to concentrate on pathologies, on rehabilitating youths (which is appropriate in certain instances), rather than cherishing and rewarding that which is valuable, competent and worthy.

Their program, called Teens as Resources Against Drugs (TARAD), is funded by the Bureau of Justice Statistics. TARAD was piloted at three sites: New York City (Teens Go After Worms in the Big Apple), Evansville, Indiana (Drugs Are Out in Evansville) and communities in South Carolina (Kids in the Know Say No in South Carolina).

The TARAD program of the National Crime Prevention Council uses youths to take on the community drug prevention challenge.

The concept is based on two premises: (1) teens are deeply concerned about the effects of drug abuse on their peers and on the community at large, and (2) as young people go through adolescence, they need to develop independence and a sense that their skills and accomplishments are needed and valued by their community.

Community support for TARAD is strong, as evidenced by the following project sponsors: high schools, middle schools, elementary schools, special education programs, alternative schools, youth membership organizations, nonprofit organizations, community centers, neighborhood organizations and groups, churches, colleges, hospitals, group homes, support groups, youth councils, mental health centers and police athletic leagues. In addition a wide variety of projects have been undertaken, including peer helping and mentoring, puppet troupes, awareness campaigns, drug patrols, lock-ins, establishing drug/alcohol-free organizations, drop-in or teen centers, beautification of drug infested areas, murals, newspapers, contests, videos, products, conferences, events and health fairs. The NCPC reports the following "exciting and varied results" (p. 36):

- For the communities: drug dealers moved out; communities more frequently turned to youths for assistance in policy making; a school changed its curriculum to acknowledge the value of community service, and annual abuse prevention activities are becoming part of local calendars.

- For the youths: youths found a safer, drug-free environment; they had an opportunity to be themselves, "warts and all"; they came to believe they could make a difference; they got assistance with jobs and scholarships; and they learned new life skills.

Mentoring

Under the Juvenile Justice and Delinquency Prevention (JJDP) Act, the OJJDP is authorized to fund mentoring efforts. In fiscal year 1998, Congress appropriated $12 million to support the Juvenile Mentoring Program (JUMP), including associated programs such as Big Brothers/Big Sisters. According to the OJJDP (*Juvenile Mentoring*, 1998, p. 3): "Mentoring . . . is defined as a one-to-one relationship between a pair of unrelated individuals, one an adult age 21 or older (mentor) and the other a juvenile (mentee), which takes place on a regular basis over an extended period of time."

The mentoring movement began at the end of the nineteenth century, when adults called the Friendly Visitors served as role models for poor children. During the 1970s, mentoring found its way into corporate America as a means for the ambitious employee to find success on the corporate ladder. Most recently mentoring has returned to its roots, focusing on disadvantaged youths and providing support and advocacy to children in need (*Juvenile Mentoring*, p. 3).

Gang Prevention

The Bureau of Justice Assistance (*Addressing Community*, 1998, p. xxii) states: "Communities with emerging or existing gang problems must plan, develop, and implement comprehensive, harm-specific responses that include a broad range of community-based components." Three suggested approaches are:

- Developing strategies to discourage gang involvement and membership
- Providing ways for youths to drop out of gangs
- Empowering communities to solve gang-associated problems through collaboration with law enforcement, parents, schools, businesses, religious and social service organizations, local government officials and youths themselves in a comprehensive, systematic approach

In emphasizing the importance of cooperation and collaboration, the BJA (p. 118) claims: "Approaches to local gang problems that emphasize sharing resources and forming community coalitions are based on the premise that no single organization or individual can prevent the development of gangs or their harmful activities." Furthermore (p. 119): "Team building as well as training in cultural and ethnic diversity and conflict resolution may be necessary to facilitate progress toward collaboration."

Antigang Programs

The National School Safety Center (1988, p. 35) publication, *Gangs in Schools: Breaking Up Is Hard to Do*, notes: "We do a lot of work helping separate gang members from gangs. We want to give them a shot at making something of themselves. It's not easy." The center suggests that "a positive, consistent approach to discipline and conflict prevention can achieve long-term and far-reaching results and improve the overall school climate" (p. 25). The center suggests several prevention and intervention strategies.

Behavior codes should be established and enforced firmly and consistently. Such behavior codes may include a dress code, a ban on the showing of gang colors and a ban on using gang hand signals. Friendliness and cooperation should be promoted and rewarded.

Graffiti removal should be done immediately. Graffiti is not only unattractive, it allows gangs to advertise their turf and their authority. A Los Angeles school administrator suggests that graffiti be photographed before removal so that the police can better investigate the vandalism. Evidence, such as paint cans and paint brushes, should be turned over to the police. In addition students might design and paint their own murals in locations where graffiti is likely to appear.

Conflict prevention strategies can also be effective. Teachers should be trained to recognize gang members and to deal with them in a nonconfrontational way. All gang members should be made known to staff. Teachers should try to build self-esteem and promote academic success for all students, including gang members. School-based programs can combine gang and drug prevention efforts.

Crisis management should be an integral part of the administration's plan for dealing with any gang activity that might occur. A working relationship should be established with the police department, and a plan for managing a crisis should be developed. The plan should include procedures for communicating with the authorities, parents and the public.

Community involvement can also be extremely effective in reducing or even preventing gang activity. Parents and the general public can be made aware of gangs operating in the community, as well as of popular heavy metal and punk bands. They can be encouraged to apply pressure to radio and television stations and bookstores to ban material that promotes the use of alcohol or drugs, promiscuity or devil worship.

Antigang programs include establishing behavior codes, removing graffiti, implementing conflict prevention strategies, developing a plan for crisis management and fostering community involvement.

Appendix D contains descriptions of several antigang programs.

Comprehensive Programs

Some programs offer a comprehensive range of prevention services. Among these are YouthCare and the CAR Program.

YouthCare

YouthCare is a private nonprofit agency in the state of Washington that provides services to young people in crisis. As noted in their annual report (1992, p. 30):

> To work through the challenges of adolescence and to successfully mature is not an easy task for any young person. For the children and young adults that YouthCare serves, it is often overwhelming. Many of them have encountered problems that would overwhelm most of us. They come from homes with severe difficulties; they have been abused; they have been abandoned in early childhood or later adolescence. In spite of these problems, they continue to grow and seek our help as they sort through the choices facing them. The ability to provide guidance and direction, while allowing youth to make their own choices, is a central theme of all our programming.

YouthCare collaborates with the public schools, the Catholic Community Services, the YMCA, the Seattle Mental Health Institute, the University of Washington, the Seattle Children's Home and several local health care facilities. They are supported by funding from businesses, churches, corporations, foundations and private groups. Their comprehensive programs are described in the following paragraphs (1992, pp. 10–11). (Reprinted by permission.)

The Shelter

The Shelter is a short-term crisis facility for young people from 11 to 17 years of age. Both boys and girls who are runaway and homeless can be placed for a maximum of 14 days. The Shelter accepts youths from any referral source, including walk-ins. Services to youths in placement include casework, counseling, academic evaluation and course work, drug-alcohol counseling, recreational activities and a 24-hour crisis line.

Threshold

Threshold is a transitional living program designed to aid young women, 16 to 18 years old, in making the transition from a "street lifestyle" to a more productive way of living. The primary goal is to provide a safe, home-like environment where residents receive intensive support and services to build a foundation for living within the community.

Straley House

Straley House is a residential program that assists 18- to 21-year-old young adults in their transition toward healthy independent living. The program is designed to serve a population of young people no longer eligible for youth programs, who will be underserved in the adult system. Straley House works to address the needs youths have as they begin the path to adulthood.

Orion Multi-Service Center

The Orion Center programs serve young people between the ages of 11 and 20. Services are especially designed for homeless and high-risk youths. The Orion Center offers case management; drug and alcohol counseling; mental health services; individual, family and group counseling; a school program; recreational opportunities; meals program; and referral to shelters.

Gang Prevention and Intervention

YouthCare plays an integral role in Seattle Team for Youth, a city-wide effort to provide gang prevention and intervention services. In partnership with the City of Seattle, the Police Department, Department of Social and Health Services and 11 other agencies, YouthCare works to offer positive alternatives to gang involvement to those youths who are at-risk.

These services include drug and alcohol treatment, employment workshops, job placement, tutoring, mentoring, sports and recreation, leadership training, self-esteem building and cultural activities.

Family Reconciliation Services (FRS)

YouthCare maintains a goal of strengthening and reuniting families whenever possible. Through a contract with the Department of Social and Health Services, Youth-

Care works with families in crisis. The goal is to provide counseling services to families in conflict. The program attempts to prevent the child from being placed out of the home, to reunite family if the youth has run away, to teach the family problem-solving skills and to give the family the tools needed for dealing with conflict.

Outreach

The Outreach program maintains a presence on the streets in many areas of the city and county where youths gather. The team works to establish relationships with youths to provide services, including drug and alcohol education, AIDS prevention education, counseling, referral to shelter, food and medical care.

Outreach workers assist youths in returning to or remaining with their families and school, finding housing, medical care, drug and alcohol treatment, legal assistance or other services. This effort works closely with the Orion Center.

AIDS Education

The YouthCare education and prevention team provides both education to youths in high-risk situations and training to individuals who work with these youths.

Research and Evaluation

To provide the most effective services for its clients, YouthCare regularly conducts evaluation and research of its programs. This evaluation is accomplished by formal research endeavors, periodic testing of clients to determine changes, and regular program audits that contract with independent researchers to examine the efficiency of YouthCare's services.

YouthCare WestSound Serving Kitsap County

YouthCare WestSound works with a local advisory board and existing programs to increase awareness in the community of the issues of "street youth" and to develop a continuum of services for this population, including counseling, family reconciliation services, and referral services to youth who are runaways, homeless, or involved in or at-risk for criminal activity.

The CAR Program

The Children at Risk (CAR) program seeks to divert inner-city youths from getting involved with drugs, gangs and crime by providing an intensive program of activities, which include case management, after-school and summer programs, counseling (both individual and family), tutoring, mentoring, community policing and more. As noted by Hebert (1993, p. 6): "CAR is a unique public/private partnership between the Bureau of Justice Assistance (BJA), the Office of Juvenile Justice and Delinquency Prevention (OJJDP) and the National Institute of Justice (NIJ)." Says Hebert:

> The CAR program consists of a service intervention component that includes family intervention, tutoring, mentoring, and incentives for participation; and a criminal justice component that includes neighborhood-based activities designed to reduce the prevalence of drug dealing and drug use. In addition, schools, service providers, police, and other criminal justice agencies collaborate at both a policy and service delivery level to provide a coordinated array of services and support for at-risk youth.

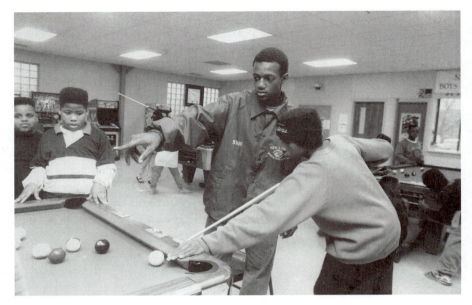

In an after-school program in New Haven, Connecticut, teenagers volunteer to work with younger neighborhood kids, keeping all involved off the streets and out of trouble.

CAR is being implemented in Austin, Texas; Bridgeport, Connecticut; Memphis, Tennessee; Newark, New Jersey; Savannah, Georgia; and Seattle, Washington. Participants must meet demographic requirements and at least one of the following high-risk eligibility criteria (Hebert, p. 8):

- School-based factors

  Student is identified as at risk by the Austin Independent School District's guidelines

  School behavior has resulted in disciplinary action

- Personal-based factors

  Experimentation with alcohol or drugs

  Involvement in drug trafficking

  Referred to juvenile court

  Special education student

  Pregnant, parent, or previous pregnancies

  Abused child

  Gang involvement

- Family-based factors

  Family members involved in the criminal justice system

  Family history of substance abuse

  Family member is a known gang member

  History of family violence

What Works?

With many programs now having several decades of experience behind them, and the road ahead appearing more challenging than ever for those involved in handling juvenile crime, the question being asked is: "What works?" The reviews, thus far, are mixed.

According to a recent study, "many favorite anti-crime programs simply don't work" ("Getting Your Money's Worth," 1998, p. 1). A research team of criminologists at the University of Maryland, led by Lawrence W. Sherman, reviewed over 500 scientific evaluations of crime-prevention programs funded by the Justice Department, with a special focus on factors relating to juvenile crime and program effects on youth violence. One result of the study was that large amounts of money are being spent on programs that do not demonstrate any positive impacts on juvenile delinquency and violence. Among the programs identified in the study that don't work (p. 8): gun buyback programs, military-style correctional boot camps, "scared straight" programs, shock probation/parole, home detention with electronic monitoring, neighborhood watch programs, the DARE program and arrests of juveniles for minor offenses.

The news was not all bad, however. Programs considered promising: gang offender monitoring by community workers and probation and police officers, community-based after-school recreation programs, drug courts and community policing with meetings to set priorities. Several programs found to be working: family therapy and parent training for delinquent and at-risk preadolescents, school-based coaching of high-risk youths in "thinking skills" and special police units that focus on high-risk repeat offenders.

Despite the harsh evaluation of some of the more popular programs for youths, the National Criminal Justice Association (pp. 10–11) states: "More and more research indicates that juvenile crime and delinquency prevention programs not only have a positive impact on troubled youth, but are a good investment when compared with the costs associated with the behavior of serious, violent, and chronic juvenile offenders." According to the NCJA (p. 11): "Programs that consistently demonstrated positive effects on youth at risk of developing delinquent behavior include those that strengthen the institutions of school and family in the life of the youth, such as smaller class sizes in early years of education; tutoring and cooperative learning; classroom behavior management, behavioral monitoring, and reinforcement of school attendance, progress, and behavior; parent training and family counseling; and youth employment and vocational training programs." In addition programs identified as holding promise included mentoring relationships, peer mediation, conflict resolution and violence prevention curricula in schools, community services for delinquent youths, restrictions on the purchase or possession of guns and enhanced motorized patrol and community policing (p. 11).

Summary

In the late 1960s, a new approach for dealing with delinquency emerged: the prevention of crime before youths engage in delinquent acts. Prevention can be corrective, punitive or mechanical. It can also be classified as primary, secondary or tertiary.

Yet another way to look at prevention is the mathematical analogy of numerator/denominator. The numerator approach focuses on individuals and symptoms, whereas the denominator approach focuses on the entire group and causes. The public health model's two-pronged strategy reduces known risk factors and promotes protective factors.

Effective prevention approaches must address the causes of delinquency. Also critical are programs aimed at preventing child neglect and abuse. Such early prevention programs should include making prevention a priority, and providing parenting education, programs for teenage parents, child care facilities and employee assistance programs. Services and education also must be provided for children with disabilities, such as the learning disabled, emotionally disturbed, mentally ill or physically or developmentally disabled. All children at risk, including runaways, habitual truants, the chronically incorrigible and those not receiving any or receiving inadequate child support, must be considered when providing prevention services.

Other prevention programs are aimed at the drug problem and the gang problem. The TARAD program of the National Crime Prevention Council enlists youths to take on the community drug prevention challenge. Antigang programs include establishing behavior codes, removing graffiti, implementing conflict prevention strategies, developing a plan for crisis management and fostering community involvement.

Discussion Questions

1. Do you support the numerator or the denominator approach to prevention? Be prepared to defend your choice.
2. Do delinquency prevention programs succeed? Do the programs deter delinquency?
3. What prevention programs are available in your area? Is there a specific target area?
4. Are all three levels of delinquency prevention applied in your area? Which one best suits your area? Why?
5. If social responses treat youths' behavior as delinquent in prevention strategies, does this cause a labeling effect? How would you handle a program so that labeling was not a factor?
6. At what types of delinquency should programs be directed? Violent youths? Status offenders? Antisocial and criminal activity in general? Gang activity?
7. List the assumptions that you feel are basic to effective delinquency prevention programs. To what extent do you feel each assumption is justified?
8. What are some contemporary attempts to prevent delinquency? Why are they effective or ineffective?
9. What kinds of programs exist in your area to prevent child neglect and abuse?
10. What kinds of programs to prevent child neglect and abuse do you think have the most promise?

References

Addressing Community Gang Problems: A Practical Guide. Bureau of Justice Assistance Monograph. May 1998.

Allen, Pam. "The Gould-Wysinger Awards: A Tradition of Excellence." *Juvenile Justice,* Vol. 1, No. 2, Fall/Winter 1993, pp. 23–28.

American Psychological Association. *Violence & Youth: Psychology's Response,* Vol. 1. Summary Report of the American Psychological Association Commission on Violence and Youth. n.d.

Berger, William B. and Graham, Alan P. "Suspended Students: A Practical Approach." *FBI Law Enforcement Bulletin,* July 1998, pp. 7–8.

Cantelon, Sharon and LeBoeuf, Donni. *Keeping Young People in School: Community Programs that Work.* OJJDP Bulletin. June 1997. (NCJ-162783)

Cullen, Francis T.; Wright, John Paul; Brown, Shayna; Moon, Melissa M.; Blankenship, Michael B.; and Applegate, Brandon K. "Public Support for Early Intervention Programs: Implications for a Progressive Policy Agenda." *Crime and Delinquency,* Vol. 44, No. 2, April 1998, pp. 187–204.

Dorn, Michael S. "Preventing School Weapons Incidents." *The Police Chief,* August 1998, pp. 28–36.

Farrington, David P. "Early Developmental Prevention of Juvenile Delinquency." *Criminal Behaviour and Mental Health,* Vol. 4, 1994, pp. 209–227.

"Fighting Crime: What Lawmakers Can Do in Safety's Name." (Minneapolis/St. Paul) *Star Tribune,* February 7, 1994, p. A10.

"Getting Your Money's Worth." *Law Enforcement News,* Vol. 24, No. 496, September 30, 1998, pp. 1, 8.

Hawkins, J. David. "Controlling Crime Before It Happens: Risk-Focused Prevention." *National Institute of Justice Journal,* August 1995, pp. 10–18.

Hebert, Eugene E. "Doing Something About Children at Risk." *National Institute of Justice Journal,* November 1993, pp. 4–9.

Helgemoe, Ray. "Teaming Up with the Boy Scouts to Reach Our High-Risk Youths." *Corrections Today,* July 1992, pp. 156–157.

Helping Communities Fight Crime: Comprehensive Planning Techniques, Models, Programs and Resources. The President's Crime Prevention Council Catalog, 1997.

Juvenile Mentoring Program (JUMP). Washington, DC: Office of Juvenile Justice and Delinquency Prevention, July 1998.

Lejins, P. "The Field of Prevention." In *Delinquency Prevention: Theory and Practice,* edited by Amos and Wellford. Englewood Cliffs, NJ: Prentice Hall, 1967.

McGillis, Daniel. *Beacons of Hope: New York City's School-Based Community Centers.* National Institute of Justice Program Focus. January 1996. (NCJ-157667)

Metropolitan Court Judges Committee Report. *Deprived Children: A Judicial Response.* Washington, DC: U.S. Government Printing Office, 1986.

National Coalition of State Juvenile Justice Advisory Groups. *Myths and Realities: Meeting the Challenge of Serious, Violent, and Chronic Juvenile Offenders, 1992 Annual Report.* Washington, DC: 1993.

National Commission on Drug-Free Schools. *Toward a Drug-Free Generation: A Nation's Responsibility.* Final Report, September 1990.

National Committee for the Prevention of Child Abuse. *Child Abuse: Prelude to Delinquency?* Washington, DC: U.S. Government Printing Office, 1986.

National Crime Prevention Council. *Given the Opportunity: How Three Communities Engaged Teens as Resources in Drug Abuse Prevention.* Washington, DC: 1992.

National Criminal Justice Association. *Juvenile Justice Reform Initiatives in the States: 1994–1996.* OJJDP Program Report. October 1997.

National School Safety Center. *Gangs in Schools: Breaking Up Is Hard to Do.* Malibu, CA: Pepperdine University Press, 1988.

"OJJDP Strategy for Juvenile Offenders Seeks Early Intervention." *NCJA Justice Bulletin,* November 1993, pp. 3–5.

Parks, Bernard C. and Lugo, Rich. "Hollenbeck Community/Police Youth Project." *The Police Chief,* August 1998, pp. 52–57.

President's Commission on Law Enforcement and the Administration of Justice. *The Challenge of Crime in a Free Society.* Washington, DC: U.S. Government Printing Office, 1967.

"Reno Calls for Crime Prevention Programs." (Minneapolis/St. Paul) *Star Tribune,* July 11, 1993, p. A1.

Slama, Julie. "SLCC Helps Teachers Deal with Violence." *The Police Chief,* August 1998, p. 38.

Smith, Robert L. "In the Service of Youth: A Common Denominator." *Juvenile Justice,* Vol. 1, No. 2, Fall/Winter 1993, pp. 9–15.

Sprinthall, Norman A. and Collins, W. Andrew. *Adolescent Psychology: A Developmental View.* New York: Random House, 1984.

Sweet, Robert W. "Preserving Families to Prevent Delinquency." OJJDP Model Programs, Juvenile Justice Bulletin, April 1992.

YouthCare 1992 Annual Report. Seattle, WA.

13 Approaches to Treatment

> In practice, treatment programs are still
> offered, but no one really believes that they
> will work, unless the young person wants to
> change. The truth is that no one really knows
> what works in treatment.
>
> —Timothy D. Crowe

Do You Know

- What is one thing that effective treatment programs often take advantage of?
- What crisis intervention capitalizes on?
- What treatment requirements are recommended by the Metropolitan Court Judges Committee?
- What service requirements are recommended by this committee?
- The committee's recommendations for establishing permanency for the child?
- What three-pronged approach to treatment is needed?
- What two agencies might form a partnership to effectively prevent further delinquency?
- What constitutes effective supervision?
- How gang-related harms might be treated?

Can You Define

abatement, desistance, holistic approach, nuisance, permanency, recidivism, tort

INTRODUCTION

The correctional portion of the juvenile justice system is most intimately concerned with treatment options, as discussed in Chapter 10. Unfortunately as stated in the opening quotation from Crowe, research is lacking or inconclusive in this area. As noted in SHOCAP guidelines for citizen action (Crowe, 1991, p. 23): "The criminological literature has consistently reported on the failure of treatment programs for more than 40 years. The failures have consistently and uniformly been associated with what to do with serious or habitual delinquents once they are identified."

Fox (1996) has referred to the problem of juvenile crime as a "ticking time bomb," while DiIulio (1995) warns of the "coming of the super-predators." Rhine (1998, p. 83) notes: "Despite its implications for community well-being, the issue of serious juvenile offenders on probation or parole supervision is often overlooked in the current 'get tough' debate." He further states:

> Effective supervision strategies must draw actively on the leverage provided by the community and other agencies that share accountability for addressing juvenile crime. Probation and parole supervision must become more firmly embedded in the communities and neighborhoods where juvenile offenders live and, in doing so, strategically refocus resources toward the paramount goal of public safety.

Although prevention and treatment are discussed in separate chapters, they are integrally related. When prevention efforts fail, if youths are found breaking the law, some intervention should be provided to prevent future offenses. Unfortunately what often follows is a cycle of crime, with the treatment failing to prevent future offenses—or recidivism. This cycle is illustrated in Figure 13.1.

As noted by Crowe (p. 22):

- Nearly all children get into trouble during their upbringing without regard to social position.

- Nearly all children grow up to be law-abiding and productive citizens, developing positive behavior through the maturation process.

- A very small number of children and adults account for the majority of serious crime.

The question for the juvenile justice system is, Where should resources be focused? Some believe resources should be focused on first-time offenders to make certain that the cycle of crime is broken for those most likely to be "rehabilitated." Others believe that youths who commit violent crimes and those who commit numerous crimes should be the top priority, since most youths will "mature" out of unlawful behavior. This issue remains unresolved.

This chapter expands on the information from Chapter 10, looking first at some theoretical concepts about treatment and some general characteristics of effective interventions. It then looks at treatments suggested for abused and neglected children. This is followed by descriptions of several alternative treatment programs being used around the country, including day treatment programs, "second chance" camps, boot camps and youth centers. The chapter concludes with descriptions of collaborative treatment efforts and treatment programs and research projects identified by the OJJDP as exemplary.

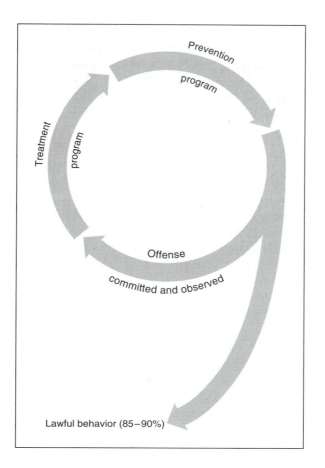

Prevention
program

Treatment
program

Offense
committed and observed

Lawful behavior (85–90%)

Figure 13.1
The Prevention/
Treatment Cycle

Treatment as Tertiary Prevention

Chapter 12 described three levels of prevention—primary, secondary and tertiary. The tertiary level focuses on preventing further delinquent acts by youths who are already identified as delinquents. That is the focus of this chapter and the challenge of the entire juvenile justice system. As has been stressed throughout this text, not any part of the system nor the system as a whole can solve the problems that come from child abuse and neglect, delinquency, crime and violence. It takes a total community effort.

One example of this prevention process is the informal adjustment program authorized by the Texas Family Code. The objectives of this program are:

- To meet the court's needs in fulfilling the intent of the family code as it relates to informal adjustment
- To provide a coordinated, comprehensive service delivery system aimed at self-rehabilitation and short-term supervision, diversion and prevention from further involvement in the judicial system
- To provide quality service to children under an informal adjustment contract

The informal adjustment contract is a six-month informal probationary period, during which a child is supervised by a probation officer or counselor. Family and child must meet certain criteria, such as good school attendance, positive attitudes toward change, a demonstrated willingness to see and use resources that can help change behavior, good attitude toward authority figures and a willingness to cooperate with the juvenile probation department. Through this agreement, children are given a second chance.

Under this program the probation officer, the parent and the child have clearly defined roles. The probation officer supervises and monitors the child's behavior during the six-month contract. Cooperation is essential for both parents and child. The parents provide emotional and financial support to the child, seek assistance from the probation officer as needed, advise the probation officer of any problems that arise, monitor the child's activities, report violations to the probation officer and provide supervision. The child must obey the rules set by the parents, attend school every day as required by law, keep parents informed of his or her whereabouts, have full-time employment if not in school and follow all rules agreed on in the contract.

The contract ends exactly six months after it is signed. The case is then closed and the file is returned to the probation department. A letter is sent to the parents advising them that the case has been closed and that they may ask the court to seal the record.

A child can terminate the contract at any time. If this occurs, however, the probation officer returns the case for a court hearing. Should the child or parent decide not to enter into an informal adjustment contract, or should the child not meet the criteria established, the case is docketed for a court hearing.

Another example of tertiary prevention is a program in Lansing, Michigan, The School Youth Advocacy Program. The program includes youths who have been institutionalized and then returned to school. It places these youths in a structured peer support group to improve their attitudes about themselves and school and to improve their academic performance, thereby reducing the likelihood that they will commit further delinquent acts.

Youths are recommended for program participation by faculty, administration, other youths and parents. They are selected for their leadership qualities, both negative and positive. Nine to 12 students participate in a group. The program has found that junior high youths are more comfortable talking about problems with peers of their own gender; thus groups are segregated by sex.

The group can decide on sanctions for any infractions by members. For example if someone in the group is caught smoking marijuana, group members decide what the consequences should be and that decision is enforced. The groups do not get involved in the daily functions and decision-making powers of the school administration or in school government or policy formation.

A third tertiary prevention program is Denver's Junior Partners with Senior Partners. This program links youths and adult community volunteers in a relationship that seeks mutual honesty, open communication and value sharing. It

This antidrug rally for junior high students is sponsored by DARE. Educational programs to keep youths off drugs are critical because the link between drug abuse and delinquency has been clearly established.

targets youths 10 to 18 years of age who may or may not be in trouble but who have been in trouble in the past and who might get in trouble again without immediate intervention.

Yet another approach uses parental involvement in court, making parents responsible for their children's actions and, in some instances, fining parents for delinquent acts committed by their children. This approach is gaining momentum in some areas.

Of course the challenge for any prevention effort remains identifying those youths at greatest risk and focusing resources on them. As Earls and Reiss (1994, p. 60) assert: "Prevention hinges on the ability to select which out of a large number of children are likely to become serious and persistent delinquents in a community." The American Psychological Association (p. 58) notes:

> Several promising techniques have been identified for treating children who already have adopted aggressive patterns of behavior. These include problem-solving skills training for the child, child management training for the parents (e.g., anger control, negotiation and positive reinforcement), family therapy and interventions at school or in the community.

Characteristics of Effective Intervention Programs

Two primary characteristics of effective intervention programs are (American Psychological Association, pp. 53–54): (1) they draw on our understanding of the developmental and sociocultural risk factors that lead to antisocial behavior and (2) they use theory-based intervention strategies that are known to change behavior, tested program designs and validated, objective measurement techniques to assess outcomes. Other key criteria identified by the American Psychological Association (pp. 54–55) include the following:

- They begin as early as possible to interrupt the "trajectory toward violence."
- They address aggression as part of a constellation of antisocial behaviors in the child or youth.
- They include multiple components that reinforce each other across the child's everyday social contexts: family, school, peer groups, media and community.
- They take advantage of developmental "windows of opportunity": points at which interventions are especially needed or especially likely to make a difference. Such windows of opportunity include transitions in children's lives: birth, entry into preschool, the beginning of elementary school and adolescence.

Effective treatment programs often take advantage of windows of opportunity, times when treatment is especially needed (in crises) or likely to make a difference (during transition periods).

The association (p. 54) suggests that adolescence is an important window of opportunity "because the limits-testing and other age-appropriate behaviors of adolescents tend to challenge even a functional family's well-developed patterns of interaction." In addition (pp. 54–55):

Antisocial behaviors tend to peak during adolescence, and many adolescents engage in sporadic aggression or antisocial behavior. Programs that prepare children to navigate the developmental crises of adolescence may help prevent violence by and toward the adolescent.

Earls and Reiss (p. 47) note that while many adult criminals were antisocial children, not every antisocial child is automatically destined for a life of crime: "In fact, relatively few delinquent children become adult criminals. Something happens in their lives that discourages them from a life of crime. This process, called **desistance,** commonly occurs during the transition between late adolescence and early adulthood." According to these authors, desistance is considered to have occurred if (p. 47):

- Offenders are diverted from serious crime to more minor violations.
- The individual rate of offending is significantly reduced.
- The time between offenses is significantly increased.

Earls and Reiss also state: "Despite years of research, no one knows why most delinquent teenagers turn away from criminal activities while a minority continue to commit offenses through adulthood."

Table 13.1
**Summary of Effectiveness
of Types of Treatment
for Reducing Recidivism
Rates among Juvenile
Offenders**

Treatment Type	Offender Status	Positive Effects Treatment/Control Recidivism Contrast (a)	Median Effect Sizes	Consistency Rating
Individual counseling	noninstitutional	.28/.50	.46	consistent
Interpersonal skills	noninstitutional	.29/.50	.44	consistent
Behavioral programs	noninstitutional	.30/.50	.42	consistent
Interpersonal skills	institutional	.31/.50	.39	consistent
Teaching family home	institutional	.33/.50	.34	consistent
Multiple services	noninstitutional	.36/.50	.29	less consistent
Restitution, probation/parole	noninstitutional	.43/.50	.15	less consistent
Behavioral programs	institutional	.34/.50	.33	less consistent
Community residential	institutional	.36/.50	.28	less consistent
Multiple services	institutional	.40/.50	.20	less consistent
Mixed Positive Effects				
Employment-related	noninstitutional	.39/.50	.22	inconsistent
Academic programs	noninstitutional	.40/.50	.20	inconsistent
Advocacy/casework	noninstitutional	.41/.50	.19	inconsistent
Family counseling	noninstitutional	.41/.50	.19	inconsistent
Group counseling	noninstitutional	.45/.50	.10	inconsistent
Individual counseling	institutional	.43/.50	.15	inconsistent
Group counseling	institutional	.46/.50	.07	inconsistent
Weak or No Effects				
Wilderness/challenge	noninstitutional	.44/.50	.12	consistent
Early release, prob./parole	noninstitutional	.48/.50	.03	consistent
Deterrence programs	noninstitutional	.53/.50	−.06	consistent
Vocational programs	noninstitutional	.59/.50	−.18	consistent
Employment-related	institutional	.43/.50	.15	inconsistent
Drug abstinence	institutional	.46/.50	.08	inconsistent
Wilderness/challenge	institutional	.46/.50	.07	inconsistent
Milieu therapy	institutional	.46/.50	.08	consistent

(a) Recidivism of treatment group in comparison to assumed control group recidivism of .50. (From Lipsey & Wilson, 1998)

Source: Ken D. Winters. "Kids and Drugs: Treatment Recognizes Link between Delinquency and Substance Abuse." *Corrections Today,* October 1998, p. 120. Reprinted with permission of the American Correctional Association, Lanham, MD.

In discussing the link between substance abuse and delinquency and the availability of intervention programs to treat each, Winters (1998, p. 119) notes: "There is some preliminary indication that desistance of delinquency behaviors during adolescence and young adulthood is associated with a discontinuation of substance use over time." Lipsey and Wilson (1998) analyzed over 200 types of delinquency intervention programs and categorized them according to their effectiveness, a summary of which is provided in Table 13.1. It is hoped that such an analysis of the treatments will help juvenile drug courts to select effective dispositions that reduce both substance abuse and **recidivism,** or repeat offending.

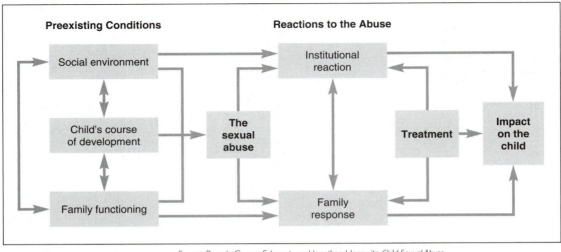

Figure 13.2
A Model of Child Abuse

Source: Beverly Gomes-Schwartz and Jonathan Horowitz. *Child Sexual Abuse Victims and Their Treatment.* Washington, DC: U.S. Department of Justice, National Institute for Juvenile Justice and Delinquency Prevention, July 1988, p. 1.

Treatment Programs for Children and Juveniles Who Have Been Abused

A model of child abuse has been developed by Gomes-Schwartz and Horowitz (1988, p. 1), reproduced in Figure 13.2. Note that the child's development and the treatment provided are influenced by the family's and institution's reaction to the abuse.

The treatment in this case is the Family Crisis Program (FCP), Division of Child Psychiatry at the Tufts New England Medical Center in Boston. The treatment approach is based on crisis theory, which begins with the assumption that at certain times in people's lives they are faced with insurmountable obstacles requiring more than the ordinary coping mechanisms.

> Crisis intervention capitalizes on windows of opportunity when the individual may be especially receptive to treatment that establishes new approaches to problem-solving.

As noted by Gomes-Schwartz and Horowitz (p. 11): "Thus, crisis intervention may not only relieve the distress of the individual, but it may also strengthen and modify the individual's capacity to withstand future stress." FCP, drawing upon crisis theory, incorporates rapid intervention, outreach, focal treatment involving 12 intensive sessions and liaison with other agencies.

The Metropolitan Court Judges Committee (1986, p. 29) states in the introduction to the recommendations for treatment and planning for deprived children:

> Although child victims frequently require help to alleviate the guilt they are experiencing about their family's problems, they are often placed into foster care without additional supports or necessary therapeutic intervention. The

lack of immediate and effective treatment and coordinated planning and resources represents serious problems. Providing an adequate number of foster homes, trained foster parents, special homes for special needs children, emergency shelter care facilities and other alternatives prior to termination of parental rights are also critical. After termination, providing resources for the treatment and subsequent adoption of deprived children is the wisest investment society can make. An abused or neglected child, whether removed from the home or remaining in the home, needs assistance which is often not provided.

Although 80 percent of all substantiated cases of abuse or neglect receive "casework counseling," given the excessive caseloads, this response must be seen as more paperwork than counseling. (The ratio of cases to workers in some large jurisdictions has exceeded an unrealistic 150:1, allowing less than an hour per month for each deprived child.)

Treatment Recommendations of the Metropolitan Court Judges Committee

The committee made the following recommendations (pp. 30–34):

- *Immediate treatment.* Treatment of abused and neglected children must be immediate, thorough, and coordinated among responsible agencies.

- *Family focus.* Treatment provided to children through court or agency intervention should involve the entire family or focus on family relationships and should stress the primary responsibility of the parents for their children's welfare and protection. Family involvement, where at all possible, should be stabilized rather than disrupted as a result of intervention and treatment.

- *Parental responsibility.* Child protection agencies and the courts should require parental responsibility for children's well-being.

- *Positive parental behavior.* Judges must have authority to order treatment for the parents, to require other positive conduct and to impose sanctions for willful failure or refusal to comply.

- *Substance abuse.* Substance abuse treatment, if appropriate, should be mandated for parents and their children.

- *Mandated treatment.* Judges must have the authority to order the treatment determined necessary and should regularly review the efficacy of such treatment.

- *Youthful sex offenders.* Judges must require appropriate treatment for youthful sexual offenders, many of whom have been victims of sexual abuse. The cycle of young victims of sexual abuse later becoming perpetrators of sexual abuse must be broken. Unless intensive intervention and effective treatment of such youthful sexual offenders is provided, the cycle will continue.

Treatment requirements recommended by the Metropolitan Court Judges Committee include immediate treatment, family focus, parental responsibility, positive parental behavior, treatment for substance abuse, mandated treatment and treatment for youthful sexual offenders.

Service
Recommendations

The committee also made recommendations for the provision of services to juveniles (pp. 30–34):

- *Qualified treatment personnel.* Child protection caseworkers must be screened, trained, and certified to improve child protection services and treatment. People who work with deprived children should undergo detailed background investigation.

- *Volunteer assistance.* Screened, qualified, and trained volunteers should be used to enhance the quality of services.

- *Foster homes.* A sufficient number of foster homes, adequately reimbursed and provided access to treatment and support services, should be established. Strict screening, improved recruiting, professional training, licensing requirements and adequate compensation will encourage quality foster care.

- *Foster care drift.* Frequently moving children from foster home to foster home is detrimental to children's physical and emotional well-being and must be reduced.

- *Children with special needs.* Specialized foster homes and foster parents should be available for children with special needs. Older, minority, disabled, or seriously abused children require particular care, with specialized foster homes, trained foster parents, and continuing agency assistance tailored to their needs.

- *Homeless children.* Homeless and runaway children must be provided proper emergency shelter facilities as well as necessary services. Much of the problem of at-risk or exploited children could be alleviated by improved and expanded emergency shelter facilities, with necessary services and counseling. Children who are "broke and on the streets" are particularly vulnerable.

In providing services, the Metropolitan Court Judges Committee recommends that treatment personnel be well qualified, that volunteer assistance be used, that quality foster homes be available, that foster care drift be reduced, that children with special needs be provided special foster homes and that shelters be established for homeless children.

Permanency
Recommendations

The final set of recommendations made by the committee dealt with planning for **permanency** for children, that is, assuring the most lasting placement or solution possible: "The Court must find a way to provide a permanent and loving home for the child" (pp. 33–34).

- *Termination of parental rights.* When there is clear, convincing evidence that the parents' conduct would legally permit termination of parental rights, and it is in the child's best interests to do so, termination should proceed expeditiously. The immediate availability of adoptive parents should not be required to terminate parental rights.

- *Alternative permanent plans.* When reunification is not possible or termination of parental rights is not in the child's best interests, courts should consider other permanent plans. In some cases, terminating a parent's rights is inappropriate and the court should examine such alternatives as:

  - Long-term custody—in a homelike setting such as placement with relatives, substitute or extended families, and foster grandparents;
  - Permanent or temporary guardianship—after a finding of dependency and removal; or
  - Any other solution short of termination leading to permanency for the child.

- *Expedited adoption process.* When needed, adoption should proceed as quickly as possible. Foster parents should be able to adopt their foster child.

- *Subsidized adoptions.* Subsidized adoption programs should be more widely available and used for special needs and hard-to-place children.

In planning for permanency, the committee recommends that when necessary, parental rights may be terminated, that alternative plans should be made if parental rights are not terminated and that the adoption process be expedited, including providing subsidized adoption programs for hard-to-place children.

Diversion Alternatives—Community-Based Treatment Programs

Zachariah (1992, p. 202) stresses that: "The ideal placement maintains a balance of community protection, juvenile accountability and juvenile development." He lists the following as options currently available in most jurisdictions:

- Intensive community supervision (at least twice a week)
- Tracking (hiring staff to exclusively monitor juveniles)
- Electronic monitoring
- Report centers (set up in accessible locations)
- Home detention
- Home tutoring
- Mentor tutoring
- Day treatment
- Evening and weekend programs (providing tutoring, recreation, work and treatment services)
- Work and apprenticeship (to develop a work ethic, a sense of responsibility and a feeling of accomplishment)
- Restitution (in services or in cash)
- Community service (cleaning up parks, working in nursing homes, etc.)
- Volunteers (to tutor youths and supervise work and recreational activities)

Earls and Reiss (p. 51) point out: "Numerous studies have established that incarcerated offenders are likely to return to crime if they are released to socially disorganized communities." Indiana has developed a continuum of alternative programs designed to provide services for offenders ranging from shoplifters to murderers.[1] Payne and Lee (1990, pp. 103–104) outline these "alternatives that work":

- **Project Challenge:** Project Challenge is a six-week program aimed at breaking the behavior cycles that lead youths to trouble. It includes a three-week wilderness camp that encourages youths to trust themselves and their peers, and provides vocational, family and individual counseling.

- **Ivy Tech:** Ivy Tech is part of the state's technical school system. It offers vocational education for troubled youths who are functionally illiterate or in need of remedial education or extra attention in the classroom. Students learn skills such as auto mechanics, welding or how to use computers. Many students then find jobs in the community.

- **Electronic Surveillance:** For four years, electronic surveillance has allowed Marion County to make sure that students are home when they are supposed to be. The devices allow them to assume responsibility while ensuring community safety. Costs are relatively low.

- **Run, Don't Run:** Run, Don't Run is aimed at youths who have literally run from encounters with law enforcement officers. Developed by the juvenile court with the Indianapolis Police Department and the Marion County Sheriff's Department, the program is intended to establish respect between young offenders and law enforcement officials. Youths learn from police officers and a judge or magistrate how fleeing, resisting and striking police officers influences the officers' actions.

- **Visions:** Visions is designed for the serious first referral or repeat offender who comes into contact with the court system. Youths are admitted to the juvenile detention center for one night, followed by a morning lesson about the juvenile justice system. That afternoon, juveniles tour the Indiana Boys/Girls School and the Marion County Jail.

- **Operation Kids CAN (Care About Neighborhoods):** Operation Kids CAN began in the summer of 1987, when more than 200 youths on probation picked up 3.5 tons of neighborhood trash. The program has now joined forces with the Indianapolis Clean City Committee. Youths spend mornings learning about the juvenile justice system. Then, they work in structured community service projects such as cleaning vacant lots and picking up garbage.

- **Garden Project:** In the Garden Project, youths and their parents plant vegetables and flowers during the summer. The program shifts in winter to craft projects.

---

[1]Reprinted from the October 1990 issue of *Corrections Today*, with the permission of the American Correctional Association, Lanham, MD.

- **National Corrective Training Institute (NCTI):** NCTI instructors have small group discussions with youths charged with misdemeanors. They talk with children about values, attitudes and behavior.

- **Paint It Clean:** Paint It Clean requires youths associated with destructive gang activities to paint over gang graffiti in local neighborhoods, parks and buildings. Under the supervision of court staff, Paint It Clean helps eliminate gang claims to territory and allows communities to reclaim their neighborhoods.

- **Summer Youth Program:** The Summer Youth Program gives youths the chance to go canoeing, horseback riding, camping, hiking, caving and on a field trip to the Indiana Amusement Park. Probation's Dispositional Alternatives Department also sponsors monthly field trips throughout the year.

- **Basketball:** The court and the Twilight Optimist Club sponsor a basketball league for youths. This collaboration gives juveniles the chance to participate in structured recreation with positive role models.

- **Near Peer Tutoring:** The Near Peer Tutoring program targets junior high school probationers having trouble in at least one class. High school honor students and adult volunteers tutor youths weekly at neighborhood probation offices.

Project New Pride

A model of community-based services that mirrors the Youth Service Bureau concept is Project New Pride, which started in Denver, Colorado, in 1973. This program is geared toward the violent and serious offender rather than the minor offender and nondelinquent. The specific goals of the program are to work hard-core delinquents back into the mainstream and to reduce the number of rearrests. The program focuses on getting the youths back in school and on getting them jobs, and it uses a **holistic** (treating the whole person) **approach** to working with hard-core delinquents. As noted in a program description (*Project New Pride,* 1985, p. 7):

> All facets of the child's life must be examined and all treatment services must be coordinated to ensure the greatest benefit for the youth. Raising a youth's academic performance is not sufficient if the family income is so low that he or she is hungry; warning a girl of the penalty for prostitution is not sufficient if she has no job skills; getting a job for a youth is not sufficient if he or she doesn't know how to apply for another job later; enrolling a youth in the school is not sufficient if he or she needs professional help with a severe emotional disturbance. New Pride youths usually suffer from a combination of problems. It takes a combination of services to help them. New Pride achieves "one-step programming" through intensive supervision from the youth's intake through the end of his or her involvement with the program.

The staff philosophy of New Pride programs, expressed in the greeting to youths at the door, aptly describes the theory behind the unique operation of Project New Pride:

> If we fish for you,
> You will live for a day.
> If we teach you to fish,
> You will live for a lifetime.

The seventeen-year-old student in this biology class in the Hartford Youthful Offender Program is a former heroin addict. She says that without the program, which gives her a chance to earn her General Equivalency Diploma (GED), she would be back on the street or spend the rest of her life in jail.

Foster Homes

Foster homes are an important diversion alternative for many youths, both those who are victims and those who have been victimizers. Berquist (1994, p. B8) describes one such home, run by Dianne Jensen, which has had success with teenagers with emotional and behavioral difficulties. Jensen dislikes the term *foster home,* feeling that she provides a true home to those who come to live with her. According to Jensen: "Love is the catalyst that can help juveniles develop trust and motivation for success." Love, plus strict rules firmly enforced and efforts to enhance the youths' self-image are keys to Jensen's success.

Intensive Supervision/ Parole/Probation/ Aftercare

To help juveniles who are identified as high-risk recidivists, Altschuler and Armstrong (1990, p. 170) developed a framework for aftercare based on five principles:

- Preparing youths for gradually increased responsibility and freedom in the community
- Helping youths to become involved in the community and getting the community to interact with them
- Working with youths and their families, peers, schools and employers to identify the qualities necessary for success
- Developing new resources and supports where needed
- Monitoring and testing youths and the community on their abilities to interact

Altschuler and Armstrong (p. 170) caution that assessment is a critical first step in determining if intensive supervision is a viable alternative because "ample evidence suggests that subjecting low- or moderate-risk offenders to intensive supervision may lead to increased technical violations and subsequent unnecessary incarceration."

Day Treatment Programs

Day treatment programs are becoming more numerous and more popular as a diversion alternative, as attested to by the first national conference on day treatment held in March 1993. Day treatment programs are designed around school settings or evening and weekend reporting centers. They have been found to be a cost-effective alternative to the more costly residential programs for status offenders.

Alternative Schools

The Robert F. Kennedy School is a secure treatment facility in Massachusetts for hard-core delinquents. Konitzer (1993, p. 213) says: "The school's primary mission is 'to effect optimal growth and development of each resident in order to guarantee successful reintegration into the community.' " The school has an academic program and a treatment regime. The treatment regime uses the "milieu therapy" approach, meaning every interaction between juveniles and staff is considered therapeutic. The program also offers counseling to families of the juveniles in the program.

Giddings State Home and School, a "way station for young criminals" that houses the "worst of juvenile offenders," is described by MacCormack (1993). More than 100 of the 320 offenders are in for capital murder, murder or voluntary manslaughter. Another 100 are in for attempted murder, and many of the rest for crimes against the person such as rape or kidnapping. Stan DeGerolami, the assistant superintendent, says: "We punish kids by confining them to this facility and making them answerable for what they do here and accountable for what they did to get here." The underlying belief is that these young offenders have been "socialized" into who they are and that the school can "resocialize" them to fit into society. As noted by MacCormack (p. 1A): "All are here on the theory that youthful offenders, even the most coldly criminal, are susceptible to rehabilitation."

Youths assigned to Giddings eventually leave for either freedom or prison. DeGerolami further notes: "We don't want to release kids who are dangerous. I don't want a kid to leave here and rape my daughter or assault my mother, so we make our recommendations very carefully."

Youth Centers

A youth center in Beloit, Kansas, is the only facility in Kansas for female juvenile offenders. One major challenge it faces is that 55 to 60 percent of the offenders admit to having been sexually abused. As noted by Moore (1991, p. 42): "Sexual abuse itself does not lead to delinquency; it is more the way in which a youth deals with the sexual abuse." The Beloit youth center has identified several factors that appear to have a significant role in fostering delinquent behavior (Moore, p. 42): anger and aggression toward others; alienation, resulting in withdrawal from positive relationships; distrust of authority and adults; self-blame; substance abuse and running away.

The voluntary program at the Beloit Center is held in a small house with comfortable chairs and couches and a kitchen. What happens during the group meetings is kept confidential, and the staff is specially trained in working with sexually abused juveniles. The goals of the program include the following (Moore, p. 45):

- Restoring self-confidence and self-esteem
- Instilling the attitude of being a survivor instead of a victim
- Restoring a sense of control and power over their lives

- Restoring a sense of control over their sexuality and developing healthy sexual attitudes
- Developing an understanding of how sexual abuse has affected their lives and ways of using positive coping skills

The Southwest Utah Youth Center is a 10-bed rural detention center that is one of 14 sites using a federal program, Law Related Education (LRE). The program brings in local police officers, attorneys, judges and legislators in an effort to make the law relevant to these juveniles. The objectives of the program include the following (Weaver, 1993, pp. 174, 176):

- Give students a practical understanding of one or more aspects of law and show them how the legal system is relevant to their lives.
- Allow students to interact positively with each other, staff and community members.
- Enable students to begin to understand the need to be an effective citizen.
- Reinforce other important life skills, such as critical thinking, decision making and problem solving.
- Reinforce students' understanding of the role that laws, lawyers, law enforcement officers and the legal system play in their community.

LRE uses small group discussion, role-playing, case studies and other types of interactive learning to keep student interest. Although no statistics on recidivism are yet available, the program reports that incidents of aggressive acts and rule violations have been "reduced tremendously."

Pennsylvania has a youth center that crosses generational lines. According to Maniglia (1993, p. 146): "The center is a true multipurpose facility. It houses a secure detention facility where youths are held awaiting adjudication and disposition as well as a courtroom in which the juvenile court judge hears all cases involving children. Attached to the building, but separate from the detention center, is a shelter housing abused and neglected children . . . and status offenders."

Seniors volunteer as role models and mentors for youths housed in the secure detention center. Weisman (1994, p. 57) notes: "An institution provides some children with a first chance to be taken care of by adults who do not hit or even yell." In addition through the Teens and Tots program, youths learn parenting skills firsthand by working with the young children from the shelter.

Texas has a similar program, which uses foster grandparents in the county's juvenile detention center. As noted by Briscoe (1990, p. 92): "Even children who are sometimes hostile and aggressive work calmly and quietly in the presence of a foster grandparent."

Since the 1950s the emphasis in most residential facilities for juvenile delinquents has followed a custody/clinical model, treating delinquent youths as deviant or abnormal. This approach has met with limited success. Ferrainola and Grissom (1990) suggest that a different model, a sociological model—one that stresses a positive environment—might be more effective. They give as an example Glen Mills, Delaware County, Pennsylvania (pp. 118, 120):

> Glen Mills is the nation's most thoroughly documented program based on a sociological model. Students there are immersed in the most positive, carefully monitored and highly structured environment they will ever experience. The group culture—which is based on values of respect, loyalty, persistence, involvement and pride—is what changes the students, not any particular therapies or set of activities.
>
> Glen Mills' experience since 1974 suggests that it is not large institutions, but the custody/clinical model, which should be abandoned.

The feature of the daily experience at Glen Mills that clearly sets it apart is confrontation. Everyone in the school—administrators, staff, and student—is responsible for confronting negative behavior, never the student alone. The purpose is to instill positive norms of behavior. Peer group status is earned through positive behavior, which is also amply recognized. Students at Glen Mills are successful not only academically, with over 1,000 students earning GEDs, but also in sports, having won local, state and national championships.

Paint Creek Youth Center is a private correctional program for juveniles in New York. This treatment program centers on the concept of positive peer community and helping youths to get along with each other. As noted by Speirs (1988, p. 3): "The premise of the positive peer community is that youth need help, particularly from their peers, to learn acceptable behaviors and develop positive, supportive, caring relationships." The program also builds on the work of nationally recognized psychologists William Glasser and Stanton Samenow and their emphasis on personal responsibility.

The Paint Creek Youth Center uses a point-and-level system designed to provide immediate, clear, consistent feedback on behavior and its acceptability. Youths enter the program at the orientation level and work their way up to the top level. In addition to vocational instruction, physical fitness and recreational therapy programs are also important to the center. It has a family therapy and support component as well as intensive supervision as the aftercare alternative for the first three or four weeks following release from the program. Speirs (p. 6) concludes that the program:

> . . . represents a viable alternative to traditional forms of correctional services. It combines treatment, education, employment, life skills, and specialized counseling and support services into one coordinated approach and provides staff and residents with a secure setting through intensive staff and peer supervision and influence. The Paint Creek Youth Center offers a unique way to facilitate changes in behavior and attitudes in a segment of the juvenile population that has become both problematic and frustrating to communities across the Nation.

"Second Chance" Camps

The Eckerd Youth Challenge Program first opened in Indian Head, Maryland, in 1987 as a community-based alternative to placing delinquents in training schools. Among the principles and practices of this program are the following (Stepanik, 1991, pp. 48–50):

- Positive relationships.
- Family involvement. Youths earn home visits (furloughs) and family is encouraged to visit.

- Challenging activities.
- Structure and discipline.
- Clinical and educational services.
- Aftercare.

The program is geared to improve self-esteem and behavior by focusing on challenges specifically designed to improve interpersonal and living skills. This experiential, action-oriented program includes canoe trips, hikes, a ropes course and community service projects.

Thistledew Camp, located on Minnesota's Iron Range, is operated by the Minnesota Department of Corrections. Like any other camp, it offers fishing, swimming, trapping, rock climbing and the like, but it also involves hard work and education. The camp does not accept youths who are assaultive. Most youths have a 100-day "stay" at the camp. In the final three weeks they go through the "Challenge," which is three days spent camping alone in the woods. It is not survival training; the youths take food and water along. It does give them time to themselves to think and to just "be." Immediately after these "solos," the youths go on a week-long wilderness trek in groups of 10. As noted by one of the camp leaders: "A lot of them have never known what it's like to get through any type of problem. It's why the suicide rate among teens is so high. This teaches them that they can make it through something difficult" (Mugford, 1994, p. 4).

Florida is experimenting with Youth Environmental Service camps, better known locally as swamp camps: "The camp, modeled on the Civilian Conservation Corps of the 1930s, is the first of what White House officials envision as 'last chance' detention centers on federal lands where felons under the age of 18 will work on environment cleanup projects while providing low-cost labor to the National Park Service" ("U.S. Tries," 1994, p. A7).

The Florida camp is based at an abandoned sawmill, which serves as home for up to 20 young offenders who have been convicted of violent crimes. Supervised by counselors rather than guards, they spend up to a year cleaning trails, getting rid of weeds and trees and building boardwalks. They also receive vocational training at the camp.

Another program that focuses on giving serious, chronic offenders a last chance operates at the Fort Smallwood Marine Institute near Baltimore, Maryland, where juvenile offenders learn maritime skills. Mardon (1991, p. 33) notes: "The youths . . . are gradually given more responsibility at sea. While they learn, their confidence and self-esteem grow." The program uses a point system. Juveniles earn points for participating in discussion, attendance and leadership. They can use the points to "buy" trips and other privileges. Says Mardon (p. 34): "Underlying the program's point system is the juveniles' understanding that if they do not succeed, they are likely to wind up in prison or dead." Mardon (p. 36) shows the success of the program by noting that: "Since the program opened, about 225 youths have completed the program. Program officials say the recidivism rate is between 20 and 30 percent, far lower than the rate at most secure facilities."

Collaborative Efforts

As has been stressed throughout this text, success in reducing juvenile crime and delinquency often rests on the innovative, collaborative efforts of those closest to the issue. Following are examples of some these successful efforts.

Boston Gun Project Working Group

In 1995, in response to a widespread gang problem and the associated gun crime, Boston launched its Gun Project Working Group. According to Clark (1997, p. 4): "The gun project is a multiagency approach with several key components, some of which . . .—like joint patrols of police and probation officers who team up to ensure that young probationers are home where they belong and not roaming the streets—were already in place as part of a BPD gang task force." Recognizing that, since most of the youth violence in the city was being committed by chronically offending gang members against other chronically offending gang members, and that most gang-involved youths were already known to authorities, the project aimed to impose harsh consequences on youths who committed such serious, violent offenses. Clark (pp. 4–5) states:

> From that point, working-group participants formulated a strategy of "focused deterrence" that served as a pivotal part of the gun project—calling members of the city's 61 known gangs in for face-to-face meetings with authorities, who warned them that intergang violence would no longer be tolerated and that future outbreaks would be met with rapid and iron-fisted responses from law enforcement. . . .
>
> In August 1996, authorities made good on their threat when they launched a crackdown on the Intervale Posse, . . . the "biggest, toughest, crack-era gang in Boston," and which authorities had linked to a string of unsolved murders. "Essentially the entire leadership cadre in that gang was taken off the street in one morning," with many charged with Federal drug offenses, [one project participant] recalled.
>
> While the operation against the Intervale Posse was "far and away the most Draconian" intervention, other gangs received the unwanted scrutiny of authorities if they continued to commit crimes. After each one of those operations, the group went back out to the gangs and told them that if they wanted to avoid this kind of attention, leave your guns at home. They did—and that's really quite remarkable.

Members of the Gun Project acknowledge that the program would not be so successful without its social-service aspects. Jeff Roehm, special agent in charge of ATF's Boston field office, notes: "To have the overall program work, you have to have prevention, intervention and enforcement. It's a three-pronged, long-term approach" (Clark, p. 5).

A recommended three-pronged approach to treatment includes prevention, intervention and enforcement.

Operation Night Light

Another collaboration between police and probation agencies is seen in Boston's Operation Night Light, begun in 1992. This effort teams police and probation officers together to ensure that gang members and other high-risk offenders adhere to the conditions of their probation. According to Jordan (1998, p. 1): "The pioneers in the two agencies transformed one another's work. Police officers started practicing community corrections; probation officers began doing community crime control. Night Light served as a catalyst for getting all the relevant players onto the same field in order to better address youth violence." Jordan further notes (p. 4):

> Recent statistics indicate that Night Light has made a tremendous impact on crime in Boston. Since implementation of the overall Boston strategy in 1996, of which Night Light is a primary component, the city has experienced a 70 percent decrease in the number of people age 24 and under killed by guns.
>   . . . The quality of the collaboration starkly contrasts with the fragmentation that hobbled public safety, criminal justice, and the community 10 years ago.

Partnerships between police departments and probation departments are having success in preventing further delinquency by youths who have been adjudicated delinquent in the past.

San Diego Police and Probation Departments

On the West Coast, police and probation collaboration has also met with success. O'Rourke et al. (1998, p. 48) state: "The Coordinated Agency Network (CAN) is an innovative pilot collaboration between the San Diego Police Department and the San Diego County Probation Department. . . . CAN targets low-risk juvenile probationers for intensive and systematic supervision. The program also includes mentoring by police officers and referrals to a wide array of participating individual and family service." As these authors explain (p. 5): "CAN joins local criminal justice, community-based organizations and human service agencies in a powerful alliance to combat juvenile delinquency. Parents, service providers, schools, businesses, residents and former CAN participants provide guidance and leadership as role models for CAN participants."

One result of the program is a reduction in the peer pressure felt by many juveniles involved in CAN. As one youth participant explained: "I could tell my friends that I had to get home because I had a curfew and I never knew when the CAN officers would show up" (p. 5).

Whole Community

In December 1996 a Wisconsin gubernatorial task force released a report calling for a paradigm shift in its corrections system toward the goal of public safety (Proband, 1996). It was determined that correction's primary purpose was to use effective supervision to control the risk of harm offenders present to other persons and their property. According to Rhine (p. 85): "Where public safety serves as the paramount goal of supervision, probation and parole officers must, of necessity, form active partnerships with local police, community members, neighborhood associations, victims, and families. Effectively

Visitors gather for an open house at the new Rogue Valley Youth Correctional Facility in Grants Pass, Oregon. The prison is one of five built around Oregon to handle increasing numbers of young offenders.

controlling the risk posed by serious juvenile offenders cannot be accomplished by traditional case management alone."

_____

Effective supervision is active, local, community-based supervision.

Exemplary Programs

The following treatment programs or research projects received the OJJDP's Gould-Wysinger Award (GWA), which was described in Chapter 12.[2]

Juvenile Intervention Project, Colorado

The goals of the Juvenile Intervention Project are jail removal and deinstitutionalization of status offenders. A training program for sheriff's officers explains screening criteria and procedures. Officers who perform intake screening are trained to provide status offenders with appropriate services. The program contracts with a host home to ensure that a bed is available for status offenders. Crisis intervention, temporary holding or attendant care, and volunteer tracking and mentoring are also provided.

The program resulted in an immediate decrease in juvenile arrests and detention, and new patrol officers now participate in a special four-hour field training program. (GWA)

_____

[2]Program descriptions written by Allen (1993), director of special projects for the Coalition of Juvenile Justice and overseer of administration of the award solicitation process.

Juvenile Detention Center, Western Nebraska Juvenile Services

The Juvenile Detention Center was established to provide programming, intervention and rehabilitation services for juveniles. A 20-bed facility serving Scotts Bluff County and the surrounding area, it is the only secure juvenile detention center in western Nebraska.

The center has a transitional living program designed to provide juveniles with the knowledge, skill and experience to live independently. A family preservation component encourages the family to cooperate in the reconciliation of the offender to the family unit. A substance abuse program provides intervention and treatment. An educational program offers four types of programs: class continuation, credit work, GED programs and college. The center also offers a 4-H program, a craft program and instruction in creative writing. Opportunities to attend church services are available.

As a result of the center's programs, recidivism has been reduced by 50 percent. Acceptance of the center has grown as other communities and counties increase their use of the facility. (GWA)

Partnership for Learning, Inc., Maryland

Partnership for Learning (PFL) was established in 1991 to screen first-time juvenile offenders appearing before juvenile court in Baltimore City and to identify and assist offenders diagnosed as learning disabled. After first-time offenders have been identified, tested and interviewed, the requirements for participating in PFL are presented. Once an agreement has been executed, the child's case is postponed, and the child is matched with a tutor trained in a special reading and spelling program. Of the children matched with tutors, over 80 percent have successfully completed or are actively involved in the program and have not reoffended.

PFL is a joint project of the Office of the State's Attorney for Baltimore City, the Office of the Public Defender, the Department of Juvenile Services, the Maryland State Department of Education, the Baltimore City Department of Education, and the Maryland Associates for Dyslexic Adults and Youth. It has gained national and international attention as a cost-effective program that reduces the rate of recidivism among youthful offenders. (GWA)

Fremont County Youth Services, Wyoming

This program's goals are to improve the efficiency and the effective use of the juvenile justice system and existing services in Fremont County, to develop programs to serve county youth, to assist the county in developing policies for secure detention of juveniles as well as for alternatives to detention in the county jail, and to reduce the liability of the board of commissioners and sheriff regarding detention of juveniles prior to a court hearing. The program provides report/intake for law enforcement and the county attorney, a deferred prosecution program, a youth council coordinator, a work alternatives program, a sentencing alternatives program, presentence investigation for county courts, formal probation supervision, limited predispositional reports for juvenile court, home detention program supervision, 24-hour intake at county jails, youth advocacy, a cooperative agreement to provide staff-secure shelter care and a jail removal transportation subsidy program.

Serving hundreds of children a year in a county of more than 9,000 square miles, the program has enabled the county to address the mandates of the Juvenile Justice and Delinquency Prevention Act. (GWA)

Earn-It Project, New Hampshire

Earn-It is a victim restitution program that serves as a sentencing alternative for juvenile court and the Juvenile Conference Committee. Juvenile offenders are referred to the program for monetary and community service work placements. Earn-It arranges the work placement in an area business, nonprofit agency or municipality by matching the offender's strengths with the needs of the worksite and monitors the youth's performance.

Earn-It has worked with juvenile offenders in 17 towns within the jurisdiction of the Keene District Court. Over 80 percent of the offenders have completed their court-ordered community service obligations and restitution to their victims. Participants have performed hundreds of hours of community service work and have given thousands of dollars to victims. The recidivism rate for youths completing the program is below 30 percent. (GWA)

Juvenile Work Restitution, Alabama

Located in Tuscaloosa, this program instills a sense of personal accountability, improves behavior and reduces recidivism. Jobs are created in the public and private sectors, and juvenile offenders are matched to an appropriate job. Offenders work to reimburse victims and provide community service.

The program has helped reduce minority overrepresentation in the state school and develop greater confidence in the juvenile justice system. Recidivism has been reduced by 10 percent. (GWA)

Prosocial Gang, New York

This unique intervention program implements Aggression Replacement Training (ART) with gang members who are involved in delinquent behavior. The program is conducted at two Brooklyn sites—-the Brownsville Community Neighborhood Action Center and Youth DARES. ART improves prosocial skills, moral reasoning and anger control by channeling aggressive behavior into a positive force so gang members become a constructive influence in the community.

Four evaluations found that the ART program significantly improves the quality of the youths' interpersonal skills; enhances their ability to reduce and control anger; decreases the level of egocentricity and increases concern for the needs of others; substantially decreases antisocial behaviors; substantially increases prosocial behaviors; improves community functioning, especially with peers; and decreases criminal recidivism. (GWA)

Sex Offender Assessment, Ohio

The Sex Offender Assessment research project was created to improve the assessment and treatment of juvenile sex offenders and enhance understanding of the victimization process. The project evaluates how offenders attempt to gain a victim's trust; what types of nonsexual behaviors are engaged in prior to the abuse; and how enticements, bribes, threats, and coercion are used to obtain cooperation in sexual activity. The last part of the project is to disseminate the study findings to practitioners during a daylong, statewide workshop.

Prior to the project, little research was available to guide the assessment and treatment of adolescent offenders. The results provide professionals with critically needed information and improve caretakers' ability to treat offenders and victims. (GWA)

Study of Serious Juvenile Offenders, Virginia

This comprehensive study of serious juvenile offenders defines the population of juveniles who have been convicted in circuit court by offense and service history, compares transferred and convicted juveniles to those retained in the juvenile justice system and committed to learning centers, identifies jurisdictional variation in the transfer option, evaluates which factors influence the decision-making process for transfer-eligible juveniles, and develops recommendations for policy-makers. Study findings are available in a detailed report.

The project makes a substantial contribution toward developing an informational base from which legislators can draw in deciding juvenile justice issues. There is a commitment to continue this important research. (GWA)

Civil Remedies

Because criminal law focuses on wrongs against the state, it is frequently overlooked that virtually every crime is also a **tort,** or a civil wrong against a person or persons for which the perpetrator is civilly liable. In *Addressing Community Gang Problems,* the Bureau of Justice Assistance notes (1998, p. 153): "Gang activity . . . is . . . likely to violate several civil ordinances, and gang members can be held responsible for the harm they create by these violations. Furthermore, civil remedies can reach other people who make it easier for gangs to operate by their failure to comply with local ordinances or commercial regulations." Table 13.2 lists the types of harm caused by gangs, including civil matters and ordinance violations.

Gang-related harm may be treated by civil remedies.

One way to attack the gang problem is to redirect the focus away from the offenders themselves and onto other contributing aspects. For example Figure 13.3 illustrates the gang problem by separating it into three components: the offender, the victim and the place where the harm occurs. This model proposes that by removing one element of the triangle, we can break the cycle of gang violence and prevent future harm.

Traditionally law enforcement has concentrated on gang members, the "offender" side of the triangle. However a community-policing, problem-oriented approach focuses on the *place* and on the third parties who control those places. According to the BJA (*Addressing Community,* p. 154): "Two things can be achieved by concentrating on problem places. Particular places can be changed so

Table 13.2
**Types of Harm Caused
by Gangs**

Criminal Offenses	Ordinance Violations	Juvenile Offenses	Civil Matters
Felonies	Traffic	Truancy	Code violations
Murder	Parking	Runaway	Fire
Aggravated assault	Littering	Beyond control of parents	Safety
Rape	Vandalism	Curfew	Health
Robbery	Malicious mischief		Torts
Armed	Graffiti		Trespass
Strong-arm	Noise		Nuisance
Arson	Disorderly conduct		Waste
Burglary	Public drunkenness		
Larceny or theft	Obstruction of public passageway		
Auto theft			
Criminal intimidation			
Witnesses			
Victims			
Jurors			
Misdemeanors			
Simple assault			
Reckless endangerment			
Petit larceny			
Criminal trespass			
Criminal mischief			
Harassment			

Source: *Addressing Community Gang Problems: A Practical Guide.* Bureau of Justice
Assistance Monograph, May 1998.

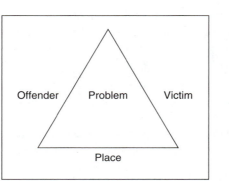

Figure 13.3
Gang-Problem Triangle

Source: *Addressing Community Gang problems: A Practical Guide.* Bureau of Justice
Assistance Monograph, May 1998, p. 154.

that gang members no longer see them as good places for gang activity. And
actions can be taken to keep gang members and potential victims from being
together at particular places at times when the victims are especially vulnerable."

One civil remedy involving property that dates back to the Middle Ages is
the legal concept of nuisance. **Nuisance** pertains to the use of property and
"briefly defined, it requires landowners to use their property so as not to injure

their neighbors' use of their properties. The concept applies to physically damaging neighboring property, reducing its value, or reducing its enjoyment" (*Addressing Community*, p. 163). Typically defined by local ordinance or state statute, public nuisances encroach on public rights and offend public order and standards of decency. Examples might include prostitution and crack houses.

Nuisance statutes commonly refer to "nuisance abatement." **Abatement** basically means doing whatever is necessary to get rid of the nuisance and bring the problem to an end. Abatement might consist of boarding up vacant houses used as crack houses or demolishing entire city blocks to remove sites commonly used for drug transactions and gang activities. Additionally, personal property may be seized and sold; hotels, restaurants and other businesses may be closed; and certain named individuals may be barred from designated properties. According to *Addressing Community Gang Problems* (p. 164): "Abatement orders have imposed specific conditions for continuing to operate a property, including establishing a system for screening tenants and installing security systems to keep gang members off a property. Abatement can be an invaluable remedy to gang-related harms."

Summary

Effective treatment programs often take advantage of windows of opportunity—times when treatment is especially needed (in crises) or likely to make a difference (during transition periods). Crisis intervention capitalizes on windows of opportunity when a person may be especially receptive to treatment that establishes new approaches to problem-solving.

Treatment requirements recommended by the Metropolitan Court Judges Committee include immediate treatment, family focus, parental responsibility, positive parental behavior, treatment for substance abuse, mandated treatment and treatment for youthful sexual offenders.

The committee recommended that treatment personnel be well qualified, that volunteer assistance be used, that quality foster homes be available, that foster care drift be reduced, that children with special needs be provided special foster homes and that shelters be established for homeless children.

In planning for permanency, the committee recommended that when necessary, parental rights may be terminated, that alternative plans should be made if parental rights are not terminated and that the adoption process be expedited, including providing subsidized adoption programs for hard-to-place children.

A recommended three-pronged approach to treatment includes prevention, intervention and enforcement. Partnerships between police departments and probation departments are successfully preventing further delinquency by some youths who have been adjudicated delinquent in the past. These partnerships enhance the level of supervision given to juvenile offenders. To be effective supervision must be active, local, community-based supervision. Gang-related harm may be treated by civil remedies.

Discussion Questions

1. Which of the recommendations of the Metropolitan Court Judges Committee do you feel are most important?
2. Do you disagree with any of the committee's recommendations? If so, which ones and why?

3. What kind of training should foster care providers have?
4. What diversionary alternatives are available in your community?
5. Does your state have any "second chance" camps for juvenile offenders? If so, have you heard anything about them?
6. How involved is your local police department in collaborative efforts with other agencies?
7. Are there any special collaborations in your local area to deal with gang violence?
8. If you were a juvenile and were adjudicated delinquent because you stole a car, what type of treatment program do you think would be most effective?
9. Of all the treatment programs discussed in this chapter, which do you feel offer the best chance for success? The least chance for success?
10. Can you think of other treatment programs that might be tried?

References

Addressing Community Gang Problems: A Practical Guide. Bureau of Justice Assistance Monograph. May 1998.

Allen, Pam. "The Gould-Wysinger Awards: A Tradition of Excellence." *Juvenile Justice,* Vol. 1, No. 2, Fall/Winter 1993, pp. 23–28.

Altschuler, David M. and Armstrong, Troy L. "Designing an Intensive Aftercare Program for High-Risk Juveniles." *Corrections Today,* December 1990, pp. 170–171.

American Psychological Association. *Violence & Youth: Psychology's Response,* Vol. 1. *Summary Report of the American Psychological Association Commission on Violence and Youth,* Vol. 1. n.d.

Berquist, Paul. "Foster Home Helping Prepare for Success." (Minneapolis/St. Paul) *Star Tribune,* April 27, 1994, p. B8.

Briscoe, Judy Culpepper. "In Texas: Reaching Out to Help Troubled Youths." *Corrections Today,* October 1990, pp. 90–95.

Clark, Jacob R. "LEN Salutes its 1997 People of the Year, the Boston Gun Project Working Group." *Law Enforcement News,* Vol. 23, No. 480, December 31, 1997, pp. 1, 4–5.

Crowe, Timothy D. *Habitual Juvenile Offenders: Guidelines for Citizen Action and Public Responses.* Serious Habitual Offender Comprehensive Action Program (SHOCAP). Washington, DC: Office of Juvenile Justice and Delinquency Prevention, October 1991.

DiIulio, John D. "The Coming of the Super-Predators." *The Weekly Standard,* November 23, 1995.

Earls, Felton J. and Reiss, Albert J., Jr. *Breaking the Cycle: Predicting and Preventing Crime.* Washington, DC: National Institute of Justice, 1994.

Ferrainola, Sam and Grissom, Grant. "Reforming Our Reform Schools." *Corrections Today,* December 1990, pp. 118–126.

Fox, James A. *Trends in Juvenile Violence: A Report to the United States Attorney General on Current and Future Rates of Juvenile Offending.* Washington, DC: Bureau of Justice Statistics, 1996.

Gomes-Schwartz, Beverly and Horowitz, Jonathan, with Cardarelli, Albert P. *Child Sexual Abuse Victims and Their Treatment.* Washington DC: Office of Juvenile Justice and Delinquency Prevention, July 1988.

Jordan, James T. "Boston's Operation Night Light: New Roles, New Rules." *FBI Law Enforcement Bulletin,* August 1998, pp. 1–5.

Konitzer, Kimberly. "Youth Facility Offers Model for Treating Juvenile Offenders." *Corrections Today,* August 1993, p. 213.

Lipsey, M. W. and Wilson, D. B. "Effective Intervention for Serious Juvenile Offenders: A Synthesis of Research." In *Serious and Violent Juvenile Offenders: Risk Factors and Successful Interventions,* edited by R. Loeger and D. Farrington. London: Sage Publications, 1998, pp. 313–344.

MacCormack, John. "Way Station for Young Criminals: Worst of Juvenile Offenders Get Chance for Rehabilitation." *San Antonio Express News,* September 26, 1993, pp. 1A, 12A–13A.

Maniglia, Rebecca. "Pennsylvania Youth Center Program Reaches Across Generational Lines." *Corrections Today,* August 1993, pp. 146–149.

Mardon, Steven. "On Board, Not Behind Bars." *Corrections Today,* February 1991, pp. 32–38.

Metropolitan Court Judges Committee Report. *Deprived Children: A Judicial Response.* Washington, DC: U.S. Government Printing Office, 1986.

Moore, James. "Addressing a Hidden Problem: Kansas Youth Center Treats Sexually Abused Female Offenders." *Corrections Today,* February 1991, pp. 40–46.

Mugford, John. "Thistledew Works to Build Up Self-Esteem." *Minnesota Sun Publications,* April 27, 1994, p. 4.

O'Rourke, George; Scott, Andrea; Lance, Debra; and Evans, Susan. "Coordinated Agency Network: Fighting Crime and Combating Juvenile Delinquency." *The Police Chief,* August 1998, pp. 48–50.

Payne, James W. and Lee, Joe E. "In Indiana: A System Designed to Accommodate Juveniles' Needs." *Corrections Today,* October 1990, pp. 100–106.

Proband, Stan C. "Wisconsin Task Force Proposes New Model for Corrections Systems." *Overcrowded Times,* Vol. 7, No. 6, 1996.

Project New Pride. Washington, DC: Office of Juvenile Justice and Delinquency Prevention, U.S. Government Printing Office, 1985.

Rhine, Edward E. "Public Safety, Community Supervision, and Serious Juvenile Offenders." *Corrections Management Quarterly,* Vol. 2, No. 1, 1998, pp. 83–88.

Speirs, Verne L. "A Private-Sector Corrections Program for Juveniles: Paint Creek Youth Center." OJJDP Update on Programs, June 1988.

Stepanik, Ron. "The Eckerd Youth Program: Challenging Juveniles to Change." *Corrections Today,* February 1991, pp. 48–50.

"U.S. Tries Ecological Tack to Counter Juvenile Crime." (Minneapolis/St. Paul) *Star Tribune,* February 19, 1994, pp. A7–A8.

Weaver, Ed Wynn S. "LRE Helps Youth Center Bring the Law to Life." *Corrections Today,* April 1993, pp. 174–176.

Weisman, Mary-Lou. "When Parents Are Not in the Best Interests of the Child." *The Atlantic Monthly,* July 1994, pp. 43–63.

Winters, Ken C. "Kids and Drugs: Treatment Recognized Link Between Delinquency and Substance Abuse." *Corrections Today,* October 1998, pp. 118–121, 163, 166.

Zachariah, John K. "Placement Key to Programs' Success." *Corrections Today,* April 1992, pp. 202–203.

14

Chapter

Rethinking Juvenile Justice:
A Global View

The historical development of the juvenile justice system has produced a magnificent monster. The time has come to face the issues and propose solutions within the framework of a total, integrated system.

—Institute of Judicial Administration, American Bar Association, Juvenile Justice Standards

Do You Know

- What areas the juvenile court has become involved in?
- What a justice model is?
- What competence refers to?
- In what two areas our juvenile justice system might be restructured?
- What country has a law against spanking children?
- What countries use panels of lay people to deal with nonviolent offenders?
- Who is responsible for the prevalence and severity of crime within a community?
- What six policy issues present a challenge for the future?
- What the objectives and elements of an effective juvenile justice system are?

Can You Define

competence, competent, coproducers of justice, John Wayne effect, paradigm, restorative justice

INTRODUCTION

The juvenile justice system, according to many, is in need of retooling, perhaps even of replacing. Critics question whether the juvenile court can serve both welfare and justice. For decades reformers have promoted the Four Ds of decriminalization, diversion, deinstitutionalization and due process. Critics note that reforms of the past decades have had little impact on violent crime or violent youths. Pressure is being applied to "get tough" with juveniles, even first-time offenders, as seen in Chapter 10 with the rise of boot camps. Some even advocate abolishing the separate juvenile justice system.

As noted by Sprott (1998, p. 399): "There is evidence in the United States . . . that small but cumulative steps are being taken to eliminate . . . separate youth justice systems." Among the changes identified by Torbet (1997, p. 1):

- The creation by some states of mandatory minimum sentences for juvenile offenders and "blended" sentences that combine juvenile and adult sanctions

- Growing pressure to publish the names of juvenile offenders

- Calls to lower the minimum and maximum ages of jurisdiction for the juvenile court

- A push to broaden the scope of offenses for which juveniles can be transferred to adult criminal court

Sprott concludes (p. 399): "The net result of these proposed and legislated changes is that the treatment of youth is becoming more similar to that of adults, with a consequent erosion of the youth justice system and the philosophies that underlie it."

According to Breed (1990, p. 70): "We have without question reached a point where the conflict between old and new policy agendas represents a watershed in the history of juvenile justice." Breed also notes: "These ideological disputes are taking place in a political context, dominated by heightened public fear of crime, media sensationalism, tightening budgets and political rhetoric that emphasizes law and order." Current dissatisfaction with the juvenile system is also described by Greenwood (p. 2):

> Conservative critics, focusing on public safety, fault the system for giving serious offenders too many chances on diversion or probation and for imposing terms of confinement that are too short. These critics often characterize juvenile facilities as country clubs and argue that some juveniles should be confined in more punitive settings.
> Liberal critics, concerned with the problems of juveniles and anxious to protect them from unwarranted State intrusions, fault the system for being too tough. Where conservative critics use the evidence of "no rehabilitative effect" to argue for more explicitly punitive sanctions, liberals use the same evidence to argue for less State involvement altogether. Liberals generally support the view that subjecting juveniles to confinement only further criminalizes them, no matter how benign the treatment.
> Another liberal group, heavily represented by defense attorneys and other youth advocates, deplores the lack of adequate procedural protections for juveniles. This group argues that many young people are "railroaded" through the system that offers no adequate protection of their rights.

This chapter presents some issues involving the juvenile justice system and some reforms that juvenile experts suggest might improve the system. As a means of broadening the perspective on juvenile justice, the chapter covers innovations in the juvenile justice systems of Sweden, England, Israel, Canada, New Zealand and Scotland. This is followed by a discussion of the Bureau of Justice Statistics–Princeton Project to "re-examine both the concepts and the methodologies involved in conceptualizing, measuring, and evaluating the performance of those agencies and actors comprising the American criminal justice system" (Dillingham, 1992, p. iii).

Juvenile Court Involvement

Juvenile justice in the United States has become more concerned with the rules than with "the best interest of the child." The juvenile court has become deluged with both criminal and civil issues: child development, psychological concepts of understanding maturity and public policy for the good of the community. It has become involved with:

- Abortion (*Bellotti v. Baird,* 1979; *City of Akron v. Akron Center for Reproductive Health,* 1983; *H. L. v. Matheson,* 1981; *Thornburgh v. American College of Obstetricians and Gynecologists,* 1986)
- School prayer (*Wallace v. Jaffree,* 1985)
- Search and seizure issues in school lockers or classrooms (*Dow v. Renfrow,* 1981; *New Jersey v. T. L. O.,* 1985)
- Interracial custody and adoption (*In re R. M. G.,* 1982; *Palmore v. Sidoti,* 1984)
- Adolescent judgment and maturity (*Planned Parenthood of Kansas City v. Ashcroft,* 1983)
- Determination that minors are "persons" entitled to protection under the Bill of Rights (*Parham v. J. R.,* 1979)
- Legal issues in terminating parental rights (*Jewish Child Care Association v. Elaine S. Y.,* 1980; *Nebraska v. Wedige,* 1980)

Juvenile courts have been involved in such issues as abortion, school prayer, search and seizure, interracial custody and adoption, adolescent judgment and maturity and legal issues in terminating parental rights.

The involvement of the juvenile court in these social and legal issues has detracted, to a point, from its primary duties of delinquency adjudication and protecting the child. This wide range of issues illustrates the courts' involvement in nondelinquent matters and its tendency to take on matters that many believe should not be legislated, or at least should not be legislated for juveniles any differently than they are for adults—for example abortion and search and seizure. In addition as Chunn (1994, p. 8) notes: "Juvenile justice wants to function as a surrogate parent, meeting the individual needs of all its children. Moreover, society expects the system to provide a lasting 'fix' to transform troubled youths into successful citizens." These varied expectations of the juvenile system leave some wondering just how many hats juvenile justice should wear.

A Juvenile Justice Model

Juvenile justice is at a crossroads. Should it become a totally adversarial system like the adult system? Or should the system be reorganized to a new order that declares that the primary objective is the punishment of crime?

Charles E. Springer, vice-chief justice of the Supreme Court of Nevada, is one strong advocate of reform in the juvenile justice system. A nationally recognized authority on juvenile justice, Springer received the Outstanding Service Award from the National Council of Juvenile and Family Court Judges in 1980. His publication *Justice for Juveniles,* published by the Office of Juvenile Justice and Delinquency Prevention, is cited extensively in this final chapter. Springer (1986, p. 4) says: "Society sets standards that determine criminal conduct. We must live up to these standards or violate them at our peril. In this case, the term 'we' includes young people, who should be held accountable for their actions and punished for their wrongs, subject to some degree of diminished responsibility." Springer (p. 2) contends that:

> The first step in doing justice for juveniles is to revise juvenile court acts throughout the country so that when juvenile courts deal with delinquent children, they operate under a justice model rather than under the present treatment of the child welfare model.

A justice model is a judicial process wherein young people who come into conflict with the law are held responsible and accountable for their behavior.

Justice Charles E. Springer is vice-chief justice of the Supreme Court of Nevada and is a strong advocate of reforming the juvenile justice system. He believes that often criminal youth do not have a problem—they ARE the problem.

This position is contrary to the social welfare philosophy of the traditional juvenile court. But as Springer (pp. 4–5) continues:

> It is not necessarily contrary to the way that juvenile court judges have traditionally handled delinquent cases. Treating and caring for youthful criminals, rather than punishing them, is simply too contrary to our experience and folk wisdom and too counterintuitive to be accepted by judges or the general public. A philosophy that denies moral guilt, abhors punishment in any form, and views criminals as innocent, hapless victims of bad social environments may be written into law, but this does not mean that it will be followed in practice.

Springer (p. 2) suggests that: "Except for certain mentally disabled and incompetent individuals, young law violators should not be considered by the juvenile courts as being 'sick' or as victims of their environments. Generally speaking, young criminals are more wrong than wronged, more the victimizers than the victims." Springer goes on to note (p. 29):

> Law violators, young and old, should be punished for their crimes. Even at a very early age, young people are not the guileless, plastic, and pliable people they are portrayed to be by those who would free them from all moral and legal responsibility. Children understand punishment and they understand fairness.

He suggests that we too often spend time trying to "diagnose the 'problem' of some young offender, when in most cases it is obvious that the criminal youth does not have a problem—he or she is the problem" (p. 33).

This hard-line, "get tough with juveniles" perspective has been supported by legislators and some state judges in the 1980s and 1990s. Often the issue is one of competence.

The Competence Issue

The concept of competence greatly influences how the legal system deals with children. Adults are presumed **competent,** that is fit or qualified to understand right from wrong. Children (i.e., minors) are presumed incompetent under the law in virtually all contexts. While children may be "heard" on behalf of themselves or may be treated as adults in a variety of circumstances, these situations are generally preceded by a qualifying process, incorporated in some specific statutory or common law exception. The statute may be specific as to whether a juvenile offender is to be tried as an adult.

Under law a person's **competence** is conceptualized as a specific functional ability.

The word *competent* is usually followed by the phrase "to . . ." rather than presented as a general attribute of a person. An adult who is deemed incompetent to stand trial for a specific offense may still be presumed competent to function as a custodial parent or to manage financial affairs. For the adult, specific incompetence must be proven case by case.

Conversely minor children are presumed incompetent for most purposes, without any concern for whether the children have the capacity to make required decisions in a practical sense. Children who are deemed legally competent for one purpose are often considered generally incompetent in other decision-making contexts. For example a juvenile offender who has been found competent to waive rights, and who has even been bound over for trial as an adult, would still be considered generally incompetent to consent to medical treatment or make contracts.

At the heart of the competence issue with juveniles is the question of knowing when an act is "wrong" and how justice can best be served. For example does the teenager who runs away from home to escape sexual abuse by a parent do "wrong"? Running away is a status offense, but is justice served by treating the youth as a delinquent? Conversely does the teenager who kills his entire family with an ax do "wrong"? Is such a youth better served by counseling, punishment or a combination?

Critics of the present system suggest that too often the runaway and the ax murderer are dumped into the same "pot"—the juvenile justice system—and that justice is often not provided for either. Restructuring the juvenile court system might provide one solution to this problem.

Restructuring

In Gilbert and Sullivan's operetta, the Mikado of Japan sings, "My object all sublime I shall achieve in time—To let the punishment fit the crime—The punishment fit the crime." In other words the wrong done should determine the response that is made. The English Children and Young Persons Act of 1969 states: "Every court, in dealing with a child or young person who is brought before it, either as an offender or otherwise, should have regard to the welfare of the child or young person." There is similar language in the Constitution of the United States. To accomplish this many argue that the juvenile court needs restructuring in two areas.

The first change often advocated is to clearly separate criminal and noncriminal acts. Noncriminal acts would be treated as civil matters. Juvenile courts, acting under the principle of *parens patriae,* do have the responsibility to intercede for children who are neglected, deprived or abused, but they might do so more effectively under a civil jurisdiction. Likewise youths who commit status offenses, particularly if they are not under the control of their parents, should not have full rein. They might initially be under the court's civil jurisdiction, with the warning that if they do not comply with the court's orders they may be declared delinquent and placed under the court's criminal jurisdiction.

The second change often advocated is to consider age more specifically. Rather than having one specific age at which a person comes within the jurisdiction of the adult courts (usually age 18), a two- or three-level approach might be more effective. Springer (p. 46) notes that: "For centuries, children were divided by the common law into three categories: children who are so young as to be generally thought of as being beyond the proper reach of criminal punishment, prepubescent children who are hard to classify in terms of criminal responsibility, and children over the age of puberty." He suggests that the same three-tiered approach should be used in our juvenile justice system (p. 47): "The answer is to set out some overlapping age brackets of diminished responsibility for all but the most vicious of youthful offenders. As has always been the case, three levels present themselves." Springer suggests that the first level might extend to approximately age 9, that the second level encompass juveniles between ages 9 and 14 or 15, and that the third level would encompass juveniles 14 or 15 and older—depending on the individual and the crime committed.

The juvenile justice system could be restructured in two areas: (1) civil and criminal jurisdictions could be separated, and within civil jurisdiction, poverty-stricken, neglected and abused children could be separated from status offenders and those who are not under the control of their parents; and (2) jurisdictional age could also be considered.

Policy Recommendations for Consideration

Lundman, a researcher who conducted a thorough review of the literature on juvenile delinquency, sets forth six specific recommendations, based on this review (Gibbons and Krohn, 1986, p. 174):

1. Traditional delinquency prevention efforts should be abandoned.
2. Diversion should be the first response of the juvenile justice system to status and minor offenders.
3. Routine probation should be retained as the first and most frequent sentencing option of juvenile court judges.
4. Efforts to scare juveniles straight should be abandoned.
5. Community treatment programs should be expanded to accommodate nearly all chronic offenders.
6. Institutionalization should continue to be used as a last resort, reserved primarily for chronic offenders adjudicated delinquent for index crimes against persons.

The Future for Neglected and Abused Children

The National Council of Juvenile and Family Court Judges, through the Metropolitan Court Judges Committee (1986), has provided a guideline for judicial response to deprived children who occupy much of the juvenile court's time. The committee has made 73 recommendations to be considered by judges, legislators, child protection agency officials and local civic leaders that will ameliorate the problems of deprived children who require public custody and protection. Several of these recommendations have been outlined in preceding chapters. The judges' concern is that there must be more than just talk about the needs of children. They believe that complex problems can be solved, but only through the commitment of government and the community, in partnership, to develop and rigorously apply all their resources and talents. As noted in the introduction of their report (pp. 5–6):

> The judges know that too often the processes of the system can exacerbate the abuse by its delays, procedures and rules which are insensitive to the feelings, perceptions and fears of children. . . . They know that agencies may override the

rights of children in their zeal to help them, taking them out of their homes on mere assertion, placing them in foster homes, sometimes of another culture or at a distance from family, school and friends. . . . The judges know also that their own authority is often limited.

The 73 recommendations cover the role of judges; court procedures; detecting, reporting and evaluating; out-of-home placement; treatment and planning and prevention issues—all areas in which changes and reform might be appropriate. Appendix E contains the specific recommendations of the Metropolitan Court Judges Committee.

Time for a Change

Sullivan and Victor (1988, p. 156), state:

> The winds of change are blowing across the nation's juvenile justice system. Traditional reforms are being replaced with a new and more conservative agenda of juvenile justice. This new reform movement emphasizes the welfare of victims, a punitive approach toward serious juvenile offenders, and protection of children from physical and sexual exploitation. Policies which favor diversion and deinstitutionalization are less popular. After many years of attempting to remove status offenders from the juvenile justice system, there are increasing calls for returning truants, runaways, and other troubled youth to juvenile court jurisdiction. In spite of these developments, there are many juvenile justice reformers who remain dedicated to advancing due process rights for children and reducing reliance on incarceration.

Clearly there is conflict and tension between the old and new juvenile justice reform agendas.

Change is usually difficult. Almost five hundred years ago Machiavelli (1469–1527), an Italian diplomat, wrote in his classic work, *The Prince* (1513):

> There is nothing more difficult to carry out, nor more doubtful of success, nor more dangerous to handle, than to initiate a new order of things. For the reformer has enemies in all those who profit by the old order, and only lukewarm defenders in all those who would profit by the new order, this lukewarmness arising partly from fear of their adversaries, who have the law in their favour; and partly from the incredulity of mankind, who do not truly believe in anything new until they have had actual experience of it.

The difficulty of change is also noted by Breed (p. 72):

> Many of us bear the scars, if not the open wounds, of previous encounters with policy and philosophy changes. Unfortunately, it is easy to bow to the inevitability of crime; to acknowledge the social injustice that causes most of it; to make claims that nothing works; to let the federal government mandate our directions and the courts to order them; and to bend to the pressures of public opinion.
>
> It's much harder to take the initiative to stand up for what is right when it is not popular; to be creative and fight mediocrity; to sense the responsibility of our current roles; to feel the intolerability of present conditions; and to seek the strength to change them.

Individuals and groups willing to take the initiative and propose reforms for the juvenile justice system do exist. Among them are Thomas R. English, Barry Krisberg and James Austin. English, director of the Oregon Council on Crime and Delinquency and president of the American Restitution Association, calls for "rejuvenating" juvenile justice. Krisberg, president of the National Council on Crime and Delinquency (NCCD), and Austin, executive vice president of the NCCD, call for "reinventing" juvenile justice.

Rejuvenating Juvenile Justice

English (1993, p. 19), in his article calling for rejuvenating juvenile justice, notes several problems with our juvenile justice system:

> If we examine the public bureaucracies in which juvenile justice programs and services are delivered, we find that they mirror the outdated, top-down management protocols of mass-production industrial economies.
>
> This approach has led to a juvenile justice bureaucracy whose hallmarks include categorical funding; large caseloads; top-down management; limited professional training; and accountability based on eligibility, rule compliance, and contract monitoring.

English suggests that juvenile justice combine ideas from the business world, including Total Quality Management (TQM) and reinvention, along with the work of the Balanced Approach/Restorative Justice (BA/RJ) group.

W. Edward Deming's Total Quality Management concept, introduced in the '50s, is perhaps best known for its zero-defect philosophy. What is of interest to juvenile justice is how Deming proposed that zero defects could be accomplished. Rather than operating with a top-down management process, where only some problems are solved, every employee, from the president to the custodian, is required to determine if what they do is helping to achieve the organization's mission. A TQM approach might make reforms in the juvenile justice system more effective. English (p. 19) notes:

> We have increased opportunities for preschool pupils but not for high school dropouts; we have established child abuse reporting but not parent training; we have implemented mastery teaching but not peer group empowerment.

In addition to using concepts from TQM, juvenile justice reformers might also borrow from the work of the Balanced Approach/Restorative Justice Project, which seeks to accomplish three objectives simultaneously: competency development and accountability for offenders and protection for the community. Community-based programs incorporating ideas from TQM and the Balanced Approach (BA) might be characterized as follows (English, pp. 17–18):

- Front-line workers are accorded wide discretion.
- A broad spectrum of responsive, convenient and timely services is provided.
- Collaboration across traditional and professional boundaries is encouraged.
- Children are viewed in the context of the family and the family in the context of neighborhoods and communities.
- Programs have deep roots in the community and are customized to meet cultural needs.
- Parental cooperation and participation are solicited.
- Establishing a relationship of trust with children and their extended families is a priority.

- A long–term prevention orientation predominates.
- The organizational milieu is based primarily on outcomes rather than on regulation.

According to English (p. 20): "We have been attempting to force the square peg of community-based programs into the round hole of professional bureaucracies." He suggests that one approach to rejuvenating juvenile justice might be to take a lead from the musical world, beginning with an orchestra. Here many different musicians and instruments combine talents to create the power of a symphony. They all play from the same musical score, but each has a specific and vital part. English takes the analogy further to include the jazz band, where individuals not only play together, but improvise, building on the original melody and creating new notes and themes. He suggests (pp. 20–21):

> We can learn from this jazz band approach as well. We must learn to work as an ensemble within each community; at the local, state, and federal levels; as public and private organizations; and as individuals and groups—each taking the lead at times and playing a supporting role at others. We must encourage innovative and reactive approaches to the problems posed by juvenile delinquency. The time has come to abandon the one-man-band approach in which juvenile justice is managed by a mega-agency and instead emulate the creative harmony and innovative improvisation of a jazz band.

Reinventing Juvenile Justice

Krisberg and Austin (1993) suggest that much more than rejuvenation is needed for the juvenile justice system. Their extensive discussion of the contemporary juvenile justice system ends with the following conclusions (pp. 109–110):

> Our analysis paints a discouraging picture. Juvenile laws are vaguely worded and inconsistently applied, permitting extensive abuses in the handling of children by social control agencies whose discretion is largely unchecked. Instead of protecting children from injustices and unwarranted state intervention, the opposite effect frequently occurs. The practices and procedures of juvenile justice agents mirror our society's class and racial prejudices and fall disproportionately on African-American, Latino, and poor people.
>   These conclusions are not new. Many practitioners within the juvenile court share this critical perspective. The vital question is, "What is to be done?" Most critics of the juvenile court continue to offer narrow reform measures that do not confront the relationship between inequities in the juvenile justice system and inequities within society. . . .
>   The quest for juvenile justice is tied inextricably to the pursuit of social justice.

For a different perspective on juvenile justice, the following pages describe how juveniles are treated in some other countries.

A Global Perspective

The United States is not alone in its efforts to control crime and violence and at the same time provide justice for its youths. This section begins by looking at the differences in how youths are treated in two countries representing the extremes.

American teenager Michael Peter Fay, 18, enters Singapore's high court for an appeal of his caning sentence for vandalism. Fay's sentence of six strokes of the cane, four months of imprisonment and a fine was upheld by the court.

Singapore and Sweden

As a starting point, consider the two extremes of Singapore and Sweden. Singapore uses caning as a punishment for those who break the law. When American Michael Fay received six lashes from a rattan cane, many Americans were outraged. Many others, however, were supportive.

Singapore's streets are safe and spotless. Nothing less is tolerated. When gum caused a subway door to malfunction, gum chewing was simply outlawed. Individual liberty in Singapore takes second place to social order.

Sweden, on the other hand, took the lead in forbidding corporal punishment of children. Sweden has outlawed force and violence against children, thereby strengthening children's legal position. In March 1979 Sweden passed an "antispanking" law.

According to Sweden's antispanking law, the parent or guardian should exercise the necessary supervision in accordance with the child's age and other circumstances. The child may not be subjected to corporal punishment or other injurious or humiliating treatment.

During the debate on the bill, one representative argued that "in a free democracy like our own we use words as arguments, not blows. . . . We talk to people, not beat them. If we cannot convince our children with words, we shall never convince them with a beating" (Salzer, 1979, p. 13).

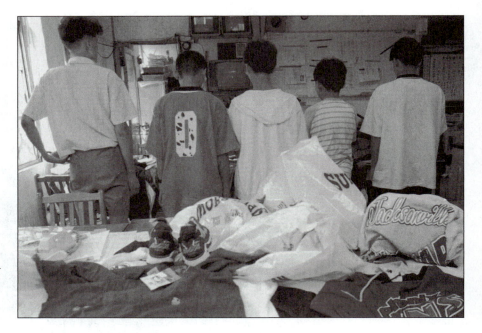

Taiwanese juveniles are held at a police station in the northern Taipei suburb of Shihlin after being arrested for stealing in this 1997 photo. Taiwan has been rocked by a series of vicious crimes committed by juveniles that has altered the perception of young people from diligent students to confused, angry misfits.

Most countries are neither as extreme as Singapore in placing social order ahead of individual liberty or as extreme as Sweden in passing an antispanking law. The United Nations, however, leans very closely to the position of Sweden. The UN's Declaration on the Rights of the Child, adopted in 1989, is the first formal recognition of the need to provide special protection for children. The right to be free from force and violence is implicit in Principle 2:

> The child shall enjoy special protection, and shall be given opportunities and facilities, by law and by other means, to enable him to develop physically, mentally, morally, spiritually and socially in a healthy and normal manner and in conditions of freedom and dignity.

Swedish juvenile justice has been influenced by social welfare authorities. Children and youths cannot be punished for crimes committed before the age of 15, the age of criminal responsibility. Instead any such cases are referred to the social welfare authorities. Fifteen is not an absolute limit, however. In practice the social welfare authorities usually assume responsibility for persons under the age of 18 who have committed serious offenses. Even in this age group, fines are the most common sanctions for minor offenses. Youths who are mentally ill or have a severe substance abuse problem may be referred to medical care or for treatment for alcoholism or drug abuse. There are two strong reasons for these exceptions. First their criminality is associated with personal difficulties or handicaps that negate the basic assumption that people are responsible for their own actions. Second the penal system lacks the resources required to deal with people having such problems.

The majority of offenders are relatively young. The largest group is the 15- to 19-year-old population. Most offenses involving youths are handled through the social welfare authorities. The police, for whatever reason, do not get involved in juvenile crime or matters of abuse, neglect and abandonment.

Article 37a in their law states: "No child shall be subjected to torture or other cruel, inhuman or degrading treatment or punishment" which is consistent with the safeguard in the antispanking law.

Canada

The Canadian juvenile justice system was revamped by the passage of the Young Offenders Act (YOA) in 1984. This act established a uniform age for legal status, defining the range of 12 to 17 years as the mandate for the youth court. The system shifted to a highly structured adversarial system resembling the adult court rather than the informal system that preceded it. As noted by Wass and Marks (1992, p. 91): "In the early '70s, the feeling was that children involved in the system would have been criminalized by the proposed bill [a similar bill which was defeated in the 1970s]. Now some 15 years later, public criticism focused on how young 'criminals' were being treated like 'children.' " The Young Offenders Act has the following operating principles (Wass and Marks, pp. 91–92):

- Young people are responsible for their illegal behavior, but are not always accountable in the same manner as adults.
- Society has a right to be protected from illegal behavior and has a responsibility to prevent crime.
- Young people have special needs.
- Young people have well-defined rights and entitlements, including the least possible interference with their freedom.
- Parents are responsible for the care and supervision of their children, who should remain in the home whenever possible.

The wide range of dispositions available under the act include community and personal service, restitution, probation, fines, open custody, secure custody and treatment orders.

New Zealand

As noted by Revering (1998, p. 167): "A concept called Police Accountability Conferencing may well be a time tested juvenile justice alternative that appears to be preventing juvenile crime—one kid at a time." He says this concept was first used by the Maori people of New Zealand hundreds of years ago to solve family, tribal and community problems. According to Revering: "Although native peoples in other parts of the world have employed similar processes, in the Maori process, the extended network of family and friends share the responsibility for a young person's behavior while involving the victims of that behavior in the process of resolution."

In New Zealand's juvenile justice system, the central component is the Family Group Conference. This lay panel was established by legislation passed in 1989 and applies to offenses committed by individuals between the ages of 10 and 18. Moore (1993, p. 4) describes the Family Group Conference process:

> The basic design of the Family Group Conference is disarmingly simple. A young person who has committed an offense against an identifiable victim is brought face to face with that victim. (There may be more than one offender or more than one victim; a single conference deals with the effects of the offense.) Both offender(s)

and victim(s) are accompanied by family members, guardians, peers, or other people with a significant relationship to the offender or the victim. These people are collectively referred to as "supporters;" they may contribute to the search for restitution and to negotiations for reparation of the damage caused by the original offense. It is this insistence on collective, community involvement in the search for reparation that sets the Family Group Conference model apart from reparations schemes run in Britain and the United States since the 1970s.

The Family Group Conference is called into session by an official of the justice system. The session itself often entails not only shame on the part of the offender, but forgiveness by the victim. As noted by Moore (p. 15): "The appropriate use of shame in civil society will be far more effective as a means of moral education than will legal retribution within the criminal justice system."

Israel

In Israel the juvenile justice system is divided into two segments: criminal and civil. Matters are referred to the juvenile court by the police, who have absolute power in matters dealing with children. The police have a special unit classified as juvenile officers. The juvenile officer handles all referrals. The matters must be related to a crime or directly related to the health, welfare and safety of the child. All crimes go to criminal court (no distinction of a juvenile court). All other matters are handled in civil court. The civil court handles divorce and foster care. There are no status offenses in Israel.

In criminal matters the police investigate, interview and determine how to refer. The police referral includes descriptions of the crime and contact with the juvenile and parents. All matters are referred to the welfare administration for disposition.

Israel shows the British influence in its juvenile justice process. All criminal and civil matters are heard by a magistrate. The Ministry of Labour and Social Affairs receives all matters, and trials and disposition are directed to the juvenile probation section. The police are youth workers in uniform. Juveniles between ages 12 and 18 are subject to the police. The police direct most cases to social services, which also has community corrections, group homes and foster care. In most cases juveniles are placed on probation. Only 2 percent of youths are placed in a secure facility. There are only two secure facilities in Israel. All citizens of Israel are subject to military law. Children who engage in armed conflict, such as stone throwers, are referred to the criminal court due to the gravity of the offense. The juvenile justice system is diagrammed in Figure 14.1.

England

In 1989 England reorganized its juvenile justice system to set up a youth court that took over matters classified as delinquency. The Children's Act of 1989 placed matters into the hands of the police for the first incident of shoplifting, vandalism and similar charges. If a youth is brought to the police station, the parents are notified. If the parents cannot or will not come to the station, a social worker is called and represents the child. If detained the child is detained in a small room with a window.

The police confront the parents of the offender and the offender in the police station, where a caution or warning against the wrongdoing is issued. The offender is released to the parents with a stipulation that the youth not commit

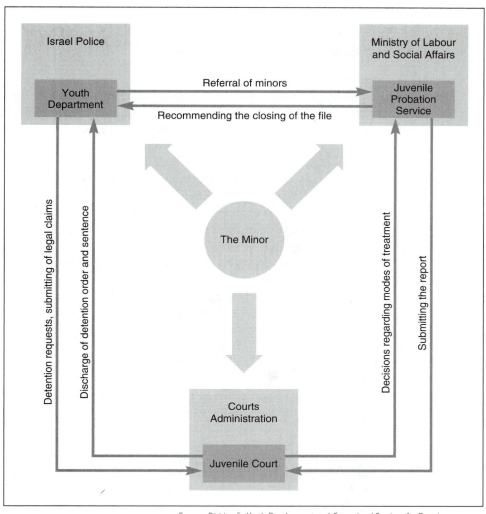

Figure 14.1
Juvenile Probation Service

Source: *Division for Youth Development and Correctional Services: An Overview.*
Jerusalem: State of Israel, Ministry of Labour and Social Affairs, July 1993, p. 20.
Reprinted with permission.

the offense again. If the youth persists in getting into trouble by violating the law, the police may refer the matter to the youth court. Before the matter is sent to the court, it is reviewed by the Crown Prosecution Service to determine if there is sufficient evidence to proceed. If there is proof, the matter is referred to a Magistrate's Court consisting of three lay people who might not have any legal background and who can come from any social status or profession.

If a legal question arises, a magistrate's clerk interprets the law for them. In England the age of reason is 10 years old, and the youth is subject to the youth court from the age of 10 to age 17. If a youthful offender receives several cautions, the police in charge send a form to the education department, social services and the probation office asking for comments and suggestions regarding the youth and the incident. The views, when received, are forwarded with the case file to the youth court for a decision. The court makes a decision called a "conditional discharge" from the court, which is in effect for 12 months. Every effort is made to avoid placing youths in detention, or as it is referred to in England, "secure accommodations."

When a youth commits a felonious act that endangers the public, such as robbery, murder, manslaughter or aggravated assault, the youth is taken to the Crown Court (adult court) without first being certified by the youth court. An example is the murder of a 2-year-old by two 10-year-olds in Liverpool. The 2-year-old was abducted from a shopping mall and taken to a railroad yard, where he was tortured and murdered by the two male 10-year-olds. The event created national and international interest. The two offenders were tried in the Crown Court in the same process afforded to adults. They were provided a defense counsel, with trial by jury, and when convicted they were placed in prison, but in a facility suitable to their age. The matter is public record when a youth is convicted, and the youth's identity can be revealed.

If the youth is at risk, such as in abuse, neglect or abandonment cases, the matter is not referred to the youth court. Instead it is referred to a body called the Inter-Agency Unit. This unit consists of a panel of police, social workers and educators who decide what is in the best interest of the child. This panel forwards its finding, if the child is a victim, to the Crown Prosecutor Service for further action, and the child is placed with social services until the matter is resolved.

Each district, such as Wales, West Yorkshire and the like, is mandated by the Children's Act of 1989. They do not all function in the same manner, however.

Scotland

The Scottish juvenile justice system is based on the concept of a "Children's Panel." The Children's Panel was developed under the Social Worker Act of 1968. This act did away with the juvenile court and replaced it with a *lay tribunal.* The idea for the lay tribunal came from a report in 1964 from the Kilbrandon Committee. This committee recommended that the juvenile court be replaced by a lay panel consisting of three people (with both men and women represented) drawn from a panel of people in the community who were aware of community affairs. The recommendation for the panel was based on the finding that children had special needs over and above those of adults and that the law courts (even the juvenile courts) were primarily concerned with determining guilt and imposing punishment, not with the well-being and welfare of children appearing before them.

As noted in the resource manual for panel members (Peacock, p. 4): "The various parts of Scotland can be characterized by pronounced local differences, arising from geographic, social, economic, political and historical factors. These will influence the manner in which the local authority exercises its responsibility."

The committee felt that several factors contributed to children's problems: The attitudes and lifestyles of their parents, their schooling, their housing conditions and their physical health could all influence children's behavior. Consequently the committee reasoned that the court when "sitting in judgment" on children's cases was faced with the difficulty of trying to do two things at once: protecting society from criminal acts by imposing suitable punishment while at the same time trying to meet a responsibility for the child's welfare and acting in the best interest of the child. The committee believed it was unrealistic for a court that handled criminal law to be combined with a specialized welfare agency for children in trouble.

The Children's Panel deals with two important issues:

- Establishing guilt or innocence
- Defining measures that will help each child

The age of reason in Scotland is eight. Children are subject to the panel from age 8 to age 17. Serious juvenile offenses continue to be heard by a Sheriff's Court (a high court similar to a district or superior court in the United States). The Sheriff's Court can also be used for appeals. Only in exceptional circumstances will the court handle juvenile matters, however.

Along with the formation of the Children's Panel, the committee suggested that an independent official, a lay person, be responsible for initially assessing all children's cases. This official was designated as the "reporter."

The format of the Children's Panel is based on the social services concept. It is community-oriented social work, with the main objective being to serve the best interest of the child.

Since the panel came into existence in 1971, children in trouble have been referred first to the reporter, who reviews the referrals. If the matter is a serious offense, the reporter takes the case(s) to a procurator-fiscal (a county/district attorney) for evaluation as to whether the matter should go before the panel or to a court of law.

When the case is referred to the panel, the contacts may come from the police, school or social workers. When the police handle a youthful offender, they interview the person about the offense. If the police, with parents, feel it is in the best interests of the child to be placed "under police supervision," the matter is handled by the police without any official referral. This happens only with matters brought to the attention of the police.

The schools also make referrals for those matters that are special to a school, such as truancy. School matters are forwarded to the reporter for a hearing. For all panel hearings, the parents of the child are notified to appear with the child at a specific date and time. When they arrive only the child sits before the panel. The parents sit behind the child. There is no legal counsel at the hearing. The child is asked to either affirm or deny the allegations presented. If he denies the allegations, the matter is automatically referred to the Sheriff's Court. If the child pleads guilty (affirms) to the matter, then the panel, in an atmosphere of a family discussion, asks the youth to explain the circumstances surrounding the matter.

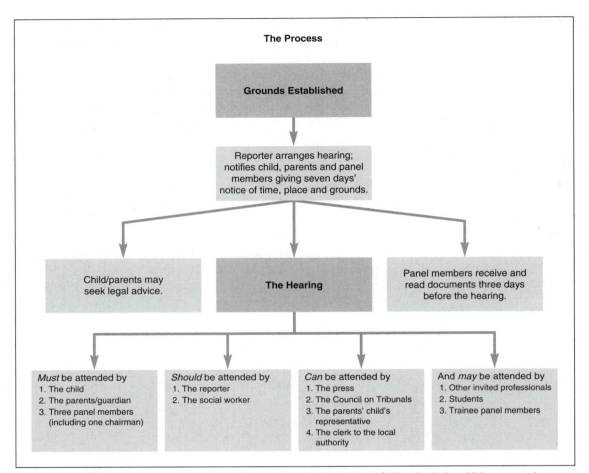

The Process

Grounds Established

Reporter arranges hearing; notifies child, parents and panel members giving seven days' notice of time, place and grounds.

Child/parents may seek legal advice.

The Hearing

Panel members receive and read documents three days before the hearing.

Must be attended by
1. The child
2. The parents/guardian
3. Three panel members (including one chairman)

Should be attended by
1. The reporter
2. The social worker

Can be attended by
1. The press
2. The Council on Tribunals
3. The parents' child's representative
4. The clerk to the local authority

And *may* be attended by
1. Other invited professionals
2. Students
3. Trainee panel members

Figure 14.2
Children's Panel Flowchart: From Establishment of Grounds to the Hearing

Note that the most usual composition of a hearing is the child, a parent, the reporter, two panel members, a panel chairman and a social worker. From June 1985, it is possible that a "safeguarder" may attend a hearing on behalf of a child. This is an important new development.

Source: Geraldine Peacock. *The Children's Hearings System in Scotland. An Introduction for Panel Members*. Social Work Services Group, The Open University, n.d., p. 33.

When the child explains, the panel asks specific questions aimed at having the child state the reasons for the offending action. When the child has finished explaining, the panel asks the child what can be done to help keep it from happening again. After the matter is fully examined, a disposition is given immediately. There is no delay in the proceeding from start to finish. In most cases the matter is referred to the social worker to follow up. There is no probation. All probation officer positions were abolished and consolidated within social services. The social worker also handles matters related to the school. Figure 14.2 illustrates the process used in the Children's Panel.

New Zealand, England and Scotland use panels of lay people to deal with nonserious, nonviolent youthful offenders.

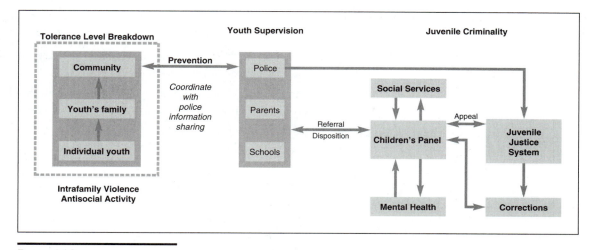

Figure 14.3
Anoka's Special Advocate Children's Panel

This Children's Panel concept has been replicated in Anoka, Minnesota, in the first program of its kind in the United States. The structure of Anoka's Special Advocate Children's Panel is illustrated in Figure 14.3.

The United Nations' Position on Children

The Declaration on the Rights of the Child that was adopted by the General Assembly of the United Nations in November 1989 states in its preamble: "The United Nations has proclaimed that childhood is entitled to special care and assistance" (Paragraph 4, p. 1). Article 3, Sub. L. states: "In all actions concerning children, whether undertaken by public or private social welfare institutions, courts of law, administrative authorities, or legislative bodies, the best interests of the child shall be a primary consideration" (p. 2).

Next consider some recommendations for "rethinking" the criminal justice system in the United States.

A Call for Change

At the beginning of this chapter, advocates of "rejuvenating" or "reinventing" juvenile justice were cited. As a part of this rejuvenation or reinvention, some are calling for a new view of justice itself—restorative justice.

Restorative Justice

Van Ness (1990, p. 62) notes: "The Western view of crime and justice has become skewed. Rather than admitting that crimes injure victims, our laws define them as only offenses against government. Contemporary criminal justice is preoccupied with maintaining public order and punishing offenders. Victims are often ignored, and the government has taken over the community's role of maintaining the peace." Van Ness argues for a return to **restorative justice,** which returns to the ancient view that justice involves not two, but four parties: offender and victim, government and community—all are injured by crime. He notes that restorative justice has three underlying principles:

1. Crimes result in injuries to victims, communities, and offenders; therefore, the criminal justice process must repair those injuries.

2. Not only government, but victims, offenders and communities should be actively involved throughout the entire criminal justice process.

3. In promoting justice, the government should preserve order, and the peace should be maintained by the community.

This concept of restorative justice is expanded and refined by the Bureau of Justice Statistics–Princeton Project, which is calling not only for a change in how justice is viewed but an entirely new paradigm for the criminal justice system itself.

The BJS–Princeton Project Call for a New Paradigm

The Bureau of Justice Statistics funded a Princeton University study group to "reexamine both the concepts and the methodologies involved in conceptualizing, measuring, and evaluating the performance of those agencies and actors comprising the American criminal justice system" (Dillingham, p. iii). This group's first publication was *Rethinking the Criminal Justice System: Toward a New Paradigm.* A **paradigm** is a pattern, a way of looking at an entire field or concept. Scientific advances often come from the ability to view things in a new light or using a new paradigm. The move from reactive, incident-driven policing to proactive, problem-oriented policing involves a paradigm shift. Such shifts are difficult and require the ability to see beyond the status quo. As noted by English (p. 16): "Inability to see beyond the status quo can lead to what may be called the John Wayne effect—'If it doesn't work, do more, and try harder, Pilgrim!'"

English notes three trends identified by the BA/RJ group that illustrate this **John Wayne effect:**

1. Increasing commitments to state institutions, especially for drug-involved youths

2. Expanded out-of-home and quasi-residential placements

3. Widespread transferring of juvenile offenders to adult court

The BJS–Princeton Project has as its key concept the democratic vision of citizens as **coproducers of justice,** a phrase suggested by Moore (p. 9): "Citizens, not judges, prosecutors, law enforcement officers, or corrections officials, are primarily responsible for the quality of life in their communities, including the prevalence and severity of crime within them. . . . Citizens in a democracy must begin by holding themselves and their neighbors accountable for public affairs."

As coproducers of justice, citizens are responsible for the prevalence and severity of the crime within their communities.

Issues for the Future

Ohlin (1998, pp. 148–153) presents six policy issues that will require new perspectives and approaches in the coming decades:

1. *Confronting the alienation of youth.* Youths' reactions to the increasing sense of isolation in our society have found expression not only in public disorder, vandalism and crime but also in the resurgence of gangs, greater substance abuse and the increased chronicity of youth offending.

2. *Building community resources.* Enhancing the role of local communities in crime prevention and control.

3. *Allocation of federal, state and local resources.* Currently in a state of uncertainty and transition, we need to learn more about the best ways to divide and coordinate responsibilities among federal, state and local governments.

4. *Employment.* The problems of employment and education contribute to the isolation and alienation of youth.

5. *Fear of crime.* Public attitude surveys indicate that the link between the fear of crime and the actual risk is not as direct as people assume. The relationships of class, race and gender to crime are potentially explosive issues that must be confronted directly. Only with cooperative, organized community programs to reduce crime will the barriers of locks, bars and dogs be replaced by a sense of safety and control.

6. *Creating cooperation.* Juvenile justice policies cannot be successfully dealt with outside the context of a more general youth policy. We must realize the need for a more comprehensive and coordinated youth policy to deal with youths alienation and delinquent acts, as well as the need for a cumulative program of research and policy analysis.

Six policy issues presenting challenges for the future are the alienation of youths; building community resources; the allocation of federal, state and local resources; employment; fear of crime; and creating cooperation.

Juvenile Justice for the Twenty-First Century

As the public calls for getting tough on violent youthful offenders, it may, in fact, be time to revisit the child-saving movement. Cullen et al. (1998) suggest:

As the United States turned into the twentieth century, progressive reformers called attention to the plight of children in urban areas and embarked on efforts, including the founding of the juvenile court, to save them. As we now ready ourselves for the next millennium, we perhaps are in another "Progressive Era" in which a child-saving movement will gain strength and create the space for policies that improve the lives of children.

The similarities between conditions that led to the Progressive Era and those existing today are described by Dionne (1996 p. 12): "Our time combines social change with moral crises, enormous economic opportunity with great economic dislocation and distress. . . . It most closely resembles the period of 1870 to 1900, which led to the Progressive Era."

In addition according to Farkas and Johnson (1997, p. 19), national data shows that the majority of Americans do not believe youths are "born bad" or are "unsalvageable." In fact over 70 percent state that "given enough love and kindness, just about any kid can be reached."

Also of significance are the comments of Bilchik (1998, pp. 89–91), administrator of the Office of Juvenile Justice and Delinquency Prevention of the U.S. Department of Justice: "As we rapidly approach the 100th anniversary of the juvenile court, it is time for us to examine how the juvenile justice system needs to operate to effectively reduce juvenile crime and victimization." He suggests: "The juvenile justice system needs to be revitalized so that it will ensure immediate and appropriate sanctions, provide effective treatment, reverse trends in juvenile violence, and rebuild public confidence in and support for the system." Building an effective juvenile justice system must be a priority for the next century. To that end Bilchik describes the objectives and elements of an effective juvenile justice system.

Objectives of an Effective Juvenile Justice System

"An effective juvenile justice system must meet three objectives: (1) hold the juvenile offender accountable; (2) enable the juvenile to become a capable, productive, and responsible citizen; and (3) ensure the safety of the community."

An effective juvenile justice system must hold offenders accountable, facilitate rehabilitation and protect the community.

Elements of an Effective Juvenile Justice System

"The most effective juvenile justice interventions are swift, certain, consistent, and appropriate. To achieve these objectives, an effective juvenile justice system must:

- Include a mechanism for comprehensively assessing a juvenile when he or she first enters the juvenile justice system to determine appropriate interventions and sanctions.
- Have the capacity to provide a range of treatment services.
- Incorporate increasingly severe sanctions and intensive treatment services when a juvenile fails to respond to initial interventions or is involved in a particularly serious or violent offense as a first offender."

Furthermore Bilchik asserts that an effective juvenile justice system does not use detention as a sanction in itself but rather as a detaining mechanism for preadjudicated youths who are at high risk of reoffending, failing to appear at court proceedings or harming themselves or others.

An effective juvenile justice system must comprehensively assess each youth to determine appropriate interventions and sanctions, be able to provide a wide range of graduated sanctions, incorporate increasingly severe sanctions and treatment services for violent first offenders and those who fail to respond to lesser sanctions, and use detention only for preadjudicated youths displaying certain risk factors.

Summary

Juvenile justice is far reaching. Juvenile courts have been involved in such issues as abortion, school prayer, search and seizure, interracial custody and adoption, adolescent judgment and maturity, and the legal issues in terminating parental rights.

Critics suggest that the system should not be so heavily involved in such "social" matters and that a justice model would be more appropriate than a welfare model when dealing with juveniles. A justice model is a judicial process wherein young people who come in conflict with the law are held responsible and accountable for their behavior. Under law a person's competence is considered as a specific functional ability.

The juvenile justice system could be restructured in two areas:

1. Civil and criminal jurisdictions could be separated, and within civil jurisdiction, poverty-stricken, neglected, and abused children might be separated from status offenders and from those who are not under the control of their parents.
2. Jurisdictional age could also be reconsidered.

Juvenile justice in other countries has many similarities to that in the United States, but also some striking differences. For example according to Sweden's antispanking law, the parent or guardian should exercise the necessary supervision in accordance with the child's age and other circumstances. The child may not be subjected to corporal punishment or other injurious or humiliating treatment. New Zealand, England and Scotland use panels of lay people to deal with nonserious, nonviolent youthful offenders.

Another way that juvenile justice might be restructured to suit the needs of our society is to adopt the concept of restorative justice and to view citizens as coproducers of justice. As coproducers of justice, citizens are responsible for the prevalence and severity of the crime within their communities.

Six policy issues that present challenges for the future are the alienation of youths; building community resources; the allocation of federal, state and local resources; employment; fear of crime; and creating cooperation. Another challenge for the future is building a more effective juvenile justice system. An effective juvenile justice system must hold offenders accountable, facilitate rehabilitation and protect the community. Furthermore an effective juvenile justice system must comprehensively assess each youth to determine appropriate interventions and sanctions, be able to provide a wide range of graduated sanctions, incorporate increasingly severe sanctions and treatment services for violent first offenders and those who fail to respond to lesser sanctions, and use detention only for preadjudicated youths displaying certain risk factors.

Discussion Questions

1. Should the juvenile justice system be reorganized to accommodate modern problems and concerns? How?
2. What would you change in the juvenile justice system in your state to be in tune with modern society?
3. Should the juvenile court be separated into different functions for criminal, civil and special needs? Why or why not?
4. Design a juvenile justice system for your state.

5. Design a juvenile justice act that all states could use.
6. Do you favor Sweden's antispanking law, Singapore's caning policy or a position somewhere in between? Why?
7. Which juvenile justice systems from other countries have elements that might be adopted in the United States?
8. Do you feel that restorative justice is a valid concept?
9. Do you believe that a new paradigm for juvenile justice is needed? What types of thinking need to be modified?
10. Can you see other examples of the John Wayne effect in the juvenile justice system or in other areas of juveniles' lives?

References

Bilchik, Shay. "A Juvenile Justice System for the 21st Century." *Crime and Delinquency,* Vol. 44, No. 1, January 1998, pp. 89–101.

Breed, Allen F. "America's Future: The Necessity of Investing in Children." *Corrections Today,* February 1990, pp. 68–72.

Chunn, Gwendolyn C. "Setting the Course for the Future." *Corrections Today,* December 1994, p. 8.

Cullen, Francis T.; Wright, John Paul; Brown, Shayna; Moon, Melissa M.; Blankenship, Michael B.; and Applegate, Brandon K. "Public Support for Early Intervention Programs: Implications for a Progressive Policy Agenda." *Crime and Delinquency,* Vol. 44, No. 2, April 1998, pp. 187–204.

Dillingham, Steven D. Foreword. In *Rethinking the Criminal Justice System: Toward a New Paradigm,* by John J. DiIulio, Jr. Bureau of Justice Statistics–Princeton Project. Washington, DC: U.S. Department of Justice, December 1992, p. iii.

Dionne, E.J., Jr. *They Only Look Dead: Why Progressives Will Dominate the Next Political Era.* New York: Simon & Schuster, 1996.

English, Thomas R. "TQM and All That Jazz: Rejuvenating Juvenile Justice." *Juvenile Justice,* Vol. 1, No. 2, Fall/Winter 1993, pp. 16–21.

Farkas, Steve and Johnson, Jean with Duffett, Ann and Bers, Ali. *Kids These Days: What Americans Really Think About the Next Generation.* New York: Public Agenda, 1997.

Gibbons, Don C. and Krohn, M. D. *Delinquency Behavior.* Englewood Cliffs, NJ: Prentice Hall, 1986.

Greenwood, Peter. "Juvenile Offenders." National Institute of Justice Crime File Study Guide, n.d.

Krisberg, Barry and Austin, James F. *Reinventing Juvenile Justice.* Newbury Park, CA: Sage Publications, 1993.

Metropolitan Court Judges Committee Report. *Deprived Children: A Judicial Response.* Washington, DC: U.S. Government Printing Office, 1986.

Moore, David B. "Shame, Forgiveness, and Juvenile Justice." *Criminal Justice Ethics,* Winter/Spring 1993, pp. 3–25.

Ohlin, Lloyd E. "The Future of Juvenile Justice Policy and Research." *Crime and Delinquency,* Vol.44, No.1, January 1998, pp. 143–153.

Peacock, Geraldine. *The Children's Hearings System in Scotland: An Introduction for Panel Members.* Social Work Services Group, The Open University, n.d.

Revering, Andrew C. "New Juvenile Justice Alternative: Police Accountability Conferencing Has Great Potential." *Law and Order,* October 1998, pp. 167–168.

Salzer, Mark. "To Combat Violence in the Child's World: Swedish Efforts to Strengthen the Child's Rights." *Social Change in Sweden,* 1979.

Springer, Charles E. *Justice for Juveniles.* Washington, DC: U.S. Department of Justice, Office of Juvenile Justice and Delinquency Prevention, 1986.

Sprott, Jane B. "Understanding Public Opposition to a Separate Youth Justice System." *Crime and Delinquency,* Vol. 44, No. 3, July 1998, pp. 399–411.

Sullivan, John J. and Victor, Joseph L., eds. *Annual Editions: Criminal Justice 88/89.* Guilford, CT: Dushkin Publishing Group, Inc., 1988.

Torbet, Patricia. "States Respond to Violent Juvenile Crime." *National Center for Juvenile Justice in Brief,* Vol. 1, No. 1, 1997, p. 1.

Van Ness, Daniel E. "Restoring the Balance: Tipping the Scales of Justice." *Corrections Today,* February 1990, pp. 62–66.

Wass, John and Marks, Ron. "Historical Overview: Young Offenders Act Revamps Juvenile Justice in Canada." *Corrections Today,* December 1992, pp. 88–93.

Cases

Bellotti v. Baird, 443 U.S. 622, 99 S.Ct. 3035, 61 L.Ed.2d 797 (1979)

City of Akron v. Akron Center for Reproductive Health, 462 U.S. 416, 103 S.Ct. 2481, 76 L.Ed.2d 687 (1983)

Dow v. Renfrow, 475 F.Supp. 1012 (N.D. Ind. 1979), aff'd in part, remanded in part, 631 F. 2d 91 (7th Cir. 1980), reh'g en banc denied, 635 F. 2d 582 (7th Cir. 1980), cert. denied, 451 U.S. 1022, 101 S.Ct. 3015, 69 L.Ed.2d 395 (1981)

H. L. v. Matheson, 450 U.S. 398, 101 S.Ct. 1164, 67 L.Ed.2d 388 (1981)

Jewish Child Care Association v. Elaine S. Y., 73 A.D.2d 154, 425 N.Y.S.2d 336 (1980)

Nebraska v. Wedige, 205 Neb. 687, 289 N.W.2d 538 (1980)

New Jersey v. T. L. O., 469 U.S. 325, 105 S.Ct. 733, 83 L.Ed.2d 720 (1985)

Palmore v. Sidoti, 466 U.S. 429, 104 S.Ct. 1879, 80 L.Ed.2d 421 (1984)

Parham v. J. R., 442 U.S. 584, 99 S.Ct. 2493, 61 L.Ed.2d 101 (1979)

Planned Parenthood of Kansas City v. Ashcroft, 462 U.S. 476, 103 S.Ct. 2517, 76 L.Ed.2d 733 (1983)

In re R. M. G., 454 A.2d 776 (D.C.App. 1982)

Thornburgh v. American College of Obstetricians and Gynecologists, 476 U.S. 747, 106 S.Ct. 2169, 90 L.Ed.2d 779 (1986)

Wallace v. Jaffree, 472 U.S. 38, 105 S.Ct. 2479, 86 L.Ed.2d 29 (1985)

Appendix A Influences on Delinquency

Appendix A summarizes the influences on delinquency discussed throughout the book. The first column lists the various philosophies and theories set forth to explain delinquency and crime in general. The second column summarizes the general explanation of causes underlying these theories. The next six columns show how each philosophy or theory perceives specific influences on the basic causes, that is how individual factors, the family, the community, the school, the social system and the criminal justice system are related to and influence delinquency.

Philosophical Influences on Delinquency

Perspective	Causes of Delinquency	Individual	Family	Community	School	Social System	Criminal Justice System
Classical School of Criminality	People possess the ability to choose freely to do right or wrong—free will. They choose to do delinquent acts because the pleasure of the act outweighs the pain of punishment.	Free will is sole factor in considering delinquency and crime.	No influence	No influence	No influence	No influence	Purpose of punishment is *deterrence;* makes pain of punishment stronger than pleasure of act.
Positivist School of Criminality	A variety of factors influence or *cause* one to be delinquent. Since these factors cause delinquency, there is no free will. In most cases, the person has little or no control over the influence of these factors.	Biological and some psychological theories view the individual as the focal point. Causes of delinquency are within the individual or the environment acting on the person.	Control and learning theories recognize the positive influence of family on definitions of delinquency.	Learning and cultural deviance theories include or focus on the community, neighborhood or gang. They define the *subculture.*	Bonding and other control theories view school as one of the elements binding the person to the *correct* value system.	Culture sets goals and means of attaining the goals. *Strain* occurs if the means are not available.	System represents outer control. System is at fault because it labels delinquent who lives up to the label.
Biological Early Theories	Criminals are *atavists* or biological throwbacks to a primitive state. Criminals are born, not developed.	Sole factor in causing delinquency is that individual is *biologically defective.*	*Criminal families* are evidence of inherited criminal behavior.	No influence	No influence	No influence	Delinquents should be quarantined.
Inherited Crime	Children inherit a *predisposition* to violence or a central nervous system that predisposes the person to crime.	Genetic predisposition of individual causes delinquency.	Chromosomal complement is inherited.	No influence	No influence	No influence	No influence

Psychological

Theory							
Psychoanalytical	Delinquents act out inner conflicts that result from pressure caused by failing to find appropriate releases. The psychic pressure is caused by poor or faulty child rearing.	Child did not develop properly through the infantile, latency and puberty periods.	Causes feelings of insecurity, rigidity, hostility or rebellion due to deficiencies in love, attention and child-rearing.	[Not considered]	Fails to recognize and deal with problems and to develop appropriate releases of pressure.	[Not considered]	[Not considered]
Frustration-Aggression	Certain stimuli—weapons, pain, noise, temperature, odors—may cause aggression.	Influenced or acted upon by outside forces.	Failed to establish tolerance or controls to counterbalance frustrations.	Stimuli may be a function of community—overcrowding.	[Not considered]	Economic status of child/family may require that they live in certain areas where stimuli are more plentiful.	[Not considered]
Learning Theory	Based on models for the youth's behavior; he learns "appropriate" ways of reacting to situations. Delinquents learn that aggressive, violent, hostile reactions are successful, therefore appropriate.	The person is a blank slate, then learns the means of dealing with difficult, hostile and frustrating situations.	Serves as a strong model for behavior—bad and good.	Serves as a stronger model for behavior during adolescence.	Provides environment for modeling and reinforcing of bad behavior.	[Not considered]	[Not considered]
Psychological/Environmental Factors (similar to Frustration-Aggression)	Urban crowding and ambient temperature cause irritability, frustration and violence.	Individual is unwittingly acted upon by environmental factors.	[Not considered]	Population density is a function of community.	[Not considered]	Social class restricts one's ability to live in less populated, more comfortable environments.	[Not considered]
Learning Theories	Crime is learned in interaction with others.	A person is neither good nor bad but learns behavior that then directs him to certain acts or associates.	One of the primary social units where learning occurs.	Peers represent strong "significant others" from whom the person learns delinquency during adolescence and young adulthood.	Fails to reinforce definitions unfavorable to the violation of the law.	[Not considered]	[Not considered]

continued

**Philosophical Influences
on Delinquency,** *continued*

Perspective	Causes of Delinquency	Individual	Family	Community	School	Social System	Criminal Justice System
Differential Association	Criminal behavior is learned in interaction with those with whom delinquents associate and from whom they define law as favorable or unfavorable.	Learns behavior from others with whom he differentially associates.	One of the intimate personal groups in which delinquent definitions are formed.	Fails to counter the delinquent associations and definitions; also, peers represent community.	Fails to counter the definitions and associations.	Defines the needs and values that give rise to criminal (and) noncriminal behavior.	[Not considered]
Social Learning Theory	Deviant behavior is learned and reinforced through social and nonsocial reinforcers.	Influenced through operant conditioning.	Provides rewards and punishments for behavior; therefore may reinforce delinquency.	Provides rewards and punishments for behavior; therefore may reinforce delinquency.	Helps or fails to reinforce conventional behavior.	[Not considered]	[Not considered]
Labeling Theory	A youth is viewed as delinquent; therefore he sees himself as a delinquent and acts according to this social- and self-concept.	Unwittingly labeled and then perpetuates the label.	May influence the labeling process.	May influence the labeling process.	May influence the labeling process.	Acts toward the youth based on the label.	Justice system discriminates and labels under- privileged youth as *delinquent*.
Conflict Theory	Social conflict, based on authority, power and economy, results in the weak suffering at the hands of the justice system, while the rich and powerful can violate the law with impunity.	Everyone conforms and everyone deviates, so it is unfair to categorize as good and bad. Categories based on status, not behavior.	No influence except as an examples of the power/authority dynamic.	No influence	No influence	A classed society with the poor discriminated against in every way.	Pawns of the powerful and tools of the state.

Source: William V. Pelphrey, *Explanations of Delinquency: Fact or Fiction?*
Washington, DC: U.S. Department of Justice, Serious Habitual Offender
Comprehensive Action Program (SHOCAP), n.d.

Appendix B Job Description: Police-School Liaison Officer

- Is directly responsible to the Flint Police Division, Juvenile Bureau. However, is readily available to school administrators in time of need or emergency school-police matters.

- Patrols school area when called upon or as deemed necessary by the Police-School Liaison Officer.

- Contributes helpful information to the Regional Counseling Team.

- Assists Community School Director to mitigate antisocial behavior by investigating delinquent or criminal acts that take place during the evening Community School Programs.

- Serves as a resource person or counselor for all youth, school administration and staff and members of the community with school-police related problems. Also is a resource person or counselor for those youth who have personal problems in their home.

- Acts as resource person and serves on committees that provide services for youth.

- Gives presentation on police-related subjects to students in the classroom and to business and community organizations.

- Serves as a resource person to the Police School Cadet Program when called upon.

- Supervises and prepares necessary records and reports as requested by the Flint Police Division and Flint Community Schools.

- Assists in crowd control at school athletic events.

- Serves as a resource person for other police personnel.

- Refers youths into Probate Court or District Court when necessary.

- Performs other related duties as assigned or as appropriate.

- Suppresses by enforcement of the law any and all illegal threats, such as drugs and acts of violence, that endanger the children's educational program, and improves community relations with police, schools and the general public.

Source: Flint, Michigan, Police Department

Appendix C Federally Funded Programs

Program & Agency	Focus	Objective	Setting/Providers	Strategies
AmeriCorp *Corporation for National Service*	All youth	Address nation's educational, human, environment and public safety needs at the community level	Any site, communities/*community-based organizations, residents, young people, institutions of higher learning, school-based programs, senior citizens*	• Conflict resolution • Community policing • Recreational programs • Leadership skills • Tutoring • Mentoring
Child Abuse and Neglect Discretionary Activities *HHS*	Neglected or abused children	Help states develop, strengthen and carry out child protection services	Homes, schools, community centers, service facilities/*state and local governments, agencies*	• Improve detection, treatment, investigation and prosecution
Children, Youth and Families At-Risk National Initiative *USDA*	High-risk youth	Provide youth educational, community-based prevention and intervention programs	Schools, community centers, service facilities, public housing/*volunteers, state land grant universities, USDA, state and local public and private agencies and organizations*	• Child care • Educational programs (reading and science literacy) • Coalitions to coordinate efforts
Civil-Military Programs *DoD*	At-risk youth	Strengthen civil-military cooperation, and innovatively address national defense and domestic policy needs	Communities, public areas/*civilians and military services*	• Individual and unit training
Community-Based Family Resource and Support Program *HHS*	All youth	Develop/expand comprehensive, statewide system of family resource and support programs that coordinate resources among existing public and private organizations; foster understanding of diverse populations to better prevent and treat child abuse and neglect	Homes, schools, community centers, service facilities/*state family service systems*	• Interagency collaboration • Service integration • Partnership between families and professionals
Community Schools Youth Services and Supervision *HHS*	Youth aged 5 to 18 in communities with significant poverty and delinquency	Provide positive and educational activities to youth in a safe environment during nonschool hours (after school, weekend, holiday, summer)	Schools, community centers, parks/*nonprofit community-based organizations, consortia, parents, volunteers*	• Supervised recreation activities • Educational enrichment • Tutoring • Mentoring • Workforce preparation • Health care • Counseling • Substance abuse treatment

Program & Agency	Focus	Objective	Setting/Providers	Strategies
Comprehensive Gang Initiative *DOJ*	Youth involved in gang-related and violent crime	Reduce illegal drug activity, crime and violence; and improve the functioning of local criminal justice systems	Any size/*police, criminal justice agencies, human service providers, community programs*	• Cooperation and coordination among various actors • Technical assistance and training
Drug Abuse Resistance Education (DARE) *DOJ/DOI*	Students (elementary, middle and high school)	Equip students with skills to resist pressure to use drugs	Schools, community centers, public housing/*police, parents, teachers*	• Classroom instruction • Family involvement • Vocational activities • After-school activities
Drug Courts Program *DOJ*	Nonviolent offenders (adult and youth) with substance abuse problems	Offer nonviolent substance-abusing offenders intervention measures that provide sanctions and services to change the criminal behavior	Homes, secure facilities, drug courts, community treatment centers/*states, state and local courts, units of local governments, tribal governments*	• Mandatory periodic drug testing • Substance abuse treatment • Diversion, probation and other supervised release programs • Offender management • Aftercare services
Even Start *ED*	Low-income families	Break the cycle of poverty and illiteracy by improving educational opportunities for low-income families	Community centers, schools, homes/*educators, service providers*	• Early childhood education • Adult literacy and basic skills instruction • Parent education
Family Preservation and Support *HHS*	Youth in families at risk for abuse and neglect	Provide federal resources for family preservation and support services at the state level	Homes, foster care facilities, social services centers/*community-based organizations, families, state child welfare systems, local agencies*	• Home visits • Parent training • Child protective services
Family Violence Prevention and Services *HHS*	Abused women and their children	Prevent family violence and provide immediate shelter and related assistance	Service facilities, secure facilities, shelters/*states, Native American tribes, agencies, coalitions, community-based agencies*	• Shelter • Research • Training • Technical assistance • Resource center • Information dissemination
4-H Youth Development *USDA*	Youth aged 5 to 19	Help youth acquire knowledge, life skills and attitudes to become self-directed and productive members of society	Any site, community-based organizations/*adult and teen volunteers, state land grant universities, state and local governments, USDA, public and private agencies and organizations*	• Nonformal educational program in animal, plant and mechanical science; natural resources; economics, employment and careers; citizenship; recreation; culture, food and nutrition

Program & *Agency*	Focus	Objective	Setting/*Providers*	Strategies
Gang Resistance Education and Training (G.R.E.A.T.) *Treasury/DOJ*	3rd, 4th and 7th graders in areas with gang activity	Help children resist the pressure to join gangs and to resolve conflicts nonviolently	Schools, communities/ *police officers, federal agencies*	• Classroom instruction • Related activities, e.g., community service
Head Start/Early Head Start *HHS*	Youth in low-income families with children aged 5 and under or with pregnant mothers	Provide comprehensive health, educational, nutritional, social and other services to bridge the gap between economically disadvantaged children and their peers; Early Head Start helps parents fulfill their roles and move toward self-sufficiency	Homes, schools, community centers, public housing, Head Start centers/*families, parents*	• Early, continuous, intensive and comprehensive child development and family support services
Healthy Start *HHS*	Pregnant mothers or families with infants	Improve the health and well-being of women, infants and their families	Any site, single service centers/*residents, service providers, health care providers, volunteers*	• Increase awareness • Streamlining and coordination of services • Partnerships • Social services • Health services • Case management • Training • Transportation
High School Career Academics *Treasury/HHS*	High school youth	Provide an alternative to gang involvement and promote high school graduation with career-oriented jobs and college attendance	*High schools, school system*	• Gang prevention • Job experience
Improving Basic Programs Operated by Local Educational Agencies/Title I *ED*	Educationally disadvantaged children	Improve the ability of schools to help population achieve high academic standards expected of all children.	Schools/*local educational agencies*	• Upgrading entire educational program • Help students reach performance standards • Parental involvement • Professional development • Integration of academic and vocational learning • Increasing amount and quality of learning time • Counseling • Mentoring • College/career awareness

Program & Agency	Focus	Objective	Setting/Providers	Strategies
Incentive Grants for Local Delinquency Prevention Programs/Title V *DOJ*	At-risk children	Prevent juvenile delinquency through a risk-focused delinquency prevention approach implemented in local communities	Any site/*states*	• Coalitions to mobilize and direct delinquency prevention efforts • Identify known risk and protective factors • Develop and implement strategies
Intensive Community-Based Juvenile Aftercare Program *DOJ*	High-risk juvenile offenders	Reintegrate into the community juvenile offenders who are being released from institutional placement	Community centers, service facilities/*local agencies*	• Skills development • Education • Employment • Social/life skills
Job Corps *DOL*	Disadvantaged youth aged 16 to 24	Provide education, training and employment for disadvantaged youth	Workplace, secure facilities, public housing, residential settings/*corporations, nonprofit, civilian conservation centers*	• Basic education and work skills • Job placement • Support services
Juvenile Mentoring Program (JUMP) *DOJ*	At-risk youth	Support one-to-one mentoring programs for youth at risk of educational failure, dropping out of school or involvement in delinquent activities, including gangs	*Local education agencies, public and private nonprofits*	• Mentoring • Personal and social development • Tutoring and academic assistance • Vocational counseling and training
Master Building Crafts Skills Program *HUD*	All public housing youth	Increase opportunities for public housing youth and reduce the chances they will turn to crime and drugs	*Public housing*	• Skills development • GED
Maternal & Child Health Improvement Projects/Special Projects of Regional and National Significance *HHS*	All youth	Build an infrastructure for the delivery of health care services to all mothers and children, particularly those who are low income and in isolated populations	Schools, community centers, service facilities, health care facilities/*state and local health care provides, primary care providers*	• Capacity building for states • Building infrastructure and resources for primary mental health services in schools • Mental health state-of-the-art instructional materials and resources • Resource centers
Operation Safe Home *HUD*	Serious, chronic and violent youth	Combat violent and white-collar crime in public and assisted housing	Public housing/*law enforcement from various agencies*	• Coordination and strengthening of law enforcement and crime prevention operations • Coordination among HUD, federal law enforcement agencies, and Office of National Drug Control Policy

Program & Agency	Focus	Objective	Setting/Providers	Strategies
Partnerships to Reduce Juvenile Gun Violence *DOJ*	All youth	Increase the effectiveness of existing youth gun violence reduction strategies by enhancing and coordinating prevention, intervention, and suppression strategies and strengthening linkages between community residents, law enforcement and the juvenile justice system	Community-based organizations applying jointly with either a state or local law enforcement agency	• Gun violence and safety awareness • Community participation • Coordinated resources and services
Project Outreach *Treasury*	All youth	Establish positive role models for youth	*Schools, youth organizations, public housing*	• Mentoring • Personal and social development • Drug, school dropout and teen pregnancy prevention
Promotion of the Arts—Grants to Organizations *NEA*	All youth	Expand opportunities for educational experiences in the arts	*Art institutions, local art agencies, arts service organizations, tribal communities, local government*	• Arts awareness • Community partnerships
Public Housing Urban Revitalization Demonstration: HOPE VI *HUD*	Disadvantaged youth	Revitalize severely distressed or obsolete public housing development in the 40 most populous U.S. cites and in troubled housing authorities	Homes, public areas, community centers, public housing/*public and private agencies*	• Reconstruction/ replacement housing • Planning and technical assistance • Community service
Runaway and Homeless Youth Programs *HHS*	Runaway and homeless youth	Support local centers that provide immediate crisis intervention services to runaway and homeless youth and their families	Public areas, community-based centers, and shelters/*families*	• Develop or strengthen community-based centers that are outside the law enforcement, juvenile justice, child welfare and mental health systems
Safe and Drug-Free Schools and Communities Federal Activities *ED*	Students at all educational levels (preschool through postsecondary)	Prevent the illegal use of drugs and violence and promote safety and discipline	Homes, schools, public areas, community centers, communities/*school personnel, parents, community members*	• Training • Evaluation • Curriculum development • Activities that connect school with community-wide efforts
Safe Kids/Safe Streets—Community Approaches to Reducing Abuse and Neglect and Preventing Delinquency *DOJ*	Youth and families	Reduce juvenile delinquency by helping break the cycle of child and adolescent abuse and neglect	*Urban, rural, tribal communities*	• Comprehensive services • Coordinated management • Family services • Development of cross-agency strategies

Program & *Agency*	Focus	Objective	Setting/*Providers*	Strategies
SafeFutures *DOJ*	Disadvantaged and court-involved children and youth	Coordinate multiple youth violence prevention and intervention strategies into a single community-based continuum of care and graduated sanctions	Local sites/*local tribal governments*	• Concentration of efforts • Continuum of care for juveniles • Capacity building to institutionalize and sustain coordinated efforts • Outcome focus
School-to-Work Transition *DOL/ED*	All youth—college-bound, career-bound, out of school, disabled, with limited English proficiency, of diverse and/or disadvantaged backgrounds, gifted and talented	Create statewide systems that offer access to performance-based education and training programs and increase opportunities for further education	School, workplaces/*educators, businesses, students, parents*	• Classroom instruction • Work-based learning • Connecting activities • Involvement of all actors • Integrated career employment, education and learning program
Step-Up *HUD*	Economically disadvantaged youth	Provide technical assistance to housing authorities to establish construction training program	*Public housing*	• Skills development • Certification • Workforce preparation
Summer Youth Employment and Training Program/Title IIB *DOL*	Disadvantaged youth aged 14 to 21	Enhance basic education skills and provide exposure to the work world	Community centers, service facilities, worksites/*public and private agencies, local businesses*	• Summer jobs • Academic enrichment • Training • Work maturity • Employment services
Year Round Program for Youth/Title IIC *DOL*	Economically disadvantaged or hard-to-serve youth aged 16 to 21	Improve long-term employability, encourage school completion or alternative school program, and reduce welfare dependency	Schools, service facilities, institutional training settings/*service providers*	• Educational and employment skills • Commitment to community development • Leadership skills
Youthbuild *HUD*	Disadvantaged youth who have dropped out of high school	Help dropouts obtain employment skills and become economically self-sufficient	Workplaces, public housing/*educators, businesses, low-income and homeless individuals and families*	• Education and employment skills • Commitment to community development • Leadership skills
Youth Environmental Services (YES) *DOI/DOJ*	Delinquent and at-risk youth, juvenile offenders	Increase the capacity of states and local communities to treat and rehabilitate juvenile offenders, and prevent at-risk youth from entering the juvenile justice system	Public areas, secure facilities, federal land/*public and private agencies*	• Education • Job training • Housing and physical environment • Transportation • Social services • Health care • Rehabilitation

Source: *Helping Communities Fight Crime: Comprehensive Planning Techniques,*
Models, Programs and Resources. The President's Crime Prevention Council Catalog, 1997.

Appendix D School and Community Programs

The following programs were identified and described by the National School Safety Center in its publication *Gangs in Schools: Breaking Up Is Hard To Do,* copyright 1988, Pepperdine University Press. The center has granted permission to reprint its descriptions of the programs.

Each program was contacted and asked to update the information on its efforts. The descriptions that follow are a combination of the National School Safety Center's descriptions and the specific projects' updates. Addresses and telephone numbers are current as of the fall of 1998.

Andrew Glover Youth Program
100 Center St.
Manhattan Criminal Court, Room 1541
New York, NY 10013
212/349-6381

A privately funded organization, the Andrew Glover Youth Program works to protect neighborhoods in New York's Lower East Side from crime. Another objective of the Program is to steer youth away from negative and illegal activities. The Program serves a large number of black and Hispanic young people by working with police, courts, youth services, and social services to provide counseling, gang mediation, family counseling, and housing assistance.

Youth workers are in contact with kids where they spend most of their time: on the streets. The youth workers also live in the community and are available for assistance twenty-four hours a day. The program was named after a local police officer who cared about and tried to help youth and who was shot to death in the line of duty by teenagers.

B.U.I.L.D. (Broader Urban Involvement and Leadership Development)
1223 N. Milwaukee Ave.
Chicago, IL 60622
312/227-2880

Non-profit B.U.I.L.D. works with gang members on the streets, trying to involve them in athletic or social recreational events and to encourage them to participate in education and job training programs. Many of the streetworkers are "graduates" of street gangs who the organization assisted.

B.U.I.L.D. also runs a prevention program for twenty-eight junior high school students identified as at-risk for joining gangs by school and police authorities. The program includes a weekly class session and after-school activities to teach kids about the dangers of joining gangs and offers positive alternative activities. The project is supported by Chicago's social, civic and corporate sectors.

Center for Urban Expression (C.U.E.)
The Dorchester Youth Collaborative
1514A Dorchester Ave.
Dorchester, MA 02122
617/228-1748

The Center for Urban Expression steers youth into structured, goal-oriented activities with a special focus on community organizing. The Common Ground prevention club, sponsored by the Center, brings youths of diverse ethnic backgrounds together to work on a variety of projects and performances.

Community service teams may shovel snow or clean garages for community residents; others may become involved in youth leadership programs. Common Ground groups have given song/rap performances in six states and have become very visible locally through their anti-drug audio and video public service media announcements.

Chicago Intervention Network
Department of Human Services
Youth Delinquency Prevention Division
510 N. Peshtigo Court, Section 5B
Chicago, IL 60611-4375
312/744-0881 or 312/744-1820

The Chicago Intervention Network works with students of all ages and provides the schools with the following programs and services: (1) early intervention and prevention curriculum, including activities in anger management, impulse control, and empathy training; (2) twenty-week delinquency prevention sessions in eight schools; (3) attitude development sessions covering self-esteem, resisting peer pressure, and understanding and managing conflict; (4) Safe School Zone Law presentations; (5) School Watch programs; Truancy follow-up; (6) assessments on gang problems in and around schools; (7) mediation and prevention of gang violence; (8) technical assistance and information for teachers and parents on how to identify gang activity through symbols, colors, and signs; (9) help in securing Safe School Zone signs for schools; and (10) individual and group counselling for challenged youth.

Gang Awareness Resource Program (GARP)

The California State Office of Criminal Justice Planning provided grant funds for the Gang Awareness Resource Program (GARP). The Program is now in its fourth year. It places an Operation Safe Streets gang investigator deputy on the Carson High School campus in a highly visible "resident" capacity. The investigator serves the high school, as well as feeder junior high and elementary schools, through the following services: training and instruction of faculty, administrators, school police, parks and recreation personnel, community groups, parents, and civic officials on gang awareness, and coordination of information between schools and between law enforcement and schools. The investigator also establishes a partnership with the business sector for their support in the effort to eliminate street gang violence.

The bridge which GARP has built between law enforcement and the schools (both faculty and students) has led to enhanced communications, reduced gang versus gang incidents, and resulted in diminished gang activity on or about the high school campus. The GARP staff has developed and published a gang awareness pamphlet for community distribution and a pocket gang directory for school administrators and police.

The GARP deputy is in daily contact with many gang members and, as a result, has arrested many for crimes committed not only on the campuses, but also in the community. He has identified hundreds of new gang members who have not, as yet, entered the criminal justice system. He has assisted in the solution of many other crimes based upon his day-to-day contacts with students throughout the Carson city schools. The GARP deputy has made hundreds of gang awareness presentations before school staff, student assemblies, and community groups. As a consequence, both school campuses and the community benefit from reduced gang violence.

Gang Crime Section
Chicago Police Department
1121 South State Street
Chicago, IL 60605
312/747-6328

The first formal gang unit in the Chicago Police Department was formed in 1967. Known by various names over the years (Gang Intelligence Unit, Gang Crimes Investigations Division, Narcotics and Gangs Unit, and Gang Crimes Enforcement Division), it became the Gang Crime Section in 1984 and has retained that name since.

The Gang Crime Section is composed of tactical (uniformed) police and detective level Gang Crime Specialists (plainclothes) police officers. Specialists conduct follow-up investigations on gang-related incidents while tactical personnel conduct directed patrol missions in areas of the city experiencing increased gang activity.

The activity of all active street gangs is monitored by gang specialists and reported on periodically. With each arrest the files of known gang members is updated. Computer analysis of reported gang incidents and statistical analysis of arrest activity and weapon seizures is prepared by administrative personnel. The results of this analysis are used to initiate directed-missions in the most active areas of the city.

GRIP . . . Gang Resistance Is Paramount
Community Services and Recreation Department
City of Paramount
16400 Colorado Ave.
Paramount, CA 90723
562/220-2120

The GRIP (Gang Resistance Is Paramount) program, formerly known as The Paramount Plan: Alternatives To Gang Membership, stresses disapproval of gang membership while working to eliminate the future gang membership base, and to diminish the influence of gangs. The program conducts youth gang prevention workshops for parents, and provides gang resistance curricula and posters on request. Gang prevention workshops are provided throughout the community by bilingual neighborhood counselors.

A recently revised fifth grade gang resistance curriculum was introduced into the Paramount Unified School District in 1982, and continues to still be utilized today.

House of Umoja (Unity)
1410 N. Frazier St.
Philadelphia, PA 19131
215/473-5893

Known as the first urban "Boys' Town," the house has taken in more than 3,000 youths since it began in 1968. At the time of the House of Umoja's inception, the deadliest phenomenon facing the youth of Philadelphia was gang warfare. The concern of Falaka and David Fattah over their own son's involvement led them to open their home in West Philadelphia to gang members. The House of Umoja quickly developed into a communal living facility, geared toward keeping young men off the streets and giving them the education and life skills necessary to enter into society and the work force. Realizing that for many of these youths, a street gang acts as a surrogate family, providing a sense of belonging and self-worth, the Fattahs created a family system of their own.

The House of Umoja Boystown has since become one of the most acclaimed and successful youth service programs in the country. Now occupying most of the original block of Frazier Street, the stated purpose of the house is to "provide a non-traditional, community-based experience which offers a positive learning environment for young men who lack a sufficient family support structure to prevent delinquency." Umoja provides not only the basic amenities of food and shelter, but also educational and emotional support often lacking even in the most "stable" of American families.

The house's outreach program has sponsored the Black Youth Olympics, cultural exchange programs with boys from Belfast, Ireland, and local cultural programs. In the wake of the first Rodney King verdict in Los Angeles, Umoja cooperated with the Quaker Friends Society to call for peaceful response. The

House also speaks on behalf of the community at local meetings, city hearings, or any gathering where a concerned voice is required.

Youth Development, Inc. Gang Intervention Program
6301 Central Ave. N.W.
Albuquerque, NM 87105
505/831-6038

Youth Development, Inc. (YDI) is a social services organization offering more than thirty different programs to assist children, youths, and families. The different components offer education, residential counseling, corrections, prevention, recreation, and employment assistance to at-risk youths and their families.

The YDI Gang Intervention Program works on three levels: prevention, diversion and intervention. Puppetry, theater presentations and educational programs focus on preventing gang violence and activities. Diversion involves directing at-risk youths into positive activities and behaviors, while their intervention component works with gang members and court-ordered youths to stop self-destructive behavior.

A major project is a regular ten-week workshop for court-ordered gang members. Youths participate in community activities such as feeding the homeless, team building events such as a ropes course and educational programs including visiting a medium security prison. Each youth also has a counselor who works intensively with him or her on a one-to-one basis during the ten-week program.

The Gang Intervention program is successful because it focuses on working with the youths as individuals, rather than as gang members. Also the YDI program is not against gangs per se, but against gang violence and illegal activities.

Appendix E Metropolitan Court Judges Committee: 73 Recommendations

Role of Judges

1. Judges must provide leadership within the community in determining needs and obtaining and developing resources and services for deprived children and families.

2. Juvenile and family courts must have the clear authority, by statute or rule, to review, order and enforce the delivery of specific services and treatment for deprived children.

3. Judges must encourage cooperation and coordination among the courts and various public and private agencies with responsibilities for deprived children.

4. Judges and court personnel must make every effort to increase media and public awareness of the complex and sensitive issues related to deprived children.

5. Juvenile and family courts must maintain close liaison and encourage coordination of policies with school authorities.

6. Judges must exercise leadership in (a) analyzing the needs of deprived children and (b) encouraging the development of adequate resources to meet those needs.

7. Judges should take an active part in the formation of a community-wide, multi-disciplinary "Constituency for Children" to promote and unify private and public sector efforts to focus attention and resources on meeting the needs of deprived children who have no effective voice of their own.

Court Procedures

8. Juvenile and family courts, to be effective, must have the same stature as general jurisdiction courts. Judicial assignments should be based on expressed interest and competence and be for a substantial number of years.

9. All judges of all courts must ensure sensitivity in the courtroom and encourage sensitivity out of the courtroom to minimize trauma to the child victim.

10. Juvenile and family courts should have immediate and primary jurisdiction over children who have been allegedly abused to ensure protection and treatment for the child victim, notwithstanding pending criminal proceedings.

11. Adult prosecution arising out of an allegation of abuse should be coordinated with juvenile and family courts.

12. Priority must be given to abuse and neglect cases in the trial court as well as in the appellate process.

13. Juvenile and family courts must have funding to allow reasonable judicial caseloads and an adequate number of judicial officers to assure the necessary time for each case.

14. Court-appointed and public attorneys representing children in abuse and neglect cases, as well as judges, should be specially trained or experienced.

15. Court Appointed Special Advocates (CASAs) should be utilized by the court at the earliest stage of the court process, where necessary, to communicate the best interests of an abused or neglected child.

16. Juvenile and family courts should consider the use of judicially appointed citizen advisory boards to assist the court with independent screening, monitoring and review of individual placements, services, facilities and treatment.

17. A person supportive of the child witness should be permitted to be present in court and accessible to the child during the child's testimony without influencing that testimony.

18. Family members should be permitted to offer suggestions or testify in aid of the disposition of the case.

19. Evidentiary and procedural rules consistent with due process must be adopted to protect the child victim from further trauma.

20. All courts should be granted authority to issue protective or restraining orders to prevent further abuse. Such orders should be freely used and vigorously enforced.

Detecting, Reporting and Evaluating

21. All persons who work with children on a regular basis should be trained to recognize indicators of abuse, neglect or significant deprivation.

22. All persons working with children must promptly report known or reasonably suspected abuse and neglect. Communication and witness privileges must not impede the reporting, investigation and adjudication of alleged child abuse.

23. Appropriate governmental agencies, schools of medicine and social work, and the media should widely publicize in each community reliable indicators of vulnerable families, child physical and sexual abuse and child neglect.

24. Abusive or potentially abusive persons should be encouraged to acknowledge their problem, seek help and participate in voluntary treatment for themselves and their families.

25. Agencies must respond immediately to reports of child abuse and neglect and provide follow-up information to the reporter.

26. A central registry of complaints of alleged abuse and neglect must be developed and maintained in each state with mandatory reporting of data

from child protection and health agencies, as well as law enforcement and school officials, with access on a demonstrated "need to know" basis.

27. A thorough assessment of a child's problems and family is needed at all public and private intake facilities.

28. Child protection services and facilities should be available 24 hours a day to assure that allegations of serious neglect or abuse can be assessed and protection provided.

29. Reports of abuse and neglect should be evaluated immediately and, where necessary, a coordinated plan of action should be developed by law enforcement, the child protection agencies and the prosecutor.

30. Emergency removal of the child from the home must be subject to prompt judicial review.

31. The alleged offender, rather than the child, should be removed from the home, whenever appropriate.

32. A suspected child victim of abuse and the non-offending family members should not be subjected to repetitious and unsystematic interviews.

Out-of-Home Placement

33. A child should not be removed from home until consideration is given as to whether the child can remain at home safely.

34. The number, duration and traumatic impact of out-of-home placements of deprived children must be reduced by "reasonable efforts" to seek alternatives consistent with the child's need for protection and treatment.

35. Judges should evaluate the criteria established by child protection agencies for initial removal and reunification decisions and determine the court's expectations of the agency as to what constitutes "reasonable efforts" to prevent removal or to hasten return of the child.

36. In placing children, courts and child protection agencies must give consideration to maintaining racial, cultural, ethnic and religious values.

37. Programs which promote family preservation and prevention of out-of-home placement by providing early intensive services for the at-risk child and family must be developed and utilized in all communities.

38. Agreements between parents and a child protection agency which voluntarily place a child out of the home should be in writing, filed with the court and reviewed by the court within 30 days.

39. As required by federal law, independent judicial review of all placements by the court or by a judicially appointed citizen review board must be conducted at least every six months. Eighteen months following placement, the court must conduct a full hearing to review the family service plan and the progress of the child for the purpose of establishing permanency planning for the child.

40. Provision must be made for minimum standards and frequent review and inspection of all out-of-home placement facilities, staff and treatment programs.

41. A child removed from home must be returned to the family as soon as conditions causing the removal have been substantially corrected and safeguards established.

Treatment and Planning

42. Treatment of an abused and neglected child must be immediate, thorough and coordinated among responsible agencies.

43. Treatment provided to the child through court or agency intervention should involve the entire family or focus on family relationships as they impact on the child, and should stress the primary responsibility of the parents for the child's welfare and protection.

44. Child protection agencies and the courts should require parental responsibility for a child's well-being.

45. Judges, as part of the disposition for the child, must have authority to order treatment for the parents, to require other positive conduct, and to impose sanctions for willful failure or refusal to comply.

46. Substance abuse treatment, where appropriate, should be mandated for the parents and the child.

47. Judges must have the authority to order the treatment determined to be necessary and should regularly review the efficacy of such treatment.

48. Judges must require appropriate treatment for youthful sexual offenders, most of whom have been victims of sexual abuse.

49. The court should require the offender to pay the costs of treating the child victim.

50. Child victims of abuse or neglect should be eligible for victims assistance and compensation programs.

51. In child support, custody and dependency hearings, if parents have or can obtain health care insurance, the court should order coverage.

52. Child protection caseworkers must be screened, trained and certified in order to improve child protection services and treatment.

53. Screened, qualified and trained volunteers should be used to enhance the quality of services to deprived children and families.

54. A sufficient number of foster homes, adequately reimbursed and provided with access to treatment and support services, should be established.

55. Frequent movement of children from foster home to foster home is detrimental to a child's physical and emotional well-being and must be reduced.

56. Specialized foster homes and foster parents should be established in each community for children with special needs.

57. Homeless and runaway children must be provided proper emergency shelter facilities as well as necessary services.

58. When there is clear and convincing evidence that the conduct of the parents would, under law, permit the termination of parental rights, and it is in the best interests of the child to do so, termination should proceed expediously.

59. When reunification is not possible or termination of parental rights is not in the best interests of the child, courts should consider other permanent plans.

60. When needed, adoption should proceed expeditiously. Foster parents should not be precluded from adopting their foster child.

61. Subsidized adoption programs should be more widely available and used for special needs and hard-to-place children.

Prevention Issues

62. Prevention and early intervention efforts must receive a high priority, with a greater emphasis placed on providing adequate services to prevent child abuse, neglect and family break-ups through adequate education, early identification of those at risk, and family-based counseling and homemaker services.

63. Continuing education in parenting and in understanding the physical and emotional needs of children and families should be widely available in schools, health care systems, religious organizations and community centers.

64. Communities must provide special parenting education and services for pregnant teenagers as well as teenage parents, including counseling on relinquishment and adoption.

65. Adequate child care facilities and services, with training, licensing and monitoring of the providers, should be available to all parents needing such services.

66. Employer-sponsored assistance and counseling programs for family violence and child abuse and neglect, such as those used for alcoholism and drug abuse, should be established.

67. Identification and assessment of the physically, mentally, emotionally or the learning disabled child must occur as early as possible.

68. Services and education must be designed for and provided to mentally ill, emotionally disturbed and developmentally disabled children and parents.

69. Judges must assure that child support orders are expedited and vigorously enforced and urge cooperation among all components of the child support enforcement process and all federal and state government agencies which may impact on child support enforcement proceedings.

70. Persons convicted of exploiting children by means of pornography, prostitution, drug use or trafficking must be severely punished. High priorities also must be given to national efforts to curtail the availability to children of pornography and excessively violent materials.

71. Courts and communities must provide services and courts must intervene, where necessary, to assist homeless, truant, runaway, and incorrigible children. Parents must be held personally and financially accountable for the conduct of their children.

72. Courts should cooperate with schools and other agencies to substantially reduce truancy and dropouts by coordinating and providing services and assistance to the habitual truant.

73. The courts should have authority to detain, in a secure facility for a limited period, a runaway, truant or incorrigible child whose chronic behavior constitutes a clear and present danger to the child's own physical or emotional well-being, when the court determines there is no viable alternative.

Source: Metropolitan Court Judges Committee Reports. *Deprived Children: A Judicial Response.* Reno, NV: National Council of Juvenile and Family Court Judges, 1986.

Glossary

The number following the definition refers to the chapter(s) in which the term is defined.

abatement—doing whatever is necessary to get rid of a nuisance and bring the problem to an end. 13

abuse—see *child abuse*. 5

acting out—the free, deliberate, often malicious indulgence of impulse that frequently leads to aggression as well as other manifestations of delinquency, such as vandalism, cruelty to animals and sometimes even murder. 6

adjudicate—to judge. 9

adjudicated—having been the subject of completed criminal or juvenile proceedings and having been cleared or declared a delinquent, status offender or dependent. 9

adjudication—a juvenile court decision ending a hearing, affirming that the juvenile is a delinquent, a status offender or a dependent, or that the allegations in a petition are not sustained. 9

adjudicatory hearing—the fact-finding process in the juvenile justice system, where the juvenile court determines if evidence is sufficient to sustain the allegations in a petition. 9

admit—to plead guilty in a juvenile delinquency proceeding.

adult supremacy—subordination of children to the absolute and arbitrary authority of parents and, in many instances, teachers. 4

adversary procedure—a means to determine guilt or innocence that pits the defense against the prosecution in court proceedings with a judge acting as arbiter of the legal rules. Under the adversary system, the burden is on the state to prove the charges beyond a reasonable doubt. 9

adversary process—in adult court, pitting prosecution and defense attorneys against each other. The American tradition of justice regards this as the fairest means of determining guilt. Until recently juvenile court avoided this process, since the determination of guilt was not considered its primary function; rather its function was considered to be formulating a rehabilitation plan "in the best interests of the child." Demands for due process for children in the juvenile court, including the introduction of defense counsel, developed as a result of the *Gault* decision. "Adversary" versus "best interests" are shorthand ways of referring to these conflicting philosophies of the juvenile court. 9

aftercare—supervision given children for a limited time after they are released from confinement but are still under the control of the institution or of the juvenile court. 10

American Dream—the belief that through hard work anyone can become rich. 2

anomie—normlessness. 2

anomie theory—the theory that states that the motivations for crime do not result simply from the flaws, failures or free choices of individuals. The distinctive patterns and levels of crime in the United States are produced by the cultural and structural organizations of American society. Specifically American culture is characterized by a strong emphasis on the goal of monetary success and a weak emphasis on the importance of pursuing success legitimately. The American Dream contributes to crime directly by encouraging people to use illegal means to achieve goals that are culturally approved. It also promotes and sustains an institutional structure in which the economy assumes dominance over all other institutions, such as the family, education and the political system, thereby diminishing their capacity to curb criminogenic cultural pressures and to impose controls over the behavior of members of society. In these ways the American Dream and its companion institutional arrangements contribute to high levels of crime. Also known as *strain theory*. 2

antisocial personality disorder—a disorder existing in persons at least age 18 who show evidence of a conduct disorder before age 15 as well as a pattern of irresponsible and antisocial behavior since the age of 15. 6

arrest—taking people into custody to restrain them until they can be held accountable for an offense at a court proceeding. The legal requirement for an arrest is probable cause; see also *take into custody*.

arrest warrant—a court order written by a judge or magistrate authorizing and directing that an individual be taken into custody to answer criminal charges.

at-risk youth—young people with the potential and willingness to take unnecessary risks or chances outside of socially accepted norms and mores, for the purpose of self-gratification, aggrandizement, and peer acceptance. Youths who engage in at-risk behavior, including habitual truancy, incorrigibility, gang activity, drug abuse, alcoholism, suicide, promiscuity, criminal activity, tattooing or self-mutilating behaviors, vandalism, possession and use of weapons. 6

attention deficit disorder—a common childhood disruptive behavior disorder characterized by heightened motor activity, short attention span, distractibility, impulsiveness and lack of self-control. 3

beyond a reasonable doubt—degree of proof required for guilt in a juvenile court proceeding. It is less than absolute certainty, but more than high probability. If there is doubt based on reason, the accused is entitled to the benefit of that doubt by acquittal.

biotic balance—an ecological term describing what occurs when the relations between the different species of plants and their necessary conditions for survival (e.g., climate, soil condition) maintain an equilibrium. All of the organisms are thus able to survive and prosper. 2

boot camp—a correctional facility that stresses military discipline, physical fitness, strict obedience to orders and education and vocational training; designed for young, nonviolent, first-time offenders; also called *shock incarceration*. 10

Bridewell—the first correctional institution, which confined both children and adults considered to be idle and disorderly. 1

broken-window phenomenon/theory—the theory that states that if it appears no one cares, disorder and crime will thrive. 6, 11

burden of proof—the duty of proving disputed facts in the trial of a case. The duty commonly lies with the person who affirms an issue and is sometimes said to shift when sufficient evidence is furnished to raise a presumption that what is alleged is true.

caring—the ways in which individuals and institutions protect young people and invest in their ongoing development. 4

case law—law derived from previous court decisions, as opposed to statutory law, which is passed by a legislative process.

certification—a procedure whereby a juvenile court waives jurisdiction and transfers the case to the adult criminal court; also called a *waiver*. 9

child—in most states, a person under 18 years of age. 1

child abuse—any physical, emotional or sexual trauma to a child for which no reasonable explanation, such as an accident, can be found. Child abuse includes neglecting to give proper care and attention to a young child. 5

children in need of supervision (CHINS)—an adjudicatory designation available to the juvenile court

when children are status offenders or habitually act to endanger their own morals or those of others. The court may claim jurisdiction over such children, but dispositional alternatives are more limited than in the case of children adjudged delinquent.

Children's Aid Society—an early child-saving organization that tried to place homeless city youths with rural families.

child savers—groups who promoted the rights of minors at the turn of the century and helped create a separate juvenile court. Their motives have been questioned by modern writers, who see their efforts as a form of social and class control. 1

child welfare agency—an agency licensed by the state to provide care and supervision for children. An agency that provides service to the juvenile court and which may accept legal custody. It may be licensed to accept guardianship, to accept children for adoption and to license foster homes.

chronic juvenile offender—a youth who has a record of five or more separate charges of delinquency, regardless of the gravity of the offenses. 6

civil law—all law that is not criminal, including torts (personal wrongs), contract law, property law, maritime law and commercial law. The juvenile court functions under a blend of civil and criminal law.

classical view of criminality—the view that delinquents are responsible for their own behavior, as individuals with free will. 2

classical world view—the view that holds that humans have free will and are responsible for their own actions. 2

coercive intervention—out-of-home placement, detainment or mandated therapy or counseling. 10

collective abuse—attitudes held as a group in a society that impede the psychological and physical development of children. 5

common law—law of custom and usage. 1

community—a concept that refers not only to the geographic area over which the justice system has jurisdiction but also to a sense of integration, of shared values and a sense of "we-ness." 11

community policing—a philosophy that embraces a proactive, problem-oriented approach to working with the community to make it safe. 8, 11

community relations—projecting and maintaining an image of the police as serving the community, rather than simply enforcing laws. 8

competence—a specific, functional ability. 14

competent—properly qualified, adequate. 14

concordance—a high degree of similarity, as in heredity studies where identical twins were more likely to both have criminal records than were fraternal twins. 2

concurrent—something happens at the same time, or a case may be heard in either juvenile or adult court. 9

conduct disorder—a behavioral disorder characterized by prolonged antisocial behavior ranging from truancy to fistfights. 6

conflict gang—a gang that usually exists in dilapidated areas with transient populations. Poverty is a defining element of their communities, and status is achieved not through the use of business connections but with violence. The Bloods and the Crips are examples of conflict gangs. 7

conflict theory—a theory that suggests that laws are established to keep the dominant class in power. 2

consensus theory—a theory that contends that individuals within a society agree on basic values, on what is inherently right and wrong. 2

contagion—a way to explain the spread of violence, equating it with the spread of infectious diseases. 6

coproducers of justice—the role of citizens as responsible for the prevalence and severity of the crime within their communities. 14

corporal punishment—inflicting bodily harm. 1

corporate gang—a gang that is highly structured and disciplined with a strong leader; its main focus is participating in illegal money-making ventures; also called *organized gang*. 7

corrections institution—a confinement facility with custodial authority over delinquents and status offenders committed to confinement after a dispositional hearing.

corrective prevention—a prevention strategy that focuses on eliminating conditions that lead to or cause criminal behavior; also called *primary prevention.*

court, juvenile—an agency of the judicial branch of government established by statute and consisting of one or more judicial officers with the authority to decide on controversies in law and disputed matters concerned with intake, custody, confinement, supervision or treatment of alleged or adjudicated delinquents, status offenders and children in need of care.

Court Appointed Special Advocate for Children (CASA)—a volunteer guardian *ad litem* program. 9

court report—a document submitted by a person designated by the court before the disposition of cases. The report contains a social history of the child and a plan of rehabilitation or treatment and care.

crack children—children exposed to cocaine while in the womb; may exhibit social, emotional and cognitive problems. 3

crew—a group of taggers. 7

crime—an offense against the state; behavior in violation of law for which a penalty is prescribed. 6

criminal gang—a very organized, well-managed, often very lucrative gang that teaches youths the ways of the criminal business world. They use business savvy and financial acumen to achieve status, not having to rely very heavily on violence. Such gangs tend to develop in stable, low-income areas where adolescents may have close relationships with adult criminals. 7

critical theory—a theory that combines the classical free-will and positivist determinism views of crime, suggesting that humans are both self-determined and society-determined. Assumes that human beings are the creators of the institutions and structures that ultimately dominate and constrain them, and includes labeling theory, conflict theory and radical theory. 2

cruel and unusual punishment—physical punishment or punishment far in excess of that given to a person under similar circumstances and, therefore, banned by the Eighth Amendment.

custodian—a person other than a parent, guardian or agency to whom legal custody of a child has been transferred by a court, but not a person who has only physical custody. A person other than a parent or legal guardian who stands *in loco parentis* to the child or a person to whom legal custody of the child has been given by order of a court. 1

custody—a legal status created by court order that vests in a person the right to have physical custody of a child; the right to determine where and with whom the child will live; the right and duty to protect, train and discipline the child, to provide food, shelter, legal services, education, ordinary medical and dental care. Such rights are subject to the rights and duties, responsibilities and provisions of any court order.

custody, discharge from—legal release from custody. State statutes specify that a child shall be released to a parent, guardian or legal custodian unless it is impractical, undesirable or otherwise ordered by the court. The legal custodian serves as a guarantor that the child will appear in court and may be asked to sign a promise to that effect. This takes the place of bail in adult court.

custody, taking into—the term used in place of *arrest* when a child is taken by a law enforcement officer. State codes and laws prescribe that a child may be taken into custody only under the following conditions: (1) when ordered by the judge for failure to obey a summons (petition); (2) when a law enforcement officer observes or has reasonable grounds to believe the child has broken a federal, state or local law and deems it in the public interest; (3) when the officer removes the child from conditions that threaten his or her welfare; (4) when the child is believed to be a runaway from parents or legal custody and (5) when the child has violated the conditions of probation. 9

decriminalization—legislation to make status offenses noncriminal acts. 1

deinstitutionalization—providing programs in a community-based setting instead of in an institution. 1

delinquency—actions or conduct by a juvenile in violation of criminal law or constituting a status offense. An error or failure by a child or adolescent to conform to society's expectations of social order where the child either resides or visits. 7

delinquent—see *delinquent child.* 6

delinquent act—an act committed by a juvenile for which an adult could be prosecuted in a criminal court. 1

delinquent child—a child adjudicated to have violated a federal, state or local law; a minor who has done an illegal act or who has been proven in court to have misbehaved seriously. A child may be found delinquent for a variety of behaviors not criminal for adults (status offenses). 1, 6

denominator approach—placing the focus of efforts on the whole population of youths, not just on the delinquents. 12

deny—a plea of "not guilty" in juvenile proceedings.

dependency—the legal status of children over whom a juvenile court has assumed jurisdiction because the court has found their care to fall short of legal standards of proper care by parents, guardians or custodians.

dependent—a child adjudged by the juvenile court to be without parent, guardian or custodian. The child needs special care and treatment because the parent, guardian or custodian is unable to provide for his or her physical or mental condition; or the parents, guardian or custodian, for good cause, desire to be relieved of legal custody; or the child is without necessary care or support through no fault of the parents, guardian or custodian.

deprived child—one who is without proper parental care or control, subsistence, education as required by law or other care or control necessary for his or her physical, mental or emotional health or morals, and the deprivation is not due primarily to the lack of financial means of the parents, guardians or other custodians. 1

deserts—punishment as a kind of justified revenge; the offending individual gets what is coming. 1

desistance—a process commonly occurring during the transition between late adolescence and early adulthood that discourages youths from a life of crime. 13

detention—temporary care of a child alleged to be delinquent who is physically restricted pending court disposition, transfer to another jurisdiction or execution of a court order. 8

detention center—a government facility that provides temporary care in a closed, locked facility for juveniles pending a court disposition.

detention hearing—a hearing in juvenile court to determine if a child held in custody shall remain in custody for the best interests of the child and in the public interest.

determinism—a philosophy that maintains that human behavior is the product of a multitude of environmental and cultural influences. 2

deterrence—punishment as a means to prevent future lawbreaking. 1, 2, 8

deviance—behavior that departs from the social norm.

differential association theory—a theory that states that a person becomes delinquent because of an excess of definitions favorable to violation of law over definitions unfavorable to violation of law. 2

disposition—a juvenile court decision that a juvenile be committed to a confinement facility, placed on probation or given treatment and care; meet certain standards of conduct or be released or a combination of court decrees. 9

dispositional hearing—an adjudicated process by the juvenile court, either formal or informal, on the evidence submitted with a guarantee of due process of law for the child in a matter before the court, as specified in the Fifth, Sixth and Fourteenth Amendments of the Constitution (cf., *In re Gault*). 9

distributive justice—providing an equal share of what is valued in a society to each member of that society. This includes power, prestige and possessions. Also called *social justice.* 2

diversion—the official halting of formal juvenile proceedings against an alleged offender and the referral of the juvenile to a treatment or care program by a private or public service agency. 1

double jeopardy—being tried for the same offense twice. 1

due process—a difficult-to-define term; the due process clause of the U.S. Constitution requires that no person shall be deprived of life, liberty or property without due process of law. 1

EBD—emotionally/behaviorally disturbed. Usually emotionally/behaviorally disturbed youths have one or more of the following behavior patterns: severely aggressive or impulsive behavior; severely withdrawn or anxious behaviors, pervasive unhappiness, depression or wide mood swings; severely disordered thought processes that show up in unusual behavior patterns, atypical communication styles and distorted interpersonal relationships. Such children may have limited coping skills and may be easily traumatized. 3

ecological model—a sociological model used to compare the growth of a city and its attendant crime problems to growth in nature. 2

ecology—the study of the relationships between organisms and their environment. 2

educare—as defined by Attorney General Janet Reno: safe, constructive child care for all children. 4

emancipation—giving up the care, custody, welfare and financial support of a minor child by renouncing parental duties.

emotional abuse—the chronic failure of a child's caretaker to provide affection and support. 5

ephebiphobia—a fear and loathing of adolescents. 6

expressive violence—an acting out of extreme hostility, in contrast to instrumental violence. 7

extrafamilial sexual abuse—sexual abuse of a child by a friend or stranger, a non-family member. 5

fact-finding hearing—as applied in juvenile court, a hearing to determine if the allegations of the petition are supported; also referred to as an *adjudicatory hearing*.

family court—a court with broad jurisdiction over family matters, such as neglect, delinquency, paternity, support and noncriminal matters and behavior.

felony—a criminal offense punished by capital punishment or confinement for one year or more in a locked facility.

fetal alcohol syndrome (FAS)—a condition in which children exposed to excessive amounts of alcohol while in the womb may exhibit impulsivity and poor communication skills, be unable to predict consequences or use appropriate judgment in daily life. The leading cause of mental retardation in the western world. 3

folkways—these describe how people are expected to dress, eat and show respect for one another. They encourage certain behaviors. 2

foster group home—a blend of group home and foster home initiatives. It provides a "real family" concept and is run by a single family, not a professional staff. 10

foster home—an unlocked facility, licensed by the state or local jurisdiction and operated by a person or couple, to provide care and maintenance for children, usually one to four such children; see *group home*. 10

functionalism—the view that crime is a necessary part of society, providing the need for laws and courts and jobs for lawyers, police officers, judges and jailers. 2

funnel effect—a term describing the phenomena that, at each point in the juvenile justice system, fewer and fewer youths pass through. 8

gang—a group of youths who form an allegiance for a common purpose and engage in unlawful or criminal activity; any group gathered together on a continuing basis to commit antisocial behavior. 7

Gould-Wysinger Award—an award established in 1992 to give national recognition for local achievement in improving the juvenile justice system and helping our nation's youths. 12

graffiti—wall writing, indoors or outdoors. Outdoors it is sometimes referred to as the "newspaper of the street." 7

group home—a nonconfining residential facility for adjudicated juveniles intended to reproduce as closely as possible the circumstances of family life and at a minimum to provide access to community activities and resources. 10

guardian *ad litem*—an individual appointed by the court to protect the best interests of a child or an incompetent in the juvenile justice process. In some states this can only be an attorney. The appointed individual is a surrogate parent, guardian or custodian and can be replaced for the best interests of the child at any point in a juvenile proceeding. 9

halfway house—a nonconfining residential facility for adjudicated juveniles to provide an alternative to confinement; also used to house juveniles on probation or in need of a period of readjustment to the community after confinement.

hearing—the presentation of evidence to a juvenile court judge for consideration and disposition. 9

hedonistic gang—a gang that focuses on having a good time, usually by smoking pot, drinking beer and sometimes engaging in minor property crimes. 7

holistic approach—treating the whole person; by examining all facets of a child's life and coordinating all treatment services, the greatest benefit for the youth is ensured. Used with Project New Pride. 13

incapacitation—making incapable by incarcerating. 2

incarceration—placing a person in a locked facility or a secure confinement for punishment, deterrence, rehabilitation or reintegration into the community.

Index crimes—Part I and Part II crimes of the Uniform Crime Report (UCR), including homicide, non-negligent manslaughter, forcible rape, robbery, aggravated assault, burglary, larceny, arson and motor vehicle theft. 6

individual abuse—physical or emotional abuse by parents or others as individuals. 5

in loco parentis—in place of the parent. Gives certain social and legal institutions the authority to act as a parent might in situations requiring discipline or need. Schools have this authority. 4

institutional abuse—the approved use of force and violence against children in the schools and in the denial of children's due process rights in institutions. 5

instrumental gang—a gang that focuses on obtaining money, committing property crimes for economic reasons rather than for the "thrill." 7

instrumental violence—violence used for some type of gain, such as robbery; in contrast to expressive violence. 7

intake—the point in the juvenile justice process that reviews referrals to the juvenile court and decides the action to be taken, based on the best interests of the child or the public good.

intake unit—the office that receives referrals to the juvenile court and screens them, either to divert them from the system to a social services agency or to file a petition.

integrated community—a geographic/political area where people feel ownership and take pride in what is right and responsibility for what is wrong. 11

intensive supervision—a highly structured form of observation provided by probation. 10

intrafamilial sexual abuse—sexual abuse of a child by a parent or other family member. 5

John Wayne effect—the inability to see beyond the status quo: "If it doesn't work, do more, and try harder, Pilgrim!" 14

judge—a judicial officer elected or appointed to preside over a court who hears and makes decisions on matters in the best interests of juveniles and the public safety.

jurisdiction—the authority of courts and judicial officers to decide a case. 9

just deserts—see *deserts*. 1

justice—fairness in treatment by the law.

justice model—the judicial process wherein young people who come into conflict with the law are held responsible and accountable for their behavior. 1

juvenile court—a court having jurisdiction over individuals defined as juveniles and alleged to be delinquents, status

offenders, dependents or in need of decisions by the court regarding their health, safety or welfare.

juvenile justice—a system that provides a legal setting in which youths can account for their wrongs or receive official protection.

juvenile justice agency—an agency that functions for the juvenile court in investigation, supervision, adjudication, care or confinement of juveniles whose conduct or condition has brought or could bring them within the juvenile court's jurisdiction.

Juvenile Justice and Delinquency Prevention Act of 1984—a federal law establishing an office of juvenile justice within the Law Enforcement Assistance Act to provide funds to control juvenile crime.

juvenile justice process—a justice proceeding for juveniles that differs from the adult criminal process. The philosophy and procedures are informal and nonadversarial, invoked in the best interests of the child rather than as punishment. A petition is filed rather than a complaint; the matter is often not public and the purpose is rehabilitation rather than retribution.

juvenile record—a confidential document kept separate from adult records and not open to public inspection. It contains an account of behavior and antisocial activity of juveniles who appeared before a juvenile court.

labeling—giving names to things; names may become self-fulfilling.

labeling theory—the theory that views society as creating deviance through a system of social control agencies that designate certain people as deviants. This stigmatizes people; they are made to feel unwanted in the normal social order. Eventually they begin to believe that the label is accurate and begin to act to fit the label. 2

law—a method to resolve disputes. A rule of action to which people obligate themselves to conform.

learning disability—one or more significant deficits in the essential learning processes. 3

least restrictive means—a phrase referring to the use of dispositional alternatives for children.

lex talionis—a legal principle establishing the concept of retaliation, that is, an eye for an eye. 1

mala in se—acts considered immoral or wrong in themselves, such as murder and rape. 2

mala prohibita—acts prohibited because they infringe on others' rights, not because they are necessarily considered evil by nature, such as having more than one wife. 2

maximalist alarmist perspective—the view that the time has come to reject the reluctance of earlier generations to face the facts and to recognize the enormity of the developing crisis. Parents are abusing and neglecting their children in record numbers, and exploitive adolescents, pedophiles (child molesters), and other abusers are preying upon youngsters with impunity. 5

mechanical jurisprudence—the view that everything is known and that, therefore, laws can be made in advance to cover every situation. 9

mechanical prevention—prevention efforts directed toward "target hardening" to make it difficult or impossible to commit particular offenses.

medical model—the view that offenders are victims of their environment and thus are curable. 1

minimalist skeptical perspective—the view that huge numbers of honestly mistaken and maliciously false allegations are mixed in with true disclosures, making the problem seem worse than it really is and fueling the impression that it is spiraling out of control. 5

minor—a person under the age of legal consent.

misdemeanor—an offense punishable by a fine and less than one year in jail. Varies from state to state.

moniker—a name adopted by a gang member to be used in place of his or her given name. 7

mores—the critical norms vital to a society's safety and survival. Often referred to as *natural law.* 2

National Council on Crime and Delinquency (NCCD)—a private national agency promoting efforts at crime control through research, citizen involvement and public information efforts.

natural law—the rules of conduct that are the same everywhere because they are basic to human behavior. Also called *mores.* 2

neglect—a child is adjudged to be neglected if the child is abandoned, without proper care; without substance, education or health care because of the refusal of a parent, guardian or custodian to provide them; in need of supervision as a result of the neglect. 5

net widening—diverting youths to other programs and agencies rather than away from the system. 1

nonjudicial disposition—a decision in a juvenile case by an authority other than a judge or court of law. This is usually an informal method that determines the most appropriate disposition in handling a juvenile.

nonresidential program—a program allowing youths to remain in their homes or foster homes while receiving services.

nonsecure facility—a facility that emphasizes the care and treatment of youths without the need to place constraints or be concerned about public protection.

Norman Rockwell family—a working father, a housewife mother and two children of school age (6 percent of U.S. households in the 1990s). 4

norms—rules or laws governing the actions and interactions of people, usually of two types: folkways and mores. 2

nuisance—a legal concept pertaining to the use of property and requiring landowners to use their property so as not to injure their neighbors' use of their properties. Typically defined by local ordinance or state statute, the concept applies to physically damaging neighboring property, reducing its value or reducing its enjoyment. 13

numerator approach—the view that the focus of prevention efforts should be on those youths who are at greatest risk. 12

ombudsman—a person whose role is to improve conditions of confinement for juveniles and protect the rights of youths in custody. Responsibilities include monitoring conditions, servicing delivery systems, investigating complaints, reporting findings, proposing changes, advocating for improvements, accessing appropriate care, and helping to expose and reduce unlawful deficiencies in juvenile detention and correctional facilities. 10

organized gang—a highly structured and disciplined gang with a strong leader; its main focus is participating in illegal moneymaking ventures; also called *corporate gang.*

paradigm—a pattern, a way of looking at an entire concept or field. 8, 14

parens patriae—literally "parent of the country." The legal provision through which the state may assume ultimate parental responsibility for the custody, care and protection of children within its jurisdiction. The right of the government to take care of minors and others who cannot legally take care of themselves. 1

parole—supervised early release from institutionalization. 10

permanency—with regard to treatments, the idea that they will endure. 13

person in need of supervision (PINS)—a youth usually characterized as ungovernable, incorrigible, truant or habitually disobedient.

petition—the formal process for bringing a matter before the juvenile court. A document alleging that a juvenile is a delinquent, status offender or dependent, and asking the court to assume jurisdiction. The petition in the juvenile process is the same as a formal complaint in the adult criminal process. 9

petition not sustained—the judgment that a petition is insufficient; there is a lack of evidence to support any allegations submitted against the juvenile.

phrenology—studying the shape of the skull to predict intelligence and character. 2

physical abuse—the nonaccidental, or intentional, physical injury of a child caused by the child's caretaker. 5

physiognomy—judging character from physical features, especially facial features. 2

PINS—see *person in need of supervision.*

police-school liaison program—a program of placing law enforcement officers within schools to help prevent juvenile delinquency and to improve community relations. 8

poor laws—laws that established the appointment of overseers to indenture poor and neglected children into servitude. 1

positivist view of criminality—the view that delinquents are victims of society.

positivist world view—the view that humans are shaped by their society and are the product of environmental and cultural influences. 2

predatory gang—a gang that commits violent crimes against persons, including robberies and street muggings; members are likely to use hard drugs, which contributes to their volatile, aggressive behavior. 7

preliminary hearing—the initial conference that satisfies those matters that must be dealt with before the juvenile case can proceed further. At this first hearing, the judge informs the parties involved of the charges in the petition and of their rights in the proceeding. The hearing may also be used to determine whether an alleged delinquent should remain in detention or in the custody of juvenile authorities. 9

preventive detention—the confinement of youths who might pose a danger to themselves or to others or who might not appear at their trial. 1

primary deviance—the original act defined as deviant by others. 2

primary prevention—prevention that seeks to change conditions that cause crime; also called *corrective prevention.* 12

probable cause—grounds that a reasonable and prudent person would believe an offense was committed and that the accused committed the crime.

probation—a sentence that entails the release of an individual into the community under the supervision of the court, subject to certain conditions for a specific time. Only the court can provide probation. 10

probation officer—a correctional officer under the principal direction of the court. In juvenile matters handles intake and presentence investigations for dispositional hearings and assists the court in determining the proper treatment of and care for juveniles. 10

proof beyond a reasonable doubt—the standard of proof needed to convict in a criminal case. The amount of absolute certainty that the defendant committed the alleged offense (e.g., *In re Winship*).

protective factors—elements that reduce the impact of negative risk factors by providing positive ways for a person to respond to such risks. 12

psychopath—virtually lacking in conscience; does not know right from wrong. 6

psychopathic behavior—chronic asocial behavior rooted in severe deficiencies in the development of a conscience. Virtually lacking in conscience; unable to distinguish right from wrong. 6

public defender—a lawyer who works for the defense of indigent offenders and is reimbursed for services by a public agency.

punitive prevention—prevention that relies on the threat of punishment to forestall criminal acts.

radial concept—the view that growth and development do not occur in isolation but instead involve a complex interaction of family, school and community, with the family being the first and most vital influence. As children grow the school becomes a more important influence, and as youths approach adolescence, the influence of parents and teachers becomes less and that of peers more influential. All of this occurs within the broader community within which children live. 4

radical theory—the theory that crime is a product of the political economy that, in capitalist societies, encourages an individualistic competition among wealthy people and among poor people and between rich and poor people (the intra- and interclass struggle) and the practice of taking advantage of other people (exploitation). 2

recidivism—repetition of criminal behavior; habitual criminality. 13

referee—a lawyer who serves part time or full time to handle simple, routine juvenile cases. 9

referral to intake—a request by police, parents, schools or social service agencies to take appropriate action concerning a juvenile alleged to have committed a delinquent act, status offense or to be dependent.

reform school—a juvenile facility designed to improve the conduct of those forcibly detained within.

rehabilitation—restoring to a condition of constructive activity.

release from detention—the authorized release from detention of a person subject to juvenile justice proceedings.

representing—a manner of dressing that uses an imaginary line drawn vertically through the body and shows allegiance or opposition. 7

residential childcare facility—a dwelling other than a detention or shelter facility that provides care, treatment and maintenance for children. Such facilities include foster family homes, group homes and halfway houses.

restitution—making right. Restoring property or a right to a person who has been unjustly deprived of it. 9

restorative justice—the view that justice involves not two, but four parties: offender and victim, government and community—all are injured by the crime. 14

retaliation—personal revenge; the accepted way to deal with members of the tribe who break the rules. 1

retreatist gang—a gang that seeks status and success through both legitimate and illegitimate means, although they lack the skills required to be a criminal gang and also lack the risk-taking, violent edge needed as a conflict gang. Their structure tends to be disorganized and their membership quite transitory. 7

retributive justice—justice that is served by some sort of punishment for wrongdoing (*lex talionis*). 2

reverse certification—when the criminal court has exclusive jurisdiction, the transfer of the case to the juvenile court. 9

risk factors—elements existing within the community, family, school and the individual that increase the probability that a young person will exhibit certain adolescent problem behaviors, including violence. 12

runaways—youths who commit the status offense of leaving the custody and home of parents, guardians or custodians without permission and failing to return within a reasonable time. 3, 5

scavenger gang—a gang of urban survivors who prey on the weak of the inner city; crimes are usually petty, senseless and spontaneous; has no particular goals, no purpose. 7

secondary deviance—an act that results because society has labeled the offender a deviant. 2

secondary prevention—prevention that focuses on changing the behavior of juveniles likely to become delinquent. Includes punitive prevention. 12

seesaw model—a model to demonstrate the functional family, where stresses and resources are balanced, and the nonfunctional family, where stresses are greater than the resources to cope with them, resulting in an unbalanced family. 5

self-fulfilling prophecy—a prophecy that occurs when people live up to the labels they are given. 3

Serious Habitual Offender Comprehensive Action Program (SHOCAP)—a federally funded program of the OJJDP that provides guidelines to various components of the juvenile justice system and the community in dealing with serious habitual offenders. 8

serious juvenile offender—a juvenile who has been convicted of a Part I offense as defined by the FBI *Uniform Crime Reports,* excluding auto theft or distribution of a controlled dangerous substance, and who was between 14 and 17 years of age at the time the offense was committed. 6

shelter—a nonsecure or unlocked place of care and custody for children awaiting court appearances and for those who have already been adjudicated and are awaiting disposition. 10

shock incarceration—a correctional facility stressing military discipline, physical fitness, strict obedience to orders and education and vocational training; designed for young, nonviolent, first-time offenders; also called *boot camp.* 10

social contract—a philosophy that entails free, independent individuals agreeing to form a community and to give up a portion of their individual freedom to benefit the security of the group. 2

social disorganization theory—the theory that urban areas produce delinquency directly by weakening community controls and generating a subculture of delinquency passed on from one generation to the next. 2

social ecology theory—the theory that ecological conditions predict delinquency and that gang membership is a normal response to social conditions. 2

socialized delinquency—youthful behavior that violates the expectations of society but conforms to the expectations of other youths. 7

social justice—providing an equal share of what is valued in a society to each member of that society, including power, prestige and status; also called *distributive justice.* 2

sociopathic behavior—see *psychopathic behavior.* 6

station adjustment—occurs when a juvenile offenders is handled by the police within the department and released. 8

status offender—a juvenile who has committed a status offense; usually not placed in a correctional institution.

status offense—an offense by a juvenile that would not be a crime if committed by an adult, e.g., truancy, running away, curfew violation, incorrigibility or endangering health and morals. 1

strain theory—see *anomie theory.* 2

street gang—a group of individuals who meet over time, have identifiable leadership, claim control over a specific territory in the community and engage in criminal behavior. 7

street justice—a decision by police to deal with a status offense in their own way, usually by ignoring it. 8

summons—a legal document ordering a person to appear in court at a certain time on a certain date. 9

symbiosis—an ecological term describing the condition of two different organisms living together in a mutually beneficial relationship. 2

tagging—a new form of graffiti whose dominant visual impression includes words, as compared to graffiti, which leaves only a hint of words. Often added to existing graffiti. 7

take into custody—the physical apprehension by a police action of a child engaged in delinquency; see also *arrest.*

termination of parental rights—ending by the court, upon petition, of all rights to a minor by his or her parents. Parents may be judged incapable and their rights terminated because of the following: debauchery, use of drugs and alcohol, conviction of a felony, lewd or lascivious behavior or mental illness.

territorial gang—a gang that designates something, someplace or someone as belonging exclusively to the gang. 7

tertiary prevention—the third level of prevention. Aimed at preventing recidivism. Focuses on preventing further delinquent acts by youths already identified as delinquents. 12

therapeutic intervention—recommendation of an appropriate treatment program.

throwaways—children whose family has kicked them out. 3, 5

tort—a civil wrong against an individual or individuals for which the perpetrator is civilly liable. 13

training schools—correctional institutions for juveniles adjudicated delinquent by a judicial officer. 10

transfer hearing—a hearing to determine whether a juvenile alleged to be delinquent will be tried in juvenile court or waived to adult criminal court. The juvenile usually must be 16 years or older to be considered for the waiver or transfer to adult court.

turf—the area claimed by a gang. 7

Uniform Crime Report (UCR)—the FBI's Uniform Crime Reporting program. 6

violent juvenile offender—a youth who has been convicted of a violent Part I offense, one against a person rather than property, and who has a prior adjudication of such an offense; a youth convicted of murder. 6

waiver—a procedure whereby juvenile court waives jurisdiction and transfers the case to the adult criminal court; also called *certification.* 9

window of opportunity—a time when treatment is especially needed (in crimes) or likely to make a difference (during transition periods). 8

youthful offender—a person adjudicated in a criminal court who may be above the statutory age limit for juveniles but below a specified upper age limit for special correctional commitment.

youth gang—a self-formed association of youths distinguished from other types of youth groups by their routine participation in illegal activities. 7

Youth Service Bureau—a neighborhood youth service agency that coordinates all community services for young people, especially designed for the predelinquent or early delinquent.

Author Index

Subject Index

Photo Credits